THE BEST 106 INTERNSHIPS

WHAT THE MEDIA HAS SAID ABOUT
THE BEST 106 INTERNSHIPS

(FORMERLY KNOWN AS *AMERICA'S TOP INTERNSHIPS*)
BY MARK OLDMAN AND SAMER HAMADEH
(RANDOM HOUSE/PRINCETON REVIEW PUBLISHING)

"I wish *America's Top Internships* had been in the bookstores when I was in college. . . . Go to your local bookstore . . . to buy a copy of the latest, neatest reference book going for college students."
  —L.M. Sixel, *The Houston Chronicle*

"A wonderful book. . . . This is fascinating stuff. It has an insider, almost gossipy look at what really goes on in a company. . . . all sorts of intriguing lists . . . and helpful charts."
  —Michele Ross, CNN

"College ladies and gentlemen, start your resumes. *America's Top Internships* . . . rates corporate internships by such factors as busywork, pay, and quality of life."
  —Kevin Salwen, *The Wall Street Journal*

"*America's Top Internships* . . . helps you figure out whether an internship may be a step inside the door of a major company . . . or just drudgery and slavery. I just sent the book off to my son in college."
  —Terry Savage, *Chicago Sun Times*

"A witty and fun guide to the world of quasi-jobs—from unpaid gopher on 'Late Show with David Letterman' to sales rep making $675 weekly at Procter & Gamble."
  —Peter Van Allen, *Camden Courier Post*

"Not interested in an internship, you say? Any college student who doesn't see this valuable on-the-job experience as an unwritten must is living on another planet. To help find these jobs, along comes *America's Top Internships*."
  —Patricia Kitchen, *New York Newsday*

"It's an invaluable tool—very easy to read and entertaining. Anyone who is interested in getting an internship—or knows someone who should—should get this book."
  —Isobel Neuberger, WXXI-AM (Rochester, NY)

"Oldman and Hamadeh are extremely informative and their book is extremely helpful for the average student searching for the above-average internship."
  —Boston College newspaper, *The Heights*

"A really neat book; funny, well-written, and insightful. You will probably want to get your own copy."
  —*Internet 101: A College Student's Guide* by Alfred Glossbrenner (McGraw-Hill, 1995)

THE BEST
106
INTERNSHIPS

**Mark Oldman and
Samer Hamadeh**

Random House, Inc.
New York
www.randomhouse.com/princetonreview

8th Edition

Princeton Review Publishing, L.L.C.
2315 Broadway
New York, NY 10024
E-mail: comments@review.com

Copyright © 1999, 2000, by Princeton Review Publishing L.L.C., Mark Oldman, and Samer Hamadeh.

All rights reserved under International and Pan-American Copyright Conventions. Published in the United States by Random House, Inc., New York, and simultaneously in Canada by Random House of Canada Limited, Toronto.

ISBN 0-375-75637-X
ISSN 1073-5801

Editor: Russell Kahn
Production Editor: Maria Dente
Production Coordinator: Robert McCormack

Manufactured in the United States of America on partially recycled paper.

9 8 7 6 5 4 3 2 1

8th Edition

Acknowledgments

We send our appreciation to the following invaluable players:

Elizabeth "Lix" Oldman, executive editor extraordinaire, whose incisive and good-humored editing gave this book a quantum leap in quality. Her literary talent and generous accessibility ("fax me in St. Bart's") are extraordinary.

Galen Smith, design consultant "on call," responsible for designing the entire interior and part of the cover of this book. He imbued the book with his unrivalled brand of retro art.

John Katzman, a man of derring-do, approachability, and shrewdness. His encouragement and good counsel are greatly appreciated.

Jeanne Krier, an unqualified goddess of publicity and our omnipresent "Charlie" (as in "Charlie's Angels") during the book tour. She deserves a red cape with a big "S" as well as a standing "O."

The Princeton Review all-stars: Greta Englert, Scott Harris, Stephanie Martin, Robert McCormack, Chris Thomas, Evelin Sanchez-O'Hara, Neil McMahon, Ryan Tozzi, and Dave Spalding.

Thanks also to the talented and fashionable Nikki Scott.

Our gratitude goes to (in no particular order) The H Brothers (Hussam, Bassim, and Basil), Charlie "Times Square" Samuels, Jane Emery, Laura Locke, Geoff "Knows How to Survive Without His Parents' $" Martz, The NYC Meat-Eaters, Lisa Herzog, and Nascar C. Philips.

A final thank you goes to our families, whose support and inspiration made creating this book immeasurably happier.

Contents

Introduction

by
Mark Oldman and Samer Hamadeh

What in the world could President Clinton, *Today* anchor Katie Couric, and New York Knicks star Patrick Ewing possibly have in common? The same hairdresser? Backstage passes for the next Streisand concert? An insatiable appetite for curly french fries?

Nope, nope, nope.

Like many college students of their generation, all three spent a summer doing an internship. Clinton got his political feet wet interning for Senator J. William Fulbright. Couric launched her broadcasting career at a Washington radio station. And Ewing, believe it or not, interned not with a sports team but with the Senate Finance Committee, his seven-foot frame towering over the technocrats of Capitol Hill.

As common as internships were a generation ago, these days have seen an explosion, among students and employers alike, in the popularity and perceived importance of internship programs. In virtually every major newspaper and magazine, career experts are stressing how internships are increasingly a powerful conduit to the best jobs. Recently in *USA Today*, one expert went on record as saying that an internship is the "most bankable credential you can put on a resume." Even President Clinton has recognized the importance of augmenting academics with real-world experience; at a recent conference of the American Council on Education, Clinton spoke of the need to "merge instead of keep divided our notion of vocational education and academic education."

For many employers, good grades and the right college major are just not enough; they seek employees who have paid their dues in the working world. "[Internships] are a real differentiator, a real symbol of maturity and competence," according to Al Krizelman, director of employment at Raychem, a leading materials-science company in Menlo Park, CA. "Applicants who've had meaningful, substantive work assignments with outstanding companies are at a very, very significant advantage [seeking a job] here." Adds William Ardrey, senior vice president at Fiduciary Communications, an investor communications company in New York City: "Give me a history major who has done internships and a business major who hasn't, and I'll hire the history major every time."

And more than ever, organizations are looking to their own internships to find permanent employees; employment directors frequently term their internships cost-effective "bull pens" or "probationary periods" because such programs are a low-risk means to assess the merits of a potential employee. Says Mary McPherran, internship coordinator at Marvel Comics in New York City: "We get a sneak preview of what a potential employee can offer . . . so when there's a job opening, we look to the intern pool, rather than someone off the street." Indeed, a number of leading organizations offer over half of their interns full-time jobs, including the likes of Hewlett-Packard, Kraft General Foods, Ruder Finn, and Bertelsmann Music Group.

But interns can also use internships as their own "probationary period" to check out a potential employer or even a potential industry. Simply put, internships are a great way of sampling a company without committing yourself for life. "When I was in college, I interned at Levi Strauss, Lucasfilm, National Geographic Society, and CNN," reported freelance journalist Laura A. Locke. "The cumulative effect of having all these disparate experiences helped me launch my career as a journalist." For the legions of college students undecided on careers, internships are an ideal way to spark a new interest, a new career direction. Kennedy biographer Nigel Hamilton, for example, found what fired his passion while serving a *Washington Post* internship decades ago; he recently told *The New York Times*, "It was a heady experience. I was an eighteen-year-old kid, and I was in the heart of things in Washington. My interest in American politics and particularly the Kennedys began there."

But not all internships are created equal. The working world is filled with the unrewarding, sweatshop variety of internship. Yet there is hope: The years we spent researching *The Best 106 Internships* helped us crystallize a set of criteria to discern the best internships from the duds. To begin, an internship should offer its participants substantive, challenging work. Who hasn't heard of an intern who spent his summer babysitting a photocopier and juggling coffee pots? Fortunately, some organizations recognize the importance of assigning their interns real-world projects. If you intern at the *Wall Street Journal*, for example, you are assigned the same kinds of stories as an entry-level reporter. Interns at 3M are placed in laboratory, engineering, and manufacturing positions where they help improve old products (everything from Post-it Notes to diaper tape) and create new ones. And expect no menial labor at the Reebok internship, where interns receive meaningful projects and practical training in the footwear business.

Nevertheless, college students must have realistic expectations about what they will do in their temporary posts. No, CIA interns aren't enlisted as spies (as far as we've been told), NASA interns stay out of the shuttle (yet they might watch a liftoff), and interns at "Late Show with David Letterman" don't book guests for the show (although they might do research on guests already booked). And a few industries—entertainment being the most notable—have internships that invariably involve large doses of phoning, faxing, photocopying, and the like. *The Best 106 Internships* addresses this issue of "busywork" head-on, offering a graphical "busywork meter" that measures how much menial labor each program requires.

While entertainment companies like Marvel Comics and MTV clock in with typically "high" busywork, they are nonetheless "top internships" because they amply satisfy a second criterion: behind-the-scenes exposure and networking. Despite the relative drudgery of their daily work, interns at MTV and other "high busywork" entertainment houses are exposed to the inner workings of their respective organizations, sometimes observing high-level meetings, attending events, and doing lunch with top brass. *Nightline* interns, for instance, sometimes have the chance to listen in on morning strategy meetings. Moreover, top internships are often treasure troves for networking, where a motivated intern can make contacts that will last a lifetime. Some organizations even go so far as to have a formal mentor program, in which interns are assigned a permanent employee who offers advice and perhaps helps the intern secure permanent employment. Frito-Lay, for example, provides its interns with a three-tiered network, assigning each intern a "buddy" (informal advisor), a "mentor" (senior manager who offers career advice), and a "supervisor" (project consultant).

Practically speaking, no internship search should overlook the issue of compensation. Although the word "internship" is sometimes seen as a euphemism for "indentured servitude," most industries have internships that compensate their interns generously.

More than 80 of America's top internships pay their participants, and some do so surprisingly well. J.P. Morgan slides its interns a weekly salary of $865; undergrad interns at Abbott Laboratories receive as much as $625 per week; and Washington Post interns rake in over $800 a week. Furthermore, some organizations don't stop with pay. Some offer free housing (Abbott Labs, U.S. Olympic Committee, Aspen Center for Environmental Studies), paid round-trip travel (Weyerhaeuser, Procter & Gamble, Academy of Television Arts and Sciences), and even free meals (Frontier Nursing Service, Crow Canyon Archaeological Center). And some internships, especially nonpaying ones, help their interns receive academic credit for their experiences. Says Albert Rodriguez, a senior at Texas A&M who served four internships at NASA and one at Disney, "The seven [academic] units I earned doing my internships were worth about $30,000 in tuition saved."

Not only is it crucial to know what constitutes a top internship, but an internship seeker must know how to go about snaring a top internship. Not surprisingly, it all starts with timing. That is, leave yourself plenty of time to investigate internship possibilities and prepare application materials. "At school, I set aside a whole day every few weeks to work on internship hunting," says Stanford University senior Shannon Snyder, who completed a Yosemite Ranger Internship and a teaching internship at Groton prep school. "You've got to put aside your schoolwork and focus on researching internships. . . . I spent a lot of time [searching] the career center's database." And smart internship hunters don't just rely on campus career centers; they consult every possible resource—college alumni, family connections, classmates, and even professors.

After identifying eight to twelve potentially excellent internships, you should start thinking about the application process. Check all application deadlines—early applications increase the chances for securing an internship. Put together a range of application materials—at least a resume and cover letter, and, if called for, transcripts, recommendations, and writing samples. Most importantly, you must research every organization to which you are applying. This means hotfooting it to the nearest library and looking up everything you can about the organizations under consideration. "[Getting hired for an internship] is ultimately an emotional process," explains Stanford's Snyder. "You want to show that you're on the same wavelength as the company . . . [so] read all you can and get inside the company's mind." After gaining a solid understanding of an organization's history and culture, you should subtly display this knowledge in the cover letter, and, if applicable, the interview. Doing your homework on an organization—something few applicants take the time to do—will impress the intern coordinator and maximize the chances of securing a top internship.

Unlike top colleges and grad schools, which heavily favor applicants with the best grades and classes, top internships have more flexibility in hiring. To be sure, some programs impose a minimum GPA (e.g., the CIA seeks undergrads with at least a 3.0 GPA) and a few programs require a particular courseload (e.g., the auction house Butterfield & Butterfield favors art-history majors). But according to the vast majority of internship coordinators, the deciding factor, time and time again, is an applicant's attitude. Specifically, coordinators use cover letters and interviews to gauge an applicant's motivation and energy. Organizations want interns who are fired up, who willingly accept all assignments and ask for more during slow periods. Says the intern coordinator at *Rolling Stone* magazine in New York City, "We look for applicants who want to learn every aspect of magazine publishing. . . [Ones who are] inquisitive and enthusiastic, even when carrying out clerical work." Counterbalancing the "go-getter" attitude, applicants must also show they realize that as interns, they will be temporary observers, oftentimes in a sensitive, hierarchical institution. Internship coordinators highly prize interns with diplomacy and discreetness. Play up your professionalism and maturity, because, as the internship coordinator at Lucasfilm in San Rafael, California, put it, companies "don't want people with pixie dust in their eyes."

With careful planning, solid research, and a good attitude, even the best internships are within reach. But the time window for doing internships is wider than most people think. Internships are not just in the summer—the majority of organizations offer opportunities during the academic year, when competition for spots is less intense and, in cities like Washington, D.C., there's more to see "in-season." Moreover, you need not be in the cradle of undergraduate academia to be an intern. Terrific internships are available to high school students (MTV, NASA, Vault.com), recent grads and grad students (The White House, Metropolitan Museum of Art, National Wildlife Federation), and even career changers of any age (Smithsonian Institution, The American Conservatory Theater, The Center for Investigative Reporting). Like anything in life, it's what you make of it, and with internships, low-risk career openers that they are, there is ample time to make a lot.

This article is reprinted from the *National Employment Business Weekly*, © 2000, Dow Jones & Co. Inc. All rights reserved. For subscription information, call 1-800-JOB-HUNT.

Authors' Note

Since we penned the first edition of *America's Top Internships* in 1994, we have watched internships go from a resume-enhancing tool to their current status as an essential stepping-stone to career success. Now everyone is talking about internships. Students and career changers want to know how to get them, career experts want to know which are the best, and employers want to how to start or improve their own internship programs.

As the first year of the 21st century comes to a close, here are the latest developments we've seen in the world of internships:

- **More College Students Interning Than Ever Before**: This year's results of Vault.com's Annual Internship Survey underscores the growing popularity of internships. The survey comprises responses from 1,172 members of the class of 2000 at 99 colleges and universities across the nation. Vault.com found that 86% of all college seniors had completed at least one internship by graduation. By comparison, only 62% of college seniors in 1995 had completed an internship.

- **Companies Receptive to Younger (and Older) Interns**: With the labor market as tight as it is, employers are increasingly willing to hire interns outside of the traditional college student/recent graduate age-group. Employers are realizing that many college underclassmen—and even high school students—have the requisite maturity and initiative to make valuable contributions to a company. Members of the "Internet generation," these younger interns are sometimes more tech-savvy than the full-time staffers they work for. With the current scarcity of talent, employers have also been more amenable to taking on older interns. These intern "elders"— career changers in their 30s, 40s, and older—can bring valuable seasoning, perspective, and experience to an organization.

- **The Intern-net Is Calling**: While there's no shortage of people seeking internships at large, brand-name companies, the siren call of the Internet is attracting more and more people to intern at net start-ups. Who can blame them? Dot-com start-ups typically offer interns real responsibility, an exciting (perhaps even chaotic) work environment, and sometimes even that coveted currency of the digital work-place, stock options. To locate hot start-ups likely to offer internship opportunities, surf the start-up databases at such sites as garage.com, thestandard.com, vault.com, and siliconalleyreporter.com.

These are just a few reasons why right now has never been a better time to intern. So get out there and strut your stuff!

Mark Oldman and Samer Hamadeh
The Internship Informants™ and Founders, Vault.com
New York, NY
August 2000
Interninfo@aol.com

HOW TO
READ AN
ENTRY

SELECTIVITY

Selectivity measures the approximate applicant pool and number of interns accepted. Whether an organization offers its internship more than once during the year (e.g., summer, fall, and spring) or accepts interns any time (e.g., Elite Model Management Corporation), the numbers given represent the yearly total of applicants and interns.

Selectivity (i.e., percentage of interns accepted) is rated as follows:

- 🔍🔍🔍🔍🔍   <5%
- 🔍🔍🔍🔍   5–10%
- 🔍🔍🔍   10–20%
- 🔍🔍   20–30%
- 🔍   ≥30%

COMPENSATION

Compensation measures the payment interns receive, as well as any housing, transportation, and food allowances.

Compensation is rated as follows:

- 💲💲💲💲💲   ≥$500 per week for undergraduates
- 💲💲💲💲 $400–499
- 💲💲💲 $300–399
- 💲💲 $200–299
- 💲 $0–199

QUALITY OF LIFE

Quality of life measures the level of happiness and comfort interns experience working for the organization. Seminars, social activities, company culture, workspaces, cafeterias, fitness centers, freebies, etc., are considered in this evaluation. The examples in the box represent only a partial list of such factors; consult each entry's description for further elaboration.

Quality of life is rated as follows:

- 🌴🌴🌴🌴🌴   Paradise City—as good as it gets
- 🌴🌴🌴🌴   Excellent—extra efforts made to ensure interns' happiness
- 🌴🌴🌴   Fine—a standard and satisfying working environment
- 🌴🌴   Okay—no special opportunities for interns
- 🌴   Poor—no "top" internship has a poor quality of life

LOCATION(S)

Location lists cities and/or states in which the internship is located.

FIELD

Field defines the primary vocational discipline associated with the organization. See Index for other related areas.

DURATION

Duration provides time parameters for the internship. All programs are full-time unless otherwise noted.

PRE-REQS

Pre-reqs describes major requirements of the internship, including class level, minimum GPA, coursework, etc. Always consult selection for details.

Class levels are defined as follows:

"College grads of any age"—anyone with a college degree

"Grad students"—J.D., M.A., M.D., M.S., M.B.A., and Ph.D. candidates, unless otherwise noted

"Recent grads"—college grads out of school no more than 3 years, unless otherwise noted

"Undergrads"—college freshmen to seniors; "college seniors" refers to students who have completed their junior year by the start of the internship; "college juniors" refers to students who have completed their sophomore year by the start of the internship; "college sophomores" refers to students who have completed their freshman year by the start of the internship; "college freshmen" refers to students currently in their freshman year, except where incoming freshman are eligible (e.g., Frontier Nursing Service)

"High school students"—refers to students enrolled in high school during the internship

DEADLINE(S)

Deadline(s) states when to submit application materials. Because some deadlines change without notice, always confirm the dates with the organization's internship coordinator. Always consult Application Procedure for details.

THE BUSYWORK METER

The Busywork Meter measures the menial tasks (stuffing envelopes, photocopying, filing, clipping newspapers, etc.) that offer little educational reward and are typically performed for one's supervisor or other employees. The intern and coordinator interviews provided an approximation of the daily amount of busywork expected of an intern.

FOR MORE INFORMATION

The addresses given were approved by the internship coordinators as the best place to send in materials and ensure their proper review.

THE TOP
INTERNSHIPS

THE TOP TEN INTERNSHIPS IN AMERICA FOR 2001

Academy of Television Arts & Sciences

■

The Coro Foundation

■

CNN

■

Hewlett-Packard

■

Inroads

■

Northwestern Mutual Financial Network

■

Proctor & Gamble

■

Summerbridge National

■

The Supreme Court of the United States

■

The Washington Post

ABBOTT LABORATORIES

SELECTIVITY	🔍 🔍 🔍 🔍 🔍
Approximate applicant pool: 4,000–5,000 Interns accepted: 150–200	

COMPENSATION	💲 💲 💲 💲 💲
$340–$625/wk for undergrads; $490–$1,250/wk for grad students; round-trip travel; housing	

QUALITY OF LIFE	↟ ↟ ↟ ↟ ↟
Free college housing; well-organized seminars Chicago boat cruise; networking/social activities	

LOCATION(S)

Lake County, IL

FIELD

Health care products/services

DURATION

12 weeks
Summer

PRE-REQS

College sophomores, juniors, and seniors; grad
students

DEADLINE(S)

Resumes accepted between September and March 1

On a cold, dark morning in June 1984, ten scientists hopped on a jet in Chicago and flew east to Washington, D.C. Their mission was urgent: retrieve a sample of one of the world's deadliest killers, the human immunodeficiency virus (HIV), which causes AIDS. Black satchel in hand, they returned to their research site—Abbott Laboratories. Within eight months, they had developed the first U.S. Food and Drug Administration-licensed test to screen blood for HIV.

Founded in 1888 by an industrious doctor named Wallace Abbott, Abbott Laboratories has a long history of making pioneering medical advances—discovering the anesthetic Pentothal in 1936, developing commercial penicillin production in 1941, and creating an automated diagnostic test for prostate cancer in 1991, to name a few. Abbott also is a U.S. leader in sales of infant formula and a worldwide leader in sales of diagnostics products. With more than 57,000 employees, a presence in 130 countries, and sales of more than $13 billion annually, Abbott produces thousands of health care products, everything from intravenous equipment, antibiotics, medical nutritionals and anesthetics to Similac infant formula, Clear Eyes eye drops, and Selsun Blue antidandruff shampoo.

DESCRIPTION

Since the early 1990s, Abbott Laboratories' Summer Internship Program has offered students positions at its Abbott Park, Illinois, corporate offices in the following business areas: Pharmaceutical Products, Diagnostic Products, Hospital Products, and Nutritional Products. Within these divisions, students work in a variety of areas, including Research and Development (R&D), Production/Operations Man-

agement, Information Technology, Finance and Accounting, Human Resources, Engineering, and Sales and Marketing. Most of the interns are undergraduates; about 30 percent annually are M.B.A., M.S., M.D., and Ph.D. candidates.

Abbott's pharmaceutical research targets cardiovascular, neurological, infectious, and viral diseases. An intern assigned to the Research and Discovery group in the pharmaceutical products area "made scale-ups of key intermediate compounds for specific [cardiovascular] drugs." Availability of in-

BUSYWORK METER
MEDIUM
LOW HIGH
OLDMAN & HAMADEH

termediates means that the company's scientists can speed up steps on the road to making potential medicines. "The methods I used were proprietary," she said. "I utilized column chromatography, HPLC [high-pressure liquid chromatography], and all kinds of reactions, from reductions to oxidations." Returning the following summer, she completed research in neuroscience medicine, an area of the company that investigates treatments for such afflictions as epilepsy, depression, and schizophrenia. "This time," she said, "I had even more responsibility and helped to develop new synthetic methods for compounds that [Abbott is] trying to turn into effective drugs."

Marketing interns are often exposed to the company's drug-making endeavors. One intern, for example, was assigned to the Pharmaceutical Products division to prepare marketing materials for a new application of Hytrin, a drug used to treat hypertension. Hytrin subsequently received FDA approval for treatment for male prostate enlargement. "I created materials that would allow us to hit markets as soon as the approval came through. This included training packets for our salespeople and a brochure that emphasized the cost benefits of using Hytrin instead of other options such as surgery or taking [competitor Merck's drug] Proscar."

Abbott also hires interns to help further the company's commitment to energy conservation and the environment. For example, an engineering intern assigned to Environmental Services and Energy Management worked on Green Lights, a voluntary EPA project that investigates forms of energy saving. "I completed lighting surveys for all of Abbott's northern Illinois buildings and entered the data into a computer program to determine ways we could reduce our power requirements. We're now in the process of installing lower-watt bulbs… and replacing switches with 'occupancy sensors,' which turn off or on depending on the motion in the room."

Several interns are also in charge of accounting tasks.

An accounting intern in Corporate Risk Management prepared numbers for financial reports and analyzed Abbott's insurance policies in addition to completing an "international asset valuation report." "I sent out a 30-page questionnaire to each of our international sites," he said. "[The questionnaire] asked for various information that later allowed me to determine the value of each site's assets." Abbott needs the values, he explained, in order to adequately insure its assets.

During the summer, interns gather for important business events, including a career exploration conference. During the conference, managers from different areas of Abbott discuss the range of available careers. Events such as these provide an opportunity for interns to network with hiring managers and explore future employment possibilities at Abbott.

Located at Abbott Park, 40 miles north of downtown Chicago, the 480-acre Abbott Laboratories headquarters consist of more than thirty modern, red brick buildings that offer pleasing views of on-site lakes, streams, and long stretches of grass; about five miles northeast is the company's North Chicago operation. Interns work from their own desks in a friendly, cooperative environment imbued with a sense of team effort. "No matter what department you visit, you'll see that the employees enjoy being there," explained an intern. "I'm not saying that everyone is best friends, but coworkers help each other, including interns. Everyone strives toward the common goal of creating world-renowned products."

A model of corporate generosity, Abbott houses non-local, undergraduate interns free of charge at nearby Lake Forest College. Though fully furnished, the dorm rooms have no kitchens or bathrooms. But not to worry—each floor contains a large centralized bathroom. Located ten miles southeast of Abbott Park, Lake Forest is just a few blocks from Lake Michigan, where interns may congregate for sunset picnics and swimming. During the

> A model of corporate generosity, Abbott houses interns free of charge at nearby Lake Forest College.

week, a free shuttle service transports interns from their dorms to work and back again. Interns have a variety of prime resources available to them. For food, interns are welcome to purchase a campus meal plan or eat at Abbott's cafeterias, which offer enough food choices to please vegetarians, nonfat dieters, and meat eaters alike. For exercise, interns can use the mile-and-a-half track, which circles the Abbott Park facilities, as well as Lake Forest College's swimming pool, outdoor sand volleyball court, weight room, and tennis courts, all of which are within walking distance from the dorms. Interns may also buy a membership to one of Abbott's two "self-care" centers. For a nominal fee, interns are able to use weights, StairMasters, Nordic Tracks, treadmills, and Lifecycles, and to take advantage of specialized exercise instruction, a body-fat percentage test, and a blood pressure reading.

The internship program offers an assortment of organized social activities, from a welcome reception to a farewell social. Most memorable, perhaps, is the night of the cruise on Lake Michigan in Chicago, on which interns enjoy dinner, dancing, and socializing. "It's a time when you can turn off work mode and get to know the other interns on a personal level," said an intern.

Pay at Abbott depends on experience and placement within the company. Salaries range from $8.50 an hour to as much as $31.25 an hour.

SELECTION

 Applicants should be juniors or seniors by the start of the internship, though younger applicants shouldn't be discouraged—a few "exceptional" freshmen and sophomores are accepted every year. Majors preferred include science (chemistry, biology, biochemistry, pharmacology, physiology, etc.), engineering (including chemical, industrial, electrical, mechanical, and environmental), production/operations management, information technology–related majors, finance, accounting, marketing, and human resources. The brochure lists "a strong academic record" and "outstanding communication skills" as essential requirements. International applicants authorized to work in the U.S. are eligible.

APPLICATION PROCEDURE

 Abbott recruits nationwide at selected campuses. Students whose campuses aren't visited by Abbott representatives may send a resume (including GPA) indicating field of interest. Resumes are accepted between September and March 1. Early submission is recommended. Resumes are scanned into a computer database and are made available to all business areas. Top candidates are granted telephone interviews and/or on-site visits. Applications are completed at the time of interview.

OVERVIEW

 In early May, students already selected to be summer interns at Abbott Laboratories receive a handbook in the mail. Containing program background such as a calendar of events, maps of Abbott facilities and the surrounding area, a description of housing accommodations, suggestions for what to bring, and reference phone numbers, the handbook prepares interns for the vast range of experiences to be had at Abbott. By the end of the summer, a mixture of projects, lab tours, and workshops will have provided interns with a whirlwind education in health care—an industry whose products help improve as well as save lives.

FOR MORE INFORMATION . . .

■ Abbott Laboratories
College Relations
Department 39K, Building AP51
200 Abbott Park Road
Abbott Park, IL 60064-3500
(847) 935-3888
www.abbott.com

ACADEMY OF
TELEVISION
ARTS & SCIENCES
®© ATAS/NATAS

SELECTIVITY	🔍 🔍 🔍 🔍 🔍
Approximate applicant pool: 1,100 Interns accepted: 30	

COMPENSATION	💲 💲
$2,500–$3,000 stipend	

QUALITY OF LIFE	🌴 🌴 🌴
ATAS activities; intern party; mentors	

LOCATION(S)

Los Angeles, CA

FIELD

Television

DURATION

8 weeks
Summer

PRE-REQS

Undergrads; graduate students; recent graduates

DEADLINE(S)

March 15

What could Mr. Rogers, Pamela Anderson, and the avuncular host of A&E's *Biography* have in common? Truth be known, they all lust after the same woman.

Who is this enchantress, you ask? She is the 15-inch golden statue signifying television's highest honor: the Emmy Award.

The mastermind behind "Emmy" and her eponymous awards is the Academy of Television Arts & Sciences, the nation's largest organization representing the television industry. Established in 1946, the Academy has a membership of more than 10,000 television professionals. Although best known for organizing the Emmy Awards, the Academy also works on a host of other projects to enhance the appreciation of television. It sponsors the ATAS Foundation Library (part of the USC Cinema-Television Library), an extensive collection of television books, memorabilia, photographs, and scripts, as well as the ATAS/UCLA Television Archives, where a multitude of TV programs are preserved, and new ones are added regularly. The Academy also sends its members to lecture at campuses across the country through its Visiting Artists Program, sponsors contests for young filmmakers, holds a yearly Faculty Seminar for teachers, and publishes *Emmy* magazine and *Debut*, its educational programs and services newsletter.

DESCRIPTION

As part of its dedication to cultivate future TV professionals, the Academy of Television Arts & Sciences has an internship program that succeeds in providing some of the best training in the business. An impressive 75 percent of previous Academy interns move on to prime jobs in television. Alumni of the program include Emmy award-winning art directors

for *The Bold & The Beautiful* and *Days of Our Lives*; an executive producer for *Star Trek: Voyager*; a senior V.P. of production at Universal Pictures; a production executive of made-for-TV movies at Paramount Network TV; a director of creative affairs at Walt Disney Network TV/Touchstone TV; and a director of current programming at 20th Century Fox.

ATAS currently offers well-financed internships to young people from across the country in 27 categories: Agency; Animation: traditional; Animation: computer-generated; Art Direction; Broadcast Advertising & Promotion; Business Affairs; Casting; Children's Programming/Development; Cinematography; Commercials; Costume Design/Supervision; Development; Documentary/Reality Production; Entertainment News; Episodic Series; Editing; Movies for Television; Music; Network Programming Management; Production Management; Public Relations & Publicity; Sound; Syndication; Television Directing: single camera film; Television Directing: multi-camera film/videotape; Television scriptwriting; and Videotape Post-Production.

What distinguishes an ATAS internship is that interns are not merely slaves to the photocopier, as is so common in entertainment internships. Interns are paired with hosts who match their interests, from costume design to scriptwriting. Former ATAS interns confirm that intern hosts do not treat their interns as temporary secretaries. The amount of training interns receive is comparable, according to past interns, to the first few months in an entry-level position in the television industry. Although interns are expected to have some knowledge of their hosts' field when they come onboard, many interns feel that by the end of their summer they have acquired "a quantum leap in skills and knowledge" about their particular field. Says Price Hicks, the Emmy award-winning producer and long-time internship director, "There's no guarantee of job placement, but having been an Academy intern says something to most people in this town."

The Academy works so hard to ensure that interns have rewarding experiences that it's difficult to find a program alumnus who was disappointed. One intern found herself at a documentary film company that had never worked with ATAS interns before and didn't seem to know quite how to take advantage of her abilities. She was stuck at a desk answering phones instead of doing the production assistance and research work she had expected, and was frustrated at the prospect of eight weeks of secretarial duties. But the Academy responded rapidly

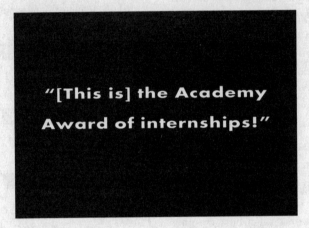

"[This is] the Academy Award of internships!"

to her complaints, and within 24 hours she was transferred to another, more experienced host. She now says she had an excellent summer.

Interns receive half of their stipend after the first four weeks of the program and the other half at its conclusion. Those interns whose permanent residences are outside Los Angeles County are given an additional $500 to assist with transportation and housing costs. Candidates for the internship program should note, however, that they may need further financial assistance to offset their summer expenses. A number of former interns who couldn't live at home during the summer feel that that they didn't fully anticipate the costs of independent living in the Los Angeles area, and urge those who haven't previously lived by themselves in southern California to "calculate your expenses carefully" well before the start of the internship.

There are some scintillating perks that accompany an Academy internship. ATAS gives free passes to first-run film screenings at the Academy Theater, and honors its interns at a massive midsummer party, the 300+ guest list which includes intern hosts, previous interns, ATAS Governors, and a sprinkling of industry bigwigs. Interns also bring home a copy of the latest publication of *Debut*, the annual newsletter by the Academy's Education department. *Debut* describes intern activities, details Academy programs, and informs interns and Academy members of former interns' accomplishments. In addition, interns attend special functions in their hosts' organization, which can range from departmental get-togethers to company-wide events like exclusive screenings of their company's latest productions. "There's definitely some glamour if you want it," reports one intern. "This is the TV business after all."

Intern alumni are assigned to current interns from the same field of interest through the Academy's Mentor Program, which can help interns deal with everything from living in the City of Angels to networking and otherwise navigating the waters of the professional world. Interns report that their mentors provide invaluable guidance, both during the program and afterward. "I'm still in touch with my mentor," says one program alumnus, "He's very generous with his connections—and has helped me land my last two jobs in the business."

Interns with various interests may be posted in several divisions during the summer. One internship alumna worked in the marketing division of Jim Henson Productions during the first month of her internship, and then spent the final four weeks immersed in their creative affairs division. The experiences were quite different. In marketing, she worked on a single project, the competitive analysis of a Henson preschool show, for which she received training in market research. She not only made a presentation of her efforts to the division after just four weeks, but her work was published in the department's booklet at the end of the summer. Her role in the creative affairs division, on the other hand, entailed writing summaries of unsolicited project proposals received from outside the company. Consequently, she found herself working on a variety of development and pre-production analyses.

New technology has created career paths in the TV and film industries that provide tremendous opportunities for students with technical and computer-related talents. With computer-generated animation featured in many productions and dominating such full-length films as *Antz* and *A Bug's Life*, the Academy stresses the importance of its internships in this area. One intern with Sony Pictures Imageworks says that the "wonderful training department" improved and added to his skills to such an extent that he was offered a job by SPI at the close of the summer. Within two weeks of the start of his internship, he was doing pre-production modeling for Sony's film *Stuart Little*, had been trained on new software, and was trusted with projects he could work on independently. After eight weeks, he had worked or met with members of the art department, software writers, visual effects technicians, digital character animators, and a host of others at Sony who considered him "just another member of the team."

Many interns find it difficult returning to school after a "totally technicolor" summer in the Academy's program. Whether or not interns are committed to pursuing a career in their internship category when the summer is over, many past interns say that the experience began and enriched their professional lives, as well as their resumes.

SELECTION

 Candidates for the ATAS internship program must be current full-time students or recent graduates (i.e., an applicant can not have graduated prior to January 1 of the year *prior* to their internship). International applicants are eligible *only* if they are pursuing a degree at a college or university in the United States. Successful applicants usually major in advertising, art, business, cinema, English, journalism, law, marketing, music, theater arts, or TV/Film, though candidates may be pursuing a degree in any field. Interns usually have had previous experiences that demonstrate their interest in a particular field relating to the television industry. The internship director stresses that, considering the professional challenges ATAS interns face, applicants with "a high level of maturity," "decent grades," and "focus" are preferred.

APPLICATION PROCEDURE

 The completed ATAS internship application must be received by March 15; this is not a rolling admission program, so applications sent "at the eleventh hour" will be accepted. Candidates can find the current official Academy application flyer at their college or university's career center or communications, film, journalism, or television department. The official application flyer will only be available from January through March of the year in which the applicant intends to intern. Application flyers can also be acquired by contacting the Academy directly or visiting the ATAS website: www.emmys.org.

Typically, candidates must submit a cover letter (with a permanent address and phone number), a resume, an approximately 300-word essay detailing professional aspirations, an official college transcript, three letters of recommendation, and the number and title of the category to which application is being made. Several categories request appropriate additions to the application, such as demo reels, portfolios, scripts, etc. The Academy urges applicants *not* to send additional materials. Category panels of eight to ten ATAS members evaluate the applications, choose three finalists per category, and send questions to the finalists with a request for videotaped responses. All of the finalists' entry materials are then sent to the host, who selects the winning intern in his or her category. Previous interns urge those considering an Academy internship not to fail to apply because they feel intimidated. The level of effort required just to be considered for an internship, explained one former intern, is designed to measure a candidate's interest in the industry.

OVERVIEW

 It isn't hyperbole when a former intern likened being awarded a place in the ATAS internship program to receiving "the Academy Award of television internships." The ATAS internship offers a uniquely powerful platform from which to launch a career in the notoriously competitive field of television. As internship director Price Hicks observes, "If you want to work in this business, then going through this program should dramatically improve your chances."

FOR MORE INFORMATION . . .

■ Academy of Television Arts & Sciences
Student Internship Program
5220 Lankershim Boulevard
North Hollywood, CA 91601
(818) 754-2830
www.emmys.org

Any die-hard *Melrose Place* fan knows that advertising is a world where Amanda Woodward-types parade around in short skirts, blackmail is an easy way to get promoted (or just as easily fired), and catfights are the common denominator. But just how close does Melrose's famed D&D Advertising come to telling it like it is? Not even close, according to those in the know. "Don't believe what you see on *Melrose Place*," admonished one intern. And he's right. Ask any real-life advertising employee what life at an agency is like and she will paint you a picture far different from the gilded portrayals Hollywood dishes out. Advertising is a professional industry expected to uphold ethical standards both in and out of the agency, a concept not included in the *Melrose Place* lexicon. No one works harder to foster a positive image for the advertising industry than the American Association of Advertising Agencies (AAAA).

AAAA is the national trade association for 525 agencies with more than 1,245 offices nationwide. Its "Creative Code," first adopted in 1924, undertakes to promote high ethical standards among its members. Its roster boasts agencies like BBDO Worldwide, Saatchi & Saatchi, Young & Rubicam, J. Walter Thompson, and Leo Burnett, to name just a few. Because these agencies are in business to help their clients wage the battle of the brands on TV and radio, in magazines and mailings, on roadside billboards, and now on the Internet, AAAA endeavors to make that fight a clean one.

DESCRIPTION

In 1973, AAAA established the MultiCultural Advertising Intern Program (MAIP). Its mission: To attract multicultural students to the advertising business for a summer and get them to stay for a lifetime. How is it doing in 2000? Mission accomplished. Today, over 60 percent of MAIP interns who seek careers in advertising go on to top agencies like Saatchi & Saatchi, Young & Rubicam, and DDB Needham. One former intern was recently hired as managing director of Spike Lee's new agency, Spike/DDB.

The program accepts 75 to 100 interns in the Account Management, Broadcast Production, Media, Art Direction, Copywriting, Print Production, Research, and Traffic departments at more than 25 sponsoring agencies across the country. Each department presents

SELECTIVITY	
Approximate applicant pool: 300–400 Interns accepted: 75–100	

COMPENSATION	$ $ $
$350/week (may vary by agency); 60 percent of housing expenses; 60 percent of one round-trip ticket between intern's home or school and internship site.	

QUALITY OF LIFE	
Seminars; Tours/field trips; Intern receptions; Alumni Association	

LOCATION(S)	
New York, NY; Chicago, IL; Detroit, MI; Bloomfield Hills, MI; San Francisco, CA; Los Angeles, CA; Philadelphia, PA; Boston, MA; Cleveland, OH; Dallas, TX; Seattle, WA; Portland, OR; Santa Ana, CA	

FIELD	
Advertising	

DURATION	
10 weeks Summer	

PRE-REQS	
Minority undergrads and grad students—see Selection	

DEADLINE(S)	
January 26	

BUSYWORK
LOW MEDIUM HIGH
OLDMAN & HAMADEH
METER

interns with a different set of responsibilities. "Account Management interns may go to client meetings and do a lot of research," said AAAA's Manager of Diversity Programs. "A Broadcast Production intern may spend time working in the editing studio and going to voice-overs and music houses." But keep in mind that no two agencies are exactly alike. Media interns at different agencies may not share the same degree of responsibility. While AAAA provides agencies with a list of goals and desired responsibilities, the agencies are the ones who structure an intern's time on the job.

One Account Management intern at Bates USA worked on the Miller Genuine Draft account. He presented the latest sales figures and predicted future sales patterns during a meeting of his account group. "It was fast-paced and intense. The account was in review and each new article of bad press turned up the pressure a notch," he said. "I assumed I would be chained to a copy machine. My team rarely handed down their busywork to me." Not so of every intern's experience, though. "Most of my work was busywork," said another intern in Account Management at Hill, Holiday. "But even from that I was able to learn things. When I photocopied, I read the materials. From that I learned how to fill out work order forms and [write] copy."

Interns in the Copywriting and Art Direction departments help develop the ideas, images, and words that go into commercials and ads. Besides strong writing skills, copywriters need to have, as an intern put it, "a love affair with words." Art directors are the ones who add visual flair to those words to create the finished product. When these two departments work in sync, the end result creates a lasting impression in the minds of consumers. Ever seen the "Just do it" ads for Nike, or the thirst-inducing "Got Milk?" commercials? These departments are the creative force that brings those ads and commercials to life. The messages get out thanks to the Media department. Media department interns assist staff in positioning the commercials and ads in places where the right people will see them. According to the Manager of Diversity Programs, the Media department is an exciting place for interns. "The Media department is [a] department that tends to get a lot of perks," she said. "Interns will probably be invited to luncheons and get free tickets to things like movies and other events." But interns in any department are bound to meet with some amount of busywork in exchange for the perks. Like the intern who took advantage of her copy-machine command post to actually learn some tricks of the trade, a Research department intern found some valuable down-time in his busywork. "It could be really intense. I had a lot of responsibility, and the busywork I did have gave me a chance to catch my breath…sometimes."

During the internship, office accommodations for interns vary widely from agency to agency. Some interns sit in cramped cubicles while others score a corner office overlooking Manhattan. Seldom, however, will interns find themselves without access to phones and computers. And office supplies at some places are free-flowing, said one intern. Despite what some interns may lack in office space, they gain in living accommodations. AAAA subsidizes housing and travel expenses for all interns who do not live in the area of their internship. AAAA pays 60 percent of both housing costs and a round-trip between the intern's home and their internship site. This is a big perk when you consider the chance interns have to explore a new city and work in a fast-paced, creative industry. But be forewarned—interns are not able to choose the city in which they intern, nor can they choose the agency or department at which they work. Interns can request to be assigned to a particular city or department but there are no guarantees. Placement decisions are made by AAAA and participating agencies based on availability.

Weekly seminars are a highlight of the internship experience for interns in New York, Chicago, and Detroit. Seminars give interns a chance to get together to compare notes, visit top agencies in their area, and rub elbows with important industry professionals. During a seminar in New York last year, interns watched the filming of a *Days*

> Besides strong writing skills, copywriters need to have, as an intern put it, "a love affair with words."

of Our Lives episode. "We try to make [the seminars] creative," said the Manager of Diversity Programs. One intern felt that the seminars were informative but focused too often on the personal grievances of a few individuals. "These problems were addressed to the group in meetings. If anything, it looked like AAAA could have devoted more time to deal with these problems privately."

To top off their whirlwind experience, interns in New York, Chicago, Detroit, Boston, San Francisco, and Los Angeles are also treated to a graduation ceremony in their city at the end of the summer. Although it does not involve as much pomp-and-circumstance as a college ceremony, interns can expect dinner and, depending on the host, some entertainment. A sponsoring agency last year turned their cafeteria into a wine and cigar bar and hired a stand-up comedian. Intermixed with all the wining and dining of graduation, interns give final presentations on why an agency should hire them.

True to its mission to bring more students of color into advertising, AAAA recently enlisted the help of past interns now working in the industry to establish the AAAA Alumni Mentor Association. Still in its early stages, the Alumni Mentor Association seeks to bring together current interns with a professional mentor. Mentors answer questions about the real world of advertising and serve as a source of inspiration for interns who dream of following in their footsteps. Said a former intern, "I think it's a wonderful idea. My mentor has been a fountain of information. Everyone deserves to have someone like that." There are Alumni Mentor Associations in New York, Chicago, and Detroit, and AAAA hopes to introduce one on the West coast soon.

SELECTION

 College juniors, seniors, and graduate students with a minimum GPA of 3.0 are eligible to apply. The program seeks multicultural students of all majors who demonstrate a commitment to a career in advertising. Applicants must be citizens or permanent residents of the United States and be willing to relocate to agency offices located across the country. The majority of interns are placed in AAAA sponsoring agencies in Chicago, Detroit, New York, and San Francisco, but past interns have also worked in Boston, Cleveland, Dallas, Los Angeles, Portland (Oregon), and Seattle.

APPLICATION PROCEDURE

 Candidates must submit the MAIP application, two essays, two letters of recommendation, and a current college transcript by the January deadline. Applicants pursuing art direction or copywriting may also submit creative samples. Although colorful and inventive applications could help "maybe" candidates gain a spot in the coveted "yes" crowd, the Manager of Diversity Programs says "there's no need to go overboard. You still have to meet all the program requirements." During the interview process, semifinalists are interviewed in person—no exceptions—by a member agency in their area who acts as a liaison for AAAA. After the interview process, AAAA compiles all the information on its applicants, puts this information in binders based on applicants' department(s) of interest, and sends these binders off to agencies. Sponsoring agencies then rank their intern choices, AAAA works some magic, and… presto! A match.

OVERVIEW

 What better place for multicultural students to get up close and personal with the world of advertising than through an American Association of Advertising Agencies internship. As an organization dedicated to increasing the presence of multicultural professionals in advertising, AAAA provides its interns with practical work experience, invaluable contacts, and the skills they need to get hired. Says an intern: "AAAA interns are well-known and respected [in the industry]." Throw in the weekly seminars, subsidized housing and travel costs, and the thrill of having a new city as your stomping ground, and it is little wonder that so many AAAA interns say "yes" to careers in advertising.

FOR MORE INFORMATION . . .

■ Multicultural Advertising Intern Program
American Association of Advertising Agencies
Attn: Tiffany R. Warren
405 Lexington Avenue, 18th Floor
New York, NY 10174-1801
(800) 676-9333
(212) 573-8968 (fax)
www.aaaa.org/initiatives

You are a physician, kidnapped by Federal DEA agents in April 1990 for your alleged participation in the torture-murder of a DEA agent. Though held in prison for over two years, you didn't do it. Who will fight for you?

Your teeth have that "not-so-fresh feeling" that says your six months are up; it's time to go in for a cleaning. However, the dentist turns you away, refusing to treat an HIV+ client. What recourse do you have?

You are a 911 operator, female, who has been sexually harassed repeatedly and, indeed, stalked by a male LAPD officer. In spite of a long pattern of sexual harassment inside the LAPD, the department does not take action with regard to your complaint. Whom are you going to turn to for help?

The ACLU, American Civil Liberties Union, that's who.

Founded in 1920 and headquartered in New York City, the ACLU is the nation's oldest and largest nonprofit organization devoted to preserving and expanding Americans' rights and freedoms. Filing more lawsuits than any other organization in the United States with the exception of the federal government, the ACLU covers a litany of social concerns that reads like a who's who of hot topics facing the nation today, from affirmative action and the rights of minors to drug legalization and the abolition of the death penalty.

DESCRIPTION

 Internship opportunities are available at virtually every ACLU office—New York City headquarters, the Washington National Office, regional offices in Atlanta and Denver, and more than 50 affiliate offices

in every state in the nation. In New York and Washington, 10 to 15 interns in each office work in the Legal Department or on the following ACLU projects—AIDS, Lesbian/Gay Rights (law students only), Women's Rights (law students only), and Workplace Rights in New York, and National Security Studies/Litigation, Privacy and Technology, Capital Punishment, Church-State, Reproductive Freedom, Public Education, Publicity, and National Prison in D.C. Other ACLU outposts take one to two interns each in legal or administrative ca-

SELECTIVITY	
Approximate applicant pool: 100 Interns accepted: 2 in NY HQ; many more nationwide	

COMPENSATION	$
None	

QUALITY OF LIFE	🕴 🌴 🕴
Brown-bag luncheons with ACLU directors; casual dress; limited resources	

LOCATION(S)	
New York, NY (HQ); Atlanta, GA; Washington, D.C.; and more than 50 affiliate offices in almost 50 states	

FIELDS	
Law; Public policy	

DURATION	
10 weeks Summer, Fall, Spring	

PRE-REQS	
Undergrads; recent college grads; law students	

DEADLINE(S)	
Summer .... March 1　　Fall .... September 1 Spring .... November 1	

pacities, depending on need. Interns are usually paired with ACLU attorneys, who assign projects and tasks involving factual and legal research, trial preparation, and/or asylum applications relevant to the attorney's caseload.

Most undergraduates at the ACLU, particularly those in the affiliate offices, intern in Field/Legislative and Development. Responsible not only for fielding questions posed to the ACLU about its activities, Public Affairs interns also perform much of the case research that is the backbone of the ACLU's successes. Helping to develop studies on the impact of legislation, case law, and public policy, Public Affairs interns investigate case issues, pursue relevant interviews, and gather critical data. After weeks of research, one intern found her signature pieces of statistical work and graphical representations in the ACLU newsletter, a quarterly update of the organization's goings-on across the country. Another gained an understanding of international law when she researched school prayer policy in other countries and compared it to American law.

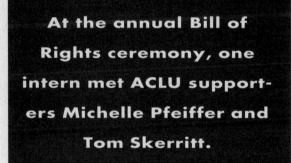

At the annual Bill of Rights ceremony, one intern met ACLU supporters Michelle Pfeiffer and Tom Skerritt.

In Field/Legislative, interns assist the department with its overarching mission—grassroots organizing and galvanizing of the general public with regard to issues and policies that affect them. As staff members, interns research and produce briefing sheets on pertinent community issues, write lobbying letters, and develop speech materials. These documents are then used by the ACLU in testimony to government and at community-based forums that update members on current issues facing the organization. One intern in Los Angeles experienced the ACLU in full swing during the Proposition 187 brouhaha concerning illegal immigrants, education, and health care, as well as the "three strikes, you're out" legislation. "I couldn't believe the tension in the room as the voting was being tallied," she said. "It was such a disappointment [to see Prop 187 succeed]. I didn't expect to lose."

Because the ACLU is a nonprofit organization, Development is probably one of the most crucial departments at the organization. Responsible for helping to raise funds for operating costs, Development interns "do whatever [their] creative minds can come up with" to help bankroll the ACLU's efforts: drafting letters, organizing, and staffing fund-raising events, for example.

The ACLU also fields an externship/summer law-clerk program for law students. Students accepted into this program have the opportunity to "get their hands dirty" in the brunt of the ACLU's work. Gaining first-hand experience in the broad spectrum of civil liberty cases in which the ACLU is involved, externs and law clerks help research and prepare legal materials and fact investigations, interview clients and witnesses, handle expert witnesses, and occasionally accompany lawyers to court. Past externs and clerks have worked on such cases as *AIDS Project Los Angeles v. Western Dental Services, Incorporated* (discrimination against HIV+ patients in dentistry), *Robalino v. City of Los Angeles* (sexual harassment and stalking), and *Tailfeather v. County Board of Supervisors* (indigent health care). Due to the nature of the ACLU's cases, however, many of them are long, drawn-out court battles, meaning that most externs/law clerks do not get to see their cases go to trial. One lucky clerk who did get to accompany his attorney-mentor to a Federal circuit court said, "It was an incredible experience. I knew exactly where my months of research had gone and what it could do for our client. Immensely gratifying." There are times, though, when extern/clerks' work can be disheartening. Underfunded, underpaid, understaffed, and overworked, as the common complaints go, externs/clerks find strength in "knowing that they are doing good for someone, somewhere." That, along with a "very friendly and supportive" staff, carries them through to the next task. "It's like a family there," said one.

"[ACLU staff members] were there to help me out when I needed it."

If you are looking for a corporate atmosphere, a private cubicle with computer and fax, and a company gym, this internship is not for you. As a nonprofit, the ACLU funnels funds wherever they can do the most good for the largest number of people—that is, to ACLU cases. While tangible perks are essentially nonexistent, interns cite as invaluable the "experience" and "the knowledge that you are working for the defense of civil liberty across the country." Moreover, the ACLU offers weekly brown-bag lunches, where interns talk with ACLU lawyers about current cases, the issues involved in the cases, and the positions and strategies necessary to win the cases. One intern described the lunches as "the best of both worlds—I got hands-on experience in the field and a weekly discussion seminar about what other people were doing." The ACLU also hosts an annual Bill of Rights ceremony, where one intern met Michelle Pfeiffer and Tom Skerritt, both ACLU supporters.

The ACLU provides what has been affectionately called a "comfortable mess." In constant motion, with a multitude of issues and policies at hand at any one time, the ACLU is "controlled chaos," giving the feeling that "something really important, something historical, could happen at any moment, and people are rushing to get to that moment in time, constantly trying to keep on top of things." As for personal working space, you must "make your own," but there seems always to be an open desk, a table in the law library, or a couch available. Dress is very casual, a bonus for many of the interns initially expecting to pay a visit to George Zimmerman for formal business attire. Aside from court appearances, jeans and shorts seem to be the wardrobe of choice; comfort is the key.

While generally satisfied, ACLU interns make a few complaints. Some interns feel the pinch from the lack of pay: "If you're considering the ACLU, you'd better have a big bank account" or "generous parents."

SELECTION

 ACLU interns are as diverse as the issues represented by the ACLU (one intern was a fine arts major; another was studying biological sciences). The internship program is open to undergraduates, recent college graduates, graduate students, and college grads of any age. "The ACLU doesn't care about your major, they care about you," said one intern. "What the ACLU wants in a person is the ability to pick up the ball and run with it." Creativity, initiative, assertiveness, a certain degree of autonomy, and the ability to see a project through to the end are highly valued. Because of the competition involved in some of the larger offices (read: New York and Washington, D.C.), "you'd better have a damn good reason for wanting to be there," said one intern. "They don't want resume-fillers; they want people genuinely interested and excited about the ACLU's work and who want to do what the ACLU does." Such interns are attracted to the ACLU for personal reasons, for "pro-humanity...fighting for people, for the underdog, for people without a voice." But people getting the most out of the experience are generally open-minded about the cases that come across their doorstep, despite personal convictions. International applicants are eligible.

APPLICATION PROCEDURE

 You must apply directly to the ACLU office in which you want to intern. The deadline to submit materials is March 1 for summer positions, September 1 for fall, and November 1 for spring. Interns should send a resume, a cover letter, and a nonfiction writing sample of about five pages directly to the office of interest. There is no application form. While phone interviews are acceptable, the ACLU prefers to interview intern candidates in person.

OVERVIEW

 While the ACLU's individual offices and internship programs are as diverse as the cities in which they are located, they all share the same ACLU shingle. Wherever you may go, therefore, the ACLU is by far, in the words of one intern, "the best place to be—at the forefront of a lot of the legal issues of today, improving society, making a difference, sleeping better knowing that someone's fighting those battles for us. This is one of the few places where you can get up in the morning, pick up the newspaper, get angry about some story, and do something about it."

FOR MORE INFORMATION . . .

■ Apply directly to your local ACLU office. Call (212) 549-2610 for information on interning at the corporate office.
Internship Coordinator
125 Broad Street
18th Floor
NY, NY, 10004
www.aclu.org/students/intern.html

SELECTIVITY	🔍🔍🔍
Approximate applicant pool: 75 Interns accepted: 9–13	

COMPENSATION	$
Some stipends available	

QUALITY OF LIFE	🏃🏃🏃
Theater tickets; comfortable offices; long workdays	

LOCATION(S)	
San Francisco, CA	

FIELD	
Theater production	

DURATION	
August/September to June/July (Theater Season)	

PRE-REQS	
Undergrads; college grads of any age	

DEADLINE(S)	
April 15	

George M. Cohan is quoted in Fred J. Ringel's book, *America as Americans See It*, as saying: "When you are away from old Broadway, you are only camping out." If we are to believe Mr. Cohan, then for the past quarter-century San Francisco's American Conservatory Theater has been staging one hell of a camp-out. A.C.T. is one of the nation's largest regional companies, each year offering nine productions performed by some fifty actors. The theater's annual audience of more than 450,000 enjoys a mix of classic drama, contemporary plays, and new work by emerging talents. Recent seasons have included such shows as *Uncle Vanya*, *Rosencrantz and Guildenstern Are Dead*, *Pygmalion*, and both parts of *Angels in America*. A.C.T. also runs an acting conservatory of seventy full-time students and is the only American theater independent of a college to have a fully accredited conservatory.

DESCRIPTION

The A.C.T. internship requires a serious commitment. Mirroring A.C.T.'s theater season, the internship spans a good eight months, from late summer to the following spring. Moreover, interns work long days, sometimes running over ten hours long, which precludes any other employment. But for those willing to make this kind of sacrifice, valuable training in theater arts awaits. Interns are placed in the following departments: Production Management, Stage Management, Properties Construction, Scenic Design, Sound Design, Lighting Design, Makeup and Wig Construction, Costume Rentals, Costume Construction, and Production Department (on a show-by-show basis).

When the internship program began in 1976, the first department to hire interns was Stage Management. The theater's nerve center, Stage Management is charged with supervising rehearsals and procuring stage-related materials from other departments. Working alongside the stage manager and an assistant stage manager, interns are integral members of the Stage Management team. For four mainstage productions during the season, they carry out a range of tasks, such as making prop and costume lists, communicating messages between departments, and helping out at rehearsals. It's a superb education in the dynamics of stage management, but one that is extremely grueling. Said one intern: "Rehearsal hours varied. Some days we worked from 10:00 A.M. to 7:00 P.M., others from 1:00 P.M. to 11:00 P.M. You had to be ready to deal with irregular rehearsal hours, and do so six days a week." If it's any consolation, the time Stage Management interns spend at A.C.T. earns membership credits toward joining the Actor's Equity Union.

There's plenty to do at A.C.T. besides stage management. Lighting Design interns draft designs for special effects, maintain records, attend production meetings, and, on occasion, act in the repertory designer's absence. Then there's Makeup and Wig Construction, where interns work in the repertory makeup shop on special projects under the direction of A.C.T.'s wigmaster (really; that's her title). Those with a background in drafting are eligible to work in Scenic Design, where interns draft and make scale models of the sets and props used in A.C.T. shows. Says one Scenic Design intern: "One of the shows I worked on was the *Imaginary Invalid*. The prop I helped design was quite complicated. I did working drawings of a piece of moving furniture that [the protagonist] used as his whole world—attached to the contraption were a toilet, medicine cabinet, and chair."

Those with a passion for costumes will be happy to know that A.C.T. hires interns for its Costume Rentals department. Interns in Costume Rentals help maintain A.C.T.'s huge stock of costumes as well as rent outfits to corporations, other theaters, and the public. Because most of the work in this department involves renting costumes to outside parties, interns have little to do with the shows A.C.T. is producing. It's no tragedy, though—interns have a lot of fun helping the public put outfits together. "People would call us needing clothes for a costume party. We'd work with them to find the right getup. It could be virtually any theme: a Victorian tea party, a Renaissance dinner—even a party spoofing *The Andy Griffith Show*. Whenever business is slow, interns in

> **Interns in Costume Rentals help the public put together outfits of virtually any theme: Victorian, Renaissance . . . even "Andy Griffith."**

Costume Rentals are encouraged to work on creating a new costume for A.C.T.. "[The rental staff] allowed us to design and build any costume we dreamed up—so long as it was not already in stock. Using A.C.T. materials and machines, I built a harlequin costume made out of lycra."

Until 1989, A.C.T. operated out of San Francisco's historic, 1,400-seat Geary Theater, but the rattle and roll of the Loma Prieta earthquake left the theater badly damaged. In the best sense of "the show must go on," A.C.T. performed in three rented theaters located throughout the city until its return to the renovated Geary Theater in early 1996. A.C.T. headquarters is situated on the top three floors of a high-rise building in downtown San Francisco. Housing A.C.T.'s administrative offices and conservatory, headquarters is a "triumph of open-space planning," with floor-to-ceiling windows and patios that are often the site of Friday afternoon cookouts. The "shop-oriented" departments—Scenic Design and Costume Rentals—are separate from headquarters, located in the "fringe" neighborhood of Potero Hill.

Even if A.C.T. interns were given a lot of perks, the season is so busy that there probably wouldn't be enough time to enjoy them. Nevertheless, there is usually opportunity to take advantage of a few privileges. Interns receive complimentary tickets to A.C.T. productions, including preview and opening night performances. Tickets to the Berkeley and San Jose Repertory Theater productions are also available, as A.C.T. has a reciprocal arrangement with these theaters. And then there's always the chance of running into William Hurt, John Turturro, Jean Stapleton, or any other of the big-name actors who grace A.C.T.'s stage.

SELECTION

 Because A.C.T. internships span several months, they are typically undertaken by undergraduates on a leave of absence from school or by recent graduates. But the intern coordinator stresses that the internship is open to college graduates of any age; past interns, for example, have included a few older participants looking for a career change. Most departments require previous experience in their area of production, but an enthusiastic and sincere personality may compensate for a lack of experience in some cases. Says one A.C.T. stage manager: "My top priority in hiring Stage Management interns is finding people who are supportive and caring. Previous stage management experience is not essential—I can teach anyone to do a prop list." International applicants are eligible.

APPLICATION PROCEDURE

 Applications are due April 15. The application process is nothing short of arduous, requiring one to submit (1) a personal statement (500 words or less), (2) an application form, (3) a resume, (4) three letters of recommendation, and (5) a $10 nonrefundable application fee. Additional materials may be required by specific departments. After the intern coordinator sorts applications based on the department preferences they list, departments select a few applicants to interview, either in person or by phone.

OVERVIEW

 This is an exciting time to be at the American Conservatory Theater. Though A.C.T. has been known over the years for its traditional approach to theater, its new artistic director, Carey Perloff, is infusing energy into the 33-year-old regional theater. In her inaugural season as director, which *The New York Times* said "[shook] up unshockable San Francisco," she jostled the establishment by staging the Vatican farce *The Pope and the Witch* and a production of *The Duchess of Malfi*, which featured the duchess in full frontal nudity.

A.C.T. interns get to go along for the ride, experiencing A.C.T. at a time of ferment and controversy, while working closely with top professionals as they design, manage, and construct the repertory pro'uction. But the experience is not for the lazy or luxury-loving. Interns must be willing to roll up their sleeves and work a rigorous schedule no different from that of permanent staff. One intern said it best: "If your interest is theater, you'd be hard pressed to find a more practical and intense experience."

FOR MORE INFORMATION . . .

■ American Conservatory Theater
   Susan West, Internship Coordinator
   30 Grant Avenue
   San Francisco, CA 94108
   (415) 834-3200

Bork. Gingrich. Kristol. Kirkpatrick. Perle. Cheney. Novak. D'Souza...

A hypothetical cast list for *Revenge of the Republicans*?

Not even close.

These are but some of the intellectual and political superstars in residence at Washington's American Enterprise Institute. Founded in 1943, AEI is a think tank committed to research on government policy, economies, and American politics. Although it calls itself a nonpartisan institution, few would disagree that AEI has a preponderance of conservative thinkers. From the "brilliant and bearded" Robert Bork to young gun Dinesh D'Souza (author of the bestseller *Illiberal Education*), AEI is a bastion of red-blooded conservatism. But to be fair, the institute is not without its share of centrist scholars, most notably Bill Schneider and Norman Ornstein, both telegenic purveyors of political wisdom.

DESCRIPTION

 AEI interns are assigned to a "resident scholar" who is conducting research in one of three areas: economic policy, foreign and defense policy, or social policy and politics. In their applications, interns may specify a preference for a particular area and even a scholar within that area. Positions are also available in Publications Marketing, Marketing, Public and Media Relations, Publications, Seminars and Conferences, and *The American Enterprise* magazine.

Interns working under the aegis of a scholar typically report to the scholar's research assistant for daily assignments. Responsibilities vary with each scholar, but certain tasks are common to virtually every

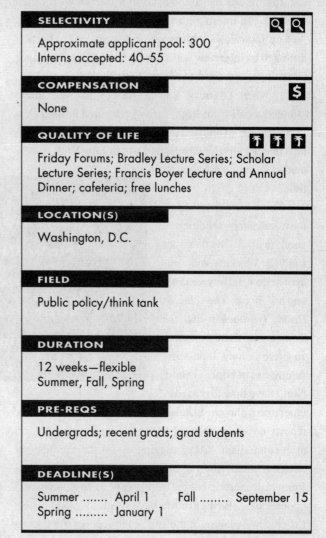

SELECTIVITY		
Approximate applicant pool: 300 Interns accepted: 40–55		
COMPENSATION		$
None		
QUALITY OF LIFE		
Friday Forums; Bradley Lecture Series; Scholar Lecture Series; Francis Boyer Lecture and Annual Dinner; cafeteria; free lunches		
LOCATION(S)		
Washington, D.C.		
FIELD		
Public policy/think tank		
DURATION		
12 weeks—flexible Summer, Fall, Spring		
PRE-REQS		
Undergrads; recent grads; grad students		
DEADLINE(S)		
Summer .... April 1 Fall .... September 15 Spring .... January 1		

intern. The least exciting of these is clipping newspaper articles on subjects relevant to the scholar's research. "Every day I looked through several newspapers and cut out articles of interest to my [scholar]. It wasn't the world's most challenging work, but it made me savvy of world affairs."

The bulk of interns' time is spent carrying out research for their scholar's upcoming books and papers. Research responsibilities include canvassing the in-house library for books and journals, telephoning academics and government agencies for information, and photocopying and filing articles for later use. Interns are also asked to arrange interviews for their scholars. An intern with Dinesh D'Souza, for example, "set up interviews with noted professors and experts… arranged an interview with [former NAACP lawyer] Jack Greenberg and tried to arrange one with Rosa Parks." Once, when D'Souza was in New York, the intern "fielded a call from *Nightline*, who wanted to interview D'Souza that evening… [A]fter making a bunch of anxious phone calls, I tracked him down in New York, and he made it on *Nightline* in time."

Sometimes interns perform research requiring a good deal of synthesis or analysis. Working with resident fellow Jeffrey Gedmin on his book *The Hidden Hand: Gorbachev and the Collapse of East Germany*, an intern skimmed and wrote summaries of books Gedmin didn't have time to read. Another intern, this one in Judge Bork's camp, wrote summary reports on issues relevant to Bork's upcoming book on multiculturalism. "After digging up all the articles and books I could find on political correctness, I wrote a summary report describing the views of its proponents and opponents… [Bork] liked to have several viewpoints, so I'd give my analysis at the end of the report. Whether he used it or not is a different story."

When a scholar's book is near completion, interns often help with fact-checking and proofreading. An intern who double-checked the footnotes on Joshua Muravchik's *Exporting Democracy* said: "It wasn't as tedious as I expected. In the process, I got to read [Muravchik's] compelling argument on why the spread of democracy should form the core of American foreign policy." Working with Robert Hahn on a paper about energy policy, another intern read over the statistics Hahn cited and made sure everything added up. "I definitely had input in the project," he said. "If something didn't make sense when I reworked the numbers, I pointed it out and [Hahn] checked it out." All this work doesn't necessarily go unacknowledged: Interns are happy to find that their efforts are occasionally credited in the finished book or paper. Said an intern whose work designing charts and graphs was acknowledged in a paper published by the *Yale Law Journal*: "It's nice to get credit for the work I did. It's tangible evidence of my tenure at AEI."

Part of the attraction of an AEI internship is the proximity it affords to renowned conservative thinkers. "If you're conservative," said an intern, "there's no better connection to the higher world of political thought." Scholars are surprisingly accessible: "All you need to do is make an appointment, and you can go in and talk to a scholar. If you're writing an honors thesis for school, this is your chance to interview a great mind on the subject." But some of the best interaction with scholars occurs at random. "No matter where you go," said an intern, "there's potential for engrossing conversations. I remember running into a scholar in the bathroom and having a great conversation on foreign policy." Even elevators are fertile ground for contact with scholars. On the first day of the Clarence Thomas–Anita Hill hearings, one intern had an elevator ride she won't soon forget. "Behind me in the elevator was Judge Bork, who said to me, 'Now I'm no longer the most maligned Supreme Court nominee.' [A]fter he exited the elevator, Jeane Kirkpatrick got on. She was talking with a friend about how to pronounce 'harassment' and turned to ask my opinion. I suggested it was pronounced 'HAIR-as-ment,' not 'her-ASS-ment.'"

If chance encounters aren't enough, there are more formal ways of tapping into scholars' wisdom. Interns are invited to attend the weekly, hour-long Friday Brown Bag Lunches, where scholars speak off-the-record about their latest research. Past luncheons have been hosted by virtually all of AEI's leading lights, including Robert Bork, who often reviews the past Supreme Court term, and Norman Ornstein, who loves to lecture on voting trends. Interns may also attend the Bradley Lecture Series, a set of 10 evening lectures given by "non-AEI people who are influential in the world of ideas"; George Will, Alan

> **"Judge Bork said to me, 'Now I'm no longer the most maligned Supreme Court nominee.'"**

Bloom, and Charles Krauthammer are but a few of the distinguished Bradley lecturers of recent memory. AEI also provides a dinner each semester in which scholars give a lecture. Newt Gingrich gave the lecture at the intern dinner during the summer of 1999.

Located across the street from the National Geographic Society and a stone's throw from the Farragut North Metro stop, AEI is in a "good business-oriented neighborhood." A "big brass AEI" adorns the outside of the organization's "modern but tacky" 12-story building. AEI occupies the building's top three floors, which are decorated with photos of the scholars and posters of AEI-published books. The library prominently displays an old campaign poster of Richard Nixon and Dwight Eisenhower, prompting one intern to quip, "You know you're not in Berkeley anymore." Interns are assigned a cubicle or "some sort of cubbyhole" within easy reach of a phone and an IBM computer. The top floor boasts a subsidized cafeteria with "decent sandwiches and burgers" as well as a fancy dining room for scholars and staff.

SELECTION

 The program is open to undergraduates of any level, recent graduates, and graduate students. Candidates from any academic background are welcome to apply, but those interested in working with economic-policy scholars should have some knowledge of economics. International applicants are eligible.

APPLICATION PROCEDURE

 The deadline for the summer internship is April 1; for the fall internship, September 15; and for the spring internship, January 1. The intern coordinator says these deadlines "are not set in stone"; she often accepts applications submitted a week or two after the deadline. Required materials include a cover letter (specifying preferred program area or department), resume, transcript, and writing sample of at least 500 words. After screening the initial applicant pool, the intern coordinator or a research assistant interviews a selection of finalists, either in person or by phone.

OVERVIEW

 Think of the AEI internship as offering students two golden keys. The first key, used by all interns, provides access to excellent research opportunities with distinguished scholars and gets students into a wealth of AEI-sponsored seminars and lectures. The other key, used only by interns with initiative and ambition, opens up other additional opportunities for research and networking. In one intern's words, "You'll never again be around such an all-star cast of great conservative thinkers. This is your chance to take the bull by the horns—knock on a few doors and get to know a few of these gurus."

FOR MORE INFORMATION . . .

■ American Enterprise Institute
Director of Human Resources—Internships
1150 Seventeenth Street NW
Washington, DC 20036
(202) 862-5800
www.aei.org

ARTHUR ANDERSEN

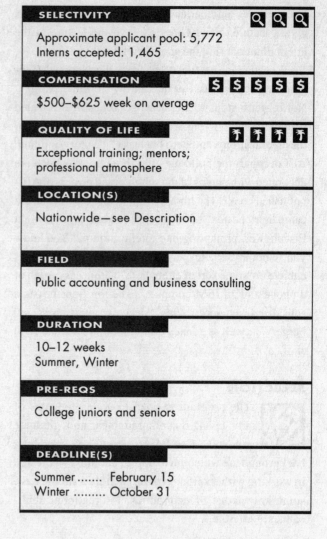

These days, accounting majors can learn the tricks of the trade from several introductory accounting textbooks, written by such big-wheel professors as Kaplan, Anthony, Weygandt, and Horngren. But back in the early 1910s, students of accounting in the United States were limited to only one available textbook, appropriately titled *Complete Accounting Course*. While this book represents an important accomplishment in the history of accounting, its author is less known for his writing than he is for establishing a small Midwestern accounting firm in 1913. That author's name is Arthur Andersen, and the company bearing his name has since grown into a global powerhouse.

Arthur Andersen's vision is to be the partner for success in the new economy. The firm helps clients find new ways to create, manage, and measure value in the rapidly-changing global economy. With world-class skills in assurance, tax, consulting, and corporate finance, Arthur Andersen has more than 70,000 people in 84 countries who are united by a single worldwide operating structure that fosters inventiveness, knowledge-sharing, and a focus on client success. Since its beginning in 1913, Arthur Andersen has realized uninterrupted growth, with 1999 revenues of more than $7 billion. Arthur Andersen is a business unit of Andersen Worldwide.

DESCRIPTION

Since around 1950, the Arthur Andersen Internship Program in the U.S. has offered students entry-level positions in Audit & Business Advisory Services, Tax & Business Advisory Services, and business consulting. "The office's goal... is to replicate the same experiences and situations that a new hire would have during the first year," says the coordinator. The following offices routinely hire both winter and summer interns: Albuquerque, Atlanta, Baltimore, Birmingham, Boston, Charlotte, Chicago, Cincinnati, Cleveland, Columbus, Dallas, Denver, Detroit, Greensboro, Hartford, Houston, Indianapolis, Kansas City, Lancaster, Long Island, Los Angeles, Louisville, Memphis, Miami, Milwaukee, Minneapolis/St. Paul (the Twin Cities), Nashville, New Jersey, New Orleans, New York, Oklahoma City, Omaha, Philadelphia, Phoenix, Pittsburgh, St. Louis, San Antonio, San Francisco, San Jose, Seattle,

SELECTIVITY
Approximate applicant pool: 5,772
Interns accepted: 1,465

COMPENSATION
$500–$625 week on average

QUALITY OF LIFE
Exceptional training; mentors; professional atmosphere

LOCATION(S)
Nationwide—see Description

FIELD
Public accounting and business consulting

DURATION
10–12 weeks
Summer, Winter

PRE-REQS
College juniors and seniors

DEADLINE(S)
Summer .... February 15
Winter .... October 31

Stamford, Tampa, Tuscon, and Washington, D.C.

Interns in Tax help out with about a half-dozen projects, from researching inquiries of the local and state tax boards to preparing corporate, partnership, and individual tax returns. Interns in Tax might also work on appraisal and valuation projects, helping to price clients' tangible and intangible assets, and in corporate tax consulting, where they help improve clients' corporate structures and accounting methods in order to minimize corporate taxes. One Tax intern worked on a client's 1040—a number dreaded by most hardworking Americans. Looking over the client's broker reports, he made sure that the client had reported every dividend but had not reported nontaxable items such as principal payments or interest from tax-exempt securities. "I sifted through her files and prepared the work papers for Text Processing, the department that fills out the actual return." In the course of their projects, interns often do research at Arthur Andersen's libraries. "One of our clients was being audited by the State Franchise Tax Board," explained an intern. "The board disagreed with us over the nature of the company's income, and I spent some time at the library searching for relevant legal cases." Tax interns are also involved with the creation of compensation packages. "An executive we were representing wanted to improve his cash flow so that he could pay off his mortgage. We came up with lots of options to present to his board of directors, and I created a spreadsheet that enumerated all the options' present values," recalled an intern.

During audits, Arthur Andersen reviews the books and accounts of its clients—from manufacturers and hospitals to advertising firms and professional sports teams. Assigned to audit teams off-site at clients' offices, each Audit intern examines one or more sections of the balance sheet—cash, accounts payable, stockholders' equity, etc.—to "obtain reasonable assurance about whether the financial statements are free of material

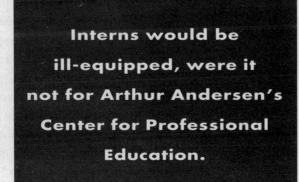

Interns would be ill-equipped, were it not for Arthur Andersen's Center for Professional Education.

misstatement," as Andersen writes in nearly every annual report it audits. Interns also work on Audit projects in operational consulting (concerned with enhancing client business practices to improve profitability), information-systems consulting, bankruptcy recovery, and litigation support. One Audit intern, assigned to a manufacturing firm, worked on inventory: "The firm had already counted the items in its plants, so I went through Andersen's checklist to make sure the firm's book-to-physical adjustment was correct." Another Audit intern was assigned to a large cosmetics company. After setting up Andersen files according to the special procedure for labeling and indexing, he audited cash, investments, and fixed assets. "I had to do everything from interviewing employees about processing cycles to getting summaries of bank accounts," he recalled. Required to investigate the company's refrigerated warehouse in Pennsylvania, he remembers "putting on a heavy down jacket" and counting boxes of vials in a –40°F cold room. "Boy, was I freezing," he said.

During the winter, interns experience what the accounting industry calls the "busy" season, the three months preceding two IRS due dates: March 15 for corporate tax returns and April 15 for individual returns. "You'll definitely work on more projects during the winter," affirms an intern. "Companies are busy doing year-end inventories, and individuals are scrambling to get their returns in on time."

In between assignments, there's a bit of busywork—looking up industry statistics on CD-ROM, arranging files, photocopying, and running documents from one department to another. For most interns, these tasks are assigned during the first week or two of the program. "I got the feeling it was a test of sorts," surmised an intern. "The managers want to see if the photocopies you make and the files you put together are complete and legible. After all, clients look at these things, and if you prove that you're careful, managers will give you great assignments." Besides gaining more responsibility, interns who are happy to attend to some busywork will familiarize themselves with the office. "You may be the lowest man on the totem pole for that one week or so," said an intern, "but it's a great way to start before you're thrown in the fire. In addition to learning how to use the computers and how to create a Lotus spreadsheet, you meet your co-workers."

Since most interns have yet to experience classes in audit or advanced tax (senior-year courses), one might think that they are unprepared to tackle their assignments. "What I learned in school was helpful the first two days only," confirmed an intern. Actually, interns *would* be ill-equipped, were it not for the organization's Center for Professional Education, hidden away in St. Charles, Illinois. At this former women's college, the firm trains interns, new hires, and employees to the tune of $340 million every year, an amount that allows Arthur Andersen to remain the world's leading employee educator. Audit interns go to the St. Charles school for two weeks. Tax interns spend a few days at the firm-wide orientation and the Tax Intern Leadership Conference. Both groups live in well-furnished dorm rooms, most without TVs, so ample time to socialize with peers is available. Instructed by experienced partners and managers, interns learn the various ins and outs of Arthur Andersen accounting procedures—balance sheets, audits, and tax returns. "Without the training," said an Audit intern, "it would have been much more difficult to grasp Arthur Andersen's standard procedures for audits. I would have had to ask my manager too many questions, distracting him from his job, and we would have had to bill the client for that extra time."

Informally known as the "campus," the Center for Professional Education comprises 151 acres on the Fox River. Though the center offers standard city conveniences such as a hair salon, a dry-cleaning shop, a cafe, and a bar, there's plenty of rusticity to balance them out: a vast woods, the Fox River, and jogging trails snaking through the forest. After the usual 8-hour day of classes, interns may release their tensions by playing basketball, tennis, volleyball, softball, or soccer. The center also offers two putting greens and a fitness center informally known as the "sweat shop." Moreover, shuttles go into St. Charles and Chicago, approximately 45 minutes away, every weekend.

Back at the office, the training continues. Interns are often assigned not a single mentor but a team of them—usually a partner, a manager, and two seniors. During and after every assignment, a member of the team sits down and evaluates the intern's work. "The first time I did 'receivables'—probably the toughest of the balance sheet items to do—my senior walked me through it," said an Audit intern. "[A]nd every time I finished a section, the senior would look over it and make suggestions or corrections." Even when mentors take interns out to lunch (a common occurrence) or mingle among interns at office social functions, they help interns augment their education. "By talking to the bosses, I learned everything from the value of networking to the kinds of work partners and managers do," explained an intern.

Because they work mainly in the office, Tax interns sit at their own cubicles, two to an IBM PC. Audit interns, on the other hand, are almost always off-site; they share areas of workspaces and phones with other interns. Professionalism mandates that all employees, including interns, wear business-appropriate attire. However, most Andersen-ites know when to shed their business attire for more casual garb; employees get together to socialize at happy hours, watch major league baseball games, and exercise at the local gym.

Interns' salaries vary from site to site. Depending on experience, overall economy of the city in which the office is located, success of the office, and cost of living, each intern may make anywhere from $500 to $625 per week on average, plus overtime pay. "A person working in New York will obviously make more than one working in Seattle," says the coordinator.

SELECTION

The internship is open to college juniors and seniors. Generally, a minimum of 12 units of accounting coursework is required for applicants. While many interns are accounting majors, students in finance, economics, and other various majors sometimes participate in the program. International applicants are eligible.

APPLICATION PROCEDURE

The deadline is February 15 for summer and October 31 for winter. Note that the number of students applying to the summer internship is much higher than the number applying for the winter positions. Therefore, your chances might be higher if you can take part in the winter session. Working through campus placement offices, recruiters interview students throughout the country. Candidates whose campuses aren't visited by Arthur Andersen should send a resume and cover letter to the desired office; only in the event that applicants are unable to locate a specific office's address and phone number should they contact Arthur Andersen's headquarters. Top candidates are invited to the offices for interviews; long-distance applicants are flown in.

OVERVIEW

Since 1981, *Public Accounting Report* has polled accounting department chairs at over 100 U.S. colleges and universities. For twelve consecutive years, the professors have ranked Arthur Andersen number one overall for new graduates starting careers in public accounting. What holds true for recent graduates holds true for undergraduates. Arthur Andersen interns receive an in-depth introduction to public accounting and tax, full exposure to partners and managers, intimate contact with clients, and an impeccable level of training. Moreover, completing the internship dramatically improves interns' chances of being offered permanent employment: approximately 80 percent of interns return to the firm.

FOR MORE INFORMATION . . .

■ Contact the Director of Recruiting in the office where you would be most interested in working. A listing of our office locations can be found on www.arthurandersen.com under "Locations."

hat is Aspen best known for? Is it champagne skiing, the Aspen Music Festival, and Jack Nicholson?

Maybe, but it's also a place where mountain lions and elk roam the three surrounding wilderness areas, a place where golden eagles and big horn sheep grace the high country. In fact, the city that *Snow Country* magazine rated as the second best ski resort in the United States is located within a natural paradise. Positioned at the edge of Hallam Lake at an elevation of 7,900 feet is the city's wildlife sanctuary, a naturalists' mecca called the Aspen Center for Environmental Studies (ACES).

Since its founding in 1968 by Aspen resident Elizabeth Paepke, the staff at the private, non-profit ACES has been educating people about stewardship, conservation, and environmental ethics. Managing the 25-acre Hallam Lake preserve and another 175-acre natural area, ACES offers naturalist-guided walks and natural history programs for both adults and children. It also runs the Environmental Learning Center, which houses the Scott Field Laboratory, Pinewood Natural History Library, Gates Visitor Center, and a bookstore known as the Den.

SELECTIVITY	🔍🔍🔍🔍
Approximate applicant pool: 200 Interns accepted: 12	

COMPENSATION	💲💲
$125/week plus housing	

QUALITY OF LIFE	🌴🌴🌴🌴🌴
Free housing; mountain surroundings; Free nature classes	

LOCATION(S)
Aspen, CO

FIELD
Environment/nature

DURATION
12–13 weeks Summer

PRE-REQS
College juniors and seniors; recent grads; grad students

DEADLINE(S)
March 1

DESCRIPTION

Interns' responsibilities include just about everything related to maintaining the center: outdoor maintenance (i.e., planting trees, repairing the boardwalks around the marshy preserve, and pulling non-native plants), handling the nonreleasable raptors for birds of prey programs, doing informal interpretation as the "on-site" naturalist in the visitor center, teaching natural history classes for kids and adults, and leading nature walks.

During the summer, the center offers more than a dozen programs taught by interns, so interns may find themselves doing anything

BUSYWORK
LOW MEDIUM HIGH
N/A
OLDMAN & HAMADEH
METER

from leading a group of adults on a sunset walk by Hallam Lake to taking children on an animal tracking adventure. The walks and programs make visitors aware of the unique flora and fauna of the Rocky Mountains, as well as the fragility of the ecological communities in which they live. "Our overall goal is to spread environmental awareness," said an intern, "not by bombarding visitors with a bunch of facts, but by encouraging them to look around and reexamine their relationship to plants and animals."

Interns describe their role in the center's environmental mission as "challenging" and "intense." Often spending several hours each week in the center's library, they research such topics as Rocky Mountain wildflowers, endangered species reintroduction, and porcupines. Working with a list of scheduled programs and classes, interns use their expertise and creativity to design and carry out the rest. For example, a recent intern taught a four-hour kids' class called "Marvelous Mud," incorporating marsh-land insects and other invertebrates, plaster track casting, and face painting with sandstone mud.

Once a converted barn, ACES was razed in 1988 to build the Environmental Learning Center, which affords spectacular views of the lake. One room inside the new center is home to a bookstore and information desk. Another room contains a laboratory, equipped with microscopes, and an indoor trout stream stocked with Colorado cutthroat trout. Next to the lab is the center's library, and across the hall is a large classroom used for some of ACES' programs.

> An intern in charge of the indoor exhibits took care of the center's collection of Madagascar hissing cockroaches, a tarantula, western box turtles, and a boa constrictor.

Outside of the lab, at the edge of the upper pond, is a small hatchery for propagating Colorado cutthroat. In conjunction with the Colorado Division of Wildlife, ACES is one of only a few sites attempting to propagate, and eventually release into the wild, Colorado's only native trout. Connecting the upper pond to Hallam Lake are a couple of spawning beds from which breeding trout are taken each spring to gather fertile eggs. Interns are actively involved in most every step of the process from caring for the eggs to cleaning the troughs where fry live and raising brine shrimp to feed the young trout.

Behind the center is the Birds of Prey building, home to a handful of hawks, eagles, and owls. All of the birds have permanent injuries and are not releasable to the wild—for instance, the golden eagle has a repaired broken wing that does not fully extend. "We have her here for teaching purposes, to show people the beauty—and importance—of the eagle," said an intern.

One would expect a wildlife preserve of ACES' size to contain all sorts of animal and plant species, and the Hallam Lake area is definitely no disappointment. A rich diversity of shrubs, wildflowers, and trees cover the meadows, forested areas, and wetlands. Prairie smoke, bog orchid, and bittersweet nightshade are a sampling of wildflowers, while balsam poplar, blue spruce, and cottonwood make up a few of the tree species. Hikers often spot wild animals, including muskrats, beavers, mule deer, coyotes, red foxes, yellow warblers, pine martens, weasels, and the occasional black bear, from the trail's edge or the marsh overlook platform. Waterfowl flock to the lake in large numbers, where visitors can observe Coleman's snipe, green-winged teal, kingfishers, and great blue herons. Bird Hollow is the place to see woodland birds such as brown creepers, juncos, and downy woodpeckers. And two riverside platforms afford overlooks to the Roaring Fork River.

Other wildlife is best viewed from higher vantage points. Aspen Mountain, at an elevation of 11,300 feet, is the place to go. To get there, visitors ride the gondola to Aspen Mountain's nature tour and information desk at the sundeck. The desk is staffed by ACES interns, and is equipped with a telescope that allows visitors to scan the surrounding alpine peaks for bighorn sheep, elk, mountain goats, bear, and eagles.

ACES interns are housed in accommodations within walking distance of the center, and convenient to the amenities of the town. Half of the team lives in the U.S. Forest Service bunkhouse, a comfortable lodge with all the modern accouterments. The other half of the intern crew is housed in a condominium owned by ACES, located at Hunter Creek. Aspen has two supermarkets, and interns often cook and eat together, forming friendships that the center's "communal atmosphere" encourages.

The center of the town of Aspen is only a five-minute walk from the ACES preserve. A mecca of endless cultural activities, Aspen offers the Aspen Music Festival, Dance Aspen, the Jazz Festival, and a variety of free concerts and performances in downtown parks. A wide array of outdoor sports and activities—mountain biking, rock climbing, and kayaking, for example—is also easily accessible. Home to wealthy residents, Aspen boasts expensive restaurants and bars. "Although they're expensive, the clubs are always filled with college-aged people having a fun time," said an intern. "And there are lots of cool, inexpensive places to dance and eat, too." Aspen's glitzy reputation attracts a bevy of celebrities, many of whom are impassioned about the environment. "Al Gore once stopped by ACES," said an intern, where he signed copies of his book, *Earth in the Balance*. "Jack Nicholson's house is across Hallam Lake; and Chris Evert Lloyd enrolled her two kids in our Little Naturalist program last year."

As part of the benefits ACES interns receive, they may take a one-day Naturalist Field School free of charge as a paid day of work. Interns become the professor's special assistant for the class they have chosen to take, allowing for more in-depth learning and discussion with the professor. The dozen or so courses that are offered teach interns different ways to appreciate nature and render even the most ardent city-slicker more environmentally aware. Students learn how to identify tundra plants and their unique communities in "Plants of Independence Pass" or how to fish in "Fly Fishing" at the nationally known Roaring Fork River.

SELECTION

 College juniors and seniors as well as recent graduates and graduate students are eligible to apply, though the bulk of interns have received college degrees by the start of the internship. The center strongly prefers students who are majoring in the natural sciences (i.e. biology), environmental studies, interpretation, or related fields. Knowledge of Rocky Mountain flora is helpful and first-aid certification is required. Following the internship, some interns are offered the opportunity to stay on at ACES to work as a winter naturalist or as an environmental educator.

APPLICATION PROCEDURE

 The deadline is March 1. Applicants need to obtain an application packet either by requesting one to be sent through the mail, or by printing it from ACES' web site. The application consists of a form to fill out (address, education, references, etc.) and a list of ten questions to answer, and requires a current resume. After the interpretation director sifts through applications, top candidates are interviewed over the phone.

OVERVIEW

 Espousing informed and active participation in the protection of natural resources, the non-profit Aspen Center for Environmental Studies recruits interns to help educate the public about the environment. Working at Hallam Lake, interns are exposed to Rocky Mountain plants and animals, riparian flora and fauna, and birds of prey such as golden eagles, hawks, and owls. After spending a summer leading interpretive walks, learning animal rehabilitation, and teaching children about the environment, interns are sure to leave with a newfound appreciation of nature and teaching.

FOR MORE INFORMATION . . .

■ Aspen Center for Environmental Studies
100 Puppy Smith Street
Aspen, CO 81611
(970) 925-5756
(970) 925-4819 (Fax)
acesone@rof.net
www.aspen.com/aces

THE ATLANTIC GROUP

So you want a job in rock and roll, but your guitar playing is better suited to Eddie Munster than it is to Eddie Van Halen.

Have you ever thought about getting involved behind the scenes? Working for a record company is an excellent way to combine an interest in music with non-musical skills. If you want to be "in the know" about the latest releases and upcoming concerts, while using your creativity to market developing artists, Atlantic Recording Group's College Marketing Internship Program may just be playing your tune.

Founded in 1948, Atlantic Records is part of the Warner-Elektra-Atlantic (WEA) partnership. Under Atlantic's umbrella are several smaller labels that are managed by Atlantic. Music legends like Ray Charles; Crosby, Stills, Nash, and Young; Led Zeppelin; and Aretha Franklin helped Atlantic to grow in the 1960s and 1970s, while newcomers Collective Soul, Hootie and the Blowfish, and Brandy are at the heart of the label's current roster.

SELECTIVITY	🔍 🔍 🔍 🔍
Approximate applicant pool: 1,000 (Interns), 500 (Reps) Interns accepted: 115–120 (Interns), 45–50 (Reps)	

COMPENSATION	$
Interns—None; Reps—Approximately $85–$150/mo for reimbursement of expenses	

QUALITY OF LIFE	🌴 🌴 🌴
Free CDs & concert tickets; possible travel on concert tours (Reps); flexible hours (Reps)	

LOCATION(S)
Interns—Los Angeles, CA; New York, NY; Nashville, TN; Reps—39 colleges in 27 states (AZ, CA, CO, CT, FL, GA, IL, IN, KS, LA, MD, MA, MI, MN, MO, NV, NJ, NY, NC, PA, SC, TX, UT, VT, VA, WA, WI)

FIELD
Music

DURATION
Interns—8–12 weeks (Summer, Fall, Spring); Reps—One year minimum; Part-time available

PRE-REQS
See Selection

DEADLINE(S)
Interns ..... Rolling; Reps ...... Open

DESCRIPTION

Like most record companies, Atlantic accepts interns in a variety of departments year round. Approximately ninety interns work at Atlantic's New York headquarters in Publicity, Promotion, Artist Relations, Product Development, Video Promotions, and Advertising. Summer interns may also work in Accounts Payable, Royalties, Legal Affairs, and Customer Service. In Los Angeles, twenty-five interns work primarily in Promotions, Media, Artist Relations, and Artists and Repertoire. The Nashville office uses one or two interns in administrative positions.

Publicity interns answer phones, organize CDs and artist bios for mailing to magazines and newspapers, and clip album and concert reviews, as well as artist interviews, from newspapers. In Advertising, interns tag Atlantic ads in magazines, organize magazine advertising rate information, mail out ads to publications, and occasionally assist the Art Department with the design of ads. Promotion interns communicate with and organize mailings of promotional CDs and marketing materials to radio stations. Interns in Artist Relations assist with the company's effort to ensure that current artists are happy and well cared for, while Artist and Repertoire (A&R) interns assist in the label's acquisition of new artists.

The jewel of Atlantic's internships, though, is the College Marketing Internship Program. Created in 1992 as part of Atlantic's Progressive Marketing Department, this program was designed to increase visibility and awareness of Atlantic's developing artists on a street level by implementing low-cost "direct-to-consumer strategies." Interns, called "college reps," work on and around their campuses promoting Atlantic artists—especially those artists with a college-age or more "alternative" appeal. Reps create and implement their own marketing strategies, with minimal supervision but tons of support and encouragement from the home office in New York.

College reps acquire hands-on experience in several key areas of the music business, including retail sales, marketing, publicity, concert promotion, and artist relations. Reps work closely with local retailers to promote Atlantic artists by putting up posters in record stores, coordinating in-store promotions and planning "listening parties," at which local press, promoters, and retailers have a chance to preview new releases. Reps also work with local newspapers and magazines to advertise and review artists' concerts and new releases. When an artist gives a concert or makes an in-store appearance, the local rep ensures that the event is well-publicized, that there are plenty of CDs in stores, and that the venue is suitably decorated with posters, or "flats." Happily, Atlantic encourages reps to meet the artists on tour dates to show the label's local support.

While a few ideas for events and promotions come from the label, reps are allowed to discover their own strengths and encouraged to "go with it." A rep with a knack for public relations, for example, might focus on the print media while someone with a taste for sales might spend more time with a retailer. Reps ascertain the most effective types of promotion and most marketable styles

> So you want a job in rock and roll, but your guitar playing is better suited to Eddie Munster than it is to Eddie Van Halen.

of music for their territory and plan projects accordingly. Atlantic is quick to provide any and all materials needed to follow through, including promotional CDs, posters, and artist photos and bios.

The amount of time a college rep spends on projects varies greatly from week to week. Although most interns average 15 to 20 hours per week, Atlantic is more interested in encouraging good, creative, successfully implemented ideas than enforcing any sort of strict time commitment. To some degree, the timing of projects and the number of activities in which an intern is involved are determined by the timing of activity at the label. When an artist releases a new album or plans to give a local concert, the workload and time investment for the rep increase. During slower periods, reps try to keep interest for Atlantic artists high in their community. Said one rep: "I liked the flexibility of hours, which allowed me to work on projects in the evenings and on weekends." Other reps commented that Atlantic was very sensitive to school workloads.

While it is not required, some reps travel in conjunction with their work. One rep attended music industry conventions in Austin, Los Angeles, and New York. Though reps pay their own way to meetings in other cities, several interns suggested that attending conventions and visiting Atlantic's offices are excellent ways to network with other Atlantic employees as well as with other people in the music business.

No music industry internship would be complete without a healthy supply of free merchandise, and Atlantic's college rep program is no exception. Reps receive plenty of free CDs, concert passes, and other promotional items, like key chains and stickers. Moreover, because projects are often planned around tour and CD release dates, reps are always kept in the loop with hot insider artist information. Opportunities also arise to meet artists on local stops. One rep was excited to meet Nine Inch Nails backstage at a local concert.

Although reps need not interact with the home office on a daily basis, most call New York once or twice per week to check in. College reps must also check their email account a few times per week. On a monthly basis, reps submit a fairly detailed (but informal) report on their progress. No other written work is required, but interns are encouraged to keep a scrapbook of their work (including, for example, press clippings of events they coordinated) for prospective employers upon graduation from college.

College reps are not paid for their work, but they are reimbursed for any internship-related expenses they may incur. College credit is available through most colleges. One rep admitted: "It would be nice to get paid, but this is a golden opportunity." Of note, some students interning in other departments in the New York office have arranged for a small hourly wage; the Los Angeles office offers only college credit.

Reps who choose to continue in the music business after graduation can often find positions within the industry. According to Linn, "The College Marketing Department will assist graduates who have displayed outstanding effort in finding jobs in the music industry. So far, every graduating college rep who wanted to work in the music industry has landed a job at places like Atlantic, Elektra, Interscope, Jam Productions, Sub Pop, and Virgin." Those who decide against pursuing a career in the music business do not leave empty-handed: the business experience reps earn and communication skills they develop through this program are highly transferable to other careers.

SELECTION

 The college rep program is open to college freshmen, sophomores, and juniors as well as first-year graduate students. Atlantic prefers individuals who can stay with the program for a year or more since the success of many of the reps' projects will depend on developing good relationships with local press and retailers as well as fine-tuning projects and efforts through some trial and error. The New York, Los Angeles, and Nashville internships are open to high school students and undergraduates.

Atlantic looks for individuals who are creative, outgoing, motivated and who don't take themselves too seriously. People who are typically the best fit for Atlantic's internships are those "into music and interested in the music industry." While there is no expectation that applicants will know the ins and outs of the business before beginning the internship, many for the college rep program do already have some knowledge of the music industry or are at least somehow connected to the local music scene. International applicants are eligible.

APPLICATION PROCESS

 For the college rep program, applicants must submit a cover letter and resume. Phone interviews are the norm.

Applicants for internships in the New York, Los Angeles, or Nashville offices must submit a resume and cover letter directly to the office in which they're interested in working. Part- and full-time positions are available and become open throughout the year in many departments. In-person interviews are conducted with department heads. Applicants must obtain a letter from their college verifying that they will receive academic credit for the internship.

OVERVIEW

 While there is much to be learned by interning in the home office of a record company, for some people interested in the music industry, temporarily relocating to New York or Los Angeles for an internship is not realistic. Atlantic's College Marketing Internship Program allows college students to gain hands-on experience in the music industry while staying in their immediate geographical area. College reps set their own schedules and are bound only by their own creativity and amount of time and effort they want to spend on projects. For those considering a career in the music business after graduation, this program not only provides important experience but also a key network in the industry.

FOR MORE INFORMATION . . .

■ Internship Coordinator
Atlantic Records
1290 Avenue of the Americas
New York, NY 10104
(212) 707-2000

■ Human Resources
Atlantic Records
9229 Sunset Blvd.
Los Angeles, CA 90069
(310) 205-7450

■ Atlantic Nashville
20 Music Square East
Nashville, TN 37203
(615) 733-1880

■ College Marketing Internship
Atlantic Records
1290 Avenue of the Americas
24th Floor
New York, NY 10104
(800) 677-7027

■ www.atlantic-records.com

BATES USA

SELECTIVITY	🔍 🔍 🔍 🔍
Approximate applicant pool: 75 Interns accepted: 5–10	

COMPENSATION	$
None; Possible bonus stipend	

QUALITY OF LIFE	🏃 🏃 🏃
Chrysler Building; Quality cafeteria; Two interns to an office; Intern Answer Book	

LOCATION(S)	
New York, NY	

FIELD	
Advertising	

DURATION	
10–12 weeks; 2 to 4 days/week Summer, Fall, Spring	

PRE-REQS	
College juniors and seniors; grad students Overall GPA 3.0 or higher	

DEADLINE(S)	
Rolling	

It seems simple enough: Distinguish a brand from its competitors and the public will buy it. But not until Bates USA (formerly Backer Spielvogel Bates) coined the term "Unique Selling Proposition" in the late 1970s did the idea become a hot topic in advertising agencies across the country.

As defined by Bates USA, a unique selling proposition (USP) is "a motivating idea, uniquely associated with a particular brand, residing in the mind of prospects." USPs have been the basis for a number of enormously successful ad campaigns, including those by Bates USA—"Soup is Good Food" (Campbell's Soup) and "Get Out of the Old, Get into the Cold" (Miller Genuine Draft)—as well as those by other firms—Bozell's "Something Special in the Air" (American Airlines) and N.W. Ayer's "The Right Choice" (AT&T).

Small wonder that an agency like Bates USA would invent an industry catchword. As the world's fifth largest advertising agency, it's no stranger to leading the pack. Headquartered in New York's Chrysler Building, Bates USA currently holds a roster of over 2,200 clients, including such high-profile companies as Wendy's, Magnavox, Campbell's Soup, Uncle Ben's, and Hyundai Motor America.

DESCRIPTION

All interns at Bates USA are placed in Strategic Planning, the department that researches consumer attitudes and trends. As Bates USA's director of Strategic Planning explained in the 1991 issue of *Casro Journal*, the concept of strategic planning "is based on the understanding of values, attitudes, and behavior that connect the target audience to a particular brand, company, or category. . . . [This] understanding is grounded in research that . . . goes beyond that satisfaction of needs to address hopes, aspirations, and sometimes, even dreams." By gaining insight into what consumers really want, Strategic Planning sets the foundation upon which the rest of the agency's departments can build.

Although there's a modest amount of busywork—"occasional photocopying and faxing"—interns report that it is kept to a minimum. "I was never asked to fetch coffee or pick up laundry. It seemed like I spent most

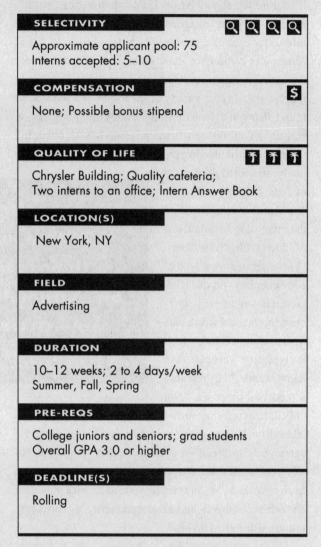

of my day thinking." Question: What do interns spend time thinking about? Answer: The challenging research projects they are assigned during the internship. One intern, for example, analyzed how "quality of life" and "consumer confidence" have changed over the years for the average American. Gathering economic and demographic data from a variety of databases and reports, he found that quality of life has steadily improved while consumer confidence in brand products has declined. His findings contributed to a report that the department eventually presented to a group of *Time* writers.

Another intern studied the increasing popularity of products with private labels. "I investigated what type of consumer buys private label products—[that is,] merchandise labeled with a particular store's name, which is typically cheaper than name brands." His research served two purposes: "Not only did this information help the department keep private labels from hurting clients' business, but it also helped the agency advise clients on when and if they should get into using private labels." He presented his conclusions in the form of a "deck," a slide presentation to the vice president and other executives, and a research paper, "which future interns will follow up on."

Some projects deal less with research on consumers and more with background information for the department. One such assignment had an intern create a report on what experts are predicting for the environment, economy, religion, and other global issues. "I've never worked so hard," she said. "I must have read or skimmed at least fifteen books. I gleaned dozens of predictions from magazines like *The Futurist* and books like *Global Outlook 2000* and *The Art of the Long View*." Another project involved compiling an index of sources from other interns' work "so future interns will know where to look when they start their projects." She found phone numbers and addresses for a wide range of arcane but useful industry associations, from the National Pet Food Association to the Cosmetic, Toi-

letry, and Fragrance Association.

Aiding interns in their research is an extremely powerful tool—GLOBAL SCAN. Developed and used exclusively by Bates USA, GLOBAL SCAN is a database that stores demographic and attitudinal information on consumers from around the world. The data comes from thousands of surveys Bates USA administers to consumers on attitudes, interests, and product usage. With GLOBAL SCAN, one can manipulate information on consumers in innovative ways. For example, an intern used GLOBAL SCAN to track the behavior of pet owners. "From looking at consumer responses to questions like, 'Do you let your dog or cat go anywhere in the house?' I pinpointed which types of people are more apt to treat their pets like human beings. These are the kind of people who would buy a more expensive brand of pet food, and thus are ideal targets for our clients who manufacture high-end pet food."

Because they are limited to just one department, interns would benefit from opportunities exposing them to the other areas of the agency. Said one intern: "Bates USA is a big company. The internship keeps you pretty isolated from the other departments. I would have liked to have spent a day in Media, Creative, and Account Management." Though no such opportunity exists, interns are welcome to attend the informational presentations the Bates USA staff sometimes holds for outside groups. They may also observe focus groups. "It's fascinating to watch the in-house moderator elicit answers from the [focus] group panels. I'd watch behind a one-way mirror and sometimes take notes that the moderator would later look at."

The best internship programs go to lengths to ensure that their interns adjust to life on the job. Bates USA comes through with flying colors in this respect. Interns report that the internship coordinator is an invaluable resource: "She's totally dedicated—she'd drop everything to help us." Moreover, every intern receives an official "Intern

> Aiding interns in their research is an extremely powerful tool—GLOBAL SCAN.

Answer Book," an 80-page spiral book detailing all aspects of the agency and the internship. Want to know Bates USA's newest clients? It's in there. Trouble with the fax machine? Check the "How Do I . . ." chapter. Writing problems? Consult the "Writing Hints" section.

"I work in a landmark," said an intern, and he's right. Bates USA occupies several floors of New York's majestic Chrysler Building, whose sleek Art Deco spire is known the world over. Decked out in gray and maroon colors, the floor where interns work is reportedly "buzzing with activity." Like most ad agencies, some offices are "littered with promotional ornaments"—such as knickknacks from Wendy's and Campbell's Soup as well as "a giant, stuffed M&M." As far as interns' accommodations go, Bates USA deserves kudos, for interns are only two to an office and have a stunning view of New York. And when hunger pangs strike, there's a Bates USA cafeteria that reportedly serves up "good meals for $5."

Bates USA likes to balance work with a few opportunities for play. Once a month, employees congregate after work in a large conference room, where cocktails and a "goodly amount of finger food" is had by all. Moreover, the Strategic Planning department habitually holds a catered picnic in Connecticut. Said one past picnic-goer: "It's a blast. Everyone relaxes and has fun. There was an egg toss. And, of course, there's plenty of Miller Genuine Draft to go around."

Although the program provides no salary, interns who consistently go the extra mile may be eligible for a bonus. Says the coordinator, "Interns who voluntarily arrive early and work late are sometimes given a bonus stipend of about $200. But this policy is not set in stone, and it's applied on a case-by-case basis."

SELECTION

The program is designed for college juniors and seniors and graduate students. Bates USA seeks candidates with "exceptional writing and communications skills" and an overall GPA of 3.0 or higher. International applicants are eligible.

APPLICATION PROCEDURE

Although there are no strict deadlines, the intern coordinator advises summer applicants to apply by late May, fall applicants by late August, and spring applicants by late December. The application process is relatively painless: Simply send a resume and a writing sample. The intern coordinator conducts interviews over the phone or in person. Interns are chosen a few weeks later.

OVERVIEW

Bates USA is a biggie, no doubt about it: It's a big agency in a big skyscraper in a big city. And with challenging projects and unique research tools, Bates USA's internship offers big responsibility, and for most, big satisfaction. Now, who says size doesn't count?

FOR MORE INFORMATION . . .

■ Bates USA
Internship Program
The Chrysler Building
498 7th Avenue
New York, NY 10018
(212) 297-7000
Fax: (212) 297-7761

BERTELSMANN MUSIC GROUP

SELECTIVITY	🔍 🔍 🔍 🔍
Approximate applicant pool: 360 Interns accepted: 30	

COMPENSATION	💲 💲
$5/hour plus $220/month for field expenses	

QUALITY OF LIFE	🌴 🌴 🌴
Promotional freebies; meetings and conferences; possible tour work	

LOCATION(S)	
Several cities nationwide—see Description	

FIELD	
Music	

DURATION	
Ongoing; 1 year to $2\frac{1}{2}$ years; 20 hours/week	

PRE-REQS	
Undergrads and grad students Others eligible—see Description	

DEADLINE(S)	
Rolling	

Mention BMG to students and it brings to mind a record-of-the-month club. Why shouldn't it? Magazines like *Rolling Stone* and *TV Guide* are constantly running ads for the BMG "Eight CDs for the Price of One" offer.

But the BMG Music Club is just the tip of a very large, very successful iceberg. Owned by German entertainment empire Bertelsmann, the Bertelsmann Music Group is composed of a variety of record labels, such as Arista Records, Zoo Entertainment, and RCA Records, as well as BMG Distribution, one of the world's most powerful record distribution systems. Generating more than $2 billion in sales annually, BMG is home to international superstars (Whitney Houston, Kenny G, Annie Lennox, Lisa Stansfield), country favorites (Clint Black, Alan Jackson, Aaron Tippin), rap acts (SWV, TLC, and KRS-ONE), and alternative bands (The Charlatans, Matthew Sweet, and Rollins Band).

DESCRIPTION

Established in 1989, BMG's Alternative Marketing Program hires students to serve as regional marketing representatives; the majority of reps promote the company's alternative (or college-market) artists, but about one-third are assigned to urban and R&B music. Twenty students are spread out among BMG's sales offices, located in Atlanta, Boston, Chicago, Dallas, Detroit, Los Angeles, Minneapolis, New York, San Francisco, Seattle, and Washington, D.C. The remaining students work out of their homes in one of nine "smaller but musically hot cities" such as Athens, GA; Austin, TX; Chapel Hill, NC; Denver, CO; Philadelphia, PA; Portland, OR; San Diego, CA; St. Louis, MO; and Tampa, FL. Home-based interns are loaned a fax machine and receive use of the company's phone card.

Whether based in a sales office or in their homes, interns spend much of their time in the field. Charged with tracking the sales of BMG's alternative artists, interns make frequent visits to record stores. "A big part of the job is checking up on local mom-and-pop record stores and seeing how our artists are selling. I'd find out exactly how many CDs and tapes of an artist were sold and report the numbers back to the local field-marketing manager." Interns also use these "retail visits" to spread the word about BMG bands: "Wherever I went, I handed out lots of stickers, promotional CDs, and concert tickets. I also dropped off 'point of purchase' material like posters and displays. . . . It helped build a relationship with retail stores and get them interested in BMG bands."

Because interns' chief objective is to get alternative artists known to college audiences, they must also visit local college radio stations. As with retail stores, interns track album popularity and spread the word about new acts: "The [radio] stations knew me as the local BMG promotion guy. I'd find out which BMG artists were getting the best listener feedback. And I'd drop off loads of CDs and knick-knacks." Interns are free to dream up promotions with the radio stations. Whether persuading college newspapers to do a write-up on a particular band, giving away CDs and souvenirs at a local club, or planning a special event for students (e.g., a bowling night), interns are constantly publicizing BMG bands.

Besides visiting record stores and college radio stations, interns have a number of other responsibilities. Some interns set up "listening parties," where local press, retail, and radio people meet at a club to hear a new album. At a listening party for The Church's "Priest=Aura" release, for example, an intern rented out a "cool coffeehouse" and "stocked the room with music, videos, and a live psychic." Others arrange publicity activities for a band when it comes to town. For such groups as The Charlatans, Dharma Bums, Straight Jacket Fits, and Box Car, an intern escorted band members to local record stores, where they met the public and signed CDs.

Once interns have proven themselves, they may be allowed to accompany a band on a particular leg of its tour. An intern working out of the Atlanta office got to "go on tour" with The Church, Peter Murphy, Pop Will Eat Itself, and the Hoodoo Gurus. She elaborated: "Sometimes I went to all of the gigs a band was playing in my region; other times I just saw one or two shows. I'd work back-

stage, making sure the right people had [backstage] passes and taking radio and retail people around to meet the band."

Another unique facet of the BMG internship is the chance it gives interns to provide input on new acts. If they come across a promising local band, interns are encouraged to send the manager of Recruiting and Development a demo tape and a memo detailing what makes the band special. The manager then circulates the material to the A&R (or talent scout) departments at BMG-owned labels such as Arista, RCA, and Zoo Records. Although these referrals have yet to lead to a band being signed, the process is beneficial because interns receive feedback about their recommendations. Says the coordinator: "Interns are sent a letter explaining, as is usually the case, why a particular band is not up to BMG's standards. It's a great way for interns to see what discovering talent is all about."

BMG makes a point of having interns participate in regional meetings and important music conventions. Said one intern: "I was always welcome to accompany [the marketing manager] when she hosted a dinner with local retail people. I was definitely in the loop." A few times a year, interns are flown to music conventions around the country, including Jack the Rapper in Atlanta.

BMG has two other internship opportunities worth noting. Recently created, the first program enables ten students to spend the summer interning for BMG Direct, the division that operates the BMG Music Club. Placed at the company's midtown Manhattan headquarters, interns work in Marketing, Graphic Design, Music Product Merchandising, and Finance. The program offers luncheons with executives, a group project, and a generous $350/week salary. The program is open to college seniors only, and the application deadline is rolling.

The other internship opportunity allows interns to spend a semester working for BMG's RCA, Arista, or Zoo record labels. Interns are placed in the usual record-

> One intern said she walked away with "enough promotional posters, stickers, and T-shirts to decorate a small museum."

label departments, including Marketing, Finance, Sales, A&R, Artist Development, and Creative Services. Although no pay is offered, the program is open not only to college students, recent grads, and grad students but also to college grads of any age. Applications are accepted on a rolling basis.

No matter what program they choose, interns are tapped into the unofficial currency of the music industry: free promotional items. Small wonder that interns are inundated with a slew of CDs, concert tickets, and party invitations: "There's always plenty of goodies left over after you distribute some to stores and radio stations." Another intern said she walked away from the internship with "enough promotional posters, stickers, and T-shirts to decorate a small museum."

On the whole, interns are quite pleased with BMG. An intern who had also served internships at a variety of record labels said, "Unlike the fast-moving, perform-well-or-perish ethic at many record labels, BMG is more of a solid corporate entity. BMG really wants to promote people from within. There's a sense you're being bred for bigger and better things." Another added: "I never felt insignificant or like I was being used. If anything, BMG management bent over backward to give me freedom to publicize bands as I saw fit."

SELECTION

The program seeks undergraduates, ideally sophomores and juniors, but sometimes freshmen and seniors. Graduate students may also participate as long as they are one or two years from graduation. Students of any major are welcome to apply. As the job involves a good deal of traveling, applicants (excluding those who want to work in New York) should have access to a car. Applicants are chosen based on "creativity," "intellectual abilities," "social abilities," "passion for music," and "experience in the music business." Although the internship is geared toward alternative music, a past intern says that "applicants need not be 'Joe Alternative'—a dude with 12 earrings and a leather jacket. A solid interest in all types of music will do just fine." International applicants are eligible.

APPLICATION PROCEDURE

As openings in the Alternative Marketing Program occur sporadically, applications are accepted on a rolling basis. Applicants must submit a resume and cover letter. When intern positions are available, the manager of Recruiting and Development flies out to different cities around the country to interview top candidates; interviews take place at a BMG sales office or a hotel suite.

OVERVIEW

As a Texan once said, "Breakin' into the record business is harder than eatin' Jell-O with chopsticks." While most record labels have internships, they are often unfulfilling excursions into a dungeon of disorganization, no pay, and indentured servitude. BMG's Alternative Marketing Program is the ideal antidote: structured responsibilities, decent pay, and practical experience in marketing. BMG is committed to using the program to develop executive talent while interns are still in school—every year, at least 50 percent of interns are given full-time positions at BMG.

FOR MORE INFORMATION . . .

■ Bertelsmann Music Group
Alternative Marketing Program or BMG Direct or
RCA/Arista/Zoo Records
Manager of Recruiting and Development
1540 Broadway, 38th Floor
New York, NY 10036
(212) 930-4000
Fax: (212) 930-4862
www.bmg.com

BOEING®

SELECTIVITY	🔍 🔍 🔍 🔍 🔍
Approximate applicant pool: 6,000 Interns accepted: 100–250	

COMPENSATION	$ $ $ $ $
$500/week plus travel allowance $1500 housing allowance	

QUALITY OF LIFE	🌴 🌴 🌴 🌴
Nearby lakes; sleek fitness centers; flight simulator; social activities	

LOCATION(S)

Seattle, WA; Wichita, KS; Philadelphia, PA; Huntsville, AL; St. Louis, MO; Southern California

FIELD

Aircraft and space systems design and manufacturing

DURATION

8–12 weeks (Summer)
6 months (Winter/Summer or Summer/Fall)

PRE-REQS

College sophomores, juniors, and seniors

DEADLINE(S)

January 31

The number 7. There's something magical about it. "Let's see a 7!" gamblers yell at the beginning of a craps round. Jazz musicians invoke it as a symbol of good luck, as in "Lucky Seven," by Malta, or "Seven Years of Good Luck," by Joe Sample. And, since 1958, Boeing has used the number to describe the company's series of airplanes—707, 727, 737, 747, 757, 767, and 777. Today, as luck would have it, Boeing is the world's largest manufacturer of commercial jets. Its airplanes are used by all the major U.S. airlines, from American to United.

Not bad for a company that produced its first plane in a boathouse. When founder and timberman William E. Boeing took the bumpy test flight of that first plane in 1916 (only 13 years after the Wright brothers' first flights), few envisioned how far the company would go. Nearly bankrupt in the early 1920s, Boeing survived and went on to operate mail routes, manufacture the first passenger airliner, and produce the B-9 bomber—all by 1931. Since then, the company has manufactured the B-29 Superfortress, from which hundreds of American bombs were dropped to help end World War II, and the B-52, which was used in Korea, Vietnam, and the Persian Gulf. Moreover, the nuclear-war deterring Minuteman missile, the President's palatial *Air Force One*, the B-2 Stealth bomber, and the Saturn V boosters, which sent the first men to the moon in 1969, were built by Boeing. All these feats justify the company's 75th anniversary slogan: "Making history every day."

DESCRIPTION

From the mid-1970s until 1985, Boeing informally brought in summer engineers to work on company projects. But in 1985, the com-

pany restructured the program, opening it up to students studying other disciplines and offering good salaries, training programs, and social activities as well. It was a good move, because in 1992 the National Society of Black Engineers selected the Boeing intern program as the number one internship in the nation. The program recruits more than 100 students each year to work in Seattle's Information and Support Services, Defense and Space, and Commercial Airplanes divisions. The latter places interns in such groups as Hydraulics Systems,

Aerodynamics, Windtunnel, Avionics, Flight Deck, Flight Test, Mechanical and Electrical Systems, and Landing Gear. Approximately 20 similar positions are available in Boeing's Philadelphia, Huntsville, and Wichita sites.

As a member of the Cargo unit of Payloads, an intern worked on caster assemblies (the manual conveyer belts inside a cargo jet). "I checked designs to make sure the assemblies would fit and to see if certain parts would be able to withstand various stresses." But reading these designs proficiently required that she study Boeing's drawing system; the newfound knowledge helped her on the next project. "Because of an FAA directive, Boeing had to modify some existing parts. So I researched old drawings to determine which airplanes had used the offending parts. Then I put together a modification kit—all the pieces plus instructions—to send out to our former clients."

Some interns are assigned to the company's 777, a wide-body twin-engine jet; smaller than the immense 747 but larger than the 767, this new aircraft services from 375 to 400 passengers. In addition to offering wider seats and more legroom, the 777 contains the newest in digital entertainment and communications gizmos—optional stereo, telephone, television, and movies at each seat.

During a recent summer, the 777 Stability and Control group hosted an intern. She spent the first three weeks of her summer working on a windtunnel test of a three-foot 777 model. "We conducted the tests in a low-speed tunnel at the University of Washington," she said. "I collected data and then analyzed it on the computer to extract aerodynamic parameters like the pitching moment, the lift, and the drag." Such information helps Boeing to see if the plane can withstand powerful gusts of wind, she explained. "I spent the rest of the summer figuring out how the plane could counteract wind forces. For example, I determined how much tail movement is needed to compensate for a pitching moment [that is,

when a plane starts rocking back and forth like a hobby horse]."

Boeing placed another intern in the 777 Hydraulics Systems group, which designs the electronics system controlling the hydraulics. Considered a full-fledged team member, the intern frequently attended planning meetings. "We'd discuss ways to reduce costs and manufacturing time, among other things," he said of the meetings. "Every two weeks, I'd make a presentation on what computer circuits the lead engineer and I were using in the hydraulic system's control box. There is no canned solution to these design problems, so I had to defend what I came up with." During the course of the sessions, he was also encouraged to offer solutions to what he perceived as problems in other engineers' design work. "I was taken seriously whenever I had thoughts to offer," he said. "Interns are no less a part of Boeing's mission than anyone else."

But planes consist of more than their hidden circuits and sophisticated controls. Boeing engineers must also design kitchens and safety equipment. Some interns end up in less technical groups such as Galley Configurations, the department that oversees the design and layout of aircraft kitchens. "I went over designers' work to make sure Boeing's electrical and water systems were compatible with the galley designed by the suppliers," said a Galley intern. "And to make sure I knew what I was doing, I checked my work with several employees working on galley designs."

An intern in Emergency Escape Systems worked on Boeing's "emergency slides," the inflatable yellow tubing that uncurls like a New Year's party noisemaker. "We wanted data on parameters like people's time-to-door, time-to-slide-down, time-to-get-off-the-slide. And we wanted these for people of all ages. But Boeing had videotaped tests for these parameters before and didn't want to subject anyone to more tests." Because of the risk involved, she explained, the use of people in tests is discouraged. "So I reviewed the videos from previous

> "This ain't no propeller job; it's the 747 of internships!"

tests and extracted data by analyzing people's reaction times in those tests," she said. She also determined slide-deployment time in sub-freezing weather: "We put the slide in the cold room at –40°F for several hours, and then I timed how long it took to open up."

Boeing kicks off the summer with an orientation at which interns receive a schedule of events, including optional presentations, plant tours, volleyball matches, and trips to Seattle Mariners baseball games. A week or two later, various illustrious speakers are recruited each year to welcome the interns. Past speakers include Seattle Mayor Norm Rice and Boeing President Phil Condit. Afterward, interns visit booths offering information on Boeing's bowling, parachuting, karate, and basketball clubs. Information is also available on "Project Compute," a tutoring program that helps disadvantaged junior high and high school students become computer literate, and in which many interns have participated in the past.

Once the summer gets under way, the company's aeronautics, mechanical, electrical, and civil engineering interns (about 50 percent of the intern class) learn how to design an airplane. Every Wednesday morning for four hours, they attend a design engineering class. Different managers make a presentation each week; in 1993, the first speaker offered a humorous start to the 7:30 A.M. meetings: "Our planes are great, big, expensive, flying Greyhound buses," he told the early risers. Afterward, interns divided into groups of ten, working for 30 to 45 minutes to solve a design problem. A hammer, a block of wood, and 25 nails were given to each group, and with only those materials, they were asked to design a tie rack. "It's only a warm-up for the more difficult airplane problems later on," remarked an intern who had worked on the tie-rack problem the previous summer, "but even designing a functional rack is harder than it sounds."

Four or five times during the summer, interns spend a day touring Boeing's facilities. Tours find interns inside airplanes, at test areas, or in the delivery center. But none of these sites gets interns lathered up like the Flight Simulator trip. Walking through the simulator building's hallways, interns sense the history of the place: hundreds of framed airline logos, many from defunct companies, hang alongside pictures of Boeing planes. At the simulators, interns see large metal boxes, each on six robotic legs, looking more like the Imperial Walkers from *Star Wars* than mock airplanes. Interns are given five minutes to test-fly these "great big video games." Said one intern: "I felt every bump and jerk. . . . It made me so dizzy that the ground was still moving when I got out." Another intern freaked when his copilot turned off one of the engines: "I forgot that I was in a simulator and thought we were going to crash; my sweaty palms were barely able to open up the rudder to compensate for the tilt."

Seattle's proximity to Puget Sound and the Cascade Mountains makes for cool, sunny summers. Opportunities to enjoy outdoor life abound, with sailing, rock climbing, fishing, and kayaking popular among interns. In addition, each Boeing plant has a fitness center, with Nautilus weights and stationary bikes. The Everett Fitness Center, built in 1992, is probably the sleekest. With outdoor running trails, basketball, volleyball, weight machines, dozens of StairMasters, a modern locker room, and a carpeted track (*carpeted*? go figure), it rivals the facilities of most large universities. And at a fee of $15 per month, membership is a bargain.

At a company as large as Boeing, there are bound to be some choppy landings. "You're at the mercy of the system, sometimes waiting for days to get information you need because you often have to go through several channels," said an intern. Some others mention that even with all the freedom interns have to learn about the company, "there's limited time to explore—our work is demanding."

Most interns stay for 10 to 14 weeks in the summer before returning to school. Some, however, elect to work as part of the co-op program, augmenting their summer experience with either a spring or fall stint. But whether they spend 12 weeks or six months, most interns are incredibly satisfied: "This ain't no propeller job; it's the 747 of internships!"

SELECTION

Boeing seeks college juniors and seniors. Though the company does not adhere to any particular GPA cutoff, it is looking for students actively involved in extracurricular activities such as campus engineering societies. Approximately 85 percent of interns study engineering and computer science. But positions for those studying accounting, information systems, public relations, communications, marketing, and other fields also exist. International applicants are eligible.

APPLICATION PROCEDURE

The deadline is rolling. Students can begin applying as early as the fall for the co-op and summer programs but should send in materials no later than January 31. Boeing recruits at dozens of universities' career fairs, where students may make inquiries or submit resumes. The company also makes appearances at the annual meetings of the Society of Women Engineers, the National Society of Black Engineers, American Indians Science and Engineering Students, and the Society of Hispanic Professional Engineers. Applicants should send a resume and a cover letter detailing the classes that they will complete by the start of the internship. Managers normally contact finalists by the end of May for phone interviews and offers.

OVERVIEW

Bowing (pronounced BO-ing). It requires one person, one horsehaired wooden rod, and one stringed musical instrument—three pieces to create a melodious sound. But unlike musical bowing, the company Boeing needs 110,000 people, several factories, and millions of manufactured parts. What are the odds that these elements can come together to produce world-class commercial jets, defense planes, and spacecraft? And still capture top billing in the industry? A long shot, you'd think. But Boeing reigns supreme. Why? In part because of well-trained and unusually dedicated employees, many of whom are former interns. With solid projects, weekly design classes, and an unbelievably realistic simulator at their fingertips, interns are exposed to a bevy of possibilities. Any way you spell it, Boeing is a sure bet.

FOR MORE INFORMATION . . .

■ Boeing College Relations
P.O. Box 37071
MS 6H-PR
Seattle, WA 98124
(425) 234-1957
Fax: (425) 237-5906
submit.resume@boeing.com
www.boeing.com/employment

Chicago Zoological Society
Brookfield Zoo

Minutes after the Chicago Bulls won their second NBA championship, a sow on display at the Brookfield Zoo gave birth to 13 piglets. The staff immediately named the babies after the team's owner, manager, and Michael Jordan, Scottie Pippen, and other players. The event made CNN.

This wasn't the first time that the Brookfield Zoo had generated press. In the summer of 1983, amidst great fanfare, Marlin Perkins of TV's *Wild Kingdom* visited the zoo to unveil a new section of the world's largest indoor mixed species exhibit, Tropic World. In May 1991, two Moscow Zoo walruses, stricken with life-threatening sinus infections, were flown to Brookfield Zoo for treatment. After complicated tusk surgery, the two walruses regained their health and made the Brookfield Zoo their new home. The Moscow pair proved a welcome addition following the loss of Brookfield's famous walrus and most popular animal, Olga, who had lived there since 1962. In December of 1994, Brookfield Zoo again received international attention when Chicory, a 9-year-old Western lowland gorilla underwent brain surgery to successfully remove a life-threatening tumor. This procedure, the first of its kind, was done at Loyola University Medical Center with a combined effort of their neurosurgical team and the Zoo's veterinary staff.

DESCRIPTION

Since the late 1970s, students pursuing zoo careers have been able to intern at Brookfield Zoo. The program offers hands-on experience in many departments: Seven Seas Panorama, Australia House, Department of Animal Health, the Children's Zoo, Conservation Biology's Mouse Colony Research, Bird Department, Primates, Nutrition, Fragile Kingdom, Habitat Africa, Living Coast, Reptile House, and The Swamp.

The Brookfield Zoo's intern program strives to teach the art of zookeeping—that is, maintaining animal health and well-being. In addition, interns also interact with visitors, directing them to exhibits and answering questions about the animals. They also assist people in finding special demonstrations or in understanding zoo services like the Parents' Program.

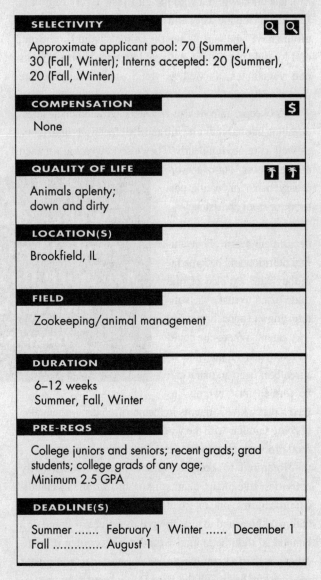

SELECTIVITY 🔍🔍

Approximate applicant pool: 70 (Summer), 30 (Fall, Winter); Interns accepted: 20 (Summer), 20 (Fall, Winter)

COMPENSATION 💲

None

QUALITY OF LIFE 🌴🌴

Animals aplenty; down and dirty

LOCATION(S)

Brookfield, IL

FIELD

Zookeeping/animal management

DURATION

6–12 weeks
Summer, Fall, Winter

PRE-REQS

College juniors and seniors; recent grads; grad students; college grads of any age; Minimum 2.5 GPA

DEADLINE(S)

Summer .... February 1 Winter ...... December 1
Fall .... August 1

BUSYWORK METER
LOW MEDIUM HIGH
N/A
OLDMAN & HAMADEH

An intern in the Mammal Department's Hoofed Stock section worked with the giraffes. "Every morning, I raked the outside yards and replenished the hay rack with alfalfa hay," she said. "Then the animals would come out, and I would clean their stalls and prepare chopped fruits and vegetables, as well as weigh out the appropriate amount of grain."

Zookeeper interns also cleaned cages and enclosures, climbing into exhibits to scrub and disinfect walls and floors, as well as removing debris. They also keep a log for each animal, noting out-of-the-ordinary behavior, eating patterns, or stool consistency.

Interns in the nutrition department learn about animal nutrition and become familiar with "tricks of the trade' used to make diets interesting and appealing to finicky eaters. Where else could an intern use a fajita slicer to shred beef heart so that it can be formed into "worms" to feed a picky kiwi? Interns in the nutrition department also become familiar with the workings of the commissary, the food procurement, storage, and distribution process.

Required to keep a journal, interns record daily activities, live births, deaths, immobilization, and medical procedures; one intern also learned how to veil medications: "I learned to hide the pill in a piece of bread or a banana so that the animal would not recognize it." Another watched a veterinarian use a blow dart to administer medication. Interns in the Bird Department may participate in on-site behavioral studies of three species of Hawaiian honeycreepers housed in the Zoo's Perching Bird House. These species serve as models in the studies in an attempt to help save many endangered birds of Hawaii.

Some interns work on a special project in lieu of or in addition to the journal. One intern made use of the zoo's library to research a paper comparing the anatomies of the giraffe and its cousin the okapi. Another intern's paper explored the possibilities of "dusting" insects with mineral-enriched oils and powders in order to improve mineral intake of insect-eating animals. A third intern developed a behavioral-enrichment device for Walter the Warthog. Favorite food tidbits, scents of food extracts, and textures like sandpaper and Astroturf were incorporated into the device to appeal to Walter's senses of taste, touch, and smell. According to the intern, "Walter really liked the feel of Astroturf! He spent lots of time rubbing his nose on it!"

Interns are assigned a mentor and receive written evaluations throughout their internship. A final evaluation, congratulations letter, and certificate of completion is presented to each intern.

Situated on 215 acres, the world-renowned zoo houses 2,500 animals representing more than 400 species of mammals, birds, reptiles, invertebrates, and amphibians and boasts realistic exhibits designed to promote animal conservation. There's Habitat Africa, offering an innovative safari featuring giraffes, zebras, African wild dogs, and exotic birds and reptiles. One can watch the dolphin shows at the 2,000-seat indoor dolphinarium. And there's Tropic World, one of the world's largest indoor mixed-species zoo exhibits, equipped with a walking path for viewing monkeys, apes, and exotic birds living in simulated rainforests. If that's not enough, one can also test the flying-strength machine at the "Be A Bird" exhibit and play with computer games teaching bird anatomy.

Interns receive a group tour of all the animal areas. "Right from the start of the internship, participants in the program receive exposure to the behind-the-scenes management of the zoo," explained the internship coordinator. "They soon realize that they play an important part in making the Brookfield Zoo run." Interns also have access to visiting specialists who give informed presentations to the staff covering varied topics from rainforest conservation to species preservation around the world. "I heard talks on animal contraception and on zoo exhibit repair," reported one intern. Other lunchtime talks have dealt with conservation techniques and tiger habitats.

> "Walter (the warthog) really liked the feel of Astroturf! He spent lots of time rubbing his nose on it!"

But even the greatest animal lovers feel some frustration. Some are chagrined to learn that zookeeping is not a glamorous profession and involves strenuous physical labor. "Cleaning can become boring and routine," said one intern. Animal diehards, on the other hand, realize the importance of cleaning exhibits: "The longer you stay, the more you realize that cleaning allows keepers to see the animals grow and adapt." Some are disappointed in not having access to certain animals like those in the Reptile House or Pachyderm House. "I wasn't allowed to work with the bats because a series of rabies shots is required," lamented one intern.

SELECTION

All applicants must have completed two years of college prior to the start of the internship and must have at least a 2.5 GPA. That means that college juniors and seniors, recent college grads, grad students, and career changers are all eligible. While neither previous zoo experience nor a science background is required, applicants must possess a serious career interest in animals. Many of the interns who work with animals, however, are majoring in life sciences like zoology, biology, animal science, or veterinary medicine. Insider's tip: Fall and spring terms are usually undersubscribed, and applicants for those periods often see less competition. International applicants are eligible.

APPLICATION PROCEDURE

Applications for a summer internship must be received by February 1, for a fall internship by August 1, and for a winter internship by December 1. Applicants must submit the application form (send away for this early), a resume, transcript, two letters of recommendation, and a cover letter describing what they wish to gain from the experience and how that experience will relate to past experience and career goals. For more information on zookeeper internships, as well as internships in non-animal departments (e.g., Education, Graphic Arts, Exhibit Design, Marketing, Horticulture, Water Quality and Public Relations), request the intern program brochure. Applicants selected from the initial screening are invited to interview on-site.

OVERVIEW

While many large zoos around the country offer internships in animal research (usually laboratory experiences that can lead to graduate work in genetics, immunology, or physiology), the Brookfield Zoo provides interns with a down-and-dirty introduction to zookeeping. "Interns are involved in all aspects of captive animal management from day one," says the coordinator, "working next to the keepers and contributing just like any other employee." And for those who don't want to pursue graduate studies in animal fields, the experience allows students to don a zookeeper's hat for a couple of months.

"Zookeeping is one of the few animal-related professions where a bachelor's degree is sufficient," said one. "But you must have hands-on animal exposure in order to land those jobs, and the Brookfield Zoo—a world-class zoo, comparable in prestige to the San Diego Zoo or the National in D.C.—gives you that exposure." No wonder, then, that about 10 percent of former interns eventually become zookeepers. The internship truly is, in the words of the coordinator, "an opportunity for future zoologists to get their feet wet—in more ways than one!"

FOR MORE INFORMATION . . .

■ Brookfield Zoo
Intern Program Coordinator
3300 South Golf Road
Brookfield, IL 60513
(708) 485-0263 ext. 459
Fax: (708) 485-0986
www.jarizzo@brookfieldzoo.org

"Think tank"—it once referred to the American military's guarded, soundproof rooms, those in which war strategies were formulated during World War II. In the 1950s, the military attached the term to its contract research organizations, such as the RAND Corporation and the Urban Institute. But by the 1960s, "think tank" was a term used by the public to describe various private research groups. It proved a fitting descriptor: Those ensconced in policy-research institutions are at once isolated and publicly displayed, like fish in a fish tank. Indeed, researchers working under the auspices of such institutions often appear on television or meet with government leaders to proffer opinions. This is certainly the case at one of America's most prestigious think tanks, the Brookings Institution.

Founded by woodenware tycoon Robert Brookings in 1916, the Brookings Institution espouses a decades-old mission—that is, "to bring knowledge to bear on the current and emerging public policy problems facing the American people" such as welfare reform and the budget deficit. Although considered predominantly liberal in ideology, Brookings consistently publishes middle-of-the-road books such as Alice Rivlin's *Reviving the American Dream* and Thomas Mann's *Renewing Congress*, earning the institute "a reputation for scrupulous objectivity and distinguished scholarship," as *The New Republic* wrote on the organization's 75th anniversary.

DESCRIPTION

The Brookings Institution offers students formal internships in Governmental Studies, a program that researches "how—and how well—American government functions." Paired with a Senior Fellow, interns work full- or part-time, depending on the Senior Fellows' needs and intern availability. Interns assist in the following research areas: budget appropriations, Congress and the presidency, criminal justice policy, domestic social regulations, entitlements and health policy, environmental justice, race and poverty, and welfare reform.

One former intern did statistical computer work for a Fellow's book, entitled *The Disappearing American Voter*. The book described the decline in voter turnout over the last several decades, starting with the 1960 presidential election. "The National

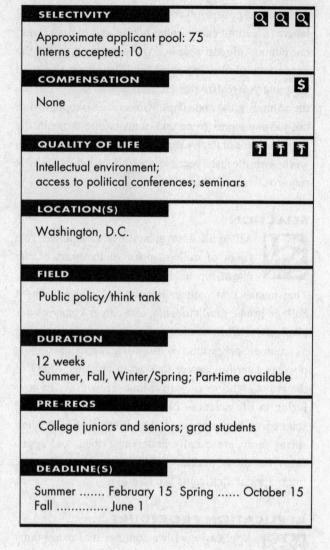

SELECTIVITY			
Approximate applicant pool: 75 Interns accepted: 10			

COMPENSATION	$
None	

QUALITY OF LIFE	
Intellectual environment; access to political conferences; seminars	

LOCATION(S)
Washington, D.C.

FIELD
Public policy/think tank

DURATION
12 weeks Summer, Fall, Winter/Spring; Part-time available

PRE-REQS
College juniors and seniors; grad students

DEADLINE(S)
Summer .... February 15 Spring ...... October 15 Fall .... June 1

Election Service sent us some computer tapes that contained voter demographic information," he said. "I wrote a program, using a statistical language that read the tapes. The program placed data from the tapes into categories such as race, age, occupation, party, and geography." The intern also searched the Brookings library for information on state voter laws. "I helped the Fellow create a database that encapsulated each state's voter laws as yes or no answers to four or five questions, such as 'can voters register by mail?' " By the end of the internship, the first few chapters of the book had been laid out. "They dispelled some of the widespread myths used to explain why people don't vote."

A few interns work for Steven Hess, described by *Mother Jones* as "a well-known scholar and longtime Republican party activist [who] logged 1,294 calls from 183 separate news organizations during 1988 alone." Hess's popularity stems from his well-known research on how the U.S. media cover foreign policy issues. As part of the effort, his former interns coded newspaper articles and surveys of foreign correspondents. Said one intern: "I handled *The New York Times*, reading each international news story carefully for salient points. Then I used an established list of numbers to code each article's elements: country, population, religion, and subject. I also sifted through the surveys, coding correspondents' responses to questions we asked on the countries they cover and on their thoughts about media coverage."

Because each Fellow already relies on a research assistant (RA) to complete the bulk of research, interns are often assigned clerical work. "Most of us come in bright-eyed and eager; we get a dose of reality pretty quickly." Depending on the Fellow's disposition, some interns do "bare-bones, less analytical research" while others dive into the heart of a project, doing substantial analysis. But tedious tasks such as photocopying, filing, and locating journal articles in the library need not discourage interns. "What you're photocopying often con-

> On the first floor, a portrait of an exceedingly contemplative-looking Mr. Brookings hints at the mental might mustered upstairs.

tains fascinating information," explained an intern. "If you think long and hard about that information and then make insightful comments, the Fellow just might be impressed."

Despite their low status (they're a notch below RAs), interns find that all of Brookings' resources are open to them—such as Brookings' library, the Library of Congress, and the National Archives. Interns may even use these resources to work on their own research projects. "I was writing a political science class paper on U.S. policy toward China during the post–cold war era," said an intern, "so I interviewed Brookings' China expert Harry Harding, who gave me some articles he had written on the subject. And he explained that because China's economy is growing fast, creating good opportunities for American businesses, the U.S. should grant China most-favored-nation status."

Students sing Brookings' praises "because of the incredible collegial environment, like an undergraduate department brimming with professors," said one intern. Many interns say that it's like a university and that Brookings fosters an environment of intellectual stimulation. Bimonthly Brookings-sponsored events have included conferences on such topics as NAFTA and speeches by the president of Turkey, King Hussein and Queen Noor of Jordan, and the ambassador to Hong Kong. Many of these activities, well attended by the press and government officials, are open to Fellows, staff, and interns alike.

Interns who want more of the academic or political talks are happy to learn that they may choose from among brown-bag, research-in-progress, and Friday lunches. The brown-bag lunches typically feature RAs talking about research projects; each week's sponsoring department posts flyers announcing the topic and advertising cookies to entice potential participants. (Baked on the premises in Brookings' cafeteria, these chewy morsels, chocolate-chip and oatmeal alike, draw a large following.) At the research-in-progress lunches, senior fellows or Ph.D. students on one-year, paid Brookings fellowships give research status reports. "One week, we heard about the AEI (American Enterprise Institute)-Brookings joint study on the public's image of Congress," said one intern. "Contrary to popular belief, the scholars concluded that Congress was actually doing an adequate job." Finally, every Friday at half past noon Senior Fellows gather to discuss various world issues. Seats for interns are available on the fringes—where "it's like being at the Master's [golf tournament]: say nothing and listen carefully." Interns can listen to Fellows debate topics such as the presidential election campaigns, the Contract with America, and the Bosnia peace talks. "At times, the discussions get pretty heated," said one intern. "Brookings is supposed to be nonpartisan, but Fellows usually don't make much of an effort to conceal their leanings, be they conservative or liberal."

Occasionally, interns are allowed to observe luncheons the program director organizes for the media and political scientists At the spring 1993 luncheon, interns listened to Gene Sperling, the deputy assistant to the president for economic policy. A Brookings RA for Steven Hess from September 1981 to August 1982, Sperling talked about his current role in White House economic policy. Interns learned that as part of President Clinton's National Economic Council, Sperling plays a large role in formulating strategies on deficit reduction, taxes, investment, and enterprise zones. "Even though we didn't get to ask him questions, it was thrilling to hear his insights," said an intern who attended.

Brookings' eight-story, sandstone building is located on embassy-lined Massachusetts Avenue. Inside, Brookings is described by interns as "stodgy and academic" compared with the more modern American Enterprise Institute. On the first floor, a portrait of an exceedingly contemplative-looking Mr. Brookings suggests the mental might mustered upstairs. Yet scholars are surprisingly "relaxed and informal, frequently available to answer questions about research, graduate schools, or political issues."

SELECTION

 The Governmental Studies Program seeks college juniors, seniors, and graduate students in political science. Even so, history, public policy, and law students have been known to intern at Brookings. The brochure states that "attention to detail is essential; some research experience and library skills are helpful."

APPLICATION PROCEDURE

 The deadline to turn in materials for the Governmental Studies Program internship is April 1 for the summer term, August 1 for the fall term, and December 1 for the winter/spring term. Students must submit a resume, cover letter, transcript plus course descriptions for all political science credits, two letters of recommendation, and a writing sample (3 to 5 pages), preferably from a political science course, to the address below. "Heavy-duty students apply here," said the coordinator. "Most have high GPAs and express an interest in a particular scholar's research, described in our brochure." After the coordinator screens resumes, Senior Fellows conduct phone interviews with a selection of finalists.

The Brookings Institution also offers research internships in Economic Studies and Foreign Policy Studies. Executive Education internships are available in the Center for Public Policy Education and the Government Affairs Institute. Communications internships are available with the Publications/Marketing office and the Public Affairs office, and an information systems internship is available in the Social Science Computation Center. Call the Brookings Job Line or access the Brookings World Wide Web page for more information. International applicants are eligible.

OVERVIEW

 Interns at the Brookings Institution have an "opportunity to work with the field's premier scholars—those who influence policy through careful study and analysis," as a brochure puts it. Paired with Senior Fellows, interns learn independent research techniques and leave with a heightened understanding of American government. One wouldn't expect anything less from the place the press has repeatedly deemed "the granddaddy of all think tanks."

FOR MORE INFORMATION . . .

■ The Brookings Institution
Internship Coordinator
(Name of Program)
1775 Massachusetts Avenue NW
Washington, DC 20036-2188
Job line: (202) 797-6096
http://www.brook.edu/admin/internships.htm

BUTTERFIELD & BUTTERFIELD

Fine Art Auctioneers and Appraisers since 1865

Ever wonder where you could pick up a few Solomon Island money rolls? How about where to go for Peruvian pre-Columbian ceramics? Where does one find Native American beaded bandoleer bags, anyway? Take heart, eager collector. Butterfield & Butterfield may be your destination.

Founded in 1865 on the present site of San Francisco's Transamerica Building, Butterfield & Butterfield is the largest and oldest full-service auction house in western America. It runs a dizzying array of fine-art and antique auctions, selling everything from paintings to fine wine. It also offers a host of appraisal services, assessing single items or entire collections, for individuals or museums.

DESCRIPTION

A range of departments accepts interns: Painting, Asian Art, Prints, Fine Photographs, Furniture and Decorative Arts, American Indian/Ethnographic Art, Oriental Rugs, Catalogues/Marketing, Public Relations, and Marketing. Most departments hire only one intern, although the busiest divisions, Furniture and Decorative Arts and Asian Art, usually hire two each. Interns are required to work only two days a week, and thus the program allows a good deal of scheduling flexibility.

In every department, interns assist the director and other specialists in preparing for upcoming auctions. Although the program strives to keep busywork at a minimum, interns find themselves undertaking a fair amount. Be it typing letters to auction-goers, keeping track of photographs of art pieces, or photocopying auction contracts, interns spend part of their time carrying out clerical tasks. They also spend time

SELECTIVITY	🔍 🔍 🔍
Approximate applicant pool: 300 Interns accepted: 35–45	

COMPENSATION	$
$10/day stipend; Course credit	

QUALITY OF LIFE	⬆ ⬆ ⬆
Previews and appraisal clinics; free parking; hands-on contact with objects	

LOCATION(S)
San Francisco, CA, Los Angeles, CA, and Chicago, IL

FIELD
Auction and appraisal

DURATION
10 weeks Summer, Fall, Spring; at least 15 hours/week

PRE-REQS
See Selection

DEADLINE(S)
Summer .... March 30   Fall .... July 30 Spring .... December 15

caring for the art and antique pieces that come through their office. Duties in this area include tagging the pieces for identification purposes, writing condition reports, and unpacking the pieces.

Interns often find that their work affords them a terrific education about a type of art or antique. Most departments have a large collection of books on a particular field, and interns are often asked to use them to determine what similar objects have sold for in the past. Interns also research the cultural histories of items that will be sold at auction, gaining

BUSYWORK METER
MEDIUM
LOW HIGH
OLDMAN & HAMADEH

insight into the historical context from which an object comes. Said one intern: "I learned so much about the pieces in my field—what makes them valuable, why they're historically important, who owned them." In their free moments, interns are encouraged to pick their supervisor's brains and to learn as much as possible about the pieces that pass through the office.

Whereas most interns focus primarily on the art pieces particular to their departments, Catalogues/Marketing interns are steeped in the art of pre- and post-auction publicity. Although these interns do not gain in-depth knowledge about a particular field of art, they like working in Catalogues/Marketing because "it exposes you to all of the other departments, as opposed to working in, for example, the Painting department, where that's basically all you see."

Every other Monday morning Butterfield invites the public to bring in art and antique pieces for appraisal. Interns are invited to assist at these Monday appraisal clinics, helping visitors unpack and display the objects they bring in. For many interns, the best part of appraisal clinics is simply the opportunity to sit down and observe an appraiser in action: "Watching the appraisers, you really got a sense of what's desirable in an antique. Examining firearms, for example, they would look for things like engravings, silver barrels, and gems in the handle." Interns are also encouraged to accompany appraisers and department directors on appraisal calls. Visiting all sorts of homes in the Bay Area, from modest apartments to chichi estates, interns get a sense of how art and antiques are displayed in the real world. Said one: "House calls were great. I went on about four of them. On one we inspected an entire room of African art. It was fascinating to see all those pieces laid out in a person's home."

A week or so before every auction, Butterfield runs a few preview sessions in which the public can inspect the pieces coming up for auction. Interns are often called upon to help out at these auction previews. Their main task is to display the art objects and answer questions about them. "It's not too difficult," said one intern. "You take the pieces out of their locked cases and field questions about them. If you get stumped, you can always ask an appraiser or refer to the catalog."

Clinics and previews are interesting, but in terms of sheer drama, nothing beats the main event—the auction. Expectant collectors crowd the auction room. A video screen displays each "lot" (a single item or group of items) as it comes up for sale. The auctioneer starts the bidding, usually at about one-third to one-half of the estimated value of the lot, as listed in the catalog. Participants hold up numbered cards when they want to bid on the lot. Tension builds until the final bid is placed, the auctioneer brings down the hammer, and the lot is "knocked down" (sold to the highest bidder).

Interns enjoy being in the charged atmosphere of auctions. At the very least, auctions provide fascinating people-watching: "Depending on what was being auctioned off, you saw all types of people—timid first-timers, impassioned novices, and seasoned veterans." Interns also help out during auctions. Some are merely gofers, retrieving documents and handling pieces of art. A few do phone bidding for parties who are unable to attend the auction, although this job is usually performed by the regular staff; interns who phone bid can't help but get caught up in the excitement of relaying a bidder's wishes: "You'd call a client from the auction room and hold up his or her numbered card when directed to. Sometimes thousands of dollars were involved. It was a big adrenaline rush."

Interns can look forward to a tiring but educational orientation day. They are sent to the main departments, spending time at Customer Service, Receiving, Art, Fine Arts, Catalog Subscription, and the Front Desk. Every effort is made to educate them about the steps needed to produce a successful auction. At one point, interns are shown a video detailing the proper ways to handle art objects. Orientation is usually held on an auction day and culminates in the

> "It sounds funny, but you get to play with wonderful objects. It's the ultimate hands-on experience for someone interested in art."

opportunity to view an actual auction.

Although most interns work at Butterfield's San Francisco headquarters, for each session a few are placed in the company's Los Angeles office. The Butterfield headquarters is located in an older neighborhood of San Francisco that has an abundance of galleries, showrooms, and cafes nearby. The Butterfield building is described as "clean but warehouselike." The main showroom is spacious, but, one intern sniffed, "not as plush as those at New York houses like Sotheby's and Christie's." Interns sit at cubicles in the offices upstairs. They describe the office environment as "friendly," "supportive," but "high pressured" on auction days. One warns that a few employees take their job a little more seriously than they have to.

When asked about perks, interns agree that a main benefit of being at Butterfield is the opportunity to handle and inspect all sorts of valuable antiques, the kind that are typically ensconced in glass or behind a velvet rope in a museum. "It sounds funny, but you get to play with wonderful objects. It's the ultimate hands-on experience for someone interested in art," remarked an intern. Other benefits include the occasional in-house lecture, such as a talk on jades by the director of the Asian department, and free parking, a scarce commodity in San Francisco. Interns also enjoy scoping out the celebrities who occasionally surface on auction day: "One day I saw Aaron Spelling buying some pretty fancy jewelry."

Butterfield's $10 daily stipend is no gravy train by any stretch of the imagination, but it at least covers the cost of daily transportation. Interns for whom money is no object are happy to learn that they can bid in the auctions. Said one intern: "If they want to, interns can bid on the sales. Working here, you hear insider tips about what's hot and what's not, and thus interns who have the means to bid are a step ahead of the game."

SELECTION

The program is open to junior and senior undergrads, graduate students, and college graduates of any age. Interested parties should have taken at least two semesters of art history (approximately 30 units). But, according to the intern coordinator, the program occasionally accepts candidates with no art history experience, usually for positions in less art-oriented areas like Cata-

logues/Marketing. Desired qualities in applicants include "a strong interest in fine arts," a "high degree of motivation," an "ability to work well with people," and "strong research skills." And, one intern added, participants "shouldn't be afraid to get dirty, because handling the various pieces of art sometimes requires you to get on your knees and brave the dust and grime."

APPLICATION PROCEDURE

Designed to coincide with academic semesters, the program has the following application deadlines: summer, March 30; fall, July 30; and spring, November 30. Students should write to the Internship Coordinator for an application. After submitting an application and resume, highly qualified candidates are invited to the auction house for interviews with the internship coordinator and the head of the department that interests them. Personal interviews are required.

OVERVIEW

There are good reasons to spend a few months at Butterfield & Butterfield. Interns there receive a dual education, learning in general about the auction business and in particular about a type of art or antique. They do so at a renowned auction house, but one that is considerably more intimate than its eastern counterparts. Individuals interested in art and antiques should bear in mind the advantages of working in an auction house over a museum or a gallery. Not only does an internship with Butterfield allow you to handle pieces that would otherwise be inaccessible but it also puts you in an environment of perpetual change and variety. As one intern said: "In the art world, museums move at 10 mph. Galleries at about 60 mph. And auction houses, with their never-ending stream of events, at 250 mph."

FOR MORE INFORMATION . . .

■ Butterfield & Butterfield
Internship Program
7601 Sunset Blvd.
Los Angeles, CA 90046
(213) 850-7500 ext. 219
Fax: (323) 850-1437

THE CARTER CENTER

Baseball greats become coaches. Professors become professors emeriti. Tennis stars become TV commentators. But what the heck do presidents do after their glory years? For James Earl Carter, the answer was easy. In 1982, "Jimmy" founded The Carter Center, an action-oriented arm of Emory University working to improve the quality of life for people around the world. Guided by Carter and staffed with distinguished professors and former diplomats, The Carter Center works with world leaders and dignitaries to promote democracy, resolve conflicts, protect human rights, eradicate disease, and improve agriculture in developing countries.

DESCRIPTION

In 1984, undergraduate and graduate students of international studies at Emory University participated in The Carter Center's inchoate internship program. The Center was still in its infancy at that point, working strictly on Middle East issues. By 1986, however, it had attracted more fellows and programs, and had constructed several new buildings, including the presidential library and museum, on a 35-acre park overlooking downtown Atlanta. That year, the Center introduced the official internship program, primarily for Emory students. A small number of students from around the country could participate as well.

Interns now work in one of the many programs in place at the Center: Latin American and Caribbean, Global 2000 (a large-scale project to improve health care and agriculture in developing countries), Mental Health, the Global Development Initiative (a program to help developing countries receive financial aid from the world's donor

SELECTIVITY	
Approximate applicant pool: 100 Interns accepted: 30	

COMPENSATION	$
None; Financial aid may be available	

QUALITY OF LIFE	🏃 🏃 🏃
Well-organized orientation, training, retreat, and lecture series; beautiful setting; intellectual atmosphere; possible travel; access to high-level meetings; fitness facility; cafeteria; free parking	

LOCATION(S)
Atlanta, GA

FIELD
Foreign affairs, health, and public policy

DURATION
12 weeks Summer, Fall, Spring

PRE-REQS
College juniors and seniors; recent grads; grad students

DEADLINE(S)
Fall .... June 15   Spring ...... October 15 Summer .... March 15

nations), and Conflict Resolution. Positions are also occasionally available in administrative offices such as Public Information, Development, and Conferencing.

Daily activities depend on the program to which an intern is assigned, though most programs allow interns to research specific issues, monitor daily events pertaining to their program, and write articles for in-house publications. One intern in Public Information, for example, helped research mailing lists, mailed out information packets, and helped the department run press conferences. "One day I helped set up for an

Atlanta Project press conference featuring a satellite appearance by Michael Jackson," he reported. "I signed in press people, distributed packets to them, and then stayed to listen to the questions asked of President Carter." Another time, he was responsible for escorting Ted Koppel's camera crew to the interview site, making sure that they had everything needed for a *Nightline* interview of Carter.

In other departments, like the international Conflict Resolution Program, interns personally monitor the daily conditions of two to three conflicts and provide weekly updates to the ICRP team. "I would use LEXIS-NEXIS, newspapers, journals, books, and interviews to probe into particular countries' activities," said an intern. "I learned a lot about conflicts and became an expert on the things going on in those countries, so much so that I was able to offer ideas on how The Carter Center could become involved in the peace process." In the human rights field, interns contribute to interventions on behalf of victims of human rights abuses by providing background research and writing initial drafts of letters from President Carter to government officials.

> "I learned a lot about conflicts and became an expert on the things going on in the countries I researched."

A variety of programs contributes to the Center's broad-based humanitarian agenda. Even an obscure disease such as "river blindness" is addressed. The Carter Center currently oversees distributions of the drug Mectizan, which protects individuals from contracting the disease. A former intern worked on a computer program to store organizations' applications for the drug. He said: "The computer had to be up and running. The speed with which we could approve the applications hinged on that. So, in that respect, my work had the potential to make a real impact."

In addition to the special projects in which interns are involved, interns often interact with important players on the international scene. Occasionally, interns are allowed to observe policy discussions. One of the largest occurs at the Center's annual consultation of the International Negotiation Network, headed by President Carter. "I saw foreign dignitaries, like Javier Perez de Cuellar, the former Secretary General of the U.N.," said one intern. "We watched firsthand as he and other world leaders conversed; then they and Carter Center representatives dispersed into private, small groups to brainstorm resolutions to international conflicts."

On the whole, interns relish the exposure that comes with being at a policy-making organization. They might peruse drafts of policy proposals or watch high-level policy discussions involving former and current world leaders. But such opportunities are not daily occurrences. "Just realize," cautioned the coordinator, "that in addition to research on countries, abuses, and conflicts, there are the day-to-day clerical tasks." By the coordinator's estimate, filing and photocopying absorb 35 percent of interns' time.

Most work takes place inside four modern circular buildings, interconnected to facilitate communication among the Center's diverse programs. A fifth pavilion houses The Jimmy Carter Library and Museum and the Center's cafe, where interns and staff members receive a 10 percent discount. To provide a respite from the fast pace indoors, the Center boasts an "absolutely beautiful" Japanese garden, two ponds, grassy hills, a small hardwood forest, flower gardens, and a fully equipped exercise room.

The internship is unpaid. Most students elect to receive academic credit through their schools; a few make financial arrangements through their college's financial aid office. Although the internship usually lasts for three months, interns may be able to stay for shorter or longer periods.

SELECTION

The Carter Center is looking for students who are at least juniors with extensive coursework in their majors. It also seeks a few recent grads and graduate students each term. Foreign language ability and computer literacy prove particularly helpful. Travel abroad and familiarity with history and economics are good preparation for many programs but are not required. Past interns stress the importance of having a "strong work ethic" and "an ability to quickly familiarize yourself with the background of your project." International applicants are eligible.

APPLICATION PROCEDURE

The deadline is June 15 for fall, October 15 for spring, and March 15 for summer. Applicants are required to submit a short essay (150 to 200 words) explaining their interest in international studies or in specific Center programs, their expectations of and objectives for the internship, and the relationship these have to career goals. A writing sample, a transcript, a resume, and two letters of recommendation must accompany the completed internship application form. The internship coordinator makes an initial screening of applications and refers them to the program directors, who make final choices.

OVERVIEW

In the Mother Goose nursery rhyme "Tweedle-Dum and Tweedle-Dee," the two boys for whom the poem is named argue over a broken rattle. Moments before they are about to fight, a powerful crow flies overhead and dissuades them from battle. An influential force in international dispute resolution, The Carter Center is a crow of sorts, working to mediate between opposing factions and promote peace. For a young organization, The Carter Center has also been especially effective in the movements to immunize children, strengthen new democracies, remove the stigma associated with mental illness, eradicate Guinea worm disease, and modernize farming in developing countries. An internship at The Carter Center allows students, through research projects and observation, to gain a deep understanding of a few of these problems. In the process, interns have the opportunity to learn from internationally respected thinkers and watch policymakers at work. You might think of the Carter Center internship as three months in the nest of that powerful crow of international and domestic public policy.

FOR MORE INFORMATION . . .

■ The Carter Center
Internship Program
One Copenhill Avenue
Atlanta, GA 30307
(404) 420-5151

Center for Investigative Reporting, Inc.

In 1977, freelance journalists Lowell Bergman, Dan Noyes, and David Weir founded the Center for Investigative Reporting (CIR) with the belief that the media needed a nonprofit, independent organization committed to investigative reporting. Since its founding, CIR has pursued "hidden stories…the hard stories, hard to assemble, and hard to tell." In 1990, for example, PBS's *Frontline* aired a one-hour CIR documentary titled "Global Dumping Ground," summarizing three years' worth of CIR stories on the international hazardous waste trade. The CIR stories had already persuaded the U.N. to pass a resolution restricting international transport of toxic material. But the broadcast now convinced China and other countries to ban toxic waste imports. Consequently, it's no surprise that media outlets such as *60 Minutes*, *20/20*, CNN, the *Los Angeles Times*, and *The Washington Post* have relied on CIR to produce similar stories for them. Or why the industry has honored the Center with over a dozen awards, most notably an Alfred I. du Pont–Columbia University Award for Broadcast Journalism, a George Polk Award for National Television Reporting, the Investigative Reporters and Editors Award, the National Magazine Award, an Emmy, and several Best Censored Story awards.

DESCRIPTION

CIR's brochure lists the internship's primary objective as "to teach investigative reporting skills to novice reporters." This has been the organization's credo ever since its start—back then, reporters occasionally hired an intern or two to assist in story research. Those interns learned so much about reporting that in 1983 CIR developed the present program; it gives students and

SELECTIVITY	🔍🔍🔍🔍
Approximate applicant pool: 200 Interns accepted: 8–10	

COMPENSATION	$
$200/month	

QUALITY OF LIFE	🌴🌴🌴
Seminars; meetings with journalists	

LOCATION(S)
San Francisco, CA

FIELD
Investigative journalism

DURATION
6 months Winter/Spring, Summer/Fall; Part-time available

PRE-REQS
Undergrads; grad students; college grads of any age

DEADLINE(S)
Winter/Spring .... December 1 Summer/Fall .... May 1

nonstudents alike a chance to moonlight as journalists for a minimum of 15 hours per week for 6 months.

After a half-day orientation to CIR procedures and administration, interns are paired with senior reporters. Under the guidance of these senior journalists, interns gather information for stories; they make phone calls, conduct interviews, search through public records, and organize library or online searches as part of the research effort.

One intern worked on CIR's 1992 documentary "Your Loan Is Denied," an investigation of mortgage-lending discrimination in Chicago. The investigation discovered widespread racism at the root of a disparity in lending practices. "The vacuum created when large banks discriminate against certain clients is often filled by fraudulent mortgage lenders, who charge exorbitant interest rates," said the intern. "I researched stories on LEXIS~NEXIS and sifted through Uniform Commercial Code filings to find the names of companies who might be engaging in illegal practices." The intern stayed with CIR long enough to see his research pay off; the documentary aired on PBS's *Frontline* at the end of his internship. "It was rewarding to see the people I had tracked down being interviewed on the show."

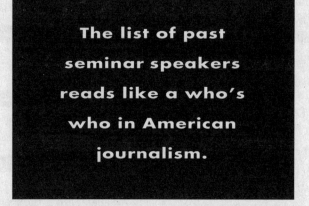

The list of past seminar speakers reads like a who's who in American journalism.

Another intern worked on a reporter's investigation of Soviet nuclear submarine accidents. "I looked through documents, interviewed people over the phone, even drove down to Stanford to attend a conference of nuclear physicists," he said. "I interviewed several of them, including a Nobel prize winner. It was pretty heady stuff for a 21-year-old."

In addition to doing reporters' legwork, interns learn investigative techniques, ethics, and writing at weekly seminars—"the most enlightening luncheon meetings you can imagine." Some seminars teach interns how to use outside resources such as City Hall, where interns visit the tax assessor's office. "When reporters want to find out who owns a particular property or building," explained the coordinator, "they need to get their hands on the city's tax records." At another seminar, interns learn about Freedom of Information Act requests. "We learned how to expedite the filing process, how to appeal if you get a negative response, and how to use documents from several agencies to piece together information needed."

Other seminars focus on building journalism skills. At one, interns learn how to use online databases like LEXIS~NEXIS and Dialog. At another, a lawyer exposes interns to legal issues in journalism. "To destroy your notes or not to destroy your notes. That is the dilemma

reporters face," said an intern. "Your notes might come in handy if you need to defend yourself, but they might reveal secret sources, too." And at a third seminar, interns hear tips from a private investigator: "He taught us how to locate missing persons and how to get information that average people cannot."

In between touring and building skills, interns interact with prominent local and national producers, reporters, and journalism instructors as well as journalists visiting from foreign countries. The list of past seminar speakers reads like a who's who in American journalism: *Rolling Stone* columnist Bill Greider, *The Nation* editor Victor Navasky, muckraker Jessica Mitford, *San Francisco Examiner* reporters Steven Chen and Ricardo Sandoval, screenwriter Judy Coburn, public broadcast executive and CIR cofounder David Weir, *The New York Times* West Coast bureau chief Jane Gross, and UC Berkeley School of Journalism's Tom Goldstein and Ben Bagdikian. One seminar featured Mark Hertsgaard, author of *On Bended Knee*: "We sat mesmerized for an hour as [Hertsgaard] explained how the media of the 1980s had caved in to the Reagan administration."

While working as assistants, interns are encouraged to research and write their own stories. The intern who worked on "Your Loan Is Denied" wrote a spin-off on San Francisco business loans: "I pitched the idea to the San Francisco radio station KQED 88.5 [which] aired it as a five-minute feature story." Another intern published a story in *The San Francisco Bay Guardian* on recent Rehnquist Supreme Court decisions, which he claimed were eroding press rights. "A majority of the justices construed the First Amendment in the narrowest possible terms," he wrote, "allowing contract and libel law to intrude on and even topple key precedents protecting the free press." A third intern interviewed antiwar activist Brian Willson about his involvement with the Bay Area Peace Navy. "I sat in a boat with Willson and a Nicaraguan boy named Erick and watched the Peace Navy protest war on the seas," she said. Published in *The Progressive*, her story described in poignant detail the man and boy's "special interest in peace"—Willson lost his legs in 1987 when a train ran over him during a protest at a naval weapons base; Erick was badly disfigured when bullets hit his face and shoulder during a Contra ambush in 1988.

One intern even "broke" a story—that is, made it publicly available for the first time. Fluent in Spanish, the intern came across a reference about Mexican death squads in a Mexican magazine. "I read about a purported ex-soldier hiding out in Canada and contacted his attorney. The soldier claimed to have executed between fifty and sixty people in the 1970s, and the Canadian government believed him." Certain Mexican government and army officials, whom the intern interviewed, corroborated the story. "Though there had been accusations of this sort of activity for years," he said, "no one had before brought the truth to light. My story was picked up by the Knight-Ridder wire and published in *The New York Times*."

Clearly, with publication come many benefits for the intern. Full credit and exposure is one. Financial compensation is another: those who write stories under the watchful eyes of CIR's editors take home 85 percent of what an outside news organization pays for the piece.

In a nondescript building two blocks south of Market Street, CIR's headquarters sits at a scenic vantage point; from windows on the east side, one has a clear view of the Bay Bridge and what's left of the Embarcadero Freeway after 1989's Loma Prieta earthquake. Industry awards, magazine covers, and stills from documentaries adorn the walls like medals honoring journalistic battles well fought. A large open area near the editorial offices houses the interns, their desks, and phones. At their fingertips is a small library and "thousands of connections."

Interns describe the working environment as "unrestricted," "calm," and "morale boosting." Because CIR is a nonprofit organization, and therefore competes for neither commercial income nor ratings, reporters take their time researching nonsensationalistic stories and writing serious, in-depth pieces. Observed one intern: "The place breeds earnest and sincere reporters who uphold the philosophy 'if we keep an eye on government and business, we can change society for the better.'"

Former interns are bent on changing the internship for the better, too. A few criticize some reporters' ineffectual mentoring. "My assigned reporter was sometimes flaky and disorganized," said one. "Occasionally, she not only kept me out of the loop on the progress of the story but also made up work to appease me." Some also point out that grunt work is compounded by interns' having to answer phones one or two hours per week. Interns also fret that the stipend is "impossible to live on." However, loyalty is strong. All acknowledge that the exposure is worth far more than any monetary compensation. And one former intern felt so indebted to the program for boosting his journalism career that he returned years later to conduct a seminar on foreign correspondents and international news.

SELECTION

 Anyone is eligible to apply, from high school seniors to college students to baby boomers thinking of career changes. CIR seeks neither a minimum GPA nor any particular major; a bioengineering major with an interest in writing was once hired to help out on a genetic engineering story. But writing ability is important. "If you're not published, just make sure you send in vivid writing samples that avoid academic or stuffy tones," said the coordinator. International applicants are eligible.

APPLICATION PROCEDURE

 The deadline is December 1 for the winter/spring term and May 1 for summer/fall term. Applicants should submit a resume, cover letter describing their interests and background, and several writing samples or published clips, though being published is not a requirement. Top candidates are asked to provide two or three personal references after a phone or on-site interview.

OVERVIEW

 Take a look at CIR's logo. It fits this non-stop investigative news agency—the ink is always flowing. Reporters have written more than 1,000 in-depth stories since the organization's inception, thanks to significant assistance from interns. Researching important stories, interns obtain vital information—from the inside scoop from people affected by the story to critical clues from places like City Hall. For tips on how to improve their reporting skills, interns attend seminars hosted by journalists. Some interns even write their own stories, the most scintillating of which are purchased by the media. For most participants, the internship launches a promising career in reporting. Former CIR interns are presently at *The Washington Post*, *Los Angeles Times*, ABC, CBS, Reuters, National Public Radio, and CIR itself. Moreover, an intern from 1982—Katherine Ellison—shared the 1985 Pulitzer Prize for a story on the U.S. holdings of then-Philippines president Ferdinand Marcos. As one CIR intern put it: "No matter what type of reporting you do in the future, the CIR laboratory gives you a solid foundation in the investigator's art."

FOR MORE INFORMATION . . .

■ Center for Investigative Reporting
c/o Communications Director
500 Howard St., Suite 206
San Francisco, CA 94105-3000
(415) 543-1200
cir@igc.org
www.muckraker.org

SELECTIVITY	🔍 🔍 🔍 🔍
Approximate applicant pool: 500 Interns accepted: 50–60	

COMPENSATION	$ $ $
$440–$640/wk (undergrad); $640–$840/wk (grad); round-trip travel	

QUALITY OF LIFE	🏃 🏃 🏃 🏃
Tight-knit culture; speaker series; Co-op Association; employee benefits	

LOCATION(S)
Langley, VA; Washington, D.C.; and other sites

FIELD
Government

DURATION
Fall, Spring, Summer

PRE-REQS
See Selection

DEADLINE(S)
November 6–9 months prior to work (grad)

"**H**ave you or any members of your family ever been employed by an agent of any foreign country?"

"No."

"Have you ever been a member of a group that is totalitarian, fascist, communist, or subversive?"

"No."

"Have you ever used marijuana?"

"Well, umm…"

The armband is getting a little tight. The room, a little stuffy. Your head, a little light.

But hey, if you want to intern at the CIA, you have to submit to the "black box."

The CIA has good reasons to ask internship candidates, as well as all other personnel, to take a polygraph test. As the agency charged with guarding America's national security, the CIA must take rigorous precautions. And lie-detector tests are just the beginning. CIA headquarters is surrounded by a 12-foot-high barbed-wire fence, patrolled by armed guards. An entire division of the agency, which is involved directly in espionage and other covert activities, is shrouded in total secrecy; the in-house phone book makes no mention of the thousands of employees who work in this division. And there are offices at the CIA deemed so sensitive that they are guarded by an agency policeman in a glass cage, a turnstile, and a combination lock.

DESCRIPTION

The CIA offers two types of internships: the CIA Internship Program and the Graduate Studies Program. As participants of both have similar projects and share the same privileges, the following description applies to both programs, except where otherwise noted.

BUSYWORK METER — LOW MEDIUM HIGH — OLDMAN & HAMADEH

Interns are assigned to one of three divisions: the Directorate of Science and Technology (DS&T), the Directorate of Intelligence (DI), and the Directorate of Administration (DA). A fourth division, the Directorate of Operations (DO), is the clandestine branch of the CIA, involved with collecting foreign intelligence through its network of "human agents" (a.k.a. spies); you guessed it: the DO is off-limits to interns.

The DS&T develops and operates the technical systems used in collecting intelligence. Video and image enhancement, chemical imagery, advanced antenna design, electro-optics, and satellite communications are but a few of the technologies DS&T covers. Those with backgrounds in computers, engineering, and hard sciences are the most likely candidates for DS&T work. An engineering major, for example, worked in the office of SIGNIT (signal intelligence) Operations. Although the substance of what he did is classified, in general terms he helped design equipment to collect and analyze signals. He said: "If, for instance, an operation overseas needed equipment to interpret a set of signals, we'd work with them to develop such a system."

Another DS&T office using interns is the National Photographic Interpretation Center (NPIC). After receiving training in photographic analysis, interns scrutinize photos from such sources as satellites and spy planes. Sitting at special optical contraptions (picture a heavy-duty microscope attached to a giant microfilm machine), interns scan photographs for basic intelligence data—military forces, military equipment production, natural disasters, etc. "I'd examine photographs taken at various times, looking for changes and trends," said one intern.

After information is collected, the Directorate of Intelligence (DI) gets to work analyzing it. The DI has five offices charged with observing a particular region of the world: the Office of Slavic and Eurasian Analysis, the Office of European Analysis, the Office of Near East and South Asian Analysis, the Office of East Asian Analysis, and the Office of African and Latin American Analysis. An intern in the Office of East Asian Analysis studied the political activities of China. "Using all sorts of resources, including Chinese newspapers translated by the agency, I kept tabs on the maneuverings of the Chinese government." He wrote a series of reports summarizing his research, including a paper on China's fourteenth Party Congress. "The bottom line," he said, "is to help the agency anticipate a government's next move." An intern in the Office of Slavic and Eurasian Analysis analyzed

political crimes and military movements in the former Soviet Union. Her analysis found its way into an in-house bulletin disseminated to members of the intelligence community on a "need-to-know basis."

In addition to regional offices, the DI has six functional offices, such as the Office of Scientific Weapons Research and the Office of Imagery Analysis. In the latter, interns examine satellite photographs and summarize their findings in written reports, some of which end up on the desks of top government officials. "Our customers are America's policy-makers," said an intern. "The analysis our office does is at the request of people like the president, vice president, and members of Congress."

The third division hiring interns, the Directorate of Administration (DA), places interns in offices carrying out the agency's daily administrative responsibilities. Drawing on students from a wide range of academic backgrounds, the DA involves interns in support areas like finance, human resources, journalism, graphic arts, and photography. An intern in the Office of Logistics, for example, helped procure office equipment for the CIA. Arranging "a slew of classified and unclassified contracts with equipment vendors," he spent the better part of his day phoning vendors and completing paperwork. Compared to the work interns do in the DS&T and DI, it's easy to see how some interns in DA find their jobs "less exciting and less uniquely CIA."

But the CIA is legendary for allowing employees to change jobs. If interns find their assignments unrewarding, chances are they will have the opportunity to switch jobs or offices. "The agency is more flexible than you'd expect," said an intern. "It will go to great lengths to make sure its employees are working at full capacity."

Working at an organization as clandestine and famous as the CIA is a mixed blessing. Interns have to get used to the fact that the nature of their work is almost always secret. Said one: "Nothing here leaves the office.

> "There's a mystique here that permeates everything you do and everyone you meet."

Ever." But just being at the CIA is a kick. "There's a mystique here that permeates everything you do and everyone you meet," said one intern. Interns in technical positions marvel at the advanced equipment to which they are exposed; as a brochure put it, the CIA "work[s] somewhere beyond the state of the art." Others are impressed with the steady flow of up-to-the-minute information the agency acquires: "We have access to news well before newspapers do."

The atmosphere at the CIA is like no other. Employees are fiercely loyal to the agency. Said one, "We come to work knowing that people's lives depend on what we do. There's a feeling here that we're all in this together. There's something intangible about it, but [this feeling] binds us together." Interns, too, speak well of the working environment: "The people I work with show a lot of professionalism, but they also have a lot of heart. We all depend on each other. . . . [I]t creates a tight-knit environment."

The CIA runs a summer speaker series for its interns. Held in the agency's bubble-shaped, 500-seat auditorium, the series invites various department heads to address the interns. Interns may also attend the "town meetings," which brief employees on CIA policy. Town meetings are led by a top dog of the agency, often a deputy director of one of the divisions, the general counsel, or the director of the agency.

Interns work in various locations in Virginia and Washington, such as in Reston, VA; Vienna, VA; or the CIA headquarters in Langley, VA. The last is the real McCoy when it comes to what one would envision the CIA compound to be. Eight miles from downtown Washington, CIA headquarters is nestled in the woods of suburban Virginia. Two fortresslike administration buildings sit at the end of a long, restricted thoroughfare. In the lobby, a huge CIA seal adorns the floor, as was depicted in a scene from the movie *Patriot Games*. Hallways inside the CIA buildings evoke a hospital-like sterility; shoes clank against the floors with austere authority. Small exhibits are interspersed throughout the buildings, including one that displays a chunk of the Berlin Wall. Bathrooms are of the typical institutional variety, except that each boasts a scale for employees to weigh themselves; "the agency wants its people in good shape," said an employee.

To further this goal of employee fitness, the CIA has a few gym facilities, each with the standard fare of Nautilus machines, StairMasters, and aerobics classes. Headquarters also has a great jogging path that snakes through the compound's woods. For the team-oriented, there's an intramural sports program (softball, flag football, men's basketball) open to all employees.

Most CIA interns elect to live in CIA-designated apartments located in Fairfax and Reston, VA. Four interns typically live in the two-bedroom apartments.

As CIA brochures will attest, generosity is the operative word when it comes to employee benefits. This spirit applies to interns, too. They are reimbursed for travel to and from Washington, whether traveling by car, train, or plane. A Co-Op Association exists to help interns plan tours of Washington and other off-hours activities. Interns receive the same benefits as permanent employees, including accrual of annual and sick leave, enrollment in health and life insurance plans, participation in carpools, and use of medical services. Job-related internal training in such subjects as computers, foreign languages, and leadership skills is also available to interns.

Salaries are paid according to percentage of coursework completed. College seniors thus earn more than juniors, and so on. Students studying a hard science or engineering will receive a slightly higher salary than business or liberal-arts majors.

SELECTION

 The CIA Internship Program is open to college juniors and seniors; particularly minority and disabled students. The Graduate Studies Program is available for minority and nonminority students entering their first or second years of graduate study. Applicants must be U.S. citizens and over the age of 17 1/2 at time of application, have a minimum GPA (3.0 for undergrads), and successfully pass medical and security screening (including a polygraph test). Although other areas of study may be applicable to the agency's needs, the CIA generally looks for students in the following majors: accounting and finance, business administration, cartography/geography, computer science, economics, engineering, hard sciences (chemistry, physics, etc.), international studies, languages (particularly non-Romance languages), mathematics, and political science.

APPLICATION PROCEDURE

 Apply E-A-R-L-Y! The deadline for undergraduate applicants is in the previous autumn; graduate applicants should apply six to nine months prior to the desired work period. It takes the CIA at least six months to run a thorough background check on its applicants. Applicants should submit a cover letter and a resume. The CIA Employment Center responds within 45 days to those judged to be the best candidates. Footing the bill for transportation and hotel expenses, the CIA invites these applicants to interview with the hiring office. Those who make it past the initial interview are asked to return to the CIA for a physical examination, psychological profile, and polygraph test.

OVERVIEW

 CIA. There are few three-letter combinations that carry more weight on a resume. At the very least, employers know that CIA interns have passed the electronic scrutiny of the "black box." But interning at the CIA is not for everyone. Despite Hollywood's portrayal of CIA work as glamorous and dangerous, the CIA internship offers little in the way of international intrigue. Nevertheless, interns do get challenging assignments. And they receive an insider's look at what *Newsweek* has deemed the most secretive and tightly knit organization in American society. But interns must be prepared to work in a highly bureaucratic environment, one that prizes discreetness and loyalty. Many do, and every year upward of 40 percent of all interns are offered permanent jobs at the CIA.

FOR MORE INFORMATION . . .

- Central Intelligence Agency
  CIA Recruitment Center
  P.O. Box 4090
  Reston, VA 20195

Chevron

SELECTIVITY	🔍 🔍 🔍
Approximate applicant pool: 1,000 Interns accepted: 100	

COMPENSATION	💲 💲 💲 💲 💲
$400–$700/wk for undergrads; $800/wk for grad students; round-trip travel; allowance for temporary-lodging	

QUALITY OF LIFE	🌴 🌴 🌴 🌴
Orientation; Chevron fitness centers & cafeterias; Summer Intern Day; special tours	

LOCATION(S)	
Bakersfield, Concord, El Segundo, Richmond, San Francisco (HQ), and San Ramon, CA; New Orleans, LA; Pascagoula, MS; Houston, TX	

FIELD	
Chemicals; Oil & gas	

DURATION	
Intern—12 weeks (Summer) Co-op—at least two 3-month sessions (ongoing)	

PRE-REQS	
Undergrads; recent grads; grad students; college grads of any age	

DEADLINE(S)	
Rolling (until on-campus interviews in January)	

Quick.

Who opened the first service station in the United States?

Answer: Chevron, in 1907.

What kind of fuel did Charles Lindbergh use when he crossed the Atlantic Ocean in 1927?

Answer: Chevron Red Crown aviation gasoline.

Who almost single-handedly supplied the Pacific Theatre of Operations during World War II with fuels and lubricants for its planes, ships, and tanks?

Answer: Chevron.

What is the hands-down fuel of choice among professional fire-spitters?

Answer: Chevron Supreme.

Well, maybe not. But it might as well be, as Chevron is the largest refiner and marketer of petroleum products in the United States and one of the world's largest petroleum companies. Its activities range from discovering, producing, transporting, and marketing oil, natural gas, and chemicals, to maintaining ancillary businesses in real estate development, mining, coal, and precious metals. Headquartered in San Francisco, Chevron employs 55,000 people worldwide in more than 100 countries and generates more than $40 billion in annual sales.

DESCRIPTION

Chevron offers internships in its refineries, engineering groups, petrochemical plants, oil field producing groups, computer services groups, research organizations, and finance and human resource functions. Interns work in various areas, including Upstream Operations (i.e., petroleum exploration and production), Downstream Operations (i.e., refinery products), Refining, Marketing (M.B.A.s only), Finance (M.B.A.s only), Human Resources (grad students only), Computer Science, and Accounting. Any way you hack it, however, all Chevron interns receive substantive assignments and work closely with other Chevron employees. As one intern put it, "Here, you don't do anything by yourself."

One Downstream Operations intern who worked in Plant Support was assigned three summer projects. In addition to testing

BUSYWORK METER
LOW · MEDIUM · HIGH
OLDMAN & HAMADEH

and installing a new flow meter in the plant, he designed a vapor-type sump cover for an open oil-sump (that is, reservoir), to prevent vapors from escaping. His last project involved finding the optimal material for building a curtain for another vapor-containment system. Referring to a draftsman he worked closely with, the intern said: "He took my ideas and put them in a drawing. Then I met with construction personnel who did the actual construction work. Although I had to get used to the refinery environment, trying to work and interface with a lot of busy people, it was neat to see my designs become actual working parts of the refinery."

An intern who worked in Marketing spent her summer coordinating orders for lubricants from Latin American customers. In addition to maintaining customer contact on a daily basis, she placed orders with the plant and arranged for the orders to be shipped. "Early in the summer," she explained, "I needed a lot of help from my direct supervisor, but by the end of the summer, I was actually handling my supervisor's workload when he went on vacation or a business trip. In sum, I learned a good deal about the corporate world, corporate politics, and teamwork."

Another Marketing intern with a civil engineering background spent his summer working on support projects for environmental engineers. For each project, he prepared bids for environmental work and worked with local, state, and federal regulators. One of his projects, for example, involved "trying to reduce the number of permits needed" for clean-up sites. Because more than 15 sites were involved, he estimated a potential savings to the company of over $100,000. "Although I did not work as a civil engineer," he said, "I learned that it does take a strong technical background to understand what consultants are giving you."

In Engineering, an intern spent his summer doing performance studies on existing equipment, as well as technical-economic studies on new equipment. One study centered around a new bearing design that Chevron was considering putting on some of its equipment. Another study concerned various rotating equipment in the refinery, like compressors, turbines, and pumps. He said: "I had a really good mix of assignments, involving a good amount of hands-on engineering."

A Human Resources intern helped design a comprehensive program of training modules for Chevron's quality improvement process. The modules would allow organizations within Chevron to explain the concept of quality improvement to employees, and how to apply it to their jobs. Spending the first part of the summer shadowing her supervisor while the supervisor presented the quality improvement process to in-house clients, the intern later worked with an outside consultant in designing five total training modules. "Between working with the internal quality-consultants and external training specialists, I was able to get a broad overview of how quality-improvement principles and training practices can be applied to organizations," she said. "I was very involved in the design and the creation of the program…. I got to work with an outside organization… with very experienced training professionals…. I was able to see how a lot of the principles I was learning in my coursework could be applied to the corporate world and used to solve tangible business problems."

Dress varies with work location and department. For the most part, interns dress casually, although those working at corporate headquarters dress in suits or skirts. At the refineries, an outfit of coveralls, hard hats, and safety boots is the norm.

Chevron interns enjoy a flood of benefits. One intern commented that a "big company like Chevron can put more into resources… for interns, and that shows." Although Chevron does not provide interns with housing, it does offer interns a temporary-lodging allowance and assistance in identifying potential roommates.

> One intern journeyed to Central America to do research on underground storage tanks.

Interns also receive free round-trip travel, as well as access to Chevron fitness facilities and subsidized cafeterias. For their professional development, interns participate in an orientation and in Chevron's Performance Appraisal Process (PAPR), a formal evaluation affording interns feedback on their communication skills, productivity, and leadership abilities from their supervisors. At the end of the summer, many interns also give project presentations to senior managers.

Social activities are plentiful as well. Interns participate in numerous planned activities, such as baseball games, picnics, group dinners, barbecues, and slide shows. For interns at headquarters, there's also a day for lunch, a boat cruise on San Francisco Bay, and a tour of Chevron oil ships docked at the Port of San Francisco. In addition, interns have the opportunity to socialize and meet Chevron executives at Summer Intern Day, an event featuring a question-and-answer "Family Feud" game on Chevron facts and trivia.

Interns have the opportunity to familiarize themselves with Chevron through tours of various company facilities. Interns from the around the country, for example, have the option of visiting corporate headquarters in downtown San Francisco and attending presentations given by senior managers. Interns may also go on "piggy-backs," that is tours of nearby refineries and research locations.

Travel is occasionally part of the Chevron intern's worklife. One Marketing intern, for example, traveled to a plant and took a tour of the refinery to familiarize herself with various blending and packaging processes and learn about "what [I] was selling." Two summers later, she "traveled to Central America and did research on underground storage tanks…. I went to Guatemala for four days and El Salvador for three days." A Human Resources intern who had worked on various projects with a consultant later flew to St. Louis, MO, to meet with outside consultants.

Interns comment favorably on the supportive atmosphere at Chevron. "Everybody always took an interest in me and in what I did. I was always included," said one intern. Said another intern: "I pretty much handled [the] projects by myself, but it required continuous [input] from folks in my group." One intern likened the work environment to a tennis team: "When you're out there on a court, you're out there playing as an individual… but you know you have a team behind you."

Indeed, say some interns, all this support is welcome, considering how challenging most intern projects are. "You're definitely not treated like a gofer or secretary," reported one intern. "You're expected to handle a project from start to finish…from the initial conception to the designing to the materials purchasing to the site preparation to meeting with the contractors to the actual construction and design to the post-construction critique analysis."

SELECTION

Chevron's summer and co-op positions are open to undergraduates, recent college graduates, and graduate students majoring in engineering (chemical, mechanical, electrical, or petroleum), geology, computer science, accounting, marketing, finance, or human resources. Engineering, computer science, and accounting interns must be at least college juniors (at least college sophomores for petroleum engineering positions). Finance, geology, and human resources interns must be at least college seniors. Co-op positions target sophomore engineers and computer scientists. International applicants with F-1 visas are eligible.

APPLICATION PROCEDURE

Applications for Chevron's summer and co-op internship programs are accepted on a rolling basis until on-campus interviews in January. Students should arrange an on-campus interview or submit a resume, college transcript, and cover letter indicating the type of work and location desired. Decisions are made following campus interviews and after considering field of study, academic record, and overall qualifications.

OVERVIEW

 Those looking for an action-packed summer will have plenty to look forward to at Chevron. In addition to gaining an overall view of the oil refinery business, interns are also "challenged in areas they might not have experience in." They work closely with a group of people who differ widely in age, expertise, and experience. Willingness to learn, ask questions, and work with others is crucial, but the rewards are plentiful. Substantive assignments, a tight-knit group of interns and colleagues, and a supportive atmosphere are some of the advantages of Chevron life. For interns who perform well, this life doesn't have to end when the internship does: Each year, up to 40 percent of new hires are former Chevron interns.

FOR MORE INFORMATION . . .

■ Chevron Corporation
Employment Services
575 Market St.
San Francisco, CA 94105
www.chevron.com

CNN is also known as TTU—Ted Turner University—because it nurtured the careers of many who have gone on to become some of the strongest anchors, correspondents, and producers in broadcast news. Bernard Shaw, Katie Couric, and Christiane Amanpour all began their ascent to stardom with jobs at the world's first twenty-four-hour broadcast news company. In an era of severe cutbacks by broadcast news companies, CNN continues to open bureaus (such as the one in Cuba) and keeps its newsrooms staffed with some of the most experienced journalists in the world.

The Cable News Network has become much more successful since its launch in 1980, when many at the broadcast news networks dared to call the upstart southern cable company "Chicken Noodle News." CNN's reputation was made during the Persian Gulf War, when it reportedly often was the first to inform even President Bush of military developments. Despite a few missteps, such as an unsubstantiated claim in 1998 that the U.S. government used nerve gas on American defectors during the Vietnam War, CNN continues to top the list of America's most trusted news sources.

DESCRIPTION

CNN's internship program varies widely among its many departments and domestic and international bureaus. Interns at CNN's Atlanta headquarters have access to the full range of seminars, training classes, and the opportunity to do on-air packages with the CNN "Newsroom" show. Many domestic and international bureaus do not have full-time intern coordinators, and some interns have had to show some initiative to ensure that they have enough work to do. Generally, interns may work full- or part-time for 12 weeks, although a few hours and weeks may be added or subtracted depending on the intern's needs.

Most of CNN's major channels and popular shows come out of CNN's Atlanta headquarters, and interns may work in any of the

---

SELECTIVITY

At Atlanta Headquarters: Approximate applicant pool: 500 (summer), 100 (each fall/winter/spring quarter) Interns accepted: 100+ (summer); approx. 40+ (each fall/winter/spring quarter)

COMPENSATION $

None

QUALITY OF LIFE 🕴 🕴 🕴 🕴

Seminars; extensive training; cafeteria; comfortable offices; casual dress; luncheons with executives; possible production experience; international flavor

LOCATION(S)

Domestic Bureaus: Atlanta, GA; Boston, MA; Chicago, IL; Dallas, TX; Detroit, MI; Los Angeles, CA; Miami, FL; New York, NY; San Francisco, CA; Washington, D.C.
International Bureaus: Amman, Jordan; Bangkok, Thailand; Beijing, China; Berlin, Germany; Brussels, Belgium; Cairo, Egypt; Frankfurt, Germany; Jerusalem, Israel; London, UK; Manila, Philippines; Mexico City, Mexico; Moscow, Russia; Nairobi, Kenya; New Delhi, India; Paris, France; Rio de Janeiro, Brazil; Rome, Italy; Santiago, Chile; Seoul, South Korea; Tokyo, Japan.

FIELD

Television News

DURATION

Approximately 12 weeks

PRE-REQS

College juniors and seniors; grad students

DEADLINE(S)

July 1 for fall (September–December)
November 1 for winter (January–April)
January 1 for spring (April–June)
March 1 for summer (June–September)

BUSYWORK

MEDIUM

LOW HIGH

OLDMAN & HAMADEH

METER

units: *CNN International* (CNNI), *CNNfn* (financial news), *CNN Newsroom Show* (news programs designed for use in the class room), *Headline News* (a half-hour news format that runs 24 hours), *CNN en Español*, *CNNSI* (a collaboration between CNN and *Sports Illustrated* magazine), *CNN World Report*, *TalkBack Live* (CNN's daily talk show, held in the CNN Center's atrium), and *NewsStand* (three one-hour weekly collaborations between CNN and *Fortune* magazine, *TIME* magazine, and *Entertainment Weekly* magazine). A few units are usually much in demand, with good reason: Bookings (which researches, locates, and works with the often famous guests who appear daily), *NewsStand* (which does long-form pieces), Political (assisting on the popular *Inside Politics* show, election coverage, and general political news), and *CNNSI* (despite its abysmal ratings, it is a fun department for sports fans).

> **"I worked on the forty-second floor and had a spacious cubicle, with a computer, phone, and terrific view of most of New York . . ."**

Atlanta is not only home to CNN's corporate and broadcast news headquarters, CNN's most extensive intern training is available there. Weekly seminars and training sessions and occasional executive luncheons punctuate departmental work, which can vary from tape-fetching to researching, depending on the departmental supervisor. During a typical week, interns may attend a weekly seminar to discuss career opportunities or producing techniques with senior producers, receive training on how to direct a live show, do textual or visual research for their department at CNN's library, and have lunch with CEO Tom Johnson. Most interns in CNN's non-corporate units emerge from their three-month internship with the skills necessary to be a production assistant.

At CNN in Atlanta, 20 lucky interns per quarter are chosen by lottery to work on four segments, three to four minutes long, that are then broadcast on the CNN *Newsroom Show* (created for students and broadcast on CNN early in the morning). The five interns assigned to each segment choose the topic, do the research, interview subjects, perform voice-overs and on-air stand-ups, write the script, and observe the editing and post-production processes. (Only one person can

do the voice-over and stand-ups, which necessitates a usually tense coin-toss.) The intern-created segments are directed by the internship coordinator under the supervision of "Newsroom's" senior and executive producers, and provide interns with an extraordinary opportunity to do hands-on reporting and producing.

Departments that are not involved in news gathering or production at CNN are not as strong as broadcast news units; an advertising firm, for example, might provide a better internship experience than CNN's advertising department. Former interns for corporate departments attest to the fact that the seminars, formal training, mentoring, and newsroom excitement that characterize the broadcast news internships often are mediocre, if they exist at all. However, interns interested in online services, advertising, post-production (editorial, audio, and graphic services), public relations, radio, sales, and marketing have plenty of departments to choose from at CNN in Atlanta. (A comprehensive list of these departments may be obtained by calling or writing to the intern coordinator at CNN in Atlanta.)

Unlike the broadcast news networks and other 24-hour news channels, CNN is not known for cutthroat competition among frantic employees. Despite the lay-offs at *Headline News* within the last several years, many people who work at CNN (particularly those in Atlanta) started and expect to end their careers at this company, which is known for its loyalty to its employees. Many departmental supervisors, producers, reporters, staff members, and on-air talent enjoy working with and advising interns. Each semester, an anchor gives an intern seminar on anchoring and invites the interns to "shadow" them, offers one-on-one career advice, and critiques their resume tapes.

At first sight, CNN's Atlanta headquarters appears to be a mall. Fast food and somewhat upscale restaurants, a couple of souvenir stores, a post office, and a cinema dominate the first floor of CNN Center. The set for *TalkBack Live*, CNN's daily talk show on issues of the day, and the Turner Store, well-stocked with overpriced T-shirts and mugs emblazoned with the logos of Ted Turner's various channels, attract crowds of tourists. The Omni Hotel connects the eastern sides of CNN's North and South Towers, and prompts weary CNN staff members to joke that they could literally live at CNN Center. Those who go on the lucrative CNN Studio Tour get a glimpse of the many floors upstairs—the humming newsroom, the Hard News Cafe (which supplies the overworked staff with vittles 24/7), and the multitude of departments that make CNN and its many offshoots possible.

Although Atlanta often feels more like a big town to those who are not from the South, it has a substantial social scene of young, diverse, and increasingly cosmopolitan professionals. CNN provides interns with free mass-transportation passes and assistance in locating temporary housing. Downtown Atlanta and nearby Buckhead entertain locals and visitors with year-round cultural events (especially concerts), a terrific nightlife (aided by a hopping music scene), lots of restaurants, and ample shopping.

A few of CNN's other domestic locations stand out. The New York and Los Angeles bureaus are notable for containing sizable numbers of producers who work on CNN's entertainment shows (*Showbiz Today* and *Entertainment Weekly*). CNN in New York is also the center of *CNNfn*, the financial network, which is known for the show *Moneyline*. CNN's bureau in Washington, D.C., ranks a close second to CNN Headquarters among political junkies. The D.C. bureau is known for its cadre of young, savvy producers who know the capital inside and out. They create the daily *Inside Politics*, a Beltway-centered show that regularly features, and is followed by, movers and shakers in national politics.

CNN's bureaus overseas tend to be small outposts of the CNN empire, and as such can offer only a limited experience for interns. The staffs in small bureaus tend to be tiny and familial, and less corporate in character than the big American bureaus. Internationally, London and Rome seem to gain the highest marks among former interns. The London bureau is favored by English-speakers for obvious reasons, and also because the UK and surrounding area tend to generate news on a daily basis that is picked up by CNN US and CNN International. Although the Frankfurt bureau is intended to replace the Rome bureau as CNN's center on the European continent, Rome remains a vital center of operations. Students accepted by an international bureau must provide their own transportation.

SELECTION

 College juniors and seniors of all majors and nationalities are invited to apply, and those with a demonstrated interest in journalism and/or broadcast news are preferred. Those involved in a campus newspaper, radio, or TV station, and anyone with previous internships in media have a better chance of acceptance to news departments. Applicants interested in interning for a show or unit that has a particular focus, such as *Inside Politics* or the medical unit, have a greater chance of acceptance if they have an academic background or extracurricular experience in that subject. Similarly, media departments (advertising, PR, etc.) tend to prefer applicants with relevant experience who intend to pursue careers in those areas. The competition for summer internship positions is intense, and a smaller percentage of applicants are accepted than are accepted for the academic year internships. Candidates who attend colleges and universities near a bureau are encouraged to apply for fall, winter, or spring quarter internships.

APPLICATION PROCEDURE

 Considering the size of the application, it's wise to begin the application process at least a month prior to the deadline. Applicants must contact the bureau at which they would prefer to intern to obtain a copy of the internship application. (Those who wish to intern at CNN's new bureau in Frankfurt, Germany, should contact the Berlin bureau for contact information and an application.) Each application must be accompanied by an essay, a current resume, two letters of recommendation, and an official college transcript. Essays tend to be about 400 words long, and should describe both professional goals and how the applicant hopes to benefit from the internship program. One letter of recommendation needs to come from the applicant's faculty advisor or major department professor. A letter of acknowledgment will be sent to applicants within three weeks following the application deadline. Although some departments occasionally call applicants, as a rule there is no interview required for intern candidates.

OVERVIEW

 The leader in 24-hour broadcast news also has the premier internship program in the business. Interns emerge from CNN's program with production assistance and researching experience; those who seek a career in broadcast news would do well to intern with the Cable News Network. CNN also looks favorably on its former interns when hiring for entry-level positions (i.e., video journalists, production assistants, researchers). The diversity of CNN's departments, from Public Relations and Sales to *Entertainment Weekly* and *Business News* units, means that those interested in almost any area can learn about their field with the guidance of top professionals.

FOR MORE INFORMATION . . .

- **Domestic Bureaus:**
  CNN Atlanta Headquarters
  Willie Jenkins
  Internship Coordinator
  CNN Human Resources
  4th Floor North Tower, One CNN Center
  Atlanta, GA 30303
  404-827-3776

- CNN Boston Bureau
  637 Washington St.
  Suite 208
  Brookline, MA 02446
  617-264-9905

- CNN Chicago Bureau
  435 North Michigan, 7th Floor
  Chicago, IL 60611
  312-654-8555

- CNN Dallas Bureau
  1201 Main Street, Suite 1525
  Dallas, TX 75250
  214-747-1440

- CNN Detroit Bureau
  7441 Second Blvd.
  Detroit, MI 48202
  313-871-3245

- CNN Los Angeles Bureau
  6430 Sunset Blvd., Suite 300
  Los Angeles, CA 90028
  213-993-5000

- CNN Miami Bureau
  1200 Biscayne Blvd., Suite 101
  North Miami, FL 33181
  305-891-3582

- CNN New York Bureau
  5 Penn Plaza, 20th Floor
  New York, NY 10001
  212-714-7800

- CNN San Francisco Bureau
  50 California Street, Suite 950
  San Francisco, CA 94111
  415-434-1661

- CNN Washington, D.C. Bureau
  820 First Street, NE
  Washington, D.C. 20002
  202-515-2913

International Bureaus:
- CNN Amman Bureau, PO Box 35070
  Jordan Ins. Co. Bldg., 6th Floor
  Third Circle, Jabal Amman
  Amman, Jordan
  9-62-665-0412

- CNN Bangkok Bureau
  93/1 Wirless Road
  Diethem Building, Tower A, Suite 1503
  Bangkok 10330, Thailand
  662-254-2016

- CNN Beijing Bureau
  9-2-82 Ta Yuan
  Diplomatic Compound
  Xin Dong Lu, Beijing, China
  861-532-6013

- CNN Berlin Bureau*
  Taubenstrasse 1
  10117 Berlin-Mitte,
  Germany
  49-30-2-019-0650

- CNN Brussels Bureau
  550 Chaussee de Lovain
  7th Floor, Box 3
  1030 Brussels, Belgium
  322-735-0971

- CNN Cairo Bureau
  1127 Corniche El-Nil
  Cairo, Egypt
  202-578-0661

- CNN Jerusalem Bureau
  c/o Jerusalem Capital Studios
  206 Jaffa Road, PO Box 13172
  Jerusalem, Israel 91131
  97-2-238-1782

- CNN London Bureau
  CNN House, 19-22 Rathbone Place
  London W1P 1DF, United Kingdom
  44-71-637-6800

- CNN Manila Bureau
  Rm. 200-VIP Bldg. 1140
  Roxas Blvd., Ermita
  Manila, Phillipines
  63-258-8905

- CNN Mexico City Bureau
  Avenida De Las Fuentes 95
  Techmachalco
  Est de Mexico, CP 53970
  Mexico City, Mexico
  525-294-2293

- CNN Moscow Bureau
  Kutuzovsky Prospect 7/4
  Apartment 256/258
  Moscow, Russia
  70-95-243-0909

- CNN Nairobi Bureau
  Koinange Street, Chester House Bldg.
  First Floor Press Center
  Nairobi, Kenya
  East Africa
  25-4-233-0273

- CNN New Delhi Bureau
  F 162 Malcha Marg
  New Dehli 110021, India
  91-301-0538

- CNN Paris Bureau
  25 Rue de Ponthieu
  75008 Paris, France
  331-428-9233

- CNN Rio de Janiero Bureau
  PCA. ALM. Belfort Viera
  #12 Apt. 1501, Leblon
  Rio de Janiero, Brazil 22440
  55-21-259-5407

- CNN Rome Bureau
  Via Col di Lana 8
  Rome 00195, Italy
  396-322-2311

- CNN Santiago Bureau
  Los Espanoles 1986, Providencia
  Santiago, Chile
  562-233-4000

- CNN Seoul Bureau
  2nd Floor, Economic News Agency Bldg.
  111 Chung Hak Dong Congroo-Ku
  Seoul, South Korea
  (no phone calls please; contact CNN's Atlanta
  Bureau for the application)

- CNN Tokyo Bureau
  659 Bldg., 2nd Floor
  6-5-9 Roppongi, Minato-Ku
  Tokyo 106, Japan
  813-3470-4121

*Also contact for information about the
Frankfurt Bureau internship program.

Bitters. Kvass. Ale. Lager. Pilsner. Mead. Stout.

Americans have been enjoying combinations of grains, water, and yeast for more than 350 years, ever since the Pilgrims landed at Plymouth Rock one November day in 1620, beer on board. By then, humans had been consuming beer for over 10,000 years, hypothesize historians, who think that the concoction was discovered accidentally when some nomads' grain, coming into contact with warm water, fermented to create a primitive beer. Since its discovery, claims Washington's Beer Institute, beer has been carried onto Noah's ark, has played a role in Chinese religious rituals, and has been scrutinized for quality by the Egyptian pharaohs' royal beer inspectors. In modern times, Coors Brewing Company has also played an influential role in beer history.

In 1868, a Prussian brewery apprentice named Adolph Coors found his way to the United States. Arriving in Golden, CO, in 1873, he founded a brewery with a partner whom he bought out seven years later. Today, Adolph Coors is gone, but his descendants run the operation, and Adolph Coors Company ranks among the Fortune 500 of American industrial corporations. Adolph Coors' vision helped make his company the third largest brewer in the United States, next to Anheuser-Busch and Miller, and make beer as popular as it is today.

DESCRIPTION

The Coors Corporate College Internship Program started formally in 1983 when it invited 22 students to experience life at the world's largest single-site brewery. Before that, only children of employees could secure a summer job at the beer-production company. Now, from 20 to 40 college students every year participate in the programs offered: Purchasing, Engineering, Sensory Analysis, Project Management, Accounting, Biology/Microbiology/Chemistry, Human Resources, Wellness Center/Recreation, and Journalism/Public Relations. However, internships in all of these departments are not available every summer.

Coors believes staunchly that its internships must contain a strong learning component. Said the coordinator: "We don't believe that the interns should have to file or simply observe a boss at work. Coors works very hard to make sure that its interns are exposed to assignments that ensure a solid learning experience."

SELECTIVITY

🔍 🔍 🔍 🔍 🔍

Approximate applicant pool: 900
Interns accepted: 20–40

COMPENSATION

💲 💲 💲 💲

Varies by grade level and major, but compensation is competitive

QUALITY OF LIFE

🌴 🌴 🌴 🌴

Entry-level projects; mountain recreation; wellness Center; intern picnic

LOCATION(S)

Golden, CO

FIELD

Consumer goods (beer)

DURATION

9–12 weeks
Summer

PRE-REQS

College sophomores, juniors, and seniors; grad students must be returning to school for at least one term

DEADLINE(S)

March 1

Occupying about seven square miles of space, Coors is situated between two foothills in the quaint town of Golden. Nestled against the Rocky Mountains about 30 minutes from metropolitan Denver, Golden and its environs offer exciting recreational opportunities like skiing, horseback riding, mountain climbing, and rafting. The brewery itself, whose gray concrete architecture reminds some interns of a "prison, Alcatraz style," is almost three-quarters of a mile long on one side. Inside, one finds vats, a maze of piping, a red-tile floor made out of Coors Ceramics products, and plenty of brew kettles and fermenters. Surrounding the brewery are an engineering facility, a can-manufacturing facility, construction offices, storage rooms, and an exercise complex called the Wellness Center, which interns may use free of charge. Housed in a renovated 23,000-square-foot Safeway store at the entrance of the brewery, the Wellness Center has weights, Eagle equipment, StairMasters, bicycles, treadmills, and a $\frac{1}{8}$-mile running track.

Interns enjoy other perks, too. For lunch, there's the subsidized cafeteria, where interns can eat for about $3. They may purchase beer at a discount from the company store, if they are 21 or older. Interns are afforded a 25 percent discount on all logo items, such as caps and pins.

Most interns spend nine or more weeks at the brewery, during which time there are clearly many things to see and do. Then there are the periodic team or one-on-one meetings held by each department. Moreover, twice in the summer, interns are formally evaluated. Concluded one intern: "On a scale of one to ten, I would have to rate my experience a ten. I was a project manager from day one, doing everything, even though project managers usually have lots of previous industry experience."

> **Interns may purchase beer at a discount from the company store, if they are older than twenty-one.**

SELECTION

 Generally, Coors seeks team players with excellent written and oral communication skills. Eligibility requirements, however, depend on the position sought. Students in Purchasing must be seniors with a 3.0 GPA in purchasing or a closely related major. Engineering applicants may be from any engineering discipline but must have already finished their junior year by the start of the internship and must have at least a 2.4 GPA in engineering. Students in Sensory Analysis must have completed their junior year in a food science program. Project Management applicants must be seniors or graduate students in construction management. Prospective Accounting interns must have finished their junior years in accounting or finance. Interns in Biology/Microbiology/Chemistry may be juniors or seniors in those fields. The Wellness Center and the Public Relations positions are nonpaid, credit-only (six to twelve semester units), for juniors or seniors. The Wellness Center positions are for students in wellness, recreation, or related fields. The Public Relations positions are for students (including outstanding sophomores) with strong journalism experience or coursework. International applicants are eligible.

APPLICATION PROCEDURE

 The deadline for submission of required materials is March 1. Applicants must send a resume and cover letter to the address below, or apply at www.coorsjobs.com. Top local-area candidates are usually invited for on-site interviews. Long-distance candidates are interviewed by phone. Those hired are required to undergo a drug test and sign a Coors Brewing Company Confidentiality Agreement.

OVERVIEW

 Of the top three beer companies in the United States, only Coors offers undergraduates a formal internship program. Thirty minutes from Denver, the company taps interns into beer processing and administration, distilling its internship philosophy to this: Talented students deserve important projects. As contributing members of the Coors team, interns present their work to a group of high-level managers or submit lengthy reports at the end of the summer. According to the program's coordinator, "Part of the objective with the intern program is to develop and then ultimately consider graduates for full-time opportunities." But don't think that just because you landed an internship position for the summer you're guaranteed the key to the executive washroom. You've got to work hard and prove yourself to be a person who can learn and grow within the Coors environment even to be considered for a regular, full-time position.

FOR MORE INFORMATION . . .

Coors Brewing Company
P.O. Box 4030
Dept. NH210
c/o College Recruiting Representative
Golden, CO 80401
www.coorsjobs.com

SELECTIVITY	
Approximate applicant pool: 300–400 Interns accepted: 60	

COMPENSATION

$3,500 tuition; grants, scholarships, installment plans, and tuition loans are available

QUALITY OF LIFE

Variety of organizations
Focus weeks; weekly seminars

LOCATION(S)

San Francisco and Los Angeles, CA;
St. Louis, MO; New York, NY; Pittsburgh, PA

FIELD

Public Service

DURATION

9 months
September–June

PRE-REQS

College grads of any age or equivalent experience

DEADLINE(S)

Early February. Call to verify.

Every group has its ultimate challenge; an experience that defines those who participate as among the most talented in their field. Track and field enthusiasts have the decathlon. Whiz kids have the Odyssey of the Mind competition. Fitness freaks have the Iron Man Triathlon. And aspiring public servants have the Coro Fellows Program.

According to its promotional literature, the 58-year-old Coro Foundation "offers the kind of hands-on experience that most graduate schools only talk about." Every year, each of the five regional Coro centers picks 12 college graduates and subjects them to a rigorous 9-month series of internships, interviews, public service projects, and seminar meetings. The Coro Fellows Program, in the words of its brochure, "provides its participants with the opportunity to step out of their schooling or careers . . . to experience new environments . . . to learn from the best . . . to discuss and analyze experiences with colleagues . . . to be challenged by demanding and changing situations."

DESCRIPTION

 The odyssey commences in September, when Coro Fellows begin the first of a series of six internships, each three to four weeks in duration. Some internships find Fellows carrying out a high-level project, while others are more of an observer's post, where Fellows conduct interviews with the key decision makers of an organization. By the time it's all over in June, Fellows will have interned in a government agency, a corporation, a community organization, a labor union, a media organization and a political campaign. The Fellows interviewed for this passage were affiliated with Coro's Northern California Center and thus completed internships with organizations in the San Francisco Bay Area; Fellows affiliated with the other Coro centers—Los Angeles, St. Louis, Pittsburgh, and New York—serve internships in their respective regions.

The government internship finds Fellows working in state or local government. One Fellow worked with Anna Eshoo, a county supervisor in San Mateo. In addition to "designing a program where kids from San Mateo could spend time in county departments to learn about government," she wrote a brochure that pulled together information about county services. Assigned to San Francisco's Department of Health, another Fellow did a project coordinating the agency's services for at-risk youth; "I made recommendations on how [the department's] services can be better integrated." The highlight of one Fellow's year was interning in the office of then-mayor of San Francisco Dianne Feinstein, herself a Coro alumna. "I rotated through different areas of the office and did small projects. But the real thrill was getting to shadow her in whatever she did." Like many officials who sponsor Coro Fellows, Feinstein was unusually accessible to the Fellow: "[Feinstein] would sometimes just let me sit in her office while she carried on with her business. . . . It's so rare that a politician would give her young intern such close contact."

> A recent Coro class included a professional dancer, a speech and debate champion, and a third-degree black belt in Chinese boxing.

For their corporate internship, Fellows are placed in one of the region's larger corporations. Chevron USA was the destination of one Fellow, who spent much of her time interviewing 100 of the company's employees. Another Fellow found herself at Wells Fargo Bank, where she worked with the vice president in charge of branch banking. "My main project was researching and writing a report on the potential for adding future [bank] branches in [San Francisco's] South of Market district. My recommendations were based on the growth of businesses and housing in this [formerly depressed] area." A third Fellow was sent to McKesson Associates, a "huge Fortune 500 company that acts as a distributor for things like beverages and pharmaceutical products." Working with the head of public affairs, he wrote a memo on recent legislation regulating the sale of bottled water. He also conducted several interviews with employees, including the CEO: "I got an unprecedented 45 minutes of the CEO's time. My boss later told me to consider myself lucky: The

CEO had never given *him* 45 minutes of time!"

Fellows are placed in a wide range of community organizations. Assigned to an environmental advocacy group called Friends of the Earth, one intern wrote several articles for its newspaper, *Not Man Apart*. Another Fellow was sent to the San Francisco chapter of Planned Parenthood, where she prepared a report briefing the executive director on how the group's operations would change when parental consent laws went into effect. The internship taught her "what working at an organization under siege feels like—you have to take extra security measures like signing in and watching for suspicious packages." A nonprofit group called Asian Incorporated was the assignment of another Fellow. "Asian Inc. is dedicated to improving Asian businesses in San Francisco," he said. "I helped the group coordinate a conference of the Asian American Business Association. I handled the nuts and bolts—like contacting an assortment of Asian professional associations and arranging for state officials to speak at the conference."

The labor union internship is typically a week shorter than the other experiences, and it emphasizes observation over practical work. Assigned to the San Francisco Building and Trades Council, one intern was "virtually attached to the head of the union," with whom he attended "sensitive contract negotiations on issues relating to plumbers, carpenters, and iron workers." Another Fellow was sent to SCIU 790, a union for service workers like school cafeteria employees and groundskeepers. In addition to doing some legal research on labor contracts, he shadowed the head of the union: "At the end of the internship, I sat next to him during the contract negotiations with the city of San Francisco. It was pretty amazing to have this kind of access."

The final internship assigns Fellows to a political campaign. A Fellow from 1984 helped out at the Gary Hart for President campaign, serving as the liaison between the state office and the local campaign offices in Northern California. In 1988, another Fellow coordinated local phone bank operations for the Dukakis campaign. "I set up phone banks throughout San Francisco, soliciting volunteers and preparing scripts for them to read." A third Fellow, a self-described "diehard Democrat," was surprised to be assigned to the 1986 campaign to elect Republican Tom Heuning as San Mateo county supervisor. He recalled: "Heuning knew that we had little in common ideologically, and said something like, 'I bet I wasn't your first choice.' [B]ut it worked out well—I passed out [campaign] literature for him when we walked precincts together, and I accompanied him to meetings and receptions."

In addition to completing internships, Fellows carry out two public service projects. At midyear, Fellows divide into groups of three or four and spend several weeks developing a policy-oriented project. Recent projects include a published report on the impact of Bay Area media on ethnic communities, a televised documentary on Mexican-American immigration, and a published manual on AIDS in the workplace. Said one Fellow: "It's exciting—projects typically receive some kind of formal recognition, whether they are published in a journal or shown on television."

Late in the year, Fellows complete an individual public-service project on a topic of their choice. Said a Fellow: "It's a chance to apply the skills you've learned and explore future professional interests." One Fellow did a case study analyzing the effectiveness of the California Employment Training Panel, a state organization that "sponsors businesses to retrain workers rather than lay them off." Another Fellow wrote a marketing plan for an energy information center. "I suggested ways the center could market itself better—such as through the newspaper, radio, and direct mail…. [T]he center heeded my recommendations, and use of the center ended up increasing dramatically."

Once a week throughout the program, Fellows meet at the Coro center for a daylong seminar. The seminar is designed to give Fellows a chance to exchange views and find out how everyone is faring in his or her internship. It also has an educational component, as Coro staff and special guests lecture on subjects like public speaking, research skills, and how to deal with the media. Past guests have included the speaker of the California State Assembly, the president of the San Francisco Planning Commission, and CEOs of Fortune 500 companies.

Interspersed throughout the nine months are several "focus weeks," designed to give Fellows intensive exposure to such areas as politics, communications, media, and entertainment. One focus week might find Fellows spending six days in Salinas Valley, learning about California's important agricultural base; another might bring Fellows to Sacramento, where they meet with state legislators, executive branch officials, and journalists covering the capital. During a focus week on negotiation, Fellows attended a workshop given by the renowned sports agent Leigh Steinberg. Said one Fellow: "Steinberg lectured on the art of negotiation and how it's so important to thoroughly research your opponent before negotiation begins. . . . Afterward, we divided into groups for mock salary negotiations. My partner and I represented a fictional athlete, and using [Steinberg's] techniques, we landed the athlete a pretty good deal."

Besides unparalleled practical and educational opportunities, the participants themselves are a glowing benefit of the Coro program. Said one Fellow: "Coro carefully selects its Fellows from a highly qualified pool of applicants—and it shows. Each of the 12 Fellows has done something special to get selected." Added another: "There was a common theme of excellence [among the Fellows]. At the same time, the Fellows bring to the program an incredible diversity of backgrounds." Indeed, a recent Coro class included a professional dancer, a speech and debate champion, a former senior class president of San Diego State University, a professional journalist, and a third-degree black belt in Chinese boxing.

Nine months with Coro is less expensive than a year of graduate school, but it's still significant—tuition for the Fellows program is $3,500. But scholarships funded by outside foundations and individuals are available, as are installment plans and tuition loans administered by Coro. And as the 60-hour-a-week program precludes outside employment, grants up to $12,000 are available, based on financial need, to assist with living expenses.

SELECTION

The program is open to anyone with a bachelor's degree. Coro stresses that Fellows "come from all academic disciplines, careers, racial and ethnic groups, and socioeconomic backgrounds." Although recent classes have ranged in age from 22 to 40, most participants are in their twenties. International applicants are eligible.

APPLICATION PROCEDURE

Applications must be submitted by mid-February. Candidates must apply to only one Coro center—San Francisco, Los Angeles, St. Louis, Pittsburgh, or New York. Required materials include completed application forms and written essays. Personal interviews are conducted at a Coro office. Twenty-four to 30 finalists per center are notified in February and invited to participate in a daylong selection process the following month. Coro sends out decision letters in April.

OVERVIEW

When interviewed about his time as a Coro Fellow, a participant from ten years ago recalled his experiences in crystal-clear detail. Commenting on why the memory is still so vivid, he said: "It's testament to how important those nine months were to me." This attitude is shared by the vast majority of former Coro Fellows, who consider their fellowship a powerful springboard to rewarding professional careers. The Coro alumni network is among the nation's most productive and prestigious. And of Coro's more than 3,500 graduates, over 75 percent now work in the public sector. Among these alumni are Senator Dianne Feinstein, Representatives Vic Fazio and Jerry Lewis, an associate justice of the California Supreme Court, and a member of the California State Assembly.

FOR MORE INFORMATION . . .

■ The Coro Fellows Program
Northern California Center
220 Sansome Street, 4th Floor
San Francisco, CA 94104
(415) 986-0521

■ The Coro Fellows Program
Southern California Center
811 Wilshire Boulevard
Suite 1025
Los Angeles, CA 90017-2624
(213) 623-1234

■ The Coro Fellows Program
Midwestern Center
1730 South 11th Street
St. Louis, MO 63104
(314) 621-3040

■ The Coro Fellows Program
Eastern Center
42 Broadway
18th Floor
New York, NY 10004
(212) 248-2935

■ The Coro Center for Civic Leadership
425 Sixth Avenue, 17th Floor
Pittsburgh, PA 15219-1819
(412) 201-5772

CREAMER DICKSON BASFORD
A EURO RSCG AGENCY

Picture it: It's a not-so-quiet, average day in the life of New York City. A gentle zephyr glides through the streets and alleys, steeped with the scent of baked pretzels, shuffling the news of yesterday along the pavement. Taxis honk, babies cry, and business deals are cut by the minute in the surrounding buildings. The planets are all moving in their respective spheres, and everything is right with the world.

Up above, a large dirigible with "Pizza Hut" painted in iris tones floats slowly across the pale summer sky. A cry goes out; the beefy blimp is falling! Disaster is about to strike! Slowly but surely, the craft is losing air, imperiling the lives of those below. Thinking quickly, the pilot maneuvers the failing airship to a nearby rooftop where the ship lands and deflates over the side of the building.

In a brutal, international game of telephone, France reports a casualty from the crash; the Chinese press begins to tally a body count. One small deflation becomes a global incident, the picture of a gray flapjack sagging over the side of a New York skyscraper gracing newspapers around the world.

Is this a visit from the ghost of Hindenbergs Past? A scene stolen from "Black Sunday"? Neither, actually. It is but one of the small PR snafus the public relations firm of Creamer Dickson Basford has handled over the years.

The North American anchor of Eurocom Corporate & PR, a US/Pan-European group which ranks among the top five international public-relations firms, Creamer Dickson Basford is one of the top ten public relations firms in the nation. Handling such products as Coors beer, Skippy peanut butter, Panasonic electronics, Ethan Allen furniture, and Pizza Hut pizza, Creamer Dickson Basford has sought to "become and remain the quality alternative—the public relations firm that 'thinks differently' and offers bold new ways for major corporations and organizations to reach their business goals."

SELECTIVITY
Approximate applicant pool: 400
Interns accepted: 10–15 (NY); 2–4 (MA); 2–4 (PA)

COMPENSATION
$250/week

QUALITY OF LIFE
Private workspace; professional development seminars; lunch with CDB's chairman; casual dress on Fridays

LOCATION(S)
New York, NY (HQ); Irvine, CA; Corona, CA; Pittsburgh, PA

FIELD
Public relations

DURATION
12 weeks
Summer, Fall, Spring

PRE-REQS
College seniors; recent grads; grad students; college grads of any age

DEADLINE(S)
Summer .... March 1
Fall and Spring ..... Rolling

BUSYWORK METER
LOW MEDIUM HIGH
OLDMAN & HAMADEH

DESCRIPTION

 Established in 1987, CDB's internship program seeks to "take a leading role in training the next generation of public relations practitioners" and prides itself on being one of the very best internships in the public relations industry. Assigned to one or more business accounts, interns are placed in all of CDB's operating groups: Creative Services, Food & Consumer, Corporate Financial, Business-to-Business, Healthcare, ChemTech, and International. Within these groups, interns spend approximately 60 to 70 percent of their time working on accounts. And as members of account teams, interns are not just "gofers," wage slaves with the scarlet letter "I" emblazoned on their blouses and Brooks Brothers oxford shirts. Rather, they are an integral part of the marketing effort. Said one intern: "I didn't really feel like an intern. The people in the office are sympathetic to your position as an intern and value you as a resource, as a person who has good ideas."

> **The new-business project gives interns the opportunity to create an entire campaign from the ground up.**

The duties and responsibilities assigned to interns reflect the trust and value CDB places in its interns. On a daily basis, interns are expected to aggressively conduct research and make media phone calls—tasks that are necessary for the development and implementation of creative and effective marketing strategies for client's products and services. Interns also participate in their group's creative brainstorming sessions concerning new products, write press releases, and pitch clients' products to newspapers, magazines, and television networks. Said one intern: "It was on-the-job, baptism in fire, but Creamer Dickson helped me hone my salesmanship skills as well as the skills needed to produce a winning idea and then execute and deliver it to as many people as possible." Indeed, one intern built up publicity for Coors Light that culminated in stories in *The Wall Street Journal* and *USA Today*. Another intern worked with Skippy peanut butter

to promote its summer in-line skating clinic, drawing a sizable crowd.

One intern had the "experience of [his] life" dealing with the Pizza Hut "Bigfoot" pizza campaign. The public relations strategy CDB developed centered on a "Bigfoot Blimp" tour involving an airship traveling the country promoting Pizza hut's new line of pizza. Selling the idea to a number of media, he eventually captured the attention of the *Late Show With David Letterman*. By selling the screen space of the blimp to *Late Show*, the four color "Bigfoot" logo was broadcast to millions of homes throughout the American market, in essence generating free advertising for Pizza Hut. However, as the blimp entered New York City in the summer for the last leg of the tour, it began to leak air and deflate, leading to the situation described in the opening earlier. With the image of the blimp oozing its plastic gray carcass over the side of the skyscraper reaching nearly every newspaper and evening news broadcast in the country as well as international news reports, this intern had to quickly educate himself in the art of crisis communications. Turning lemons into lemonade, he fueled the publicity fires with press releases to major New York newspapers, CNN, CBS, and NBC and tracked the international wires for their perceptions (and misperceptions) of the incident.

The central tenet of the CDB internship seems to be that of learning by doing, and the interns have the opportunity to do just that. Toward the end of their tenure at CDB, interns work together, independently of CDB employees, on the development of a new business program. A main drawing card of the CDB internship, the new-business project gives interns the opportunity to create an entire campaign from the ground up and then present their work to the client, who sometimes implements the ideas. Though employees do meet with the interns during their project and are available for consultation, the final product is solely the child of the summer interns and is a great addition to a growing professional portfolio. Describing it as "one of the most nerve-racking experiences" of the internship, one intern said: "Everybody knows about it; both the interns and the people in the office talk about it. It's a lot of pressure, but a fantastic learning experience." A recent intern project involved an awareness enhancing program targeting the annual Matrix Awards for Women In Communications (WIC). The presentation was so well-received that the interns presented the program again to WIC's board of directors.

Every week, CDB holds summer seminars for its interns, adding another facet to the comprehensive public relations education that the firm provides. Run by senior management, the interactive professional-development seminars investigate topics such as "Creativity in Public Relations," "Charting Your Own Career Path In Public Relations," and "The Marketing Decision-Making Process." Included in this battery of seminars is the opportunity to "talk shop" with the people in the business and learn about the actual ins and outs of public relations, including a luncheon with CDB's CEO and chairman, who discusses how to generate new business. At the end of the year, each intern is given the opportunity to go through a "mock" interview with members of senior management; one intern was "lucky" enough to draw the CEO as one of his interviewers. Looking forward to getting interns involved in public relations, CDB "views everybody as a potential employee" and occasionally hires former interns into positions within the organization.

The office environment in which all of this happens is "a comfortable, but busy one, though there is always the feeling that something very important is going on at all times, that something big is about to break onto the scene." Each intern does get his or her own work area, telephone, and computer, though the hustle and bustle of the workplace seem to keep everybody moving. "There is always something going on, something happening, people moving around. The office is always in fluid motion." To interns' benefit, CDB subscribes to an "open door" policy (except when important meetings are in progress), allowing interns to interact freely with seasoned employees, seek their advice on tasks and projects, and learn from their experiences in the field. " I knew that if I had a problem with my current assignment," reported one intern, "that there would always be someone around the corner that I could ask a question." Given the high-profile professionalism involved in public relations, business dress is dictated, with the exception of Fridays, when casual dress is allowed.

CDB is located on the 27th floor of the Paramount Plaza building in the heart of New York on Broadway. A strong drawing card for interns, the charms New York offers a college student are nearly endless, and CDB knows it. The internship coordinator organizes various day tours for interns to introduce them to New York and all of its resources, including the Metropolitan Museum of Modern Art, the Guggenheim, Rockefeller Center, and New York Public Library. And for sports enthusiasts, CDB fields a softball team. Though "we had the losingest record in the league," said one intern, "we probably had the most fun."

SELECTION

 Although CDB's internship program is open to college seniors, recent college grads, grad students, and college grads of any age of all backgrounds and majors, CDB looks favorably on people who have some working knowledge pertinent to the field of public relations (e.g., those majoring in or who majored in public relations, business, communications, or a related field). But applicants with drive and enthusiasm should not be dissuaded. In addition to academic major, CDB looks at an applicant's extra-curricular activities and experiences outside of the classroom. "We want someone who is not just going through the motions of a college education," says the coordinator, "but aggressively pursuing experience affording written and verbal communication skills." According to former interns, CDB also seeks well-rounded people who can "create an idea and run with it independently... real go-getters."

APPLICATION PROCEDURE

 The deadline to apply is March 1 for the summer and rolling for fall and spring. Regardless of the location in which they wish to intern, applicants must submit the following materials to the New York office: resume, cover letter, writing samples, recommendations, and "anything else that will persuade us to hire you," says the coordinator. Applicants who make the final cut can expect to take a CDB writing test to evaluate their strengths and weaknesses in such areas as editing and press-release writing. According to the internship coordinator, it is an evaluative tool that CDB uses to assess interns' career goals and how CDB can help to achieve them.

OVERVIEW

 A Creamer Dickson Basford brochure states: "In order that people may be happy in their work . . . they must have a sense of success in it." This spirit extends to CDB's internship program, where interns are made to feel an integral part of the agency's work. Working in teams on a new business project and assisting account teams with important research and brainstorming work, interns can gain a sense of success not only in what they achieve, but also in what a future in PR can offer.

FOR MORE INFORMATION . . .

■ Internship Program
Creamer Dickson Basford
350 Hudson Street
5th Floor
New York, NY 10014
(212) 367-6800

CROW CANYON
ARCHAEOLOGICAL
C E N T E R

In the late thirteenth century, the Ancestral Pueblo Indians mysteriously abandoned their villages located in what is now southern Colorado. Was their departure due to the drought of 1276? Was it for religious reasons? Did warfare drive them away?

Organized in 1984, Crow Canyon Archaeological Center is dedicated to exploring the question of why the Ancestral Pueblo abandoned the Mesa Verde region. Crow canyon archaeologists and volunteers conduct research in ancient villages near the town of Cortez. Although it is a place where adult volunteers pay to dig, Crow Canyon runs a serious institutional research program. With a staff of 14 professional archaeologists, the center has received grants from the National Science Foundation, the National Geographic Society, and the National Endowment for the Humanities and the Colorado Historical Society. In 1992, it was the recipient of the President's Award for Historic Preservation, the nation's highest honor to a private organization dedicated to the preservation of America's heritage.

SELECTIVITY	
Approximate applicant pool: 130+ Interns accepted: 8–12	

COMPENSATION	
Room, board, and weekly stipend (approximately $50); maximum $350 travel reimbursement	

QUALITY OF LIFE	
Beautiful location; Tex-Mex meals; Seminars	

LOCATION(S)	
Cortez, CO	

FIELD	
Archaeology; Public Education	

DURATION	
10–12 weeks (See Application Procedure)	

PRE-REQS	
College juniors and seniors; grad students Previous field experience for field internship	

DEADLINE(S)	
Early March (see application for specific date)	

DESCRIPTION

 Crow Canyon's archaeological research is performed at various locations within a 35- to 45-minute drive of the Crow Canyon campus. Research focuses on thirteenth-century Ancestral Pueblo occupations in the Mesa Verde region and seeks to understand community organization, dynamics, and abandonment through archaeological survey, testing, and excavation.

Assisting the professional archaeologists are field interns who work at the site in a variety of capacities. First and foremost, they excavate, using a trowel and whisk broom to remove artifacts for analysis. "It was your basic excavation process," said one intern.

"After digging up a chunk of soil, we'd screen out the dirt to catch any artifacts." Working closely with professional archaeologists, interns get the experience and guidance that help them to hone their archaeological skills. "Digging under the supervision of experienced professionals, I developed and refined my field techniques well beyond what I expected," said one intern. During a workday, field interns write narrative notes and fill out computer-coded forms indicating where each artifact was discovered. Occasionally, they take photographs and draw sketches of site areas as well.

BUSYWORK
MEDIUM
LOW HIGH
N/A
OLDMAN & HAMADEH
METER

Another responsibility of field interns is to teach lay participants archaeological techniques. Said one intern: "We supervised the paying volunteers during excavation, making sure they didn't miss any artifacts when they dug." Because a few volunteers come to the site expecting to unearth treasures of yore—the so-called Indiana Jones syndrome—interns have to remind participants that artifacts found during excavations are seldom glamorous. One finds mostly bones, pottery shards, and stone debris. "It's not what you find, but what you find out," as one intern put it.

Crow Canyon also hires interns to work with researchers in the laboratory. Lab interns gain experience in processing and analyzing a wide variety of archaeological artifacts and samples. They also work in laboratory administration, collections management, and database management. Many lab interns are able to identify and gather data for advanced undergraduate and graduate research papers. Like field interns, lab interns work closely with lay participants showing them how to wash, sort, catalog, and analyze artifacts.

A third internship area at Crow Canyon is Environmental Archaeology. In this department, interns work closely with researchers analyzing and interpreting many of the prehistoric plant remains collected from the excavated sites. "The [Environmental Archaeology] project gives archaeologists a better idea of how the Ancestral Pueblo altered their environment before they abandoned the Mesa Verde region," said one intern.

Four hundred miles southwest of Denver and ten miles from the entrance to Mesa Verde National Park, Crow Canyon is situated in one of the most pristine natural areas in America. The Crow Canyon campus is a picture of southwestern beauty. Adobe architecture is everywhere and hiking trails snake through the juniper-covered terrain. Sweeping vistas of mountains and "incredible geological formations" are part of the area's natural beauty. Sunny weather is the norm, and uncomfortably warm temperatures are rare, even in midsummer.

Housing is either in rustic cabins or tents. "It's not that bad," said one intern. "But it gets a little cold sometimes. More than once I woke up with frost on my body." Heat-seeking interns, rest assured: Winter-month participants are housed indoors. Conditions are not so primitive that interns must use the bushes as a bathroom; toilets and hot shower facilities are provided in a bathhouse near the tents. Despite these rugged accommodations, most interns like their home on the hill, viewing it as a comfortable retreat from the bustle of daily work.

> **Homemade salsas, luscious guacamole, gourmet tacos, and the house specialty— blue-corn chicken enchiladas—are enough to make one give up Taco Bell for life.**

Thanks to the paying volunteers, everyone eats well at Crow Canyon. The resident chef serves up three delicious meals every day. Homemade salsas, luscious guacamole, gourmet tacos, and the house specialty— blue-corn chicken enchiladas—are enough to make one give up Taco Bell for life. Interns are grateful for this unexpected culinary bounty: "The food was terrific. With the adult volunteers in residence [Crow Canyon] really pulls out all the stops."

If they play their cards right, interns leave Crow Canyon with an education in southwestern culture. Every so often, the center sponsors workshops that interns are welcome to attend. Native American artisans give presentations in basketry, twill weaving, flute playing, jewelry making, and other southwestern specialties. "I attended a workshop on basketry and learned how weavers used yucca fibers to create sandals and twine. It shed light on how the Ancestral Pueblo clothed themselves."

Interns get the weekends off, and there's plenty of places for them to play. The closest city is Cortez, a rustic town with little more than a Wal-Mart, a gym, and a few bars. Durango, a lively college town, is a 45-minute drive away. Another popular destination, Telluride, can be reached by car in 90 minutes and features superb skiing in the winter and a film festival in the summer. For those interested in furthering their archaeological education, nearby Mesa Verde National Park features Ancestral Pueblo cliff dwellings and spectacular prehistoric rock art.

SELECTION

 The program accepts college juniors and seniors as well as graduate students. Students interested in the field internship must have previous field experience. Lab and Environment Archeology positions require no field experience, but some coursework in archaeology, anthropology, ethnobotany, botany, or museum studies is desirable. International applicants are eligible.

APPLICATION PROCEDURE

 The application deadline is in early March. Internships are generally offered four times a year: mid-May to early August, early August to mid-October, mid-October to mid-December, and early January to mid-March. Write to Crow Canyon for exact dates. Interested parties should submit a completed Crow Canyon application—a three-page questionnaire that asks about academic coursework, related work experience, reasons for wanting the job, and three references (phone numbers and addresses). A resume is desirable but not mandatory. Informal phone interviews may be conducted. After an initial screening, finalists are determined. Be forewarned: The intern supervisors call the references of each finalist, so references are critical. They can make the difference between two candidates who are equally qualified on paper.

OVERVIEW

 The Crow Canyon internship is an all-around winner. Interns work closely with experienced professionals excavating and recording artifacts, processing and analyzing lab samples, or conducting studies of past and present environments. Along the way interns sharpen their archaeological skills and gain teaching experience. Add to this bounty of benefits a gorgeous campus, gourmet southwestern meals, and enriching extracurricular opportunities—and you've got an experience worth getting dirty for.

FOR MORE INFORMATION . . .

- Crow Canyon Archaeological Center
  Internship Program
  23390 County Road K
  Cortez, CO 81321
  (970) 565-8975
  www.crowcanyon.org
  mromasco@crowcanyon.org

elite
John Casablancas

The face of Cindy Crawford graces the covers of *Vogue* and *Cosmopolitan*. Iman dances in husband David Bowie's new MTV video. Paulina Porizkova's face promotes the new line of makeup at the local department store's Estée Lauder counter. The first few pages of *GQ* find voluptuous Anna Nicole smiling sensually for Guess Jeans. What do all these women have in common? Are they the 5'10" Society? Do they have an exercise videotape on the shelves of the local video store or an ability to mesmerize most of male America? Perhaps they share all of these things but the one very important common denominator among them is that they all have relied on Elite to catapult them to supermodel status.

Why Elite? In 1971, a young European man named John Casablancas opened his first Elite in Paris. Back then, top American agencies like New York's Ford and Wilhelmina sent him their hot new prospects. Under his guidance, the fledgling models became Europe's stars. Once world-famous, the models returned to the United States and posed for the country's top fashion magazines. They rarely returned to Europe. Frustrated by an inability to retain the women whose fame he fostered, Casablancas resolved to open an agency in the United States, and in 1977, Elite set up shop in the Big Apple. Focusing on editorial and upscale catalog clientele, today Elite continues to attract the industry's crème de la crème. No fewer than six of the world's top ten models, featured on the cover of *Vogue*'s April 1992 "100th Anniversary Special," worked for Elite.

DESCRIPTION

Since 1985, Elite has allowed college students to observe first-hand the inner workings of one of the most prestigious modeling agencies

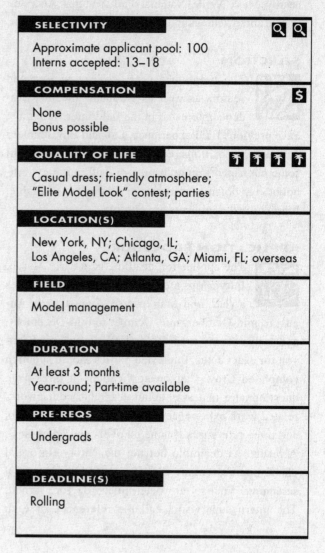

SELECTIVITY	🔍 🔍
Approximate applicant pool: 100 Interns accepted: 13–18	

COMPENSATION	$
None Bonus possible	

QUALITY OF LIFE	🌴 🌴 🌴 🌴
Casual dress; friendly atmosphere; "Elite Model Look" contest; parties	

LOCATION(S)

New York, NY; Chicago, IL;
Los Angeles, CA; Atlanta, GA; Miami, FL; overseas

FIELD

Model management

DURATION

At least 3 months
Year-round; Part-time available

PRE-REQS

Undergrads

DEADLINE(S)

Rolling

in the world. Interns work out of the New York, Chicago, Los Angeles, Atlanta, and Miami offices, as well as several overseas locations (see "For More Information...") in the Scouting, Model Management, New Faces, and Elite divisions, assisting employees in every capacity, from the clerical duties to the actual work of the booking agents. While the New York office takes on five to ten interns per year, the others hire only one to two each.

Naturally, interns don't assume the responsibilities of Elite booking agents until well into the internship. During the first few weeks interns answer phones and open mail, sifting through unsolicited photographs and creating "Yes" and "No" piles for the scout to peruse later. Interns also accompany some of the models to their first-time appointments with clients (referred to as "go-sees" in model-speak). Energetic interns "willing to do whatever needs to be done," as the vice president told us, "will eventually take on some of the bookers' tasks, maintaining day-to-day contact with the models and scheduling assignments."

Some interns rotate through all the departments, getting an overview of the model management business. Most, however, spend a significant portion of their time in just one division. One intern, assisting the director of Scouting, found herself actually scouting within the first week. "In between answering mail and handling the phones," she said, "I evaluated from 10 to 25 prospective models at the open calls that Elite holds four times a week." She elaborated: "I held their potential careers in my hands. If I thought that they looked right, I would schedule a test shoot—simple, clean photographs, some black and white, some color. Otherwise, I had to learn to turn them away gently." In addition to running the office and interviewing potential models, interns in Scouting might also assist in locating new talent. "I corresponded with other agencies nationwide and arranged to bring in their models to New York for a couple weeks of testing," explained another intern. "I would also acquaint the girls to the city once they arrived, as well as field telephone calls from concerned parents."

An intern in Model Management spent the initial part of his summer sorting mail, pulling models' cards, and photocopying "futures" (models' schedules) for the accounting department's use. While such work might sound monotonous, the intern pointed out: "Those activities helped me to learn models' names and faces and to understand the way business is done." Interns in this department also put together composite cards for new faces and make "go-see" appointments for Elite's models. One diligent, enthusiastic intern eventually worked his

way up to a spot at the spirited octagonal bookers' table—equipped with a phone, drawers, and all the models' calendars spread out before him. "It's like sitting at a lively Thanksgiving dinner with six or seven of your family members," he said. There, he learned how to book work for the models. "Eventually," he said, "I even recommended certain models for our clients. It got to the point where clients thought that I was just another booker."

Most Elite interns also work on the agency's annual "Elite Model Look" contest, a highly touted nationwide search for new models. Cindy Crawford was a finalist in 1988's contest. According to the organization, in the most recent contest, more than 300,000 women sent in their pictures, with the hope of becoming one of 10 to 15 finalists. One of the interns sifted through thousands of applications, helping to determine which would be retained. Another served as a gofer at the actual Look of the Year show. "I just stood there and whenever someone asked me to do something, like find a participant for her photo shoot, I took care of it," he said. "I didn't do anything specific, but to be [at the show] was amazing…. Over 60 models from around the world were there, and Fox filmed it."

Two floors of a converted five-story townhouse in Manhattan house Elite's headquarters. Adorning the walls of the reception area, dozens of magazine covers flaunt Elite models. Beyond, one finds sleek, modern hallways and rooms, as well as an intense yet friendly atmosphere, where "most everyone gets along," several interns said. Employees work together in "a laid-back environment, not a suit-and-tie place," as one described it. But another conceded that "while the atmosphere is often spirited, it's sometimes also stressful—phones are ringing off the hook, models are coming in and out, and people are running around trying to get everything done."

Interns, especially those in New York, enjoy a panoply of perks. For example, they occasionally accompany

> Interns are invited to join Elite at weekly parties and promotional events put on by fashion designers, music industry gurus, movie bigwigs, or Elite itself.

the director of Scouting to client dinners. Interns are also invited to join Elite employees, models, and their families at weekly parties and promotional events put on by fashion designers, music industry gurus, movie bigwigs, or Elite itself. "I went to a big party at the Banana Café for all the Elite models appearing in the spring fashion-show," said one New York intern. "About 100 people attended, and I mixed with agents, models, and photographers. I made many contacts that night." Those who intern for two or more terms might find themselves traveling to scout at an upstate New York convention or at the nearby Waldorf Astoria Hotel. Anyone looking to sidle up to the office's superstars, be forewarned: These women are very busy and they don't stop in often.

To be sure, most interns do a fair share of the grunt-work. But they appreciate the opportunity to work at an epicenter of the modeling business. "Reading the faxes and files was fascinating," one intern said. "Plus, I learned how to talk to models, to clients, and to photographers." Interns do complain about the lack of pay, however: "You can't live that way in New York." Still, interns are expected to work at least five half-days or three full days per week. The reward for hard work? Possibly a farewell party and a bonus check of a few hundred dollars at the conclusion of the internship.

SELECTION

 Undergraduates of any level are eligible to apply. No area of study is excluded; past interns have majored in political science, women's studies, fashion merchandising, business, and advertising. For overseas offices, applicants must be fluent in the local language. International applicants are eligible.

APPLICATION PROCEDURE

 Internships are available year-round, and materials may be submitted at any time to the desired office. Send a resume and cover letter, but be personal. The vice president is quick to point out that "your personality must come out in these typically bland documents." Applicants who reach the final round participate in telephone interviews.

OVERVIEW

 Elite arguably occupies the premier position among the world's modeling agencies. There might not be a better internship for those who wish to work permanently in modeling or who simply want impressive material for cocktail party conversation. Claimed one intern: "Elite is the most influential agency in the business, representing the most famous models." Compared to competitor Ford's five agencies, Elite manages nearly 50 modeling centers and operates out of 16 agencies worldwide. Following a summer stint, one former intern took a permanent position with Elite. Another went to work for Ford. One was named director of model relations at a prestigious scouting firm. Still others have moved into related fields—entertainment or fashion merchandising. But all are quick to say that they will never forget the experience. "I would love to be an Elite intern forever," concluded one.

In 1998 four of the five New York interns were hired as full-time employees.

FOR MORE INFORMATION . . .

■ Elite Model Management
111 East 22nd Street
New York, NY 10010
(212) 529-9700

■ Elite Model Management
345 North Maple Drive #397
Beverly Hills, CA 90210
(310) 274-9395

■ Elite Model Management
212 West Superior St.
Suite 406
Chicago, IL 60610
(312) 943-3226

■ Elite Model Management
One Buckhead Plaza
3060 Peach Tree Road, NW
Suite 1465
Atlanta, GA 30305
(404) 674-9500

■ Elite Model Management
1200 Collins Avenue
Miami Beach, FL 33139
(305) 674-9500

■ Overseas:
Rio de Janeiro, Brazil: 55-21-511-3437
Sao Paulo, Brazil: 55-11-816-4355
Toronto, Canada: (416) 979-9995
Copenhagen, Denmark: 45-33-151-414
London, England: 44-171-333-0888
Paris, France: 33-1-4044-3222
Hamburg, Germany: 49-40-440-555
Munich, Germany: 49-89-341-336
Hong Kong: 85-2-285-05550
Milan, Italy: 39-2-481-4704
Tokyo, Japan: 81-3-3587-0200
Amsterdam, The Netherlands: 31-20-627-9929
Barcelona, Spain: 34-3-418-8099
Madrid, Spain: 34-1-310-2777
Fribourg, Switzerland: 41-37-224-815

A decade or so ago, in a section of Chicago known as the South Side, newspapers, cardboard, and junk mail would pile up like so many leaves on an autumn day. If they didn't litter the roadsides, they'd pack the nearby landfill.

In came Michael Finn, a 1981 graduate of Northern Illinois University. In 1982, he did an internship with Chicago's Neighborhood Institute, working on a South Side recycling program to demonstrate that recycling efforts could promote economic development. Seeing an opportunity to make recycling a career, he and his supervisor left the Neighborhood Institute in 1984 to found Recycling Services, Inc. Now a $4 million company, Recycling Services collects, sorts, and bales wastepaper for paper mills.

But who provided Finn with the internship that gave him the experience necessary to embark upon such an environmental endeavor? A nonprofit group called the Environmental Careers Organization (ECO). Its story begins in 1972, with a recent college graduate named John Cook. Realizing that the environmental movement was gaining steam and that few people were adequately prepared to tackle environmental problems, Cook founded ECO to "protect and enhance the environment through the development of professionals, the promotion of careers, and the inspiration of individual action." Though it sponsors an annual environmental conference, publishes books on environmental careers, and maintains environmental-career libraries, its main business is finding and creating environmental internships. Twenty-odd years later, ECO has nearly 6,000 alumni.

SELECTIVITY

Approximate applicant pool: 3,000
Interns accepted: 600

COMPENSATION

$200–$800/week
Average Salary: $425–$450/week

QUALITY OF LIFE

N/A

LOCATION(S)

Nationwide—see Index

FIELD

Environment

DURATION

12 weeks–2 years
Year-round

PRE-REQS

DI: minority undergrads, recent grads, grad students
EPS: college juniors and seniors, grad students, college grads any age

DEADLINE(S)

Rolling

DESCRIPTION

ECO (pronounced "EE-ko") places over 600 students annually in two programs—approximately 460 students year-round in the Environmental Placement Services (EPS) program and 160 minority students, primarily during the summer, through its Diversity Initiative (DI) program. Forty percent of all interns are graduate students, 40 percent are recent graduates, and the remaining 20

BUSYWORK
LOW MEDIUM HIGH
OLDMAN & HAMADEH
METER

percent are undergraduates. Projects last 6 months on average and are available in a majority of states.

Approximately 175 organizations sponsor ECO interns. Many of the internships, according to ECO, aren't established programs open to the general public but are specially arranged; in other words, by soliciting environmental professionals whose projects could use interns, ECO creates environmental internships. "We're specialized, and we understand the environmental language," says ECO president John Cook. "We can place a student who wants to work in wetlands ecology with a position in wetlands ecology." Almost every type of environmental career is covered, as both EPS and DI place students within corporations, environmental consulting firms, governmental agencies, and nonprofit organizations like the Natural Resources Defense Council, Environmental Defense Fund, and the Nature Conservancy. According to Cook, 10 to 20 percent of the placements are with the U.S. Environmental Protection Agency (EPA).

As members of ECO, past and present interns can count on ECO for guidance and career advice.

Corporations sponsoring interns include IBM, Ford, Boeing, and Polaroid. Placed in departments like Environmental Health & Safety, interns often help their sponsors compile reports that satisfy local, state, and national regulatory or compliance boards. An intern for Pacific Gas & Electric (PG&E) in San Francisco was placed in Qualifying Facilities Contracts, a PG&E department in charge of evaluating the power produced by alternative-energy sources such as solar facilities and wind farms. According to a law dating back to the Carter administration, she explained, PG&E was required to purchase alternative power from sources that qualified under the Carter program. "I updated contracts," she said, "checking to see if our contracted facilities were fulfilling their reporting requirements." She also determined what type of energy each of the producers was creating and what percentage of the total energy distributed by PG&E was alternative energy. "By the end of the summer, I had a greater understanding of the private side of energy issues and the economics of power producers," she said.

Approximately 15 percent of interns are placed with environmental consulting firms, companies that recommend and implement solutions to environmental problems for clients—usually corporations, government agencies, and cities. Assigned to CH2M Hill in Deerfield Beach, FL, an intern spent approximately one-third of his time collecting water and soil samples in the field. "Sometimes I dipped a jar in the water or soil and capped it," he said. "Other times, I set up the automatic sampling machine, which takes a weighted average of measurements made every half hour [or so]." After samples were analyzed by CH2M Hill's laboratories, he wrote reports, using charts to present the data—information on water levels, chemical composition of the samples, and extent of contamination. "By the end of the internship," he said, "I definitely had gained a good sense of how science and technology are used in practice to solve environmental problems." Another intern, this one at Environmental Research and Technology, Inc., in Boston, tracked energy regulations for the Department of Energy and studied circulation patterns of people in a local park. "I made so many contacts [at ERT]," he concluded, "that my job hunting a few months later was significantly easier."

Over half of all interns work for local, state, and federal agencies. Past interns have studied how a local government can better regulate air pollution from automobiles, investigated undersea corals for the U.S. Geological Survey, monitored salmon and bald eagles for the city of San Francisco, assessed the level of metals contamination at the site of a former treatment plant in Seattle, and developed solid-waste management and recycling programs for an Ohio sewer district. An intern with the EPA in Washington, D.C., during the summer of 1993 was assigned to the EPA's Energy Star Computers project, an effort to encourage computer companies to create energy-saving computers. "Because a large percentage of people leave their computers on 24 hours a day, seven days a week," she elaborated, "the EPA wants computer makers to manufacture energy-conscious computers—[for example, ones that] automatically turn off if left idle for 30 minutes." Working on a campaign to sign up as many computer companies as possible, she sent out agreements to interested executives, whose companies became part of the project once the completed forms were returned. "I helped sign up nearly 100 companies," she said. She also attended a press conference led by EPA administrator Carol Browner and Vice President Al Gore, which was attended by representatives of 24 major computer companies. "[The summer] certainly proved to me that [America] can grow economically while . . . conserving energy," she concluded.

Though ECO's primary function is to provide students with internships, it's more than a clearinghouse. It also maintains contact with interns throughout their experience, intercedes on their behalf should problems arise, and organizes a social event or two. At the beginning of the internship, the program director and staff at ECO's five offices—in Boston, Cleveland, Seattle, San Francisco, and Tampa—contact their interns to welcome them to the program. After that initial call, ECO officials attempt to make on-site visits to meet interns over lunch. Each ECO office occasionally hosts an informal reception, dinner, or picnic where interns meet one another, ECO sponsors, and ECO alumni and hear about other ECO projects. "The networking opportunities [at these functions] are prime," said an intern. Throughout the summer, interns receive additional phone calls from ECO staff checking on interns' progress. "It's great that ECO takes time out to keep communication lines open," said an intern. "That way, sponsors and interns know what to expect."

As members of ECO, past and present interns can count on ECO for guidance and career advice. Alumni get *Connections* magazine, ECO's newsletter to keep alumni informed of ECO's programs. "It keeps me tied into the organization," says an intern from 1973. "Reading about other experiences gives me a benchmark against which to compare an internship program that I run [as president of the Quebec-Labrador Foundation and its Atlantic Center for the Environment]." At each of ECO's offices, interns

are welcome to use the career library to search current job listings. They can also attend the organization's annual Environmental Career Conference. Typically held in the fall, the conference provides an overview of job opportunities in the environmental industry and features a keynote address—recent speakers include Paul Hawken, of the upscale garden-shop chain Smith & Hawken; Eugene Hester, deputy director of the U.S. Department of Interior; and Thomas Grumbly, assistant secretary of the U.S. Department of Energy. To participate in the conference, interested alumni and interns must pay an admission fee (approximately $50) as well as travel and lodging expenses. But for the price, attendees get two days' worth of workshops, career advice, a career fair, and panel discussions on topics such as forestry, parks, law careers, and graduate schools. The conference also offers special sessions for minorities looking for employment in the environmental industry.

SELECTION

 ECO's EPS program seeks college juniors, seniors, and graduate students as well as career-changers and those who have recently completed their BS, MS, or Ph.D. degrees as applicants. DI targets minority undergraduates of any level, recent graduates, and graduate students—primarily those of African American, Hispanic, Asian/Pacific Islander, and Native American descent. Any major is acceptable—approximately two-thirds of interns have science and technology backgrounds, while one-third are concentrating in liberal arts. International applicants eligible.

APPLICATION PROCEDURE

 The deadline is rolling. Applicants to the EPS program are encouraged to apply at least three months before they are available to intern. Regardless of where they wish to work, students need submit only one application. Both programs require a completed application form (there's a different one for each program), which asks for a writing sample, resume, and list of relevant courses. Applications are kept active for 12 months after receipt. After ECO screens the applications, it recommends to each sponsoring organization approximately five applicants per position to interview.

OVERVIEW

 According to research done by San Diego's Environmental Business International Inc., nearly 500,000 new jobs will be created by the environmental industry in just a few years—that's a world of opportunity for those interested in the environment. Students who want to explore these positions should check out the Environmental Careers Organization. Providing career advice, networking opportunities, and oftentimes internships inaccessible to the general public, the Environmental Careers Organization prepares students to become the next generation of environmental scientists and engineers, chemists and biologists, teachers, recycling coordinators, eco managers, and environmental lawyers.

FOR MORE INFORMATION . . .

■ The Environmental Careers Organization
179 South St.
Boston, MA 02111
apply@eco.org
www.eco.org

SELECTIVITY	🔍 🔍 🔍
Approximate applicant pool: 300 Interns accepted: 75–100 annually	

COMPENSATION	$ $ $
$5,000–$9,000 grant	

QUALITY OF LIFE	N/A
N/A	

LOCATION(S)	
Nationwide—see Description	

FIELDS	
Environmental policy; management; science; public relations and communications; and computer programming and development	

DURATION	
10–14 weeks Fall, Winter, Spring, Summer 1-year grants and part-time available	

PRE-REQS	
Undergrads: minimum 3.0 GPA, at least 4 courses in environmental studies Grad students: minimum of one semester completed	

DEADLINE(S)	
Generally in December	

A grim specter has crept upon us almost unnoticed . . .

So wrote marine biologist Rachel Carson in 1962 in the now-classic *Silent Spring*. Her book, says Vice President Al Gore in his *Earth in the Balance*, "eloquently warned America and the world . . . of the dangers posed to migratory birds and other elements of the natural environment by pesticide runoff." It was her admonishment that touched off a series of national protests and government actions, from a 1962 special panel investigation of pesticides by President Kennedy's Science Advisory Committee to the first Earth Day, held in 1969. By the time President Nixon signed the 1970 National Environmental Policy Act, which mandated that federal agencies submit Environmental Impact Statements whenever projects might affect their surroundings, the 1970s had been heralded as "the decade of the environment."

But no environmental decade could be complete in Nixon's eyes without a powerful body to enforce government environmental mandates. So on July 9, 1970, he created the U.S. Environmental Protection Agency (EPA), with an initial budget of $900 million. Today, the EPA's budget has ballooned to over $6 billion, and its enforcement arm—capable of implementing a host of penalties, from fines to criminal lawsuits—extends to 14 major laws, including the Clean Air Act, the Clean Water Act, and Superfund.

DESCRIPTION

In 1987, the EPA created the National Network for Environmental Management Studies (NNEMS) program—pronounced "nemz"—in order to give students exposure to environmental pro-

fessions. Three years later, the 1990 National Environmental Education Act created the Office of Environmental Education (OEE) to foster environmental education, and in 1991 the OEE took over the NNEMS program. Work is available in the following areas: Environmental Policy, Regulations, and Law; Environmental Management and Administration; Environmental Science; Public Relations and Communications; and Computer Programming and Development. Eighty percent of interns work full-time during the summer, the remaining 20 percent work full- or part-time during fall, winter and spring. Opportunities are available at EPA headquarters in D.C. and at the ten EPA regional offices, located in Boston, New York, Philadelphia, Atlanta, Chicago, Dallas, Kansas City, Denver, San Francisco, and Seattle. The EPA also offers research projects in its laboratories in Research Triangle Park, NC; Duluth, Minnesota; Ann Arbor, MI; Las Vegas, NV; Ada, OK; Corvallis, OR; Gulf Breeze, FL; and Athens, GA.

The EPA's Region Three office in Philadelphia sponsors several students every year. One undergraduate was placed in the office's Water Management Division to investigate farm pollution regulations in relation to animal wastes. "When farmers' animals make waste in tributaries that traverse farms, the wastes pollute the drinking and recreational water sources downstream. We were trying to figure out what should be the EPA's role, versus state and city roles, in remedying those waters polluted by animal wastes." Because it's difficult to determine who is responsible for the pollution, she explained, the EPA currently helps fund farmers who use best management practices (BMPs)—such as manure holding tanks, which prevent cow dung from getting into waterways. "But I didn't think that was enough," she said. "A report I wrote at the end of the summer also called for a joint effort of the federal, state, and local governments to educate farmers on acceptable water uses."

"If you're looking to save the world, you won't . . . But you can make an impact."

Sometimes a sponsoring office allows its NNEMS intern to perform research out of his or her home. That's what happened in the case of a New York student who received a project from the EPA's Boston office on nitrogen loading in Long Island Sound. "I went to Boston for three days in the beginning to get briefed on the project. The critical question was—will BMPs such as wetlands, detention ponds, and infiltration ditches reduce the Sound's high nitrogen levels?" To find an answer, she read articles and EPA reports on the effectiveness of such BMPs. "I solicited the opinions of several experts and asked them to send me relevant maps and models." Four months later, she attended a meeting of the Long Island

Sound Study Group to present her findings to members of the EPA, New York City officials, professors, and concerned citizens. "I concluded that the nitrogen buildup is so huge, we might have to put BMPs in residential areas. Now imagine asking some residents in Stamford, CT, to move out so that we can dig a detention pond where their homes are."

Another intern, assigned to the Boston office's Indoor Air section researched residential air quality. "Most indoor air studies focus on the office and known hazardous materials. I felt that the home harbors a number of potentially hazardous substances as well . . . cleaners and paint thinners, for example." After researching various household products, she realized that the EPA should "work cooperatively with industry to label products that contain possibly carcinogenic materials."

Interns sometimes travel in order to better investigate the regions involved in their research. The intern researching animal waste pollution, for example, visited a nearby lake. "Six EPA employees, a water quality expert, and I went out on a boat to the middle of Lake Nockamixon. We ran water quality tests, lowering various equipment into the water in order to determine how much pollution there was." Back on land, she visited some farmers near the lake. "We interviewed them about the steps they were taking to prevent animal waste pollution. I was in charge of filming the interviews on our video camera."

Because environmental issues are often contested and solutions not readily available, interns' final reports often generate disagreements. The intern who did the animal waste study, for example, was convinced that waste could potentially be a major source of pollution. Others didn't share her opinion. "The USDA issued an animal waste report that contradicted mine—they concluded that the animal waste problem was confined only to a few 'hot spots' [i.e., concentrated areas of pollution]—and they asserted that the contribution of animal waste is minor when compared with other sources of pollution."

Despite differing opinions about environmental issues, intern reports are often praised as fresh and interesting. "As a student, you come in with an open mind and are potentially more critical than EPA employees because you aren't biased by any politics," explained an intern. "The people working in my office appreciated such candor." The intern who performed research for the indoor air report, for example, discovered that while many EPA employees were wary of her proposal, at least one person extolled her tenacity. "I attended an EPA meeting half a year later to answer questions about my paper, which by this time had been widely distributed around the agency. After I finished, one person came up to thank me for getting the ball rolling."

Because NNEMS projects aren't designed to be accomplished by team effort, interns must tackle research completely on their own. Nevertheless, those who "fight to the finish" can make an impact. Recipients of NNEMS fellowships receive a stipend based on their level of education and the duration and location of the project. For fiscal year 2000 NNEMS stipends begin at $5,000 for entry-level undergraduates and go as high as $9,000 for graduate students for a three-month full-time fellowship. But some interns complain that the stipend is on the low side. Spread out over the life of the work, the money (after taxes) doesn't go a long way. "Most of these projects end up growing into something bigger than you initially envision," said an intern. "In the end, the money is just not enough to cover the time you must spend to solve the problem."

SELECTION

 The internship is open to undergraduates of any level and graduate students. While graduate students must only have completed at least one semester of graduate studies, undergraduates must have taken at least four courses in environmental studies—hard sciences, engineering, or resource management—and must have at least a 3.0 GPA. Any major is eligible, but students must show a strong interest in environmental issues.

APPLICATION PROCEDURE

 The deadline is generally in December for receipt of materials. The NNEMS program catalog explains that students may apply for agency-sponsored projects. Students must specify the project they are seeking, as described in the NNEMS catalog. For each project, the application requires the NNEMS research proposal page, a resume, a letter of recommendation from a professor or academic advisor, and an official transcript. Students may submit more than one application, though each application submitted must include a photocopy of itself. More than 250 colleges and universities' career centers receive NNEMS brochures and program catalogs. Students attending universities that do not receive the materials should ask their school's career center to request them by writing to the address listed below. Detailed NNEMS information and application materials are available on their website.

OVERVIEW

 The EPA is one of America's greatest allies in the fight to improve the environment. Fortunately for college students, a congressional law mandates educational programs in environmental studies. Called NNEMS, the EPA's program affords students the opportunity to analyze real environmental problems. Circulated among EPA personnel, interns' final reports often generate valuable information. But to get there, interns must invest long hours researching their topics. And their reports sometimes generate disagreement and succumb to bureaucratic foot dragging. "If you're looking to save the world, you won't," concluded one intern. "But you can make an impact."

FOR MORE INFORMATION . . .

■ Environmental Protection Agency
NNEMS National Program Manager
US EPA (1704)
401 M Street SW
Washington, DC 20460
(202) 260-5283
www.epa.gov/enviroed/students.html

SELECTIVITY	
Approximate applicant pool: 2,000 Interns accepted: 75–100	🔍 🔍 🔍 🔍 🔍

COMPENSATION	
$390/week	$ $ $

QUALITY OF LIFE	
Lunch with FBI director; firearms training; field trips	🏃 🏃 🏃

LOCATION(S)

Washington, D.C. and Quantico, VA

FIELD

National security and criminal investigation

DURATION

10 weeks
Summer (June–August)

PRE-REQS

College juniors; grad students
U.S. citizenship; Background check

DEADLINE(S)

November 1

In 1971, accountant John Emil List murdered his mother, wife, and three children at their Westfield, NJ, home. Despite an international search, he disappeared. Eighteen years later, the case was still unsolved; so the FBI Special Projects Unit used advanced technology to create a clay bust depicting what List, now probably bald and wrinkled, would look like. Within hours of the bust's appearance on the TV show *America's Most Wanted*, List was apprehended. He is now serving five consecutive life sentences.

Since its founding in 1908, the FBI has been responsible for tracking down and arresting criminals like List. Its efforts have helped immortalize some of history's most notorious criminals, including Al Capone, Pretty Boy Floyd, Baby Face Nelson, and Machine Gun Kelly. Currently, the FBI enforces over 260 federal statutes—organized and white-collar crime, bribery, copyright matters, bank robbery, kidnapping, terrorism, civil rights violence, and drug trafficking. About 10,000 Special Agents and 13,000 personnel contribute to this enforcement effort. These men and women have a computerized network of crime information, DNA profiling techniques, millions of fingerprint cards, and the lofty ideals emblazoned on the FBI seal—Fidelity, Bravery, Integrity—to lead them in their mission.

DESCRIPTION

 The FBI Honors Internship Program was started in 1985 to expose college students to the Bureau and its mission. Interns are placed in Washington, D.C. at FBI headquarters or at the FBI Academy in Quantico, VA, the Engineering Research Facility, or the Forensic Science Research and Training Center. Interns

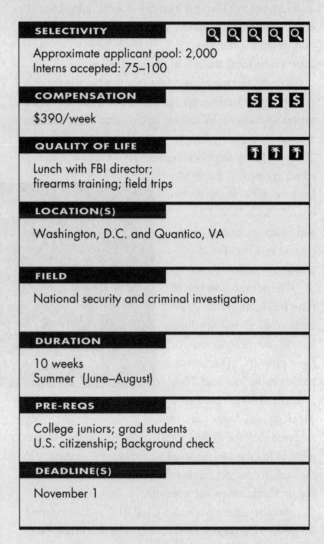

work in units such as Behavioral Science Services, Criminal Informant, Accounting and Budget Analysis, Legal Forfeiture, European/Asian/Money Laundering, Undercover and Sensitive Operations, and Audit. Unfortunately, interns cannot designate preferences for unit or location. Assignments are based on academic major and bureau need.

The internship starts with a two-day orientation during which interns listen to an overview of the FBI, tour headquarters, receive summer assignments, learn about employee benefits, and discuss security. The

FBI director makes a brief speech, and interns are officially sworn in. They get a notebook containing interns' names and phone numbers, maps of D.C., and information on public transportation. Introductions to division supervisors mark the end of the orientation.

Prospective interns should realize that they do not play Agent Clarice Starling, the gun-toting girl-wonder from the movie *Silence of the Lambs*. "Interns aren't here to make arrests or do surveillance," explained the coordinator. "Besides being terribly dangerous, it would be inconvenient; eventually, they might have to give testimony in court." So in lieu of danger and glamour, interns do important research for investigations.

The sensitive nature of most FBI work precludes interns from giving anything but vague descriptions of their projects. One intern, placed in the Mexican Traffickers Unit, compared Mexican and American criminal justice systems. "My research took me to the Library of Congress, the Department of Justice, and the Mexican Embassy," she said. "In the end, my project furnished agents with an understanding of Mexican law enforcement."

Another intern worked in Civil RICO (Racketeering Influenced Corrupt Organizations). The unit investigates Mafia corruption of labor unions. "I researched complaints filed with the bureau," she said. "Then I analyzed a complaint's validity, based on the amount of information available in FBI files. The files were restricted, so a supervisor had to be with me when I checked them out from the library. At the end of the summer, I compiled the researched complaints into a booklet that the unit could use for further investigation and possible litigation."

There are as many intern projects at the FBI as there are confiscated guns. An intern in Behavioral Science Services researched the usefulness of hypnosis on witnesses. One in Forensic Science Research used electrophoresis techniques to separate pieces of DNA. A Language Services intern worked with translation experts to translate foreign documents. An intern in Audit traveled to Houston, Texas, to assist in a week-long audit of the local field office.

Several graduate students intern at the organization. One law student found himself in Legal Forfeiture, the unit in charge of seizing money and property of suspected drug dealers. "I researched the Eighth Amendment to see if these seizures jibed with the provision against cruel and unusual punishment," said the soon-to-be lawyer. "I also wrote a lot of legal briefs. Overall, my internship was similar to a clerkship with a judge, because the unit's Special Agents often made administrative law rulings on FBI promotion, transfer, or disciplinary policies."

The majority of interns works at the D.C. headquarters, called the J. Edgar Hoover Building. A sprawling, 11-story structure, Hoover's namesake stands as a testament to law and order. In addition to housing most of the units, the building holds the Special Operations Center, which is on alert 24 hours a day in case of a national crisis. Most interns work out of their own cubicle, equipped with "modular furniture" and often a computer. Linoleum-floored, white-walled corridors, "drab" carpets, and "gender-neutral office colors" are sure to offer little distraction from the work going on.

Occasionally throughout the summer, interns meet with senior management. An assistant director from one of the ten divisions like Laboratory, Identification, or Criminal Intelligence may lecture on his division's mission, or agents may speak on career opportunities within the bureau. Interns also meet as often as possible after-hours with their mentor—an FBI field agent or professional-support employee, whom they share with four other interns.

Approximately once every two weeks, interns make an organized trip. The Baltimore field office is a typical destination. The secluded Quantico Academy—thirty buildings on more than 400 acres—is another. A training

> Interns whose hearts are set on brandishing a gun receive a half-day of firearms training.

ground for new agents, the academy features Hogan's Alley, a simulated town with a bank, pool hall, and hotel. Here, agents-in-training shoot blanks at actors pretending to be criminals. Though interns rarely see the alley in action, they do learn about FBI training techniques. Interns also visit the academy's Engineering department to see classified equipment: "These gadgets looked like Q's inventions from the James Bond movies." The interns hear the Behavioral Sciences "spook squad," a group of world-class homicide experts, speak on serial killer cases, and watch a demonstration on how to free hostages from terrorists. This show is put on by the Hostage Rescue Team, considered by some to be the best SWAT team in America.

Several perks keep interns happy. Accrued sick and annual leave entitle them to two-and-one-half paid vacation days during the summer. They have access to the FBI gym, where they are likely to encounter agents shaping up for annual physical fitness tests. They may also purchase T-shirts, mugs, and caps from the FBI Recreation Association and gift shop, both of which are inaccessible to the public.

Like other employees, interns may prearrange a guided tour of headquarters for visiting family members. Displayed on the tour are antique toys—fake handcuffs, FBI agent badges, pistols, and uniforms from the 1920s and 1930s. Back then, these toys suggest, kids loved to dress up like G-men and apprehend "criminals." Not surprisingly, many FBI interns wouldn't mind playing cops and robbers, too. But the closest they'll get is a Ride-Along with D.C.'s metro police. "At least then they can feel what it's like to wear a bulletproof vest," said the coordinator. For those whose hearts are set on brandishing a gun, though, there is hope: Interns receive a half-day of firearms training. "They fire the .38 Smith & Wesson revolver, the semiautomatic 9 mm Sig-Sauer model P226 pistol used by our agents, and the fully automatic H & K MP5 assault weapon, used by SWAT teams," said the coordinator. "A firearms instructor monitors them, and they leave with a videotape, a photograph, and their bullet-ridden target."

Not all shooting is directed at paper targets; interns also take a few shots at the program. Some interns were frustrated that their writing was found unacceptable: "We

were not taught how to write in 'bureau-ese'." A few others bemoan the occasional wimpy project. "My year, two interns were given mostly secretarial assignments," one said. She blamed the situation on poor placement and charged the bureau with indifference: "A request for transfer was shrugged off without the FBI's batting an eyelash." To discuss such concerns, interns meet formally with management once or twice during the summer.

During the final week of the program, the FBI director hosts a closing lunch. After answering interns' questions, he joins them for a group photograph. This photograph, combined with a yearbook and a certificate, provides proof that the student was, however briefly, part of the FBI's shadowy world.

SELECTION

 The FBI seeks undergraduates with three years of college under their belt and a few graduate students (JD, MBA, master's, and PhD candidates) who will be returning to school after the internship. A minimum 3.0 GPA and U.S. citizenship are required, but all majors are eligible. Thoroughness in completing the application, academic achievement, work experience, and academic major are all important "but you must show an interest in law enforcement." Extensive arrest records or use of cocaine is a no-no.

APPLICATION PROCEDURE

 The deadline falls on November 1 every year to allow time for the FBI's thorough background investigation. Submit an official academic transcript, a resume, one letter of recommendation from a dean or department head, a recent photograph, a 500-word essay explaining reasons for applying to the program, and the one-page FBI Preliminary Application. All materials must be turned in to the nearest FBI field office (check your local phone book or call the jobs hotline below for more information). Applications are initially screened by these field offices, who nominate top candidates to Headquarters. Headquarters makes final selections, but the ordeal doesn't end there. Selected applicants must complete the bureau's Application for Employment (an 11-page monster), a background investigation, a drug test, and an interview at their sponsoring field office. All interns will be polygraphed for security related issues and drug usage. Interns will not be processed further if they are not in compliance with the FBI's drug policy.

OVERVIEW

 Scotland Yard, Japanese National Police, Royal Canadian Mounted Police, and Interpol are among the world's top criminal investigation organizations. But the king of them all is the FBI. Luckily for America's students, this leader of law enforcement takes on interns. Internship participants work on projects related to ongoing investigations. They have access to Special Agents. They take tours of field offices, DNA labs, and the Quantico Academy. Moreover, former Honors interns are heavily recruited to serve as technical support personnel after graduation or as FBI agents after three years of work experience. Aside from setting the nearest town ablaze and fleeing the country, there's no easier way to make it on the FBI's Most Wanted list.

FOR MORE INFORMATION . . .

■ Contact the FBI office nearest your school (look in the phone book)

■ Job hotline: (202) 324-3674
www.fbi.gov

THE FUND FOR THE
FEMINIST MAJORITY

The scene is the back room of a local church. The time is early morning. Several dozen community members speak in hushed tones, organizing to blockade the area's abortion clinic. They are members of Operation Rescue, and they uphold the rights of the unborn fetus. One of them notices the time and the group moves toward the door. What they don't notice is the plain-looking woman who has already headed for her car, who now calmly calls out from her car phone. Who is she? Impersonating a right-to-lifer, she's a pro-choice advocate working with the Feminist Majority's Clinic Defense Project to mobilize readied forces throughout the city. When Operation Rescue gets to the clinic, it finds several hundred demonstrators—a veritable human shield—blocking its path. People are pushed, punched, and kicked, but women can still walk in. Chalk up another victory for the Feminist Majority.

Founded by TV producer and philanthropist Peg Yorkin and former National Organization for Women (NOW) president Eleanor "Ellie" Smeal in 1987, the Feminist Majority wasn't always so controversial. The organization initially set out to encourage more women to run for public office. In its first year, two dozen women traveled the country, setting up campaign rallies in twelve major cities, much like Republicans and Democrats do every four years. The plan succeeded, inspiring dozens of feminists nationwide to run for local and national office. Today, the Feminist Majority still espouses its more-women-in-public-office philosophy. But it has added to its agenda an Empowering Women campaign, a Rock for Choice project, abortion clinic defense, lobbying, and women's rights research.

SELECTIVITY

Approximate applicant pool: 300
Interns accepted: 20

COMPENSATION

Stipend possible

QUALITY OF LIFE

Substantive projects; travel opportunities; lobbying on Capitol Hill (D.C.)

LOCATION(S)

Los Angeles, CA; Arlington, VA

FIELD

Women's rights/think tank

DURATION

2 months minimum
Year-round; Part-time available

PRE-REQS

High school students; undergrads; grad students

DEADLINE(S)

Rolling

DESCRIPTION

Since 1987, the Feminist Majority has given students the opportunity to tackle feminist issues on a national level. One of the women touring the country for those first campaign rallies, in fact, was a junior from a New Jersey state college. One morning she got a call from a woman she had met during an ERA campaign a year earlier. "How would you like to join Ellie Smeal's Feminist Majority?"

BUSYWORK METER
LOW MEDIUM HIGH
OLDMAN & HAMADEH

Six days later, the college student was on a plane heading to Los Angeles. Fortunately, today's prospective interns get a little more time to think about it. Before starting, interns sit down with the coordinator to figure out which Feminist Majority research project best matches their interests.

Students may intern part- or full-time, for a period of eight weeks to a year. In any case, interns monitor press conferences and congressional hearings and analyze policy. They also work on current campaigns such as Feminization of Power, which strives to place feminists in public office or college-campus leadership positions, and Empowering Women, which encourages women to seek top positions in their professions. Interns also write position papers and engage in research, exploring such areas as abortion, sexual harassment, gender balance, and RU 486 (the French abortion pill that may be taken up to nine weeks after conception).

One intern analyzed the legislative processes in 23 states. "We wanted to know how to get issues on the ballot," she said. "In order to bring such issues to a vote, we needed to understand how the law is structured in each state." The intern also researched reapportionment—the federal distribution of boundaries for use as congressional districts. "[The Feminist Majority] wanted to influence the reapportionment process in order to form a 'woman's district,' which could then elect a female candidate." Though she found several areas with a majority of women, the organization could not influence the government to redraw the boundaries. However, her research was not conducted in vain: "My work showed us that we need to focus our energies on recruiting women candidates."

As part of the Feminization of Power campaign, another intern compiled demographic statistics on New York, using Excel to record the political parties to which the state's residents belonged. "It's tedious to sit in front of the computer and punch in what seems like useless data, but such information helps us put more women in elected office," said the intern. "It allows us to figure out whom we need to target in each district in order to win." She also created a press book for the Rock for Choice project, a series of rock concerts (Red Hot Chili Peppers, Pearl Jam, etc.) that raise money for the Feminist Majority's abortion rights campaigns.

As one would expect, most interns are women. But men are welcome, and a few have served as interns. One male intern, in addition to becoming involved in the Feminization of Power campaign during the 1992 elections, oversaw part-time interns. "I had to make sure that they were making good progress in whatever they were doing—be it arranging fund-raising walkathons, researching government funding of abortions, or compiling information on female candidates." He also served as the administrative liaison to the Women's Advisory Council to the police commission. "I wrote letters, coordinated presentations, put together phone lists, and created memos…. [A]nd I did research on gender balance in the police force, looking at recruitment policies and hiring strategies." He made such a thorough examination, that back at school, he "consulted the [local] police force, which was revamping hiring practices."

The Feminist Majority applies pressure to anti-abortion movements in major cities like New York, Atlanta, Chicago, and Houston. Occasionally, interns participate in these efforts. Bankrolled by the Feminist Majority, they travel to the sites to organize clinic defenses: "I mobilized local abortion rights groups and arranged advertising to inform more people about our cause." Back at home, staff and interns sometimes stage their own protests. In D.C., the interns occasionally organize intern lobby days and, depending on the piece of legislation pending at the time, spend an entire day lobbying congresspeople.

> The organization is so intimate that regular contact with the top brass is commonplace.

Some interns are frustrated by the Feminist Majority's nonprofit status, which makes it difficult for the organization to do sophisticated research. "One of my projects was stonewalled because of low funding," said one intern. Limited funding also prevents interns from receiving any sort of compensation (save a few who get small stipends) and means that the office can afford few secretaries. So interns sometimes photocopy, file, and stuff envelopes. They also put together press packets and make phone calls. "In order to compile state-wide election results one season," one intern said, "I called [the office of] each state's secretary of state until I was blue in the face."

Interns are encouraged to seek the help of staff and to speak their minds on research projects and campaigns. "Besides including us in regular strategy sessions, people here want us to tell them what we think," said one intern. "They want to hear the student perspective." Said another: "It's such a small group that you can always knock on someone's door and make suggestions." The organization is so intimate, in fact, that regular contact with the top brass is commonplace. "The executive director and the chairman of the board were always available if I had questions or needed advice," said an intern.

SELECTION

 The Feminist Majority welcomes applications from high school, undergraduate, and graduate students who display strong interest in women's issues. Students of any educational background are eligible; past interns have pursued degrees in journalism, women's studies, public policy, government, and history. International applicants are eligible.

APPLICATION PROCEDURE

 The deadline to submit materials is rolling. Applicants must send a resume, cover letter, and writing sample of two to ten pages (an academic paper is sufficient) to either the Los Angeles or D.C. office. Finalists are given phone interviews.

OVERVIEW

 In 1987, in a large theater off Los Angeles' Wilshire Boulevard, California state senator Diane Watson and actor Ed Asner were among the keynote speakers who had gathered at the Feminist Majority's first event—a Feminization of Power rally. "We are working too hard to convince legislators to adopt our positions," they said. "Let's just put ourselves in public offices nationwide." The audience erupted in applause. Today, the Feminist Majority is one of the few feminist organizations embracing a national perspective. Grooming interns as the feminist movement's future leaders, it exposes them to abortion laws, RU 486, sexual harassment issues, and women's rights. It allows them to mingle with dedicated staffers and feminist greats like Ellie Smeal. It even sends some of them to cities around the country to organize defenses of abortion clinics. "What a fantastic experience," said an intern. "It prepared me for a lifelong career in feminism."

FOR MORE INFORMATION . . .

■ The Feminist Majority
8105 West Third Street
Los Angeles, CA 90048
(213) 651-0495
(213) 653-2689 (fax)

■ The Feminist Majority
1600 Wilson Boulevard
Suite 801
Arlington, VA 22209
(703) 522-2214
(703) 522-2219 (fax)

SELECTIVITY	🔍 🔍 🔍 🔍
Approximate applicant pool: 3,500–4,000 Interns accepted: 1,000–1,200	

COMPENSATION	$ $ $ $ $
$2,235–2,890/mo for undergrads; $3,470–5,325/ mo for grad students; round-trip travel; free housing (Dearborn) or housing allowance (non-Dearborn)	

QUALITY OF LIFE	↑ ↑ ↑ ↑ ↑
Orientation and seminars with division heads; job counseling; fFitness center (Dearborn only); demonstrations (auto assembly, crash test, etc.)	

LOCATION(S)

Dearborn, MI, and numerous cities in southeast MI

FIELD

Automobiles and automobile components

DURATION

14 weeks
Summer

PRE-REQS

Undergrads; grad students

DEADLINE(S)

April 1

It was 1908 when the sturdy steel vehicle first made its debut on American roads. It had a four-cylinder, twenty-horsepower motor, full-leather upholstery stitched in a diamond-tufted pattern, cushy sofa seats, gas lamps, and it came in red, green, or black. At $850, the Model T was one of the first automobiles which was produced using standardized parts and assembly-line methods and which the average American could afford to buy. The Model T was a phenomenal success. More than 10,000 were sold the year the car first appeared; within six years, 250,000 had been unloaded; and by 1927, when the Model T left the production line for good, more than 15 million had been sold, making it the second-bestselling model of all time.

These days, Ford continues to produce a variety of well-known cars—notably the Mustang, Explorer, Bronco, Escort, Taurus, and Probe as well as the Lincoln Continental and the Mercury Sable. Since its founding in 1903, Ford has evolved into the world's third-largest industrial corporation and second-largest producer of cars and trucks. The company sells almost 6 million vehicles each year, generating sales in excess of $100 billion.

DESCRIPTION

Established in 1953, Ford's internship program was recently revamped as part of the company's global restructuring program known as "Ford 2000." Five departments are open to interns: Product Engineering & Manufacturing, Finance, Purchasing & Supplies, Sales & Marketing, and Employee Relations. Placed in one of the company's many teams, the exact size and composition of which vary with department, each intern is given an assignment and a work plan for the summer. Since Ford tends to organize its teams by product, a typical team might consist of research and development engineers, purchasing agents, design and assembly engineers, and sales managers. Because approximately 90 percent of Ford's summer interns work in engineering functions, the following description focuses on

Product Engineering & Manufacturing internships.

One Product Development intern worked in the Vehicle Engineering Department on export "homologation" (i.e., making the American product compatible with Japanese standards). He explained: "In Japan, [consumers] require a full-size spare tire. But then the carpeting in the trunk doesn't fit. So you have to replace it with some carpeting that does fit over the big tire." The intern spent a lot of time in the plant interfacing between the design engineers and the assembly engineers, identifying possible issues of concern, such as whether the parts were easy to assemble and whether the parts from the American and Japanese models were easily distinguishable.

But Product Development involves more than simply working in the plant. Later in the summer, "in an effort to evaluate the [Mustang] seat designs," one Product Development intern "got together a group of fifteen to twenty Mustang employees, all of different sizes and shapes, and six or seven vehicles with different seat designs, and we spent two days driving around the state of Michigan. [We took] turns switching drivers every two hours, and at each pit stop we evaluated the seat designs for comfort and appearance." Now, "when I sit in a seat, I notice all the things that I never picked up on before."

Another Product Development intern worked on a crash-test program for the introduction of the new Ford Aerostar. He explained: "I was responsible for coordinating the prototype production of Aerostars. On a typical day, I'd find out what we still needed for the vehicles, and then I'd order parts or talk to mechanics." Although he had a desk with a telephone and voice mail, he spent most of his time at the prototype shop or at assembly plants outside the office.

As Ford also offers a co-op program, some interns work spring or fall semester in addition to a summer term. One Production Equipment co-op intern worked on three separate projects during her six-month tenure. She spent the first part of her summer helping a manufacturing

engineer develop new fixtures for a heater core. Her second project involved researching quality-control methods, in preparation for Ford's Total Quality Excellence Award, presented to a particular division for exemplary safety and quality-control practices. Her final project consisted of tracking the budgets of various projects within a facility.

Ford interns are always busy with one responsibility after another, but the friendly, open atmosphere helps alleviate a great deal of the anxiety which an intern might expect to feel upon receiving his or her first assignment. "The people I worked with were always willing to help me," reported one intern. Another intern appreciated the respect she was shown by her supervisor and immediate staff: "I felt no different than a real Ford employee. I dealt with suppliers and other engineers just like everyone else in the group."

At Ford, "people skills" are considered important. The overwhelming consensus among employees is that interns who are unafraid to ask questions, and who are passionate about their work, will learn much and enjoy themselves enormously. One intern did complain, however, that, "some hourly people don't take you seriously if you're an intern. [But the] salaried people and management are very encouraging."

Most interns work in Dearborn, home of Ford's world headquarters, Research and Engineering Center, and various manufacturing and assembly operations. "Dearborn and Ford are sort of synonymous," noted one intern. Although the city is mostly industry-based, with "a lot of buildings… [and a] lot of industrial parks," there is also a large residential population. "Dearborn has its own little downtown section. [It's] definitely a city. It's got some cute little stores and restaurants," reported another intern. Located just ten minutes from downtown Detroit, Dearborn also provides easy access to many of Detroit's attractions. Dancing, ethnic restaurants, and blues clubs are all readily available in Detroit's "Ware-

> **One intern spent two days driving throughout Michigan evaluating Ford Mustang seat designs.**

house District and Downtown."

Upon arrival, interns attend an orientation and an ice-cream social. Later in the summer, they have opportunities to attend speeches by executives. On the job, interns participate in performance evaluations, are eligible to receive job counseling, and may attend seminars held by division heads.

Other diversions await Ford interns. They have the option of touring a body assembly plant, a components facility, a test track, and a wind tunnel. They may also choose to attend a crash-test demonstration. Other opportunities open to interns include Ford's summer softball league, museum visits, and tickets to the Detroit Grand Prix. Moreover, not far from Dearborn is Greenfield Village, which houses Henry Ford's original childhood home, Thomas Edison's lab (the two were close friends), a blacksmith shop, and a replica of a schoolhouse. Other local attractions include the Henry Ford museum and Cedar Point amusement park.

Ford goes out of its way to make life easier for its interns. All interns are reimbursed for round-trip transportation expenses. Those interns working at and living more than 50 miles from Dearborn also have the option of receiving free housing in fraternity houses or apartment complexes at the University of Michigan at Ann Arbor, located about 35 to 40 minutes from Dearborn. Or, they can opt to receive a stipend and find their own housing. Students living in the provided housing and working in Dearborn (60 percent of interns) receive free transportation to and from work and have access to the company's fitness center.

Interns residing in the University Towers Apartments, located in the center of the University of Michigan campus, share a two-bedroom apartment with three other interns. They have access to meeting and exercise rooms, a pool, and, for a monthly fee, cable television. Interns living in the fraternity houses share a one-room double with another intern. Continental breakfast and free maid service are provided each work day. On weekends, all interns have the option of fending for themselves in Ann Arbor or creating a home-cooked meal in the common kitchen. "To be honest," commented one intern, "most evenings I just hung out with my Ford roommates and watched TV. [But] Ann Arbor has a lot of good restaurants and a lot of summer activities. Plus, Canada is only an hour away."

SELECTION

 Although Ford tends to draw heavily from schools in the midwest due to its location, students from throughout the country are encouraged to apply. And while most Ford interns are electrical or mechanical engineers who have completed their junior year and have a minimum GPA of 3.0, the internship program is open to all undergraduates. Graduate students who are pursuing an M.S. in engineering or an M.B.A. and who have completed their first year are hired in Finance, Purchasing & Supplies, and Sales & Marketing. Communication and leadership skills, the ability to work well in teams, and willingness to relocate are also strong considerations in the selection process. Past internship experience is not as important. We "can't look for experienced people," says the coordinator, "because that's what we're trying to give [interns]." International applicants eligible. To research background information on Ford, check out the company's web site at www.ford.com.

APPLICATION PROCEDURE

 The deadline to apply is April 1. Approximately 40 percent of Ford interns are recruited directly off college and university campuses and receive half-hour, formal interviews before their resumes are passed on with recommendations. The other 60 percent of interns are either "write-ins" who mailed in their resumes or "walk-ins" who simply dropped by the office with a resume in hand. After these resumes are reviewed, selected walk-in students are contacted for on-site, half-day interviews. Write-ins who pass muster receive a half-hour phone interview. After completing interviews, College Relations sifts through interviewers' comments, and the best candidates are invited to spend a summer at Ford. Ford also offers a College Cooperative Education Program, primarily for college juniors in engineering and science, who alternate semesters studying and interning. "[The Co-op Program] is one of the best ways to end up at Ford after graduating," says the coordinator. "While we offer full-time employment to only 10 percent of summer interns, we hire approximately 90 percent of the co-ops." Interested students should contact their campus co-op coordinator for more information.

OVERVIEW

 The automobile enthusiast will find plenty to revel in a Ford internship, as the challenging projects and hands-on experience provide powerful insight into the automotive industry. And if seeing the fruits of your labors is important to you, working at Ford provides near-unrivaled opportunities to accomplish these goals. As one intern commented: "[It's especially] gratifying to work on a project you can contribute to from start to finish." Past interns are overwhelmingly positive when speaking of their Ford experiences: "I would recommend [this internship] to any student," said one intern. "There's absolutely no doubt in my mind that it was the best thing I could have done. It's an experience that no book or teacher could teach you . . . This was real-world."

FOR MORE INFORMATION . . .

■ HR Customer Operations
Ford Motor Company
P.O. Box 0520
Allen Park, MI 48101
www.ford.com

SELECTIVITY	🔍 🔍 🔍 🔍
Approximate applicant pool: 300–400 Interns accepted: 25	

COMPENSATION	💲 💲 💲 💲 💲
$375–$649/wk for undergrads; $649–$953/wk for grads $500 relocation stipend; $1,000 bonus/or previous Frito-Lay internship	

QUALITY OF LIFE	🌴 🌴 🌴
3-day intern conference; team of mentors; chip heaven	

LOCATION(S)

Plano and Dallas, TX, and other cities—see Description

FIELD

Snack food

DURATION

10–12 weeks
Summer

PRE-REQS

College juniors and seniors; grad students
Minimum 3.0 GPA

DEADLINE(S)

Application period January 1–March 31 only

Crunch, scranch, craunch, scrunch, wunch, chomp, munch.

Such were the savory sounds of success for Elmer Doolin. That first bag of Mexican corn snacks he tasted in a San Antonio cafe in 1932 spurred him to close his floundering ice cream business and start making corn chips. At night, he'd produce ten pounds an hour out of his mother's kitchen and in the daytime, he'd peddle chips from his car. This was the humble start of the Frito Company.

That same year, a Nashville man named Herman Lay discovered potato snacks and, like Doolin, he set up shop in an old touring car and H.W. Lay & Company was born.

Each creating its own particular kind of chip, the two companies became regional giants over the next three decades, Frito in the Southwest and H.W. Lay in the Southeast. Ascribing to the adage "two heads are better than one," the companies merged in 1961, setting up Frito-Lay, Inc., in Dallas.

Today, the synergy has made Frito-Lay the world's largest snack-food company, with yearly sales of over $5 billion. Using 1.6 billion pounds of potatoes and 600 million pounds of corn each year, its 40,000 employees nationwide churn out a couch potato's fantasy menu: Doritos tortilla chips, Fritos corn chips, Lay's and Ruffles potato chips, and Chee-tos snacks.

DESCRIPTION

In 1990, Frito-Lay started the Minority Intern Program to "provide outstanding students of color with significant business experiences across Frito-Lay." In 1994, Frito-Lay opened up the program to include all students. Interns are placed in Sales, Marketing, Finance, Manufacturing,

Purchasing, Logistics, Engineering, Management Systems, Research and Development, and Communications, at the corporate headquarters in Plano, TX. Other interns take field assignments in Sales, Operations, Manufacturing, and Distribution at such varied locations as Beloit and Milwaukee, WI; Los Angeles, CA; Phoenix, AZ; and Chicago, IL. About 20 percent of interns are graduate students.

Those working in technical positions develop packaging graphics, install new seasoning systems, develop hardware and software, and track seasoning-usage fluc-

BUSYWORK
MEDIUM
LOW / HIGH
OLDMAN & HAMADEH
METER

tuations (too much paprika? too much salt?). Interns in nontechnical positions evaluate competitor products, and sell and produce chips and dips. They also write articles for the company's newsletters. A Communications intern, for instance, traveled to Atlanta and Orlando to interview employees. "I was there pursuing human-interest stories and stories about new products or company events. Back at headquarters, I wrote each story in its entirety, helped brainstorm new ideas, and edited pieces—talk about responsibility!"

A Field Sales intern working out of Arizona spent half the internship on the road, riding with semi-truck drivers, making the rounds with the sales force, and setting up displays with merchandisers: "These displays were just your basic end-aisle variety, the type you see in grocery stores, but setting them up was an education in marketing." At the office, he shadowed managers and attended a meeting of the Trade Development group, which works to improve the sales operation. Not surprisingly, the people at the meeting served a few bags of chips, since chips were the topic of conversation. "There are bags of chips everywhere at this company," remarked the intern, who is now a Sales employee. "We eat them at meetings, during lunch, on breaks, and for dinner. As you might imagine, I've gained a lot of weight."

In the company's Dallas R&D facility, interns test manufacturing processes at Semiworks, a small-scale version of Frito-Lay's manufacturing plants. "Before spending millions of dollars setting up an operation at one of the plants," explained an R&D intern, "the company needs to see if it will work; that's the purpose of Semiworks." Each intern at this mock-up is involved in a number of projects. One intern helped design a "swing line," a system configured to make different types of chips by the mere switching of mechanical parts. "It's obviously more economical when you make two or more chips with the same equipment. I designed a Supremos cutter, which worked on the same [machine] used to make Sun Chips. I also designed a quick-change apparatus that could replace the Sun Chips cutter with the Supremos one within minutes. The hardest part was coming up with the concepts, but in R&D there are no wrong answers." Fabrication shops turned his designs into actual cutters that worked so well that they were implemented in operations.

The atmosphere at Frito-Lay is unusually supportive. "We want our interns to succeed," said the coordinator. "So we provide them with buddies, mentors, and supervisors that they may turn to for assistance." Buddies (fairly new employees) answer any questions interns may have. Mentors (senior managers) offer career advice. And supervisors (midlevel managers) assist interns with their projects. Yet, as available as supervisors are supposed to be, some interns claim that a few supervisors don't give their interns ample feedback: "After assigning me a project, my supervisor didn't touch base with me or track my progress until the internship was half over."

A third of the interns work at the Plano, TX, headquarters, a four-story complex shaped like the letter *A*. In the eye of the *A* is a large waterfall that cascades into a stream that flows under the middle bar of the *A* into an eight-acre lake, home to geese and monster catfish. Fishing is allowed whenever the lake is overstocked, but this happens rarely. Surrounding the building and the lake are a four-mile running track, tennis courts, a volleyball court, and a softball diamond. Inside, there's a state-of-the-art gym, fully equipped with treadmills, free-weights, StairMasters, Nautilus machines, and aerobics classes; gym membership is a nominal $1 a week.

Money is not a problem for interns at Frito-Lay. Aside from a great salary and up to $500 for moving expenses, each intern who has participated in *any* previous internship gets a bonus of $1,000 (but don't get any funny ideas; the company checks all claims). At the conclusion of the internship, interns give formal presen-

> "There are chips everywhere. . . . We eat them at meetings, during lunch, on breaks, and for dinner."

tations of their work to a group of five managers. Afterward, interns are formally evaluated on project results, demonstration of management skills, and overall performance (with ratings of outstanding, superior, acceptable, or unsatisfactory).

At the end of June, the Plano headquarters serves as the site of the summer intern conference. Interns from all over the country are flown in to listen to presentations made by senior executives. They also attend workshops on how to solve business problems, and they tour manufacturing facilities. One of the tours exposes the interns to a potato chip plant. Said one intern: "We could barely hear each other; the clanging of conveyer belts and automatic potato slicers made conversation difficult. [But] we could see the slicers, spinning around so fast that [the centrifugal force] pushed the potatoes into sharp blades located at the edge. Within seconds, the straight blades cut Lay's chips and the rippled blades made Ruffles. Then they were cooked, seasoned, and bagged." On the third and final day of the conference, interns sit for a finale dinner, which is attended by as many as thirty-five senior executives, who spend up to two hours interacting with students. "The dinner clearly signifies our belief that interns are a real investment," said the coordinator.

SELECTION

 Undergraduate and graduate students are eligible. To be considered, applicants must have finished their sophomore year, must have at least a 3.0 GPA, and must be studying one of the following disciplines: business administration or finance, any engineering, logistics, operations research, or economics. Liberal arts majors with an interest in business careers are also eligible. "By far, the biggest things we look for are initiative and management skills," said the coordinator. "We want results-oriented leaders with business experience."

APPLICATION PROCEDURE

 Students must send in a resume (GPA included) and a cover letter indicating a preference for position and location. Alternatively, students may attend Frito-Lay's winter recruiting events at campuses nationwide and participate in on-campus interviews during March. Promising students are invited to the various locations for on-site interviews. International applicants are eligible.

OVERVIEW

 "Imagination, ingenuity, and perseverance"—these traits were often attributed to Frito-Lay cofounder Elmer Doolin. These are also the qualities that the company searches for in its interns, who are sometimes called upon to undertake projects requiring innovative solutions. Such projects have included creating new graphics for packages, designing hardware for manufacturing plants, and setting up grocery store chip displays. In the middle of the summer, interns make use of their creative skills at a three-day conference. And at the end of the summer, interns judged to have the greatest employment potential—over 50 percent of them—are offered permanent jobs.

FOR MORE INFORMATION . . .

■ Frito-Lay, Inc.
Staffing Department
Dept: Intern
7701 Legacy Drive
P.O. Box 225458
Dallas, TX 75222-5458

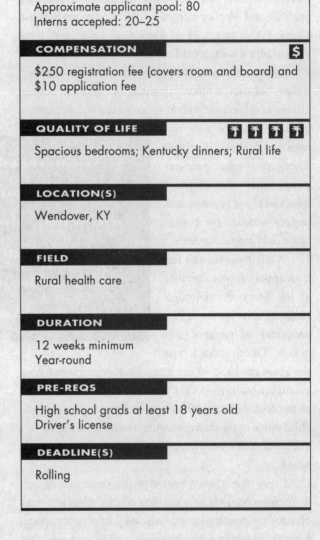

SELECTIVITY

Approximate applicant pool: 80
Interns accepted: 20–25

COMPENSATION

$250 registration fee (covers room and board) and
$10 application fee

QUALITY OF LIFE

Spacious bedrooms; Kentucky dinners; Rural life

LOCATION(S)

Wendover, KY

FIELD

Rural health care

DURATION

12 weeks minimum
Year-round

PRE-REQS

High school grads at least 18 years old
Driver's license

DEADLINE(S)

Rolling

The bearer of newborns is known as the "stork" to many American children.

But in Leslie County, KY, when children ask where babies come from, adults say the "nurses on horseback."

The nurses to which they refer work for the Frontier Nursing Service (FNS), an organization founded in 1925 by a woman named Mary Breckinridge following the deaths of her four-year-old son and infant daughter. Believing that her children had been victims of the inadequate health care system of her rural town, Breckinridge traveled to Leslie County with the goal of reducing its maternal and infant mortality rates. At that time, they were among the highest in the United States. Armed with an extraordinary degree of courage and leather saddlebags bursting with medical supplies, FNS nurses would ride around Kentucky's Appalachian region to deliver babies and care for expectant mothers.

Today, the horses are no longer in use, but FNS still provides quality health care to many of Leslie County's rural residents. In addition to delivering babies, FNS runs three rural health clinics, a women's health care center, the forty-bed Mary Breckinridge Hospital, and the Frontier School of Midwifery and Family Nursing, the oldest nursing midwife school in the United States. Now known the world over as an exceptional rural demonstration in family-centered health care, FNS has delivered nearly 25,000 babies since 1925 and has reduced the maternal and infant mortality rates in Leslie County to a percentage that is well below the national average.

DESCRIPTION

 Buried in the heart of Kentucky is a little-known but outstanding internship program for those interested in health care. Known as "couri-

ers," interns have been employed by FNS since its founding. In addition to delivering supplies, couriers assist doctors, midwives, family nurse practitioners, and nurses in one or more of the five areas: Women's Health Care, FNS Outpost Clinics, Mary Breckinridge Hospital, and Home Health Agency.

Couriers spend approximately 25 percent of their time on busywork. From 11 A.M. to 2 P.M. at least one day each week, couriers hop into one of FNS's Toyotas to make necessary pickups and deliveries. First they stop by the hospital to pick up incoming mail, medicines from the pharmacy, and supplies like gloves, and blood-drawing apparatuses. They usually spend the next three hours delivering these materials to the three outpost clinics, where they pick up outgoing mail, blood and urine samples requiring analysis, and supply orders to be delivered to the hospital. Couriers also take care of gardening, landscaping, and general office work at the FNS administrative building.

When they're not performing these "rounds," interns help out in other capacities. At the three outpost clinics, couriers help prepare exam rooms and write down patient histories and accounts of their illnesses. They also take patients' pulse, heart rate, temperature, and blood pressure and collect samples for blood, urine, and pregnancy tests.

While patients wait for their appointments, couriers at the Mary Breckinridge Hospital also jot down descriptions of patients' illnesses. Often invited into the exam rooms, couriers assist doctors and watch how exams are performed. Couriers have entertained children as the doctor checked their ears and throats, held a little child down as the doctor scrubbed coal out of the child's knee and used a stethoscope to hear a wheezing patient's lungs.

Every Wednesday, the hospital's surgeon comes in to perform various surgical procedures. Couriers may observe the doctor at work, providing they scrub up and wear a hygienic smock, white mask, and latex gloves. One courier watched the doctor insert a viewing scope into a man's colon: "I couldn't believe that I was seeing the insides of the guy's large intestine." Another courier watched the doctor perform a hysterectomy: "I felt important—[the doctor] asked me to hold the suture [i.e., the thread] while he sewed the patient together." And a third observed a cesarean section. "We gained so much first-hand experience with the patients themselves," said a courier. "It made me want to become a doctor."

> **Couriers may be exposed to country-western dancing, the music of bluegrass bands, and the bite of homegrown moonshine.**

Home Health Agency couriers travel with nurses to the homes of six to ten patients a day. Taking vital signs and assisting in bathing retarded, deaf-mute, disabled, and elderly patients, couriers learn the practices of home health care. "It was a real opportunity to help people who genuinely couldn't help themselves," said one courier. After finishing their medical duties, it's not uncommon for nurse and courier to sit down and chat with a patient for as long as 20 minutes. "I'd come back from a day of Home Health glowing," said a courier. "It's the place where you probably make the most difference in people's lives."

Couriers also assist FNS in its Literacy project. They tutor adults in English, act as teachers' aides at elementary, vocational, and high schools, and help young kids gain basic skills in reading and math. "Tutoring was rewarding because the illiteracy rate [in Leslie County] is so high," said a courier. "Getting these people interested in reading was a challenging but satisfying assignment." FNS's offices are the only buildings located in Wendover, just four miles from Hyden, a community of 500 residents. Couriers looking for the conveniences of a slightly larger town—a movie theater, restaurants, and a Wal-Mart—can drive to Hazard, located 20 miles away.

All couriers live at FNS, in the Garden House on the second floor just above the administrative offices. Couriers are given their own rooms, each with a bed, desk, and closet. The Big House, the two-story log cabin that served as Mary Breckinridge's home until 1965, houses visitors and serves three meals per day to staff and couriers. Lunches and dinners include typical Kentucky home cooking such as fried chicken, mashed potatoes with mounds of butter, pork chops, meat loaf, and corn bread. After eating, couriers are required to wash dishes and put away leftovers, which are always available for snacking. In keeping with a tradition dating back to FNS's early years, couriers host the "Monday Night Tea," a special dinner served on fine china. Before dinner, tea and sherry are served in the living room as couriers, staff, FNS doctors and administrators chat with each other. "Teas are a good opportunity to ask questions about medicine and hospital administration," said a courier.

Though couriers are busy most of the day, free time is available in the evenings and on weekends. Journal writing and reading are common activities. Often, couriers gather to watch television in the lounge of the Garden House, which has two couches, a fireplace, a VCR, and cable TV. For recreation, couriers use the Richard Nixon Recreation Center two miles away for basketball, tennis, and swimming.

An opportunity to experience rural life up close, the FNS internship can expose couriers to country-western dancing, the music of bluegrass bands, and the bite of homegrown moonshine. Couriers have the opportunity to meet famous residents like Alabam Morgan, who is all too happy to teach young people the art of quilting. "She's 70 but full of energy," said a courier. "We'd sit around with quilting bags, and she'd feed us rhubarb and fried apple pies." Then there's the 80-year-old craftsman Sherman Wooton, who shows couriers how to make stools. "We went into the woods and cut down a hickory tree with a two-man saw," recalled a courier. "Then we removed the bark and cut it into strips to weave the seats. They were sturdy, good-looking stools. Many of us are now using them in college."

SELECTION

Anyone 18 years of age or older who has completed high school is eligible to apply. No particular major or interest is required. FNS seeks people who can get along with others and who wish to help those in need. Before being officially accepted as couriers, applicants must show proof that they have a valid driver's license and a vehicle, International applicants are eligible.

APPLICATION PROCEDURE

The deadline is rolling, as FNS accepts couriers year-round. Applicants must submit a $250 registration fee, an application form (which asks for several essays), a cover letter explaining their interest in the program, and resume. Applicants are asked to bring their own cars. The coordinator conducts phone interviews with finalists.

OVERVIEW

The Frontier Nursing Service is the place to turn for students interested in medicine, nursing, midwifery, or public health. A model for rural health care, FNS provides students with a taste of Kentucky life while allowing them to observe medical procedures and assist nurses, doctors, midwives and family nurse practitioners.

FOR MORE INFORMATION . . .

■ Frontier Nursing Service
Courier Program
132 FNS Drive
Wendover, KY 41775
(606) 672-2317
(606) 672-3022

Genentech, Inc.
Genentech, Inc.
Genentech, Inc.
Genentech, Inc.
Genentech, Inc.

In 1976, venture capitalist Robert Swanson and biochemist Herb Boyers sat down to consider a bold new business exploring the commercial potential of biotechnology. They formulated a company called Genentech, and within a year company employees had created a human protein using recombinant DNA technology—the first demonstration of its kind. But the company didn't stop there. In 1982, it introduced human insulin as the first commercial product of the recombinant DNA technology and promptly licensed the insulin to pharmaceutical giant Eli Lilly for mass distribution.

Since then, the young company has remained in the forefront of biotechnology. In 1985, it earned accolades for being the first company of its sort to market a pharmaceutical—namely "protropin," a growth hormone. In 1987, it received widespread praise for creating TPA, a medicine for treating heart attacks. And in 1993, it became the only biotechnology company in the world with five marketed products, adding Pulmozyme (for chronic obstructive pulmonary disease) and Nutropin (for short stature due to Turner syndrome) to its drug mix. With these five FDA-approved products and more on the way, Genentech is upholding its mission "to diagnose, treat and cure serious human disease—and create a better way of life for millions of people."

DESCRIPTION

Genentech started its Summer Internship Program for college undergraduate and graduate students in 1987. In the beginning, virtually all positions were in Research, but the program has expanded to offer a taste of biotechnology to students from all sorts of academic majors. Now, positions are also available in Manufacturing, Business, Quality Control, Medical Affairs, Marketing, and Corporate Communications. But because the majority of interns continues to work in Research, this passage will focus on interns' research experiences.

Research interns work in laboratories alongside a research assistant or postdoctoral student and a head scientist. One intern

SELECTIVITY

Approximate applicant pool: 1,700
Interns accepted: 100

COMPENSATION

$400/week for undergrads
$490/week for grad students

QUALITY OF LIFE

Bay view; Friday Ho Hos;
daily science lectures; social activities

LOCATION(S)

San Francisco, CA

FIELD

Biotechnology

DURATION

10–12 weeks
Summer

PRE-REQS

College sophomores, juniors and seniors;
grad students
Must be returning to school in the fall

DEADLINE(S)

March 15

worked with a hormone that moderates the immune response: "I revealed the structure of the particular receptor molecule to which the hormone binds," he recalled. "We already knew that too much hormone, however, can lead to inflammation and shock in the body." Using recombinant DNA techniques, he and his team attempted to create a soluble version of the receptor. He explained: "If administered to patients with arthritic symptoms, for example, that version could render the excess hormone harmless." Another intern tested the stability of anticoagulants under different pH, temperature, and concentration conditions. "I wanted to see if [the anticoagulants] would stay together in pill form; that is, I was trying to understand the relationship between their structure and their reactivity with certain powerful digestive enzymes in the gut."

Working vigorously to bring drugs to market, Genentech involves interns in research of all of its products under investigation. Genentech is currently researching an AIDS vaccine, an insulin-like growth factor to combat physical wasting in AIDS patients, and products to treat allergies and inflammation. Research interns do not normally choose their projects; managers assign interns to laboratories that seem to be best suited to their academic and research backgrounds.

Research interns describe their labwork as intense and imbued with a great deal of responsibility. One intern recalled: "I was the sole person responsible for implementing the project. I knew from start to finish the whole plan— the DNA sequences we'd create, the mutant forms of the proteins we'd get, and the genetic engineering techniques we'd use. In the end, the team and I had completed such substantive research that our work was published in a scientific journal." To complete such tasks, most interns are supplied with their own desk and a Macintosh or UNIX computer. Given the interns' interaction with the principal scientists, it is no wonder that words like *stimulating* and *cutting-edge* are repeatedly used to describe the experi-

ence. Said one intern: "I had access to the Ph.Ds, my boss, and even his boss. They were excited to help me even though I was an intern. This is work that people with master's and doctorate degrees do."

There is serious research going on at Genentech. But one gets the feeling that although employees are highly motivated and deeply interested in science, they know how to mix business with pleasure. Spacious buildings with large windows provide a beautiful view of San Francisco Bay. Pleasing aromas emanate from the two company-run cafeterias, where one can get a great lunch for a few dollars. Moreover, each floor contains a large lounge area equipped with an espresso machine, a lunch table, newspapers, and magazines. The labs receive money for a stereo system to "blend science and rock n' roll," as one intern put it.

Interns can attend daily lectures given by top scientists from around the world and weekly lab meetings to discuss project progress and administrative concerns. In addition, there are departmental trips to Giants games, picnic sites, and local museums. Athletically inclined interns may also partake of the company-sponsored membership to a local health club. Every Friday afternoon, interns are treated to the weekly happy hour, affectionately known as the "Ho Ho." Though no one seems to recall how the name came into being, this gathering has metamorphosed into a giant party with bands, free food, and loads of beverages. Most weeks, the party focuses on a specific theme such as ecology or the Olympics. In the off-hours, interns delight in exploring San Francisco and nearby beaches and campgrounds.

Though competitive with the salaries of other biotech internships, Genentech's compensation falls short of what other technical internships offer. No one seems to mind terribly, however. "Genentech offers such a good experience," said one intern, "that I willingly rejected a much higher-paying offer to see how a great,

> **Working vigorously to bring drugs to market, Genentech involves interns in research of all of its products under investigation.**

perhaps the best, biotech company is run."

Commuting is sometimes cited as a negative aspect of the internship. Given Bay Area traffic and the fact that most interns live as far away as Berkeley and Palo Alto, getting to Genentech is a bit of a trek. Fortunately, interns may join one of the company's carpool groups or take CAL trains or BART into South San Francisco where Genentech's shuttle will transport them to work.

The Genentech experience ends quickly, so interns must work diligently to make a final presentation or provide a manuscript to be considered for publication. "In my three months," concluded one intern, "I got a feel for the whole biotech industry and observed how research fits in with production. By preparing for my talk at the end of the summer, I refined the verbal skills needed to defend my work."

SELECTION

 Genentech is looking for students who are at least sophomores and who will return to school after completing the internship. The company recruits primarily through campus newspaper advertisements and career center bulletins, although half of the students considered send unsolicited applications. An affirmative action program screens for excellent minority and female applicants. While 80 percent of interns have science backgrounds (e.g., biology, chemistry, and chemical engineering), there is room for students who are interested in science and technology but study liberal arts. International applicants are eligible.

APPLICATION PROCEDURE

 The deadline is March 15. Applicants are required to send in a resume detailing relevant laboratory and/or business skills, a cover letter, and a copy of their academic record. The company also conducts on-campus interviews at Bay Area colleges. After an initial screening of resumes, Genentech conducts on-site or phone interviews. Program participants are required to sign an agreement of strict confidentiality.

OVERVIEW

 Take scientifically oriented students, throw in cutting-edge research opportunities, world-class presentations, and a bit of San Francisco and you've got the Genentech Summer Internship Program—a unique opportunity to experience the biotechnology industry. For motivated, inquisitive, and diligent students, this program opens up many doors. One door allows interns to return a second summer. Another offers permanent employment to as many as five or ten of each summer's interns. A third clears a path to Ph.D. programs or medical schools. And a fourth attracts former interns to top biotech, environmental, and engineering firms. Concluded one intern: "As far as science training goes, it's one of the best places. You come out of Genentech and are respected for your technical skills. Academics and industry people alike know that it's a place where things get done."

FOR MORE INFORMATION . . .

■ Genentech
Human Resources
Summer Internship Program
P.O. Box 1950
South San Francisco, CA 94083
www.gene.com/careers/college/internships.html

GEORGETOWN UNIVERSITY LAW CENTER

In the heart of Washington, D.C., an intern is hunched over a computer, his face illuminated by a glowing computer screen as he conducts research for a highly prestigious law firm. Meanwhile, blocks away, two other interns are working for equally prestigious attorneys, but these college students are at a crime scene. One snaps photos while her partner takes statements. They work for Georgetown University Law Center's Criminal and Juvenile Justice Clinic.

First established in 1960, The Criminal and Juvenile Justice Clinic at Georgetown University Law Center provides high-quality attorneys for indigent criminal defendants in the Washington, D.C. area who would otherwise not be able to afford representation. Some of the attorneys that have worked for the Clinic include O.J. Simpson defense team member Gerald Uelman and CNN legal commentator Greta Van Susteren.

DESCRIPTION

In 1985, interns were added to facilitate this process, aiding the attorneys in nearly all the stages of the case, from investigation to trial. Even though the Clinic's attorneys are court-appointed, they do not receive any payment from clients or from the courts for their work; they have to rely on the interns to do the bulk of the investigative work on cases ranging from first degree murder to possession of drugs.

The internship starts with a week of intensive training at the Law Center. These 40 mandatory hours provide interns with the basic components of their job, including defense theories, narrative interviews, locating witnesses, statement writing, ethical constraints, eyewitness reliability, subpoenas, and investigative resources. Supplementary meetings focus on Fourth

---

SELECTIVITY

Approximate size of applicant pool: 400–500
interns accepted: 30 (ten each semester)

COMPENSATION

Only parking and mileage fees

QUALITY OF LIFE

Brown bag lunches;
extensive training in criminal investigations,
legal research, and criminal law; numerous tours

LOCATIONS

Washington, D.C.

FIELD

Criminal Law

DURATION

12 weeks (Summer)
14 weeks (Fall and Spring)

PRE-REQS

College juniors and seniors; recent grads; grad students; college graduates of any age

DEADLINE

Summer .... April 1
Fall .... Rolling but no later than March 15
(first round) or July 1 (supplemental round)
Spring .... Rolling but no later than December 1

Amendment issues, more in-depth investigative strategies, and a closer look at police proceedings.

After this week, however, the interns are no longer confined to a building from 9 to 5. According to the discovery rules in the District of Columbia, the prosecution does not have to turn over to the defense the names or addresses of witnesses, which effectively handcuffs the defense. Therefore, the investigation starts at the lowest level as the defense first finds out who the witnesses are and then interviews them.

BUSYWORK
MEDIUM
LOW HIGH
OLDMAN & HAMADEH
METER

A former intern noted the wide range of subsequent responsibilities: "Work includes taking written statements from witnesses, serving subpoenas, visiting crime scenes, preparing diagrams for trial, obtaining all pertinent records and documents, viewing evidence with an attorney, observing all court procedures relevant to a case, and assisting in preparing the attorney for trial." Another former intern concurred, adding that "each day was a new experience."

At the teaching clinic, the attorneys also examine the relation between their work and the justice system. The former Investigations Supervisor Christine Depies related, "We want our students and interns to develop an understanding of why we do what we do, and not just go through the motions never really understanding the reasons behind it." The Clinic's small size ensures that the interns work, according to one former intern, "hand in hand with lawyers and law students."

> **Compared to interns at other law firms, interns at the Clinic learn more about the true mechanisms behind legal work**

Several extracurricular activities are scheduled to enhance the educational experience of the students. Numerous trips are planned and the interns view the working of the criminal justice system from a different angle. In a tour of the Correctional Treatment Facility in Washington, D.C., interns not only toured the building but also engaged in "discussions with administrators in all CTF [Correctional Treatment Facility] offices and departments." Interns also visited the Maximum Security Penitentiary in Lorton, VA, and "met several inmates and asked questions [about their views on the criminal justice system]." Interns also tour St. Elizabeth's hospital, which treats the criminally insane of the District of Columbia. Police ride-alongs are also arranged for interested students. Interns will also view an autopsy and listen to a lecture given by the Chief Medical Examiner.

The only monetary compensation received is reimbursement for mileage accrued during the workday; however, numerous perks await the intern in addition to the field trips. Interns also attend a private, brown bag lunch with the Dean of Admissions. An overlooked perk, free underground parking is provided for the entire semester at a parking garage, a commodity in downtown Washington, D.C. The Investigations Supervisor will also assist students in finding housing if they are not from the D.C. area.

The Clinic, found at Second and F streets, is only a short walk from the U.S. Capitol, the U.S. Supreme Court, the Library of Congress, Union Station, and other sites. Its close proximity to the Metro also opens up the city to those who do not have a car. The Clinic has a large workroom for the intern investigators, furnished with computers, telephones, and desks. However, aside from the first training week, the workplace of the intern is not a stuffy building but rather the neighborhoods, courthouses, and police stations of Washington, D.C., Maryland, and Virginia. Because the clients represented by the Clinic are indigent, interns (as well as the law students and Clinic professors) frequently journey into the poorest areas of the city.

The working schedule, like the workplace, is constantly in flux. Each intern is expected to commit a minimum of three full days per week to the internship although preference is given to full-time applicants. Though most of the work can be accomplished within normal business hours (9 to 5), the nature of investigative work frequently requires the interns to work some weekends and evenings. In addition, because the interns are assisting trial attorneys, the work schedule for the interns becomes hectic whenever the court date approaches.

For the most part, interns are encouraged to dress casually. However, interns are regularly called upon to testify in court and are then required to clad themselves in business attire.

The interns' responses to their time at the Clinic is mostly positive. One intern labeled it "a truly incredible program." Compared to interns at other law firms, interns at the Clinic learn more about the true mechanisms behind legal work in addition to legal research training on the computer databases LEXIS-NEXIS and Westlaw. However, this internship is not for everyone. The time commitment varies from week to week and interns will have to put in long hours occasionally. In addition, the majority of the intern's time is spent out in the field, and interns travel all over the D.C. area, "from the posh sections to the slums. If you work here, you will see things that make your mouth drop open." Safety is a concern, but the Clinic heavily emphasizes safety techniques and interns always work in pairs.

SELECTION

The Investigative Internship Program is open to college juniors and seniors, as well as grad students, recent grads, and college graduates of any age. No previous experience in criminal investigations is necessary, but applicants need to have a basic understanding of the criminal justice system. References may be called to see how well "you work with strangers," "accept challenges," "work without close supervision," and "solve problems." The intern will write a great deal, so interns should be "comfortable with the written word." In addition, since "clinic attorneys expect investigators to write with a level of detail and precision that surpasses the usual level necessary for undergraduate courses," the essays in the application will be judged by "the persuasiveness and quality of thought behind the answers" and "the mechanics of the presentation."

APPLICATION PROCEDURE

Eligible applicants should write for a special application that contains a typical data sheet, two short essays, and one long essay. The Intern Supervisor will attempt to conduct a phone interview with each candidate; however, prospective interns should assume that they will not be contacted and should submit "everything that they may wish to be considered." Applications for the summer session are due April 1. Even though spring applications should arrive by December 1, students should apply as early as possible because this session has rolling admissions. The

fall term contains two rounds: The first round, which is rolling, has a deadline of March 15; positions that are not filled through this round will be filled through a supplemental round that accepts applications until July 1; the supplemental round is rolling as well. Notification occurs two weeks after the deadline

OVERVIEW

This internship is not for everyone; it requires interns to go out into the streets and get their hands dirty rather than remaining in a climate-controlled high-rise. However, this internship, which emphasizes the education of the intern, is a valuable way for interns to learn how the law and the criminal justice system impact individual citizens. As one intern related, "this was a great experience... it gives you a candid perspective on being a defense lawyer," a perspective that can be difficult to find in a room with wall-to-wall carpeting.

FOR MORE INFORMATION . . .

■ Creecy Chandler, Investigations Supervisor
The Criminal and Juvenile Justice Clinic
111 F Street, NW
Washington, DC 20001-2095
Phone: (202) 662-9575
Fax: (202) 662-9681
acc5@law.Georgetown.edu

Hallmark Cards

SELECTIVITY	
Approximate applicant pool: 2,000 Interns accepted: 30–70	🔍🔍🔍🔍🔍

COMPENSATION	
$2,500–$3,000/month for undergrads $3,800–$5,200/month for grad students	$ $ $ $ $

QUALITY OF LIFE	
Friendly culture; luncheon seminars; field trips; Crown Center; fitness center	🌴🌴🌴🌴

LOCATION(S)

Kansas City, MO (HQ);
Other locations in KS

FIELD

Greeting cards and personal
communications products

DURATION

10–12 weeks
Summer

PRE-REQS

Students entering the final year of their
undergrad or grad program

DEADLINE(S)

January 15

Take a deep breath: Can you smell it, the weeks-old potpourri, perfumed paper, scented soaps, and heady Magic Marker fumes? Memories of birthdays, perhaps even hospital visits flood your mind. You're in a greeting card shop. There's a sea of greeting cards, in every conceivable color, for every conceivable occasion. Chances are, most have a five-pointed crown on their back flap.

That crown belongs to Hallmark, the world's largest greeting card company. From its persuasive advertising slogan, "When you care enough to send the very best," to its 665-person creative staff, Hallmark is the gold standard in greeting cards. In addition to cards, it produces an extensive line of partyware and gift products, keeping the world supplied with a large selection of giftwrap, ribbons and bows, Christmas ornaments, jigsaw puzzles, and stickers. Hallmark is also a company of legendary employee satisfaction: The majority of Hallmarkers enjoy a generous string of benefits and stay with the company the better part of their lives.

DESCRIPTION

To the disappointment of many students, interns in Hallmark's Corporate Staffing Intern Program do not write Hallmark cards. Instead, interns choose from a variety of business-oriented positions like Accounting/Finance, Business Research, Engineering, Human Resources, Business Services, Manufacturing, Marketing, and Information Technology.

No matter where they are placed, a lot of an intern's time is spent searching databases, gathering documents in the corporate library, meeting with managers from various divisions, and writing reports and delivering oral presentations. In marketing, for example, interns work on projects related to the development and management of superior products and programs. One intern, for example, completed a competitive analysis of product and programs of Hallmark's chief gift channel competitors. A final report included a comprehensive analysis of product trends, model line analysis, subject matter, merchandising, and pricing, with strategic and tactical recommendations for Hallmark.

In Human Resources, an intern worked on a job-categorization project evaluating Hallmark's previous employment decisions

BUSYWORK METER
LOW MEDIUM HIGH
OLDMAN & HAMADEH

and predicting its future employment trends. She also worked with a manager on developing a strategic plan for the Management Information Systems, the division in charge of computer systems and data communications.

In Manufacturing, an intern spent several weeks comparing conventional, manually produced artwork with computer-generated art. After studying each in terms of material cost, labor cost, and time of completion, he wrote a report asserting that computer-based art was the better method, because it is less expensive and more accurate than painting by hand. Later in the summer, he helped design a system to measure productivity among employees in the photo studio. The current system measured productivity by counting the number of photos each employee shoots per day; but it didn't take into account that some jobs take more time than others. He improved on the traditional method by creating a ranking system that assigned higher values to more laborious jobs, thereby yielding a more accurate assessment of productivity. The intern found both projects to be "very satisfying, as they were real-world situations that challenged my problem-solving skills."

Interns receive a formal performance evaluation in midsummer and at the end of their tenure. "Your manager sits down with you and goes over a one-page critique he or she has written about your performance," said one intern. "A basic battery of criteria is considered: communication and listening skills." Interns are evaluated on the following skills: communications, interpersonal effectiveness, leadership/initiative, problem solving/decision making, conceptual skills, creativity/innovation, results orientation, adaptability/self development. Most interns appreciate these performance appraisals, viewing them as a source of constructive criticism and praise for a job well done.

In addition to the Corporate Staffing Internship Program, Hallmark runs a summer program (the Scholarship Internship Program) for minority students interested in creative positions. Selected from a portfolio competition, interns work with writers and editors. This program allows interns to work in Hallmark's creative areas.

Hallmark interns enjoy a wealth of extracurricular activities. Executives from various departments speak at luncheon seminars that are organized twice a month. Tours of Hallmark's production and distribution facilities are also arranged to give interns an insider's look at places like the Topeka Production Center, one of four production centers responsible for printing millions of cards each week. The intern coordinator plans several cultural and social activities, including a trip to a Royals game, a show at Kansas City's Starlight Theater, and an intern picnic. Interns agree that such outings are "a great way to get to know other interns, especially those in other departments," but a few complain that the activities "are scheduled so late in the summer that it isn't worth bothering to make friends."

Hallmark is proud of the perks it offers its interns. They can frequent the company store, where they receive a 50 percent discount on most company products. There's also a clearance store, which sells surplus items at a 75 percent deduction. All this discounted material is too good to pass up for most interns: "I bought a truckload of greeting cards and knickknacks for every friend and family member I have." Interns have access to Hallmark's Fitness Center, a decent gym offering weights, StairMasters, Nautilus machines, and a track. Other benefits include business travel accident insurance coverage, pay for necessary absence due to a death in the family or jury duty, paid holidays, and free parking.

No description of life at Hallmark is complete without mentioning Crown Center. Located adjacent to Hallmark's headquarters, Crown Center is a "city-within-a-city." Crown Center has two hotels, twenty eating establishments, six movie theaters, a full-service

> "Be it a holiday, birthday, illness, or job well done, greeting cards are the currency of communication. This is a card-happy culture . . ."

bank, a parking lot that holds more than 6,000 cars, and retail stores of every kind. "It's an orgy of modern consumerism," said one intern. Happily, Hallmark employees, including interns, receive up to 20 percent off at many of the shops in the Crown Center complex.

Hallmark's Kansas City headquarters are located in a group of modern, industrial buildings that have a slew of windows and hold an abundance of artwork, ranging from abstract paintings to sculpture. Interns are afforded the same resources given to entry-level employees, which include a cubicle and their own computer equipment.

As funny as it sounds, the atmosphere at Hallmark tends to be warm and fuzzy. Employees care about their product and they care about each other. Interns are often surprised to see how seriously the company treats anniversary celebrations: "Anniversaries, particularly those commemorating 25 years with the company, are major affairs. Free cake and coffee. Dozens of well-wishers from all over the company. Sometimes top executives show up." As would be expected at the world's largest greeting card company, anniversaries find dozens of cards making their way to the honored employee. But anniversaries aren't the only events commemorated with greeting cards. Be it a holiday, birthday, illness, or job well done, greeting cards are the currency of communication at Hallmark. "This is a card-happy culture," an intern noticed. "Cards circulate at the drop of a hat."

The intern feedback is overwhelmingly positive. Said one intern, "I waited for the day I would dread coming to work and it never came. They really take care of you here." The only complaints were in reference to factors unrelated to an intern's workday. One intern groaned about the difficulty he had finding affordable, short-term housing in Kansas City: "Hallmark put me up in a hotel for three days while I was looking for housing. But I needed more time and ended up rushing into renting an overpriced, underfurnished apartment." Another said the move to Kansas City took getting used to: "Being from California, I wasn't prepared for oppressively hot weather in the summer. Also, things here are much slower. You have to adopt a Midwestern frame of mind."

SELECTION

 The Hallmark Corporate Staffing Summer Intern Program is open to students entering the final year of their undergraduate or graduate program. According to the program's brochure, qualifications include "demonstrated academic achievement," "demonstrated leadership ability," "excellent communication skills," and "an ability to relate to a wide variety of people and disciplines." Interns stress the importance of having "skills in network and relationship building" and "the assertiveness to ask for additional projects."

APPLICATION PROCEDURE

 Although Hallmark selects most of its interns through on-campus interviews and referrals, it encourages students to send a cover letter and resume to the Corporate Staffing department. Applications are due January 15. Most interns are offered positions after a campus interview.

OVERVIEW

 The word *hallmark* dates back to 18th-century England, when official marks were stamped on gold and silver articles to signify their purity. In all the important ways, Hallmark's internship program deserves the recognition of one of these archaic hallmarks. Challenging projects, structured feedback, group outings to Kansas City, and prime perks combined are a recipe for internship success. For students interested in spending a few months with the prime mover of the sentiment business, Hallmark's got the card.

FOR MORE INFORMATION . . .

■ Hallmark Cards
Corporate Staffing/Internship Program
Mail Drop #112
P.O. Box 419580
Kansas City, MO 64141-6580
(816) 274-5111
hcolle1@hallmark.com
www.hallmark.com

THE HERMITAGE
HOME OF ANDREW JACKSON

"A man of his accomplishments... did not belong on a farm, rusticating in Tennessee.... Such a man belonged in the White House."

So said the friends of Andrew Jackson in 1821, according to biographer Robert V. Remini. They were determined to see the former governor win the White House, and they got their wish seven years later when Jackson defeated John Quincy Adams to become the seventh President of the United States. But after serving two terms as president, Jackson returned to Tennessee—and "rusticate" (look it up) is exactly what he did. Can you blame him for wanting to rusticate at his sprawling Hermitage plantation and mansion?

Preserved by the Ladies' Hermitage Association, the Hermitage today differs from what it was during Jackson's time. The stately mansion still stands, as does the beautiful garden dedicated to Jackson's wife, Rachel. But there are few traces of its role as a full-scale cotton plantation left above ground. You must dig to find them.

Since 1988 archaeological fieldwork has been performed on the grounds of the Hermitage. By exploring the foundations and other subsurface artifacts adjacent to the Jackson family mansion, archaeologists and interns reconstruct what plantation life was like at the Hermitage of Jackson's time.

DESCRIPTION

Interns work at the Hermitage for a two-week, five-week, or ten-week session. After a brief orientation meeting and a welcoming barbecue, they begin their adventure in historical archaeology. The first few weeks of a session focus on digging test pits near the mansion and gar-

SELECTIVITY			
Approximate applicant pool: 200 Interns accepted: 16			

COMPENSATION			
$250/week, free room and board			

QUALITY OF LIFE			
Farmhouse residences Earthwatch meals; sweltering weather			

LOCATION(S)
Hermitage, TN

FIELD
Archaeology; History

DURATION
2 weeks, 5 weeks, or 10 weeks Summer

PRE-REQS
College juniors and seniors; recent grads; grad students Previous field training

DEADLINE(S)
April 10

den. Said one intern: "We dug about 175 1' × 1' test pits to get an initial idea of which areas had the best collection of artifacts." After locating a few choice spots, interns spend the rest of their time opening up larger excavation units, typically 10' × 10' squares.

Trowel in hand and sweat on brow, interns are fully immersed in archaeological excavation. Such work is clearly not for everyone: "You're bending down and scraping dirt for eight hours a day. You've got to be into it." But physical discomfort is offset by the thrill of discovery. Interns unearth all sorts of artifacts, including pieces of pottery, pieces of glass, animal bones, rusty nails, glass beads and coins from the 1850s. One intern even came across a glass eye. "Every day brings a new discovery. It really makes you enjoy the digging," said one intern.

Each artifact helps reconstruct what life was like at the Hermitage of Jackson's day. Many objects point to the presence of slaves. "I found a blue glass bead. From what [the staff archaeologist] told me, blue jewelry was worn by slaves to ward off evil and sickness," said an intern. Another found an amulet in the shape of a clenched fist—an old Islamic symbol. The Hermitage staff surmised that because the amulet was probably a necklace charm worn by slaves, it suggests that not all of Jackson's slaves were Christian, as is commonly thought by historians. Even the animal bones are useful bits of evidence, because they indicate what people were eating in a given area.

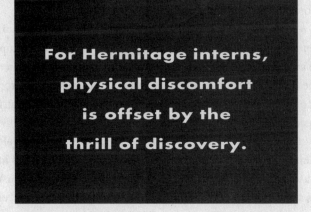

For Hermitage interns, physical discomfort is offset by the thrill of discovery.

Interns also find evidence of structures that were present at the original Hermitage. One group pinpointed the location of a few slave cabins when it uncovered a series of cellar holes and postholes. Another discovered a well-like hole filled with trash from the mid-19th century. Archaeologists hypothesize that in Jackson's time the hole was filled with snow and used as an ice house. Interns working near the garden uncovered an unnaturally narrow layer of gravel thought to be a 19th-century walkway.

An integral part of life as a Hermitage intern is interaction with the public. Hundreds of tourists visit the grounds every day, and inevitably they encounter interns hard at work excavating. Although a sign explains the basics of the project, it's up to interns to answer any questions visitors have about the excavation. "We got a lot of inquiries about what we were doing and about archaeology in general. And there were always a few tourists who asked if we were digging for gold." Despite a seemingly constant stream of questions, most interns find public interaction worthwhile: "It was fun talking with all those people—I felt like a spokesperson for the field of archaeology. It was also a great reason to take a break from digging."

There's no way around it: Life on the job is gritty and exhausting. Tennessee summers are oppressively humid, so interns begin their eight-hour workdays at 6:30 A.M. to avoid some of the afternoon heat. But, according to one intern, "It's still sometimes hot enough to melt the mercury in a thermometer." Nevertheless, if interns take frequent breaks, they'll begin to adjust to the scorching heat. The staff archaeologist said, "Although no one gets fully acclimated to outside summer work in this area, you will find after a few days of pacing yourself [that] you will more or less get used to the heat." Equally bothersome are the omnipresent insects. "This place is crawling with bugs," said one intern. "The sweat bees were the worst. They sting you in the elbow and behind the knees." Consequently, interns are advised to stock up on several cans of bug repellent.

Interns live in one of two 1930s-era farm houses located on the Hermitage property about a half-mile from the mansion. Although the houses "aren't the lap of luxury," each has a bathroom, a few pieces of furniture, and a fully equipped kitchen. Six people live in each house, with two or three to a bedroom. No air-conditioning is available (gasp), but a few well-placed fans seem to keep things cool. As expected of a Southern abode, the houses come complete with comfortable front porches. Said one intern: "At the end of the day, we'd sit on the porch, pop a beer, and watch the thunderstorms roll in. Those storms were always a relief from the heat."

A unique aspect of the Hermitage experience is that interns live and work with participants from the Earthwatch program. For three two-week sessions during the summer, Earthwatch sends a crew of paying volunteers to work on the excavation site. They come from a wide range of backgrounds and ages, and add an interesting dimension to the internship. "Earthwatch people worked alongside the interns. [The staff archaeologist] went out of his way to make sure that the two groups blended together. I found the Earthwatch people friendly and fun to be with. There was definitely a team spirit going on." This sense of community extends into the dining room as well. When Earthwatch is in session everyone gathers for dinner at one of the two crew houses. Earthwatch hires its own cooking director, making meals "elaborate and satisfying." Said one intern: "Meals are a terrific dividend of having the Earthwatch people around. In their absence, we had to go to the grocery store and make our own meals."

There's plenty to do when Hermitage life becomes stale. Memphis and Knoxville are popular weekend destinations. Downtown Nashville is just a 15-minute drive away. No stay in Tennessee is complete without checking out Nashville's Country Music Row, a collection of museums chronicling the lives of country music's biggest stars. "I liked the Elvis and Randy Travis museums the best," said one intern. If live music is desired, Nashville's Summer Lights Festival offers a mélange of country and rock bands.

SELECTION

The Hermitage accepts college juniors and seniors, recent graduates, and "early phase" graduate students. Although most have had at least one field course in archaeology, the staff archaeologist is willing to consider applicants who lack field experience but have academic backgrounds applicable to historical archaeology. In recent years, for example, the program has taken on students majoring in history and architecture. The Hermitage attracts applicants from all over the country; a student who completed two Hermitage internships says his peers hailed from Maine, California, New York, Ohio, Texas, Georgia, and Canada. According to interns, applicants should "be able to adapt easily to strangers," "enjoy working in close contact with people," and "be able to endure sweltering weather." International applicants are eligible.

APPLICATION PROCEDURE

The deadline is April 10. Submit a letter summarizing education and field experience, and a statement explaining interest in the program. Specify a session preference. Applicants must also have two professors or previous employers send letters of recommendation directly to the Hermitage. No interviews are conducted and therefore the recommendation is particularly critical. "It's important that the reference indicates whether an applicant works well with people," the staff archaeologist said.

OVERVIEW

The Hermitage offers one of the best archaeological internships available. Compensation is unusually generous for an archaeology program; interns receive free room and board, *and* an ample stipend. Supervision is unusually educational. The staff archaeologist goes out of his way to help interns perfect their excavation skills and also advises them on graduate schools and career choices in archaeology. And excavation at the Hermitage is unusually important. By digging up artifacts and other pieces of evidence, interns help archaeologists discover aspects of the workings of the original estate that would otherwise remain unknown. Excavations yield a clearer picture of the lifestyle of the Hermitage's inhabitants and the locations of its buildings. In this way, Hermitage interns help add missing pieces to a historical jigsaw puzzle.

FOR MORE INFORMATION . . .

■ The Hermitage
Internship Program
4580 Rachel's Lane
Hermitage, TN 37076-1331
(615) 889-2941

**HEWLETT®
PACKARD**

SELECTIVITY	🔍 🔍 🔍
Approximate applicant pool: 5,000 Interns accepted: 600–900	

COMPENSATION	$ $ $ $ $
$450–$700/week for undergrads; $1,000–$1,300/week for grad students; round-trip travel; relocation allowance	

QUALITY OF LIFE	🌴 🌴 🌴 🌴 🌴
"Management by Objectives"; beer busts free HP calculator; social activities	

LOCATION(S)

California, Colorado, Delaware, Georgia, Idaho, Massachusetts, New Hampshire, New Jersey, Oregon, Washington

FIELD

Computers and electronics

DURATION

10–14 weeks
Summer

PRE-REQS

College sophomores, juniors, and seniors; grad students

DEADLINE(S)

April 30

A small makeshift garage stands at 367 Addison Avenue, Palo Alto, CA.

That's where two Stanford University engineering graduates named Bill Hewlett and David Packard set up shop in 1939. Offering for sale an audio oscillator that Hewlett had invented under the tutelage of Stanford Dean of Engineering Fred Terman, the pair set out "to make a run for it." After selling eight oscillators to The Walt Disney Studios, Hewlett-Packard—the company name they came up with after tossing a coin—was well on its way.

For over a half-century, Hewlett-Packard has manufactured a diverse line of products that includes everything from high-speed frequency counters and fetal-heart monitors to the world's first scientific handheld calculator (the HP-35) and the world's first desktop laser printer (the LaserJet). With more than 98,000 employees and nearly $25 billion in annual revenues, HP now offers 23,000 electronic products and dominates its industry in several areas. It's number one worldwide in laser printers, test-and-measurement devices, patient-monitoring systems, gas chromatographs, and high-speed couplers. No wonder the garage where it all began is now California historical landmark No. 976 and recognized as the birthplace of Silicon Valley.

DESCRIPTION

Hewlett-Packard's Student Employment and Educational Development (SEED) program was formed in the early 1970s to replace a high school summer internship program called the Engineering Pool that had been in place since 1955. Today, SEED fosters "practical work experience[s] in a sophisticated technical environment." Interns may be offered positions in a wide variety of areas, including Research & Development, Manufacturing, Marketing, Field Sales, Quality, Materials, Facilities, Information Technology, Finance, and Personnel. Marketing and Finance positions are primarily open to MBA students, who make up approximately 30 percent of the intern class; the remaining 70 percent, mostly undergraduates studying technical fields, work in the other areas. Only five interns work in Sales and Personnel while over 100 interns are placed in R&D and Manufacturing. Though interns are concen-

BUSYWORK
MEDIUM
LOW HIGH
OLDMAN &
HAMADEH
METER

trated in the San Francisco Bay Area, there are positions available in Colorado, Delaware, Georgia, Idaho, Massachusetts, New Hampshire, New Jersey, Oregon, and Washington. The company runs a similar program called WEEP (Work Experience and Education Program), offering summer employment, part-time employment, and scholarship programs to high school students 16 years of age and older. For further information about this program, high school students should consult a guidance counselor or the nearest division's staffing manager.

At the Disk Mechanisms Division in Boise, Idaho, an R&D intern helped to decrease a disk-drive assembly line's "cycle time," the time it takes to go through the assembly line once. Designated head of a group of five engineers, he interviewed the line's workers and figured out the cause of bottlenecks—disk-drive tests for cleanliness. "[The tests] were taking too long," he said. "We'd connect the disk drive to a power supply so that [the drive] would spin. Then we'd put a nozzle through the slot and pump in compressed air to stir up the dust particles. Finally, we'd insert an instrument called a particle analyzer to measure the amount of dust . . . . [And] whether or not a disk drive passed inspection, employees would type the drive's ID number and the results of the test into a computer, sometimes making mistakes." It quickly became apparent to him that he had to shorten the test times and reduce the number of employee data entry errors. "I connected the compressed-air nozzle and particle analyzer to one another so that they could do their respective tasks at once. And I set up a new system, using bar codes and a scanner, to more accurately input each disk drive's ID number and status."

An intern at Sunnyvale's Personal Computer Software Division worked on developing a new release of a PC graphics product called Graphics Gallery. "It was part drawing program, part chart, so that the user could type in or import data and then graph it. I spent the first month or

> HP's "Management-by-Objective" policy means that interns may approach projects with a lot of freedom.

so learning the program by talking to its designers and going over the code. After that, I worked on fixing bugs that HP testers had discovered." Eventually, his managers became so confident in him that they asked him to implement a "device control interface," a series of screens used to configure printers, plotters, and cameras. "All the engineers hated the previous version of the interface because its code was long and complicated. So I simplified it, rewriting sections and adding features that would support new printer configurations. At the end of the summer I pulled together the work of the fifteen engineers who were developing the new version, helped administer a few tests, and then created the final disk that went to manufacturing."

At the Medical Products Group in Andover, MA, the company manufactures "transducers," devices that send out the oscillating signals in ultrasound machines. One summer intern was asked to improve the system of testing the transducers. "A transducer up for testing would be attached to a 'network analyzer,' a machine that measures the frequencies of transducer vibrations. The analyzer required calibration before each and every test, about six or seven in all." But the people on the line weren't technically skilled and had to call an engineer over to do the calibrations, a process that was delaying the testing. So, the intern wrote a program in BASIC for each of the calibrations on HP's 95L calculator. "The programs allowed the line workers to do the calibrations at the push of a button, eliminating the need to bring over the engineers."

HP believes that "each individual at each level in the organization should make his or her own plans to achieve company objectives and goals." This "Management by Objectives" policy, as HP refers to it, means that interns may approach projects with a lot of freedom. While in most cases it affords interns a great deal of responsibility, it also opens up the possibility that a few projects every summer will not be clearly defined or will be supervised inadequately. Said one intern: "Students need to ask plenty of questions of their supervisors and stay on top of things; otherwise, they'll accomplish nothing significant." Each intern also has the freedom to take HP-offered classes. "I took a two-day, in-house C-programming course and a class on presentation skills," said one intern. "Whatever your reason, HP will let you take any of its classes, just like that."

HP's Palo Alto headquarters consists of a few buildings spread out over nearly 12 acres. There's a jogging track that goes around the central building, whose four stories jut out in a staggered fashion to form what "looks like a staircase." Each floor has an open-sky atrium, used for meetings or one-on-one talks with supervisors. To the delight of health-conscious interns, headquarters (and many other HP sites) also has a fitness center.

HP is described by one intern as "family-oriented." Employees interact with one another on an informal basis. There is a "low-key, casual, no-suit-and-tie" attire that reaches even the corporate level, and there's friendly, upbeat chatter in the offices and the cafeterias. An open-door policy encourages employees and interns alike to raise any concerns they have with management or personnel. When new products are released, divisions often throw afternoon "beer busts," employee and intern get-togethers offering beer, soft drinks, music, cheese, crackers, and fruit. It's all part of "The HP Way," which Bill Hewlett once described as "the policies and actions that flow from the belief that men and women want to do a good job, a creative job, and that if they are provided the proper environment they will do so."

This so-called proper environment includes great employee benefits, to which interns are made privy. Treated like regular employees, interns receive holiday pay and medical insurance coverage. A relocation program chaired by two administrators (one for east of the Mississippi River, the other for west) provides detailed packets of housing information to simplify interns' apartment hunts.

Each site offers a one-day orientation at the beginning of the summer. In Boise, interns view a video on HP, receive badges, and learn administrative procedures. At the Bay Area orientation, they are treated to a continental breakfast and buffet lunch in between speeches given by executives, including CEO Lewis Platt. "[Platt] gave a

45-minute talk on the importance of having youthful energy at the company," said an intern. He also stressed HP's commitment to hiring summer students as permanent employees."

All summer long, HP organizes social activities for interns. Boise interns go horseback riding, camping, and white-water rafting down the Snake River ("one of the wildest rides in the country") as well as attend minor league baseball games and participate in intern volleyball leagues. Bay Area interns attend the company's annual summer picnic: "My year HP rented out Great America amusement park for an entire day; we played volleyball, ate barbecue, and rode the roller coasters."

HP's intern pay is some of the highest in the industry. Undergraduates pursuing technical degrees make from $2,000 to $2,500 per month while graduate students working in technical areas receive from $3,550 to $5,000 per month.

SELECTION

 Applicants must have completed their freshman year and must be pursuing BS, MS, MBA, or PhD degrees in one of the following fields: accounting, engineering (electrical, computer, mechanical, or industrial), computer science, information technology, operations research, finance, or business administration. "Ability to work in a team and problem-solving skills" are essential, according to the coordinator. While the program is open to everyone, it seeks to hire forty percent women and one-third minorities. International applicants are eligible.

APPLICATION PROCEDURE

 The deadline is April 30, but students may begin submitting materials as early as January 1. Required materials include a resume and a cover letter. Most students either send in materials to headquarters or meet HP recruiters at one of the sixty-five campuses the company visits nationwide. In addition to applying to headquarters, students may write directly to a specific division, each of which concentrates on a different area of the company's expertise—from desk jet components in Vancouver, WA to laser jets in Boise, ID, to workstations in the San Francisco area. Students are advised to call for the company's "Where You Can Work in HP" brochure, which describes all facility locations and functions, and/or call headquarters in March, when coordinators know which divisions need interns. To research background information on Hewlett-Packard before you apply, check out the company's web site at www.hp.com.

OVERVIEW

 These days, Hewlett-Packard is riding high. HP is the sixth largest manufacturer of personal computers. It is second only to Sun Microsystems in the production of computer workstations. Profits are up and orders are growing. As part of HP's SEED internship, students can get in on the action. Armed with a free HP calculator and empowered with the same resources as the rest of the HP workforce, interns are asked to manage projects involving products from disk drives and computers to calculators and laser printers. For their efforts, interns can look forward to one of the highest rehire rates of any internship—nearly 70 percent of eligible interns receive offers of permanent employment.

FOR MORE INFORMATION . . .

■ SEED Program
Hewlett-Packard
3000 Hanover Street
Mail Stop 20-AC
Palo Alto, CA 94304-1181
(415) 857–2092

HILL AND KNOWLTON

SELECTIVITY	🔍 🔍 🔍 🔍 🔍
Approximate applicant pool: 500 Interns accepted: 10–15	

COMPENSATION	$ $
$280/week	

QUALITY OF LIFE	🌴 🌴 🌴
Seminars and field trips; company outing; casual Fridays	

LOCATION(S)	
New York, NY	

FIELD	
Public relations	

DURATION	
10 weeks full-time (Summer) As needed (Fall and Spring)	

PRE-REQS	
College juniors and seniors; grad students	

DEADLINE(S)	
Summer .... February 28 Fall .... July 30 Winter .... October 15	

Which public relations firm represents six out of the top ten Fortune 500 companies and 35 percent of the entire Fortune 500 list? Hill and Knowlton does. Founded in 1927, Hill and Knowlton has been an agency of firsts. In the fifties, H&K became the first American public relations firm to have offices in Europe. In 1985, it was the first to expand its network to the People's Republic of China, and six years later it was the first to establish a presence in Hungary. Today, in addition to its New York headquarters, H&K has forty-eight offices and fifty-one associate firms across the country and all over the world, with offices on every continent except Africa and Antarctica. H&K's client list reads like Gordon Gekko's ideal stock portfolio, with such heavy-hitters as Kelloggs, Puerto Rico Tourism Board, GAP, and Pricewaterhouse Coopers.

DESCRIPTION

According to the internship bulletin, Hill & Knowlton's Summer Internship Program is "designed to introduce students to the day-to-day business of a public relations agency and help them develop the essential written and oral communication skills required to conduct public relations activities." Interns are assigned to work with one or two supervisors. Depending on their interest and agency need, interns are matched with particular accounts like Hiram Walker and Procter & Gamble, or are placed in specific account areas like Travel and Leisure Communications.

No matter what account they work on, virtually all interns perform a standard set of public-relations tasks. The closest they come to busywork is writing media lists, which requires one to "research the names, addresses, and phone numbers of news orga-

nizations who may be interested in your client's activities." More substantive intern work is press release writing, a one- or two-page account of a client's activities. "After researching the client in detail, I'd write up a draft of the press release which my supervisor would then edit. It took considerable effort. I would submit the press release for editing again and again until it read well." When they're not writing press releases, interns spend a lot of time composing

BUSYWORK METER
LOW MEDIUM HIGH
OLDMAN & HAMADEH

pitch letters. Designed to convince journalists to cover a client's activities, pitch letters require more creativity than press releases, according to interns. "You need to think of fresh ways to get journalists interested in a client. Your writing has to grab the reader," said one intern.

In addition to their daily tasks, interns have a variety of other responsibilities. An intern assigned to the account for Philips' Digital Compact Cassette (DCC) participated in client meetings and attended equipment demonstrations held for the press. "I went to a bunch of demonstrations for the DCC. One was at Masterdisk recording studio, where [sound expert] Bob Ludwig assessed the DCC's sound quality." An intern for Travel and Leisure Communications was sent to help out at tourism conventions in the New York area. Another intern helped organize special media events, such as a press reception in the penthouse of the Parker Meridian Hotel.

> Said an intern who attended a brainstorming session where shots of tequila were available: "You've got to know a product before you sell it."

One of the best parts of daily life at H&K are the "brainstorming sessions," where ten or so staff members get together to dream up proposals for soliciting new business. Interns are welcome at these meetings: "[Senior staff] made me feel really comfortable. There's no such thing as a bad idea. Everyone is encouraged to throw ideas on the table." For some interns, it takes time to muster enough confidence to participate: "In the beginning, I did a lot of observing. But I learned what types of issues the [senior staff] wanted to hear, and I began adding my two cents pretty regularly." To give participants a better idea of the product being discussed, samples are often passed around the conference table and (if edible) they are consumed. Sessions involve tastings of everything from spaghetti sauce to milk. Said one intern who attended a session where shots of tequila were available: "You've got to know a product before you sell it."

The highlight of a summer at H&K is the Intern New-Business Competition. Divided into teams of three or four, interns have four days to create a new-business proposal based on a hypothetical scenario involving a fictional client. One scenario, for example, required intern teams to write a media strategy for Blockbuster Video. During the competition, teams meet regularly for intense training in presentation skills. By the end of the week, the teams are ready to present their proposals to the "client," represented by a group of agency executives that may include the general manager of the office. "It's really hard-core," said an intern. "Each team has 15 minutes to describe its proposal to an audience of senior managers. We pulled out all the stops—using visuals, overheads, and video clips." After all of the presentations are given, the executives critique each performance and choose a winning team. "The winners my year proposed running a promotion where 'golden tickets' were inserted into Blockbuster boxes—similar to the golden tickets in *Willy Wonka and the Chocolate Factory*."

Beside giving interns "invaluable practical experience in creating new-business proposals," the competition serves to bond interns together. "You don't get to choose who's on your team, so you have to learn how to get along and function effectively as a team…. The people in my group ended up becoming not just colleagues, but buddies." But one intern complained that this bonding experience comes too late in the internship: "During the weeks preceding the group project, it felt like [the interns] were not relating to each other as well as we could…. It would have helped to have more social activities earlier in the summer."

In H&K's defense, there are other extracurricular events where interns can meet each other. One-hour weekly seminars are held with different senior executives to expose interns to a variety of practice specialties within the public relations profession, including financial relations, media relations, marketing, communications, and crisis communications. Field trips to the offices of publishing, advertising, radio, and/or television companies are also organized, as is a trip to a Yankees game. Once or twice a summer, interns are treated to a party in their honor, such as a catered picnic in Central Park where they watch an outdoor concert. The office has also established a sports committee which welcomes intern participation.

Formerly situated in a building interns described as "sterile as a hospital," Hill and Knowlton is now located in an office space in the Park Avenue Atrium buildings downstairs from sister ad agency J. Walter Thompson. This more intimate space has heightened professional interaction: for example, whereas brainstormings used to take place behind the closed doors of a conference room, they are now just as likely to take place in the hallways and common areas. The building itself is centrally located in midtown Manhattan, near Grand Central Terminal.

SELECTION

 The program is open to college juniors and seniors as well as graduate students. While there are no set academic criteria for selection, candidates—in the words of the internship bulletin—"must demonstrate good oral and written communication skills, a genuine interest in the field of public relations, [and] the ability to assume responsibility, prioritize and organize their work, and to think creatively." Previous extracurricular and/or work experience related to the field of public relations is also helpful. International applicants are eligible.

APPLICATION PROCEDURE

 Applications for the summer program are due February 28. Required materials include a cover letter, resume, and writing sample ("any paper demonstrating one's proficiency in writing" says the brochure). The coordinator conducts interviews with selected applicants over the phone.

OVERVIEW

 If there was ever a textbook example of an excellent internship in public relations, Hill and Knowlton's program would come pretty close. It has everything; prestige, real-world assignments, seminars and trips, and a well-organized group project.

FOR MORE INFORMATION . . .

■ Internship Coordinator
466 Lexington Avenue
New York, NY 10017
(212) 885-0410
Fax: (212) 885-0570
rmoatz@hillknowlton.com

HILL|HOLLIDAY

You won't find a copy of *Internal Affairs* at any library. But for a recent group of interns at Hill, Holliday, Connors, Cosmopulos Advertising, Inc. (known as Hill, Holliday), this 12-page newsletter was the highlight of their eight weeks at the Boston ad agency. As part of a group project, interns created a slick newsletter, complete with snazzy graphics, feature stories like "Green Marketing, the Ad Industry, and the Green Consumer" and tongue-in-cheek articles like "You Know You're Having a Bad Day When..." Few advertising agencies have the time and inclination to encourage their interns to embark on such a venture. Yet, Hill, Holliday believes its interns are capable of doing more than babysitting photocopy machines.

Founded in 1968, Hill, Holliday is one of the country's leading midsize advertising agencies. Not only does it service well-known local clients like John Hancock and Fleet, but it also handles the advertising for such national companies as Dunkin Donuts, Marshalls, Fidelity, and anyday.com. The agency has picked up its fair share of honors.

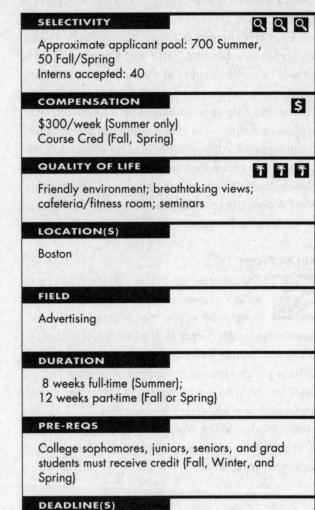

SELECTIVITY

Approximate applicant pool: 700 Summer, 50 Fall/Spring
Interns accepted: 40

COMPENSATION

$300/week (Summer only)
Course Cred (Fall, Spring)

QUALITY OF LIFE

Friendly environment; breathtaking views; cafeteria/fitness room; seminars

LOCATION(S)

Boston

FIELD

Advertising

DURATION

8 weeks full-time (Summer);
12 weeks part-time (Fall or Spring)

PRE-REQS

College sophomores, juniors, seniors, and grad students must receive credit (Fall, Winter, and Spring)

DEADLINE(S)

Summer .... March 1   Fall .... July 1
Spring .... November 1

DESCRIPTION

Unlike many advertising agencies, Hill, Holliday (HHCC) hires interns for virtually every one of its departments. Said one intern: "This policy allows students to get in-depth exposure to a particular stage of the advertising process, whether it's pitching new accounts or putting the finishing touches on an ad." Interns are placed in one of the following departments: Accounting, Account Service, Broadcast Production, Community Relations, Creative, Design, Direct Marketing, Human Resources, Market Research, Media, New Business, Traffic, and Exhibition Services.

Wherever they are assigned, interns serve as all-around assistants, helping a department with clerical work and a variety of short- and medium-term projects. In Account Service, interns support the team through daily client service. An intern in Traffic, the department that "mediates between the creative and business people," helped the Traffic manager prepare print ads to be sent to publications around the country.

One intern liked working in New Business because it's the "very first step of the advertising process—and you get to see what's involved in pitching and hopefully winning an ad account." Part of her job involved tracking down ads produced by competitor agencies. "I pulled competitors' ads from dozens of magazines and newspapers so that when HHCC made its pitch to a potential client, it could say, 'Everyone else is advertising this way . . . but this is what we can do for your business.'" She also helped type, edit, and copy the so-called leave-behinds, informational booklets that HHCC gives to potential clients after account executives make a live pitch. "For a pitch the agency was making to Weight Watchers in New York, I stayed up the entire night helping to get the information together for a leave-behind. Easy it wasn't, but when it was over I had a better perspective of how [ad] agencies pitch an account."

For some, the Broadcast department is the most exciting place to be. Interns there do "anything needed to get the production of television commercials off the ground." While there's plenty of classic busywork tasks like faxing, distributing schedules, and sitting at the phones, there are also substantive editing projects. "One of my jobs was to create video mock-ups that account executives would use to show a client what a commercial will look like when it is filmed. We called these 'steal-o-matics,' because they are pieced together from bits of TV shows, movies, and other random footage." To his delight, a piece of one of his steal-o-matics, was actually used in the finished commercial: "Footage I found of Lee Trevino was incorporated into the final version of a Spalding golf ball commercial. I liked knowing that I made a difference."

To ensure that everyone gets a sense of what's involved in all stages of an advertising campaign, the agency divides interns into groups for a special project to be completed during the course of the internship. In the past, groups were often asked to create an in-house newsletter, as described previously. These days, however, intern groups take on a real client from the agency's Community Relations department. These clients are local nonprofit organizations in need of marketing and advertising assis-

> **One had better like heights—Hill, Holliday is located 40 stories above Boston in the John Hancock Building, the city's tallest skyscraper.**

tance. Under the watchful eye of agency mentors, interns meet with their client and get briefed on a particular marketing issue. They then undertake a series of strategic planning exercises and eventually make a formal multimedia presentation of their communications recommendations to the client and agency mentors. Recent intern groups have helped launch a new corporate identity for Family Service of Greater Boston and generated a marketing platform and fundraising program ideas for The Kids Fund of Boston Medical Center. For some, the moments before the final presentation are anxiety ridden, but they soon find the audience is very receptive and unintimidating. The nonprofit clients have been impressed with the solid thinking and great ideas provided by Hill, Holliday interns, and the interns leave knowing they made a difference for a nonprofit organization.

In addition to their daily work and group project, interns have a few excellent extracurricular opportunities. Interns are welcome to accompany staff to the studio to watch a television or radio commercial being made. Said one: "I attended a recording session for a *Boston Globe* radio spot. It was fun to observe the talent and the producer run through the commercial over and over." There's also a seminar series that introduces the interns to a department head every week. "The executives gave some terrific presentations. A creative director, for example, showed us a reel of his best work and described what people in his department do to avoid creative blocks—such as throwing a tennis ball against the wall or playing pool in the Creative department."

One had better like heights because HHCC is located 40 stories above Boston in the John Hancock Building, the city's tallest skyscraper. Employees have a "breathtaking" view of the Massachusetts State House and Copley Place. The agency is spread out over five floors and has an "open-door" design whereby offices are predominantly glass and doorless to promote a community spirit. The agency has also expanded and opened an annex one block away where the Finance and Exhibition Services groups are now housed. The creative areas of the agency tend to have their share of wacky decorations, such as toy figures, sporting equipment, and a "sculpture of spaghetti with fork." Observed one intern: "I don't think you'd see this type of decor in any other industry."

Interns' nutritional and fitness needs are well taken care of at Hill, Holliday. There's a cafeteria available to all employees of the building, and word has it that the chow is cheap ("you can fuel up for under $5") and satisfying ("100 times better than my school's cafeteria"). As far as fitness goes, there's a room on one of HHCC's floors with a few exercise bikes and showers and another room with a selection of dumbbells—a far cry from Gold's Gym, but the fact that an ad agency takes exercise into account at all is praiseworthy.

SELECTION

The program seeks college juniors and seniors, but sometimes accepts outstanding sophomores and graduate students. Candidates of any academic background are welcome. International applicants are eligible.

APPLICATION PROCEDURE

The application deadlines are as follows: fall internship, July 1; spring, November 1; and summer, March 1. The summer internship runs from mid-June through mid-August, the fall internship runs from mid-September through early December, and the spring internship runs from early February through early May. Applicants should submit a resume and a cover letter (with a list of department preferences). After screening the initial applicant pool, the coordinator conducts interviews with a group of finalists.

OVERVIEW

Hill, Holliday offers interns the best of both worlds. It has the feel and energy of a small agency; people are, in the words of interns, "warm," "friendly," and "spunky." At the same time, it has the financial strength and talented people that are hallmarks of a large agency. In this rich environment, interns work alongside professionals and become familiar with a particular area of the advertising process. Assigned a group project, they also gain a sense of what it takes to see a marketing project from its inception to fruition.

FOR MORE INFORMATION . . .

■ Hill, Holliday, Connors, Cosmopulos, Inc.
Internship Coordinator
200 Clarendon Street
Boston, MA 02116
(617) 585–3715
Fax: (617) 859-4279

INROADS.

SELECTIVITY	🔍 🔍 🔍
Approximate applicant pool: 5,500 Interns accepted: 1,000–1,200	

COMPENSATION	💲 💲 💲
$240–$750/week	

QUALITY OF LIFE	🌴 🌴 🌴
Business workshops; Public service projects; Mentors; Academic counseling	

LOCATION(S)

Nationwide—see Description

FIELD

Business-career development

DURATION

8–14 weeks
At least 2 Summers

PRE-REQS

Minority high school and college students
Minimum 3.0 GPA

DEADLINE(S)

January 31

On a sweltering afternoon in August 1963, a Princeton University graduate named Frank Carr stood among more than 300,000 people at the Washington Mall. Having traveled from New York to Washington, D.C., during the wee hours of the morning, he braved the heat to listen to a man dream of the day when oppressed peoples would be "free at last."

"I have a dream that one day this nation will rise up and live out the true meaning of its creed . . . " declared the impassioned Martin Luther King, Jr.

But as a white man of privilege, Carr wasn't expected to understand King's dream. He had grown up in a family famous for its work in publishing, with the founder of Pocket Books for an uncle and a cousin named Doubleday. As a boy he had attended Andover and played varsity high-school soccer with George Bush. Yet the deeply religious Carr understood that things weren't right. "I couldn't imagine, if we were all God's children, how this inequality could exist. It must be man-made, I thought, not God-made," remembers Carr, who is now a Catholic priest.

So after a few years of these troubling thoughts, he quit his job to right what he saw as a pervasive wrong. "I didn't want special treatment for minorities," he says, "only a level playing field." Carr set out to arm young minority men and women with the skills necessary to make it in corporate America. Soon he had created an organization called Inroads.

Training minorities for management positions, Inroads provides students with internships in business, engineering, and science. Founded in 1970, the organization has grown from one office, 25 students, and 17 sponsoring companies to 48 affiliates, more than 7,000 students, and a roster of sponsors that includes most of the Fortune 1000 companies.

BUSYWORK METER

LOW MEDIUM HIGH

N/A

OLDMAN & HAMADEH

???

DESCRIPTION

Students may join Inroads as early as their junior year in high school or as late as their sophomore year in college. The Pre-College Component is offered at 13 locations (marked with an asterisk in the list that follows). Internships with sponsoring companies are offered nationwide, usually near Inroads' offices, which are located in Birmingham, AL; Phoenix, AZ; Los Angeles, San Diego, San Francisco, and Sunnyvale, CA; Colorado Springs and Denver, CO; Hartford and

Stamford, CT; Jacksonville, Miami, Orlando, and Tampa Bay, FL; Atlanta, GA; Chicago, IL; Gary and Indianapolis, IN; New Orleans, LA; Boston, MA; Baltimore, MD; Detroit, MI; St. Paul, MN; Kansas City and St. Louis, MO; Jackson, MS; Omaha, NE; Charlotte and Raleigh, NC; North Brunswick and Newark, NJ; Buffalo, New York City, Rochester, and Syracuse, NY; Cincinnati, Cleveland, Columbus, and Toledo, OH; Philadelphia and Pittsburgh, PA; Memphis and Nashville, TN; Austin, Dallas, and Houston, TX; Richmond, VA; Seattle, WA; Charleston, WV; Beloit and Milwaukee, WI; and Washington, DC.

Inroads' application process is rigorous in its requirements. Besides submitting a form that reminded one Inroader of "a college application—only a little shorter," almost all Inroads applicants have to go through Inroads's Talent Pool, 20 hours of preparation during January and February. To prepare applicants for their interviews with sponsoring companies, the workshops teach students how to interview, how to dress for success, how to write a resume, and how to research a company. "Each of my on-site visits was about four hours long, consisting of interviews with several managers," said one intern. "The Talent Pool really helped to make [the interviews] seem so familiar."

Once accepted by one of the sponsoring companies, an applicant officially becomes an Inroads intern and is offered a summer job with that company until graduation (barring release from Inroads, as described below). Although companies in certain popular fields (e.g., medicine, law, and teaching) aren't represented, Inroads has internships in nearly every industry, from advertising to utilities. Organizations such as AT&T, American Express, Shell Oil, Johnson & Johnson, Anheuser-Busch, Enterprise Rent-a-Car, Federal Express, and the Federal Reserve Banks are all part of the Inroads team. Like other sponsoring companies, they provide interns with summer salaries, two formal evaluations, and mentors. Despite corporate downsizing, which has forced some companies

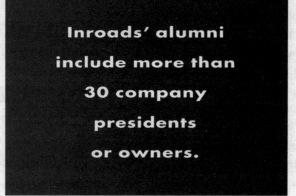

Inroads' alumni include more than 30 company presidents or owners.

to withdraw their sponsorship and reduce the number of upper-level managers who would act as interns' mentors, Inroads continues to be singularly successful. "Even though companies are downsizing, they still need talent," says Inroads President Charles Story. "And because we cover such a wide spectrum of occupations, companies can rely on us to take care of that need."

For many interns, the first summer with Inroads follows their senior year in high school. Because high school grads often aren't sufficiently skilled to tackle entry-level projects, their assignments tend to emphasize busywork. "My company didn't have much work for me to do my first two summers," said an intern who spent a virtually unheard-of six summers at Clorox. "I worked on the production line the first summer and did manual labor in the shipping department the next." But such lackluster experiences, common among freshman and sophomore Inroaders, have their purpose. They prepare interns to handle more responsibility later on. "I realized that the work I did my first two years allowed me to learn the company's culture and understand the company's mission," explained the Clorox intern. "It's important to know those things... [that understanding] allowed me to approach tougher problems [in later summers] from a seasoned employee's point of view." As a process operator during his third summer, for example, he managed the production line that churns out Clorox products like Tilex, 409, and Liquid-Plumr. "I was the sole person in charge of opening the valves and putting the correct raw materials through the mixers. It was a significant undertaking—each day, we produced a few thousand cases [of products]." During his fourth summer spent at the Clorox Technical Center (the last for the vast majority of Inroads interns), he was asked to find the optimal dimensions and cap tightness for different Clorox bottles. "It was pretty difficult. I had to ask some of the original bottle designers for assistance, but by the end I had gained a good sense of what R&D is all about."

Students who begin Inroads in their freshman or sophomore years are still afforded the same kinds of experiences as interns who commit to Inroads before college. A student who joined Inroads in his sophomore year, for example, worked his first summer on an airflow analysis at an aluminum can manufacturing plant. Spending a total of three summers with Ball Corporation, he next helped design a heating-and-air-conditioning system for which he wrote an 80-page report complete with diagrams and charts: "I did all the steps that any company engineer would have." During his final summer, he helped overhaul Ball's system for processing scrap aluminum. "It was amazing how much responsibility I had," he said in retrospect. "I realized that [my sponsor] had grown confident in me, and that was a great feeling."

Inroads helps its students to become successful managers by offering them a substantial degree of career training. Every Saturday during the summer, interns gather for a full day of workshops in topics such as time management, assertiveness, negotiation, presentation skills, and group interaction. As an exercise in decision making, for example, interns pretend to be lost in the woods and work together to figure out what to do. "You typically don't get this type of training until you've been with a company for a few years," stressed one alumna. Because the meetings are held on a Saturday, however, many Inroaders complain that their summer vacation is infringed upon. Others say that's the price one must pay for success.

In between summer jobs, Inroads provides personal coaching and academic guidance. Counselors from the various affiliate offices visit nearby campuses and schedule appointments with their Inroads students every month during the school year. Meeting one on one, the coach and student discuss how things are going. If the student is not doing particularly well in a course, they decide together whether the Inroader should hire a tutor, the costs of which are covered by Inroads.

Inroads places a great emphasis upon community leadership. Two Saturdays every summer, interns are required to participate in Inroads-sponsored projects—a charity volleyball tournament or a landscaping project at a homeless shelter, for example. "You can't forget your community," admonishes a Chicago Inroads board mem-ber. Indeed, the idea of "giving back" is an important facet in the Inroads philosophy and interns are encouraged to participate in such volunteer work as caring for the elderly, helping the Salvation Army, tutoring illiterate individuals, and coaching Little League baseball.

After completing two to four or more years of summer jobs and training, Inroaders cap off their experience with an Inroads Senior Conference. Usually held regionally, the conferences assemble college seniors for three days of social and educational activities. On one hand, they enjoy a banquet followed by dancing, and basketball, volleyball, and softball tournaments pitting Inroaders against one another. On the other hand, workshops in such topics as team dynamics and college-to-career transitions reinforce the lessons interns have learned over the past few years. "It was a lot of fun . . . a terrific way to finish Inroads," said one intern, who was honored as Inroads' Senior of the Year. "I made a lot of contacts with people from my region."

Starting in 1996, Inroads will hold a national Seniors Leadership Institute for the top third of the graduating class, with selection based on academics, work performance, and leadership achievements. (Criteria are still being worked out.) The Leadership Institute will be at the Arthur Andersen/Andersen Consulting Center for Professional Education in St. Charles, IL, and the curricula will include the kind of advanced managerial development courses the firm provides its own and client employees.

Inroads is not for the uncommitted—in fact, interns who are unable to perform to expectation are released from the program. The requirements are so tough that at the end of four years, approximately 20 percent of an Inroads class will have dropped out. The reasons are varied: unsatisfactory grades (below 3.0), poor work performance, and lack of participation in workshops, for example. However, many interns leave the program because they have changed to a major not related to business or engineering or because they have received lucrative scholarships with conflicting requirements.

But students who stick it out through the recommended four years of the program find many doors open. "You've built confidence and learned skills that will help you succeed," explained one alumna, who after completing Inroads in 1979, interviewed for full-time positions with 12 companies and received 11 job offers, including one from her sponsoring company, to which she returned. Another former Inroader, who graduated from college in 1977, is still working for his Inroads sponsor—a department store chain in St. Louis. During more than two decades of employment there, he has risen from intern to vice president. "Inroads prepared me for what to expect," he said. Anywhere from 70 to 90 percent of Inroads interns receive job offers from their sponsors, and over half accept. "I liken it to a courtship or marriage," says Inroads' president. "The more time you've spent with a company, the better your chances of success." More recently, a multilingual 1990 graduate rose to vice president in five years at an international bank, his sponsor. He's now in São Paulo, Brazil, advising corporate clients on financing.

SELECTION

 For its Pre-College Component, Inroads seeks high school sophomores and juniors. For the internship program (called College Component by Inroads), only high school seniors and college freshmen and sophomores are eligible, as Inroads requires a two-year minimum commitment. Inroads seeks African-American, Native American, and Hispanic-American students who meet one of the following criteria: 3.0 GPA or better, ACT composite score of 20 or better, SAT combined score of 800 or better, or top 10 percent of high school class. Some Inroads' affiliates have higher selection standards. Students must be interested in pursuing business or technical college degrees.

APPLICATION PROCEDURE

 The deadline to apply is December 31. Students should apply to the Inroads affiliate nearest to them. After applications are processed and applicants are interviewed by Inroads staff, approximately 50 percent of applicants are chosen to participate in Inroads' Talent Pool. Students' performance in the Talent Pool dictates whether they receive interviews with sponsoring companies.

OVERVIEW

 Minority students wishing to develop careers in the areas of business, engineering, and science would do well to turn to a career development organization appropriately called Inroads. Provided with up to four summers of top internships, year-round personal counseling, and leadership training, students leave Inroads ready to embark upon management and technology positions with Fortune 1000 companies. In the quarter century since its founding, Inroads has made a monumental impact, infusing corporate America with talented African Americans, Hispanics, Native Americans, and other minorities. Alumni include hundreds of middle managers, nearly 20 CFOs, approximately 20 corporate vice presidents, and more than 20 company presidents or owners.

FOR MORE INFORMATION . . .

■ Inroads, Inc.
 10 South Broadway
 Suite 700
 St. Louis, MO 63102
 (314) 241-7330
 Fax: (314) 241-9325
 www.inroadsinc.org

In 1971, a fledgling company called Intel dazzled Silicon Valley by unleashing the world's first "microprocessor," a silicon chip used to process computer data. Eight years later, the company convinced IBM to use the Intel 8088 microprocessor to power the IBM PC, and the precursor to today's personal computer was born.

Since its founding in 1968 by Robert Noyce, Andrew Grove, and Gordon Moore, Intel Corporation has grown increasingly more influential. In 1987, the company ranked tenth in chip production. Five years later, it had surpassed industry giants NEC, Toshiba, and Motorola to become the world's largest manufacturer of semiconductors. Intel's computer chips are currently inside 80 to 90 percent of all personal computers worldwide. Intel produces other kinds of chips as well—more than 10,000 of them. In fact, Intel technology powers everything from traffic lights, cash registers, and taxi meters to laptops, laser printers, and supercomputers.

DESCRIPTION

Every year, over 1,200 students work at Intel. Nearly half of them are summer interns; the other half work school year co-op's, interning from January to August or June to December. Positions include: Design Engineer, Product Engineer, Process Engineer, Software/Hardware Engineer, Test Engineer, Quality/Reliability Engineer, Technical Sales Engineer, Applications Engineer, Equipment Engineer, Systems Engineer, as well as Financial Analysts, Purchasing and Human Resources staff. Eight main sites offer internships: Phoenix, AZ; Sacramento and Santa Clara, CA; Hudson, MA; Albuquerque, NM; Portland, OR; Austin, TX; Seattle, WA; and a number of smaller sites.

Intel has built its success in recent years around the Pentium, Pentium II and Pentium III microprocessor families. As a leader in the global computer industry, Intel offers students a chance to gain quality career experience as an intern. You will become a full-fledged member of the Intel team, with opportunities to apply your ideas to challenging hands-on projects. In recent years Intel has grown to include thousands of diverse people at sites around the world, with a unique culture—a highly motivating, "can do" atmosphere prevails at every site. Intel's emphasis on open communication, commitment to developing a diverse workforce, and philosophy of shared rewards has made Intel an appealing place to work. Right away you'll see it's a little different than most major corporations. Everyone's idea is important and the team helps everyone succeed.

For one intern, only three months into his eight-month cooperative education experience with Intel in Santa Clara, California, the ECE/computer science major was already in the headlines. His team in the microprocessor research lab used special cooling techniques to break the 1 GHz speed barrier for a general purpose microprocessor. This was the first time the gigahertz (one billion cycles per second) frequency had been achieved in public on a standard microprocessor. The clock speed was demonstrated using a 0.25 micron Pentium III processor, before an audience of 1,500 software and hardware developers and more than 100 reporters attending the Intel Developer Forum. The demonstration consisted of a system running a CPU speed meter which registered greater than 1 GHz clock speed, while running a Microsoft PowerPoint application. "This was definitely a prototype machine," the intern said. "The night before we were still enhancing it. Our goal was to push the limits of the technology and show where the future of microprocessors is headed. It was a very challenging and rewarding experience."

A second intern was assigned to Arizona's Packaging Division. "At first I thought they were talking about cardboard and bubble wrap," said the Material Science student. She soon learned, however, that the "package" actually refers to the plastic that covers a chip and protects it from humidity and dust. That plastic is formed by a process known as "transfer molding," whereby powdered plastic is heated to create a liquid that fills the mold surrounding the chip. The liquid is then "cured" (heated, then cooled) to create the solid plastic. "I was asked to test how curing parameters such as time and temperature affect package performance," she said. After creating packages from different curing conditions, various sets of times and temperatures, she subjected them to nearly 100 percent humidity for one week and finally tested them on a circuit board. "It was exhilarating to finally determine an optimal temperature and time for the curing process."

Intel's culture is described by interns as both "intense" and "kinetic." Employees are constantly pushing to create the next line of faster, more reliable products—as if competitors were right at Intel's heels. In fact, whereas Intel used to release a new microprocessor every four years, it now plans on introducing new chip families every two years, a pace that few rivals can match. Intel continues to invest in state-of-the-art manufacturing facilities and programs that make such innovaions possible, spending $4 billion for capital additions and $2.7 billion for R&D in 1998, the highest spending of its kind among semiconductor and computer companies worldwide. Such drive forces employees to work a lot of overtime. But it also encourages them to be creative. "Intel employees are risk takers," observed an intern. "Even if their ideas are shot down by upper management, they keep trying."

As hard as people work, however, the atmosphere remains casual and friendly. There's essentially no dress code, so jeans, shorts, sneakers, and sandals keep people comfortable. In addition, employees are exceedingly willing to help interns—a tendency manifested in an open-door policy that calls for no room, except conference rooms, ever to be closed. "If you have a valid reason, you can always go talk to managers or VPs," said an intern. "Some upper managers even took the time to discuss what I should do with my career plans."

Each of Intel's sites includes a technical library, free recreation centers with courts and weights, and cafeterias

> Interns working in Intel's clean rooms must first remove all traces of perfume, hair spray, and makeup before donning a bunny suit.

with cuisine comparable to that of a good delicatessen. Each site oversees different Intel products or functions. Albuquerque, Phoenix, and Portland, for example, contain the bulk of Intel's fabrication facilities, where thin slices of silicon, called wafers, are made in "clean rooms." One thousand times cleaner than hospital operating rooms, clean rooms ensure that not a single speck of dust (disastrous to semiconductors) creeps inside the chips. To keep the environment pristine, interns working in Intel's clean rooms must first remove all traces of perfume, hair spray, and makeup before donning the typical clean-room uniform, or "bunny suit." Equipped with a helmet and a filter pack, the bunny suit filters the wearer's exhalations before releasing them into the purified space.

Like all Intel employees, interns are offered developmental courses in management, quality, and corporate values through Intel University. Senior managers, including CEO Craig Barrett, teach the college's classes. "He talked about the company's founding and how Intel tries to maintain a small-company attitude," one intern recalled. "It was exciting to hear him, because he's a high-level person." Other classes teach resume writing, interviewing skills networking, and technical topics such as hazardous chemical training, circuit analysis, and VLSI design.

The company also organizes developmental and social activities for interns. Weekly brown-bag lunches feature VPs and senior managers sharing information about the business. "It's a way of finding out what's going on in the company," said one intern. Interns are also provided with relocation options. A free relocation assistance program is available to interns that provides local housing, transportation information, a roomate service, and other area information.

Pay is commensurate with education, area of study, and experience. A freshman interning in a nontechnical area can earn approximately $2,200 per month, while a freshman in a technical area receives $2,800. Experienced seniors studying technical fields earn approximately $3,500 per month. But PhD, MS, and MBA candidates with several years of experience take the cake. They can earn up to a whopping $5,800 per month.

SELECTION

Intel seeks students of all ages, from college freshmen to PhD candidates. A minimum 3.0 GPA is required. The company targets the following majors: electrical engineering (40 percent of Intel's interns), computer science (35 percent), computer engineering (10 percent), other technical degrees such as materials science, mathematics, chemical engineering, or industrial engineering (10 percent), and business, finance, accounting, education, and human resources (5 percent). International applicants are eligible. To research background information on Intel before you apply, check out the company's web site at www.intel.com.

APPLICATION PROCEDURE

The deadline is rolling, but the majority of positions are filled by March 15. For co-ops, applications are due approximately two to three months before the start of the internship. While the company recruits at approximately 50 schools for most of its interns, students from other colleges are welcome to apply. Applicants should send /e-mail a resume and cover letter which Intel scans into its database for managers to review.

OVERVIEW

If the Intel internship were a computer chip, the chip's many transistors would symbolize the program's perks. They include interaction with management and organized social activities to some of the highest intern pay in the country, complete with bonuses and vacation time. Working intimately with the components that make nearly every electronic device tick, interns gain a firm foundation in microprocessor and semiconductor engineering. Intel strives to convert at least 70 percent of their interns into full-timers upon graduation. Considering that Intel plans on hiring at least 1,500 new college graduates annually for the next several years, landing an internship at Intel all but ensures you a future job with the king of computer chip makers.

FOR MORE INFORMATION . . .

■ Intel Corporation
   Staffing Department
   705-2 East Bidwell Street
   Suite #246
   Folsom, CA 95630
   (800) 238-0486
   collegejobs@intel.com

JPMorgan

SELECTIVITY	🔍 🔍 🔍
Approximate applicant pool: 1,300 Interns accepted: 245	

COMPENSATION	$ $ $ $ $
Approximately $865/week	

QUALITY OF LIFE	⬆ ⬆ ⬆ ⬆
Weekly training; interaction with business leaders; professional atmosphere	

LOCATION(S)

New York, NY; Newark, DE

FIELD

Investment banking

DURATION

10 weeks
Summer

PRE-REQS

College seniors; Junior Internship Program—college sophmores and juniors

DEADLINE(S)

February 1

Since the dawn of the industrial era, J.P. Morgan has served as advisor, underwriter, and lender to an impressive roster of institutions, corporations, and individuals. Morgan has survived through the major financial shifts of the past two centuries by adapting to the changing needs of its clients and the shifts in global and local economies. In 1989 Morgan became the first U.S. bank to be granted the power to underwrite securities, 10 years ahead of the Financial Services Modernization Act of 1999. The firm has recently formed partnerships with governments that are working to develop free market economies. America's fifth-largest bank, J.P. Morgan's current list of clients include, new technology companies such as Genentech, Network Solutions, and MediaOne, and such established giants as GM, BP Amoco, and Johnson & Johnson.

Morgan has continued to adapt and thrive in the current dot-com economy. Recent developments include a daily casual dress code, an aggressive corporate diversity program, expansive benefits packages (including same-sex partner benefits), and the launching of a new e-finance unit, LabMorgan. LabMorgan is Morgan's answer to technology start-ups, a work environment where new ideas are incubated, cutting-edge innovation is paramount, and colleagues can brainstorm around an indoor putting green. LabMorgan will work with Morgan's other business groups to accelerate e-finance ideas both inside and outside the firm.

DESCRIPTION

 Morgan's internship program reflects a company philosophy that values teamwork and long-term thinking. Consistently rated among the top internship programs in the country, it is a high-energy program that challenges interns with responsibility as team members and mirrors real work experience in the firm. In addition to the work, the program offers opportunities to have fun: Cultural events, presentations, receptions, and dinners throughout the summer give interns a chance to network with peers and managers and form personal and professional relationships. In addition, interns are assigned a mentor who advises them in their work and can answer questions about the

BUSYWORK METER
LOW MEDIUM HIGH
OLDMAN & HAMADEH

finance industry or about working at Morgan. Since the main objective of Morgan's internship program is to convert qualified interns to full-time hires (more than half of their interns get hired full-time), the program is designed to give both the interns and the firm information to make informed decisions about future employment.

"I was amazed at the energy level, motivation, and intelligence of the people that I met," said one former intern. "I was also impressed with the level of responsibility that young people received. It is a great atmosphere in which to work." Another intern said "The firm is disposed to stretch people in both their capabilities and their project roles." "A person is constantly coaxed out of the 'box' to not only do one's job but also learn about other areas, products, and functions."

The Morgan summer internship program looks for candidates with strong quantitative, analytic, and decision-making skills who have the ability to work as part of a team, handle a high degree of responsibility, meet deadlines, and manage and complete multiple projects simultaneously without continual supervision. Internships begin in June and usually last about 10 weeks. Nearly 250 college students entering their senior year are hired for positions in the company's New York (Wall Street or midtown) offices, with some positions available in the Newark, Delaware office, as well. Interns are assigned to one of four business groups—Investment Banking, Markets, Asset Management Services (AMS), or Internal Consulting Services (ICS)—which offer the following assignments:

Investment Banking provides a broad range of capabilities to multinational corporations, privately held companies, and governments. Internships may be in Corporate Finance/Mergers and Acquisitions Sectors such as healthcare, real estate, and natural resources and power, or in product groups such as Equity Capital Markets. Summer interns participate in a two-day training program that covers topics such as corporate finance,

> The old expression— "there's no such thing as a free lunch"—doesn't apply at JP Morgan.

risk management, and software skills. Possible intern responsibilities include assisting in developing financing alternatives for clients, or performing a financial analysis to help value a company being sold.

Markets is a collection of product and business groups that engage in sales, trading, and research activities in the world's financial markets. The Markets Summer Analyst position has assignments in areas such as derivatives marketing, syndicate, credit research, structured finance, and credit portfolio. Examples of an intern's responsibilities include helping to determine how derivatives can be used to minimize borrowing costs or helping to assess and manage credit risk across product areas. Interns gain hands-on experience in the financial markets through assignments on the trading floor, at various trading desks such as fixed income, emerging markets, foreign exchange, precious metals, equity derivatives, and proprietary positioning. The position requires appreciation of the risk/reward trade-off, an interest in current events, and an understanding of how international and local issues shape market activity.

Asset Management Services (AMS) offers financial strategies to a large client base that includes individual and institutional investors. Summer internships in AMS are divided into Private Banking and Investment Management.

Private Banking provides investment services to high-net-worth individuals by devising financial strategies, such as portfolio management, securities brokerage, fiduciary services, and liquidity management that are tailored to each client's particular needs and long-term goals. Interns work on projects that include researching and executing financial and investment analysis, or assisting with business development and maintenance for product and sales support. Candidates must show sound judgment and the discretion needed to work with highly confidential information

Investment Management manages institutional portfolios such as employee benefit plans, endowment funds, governments, and insurance companies. Interns work in portfolio management, quantitative research, or client marketing assignments such as: analyzing portfolio performance and assisting with the execution of trade orders; modeling of risk, return, and liquidity characteristics of financial instruments; and gathering competitive information and producing marketing materials for clients.

Internal Consulting Services (ICS) provides advice and services in several areas of expertise to support Morgan's business lines. ICS Generalist interns work on projects in various infrastructure groups to assess risks, analyze profitability and procedures, and improve business processes. ICS Application Delivery Specialists serve on business-aligned technology teams to design and develop software applications and enhance ongoing systems. ICS offers internship opportunities in New York and Delaware.

Junior Internships - In addition to the internships offered above, Morgan also offers 10-week junior internships to college students entering their sophomore and junior years. The aim of this New York-based program is to attract students of color, female students, and students with disabilities to Morgan, and prepare them for transition into Morgan's senior intern program and future employment with the firm. Junior interns attend a series of training sessions designed to help them acquire a broad range of business and professional skills, knowledge of Morgan's businesses, an understanding of the financial services industry, and information about senior internships and full-time opportunities at Morgan. Training includes formal computer instruction classes and access to self-instructional training materials on a wide range of topics through the firm's Learning Resource Center.

The location of J.P. Morgan's Wall Street offices means that interns spend their days in the heart of New York's historic financial district, on the southeast part of the island of Manhattan. The neighborhood is host to spectacular architecture in styles that range from neo-gothic to neo-classical, all within one city block. The New York Stock Exchange and Trinity Church lie to the west, the South Street Seaport boardwalk to the east, and the World Financial Center is just a few blocks northwest. Morgan's 47-floor tower at 60 Wall Street has an excellent cafeteria, a formal dining facility where interns and managers share meals and stories several times each summer, and offers panoramic views of the city. And just in case one has to work late, the sunsets from the upper floors are worth it.

SELECTION

 Applicants must be college students entering their senior year. If applying for the junior internship program, applicants must be college students entering their sophomore or junior years. No specific major is required for most programs, but all candidates should have strong analytical, quantitative and communications skills, and those candidates applying for technical positions should also have strong technical skills.

APPLICATION PROCEDURE

 Morgan has no formal application deadline, but applicants should try to apply by February 1. Applicants should submit a cover letter, resume, and transcript for all programs in which they are interested. (Students can interview for more than one summer intern position, but will be selected for only one.) The initial round of interviews is conducted by phone, on-campus at colleges where Morgan has a formal recruiting relationship, or at the Morgan offices at the student's own expense. If a second interview is necessary, Morgan will pay for any associated expenses. Students are encouraged to apply online at www.jpmorgan.com/careers. Morgan gives careful consideration to each candidate who applies. Offers for summer intern positions are usually extended by the middle of March.

OVERVIEW

 Students interested in both commercial and investment banking have a friend in J.P. Morgan—it's one of the only Wall Street investment firms to offer a structured internship program for undergraduates in a variety of business areas. With its assortment of receptions, lectures on banking, and projects involving finance, the internship program at J. P. Morgan exposes students to all that is quintessentially Wall Street.

FOR MORE INFORMATION . . .

■ J.P. Morgan & Co. Incorporated
60 Wall Street
New York, NY 10260
(212) 648-3900
www.jpmorgan.com/careers

WILEY

SELECTIVITY	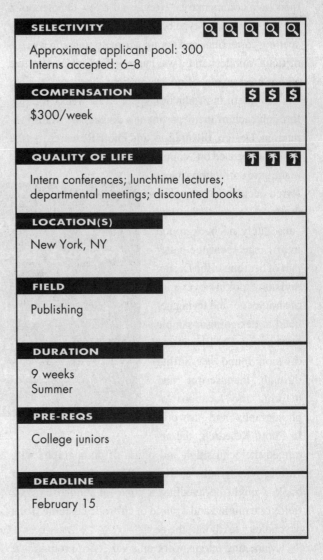
Approximate applicant pool: 300 Interns accepted: 6–8	
COMPENSATION	$ $ $
$300/week	
QUALITY OF LIFE	⚘ ⚘ ⚘
Intern conferences; lunchtime lectures; departmental meetings; discounted books	
LOCATION(S)	
New York, NY	
FIELD	
Publishing	
DURATION	
9 weeks Summer	
PRE-REQS	
College juniors	
DEADLINE	
February 15	

It's three A.M. and you're cramming for your calculus midterm. The clock is ticking, your stomach is kicking, and none of your lessons are sticking. Nothing left to do but bite your lip and curse the makers of your calculus textbook.

Chances are your cursing is directed at John Wiley & Sons, the oldest and largest independent publishing company in North America. Founded in 1807, Wiley has spent the past two centuries establishing itself as a leading publisher of college textbooks. Wiley textbooks are found in lecture halls, seminar rooms, and backpacks across the world. Specializing in mathematics, engineering, and the sciences, Wiley churns out such classroom classics as Halliday and Resnick's *Fundamentals of Physics*, Anton's *Calculus*, Weygandt's *Accounting Principles*, and Solomon's *Organic Chemistry*. Wiley's recent professional, reference, and trade bestsellers include *The Ernst & Young Tax Guide*, *The Warren Buffet Way*, and *Hard Drive: Bill Gates and the Making of the Microsoft Empire*.

DESCRIPTION

The Wiley Internship assigns interns to its Editorial, Sales, Corporate Communications, Information Technology, Marketing, Finance, or Production departments. Every department requires some busywork, but the amount depends on the requirements of an intern's supervisor. "The editor I worked with wanted five copies of everything I did—it was a real drag," said one intern. "But other supervisors were far less demanding about making copies." In any case, some interns should expect to "become a pro at the Minolta copier" by the end of their stay.

Interns assigned to the Editorial department assist a particular editor in a range of tasks. Phonework is prevalent, as interns are asked to check up on authors and remind them of deadlines. Interns also spend time on the phone finding professors willing to critique chapters of a book being written: "It really helps to a have a professor read over a manuscript and give suggestions. For a book on, say, the geography of China, I'd call geography departments at different colleges in hopes of locating a professor to read the initial chapters. If all goes well, we keep the professor on board as a consultant for the whole project." Every so often, interns also add their own commentary: "I reviewed a few chapters of a 'physics-for-poets'-type book. I'd go through it, making spelling corrections and noting where a paragraph was too difficult to understand. I was happy to find out later that the author used several of my suggestions."

An intern in Production spent a few weeks rotating through each of the department's divisions—Main Production, Design, Illustration, and Photo Research. In the first, she focused on "comparing drafts of manuscripts to make sure corrections transferred accurately to revised drafts." Because she had "absolutely no background in art," she spent the better part of her time in the Design division "looking over a lot of shoulders" and trying her hand at designing a sample book cover. The Illustration division found her sifting through manuscripts and marking the locations of photographs and artwork. In Photo Research, she arranged the acquisition and return of photographs with various photography agencies. "Depending on the textbook, I might be handling a photo of Indonesian rice fields one minute and a photo of an erotic costume [for a psychology textbook] the next."

Marketing interns work on a variety of promotional and advertising projects. One intern designed a series of flyers for display at a convention of the American Statistical Association. "I was in charge of creating flyers that would generate interest in a line of statistics books." In order to write the text for the flyers, she had to first figure out what the books were about: "These books were pretty advanced—deciphering them was no small feat. A few times I called the authors to double-check that what I had written was accurate." But the best part of the project was the chance to be creative in designing the layout: "I had to figure out ways to make the flyers eye-catching. I played around with a variety of typefaces, colors, and illustrations until I came up with something that would stand out."

> "Just in case you have to work late, the sunsets from the 47-storey building in downtown Manhattan are worth it."

Interns are welcome to attend various departmental meetings. A Marketing intern sat in on a conference where new books were introduced to representatives of Wiley's sales force. "The meeting gave me an overview of the different factors that make a given book sell well—[such as] price, audience, and packaging." Alternatively, an Editorial intern was a regular attendee at his department's biweekly progress meetings. "Everyone involved in the production process was there—marketing, design, and product managers as well as the editor. They'd discuss how a book's production was going and what changes in schedule needed to be made." These meetings are a good place to learn various bits of production lingo. By the end of the internship, I had picked up all sorts of words of the trade—[such as] *signature*, *page openers*, and *subchapter headings*."

Depending on how one looks at it, the fact that Wiley specializes in publishing textbooks can be a blessing or a bane. Said one intern: "If you're interested solely in fiction publishing, then working at Wiley will seem like a dead end." But another says: "I wasn't particularly passionate about textbook publishing before [working at Wiley], but it grew on me as my internship wore on." Some enjoy working with textbooks for sheer intellectual stimulation: "Believe it or not, it was fun to read the biology textbooks around the office—especially because I knew I didn't have to be tested on what I read." Others see their job as a rare opportunity to learn what goes into publishing a textbook: "Working here really pertains to my life. Several of [Wiley's] books—*Abnormal Psychology*, for example—I used in school. It's fascinating to see how a book you've spent a semester with is actually put together."

Unlike most internships in publishing, Wiley's program is structured to include a selection of extracurriculars. Every other Friday the Human Resources department brings interns together to discuss how their work is going. Said one intern: "Since everyone is working in different departments, the intern meetings are a good time to find out what goes on in departments other than your own." The intern coordinator also organizes a few lunchtime lectures with various department heads. "A lecture given by the head of Marketing was great. He spoke about a variety of promotional gimmicks to get professors interested in using a particular textbook. For a textbook on stress, for example, he showed us an electronic ball that screamed when you pressed it."

A smattering of fringe benefits awaits the Wiley intern. As would be expected of a publishing house, interns may purchase any Wiley book at a significant discount. Although most Wiley textbooks are a far cry from pleasure reading, they're good to have if only to "remind you of the internship" or to "pass on to younger siblings who can use the books for their classes." Wiley paraphernalia also finds its way into interns' hands, including such items as water bottles, mugs, tote bags, and "really cool T-shirts picturing a surfer and the words—A GROOVY HAPPENING KIND OF PLACE." Moreover, the company holds a picnic every summer that interns may attend. Said one intern: "The picnic is for everyone in the New York and New Jersey offices. It's held in a park in New Jersey, and a good time is had by all—there's barbecuing, softball games, and bumper boats." Interns can also take advantage of free admission to museums and discounts to Broadway shows through Wiley's Culture Card program.

Occupying seven floors of a midtown skyscraper, Wiley is located in a "bustling business-oriented neighborhood close to Grand Central Station." The office is decorated with framed covers of Wiley books and "a sea of blue carpet." Interns typically work at cubicles, but in rare cases they may have their own offices. There's a small cafeteria on the seventh floor that's open to the public but has a "special Wiley employees section." The cafeteria gets mixed reviews—one intern says it's "only good for rainy days"; another reports it's worth a visit if only for "terrific cookies and Columbo yogurt."

SELECTION

 Officially, the program is open only to college juniors, but sophomores and seniors are considered in exceptional cases. While the majority of applicants are English majors, Wiley welcomes applicants from all academic disciplines. The intern coordinator looks for applicants who "demonstrate a real interest in publishing" and "have basic computer skills." International applicants are eligible.

APPLICATION PROCEDURE

 The application deadline is February 15. Applicants need only submit a cover letter and resume. After the coordinators screen the initial applicant pool, personal interviews are conducted with finalists. In rare cases, a telephone interview may be substituted for a live appearance.

OVERVIEW

 Although structured internships in publishing are about as scarce as water fountains in the Sahara, John Wiley & Sons sees the value in introducing interns to nonfiction publishing through an organized program of projects, discussion meetings, and luncheon seminars. For students interested in a publishing house whose primary focus is textbooks and nonfiction tradebooks, Wiley is a valuable nine-week introduction to the art of the printed page.

FOR MORE INFORMATION . . .

■ John Wiley & Sons, Inc.
Internship Program
605 Third Avenue
New York, NY 10158
(212) 850-6238

JOHNS HOPKINS
U N I V E R S I T Y

Center for Talented Youth

SELECTIVITY

Approximate applicant pool: 2,000
Interns accepted: 1,000

COMPENSATION $ $ $

RA, RPA: $1,000/session
TA: $900/session; all positions—room and board

QUALITY OF LIFE

Summer-camp atmosphere;
College facilities; Field trips

LOCATION(S)

Los Angeles, CA; Palo Alto, CA; Santa Cruz, CA;
Baltimore, MD; Chesterton, MD; Frederick, MD;
South Hadley, MA; Clinton, NY; Saratoga Springs,
NY; Bethlehem, PA; Carlisle, PA; Lancaster, PA;

FIELD

Education

DURATION

One or two 3-week sessions
Summer

PRE-REQS

Undergrad and grad students
Overall GPA: 3.2 or higher

DEADLINE(S)

January 31

"**S**omebody for God's sake challenge me!"

Such are the tortured words of Daman "Math-magician" Wells, the pubescently obnoxious teenage prodigy who befriends seven-year-old Fred Tate in the movie *Little Man Tate*.

But they could be the words of any bright student who has felt limited by a fruitless educational system. Since 1980, the Center for Talented Youth (CTY) of the Johns Hopkins University has tried to fill that educational void. Committed to nurturing academic talent, CTY runs a summer school at six college campuses around the country. Preteens and adolescents who meet CTY's stringent academic standards are afforded the opportunity to study a discipline at a more advanced level than commonly available. A researcher from the Carnegie Foundation for the Advancement of Teaching called CTY "the premier program and national model for those [organizations that offer] . . . college-level courses for talented precollege age youth."

DESCRIPTION

Two kinds of CTY summer programs exist: one teaching students in grades 7 and up and the other teaching students in grades 2 to 6. The former hires five times as many staff as the latter, and as college students generally find supervising older children more challenging, the programs for older students will be discussed here. Applicants interested in working at CTY are free to apply to all programs but must indicate in the application which program they prefer. They must also specify the sites at which they are most interested in working—Johns Hopkins University (Baltimore, MD), Hamilton College (Clinton, NY), Dickinson College (Carlisle, PA), Skidmore College (Saratoga Springs, NY), Franklin and Marshall College (Lancaster, PA), and Loyola Marymount University (Los Angeles, CA). Every site runs two consecutive three-week sessions, and candidates may apply to work at one or both of them.

CTY hires resident assistants (RAs), teaching assistants (TAs), laboratory assistants (LAs), resident program assistants (RPSs), and health assistants (HAs). RAs live in a CTY dormitory and supervise the dozen or so students on their hall.

Charged with guarding students' safety and planning their recreational activities, RAs do everything one would expect of live-in chaperons: They lay down the rules and maintain order, supervise evening study halls, visit their students' classes, and generally help them adjust to residential life. In short, RAs are responsible for their students' well-being whenever the students are not in class. As one RA concluded: "It's an intense experience. You're with your kids ten hours a day."

CTY students aren't your run-of-the-mill "kids." Most took the SAT in seventh grade and scored as well as or better than college-bound seniors. "Many are bright enough at 12 to gain admission to a top college," said an RA. But among adolescents, academic talent can be inversely proportional to social adaptability, and many CTY students come from schools where they are uncomfortable and dissatisfied. Explained an RA: "Although you see a wide range of personalities, from the extremely outgoing to the introverted, students tend to be a little awkward socially. . . . [A]s RAs, we try to create an environment where they are drawn out of their shells."

RAs must be able to assume a variety of personas. First of all, they must be social facilitators. During the first week of a session, RAs sit with their students at dinner until the children feel comfortable interacting with each other. But as one RA pointed out: "It doesn't take long before the ice is broken and the kids don't need the RA hanging around their dinner table."

Another RA responsibility is akin to that of Julie McCoy from *The Love Boat*: recreation director. RAs plan and supervise activities one would find at any summer camp, such as tennis, ultimate Frisbee, painting, improvisational drama, swimming, and so on. Watching these activities, many RAs are gratified by changes they see in

their students. Remarked one RA: "You see how these kids open up in just a few weeks. One girl on my hall went from hating sports to realizing 'Hey, I'm not so bad at kickball.'"

RAs try to strike a balance between maintaining authority and establishing friendships with their charges. "In one sense, you have to be a disciplinarian. The kids need to realize that you're in charge, that when you say, 'lights out at ten o'clock,' you mean it," explained an RA. "But you also want to gain your kids' trust. You want to be their pal and—when needed—their confidant." Achieving this equilibrium is not easy. The majority of RAs are able to exert control while remaining easygoing and affable. But a few are either "strict and humorless" or a little "too chummy." One reports that the secret to his success involved employing a few tricks, such as "putting the kids to bed early when they misbehave," "using anger sparingly, to show the students that there's a line they shouldn't cross," and "explaining calmly to students why their behavior is inappropriate, rather than punishing them without ample explanation."

Amidst the charged atmosphere generated by lively and rambunctious teenagers, RAs leave CTY with at least a few humorous memories. One RA, for example, was kidnapped by his students and carried around campus, as the group sang songs to the amusement of random passersby. Perhaps the most memorable incident involved a 12-year-old who wanted to see if he could make a telephone ring using a lamp's power cord. Cutting the cord of a plugged-in lamp, the student created a power surge that shut down the power in his section of the residence hall.

While RAs and their immediate supervisors, senior RAs, comprise the residential staff, TAs and LAs are known as the "instructional assistants." As the name suggests, instructional assistants help instructors carry out the work in the classroom. They perform clerical tasks (typing, photocopying, grading, etc.), tutor individual students, and

> [One] TA tutored a student who had published a chapbook on poetry at age 16.

run evening class sessions. LAs also clean up after afternoon lab sessions and help the instructor plan labwork. Unlike RAs, TAs and LAs have the weekends off.

Instructional assistants are in the best position to appreciate their students' intellectual prowess and passion because they interact with students in class. "The first fact you realize is that these kids are really sharp," said one TA. "Having previously been a TA at a prep school, I was accustomed to bright kids. But CTY students were extraordinary. Virtually all of them were passionate about learning." Said another: "Being a TA is ideal if you're into teaching and if your instructor gives you responsibility. You teach kids who have an incredible desire and capacity to learn. There's no variable you could change to make the teaching environment better." Each student enrolls in one course per session, choosing from among offerings in mathematics, science, humanities, and writing. TAs can't help but be impressed by the heavy workloads their students undertake. "The amount of work these teenagers do is stunning. Some classes have their students read 40 pages of a college textbook nightly," said one TA. And every so often, a TA encounters a potential genius: "I knew of a 14-year-old who mastered a pre-calculus book in 12 days." Another TA tutored a student who had published a chapbook of poetry at age 16.

CTY has recently added the positions of Resident Program Assistant (RPA) and Health Assistant (HA). Each RPA (there are usually two per site) helps to run the site's central office, drives students to and from airports and various appointments, and substitutes for ill RAs and TAs. HAs help coordinate health care on the site by making sure that students take their medications, scheduling appointments, and driving students to the doctor.

As CTY sites are located at college campuses around the country, staff enjoy the resources that accompany college life. A full range of college facilities at their disposal, they make use of libraries, gyms, tennis courts, and swimming pools. Cafeterias, on the whole, tend to be mediocre, but one RA praised the food at Dickinson College. Staff members live by themselves in double rooms, a few of which have private bathrooms.

Material perks are few. Every staff member receives an official CTY "Staff" shirt to be worn in front of parents on the opening and closing days of the program. Office supplies are plentiful and TAs and LAs receive free copies of the books used in their classes.

Staff members are usually so busy with their students that off-campus forays are a rarity. Even so, some TAs arrange field trips for their classes. One took his class to a local hospital; another visited an aquarium. RAs have been known to take their students to 4th of July fireworks displays and the beach, although keeping track of 15 high-spirited teenagers off campus can be a "logistical nightmare."

Any program as comprehensive as CTY's is bound to receive its share of criticism. Several interns were frustrated with what they deemed "inadequate lines of communication" between the residential and instructional staffs. Said one TA: "Residential and instructional life are dependent on each other…[For example], if an RA fails to enforce 'lights-out' at a decent hour, many of her students will perform below par in class the next day. The instructor and TAs will be understandably concerned. But it's difficult for them to get in touch with the RAs when each group works at a different time." Another TA warned that one's experience as a TA is shaped largely by the assigned instructor. "Although most TAs and LAs found their jobs rewarding, personality conflicts do occur. . . . A few of the instructors have chips on their shoulders and make life difficult for their teaching assistants."

SELECTION

The program is open to all undergraduate and graduate students. Although they must have a cumulative GPA of 3.2 or higher, applicants need not match the intellectual ability of CTY students. Indeed, one RA applied to CTY even though a few years back "he had not made the cut to become a student." Above all, the brochure states that candidates should be "mature, responsible, and energetic." Staff members report that the program attracts people who are "confident," "outgoing," and desirous of "intellectual stimulation." International applicants are eligible.

APPLICATION PROCEDURE

 The deadline for RA applications is January 31; for TA and LA positions, the deadline is January 31. In addition to a cover letter and transcripts (from all undergraduate and graduate work), applicants must arrange for three letters of recommendation to be sent directly to CTY. If an applicant has had experience directly related to CTY (i.e., as a teacher, lab assistant, resident adviser, camp counselor, or tutor), one recommendation must be from someone who supervised such work. Those who lack related experience must secure at least one recommendation from an employer. Applicants must also submit a CTY employment application. After the application deadlines have past, the CTY administration screens out the strongest candidates. Of this selected group, those with previous CTY experience are offered positions. New applicants are then interviewed by telephone, or in person if possible, to fill the remaining openings.

OVERVIEW

 College students and graduates of any academic major, here's your chance for a rewarding summer of fun with some extraordinary youngsters. Enjoy working with teenagers? Fascinated by the highly intelligent? Long for the camaraderie and warm cheer of summer camp? CTY merits consideration. The overwhelming majority of students who have worked for CTY are glad they did.

Staff members tend to forge close bonds with one another—so close, in fact, that one summer brought together three couples who eventually married. Staff become so attached to the program that several elect to be "repeat offenders"; more than a few have returned for five or more summers, serving as RAs, TAs, and eventually instructors. In sum, CTY combines the charms of summer camp with the stimulation of academic achievement. For college students interested in supervising, teaching, and learning from highly talented adolescents, it's a well-spent summer at "brain camp."

FOR MORE INFORMATION . . .

■ Center for Talented Youth
The Johns Hopkins University
3400 North Charles Street
Baltimore, MD 21218
(410) 516-0053
Fax: (410) 516-0093
academic@jhu.edu
www.jhu.edu/~gifted/acadprog/jobs.html

The Kennedy Center

SELECTIVITY	🔍🔍🔍🔍
Approximate applicant pool: 500 Interns accepted: 30 (every three to four months)	

COMPENSATION	$
$650/month	

QUALITY OF LIFE	🌴🌴🌴
Tickets to performances; weekly seminars; Spartan workspaces	

LOCATION(S)
Washington, D.C.

FIELD
Arts management and performance

DURATION
12–16 weeks Summer, Fall, Winter/Spring

PRE-REQS
Undergrads; recent grads; grad students

DEADLINE(S)
Summer .... March 1   Fall .... June 23 Winter/Spring .... November 1

Just what *is* the Kennedy Center?

An airport in New York? A stadium in Philadelphia? A school of government in Cambridge, MA? Hundreds of elementary schools across the country? If you think about it, our whole Camelot-loving country is a Kennedy Center!

Yet, officially speaking, the Kennedy Center is one of the country's foremost performing arts institutions. Founded in 1971 as a memorial to President John F. Kennedy, the Center not only was a sorely needed addition to Washington's cultural scene, but also quickly became an arts center of national and international importance. Indeed, today the center has the drawing power to attract the country's finest music, dance, and theater companies while also providing a home to the National Symphony Orchestra, the American Film Institute, and the Washington Opera. It also runs an admirable array of educational programs and competitions for students of all ages.

DESCRIPTION

If choice is the spice of life, then the Kennedy Center Internship Program offers an industrial-sized spice rack of opportunity. Positions are available in a whopping 20 departments: Advertising, Alliance for Arts Education, Kennedy Center American College Theater Festival, Community Partnerships, Development, Education, Events for Teachers, Marketing, National Symphony Orchestra, Performance Plus, Press Office, Programming, Special Events, Youth & Family Programming, Electronic Media, Production, Finance, Member Services, Volunteer Management, and Management Information Services.

BUSYWORK METER
LOW MEDIUM HIGH
OLDMAN & HAMADEH

The Press Office is a high-profile department that most interns find stimulating. In addition to performing some requisite clerical work, Press Office interns help publicize events by compiling media lists, calling television and radio contacts, and writing press releases. Best of all, they get to escort artists to interviews at news agencies around Washington. "I'd accompany an artist or director in one of the center's hired cars. Once we got to the news office, such as *The Washington Post* or a local radio station, I'd introduce the artist and make sure the interviewer had a press release." Interns have had the opportunity to escort all sorts of VIPs, from Matthew Broderick to the head of the Joffrey Ballet.

Most positions, however, are more behind the scenes. Interns in Member Services, for example, help the Center with its campaign to recruit and renew members. A lot of the work is monotonous: "I performed 'batch balances,' tracking the money generated from membership dues…. It was very tedious." But there are also interesting assignments: "I helped organize a direct mail campaign, editing—and improving— the letters we'd send out to solicit new members."

Programming is another department where interns see both the mundane and the substantive. On one hand, interns "act as a secretary for the office, photocopying producing contracts, and answering phones." At the same time, they are directly involved in arranging the visits of incoming artists, scheduling their housing and greeting them. They also put together the paperwork enabling foreign artists to enter the country. "I helped write petitions to the government requesting visas for foreign artists— such as the National Ballet of Spain. I'd find reviews and articles testifying to the group's artistic worth."

Some interns work for a specific program. The Kennedy Center American College Theater Festival (KCACTF) is a national competition, selecting a handful of college theater groups to perform at the Kennedy Center every April. The Irene Ryan Competition (part of KCACTF) showcases 16 finalists who vie for distinction as best actor. Interns for this program have their hands full making travel arrangements for the visiting groups, preparing for the arrival of festival judges, and working with the Press Office to promote the events. Said one intern: "Preparing for the festivals was a lot of work, but it was rewarding. I was in charge of distributing tickets to the events. I also met the visiting groups at the airport and escorted them—via Metro—back to the center." The

> **Interns have had the opportunity to escort all sorts of VIPs, from Matthew Broderick to the head of the Joffrey Ballet.**

position offers a unique opportunity to schmooze: "I networked with some big-name festival judges. [Among them were] the casting director from Paramount Studios and the head of daytime casting for ABC."

Because they are spread out over 20 departments, interns sometimes feel estranged from their peers. "The Kennedy Center is a big place. We were all in our separate worlds. There wasn't much chance for interns to meet each other." Responding to this criticism, the program tries to build cohesiveness by inviting interns to bi-monthly roundtable lunch discussions and the Weekly Executive Seminar Series. At the roundtable discussions, interns talk about current issues in the arts or arts education. Recent discussions have included federal funding for the arts, *Shear Madness* (a play that has been performed at the Kennedy Center for more than 11 years), and "why have an education department at a performing arts center." At the Weekly Executive Seminar Series, interns have the opportunity to meet with senior Kennedy Center authorities and experts from other arts institutions. The series has featured speakers such as the Kennedy Center's chairman, president, and director of marketing as well as the administrative director of the Washington Opera and representatives from the National Endowment for the Arts.

Despite its reputation as a highbrow arts institution, the Kennedy Center has an office atmosphere that is reportedly "down to earth" and "friendly." Explained one intern: "The people who work there are warm and outgoing. I noticed a down-home Midwestern ethic."

Paces away from the infamous Watergate complex, the Kennedy Center is an impressive sight, perched proudly on the edge of the Potomac River. The center's grand Italian marble exterior is matched by a foyer "so big that the Washington Monument could lie inside," regal red carpet, and an 18-foot-high bust of JFK. Interns have said that the physical plant is getting "a bit run-down," but the Center has spent $50 million on improving the site over the past five years. Offices tend to be on the spartan side—"windowless, sparsely decorated, and cramped." Interns sit at desks or cubicles, each outfitted with a phone and a computer.

Kennedy Center interns enjoy a veritable smorgasbord of entertainment. They have dibs on two tickets to any event, including previews and opening nights—"I went to as many shows as I could and returned to school an unabashed culture vulture." Interns are also welcome at special events like cast parties and the annual Open House, a free festival in the fall featuring performances by local artists. Star gazers will be amply satisfied. Interns observe and sometimes meet the celebrities visiting or performing at the center. One intern had "brushes with greatness" with Mikhail Baryshnikov and Kathy Bates.

SELECTION

While the majority of applicants will be college juniors and seniors, recent graduates and graduate students are also welcome to apply. If you haven't spent the past few years studying the arias of Puccini, don't fret, the program requires no formal background in the arts. In fact, the intern coordinator says that each session sees a few interns majoring in subjects like "biology, sociology, and physical education . . . so long as they have a genuine interest in the arts."

APPLICATION PROCEDURE

The application deadlines are as follows: summer internship, March 1; fall internship, June 23; and winter/spring internship, November 1. Submit a cover letter (stating your career goals, areas of interest, and computer experience), resume, two letters of recommendation, an academic transcript, and a brief writing sample. After applications are received, they are reviewed by a committee. The committee then sends them to the appropriate department heads, who each conduct phone interviews with a handful of finalists.

OVERVIEW

Internship seekers interested in performing arts opportunities in the Washington area often narrow their search to two choices: Wolf Trap and the Kennedy Center. Both are top-of-the-heap programs that expose interns to the ins and outs of arts management. But for candidates who crave a dose of glamour with their internship, the Kennedy Center is king. A cultural beacon in the nation's capital, the center exudes an aura of prestige and grandeur. A bit of this luster rubs off on interns' resumes, helping them land juicy jobs in the arts. Internship alumni include a talent coordinator for Disney World, the general manager of New York's Ice Theater, the operations manager of the Arlington Symphony, and a cultural affairs officer in San Juan, Puerto Rico.

FOR MORE INFORMATION . . .

■ The Kennedy Center
Ms. Amanda L. Perry
Internship Program Manager
Washington, DC 20566-0001
(202) 416-8821
Fax: (202) 416-8853
alperry@kennedy-center.org
www.kennedy-center.org/internships

We know what you're hungry for.

Kraft Cheez Whiz fights cancer?

Perhaps, if we are to believe Dr. Michael Pariza, microbiologist at the University of Wisconsin in Madison. According to Pariza, Cheez Whiz contains rich amounts of a polyunsaturated fat called CLA, which wards off several kinds of cancer in laboratory animals.

Regardless of whether or not Cheez Whiz has healthful effects, the story is an example of how the products of Kraft Foods, Inc. are in the public eye. It is no real surprise that they are, since Kraft Foods is North America's largest food company. Generating sales upwards of $17 billion annually, it churns out over 2,500 products, among them such household favorites as Oscar Mayer meats, Kool-Aid, Philadelphia Brand cream cheese, Post Grape-Nuts, Velveeta, and Jell-O. Of every dollar spent on food in the United States, 10 cents goes to one of Kraft's products.

DESCRIPTION

 Kraft Foods places 90 percent of its interns, half of whom are graduate students, in one of five locations: Glenview, Illinois; Northfield, Illinois; Madison, Wisconsin; Rye Brook, New York; and Tarrytown, New York. Business divisions located in Glenview, Illinois, are the Kraft Cheese Division, the New Meals division, and the Kraft Pizza Company. The Oscar Mayer Foods Division is located in Madison, Wisconsin. The business divisions of beverages, desserts, coffee, and cereal are located in the metropolitan New York area. At Kraft Foods Technical Center, interns may conduct research on any Kraft product. At Kraft Corporate, as well as at all of the other locations, interns work in Corporate Affairs, Sales, Finance, and Human Resources.

SELECTIVITY	
Approximate applicant pool: 3,000 Interns accepted: 50–100	🔍🔍🔍

COMPENSATION	
$400–$600/week for undergraduates $800–$900/week for graduate students	$ $ $ $ $

QUALITY OF LIFE	
Training; health clubs; good lunches; company stores	🌴🌴🌴

LOCATION(S)

Glenview, IL; Northfield, IL; White Plains, NY; Tarrytown, NY; Madison, WI

FIELD

Foods

DURATION

12 weeks
Summer

PRE-REQS

Undergrads and grad students

DEADLINE(S)

March 31

Employment at Kraft gives interns a chance to work with childhood treats such as Jell-O, Oscar Mayer hot dogs, Kraft Macaroni and Cheese, and Kool-Aid. In 1991, the Kraft Foods' Technical Center changed the formulation of Kool-Aid, and an intern in the Process Development group studied the new formula's viability. "We wanted to investigate what side effects the new ingredients would have on shelf life. I analyzed the data from several previous experiments and realized that we couldn't correlate shelf life to caking [the powder's forming into a hard mass] unless we considered some other variables. So I set up a new experiment—an accelerated pantry study—whereby Kool-Aid was subjected to six weeks of harsh conditions, equivalent to its sitting in a pantry for six months."

In the Beverage division, one intern tested the materials used in drink packaging. "Our shipping boxes are made out of corrugated cardboard. I'd compress them and also subject them to various temperatures to see how strong they are." After becoming proficient with materials, he was flown to Chino, CA, where he spent half the internship supporting a plant start-up. The plant was being "configured to bottle a ready-to-drink beverage. During line trials, we noticed that bottles would sometimes break at the conveyor system's transfer points. So I did some troubleshooting, testing the bottles, the shrink wrap used to package six-packs, and the shipping container. What I finally came up with to solve the problem is proprietary and no less of a contribution than the principal scientist's."

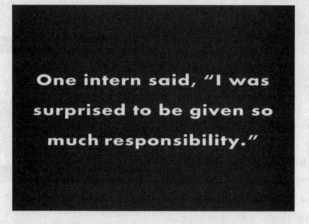

One intern said, "I was surprised to be given so much responsibility."

vised contractors to make sure that wiring designs were followed properly. "I was surprised to be given so much responsibility," he said. Nevertheless, he and a few other interns had the plant up and running by fall. "We worked 60 to 70 hours a week to get the project done, but at least the company flew me home to Chicago twice a month."

Kraft Foods is a large, decentralized company, so some interns get lost in the corporate shuffle. Said one employee: "Every year a few interns simply sit in front of the CAD machines all summer, transferring designers' hand sketches onto the computer." Yet the company is making a concerted effort these days to assign interns challenging projects. However, interns shouldn't expect a lot of guidance. Managers are often too busy with their own projects to do anything more than sign interns' paperwork and point them in the right direction. "They don't have time to hold our hands here. The burden is on us to create value; it's a lot of responsibility."

From a melting pot of academic backgrounds, interns take on a range of responsibilities at the company. One electrical engineering intern did a power survey of industrial distribution systems that deliver electricity to plant equipment. "You can't just plug in the machines and turn the switch," he said. "I had to draw electrical plans indicating the loads and where the electricity would come from." But first, he needed to observe plants in operation. "There are no plants in Glenview, so the company sent me to Texas and Wisconsin and put me up in hotels. I'd stay anywhere from a day to a week in order to learn the system. By the end of the summer, I was doing the same kind of work at the company's plant, consulting engineers."

So when he asked to return to Kraft a second summer, he was welcomed with open arms. "Though I was stationed in Glenview, I spent most of that summer in Tulare, CA, setting up process control equipment at a new $4 billion plant. I programmed the PLCs [programmable logic computers], which control the blenders, conveyor belts, etc. and monitor the operation. For example, if something gets too hot, a PLC activates a cooling mechanism." He also super-

You'll never want for social and developmental activities as a Kraft Foods intern. In the middle of the summer, some interns participate in Kraft's presentation-skills workshop. Students who participate pick up some new techniques and styles that prove very helpful for their end-of-summer presentations. Interns also undergo a full day of diversity training, a highly interactive awareness-building session. A current employee explained: "In today's corporate world, you will be facing a multitude of cultures, and you need to learn how to work with different people."

Interns also tour nearby plants, such as Kraft's largest cheese plant, in Champaign, IL. Barbecue sauce, pasta, and macaroni and cheese, in addition to Velveeta and Kraft Singles are all manufactured there. Upon entering the factory, interns are greeted by blenders, conveyer belts, and cookers all rattling and humming at once. "The conveyer belts deliver 3 by 3 by 3 [feet, that is] blocks of Velveeta to the processing area, where huge blenders mix 10,000 pounds [of the processed cheese] into a gooey mass. The blob then goes to giant-sized cookers, and a packaging machine spits out a continuous strand of soft Velveeta onto plastic wrapping every few seconds. Finally, slices are cut, organized into packages, and placed in boxes, ready for shipping."

Kraft Foods locations rate high in quality of life. Employees at the three headquarters locations enjoy subsidized cafeterias with "fantastic $3 lunches" and free health clubs, with treadmills, fitness counselors, aerobics rooms, and basketball and volleyball courts. Artwork commemorates Kraft Foods's rich history. Near the entrance to the Tarrytown Technical Center cafeteria, for example, there's a Hall of Fame wall, featuring decades of General Foods products. At the Kraft cafeteria, the company sometimes coordinates breakfast events, such as a speech by the company president and free Kraft brand food.

The company has high expectations of its interns. Midsummer, they go through a performance review. "A supervisor determines if you're reaching your goals and objectives," explained one intern, "and your rating affects whether you later receive an offer of permanent employment [30 percent return for full-time jobs]." And at the end of the summer, each intern is required to give a presentation to approximately five senior managers, including the department head.

SELECTION

 Sophomores, juniors, and seniors and graduate students are eligible to apply. Targeted majors include marketing, information systems, engineering (chemical, mechanical, industrial, electrical, etc.), accounting, finance, human resources, food science, chemistry, microbiology, biology, and biochemistry. Kraft Foods seeks leaders who have excelled in their coursework, participated in extracurricular activities, and have relevant work experience. "We expect good grades, taking into account the strength of the student's college and his or her level of participation in activities," said the staffing manager. "Of course, the more relevant experience one has, the better."

APPLICATION PROCEDURE

 (There is no set deadline, but be sure to send your resume early as most internship positions are filled by the beginning of March. Send in a resume and cover letter c/o Manager of University Relations to one of the company's addresses. "Show that you know our company and you've thought about what function you want to work in," says the staffing manager.

Kraft recruits at about 50 college campuses nationwide and advertises the location, time of presentations, and interviews well in advance. It also targets talented students at the national and local chapters of the National Society of Black Engineers, the National Society of Black MBAs, and the National Society of Hispanic MBAs. While most interns are selected through the campus recruiting process, unsolicited resumes are accepted. But the staffing manager warns: "You've got to make it stand out from the thousands that flood in."

OVERVIEW

 Kraft Macaroni and Cheese is eaten by 72 percent of U.S. college students. For some, this is reason enough to want to intern at Kraft Foods. But even if Kraft wasn't the king of mac and cheese, its internship program would still be a must-do. The Kraft Foods internship puts students in the center of the action, where they improve manufacturing processes, enhance food ingredients, implement computer systems, and assist in plant start-ups. Their reward is the realization, as one intern put it, of "a child's dream—to see and work with goodies we've eaten all our lives."

FOR MORE INFORMATION . . .

■ Kraft Foods, Inc.
University Relations
3 Lakes Drive
Northfield, IL 60093
(847) 646-2000

■ Oscar Mayer
University Relations
910 Mayer Avenue
Madison, WI 53704
(608) 241-3311

■ Kraft Foods
University Relations
800 Westchester Avenue
Rye Brook, NY 10673-1301
(914) 335-2500
www.kraftfoods.com

LATE SHOW

with

David Letterman

Every weeknight, college students on study-breaks, high-schoolers stretching their curfews, and adults all over the United States turn to a skinny, middle-aged, gray-haired, and gap-toothed fellow to bombard them with an hour's worth of neurotic, sarcastic humor. Though he and Jay "Joke-Machine" Leno of *The Tonight Show* duel mightily every night for ratings, David Letterman—along with his "Top Ten Lists" and "Stupid Pet Tricks"—has undeniably become a pop-culture icon. Much has been made of his slips (he won't be changing networks or hosting awards shows anytime soon), not so much because he has egregiously erred but because his audience has grown to expect nothing less than perfectly timed irreverence and side-splitting asides. Personally, Letterman has also weathered the scary need for heart bypass surgery. Though his self-effacing style can occasionally border on uncomfortable self-criticism, and the man definitely has unresolved issues with his mother, many would agree that no show matches the hip edginess of the *Late Show with David Letterman*.

SELECTIVITY	🔍🔍🔍🔍🔍
Approximate applicant pool: 750 Interns accepted per semester: 15	

COMPENSATION	$
None	

QUALITY OF LIFE	🌴🌴🌴
Some free Late Show paraphernalia; chance to be an extra; hectic environment	

LOCATION(S)	
New York, NY	

FIELD	
Television	

DURATION	
14–16 weeks Summer, Fall, Spring	

PRE-REQS	
Undergrads Must receive academic credit	

DEADLINE	
Summer .... March 1 Fall .... June 1 Spring .... October 1	

DESCRIPTION

The *Late Show's* internship program first earned recognition in the 1994 edition of *America's Top Internships*, and now, years later, the program has only gotten better. Although interns are no longer posted to the Audio Consultant and Pet and Human Trick departments, they may now be assigned to work with the executive producers, which is "the top of the totem poll." Interns may also spend their semester or summer in the Music, Production, Research, Writing, and Talent departments.

"Most of the staff members were interns and remember what it was like," says an alumna of the program who now works for the show full-time. A current intern says, "I found the staff to be really friendly and helpful. Your duties are always pretty easy, so it's no trouble for them to train you anyway." Interns can also work in different departments to get a variety of experiences. "Just show up with a note pad and offer to help out," advises one intern, "and someone will ask you to do something. It's a great way to meet everyone. I've scouted

BUSYWORK METER
LOW MEDIUM HIGH
OLDMAN & HAMADEH

locations with writers, answered mail, and hung out with producers all over a couple of months."

Because of the contracts between the *Late Show* and its employees (represented by guilds and unions) interns are not permitted to write for the show or use the technical equipment. Similar situations exist at most top television networks and shows and ensure that most TV interns are mired in pretty mundane duties most of the time. Still, most Late Show interns acquire or polish skills that look terrific on their resumes and assist them in future positions. "If you've been an intern at the *Late Show*," says one former intern, "you've most likely done production assistance, research, gone on shoots, assisted producers in the control room, and been a receptionist for a couple of hours a week. That's not bad."

Production and research are two of the most popular departments, and two of the largest as well. Production interns do primarily P.A. (production assistance) duties, such as fetching tapes, carrying equipment, collating and handing out scripts and revisions, and such. "You need a little physical stamina," says one, "to run around with one revision after another throughout the day." Interns learn the "nuts and bolts of how to do a show" in this department, and can regularly find themselves working with producers in the control room or running errands beneath the stage as the show is being taped.

Interning in the research department can seem "either really isolating or incredibly rewarding," says an intern. Producers turn to the interns' research to help draw up Dave's interview questions, and writers sometimes examine research materials for potential gags. Going through books, files, on-line resources, and tapes all day in search of one or two interesting facts about a guest for their biographical booklets can be tedious. If and when that bit of info makes it on-air, however, research can also be tremendously satisfying. "I learned everything I could ever want to know about John Travolta and more from the *Late Show's* files on him," says one recent intern, "about his kids, his home life, everything. I could answer any question about him from any of the producers. It was neat to hear Dave use the info I dug up with Travolta on-air."

As almost any intern will tell you, the best part of working on Letterman is getting close to the show itself, which is taped from 5:30 to 6:30 p.m., Mondays through Thursdays. Interns are now able to watch the show being taped from the control room "at least twice during their stay with us," says the intern coordinator. "They spend an entire day watching the show being created from scratch, so that they'll have an idea of what the entire process is like." Some interns get "close to the real action" on their very first day; others must wait until they've "languished in research for a month" before actually seeing the show first-hand.

> "In another skit, I played a woman in drag and pretended I was lost on my way to the Donahue show."

Another unforgettable experience is being included in a Late Show taping. "We try to give every intern a walk-on part as an extra in one of Dave's skits," says an intern alumna. "They can take home a little money [approximately $135], and have the fun of being on-air." Some experiences are more unforgettable than others. "Dave assaulted me," reports one former intern. "He pretended to choke me as part of this skit. I still have the tape of me smiling happily at the camera with Dave's hands wrapped around my throat."

Interaction with Dave himself is minimal due to scattering of departments within The Late Show headquarters in the gorgeous Ed Sullivan Theater. "A word might be exchanged here or there," says one intern, "but, although about 50 percent of interns see him at least once a day, there really isn't much chit-chat." Those who have spent a little time in the presence of Letterman himself describe him as "shy" and "uncomfortable" socially, "a nerd at heart who isn't really good at mindless chatter." The pressures of putting out at least one show a day mean that Dave is also very busy, and doesn't have much time or energy for socializing.

Contact between interns and the celebrities Dave interviews is "miniscule," says one intern. "We're not even allowed near them much." Still, some interns do have the chance to catch the eye of a superstar now and then. One intern got to "stand in the presence of Mel Gibson and Bill Cosby in the same week" and needed serious recovery time. The staff and crew depend on interns to remain professional in the presence of greatness, and apparently can become mildly irked during those infrequent occasions when an intern obviously slobbers over a celebrity.

"Don't do this internship just to get a [Late Show] jacket," warns the intern coordinator. "There's no guarantee that every intern will be loaded with paraphernalia on his or her departure from the Late Show." That having been said, this is a great internship for anyone who wants to get stuff. Not just hats, jackets, sweatshirts, and T-shirts, but the pick of the food, clothing, and "weird things" sent to Letterman and his staff by grateful fans and random companies. "We have this box in the hall of all the free goodies that pour in," says one former intern. "Every time you go by there seems to be something cool to grab."

The occasional give-away cannot substitute for the lack of compensation for Late Show interns. A number of interns live with their parents, attend school in the vicinity, or stay with friends in Manhattan. Others depend on handouts from parents, or even work at restaurants late at night and on weekends to pay the bills. The staff buys dinner for the interns on Thursdays, when interns traditionally stay late for the taping of two shows, but otherwise interns are expected to handle the high cost of New York living entirely on their own.

Because interning at the Late Show involves primarily mundane work, some interns find that, at the time, getting a jacket can seem like the highlight of their internship experience. What they may overlook, but what few alumni of the program who have gone on to work full-time at the Late Show forget, are the networking possibilities. Twenty-seven members of Letterman's staff and crew are former interns, and there is little turnover. "Most people who are here used to be interns," says the intern

coordinator. "This is a fabulous way to get a foot in the door," says one former intern who now works at the Late Show. "Interns are the number one source for our new entry-level people. Not many are willing to leave this place, but it's worth staying in contact with the staff here to grab jobs when they become available."

SELECTION

Only undergraduates whose schools will send an official letter to the Late Show stating that they will receive academic credit for a Letterman internship will be considered. International applicants are welcome to apply. Successful candidates often (but not necessarily) have some demonstrated interest in and knowledge of television programs (often through classes and/or other internships), are enthusiastic but professional in their cover letters and interviews, and are eager to work in a particular aspect of entertainment television (writing, producing, etc.).

APPLICATION PROCEDURE

Applicants should submit a cover letter and resume on March 1 for the summer internship, June 1 for the fall, and October 1 for the spring. Although the Late Show is an irreverent show, applications and interviews are expected to be strictly professional, and addenda to the application are strongly discouraged (no pictures of pets doing stupid tricks, etc.). The thirty finalists selected by the internship coordinator must pay their way to New York City for the mandatory interview with the coordinator, which is reportedly "more casual than an interview at an investment bank and less casual than talking to Letterman." Candidates must be just as businesslike when speaking to the heads of each department hiring interns for that semester, and aware that they may spend an entire day being questioned by bigwigs at the Late Show. Fifteen of the most impressive (i.e., "articulate, enthusiastic, and professional") applicants are then chosen by departmental directors to be interns.

OVERVIEW

Most graduates of the internship program say that interns "either love it or hate it." But busywork aside, anyone who is seriously considering a career in entertainment television should without a doubt try for an internship at the *Late Show*. "Even if you discover you can't stand it," says one intern alumnus, "you'll have spent a semester making invaluable contacts and watching the best in the business do their thing, and that's priceless."

FOR MORE INFORMATION . . .

■ Janice Penino
Internship Coordinator
Late Show with David Letterman
1697 Broadway
New York, NY 10019
212-975-5806
fax: 212-975-5546
www.cbs.com

THE LIBRARY OF CONGRESS

SELECTIVITY	🔍 🔍 🔍 🔍 🔍
Approximate applicant pool: 350 Interns accepted: 6–10	

COMPENSATION	$ $ $
$300/week	

QUALITY OF LIFE	🌴 🌴 🌴
Hands-on contact with artifacts; twice-weekly tours; slow computers	

LOCATION(S)
Washington, D.C.

FIELD
Library

DURATION
8–12 weeks Summer

PRE-REQS
College juniors and seniors; recent grads; grad students

DEADLINE(S)
April 1

Whose library is it, anyway?

Is the Library of Congress exclusively allocated for members of Congress? You might think so. After all, when President Thomas Jefferson created the library in 1800, he intended it to be a reference tool for congresspeople only. Today it is still used by legislators who make frequent visits to its Congressional Research Service (CRS) and Law Library.

But as taxpayers would have it, the Library of Congress is not the private domain of the Capitol Hill gang. Its 105-million-item collection of books, manuscripts, maps, photographs, and films is open to anyone 18 and older who is pursuing serious research. Those who can't make it to the national library may still access its collections by requesting an interlibrary loan, purchasing copies through the mail, or writing to the reference divisions.

DESCRIPTION

The Library of Congress started its Junior Fellows Program in the summer of 1991. Generously funded by Mrs. Jefferson Patterson, a 1939 CBS News broadcaster and member of the James Madison Council (the library's advisory body), the program is designed to introduce students to the art of librarianship. Composed of an equal number of undergraduates and graduate students, the intern class is divided among the following divisions: Manuscript, Music, Prints and Photographs, American Folklife Center, and Motion Picture, Broadcasting & Recorded Sound.

Students work within these divisions to meet "arrearage" reduction goals; arrearage is a library-specific term that refers to the library's piles of uncataloged materials stored in warehouses throughout Washington, D.C. Each intern's work is similar to an entry-level library employee's—they prepare material for display presentation or for researchers' use. Accordingly, past projects have seen interns catalog American companies' logos, review Chinese microfilms, arrange cartoon maps, process the Copland music collection, tag the NAACP's historical photographs, and organize rare Arabic imprints.

The Prints and Photographs division, recently employed an intern to help process a collection of 2,000 Civil War drawings. "Two catalogers and a curator had already done most of the work, except for some photos by an artist named Alfred Waud. During the war, Waud had followed the Army of the Potomac, a predominantly African-American unit on the Union side. A picture of the soldiers running into battle at St. Petersburg is one of his most famous," she said. Referring to a special thesaurus of visual art terms used by the Library, she cataloged the photos by subject heading. "I looked carefully at each picture before listing it under such categories as African Americans,' 'Battle,' 'Union,' and 'War' in the library's computerized subject databases. Now these [heretofore unavailable] works can be accessed by researchers."

In the summer of 1992, nearly 50 boxes, "some partially organized, others in chaos," sat in a room at the Rare Books and Special Collections division. They contained the personal papers of 20th-century typographer Bruce Rogers. An intern with an interest in printing was charged with archiving them. "In order to come up with subjects for the cataloging, I had to understand [Rogers'] life in great detail. I spent most of the summer reading everything in the boxes. I also checked to see what else the library has on the subject to get a good overview of other Rogers' cataloging schemes. Meanwhile, I numbered and described the papers, organizing them in a word-processing file for easy access by researchers."

The arrearage reduction projects often require interns to search the institution's many databases. To access the databases, they must use the institution's central workstation. "About 15 years ago, this was the most technologically advanced library in the world," said one intern. "But the library lagged in modernizing during the fast-moving computer age. The result is that there are so many commands and files that it makes our searches at times slow and torturous." Another intern explained that the problem was compounded by frequent computer breakdowns. "Sometimes we'd sit around for one to two hours waiting for the computer to come back on." Fortunately, the library is currently upgrading its systems, installing faster disk drives and larger mainframes.

Originally housed in the U.S. Capitol, the Library of Congress now comprises three buildings on the corner of Independence Avenue and Second Street SE. These facilities are named after John Adams (who signed the bill establishing the library), James Madison ("the Father of the Constitution"), and Thomas Jefferson (who donated his private stash of nearly 6,500 books to the library in 1814, thereby making a national library possible). Underneath the library are extensive catacombs leading to the subway and congressional buildings; access is restricted to those with passes—and interns get them!

The Jefferson Building is the oldest of the three buildings, and its circular Main Reading Room serves as the central point of access to the library's collections. One-hundred-sixty feet tall at its dome's apex, the Main Reading Room is a mighty display of soaring marble columns, stained-glass windows, and bronze statues of Moses, Beethoven, Shakespeare, and Newton. Forming three concentric circles around a reference area at the center, hundreds of desks allow readers to access computer databases and 70,000 reference works.

Interns start the summer by touring the Jefferson Building and listening to a discussion on the library's history in the Main Reading Room. After that, tours of divisions are offered approximately twice a week and, by summer's end, interns will have toured all 12 divisions. At the Manuscript division, they see Jefferson's rough draft of the Declaration of Independence, Washington's first inaugural address, and Alexander Graham Bell's first drawing of the telephone. In Rare Books, interns peruse the American classics: "We thumbed through *Leaves of Grass* and *Walden*, both signed by Whitman and Thoreau as gifts to each other."

On their twice-weekly tours, interns become familiar with other parts of the library, such as the Copyright Office and the Landover, MD, storage facility ("acres

> "If for no other reason, work at the Library of Congress to see and touch some of the world's greatest treasures."

and acres of books, paintings, maps, and piles of dust"). Interns also learn about the up-and-coming technologies to improve library storage and access. At the library's National Digital Library, interns hear a talk on the "virtual reality" project, designed to allow a person to—via computer—"walk" into the stacks, look through materials, and review items of interest. They see the "American Memory," a Library of Congress pilot project seeking to put American images on optical disks. They are briefed on microfilming and preservation techniques by the Preservation directorate, who oversees the microfilming of 20,000 fragile books each year. They listen to curators explain how the more unusual exhibits are prepared. In the summer of 1993, interns visited an exhibit of the Dead Sea Scrolls, the oldest surviving biblical manuscripts.

The atmosphere engenders a love for exploration. Some interns "become giddy as schoolchildren" when they make an interesting find. "These moments are treasured," explained one intern, "because our job is sometimes tedious." Interns compensate for monotonous work by poking around on their own time, since supervisors are rarely willing to allow an intern to pursue personal curiosities when there is so much cataloging to be done. "I stayed an extra one or two hours every day," said one bookworm. "I figured I might not have this chance again, so I went for it." Another intern went so far as to volunteer some Saturday hours at the reference desk: "I wanted to learn how some of the best reference librarians in the world come up with all that information." In addition, interns may borrow books on their library card; only library employees, congresspeople, and congressional staffs are eligible for one.

SELECTION

 College juniors and seniors, recent graduates, and graduate students are eligible for the program. While students of any major may apply, the majority of interns study history, American studies, languages, geography, or cartography. As for GPA, the coordinator says: "We put less emphasis on grades and more emphasis on coursework....We want people who are excited about the divisions to which they apply and about coming to the library." International applicants are eligible.

APPLICATION PROCEDURE

 The deadline is April 1. Send a cover letter (highlighting your relevant background, the division or subject area of interest, and foreign language ability, if necessary for the position), a resume (including Social Security number, address, telephone number, date of birth, and citizenship), a letter of recommendation from a professor or an employer, and an official transcript. "We emphasize the letter of recommendation when selecting students, but we also want to see a well-written, enthusiastic cover letter," said the coordinator. After the coordinator checks applications for completeness, the division chiefs match the best candidates to appropriate projects. Final selections are determined after phone interviews.

OVERVIEW

 The world's largest library, the Library of Congress gives students with a penchant for history a chance to learn archiving techniques in the company of rare manuscripts, old pictures, and antique maps. But in the process, interns must put up with slow computers and a huge backlog of uncataloged work. But persevering interns help make special collections publicly available for the first time—they may even publish articles on their work in journals like the Library of Congress' *Information Bulletin* and the American Library Association's *Meridian*. By the time they make presentations of their projects to the Librarian of Congress, most have gained a good sense of what librarianship is all about. Concluded one intern: "If for no other reason, work at the Library of Congress to see and touch some of the world's greatest treasures."

FOR MORE INFORMATION . . .

■ The Library of Congress
Junior Fellows Program Coordinator
Collection Services LM-642
Washington, DC 20540-4700
(202) 707-8253
lcmarvel@loc.gov

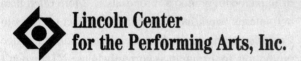

Lincoln Center for the Performing Arts, Inc.

SELECTIVITY	🔍 🔍 🔍 🔍 🔍
Approximate applicant pool: 95 Interns accepted: 2	

COMPENSATION	💲 💲 💲 💲
$500/week	

QUALITY OF LIFE	⌘ ⌘ ⌘
Spacious offices; concert tickets	

LOCATION(S)	
New York, NY	

FIELD	
Arts management	

DURATION	
12 weeks Summer	

PRE-REQS	
One year of graduate coursework	

DEADLINE(S)	
February 10	

Who celebrated a birthday with 25 army anti-aircraft lights, 18 trumpeters, and a chorus of 200 students singing Handel's "Hallelujah Chorus"? Was it the British royal family, the sultan of Brunei, or King Fahd of Saudi Arabia? Think again. It was Lincoln Center for the Performing Arts, in celebration of its 25th anniversary.

Few organizations could get away with staging such a spectacle of self-congratulation. But Lincoln Center is no run-of-the-mill institution. It is arguably the world's leading performing arts center, home to the New York State Theater, Avery Fisher Hall, the Metropolitan Opera House, the Beaumont Theater, and the Juilliard School.

DESCRIPTION

In 1968, Lincoln Center, Inc., created an internship program to provide hands-on training in arts administration. A nonprofit organization, Lincoln Center secured grants from the Ittleson Foundation and the Edward John Noble Foundation to fund a program offering graduate students high-level arts-management experience.

New interns are often surprised to learn that no prearranged project awaits their arrival at Lincoln Center. Instead, they spend their first day interviewing with key staff members, with whom they develop a few projects meeting both the needs of the organization and the interests of the intern. Emphasis is placed on creating projects that will give interns broad exposure to a range of departments, including Programming, Marketing, Finance, Operations, Planning and Development, and Education.

One intern worked on developing strategies to promote Lincoln Center's 18-month

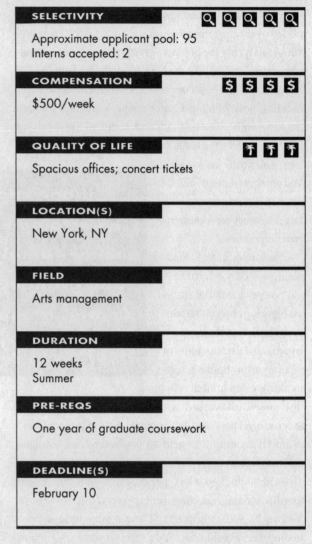

Mozart Bicentennial celebration. She put together a proposal persuading upscale retailers to publicize the Mozart Bicentennial in their stores. "It was exciting," she reported. "I went around New York soliciting support for the Bicentennial . . . talk[ing] with Godiva about making a special Bicentennial chocolate treat . . . contact[ing] Ben & Jerry's about selling a Mozart Bicentennial flavor in their New York retail stores . . . even ask[ing] the people at Rockefeller Center to play half an hour of Mozart each day at the skating rink."

Many projects focus on helping Lincoln Center in its fund-raising responsibilities. One intern helped develop a program of planned giving, whereby donors give money over time rather than straight out. "After spending weeks analyzing the planned-giving programs of comparable organizations like the New York Public Library and the Metropolitan Museum of Art, I wrote a report recommending how Lincoln Center should construct its program." Another intern examined reams of fund-raising data to determine the benefits of cultivating current donors over soliciting new ones. And another summer, a computer-savvy intern created a database tracking donations from corporations.

Promotions and fund-raising are only two of several potential areas of analysis. Figuring costs and equipment requirements, an intern investigated the feasibility of creating an in-house graphics design department. Another intern developed a plan to market the center's underutilized park-and-lock garage. A third project found an intern creating a system to implement and evaluate audience surveys.

Although they meet periodically with the intern coordinator and relevant administrators, interns stress a need to be self-motivated. "There's very little spoon-feeding here," said one. "You receive your assignment and get to work. There's no one breathing down your neck on a daily basis." Interns appreciate the respect and freedom they're given: "The staff knows that you've made it through a rigorous selection process. They know you have the ability to get the job done." Moreover, there's virtually no busywork expected of interns; "menial tasks, like stuffing envelopes, are off-limits," said the coordinator. The closest an intern came to busywork was spending a few days conducting phone interviews of current subscribers.

The program's faith in its interns is evident in the seriousness with which senior staff evaluates completed projects. At the end of the summer, interns submit their reports to management. And management listens. According to the coordinator, "There's a great track record of implementing interns' proposals…. More often than not, interns' work has a meaningful impact on Lincoln Center's operations." Indeed, the aforementioned garage promotion, for example, is currently in use. "They don't just put interns through the motions here. Senior staff examines and often implements interns' recommendations," said an intern.

In addition to projects, interns spend a week working behind the scenes at the JVC Jazz Festival, considered by many the world's foremost jazz festival, attracting the likes of the late Miles Davis, Kenny G and Santana. "Basically, we shadowed the stage manager, watching him interact with everyone from artists to ushers," said an intern. They attend preproduction meetings and work at the event itself, attending to artists and the press. During the performance, interns help out any way they can. One was asked to hold the stage door open for Kenny G, who likes to scurry into the audience during his saxophone solos. Another had the opportunity to meet Ella Fitzgerald; "it was a big thrill for me," the intern said. Interns agree that helping out at the festival "gives you a good sense of what it's like to run a concert hall."

If one cannot find entertainment during a summer amid the glamour and grandeur of Lincoln Center, it's time to throw in the towel. Interns have dibs on passes to any performance produced by Lincoln Center, Inc. including such summertime shows as "Mostly Mozart," "Serious Fun!" and "Lincoln Center Out-of-Doors." Contrary to what many think before beginning the internship, free tickets aren't readily available for Lincoln Center's constituent organizations, such as the New York City Ballet and the Metropolitan Opera. Although they share the same grounds, the constituents are independent of Lincoln Center, Inc., and cooperation between the two

> If one cannot find entertainment during a summer amid the glamour and grandeur of Lincoln Center, it's time to throw in the towel.

is, according to an intern, "much less than you'd think." It's no big deal though; most of the constituents don't perform during the summer, anyway.

Luckily for interns, the program recently vacated its former "cramped" quarters and relocated to a spacious office on the ninth floor of Lincoln Center's new Rose Building. Despite the Center's nonprofit status, the office has a distinctly modern "for-profit" look; it could be a "law firm or ad agency," said an intern. Interns work at carrels no different than the ones used by staff. Each comes equipped with computers and a full assortment of supplies.

Interns offer a few parting words of wisdom. One stressed the fact that the substance of an intern's work depends almost entirely on the project to which he or she is assigned. "Before applying," he warned, "think long and hard about the type of project you'd like to undertake. If you're selected, you'll want to convey your interests clearly to senior management. Once you're given a project, you'll work on it for several weeks, often with little supervision." Another explained that because the internship lasts only three months, interns are occasionally unable to finish their projects. He said, "I was frustrated. By the time I really learned the ins and outs of my project, my tenure drew to a close. I needed more time to see my work to fruition."

SELECTION

The program is open only to students who've had at least one year of graduate coursework in arts administration or business. Although recent years have seen a majority of MBAs in the internship, Lincoln Center is also interested in selecting other types of grad students, such as MAs / MFAs. While arts experience is not required, the intern coordinator would like to see a "demonstrated interest in and commitment to a career in arts management," as well as "strong verbal and analytical skills." International applicants are eligible.

APPLICATION PROCEDURE

Applications are due February 15. Submit a resume and a cover letter (describing qualifications and career goals). After making a preliminary screening, the coordinator invites 15 finalists to Lincoln Center for interviews. While many finalists find that interviews coincide with spring

break, those who cannot arrange or afford a trip to New York may be able to set up a phone interview. Finalists must also submit two letters of recommendation. Applicants are notified in early April.

OVERVIEW

As one intern said, "Everyone and his brother knows Lincoln Center." It's true, the Lincoln Center internship is valuable for prestige alone. But a magnetic name is only the beginning. The program carefully chooses two interns and works with them to design challenging, real-world projects. So admired is the program that the Noble Foundation considers it a model for other arts internships the foundation is funding across the country. Alumni go on to illustrious careers, some in arts management, others not. Bill Wingate, for one, interned in the late sixties, and recently served as executive director of the New York City Ballet.

FOR MORE INFORMATION . . .

■ Lincoln Center for the Performing Arts, Inc.
Internship Coordinator
Human Resources Dept.
70 Lincoln Center Plaza
New York, NY 10023-6583
(212) 875-5300
Fax: (212) 875-5185

Liz claiborne

SELECTIVITY	🔍 🔍 🔍
Approximate applicant pool: 500 Interns accepted: 50	

COMPENSATION	💲 💲
An hourly rate commensurate with experience	

QUALITY OF LIFE	⚑ ⚑ ⚑
Nurturing environment; Garment district	

LOCATION(S)	
New York, NY; North Bergen, NJ	

FIELD	
Apparel and fashion accessories	

DURATION	
3–6 months Summer, Fall, Winter/Spring Part-time available	

PRE-REQS	
Undergrads	

DEADLINE(S)	
Summer .... April 1 Fall .... August 1 Spring .... December 1	

Look inside any woman's clothes closet, and you're likely to find at least one Liz Claiborne label. That's because in a recent poll conducted by the public-opinion firm EDK Associates, a surprising 43 percent of women nationwide picked Liz Claiborne ahead of the designer labels Calvin Klein, Anne Klein, Ralph Lauren, Donna Karan, and Adrienne Vittadini. When asked why they preferred a dress or blazer from Liz Claiborne, the women cited the mid-range prices and the fact that these are "wearable, real-life clothes."

Founded in 1976, "Liz" (as the company is known in the fashion world) made the Fortune 500 list just ten years later. Only one other company founded by a woman has even made that honor roll. Its stock, which went public in 1981, increased in value nearly 60-fold by 1991. Today, Liz Claiborne, Inc., is one of the largest marketers of women's apparel and accessories in the world, selling over $2 billion worth of products annually, from jewelry and shoes to dresses and menswear.

DESCRIPTION

Liz Claiborne's New York office offers internships in the Marketing, Textile Design, Apparel Design, International Merchandising, and Sales groups of the company's clothing divisions. Liz Claiborne's New Jersey headquarters places interns in administrative departments, such as Finance, Human Resources, Management Information Systems, and Production. Regardless of location or position, interns are assigned projects and participate in staff meetings.

One intern was assigned to the Textile Design group of the Elisabeth Division, which offers clothing lines for larger women. One of her responsibilities was to keep track of the myriad fabrics available from suppliers. "I logged the fabrics into the books—about 80 fabrics per season; there are six seasons per year in the fashion industry." The large number of sample materials prompted her to establish a small fabric library: "I cordoned off a section of the wall and put the materials into categories like wools, cottons, etc.; it made fabrics easier to find later." After the company chooses one of these fabrics to use in clothing, she learned, it establishes a "hand standard." "Because the same kind of fabric can have different feels, the hand standard indicates the precise texture," explained the intern. "I sent the standard to the mill as a reference to maintain quality control." Acting as a liaison between Textile and Production, she also sent fabrics to employees involved in making sample products. "A particular fabric might come back as a dress or a blouse, depending on what the designer envisions."

Another student interned in the Creative Resources department. Besides helping make company posters, shopping bags, boxes, and stationery, he worked on the packaging for Liz Claiborne's fragrance *Vivid*. "I assisted the art directors in putting together a comp of what the final product—bottle and box—would look like," he said. "The comp is a prototype used in photo shoots and market tests before the manufacturer starts making the product." His role also required that he attend marketing strategy meetings for the new product. "But I made no comments—only observations," he said.

One intern produced a layout for a sweater idea— the shape, pattern, and colors.

On to the meat and potatoes of fashion—clothing design. One Apparel Design intern in the Collection division's knitwear group learned how sweaters are made. "The head designer was overwhelmed with work and sometimes sent design projects my way," she said. Taking on the role of assistant designer, she occasionally produced a layout for a sweater idea—the shape, pattern, and colors. "I first made three graphs, one for the front, one for the back, and one for the sleeves; the graphs indicate exactly where each stitch should go," she said. "I then wrote a preliminary spec sheet—neck size, width, arm length, and a sketch of what the sweater should eventually look like. Finally, I made two-dimensional, life-size, color versions of the sweater and 'sourced the trim' [i.e., found suppliers of buttons, ribbons, and any other accessories on the sweater]." After prototypes were made, the group sat down to decide which sweaters the company should include in its line: "My role involved displaying models on the wall and taking notes." In between layout assignments, she tran-

scribed messages sent by the Hong Kong production facilities via LINCS (Liz Claiborne International Network Computer System). She also worked with tear sheets (magazine pages ripped out by the head designer). "Sometimes, I combined aspects from several of the tops or blouses pictured and created a half-dozen or so designs to show the designer."

New York interns work in several high-rises within a few blocks of each other. The buildings are located in New York's famous garment district—several square blocks of clothing companies, fabric stores, and design shops. While the majority of interns at Liz sit behind desks outfitted with phones and computers, Apparel Design interns sit at "illuminated tables to facilitate drawing." To liven up the place, employees decorate the corridors and work spaces: "You can't walk five feet without seeing an array of magazine tear sheets, fabrics, and plants."

Perks are minimal. Interns aren't eligible for company benefits, but exposure to managers is frequent, and interns do receive a 35 percent employee discount at the outlet store, which sells inventory from past seasons, and a 40 percent discount at retail stores. At the end of the internship, an exit interview screens interns for full-time employment.

SELECTION

 College freshmen, sophomores, juniors, and seniors as well as graduate students are eligible for Liz Claiborne internships. All positions require computer skills, except for Design (where sketching ability is mandatory). The internship is relatively competitive, especially for the summer. "The quality of writing in the cover letter, the level of participation in extracurricular activities, and work experience in the fashion industry or an office definitely give a candidate an edge," said the Manager of College Relations. International applicants are eligible.

APPLICATION PROCEDURE

 Applicants must send in a resume and a cover letter indicating their area of interest. Top candidates are interviewed in New York or New Jersey, depending on their area of interest. Those who cannot arrange a trip to New York or New Jersey may be interviewed by phone.

OVERVIEW

 "You can't love a good bag enough," states a Liz Claiborne ad for handbags. Similarly, Claiborne employees care for their interns a great deal. From celebrating intern birthdays to providing interns with well-tailored projects, employees go out of their way, as one intern put it, "to make sure students gain connections and experience—the two most valuable commodities in the fashion industry."

FOR MORE INFORMATION . . .

■ Liz Claiborne, Inc.
Attn: Coordinator, College Relations
1440 Broadway, 2nd Floor
New York, N Y 10018
(212) 626-5376
Fax: (212) 626-5527

INDUSTRIAL LIGHT+MAGIC

SKYWALKER SOUND

SELECTIVITY	🔍 🔍 🔍 🔍 🔍
Approximate applicant pool: 1,000–1,500 Interns accepted: 75–90	

COMPENSATION	$
Minimum wage	

QUALITY OF LIFE	🌴 🌴 🌴 🌴
Skywalker Ranch; fitness center; seminars; parties	

LOCATION(S)
San Rafael and Nicasio, CA

FIELD
Entertainment

DURATION
10–12 weeks Summer, Fall, Spring

PRE-REQS
College juniors and seniors; grad students

DEADLINE(S)
Summer .... March 30   Fall .... July 25 Spring .... October 25

Special effects in movies have come a long way since those old Buck Rogers films, the ones that show hobby-shop spaceships, pulled by supposedly invisible wire, hurtling by. The *Star Wars* movies revolutionized special effects, making space travel and space battle seem breathtakingly believable. *Terminator 2* upped the ante, stretching technology to startling limits; who can forget the scene where the T-1000, played by actor Robert Patrick, sustains a body-splitting Samurai blow, only to regenerate his alloy body by zipping himself together like a parka. Even a recent Miller Lite commercial displayed stunning visual effects, showing a couple as they transform magically from disco dancers to punk-rockers and then to futuristic citizens.

The man responsible for all of these technical triumphs is George Lucas, the mastermind writer and director of *Star Wars*, who now presides over the cutting-edge companies Lucasfilm and Lucas Digital. Lucasfilm is one of the world's leading motion picture production and entertainment companies, responsible for *American Graffiti*, the *Star Wars* movies, the *Indiana Jones* series, as well as the television series *The Young Indiana Jones Chronicles*. Lucas Digital is involved in film effects and postproduction sound, operating through its divisions Industrial Light and Magic (ILM) and Skywalker Sound, respectively. ILM has created effects for *Small Soldiers, Men In Black, Jurassic Park, Forrest Gump*, and *Saving Private Ryan*. Skywalker Sound offers a full range of sound recording, editing, and mixing services for film, video, and theme park attractions.

BUSYWORK
LOW MEDIUM HIGH
OLDMAN & HAMADEH
METER

DESCRIPTION

 A rich diversity of positions is available at Lucasfilm and Lucas Digital. Departments accepting interns at Lucasfilm include THX, IT&S, Ranch Operations, Internet, Archives, Library/ Research, and Business Affairs. Lucas Digital interns may work in Skywalker Sound as well as in the ILM divisions of Communications, Marketing & PR, Human Resources, Feature Post-Production Management, Video Engineering, Art, Computer Graphics, Finance/ Accounting, Information Systems, and Editorial.

The work an intern performs depends entirely on the department in which he or she works. A Public Relations intern at Lucasfilm, for example, worked primarily for The Young Indiana Jones Chronicles, a weekly television show produced by Lucasfilm. To boost ratings for the show, she identified and sent press releases to special-interest groups who might be interested in a particular episode, contacting, for example, African-American groups before the episode in which young Indiana Jones travels to Africa; she also sent videotapes of the show to opinion-makers such as Hillary Clinton and Katharine Hepburn. Her other responsibilities ran the gamut from gofering on the set of a documentary about George Lucas to translating Spanish phrases for Lucas in preparation for a promo he was filming.

One computer graphics intern did everything from animation programming to software translation for a new computer. Particularly fascinating to him were the periodic department meetings in which programmers would describe past projects. He said: "A programmer who worked on the Miller Lite commercial showed us how the ad was made. Painstaking detail went into each fraction-of-a-second frame. It was amazing to see."

Some interns at Lucasfilm carry out research and marketing projects for THX, an audio system providing unbelievably realistic sound in both movie theaters and home audio equipment. "THX is an exciting piece of technology," said one intern. "With speakers carefully situated around the theater and behind the movie screen, it makes moviegoers feel as if they are in the center of the action. It increases the believability of the images they see." One intern assembled databases tracking the licensees of the Home THX Audio System and created binders cataloging information on those licensees. While such work seems far from scintillating, he was quick to point out that "despite these relatively mundane tasks, I greatly enjoyed seeing how communications theories I learned in school applied to a real-life product. My textbooks described how TV is a passive medium, how it leaves little for the imagination. Working at Lucasfilm, I saw how THX is transforming TV and movies into more active media. It increases the imagination involved."

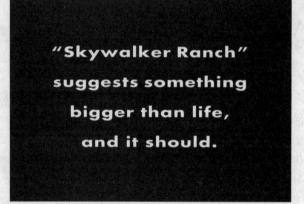

"Skywalker Ranch" suggests something bigger than life, and it should.

From day one, interns are treated to a host of activities. Orientation introduces freshly arrived students to the variety of departments. After settling into their jobs, interns are sometimes invited to "dailies," the early morning screenings of the previous day's special-effects work, open only to company employees. Said one intern: "The dailies were a great way of keeping up on the stunning film moments being made. At a daily for *Death Becomes Her*, for instance, we saw several takes of Meryl Streep with her head on backward and Goldie Hawn with a hole through her stomach." Interns are also free to attend advance screenings of Lucasfilm movies, held every so often in the company's main screening room. And, befitting a film company, free passes to local movies abound, and interns can find out about them via Email.

The best internships invite speakers to address their interns, and Lucasfilm's is no exception. Meeting every two or three weeks, interns hear words of wisdom from various department heads and executives. Past interns especially enjoyed meeting with Gordon Radley, president of the company. They found him remarkably approachable and asked him a host of juicy questions.

Chances are interns will take in a few memorable parties during their time. Described as a "lakeside hoedown" and a "good old-fashioned western picnic," the annual Fourth of July bash garners high ratings. The whole company comes out for the party, as do a number of celebrities.

Working at Lucas Digital sometimes yields a few unexpected opportunities. One student spent an afternoon assisting Robert Townsend when the actor was putting the finishing touches on his movie *Meteor Man*. The same summer, a few interns were enlisted to make voiceovers for *The Young Indiana Jones Chronicles*; according to one, he "generated assorted noises, including applause and laughing sounds, for the show's sound track."

Lucas Digital interns work at a complex in central San Rafael, an industrial city about 20 minutes from San Francisco. The "bustling" San Rafael complex has an industrial but modern feel. Offices are decorated with a variety of movie posters and paintings. An employee gym, called the Bodybay, is located on the premises, as is a basketball court. An array of restaurants is in walking distance of the complex.

Lucasfilm interns work at Skywalker Ranch, a name that suggests something bigger than life, and it should. Imagine a sprawling, bucolic estate reachable by a long, sinuous road. A corral holds an assortment of horses; longhorn steer roam the mountainside. Burgundy-colored bikes dot the compound, used by employees to shuttle between buildings. Several rustic houses sit on the premises, some holding conference rooms and offices, others housing screening rooms and production equipment. A variety of artwork decorates these houses, as do fireplaces and comfortable furnishings. Arriving at the ranch, one intern asked himself: "Is this a production company or the set of *Dallas*, turbocharged?"

Like all of the rooms at the ranch, the dining areas have a handsome, personal feel. One dining room has a solarium that employees are free to use. The food is affordable and highly regarded ("delicious meals prepared by able chefs, some of whom studied at the California Culinary Academy").

Lucasfilm interns receive a car sticker affording them access to the ranch, and even interns who do not work at the ranch are free to visit when they have free time, however rare this is.

While the ranch offers the type of Edenic workplace most people only dream about, not everyone appreciates this paradise. About 45 minutes from San Francisco in a valley of West Marin, "the ranch is unbelievably beautiful," in an intern's estimation, "but it is isolated from civilization. And because the buildings are really spread out, you don't get to see a lot of what's going on. It is isolated both geographically and institutionally." Although a few prefer San Rafael's faster-paced environment, most find it hard to forsake the ranch's breathtaking beauty and low-key atmosphere.

Although the overwhelming majority of interns' comments about the internship are overwhelmingly positive, a few reveal some on-the-job frustrations. As in all film and television internships, union rules prohibit interns from undertaking tasks done by union employees, such as building sets and mixing sound. Although he found the professional staff "extremely friendly," one intern felt occasionally resented by the union workers; he said, "The stagehands would go ballistic if you lifted a box." Another intern wished there was more positive feedback from his supervisors: "People here are so used to excellence that it seemed like they didn't give me enough time to learn the ropes. I could have used more encouragement." A few interns complained that they were notified about being accepted to the program too late: "I didn't hear from Lucasfilm until a week before my internship was to start. I had to cancel the alternative plans I had made."

SELECTION

 College juniors and seniors and graduate students are eligible to apply. All students must be returning to school full-time when the internship ends; thus, the program does not accept recent graduates. The program gives first consideration to students with an overall GPA of at least 3.3; it prefers that students have a 3.5 GPA in their major. In general, the internship has no hard and fast prerequisites, but computer literacy is required. The intern coordinator looks favorably upon applicants with previous work experience, be it "another internship or even pumping gas." Applicants with professionalism and maturity are also highly prized.

APPLICATION PROCEDURE

 Deadlines for applying to the internship are as follows: summer, March 30; fall, July 25; spring, October 25. Applicants should apply directly to Lucasfilm or LucasDigital. Send in the following items stapled together in the order given: application form, resume, cover letter, intern questionnaire, official transcripts, and two letters of recommendation (from college professors, guidance counselors, or employers). The intern questionnaire asks general questions about a candidate's academic background, vocational interests, expectations for the internship, and past accomplishments. Lucasfilm does not accept film/video tapes. After all materials have been submitted, applicants are interviewed by the intern coordinator over the phone or in person. The internship coordinator stresses that incomplete applications are not considered.

OVERVIEW

 If spending a few months exposed to the technological and creative genius of a cutting-edge entertainment company sounds appealing, Lucasfilm and Lucas Digital is for you. Interns carry out rewarding projects while enjoying a breathtaking array of extracurricular activities. They leave with "tremendous insight into the entertainment industry," not to mention "an incredible resume enhancer." It's no surprise that interns often wish to repeat the program, but Lucasfilm forbids their doing so. Said one intern: "Like Cinderella at the ball, you only get one shot as a Lucasfilm intern." With less than 5 percent of the applicants accepted, landing one opportunity at the company is difficult enough. Word to the wise: Apply early, and may the Force be with you.

FOR MORE INFORMATION . . .

■ Lucasfilm
Human Resources-Intern Department
P.O. Box 2009
San Rafael, CA 94912
(415) 662-1999
www.lucasfilm.com

■ Lucas Digital
Internship Coordinator
P.O. Box 2459
San Rafael, CA 94912
(415) 258-2000
www.ilm.com

Lucent Technologies
Bell Labs Innovations

SELECTIVITY	🔍 🔍 🔍
Approximate applicant pool: 500 (SRP)/ 2,700 (UR) Interns accepted: 80 (SRP)/ 250 (UR)	

COMPENSATION	💲 💲 💲 💲
Estimate $430–$520/wk for undergrads; Estimate $550–$620/wk for grad students; round-trip travel	

QUALITY OF LIFE	🌴 🌴 🌴 🌴
Excellent mentors; Science seminars; dorm housing	

LOCATION(S)	
NJ and PA—see Description	

FIELD	
Telecommunications research	

DURATION	
10–12 weeks Summer	

PRE-REQS	
Varies with program—see Application Procedure	

DEADLINE(S)	
Summer Research Program .... December 1 University Relations Summer Program .... January 31	

"**U**.S. PATENT NO.: 4,968,542."

Pick a few numbers, slap on a "U.S. Patent No.," and you've got yourself a patent.

Not so fast. To license an invention in America, you must pay your dues. After submitting a three-page application and a $710 filing fee, there's a delay of up to two years while the Patent and Trademark Office verifies the originality of your invention. What are the chances for success? According to the Patent Office, about 65 percent of all applicants are actually awarded patents.

Amazingly enough, Lucent Technologies Bell Laboratories has become a master of this arduous process. Since its founding in 1925 (then AT&T Bell Laboratories), nearly nine out of every ten Bell Labs applications have been approved by the Patent Office—an average of one patent every working day! It's no surprise when one considers some of the devices Bell Labs has invented: transistors, sound motion pictures, liquid crystal displays, lasers, solar cells, Touch-Tone phones, trans-Atlantic fiber-optic cables, and motion videophones.

Lucent Technologies Bell Labs employs over 4,000 scientists and 25,000 technicians who develop new products, systems, and services as well as conduct research in five areas to maintain Lucent Technologies' technological edge: microelectronics, software, image processing, speech processing, and photonics (technologies for generating, processing, and detecting light signals).

DESCRIPTION

 In 1972, Lucent Technology Bell Laboratories, then AT&T Bell Laboratories, established the Summer Research Program for Minorities and Women (SRP) in order to attract minority undergraduate students to Ph.D. programs in the sciences. The laboratory's University Relations Summer Program (UR) had already been providing structured research opportunities to college undergraduate and graduate students since 1945. Today, well over 1,200 students have gone through SRP and an even greater number through UR. While SRP students are placed exclusively in the Basic Research department and most frequently at Bell Labs' Murray Hill location, UR students work in both Product Development and Basic Research in Murray Hill, Middletown, Holmdel, Whippany, Red Hill (all N.J.), and Allentown (PA).

The hundreds of laboratories at Bell Labs are known by number. The Research Materials Science Engineering & Academic Affairs division's Solid State Chemistry Research Lab is referred to more easily as Lab 11535, and the Information Sciences Research division's Mathematics of Communication and Computer Systems Lab is Lab 11211. The numbers alleviate the difficulty of trying to remember the area, division, and lab name associated with each lab. It's a good thing, too, because interns need every brain cell in their heads to understand the research going on here.

A student in Lab 11535 "detwinned" superconducting crystals—that is, he realigned the oxygen molecules (of which each crystal is partly composed) with the other molecules in the crystal. "First I had to find suitable crystals, those without cracks or jagged edges. Since the crystals are only tenths of a millimeter on each side, it's impossible to locate imperfections visually. So I X-rayed them and then read the diffraction pattern; a non-uniform pattern indicated that there was a crack." Once located, good crystals were subjected to heating at 600° to 800°C; the heating lines up the oxygen molecules. Occasionally, however, a tiny imperfection unseen by the X-ray would cause the crystal to destruct upon heating. "Sometimes I'd open the oven door and discover a small pile of dust."

An intern in the Research Physics division was paired with a professor investigating "chaos theory"—the idea that apparently irregular or random systems, like the weather, exhibit some predictability. "[The professor] discovered that an array of solid-state devices called 'Josephson tunnel junctions' exhibit chaotic behavior," he said. "[So] if we could determine how the junctions work, we'd go pretty far in understanding how chaos works." But Josephson tunnel junctions themselves are not clearly understood and are difficult to make. Consequently, while the professor performed lab experiments on the junctions, the intern programmed a

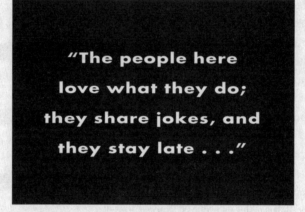

"The people here love what they do; they share jokes, and they stay late . . ."

computer to simulate them. "I developed a 600-line program using C (a computer language) to describe what was going on mathematically. As you can imagine, it took me several weeks to write the code…and plot the output using a graphing program specifically designed for chaotic systems."

Interns may be found in Basic Research as well as Product Development and not all intern projects involve heavy-duty scientific research. An intern in Software Development Tools, for example, spent the summer creating a database to categorize the 100 or so computer hardware and software products that her department utilizes in its work. "I was asked to use two programs to develop the database," she said. "One was a commercial program called INFORMIX and the other was a program that [Bell Labs] had developed called GHOST. We wanted to see if GHOST worked as well as INFORMIX did in keeping track of all the items in the stock room." But because there was no manual for GHOST, she explained, she had to read the code—several hundred pages' worth. "It filled a two-inch binder and was so complicated… I didn't really have the background to fully understand it." On top of that, her summer ended before she could make the GHOST database. "At least I learned more about computer programming and how [INFORMIX] works."

As the last two examples would suggest, student projects are often so complex that interns find it difficult to finish by the end of the summer. It's a situation ripe for frustration, so Bell Labs assigns supervisors and mentor-scientists to whom interns may turn for assistance. Many mentors are world-renowned, such as Jim West, inventor of the modern telephone microphone, and Jim Mitchell, head of the Analytical Chemistry department. But one had better schedule meetings with his or her mentor well in advance, cautions one intern: "These people are very busy."

The summer begins with a half-day orientation over breakfast followed by an information session and a speech on the advantages of attending graduate school. The highlight of the day is a talk given by Vice President of Research Arno Penzias, who welcomes the interns and answers their questions about the organization. Employed by Bell Labs since 1961, Penzias is no stranger to research: He shared a Nobel Prize in physics with Bell Labs' Robert Wilson in 1978 for his codiscovery of faint background radiation, proving that the universe was created by the Big Bang billions of years ago.

Several large five-story buildings sit at the center of Bell Labs' headquarters in Murray Hill, surrounded by meticulously maintained lawns and an abundance of trees. Inside, interns are impressed with the winding, maze-like corridors, enormous labs outfitted with top-of-the-line equipment, and an oversupply of old computers, many of which are waiting to be shipped out as donations. It is no wonder that the company's researchers are eager to spend long hours here. Remarked one intern: "The people here love what they do; they share jokes, and they stay late all the time even though there's no overtime pay." This spirit certainly rubs off on the interns, who often work 10 hours a day. "But no one lords over you; you can take a long lunch or leave early," said an intern.

Interns are encouraged to occasionally leave the confines of their labs and attend the workshops and weekly talks given at the Murray Hill location (shuttle service is provided from the other sites). Focusing on advances in technology and science, the discussions explore such topics as post-magnetic fields, planetary magnetospheres, and blackbody radiation as well as videophones, infrared cameras, and high-definition television. "Afterwards, if one of the discussions interests you, and you want to return for a second summer," said an intern, "you can go up to the speaker and see if he or she would be willing to take you on as a future intern."

For years, the company has arranged for student housing at nearby Rutgers University. Maintaining campuses in several cities, the university houses Bell Labs interns at its Busch campus, in Piscataway, NJ. Nearly 90 percent of all Bell Labs' interns live in these dorms,

priced at $300 to $400 a month, which is deducted from interns' paychecks. Typical of dorms, carpeting is often found to be "ratty" and air-conditioning not as powerful as it could be. "At least the Rutgers gym is close by and free, and we party on Friday nights," said an intern. Because the dorms are a considerable distance from the company buildings, bus transportation to and from work is provided.

At the end of the summer, interns give presentations of their work to groups of managers. Afterward, the several hundred interns gather together for the last time at the farewell picnic. One of the internship coordinators makes a few opening remarks, and then interns dive into barbecue and beverages. In between swimming, volleyball, basketball, and softball, interns exchange phone numbers and parting words. "It was a really fun day, capping off a wonderful learning experience," recalled an intern.

SELECTION

 SRP applicants must be college sophomores, juniors, or seniors. UR applicants, however, may be BS, MS, or Ph.D. candidates so long as they are available for permanent employment within two years after the internship. Only students with a minimum 3.0 GPA are considered. Both programs target those studying ceramic engineering, chemical engineering, chemistry, communications science, computer science/engineering, electrical engineering, information science, materials science, mathematics, mechanical engineering, operations research, physics, or statistics. Students majoring in other technical fields are considered by the UR program. Brochures cite a candidate's "academic achievement… [and] demonstrated interest and motivation in scientific fields" as key selection criteria. International applicants are eligible.

APPLICATION PROCEDURE

 The SRP deadline and UR deadline fall on December 1 and January 31, respectively. The company accepts applications as early as October 15. SRP candidates must submit an application form, official transcript, resume, three letters of recommendation, and a personal statement answering the four questions that appear on the application form. UR candidates need only submit a resume, cover letter, and official transcript. The best candidates are interviewed over the phone by department managers.

Lucent Technologies also administers five scholarship/fellowship programs. The Cooperative Research Fellowship Program (CRFP) and the Graduate Research Program for Women (GRPW) provide summer jobs, tuition, and living stipends to minority and female college seniors who will pursue a Ph.D. in science or engineering. The Dual Degree Scholarship Program (DDSP) provides summer jobs, tuition, and room and board to minorities and women willing to pursue two degrees at one of nine specific East Coast schools. The Engineering Scholarship Program (ESP) provides full tuition, room and board, and summer jobs to minority and female college seniors who will pursue a BS degree in computers or engineering. The PhD Scholarship Program (Ph.D.) provides tuition, living stipends, and research assignments to Ph.D. students nominated by their departments. Interested students should contact the appropriate program manager for further information.

OVERVIEW

 A Lucent Technologies Bell Laboratories internship is one of the most rigorous in its class. Applying their talents to any number of challenging research projects, interns are exposed to cutting-edge physics, electronics, and materials-science research inside one of the world's preeminent industrial research and development institutions. In addition to gaining knowledge from renowned scientists, interns might someday end up using a product on which they themselves did research. Over the nearly fifty-year history of the internship program, hundreds of interns have helped develop the Touch-Tone telephone, the Telstar communications satellite, which made cable TV possible, and the cellular telephone. Now future interns have an opportunity to make an impact on voice-controlled robot arms, digital radio, and high-definition television.

FOR MORE INFORMATION . . .

- www.lucent.com/college

SELECTIVITY		🔍
Approximate applicant pool: 50 Interns accepted: 30		

COMPENSATION		💲
None		

QUALITY OF LIFE		🌴 🌴 🌴
Casual atmosphere; freebies galore		

LOCATION(S)	
New York, NY	

FIELD	
Comic books	

DURATION	
3 to 4 months Summer, Fall, Spring	

PRE-REQS	
College juniors and seniors Must receive academic credit	

DEADLINE(S)	
Rolling	

According to Marvel Comics, 76 percent of American children between the ages of 6 and 17 have read Marvel comic books. What makes these stories so compelling to young people? Vivid colors, maybe; the exciting content, perhaps; characters of superhuman strength and ability, sure. But Marvel cites an additional reason for the success of its comic books: Marvel characters, who are bastions of unearthly brawn, suffer also from human concerns and conflicts. Originally an ostracized high school student, Spider Man, for example, is a crime fighter troubled by money, guilt, and an unappreciative public. The Incredible Hulk has extraordinary strength, but such power is driven by rage and he struggles perpetually to keep his passion in check. Living not in a fictitious city but in New York, the Fantastic Four see no need to conceal their identities and together they fight crime, but not without occasionally arguing among themselves. The Marvel formula is clear: One part supernatural ability plus one part earthly vulnerability equals compelling super heroes who are understood and appreciated by children of all backgrounds.

DESCRIPTION

The Marvel College Internship program hires about thirty interns per session, each of whom is assigned to one of the company's thirty editors. No matter where an intern ends up, there is a lot of gofer work to be done. "You basically assist an editor with any tasks that need to be done," reports an intern. Photocopying, retrieving mail, sending out complimentary comic books, filing, typing fan mail responses, and answering fan inquiries over the phone—all fall under Marvel interns' jurisdiction. When editors write new plots for a super hero, they rely on interns to ferret out the names of past characters and settings that may have relevance to the new stories. Interns, in search of these past issues, make countless trips to the archives room. To some all this is plain gruntwork; to others, particularly those who have grown up collecting comics, it is a "labor of love."

"When an editor begins to trust you, you receive better assignments," explains an intern. Some get to put editing and writing skills to use. Interns are sometimes asked to read and critique scripts sent in by comic

BUSYWORK METER
LOW MEDIUM HIGH
OLDMAN & HAMADEH

book writers. A few interns have the chance to write comic books' "letters pages," where fans' questions are answered in a "Dear Editor" format. Other interns work with layout and design materials. One intern worked with film negatives to enlarge the pages in the *Marvel Masterworks*, a compendium of early issues of Marvel comics. Others are asked to make various paste-ups, such as pasting thought-balloons onto comic strips. On an informal basis, editors consult with interns, asking their opinions on design decisions: "My editor asked my input on logos and cover designs. I liked being in the loop on such matters."

Marvel attempts to expose its interns to every stage of comic book production. Between tasks, interns are free to visit the various departments responsible for creating the comic books. Some attend plot lunches, where editors and writers meet to discuss how they want their stories to unfold. Interns receive demonstrations on the other stages of production, including penciling, whereby an artist sketches pictures based on what the plot describes; lettering, performed by an artist who hand-letters the dialog and narration; inking, which involves going over the penciled art in black india ink; and finally, coloring, in which each page receives a selection of Dr. Martin's watercolor dyes. Seeing the whole production process, interns can't help but be impressed: "I grew up thinking that comics were put together by magical elves. It was terrific to see the nuts and bolts of how the books are really made."

Part of the attraction of working at Marvel is its casual atmosphere. The editorial office looks like a cross between a law firm and an eighth grader's bedroom. Inside the modern, recently remodeled rooms one finds a smattering of super hero posters; desks that sport Spider Man and Incredible Hulk action figures; and a rubber chicken that hangs from the ceiling. "This is not your typical New York office space," says a Marvel editor. "It's a jeans-and-T-shirt office. It's a little offbeat. Creative people need comfortable surroundings." Most interns work on the tenth floor, which is considered the main editorial area. A few work in the ninth-floor editorial annex, affectionately known as "the dungeon," because it seems isolated in comparison to the bustling floor above.

Marvel has loads of freebies. Interns receive free copies of each month's comic books, averaging out to about twenty books a week. If bundles of comics aren't enough, a healthy amount of super hero buttons, T-shirts, and toy figures come interns' way.

For interns interested in a career in comic books, interning at Marvel is clearly a stepping stone to permanent employment. A long line of assistants, artists, and editors currently at the company began their careers as Marvel interns. The intern coordinator estimates that at least 60 percent of the editorial department passed through the internship program.

The most common complaint about the internship is its lack of pay. "I had to commute from New Jersey," gripes an intern, "and factoring in transportation costs, I lost money working at Marvel." Another downside to the program is the disproportionately large share of men. Although Marvel would like to see an equal proportion of male and female interns, far fewer women apply for the internship. Each session usually has only two or three female interns. On top of that, only six of Marvel's thirty editors are women. These ratios make for a distinctly male culture. "The internship needs more female interns… a woman's perspective would balance out the overwhelming macho attitude here," said one intern.

SELECTION

The Marvel College Internship selects college juniors and seniors for internships. Those who get the most out of the internship have initiative and the ability to interact well with others. "Interns able to adapt to a wide variety of personalities do well at Marvel," says one past intern.

> At Marvel, one finds a smattering of super hero posters; desks that sport Spider Man and Incredible Hulk action figures; and a rubber chicken that hangs from the ceiling.

Many interns have previous experience in drawing comics, but artistic skills are by no means required. Marvel gets its fair share of English and business majors and even a few engineering majors on occasion. Above all, in the words of the program's information sheet, interns should "be familiar with the Marvel universe of characters." Knowledge of stories and characters is no small deal at Marvel. Says the coordinator: "While a general familiarity with Marvel super heroes is fine, some of our best interns have known comic book histories as they would the Bible, able to quote chapter and verse." Marvel-savvy interns prove valuable in helping editors do research for new stories, recalling on command arcane aspects of a super hero's history, but there can be too much of a good thing. "A few of the interns were so intense about Marvel comics that nothing else seemed to matter. If their favorite characters failed, they mourned for days. We called these interns 'fan geeks.'" International applicants are eligible.

APPLICATION PROCEDURE

 The Marvel College Internship runs throughout the year and interns are hired for the summer, fall, and spring on a rolling basis. Applicants should send the intern coordinator a resume, cover letter, and a letter from their college stating that they will receive credit for the internship. The coordinator then interviews applicants, preferably in person but also by phone, to find out which Marvel comic books interest them. With this information, the coordinator attempts to have editors of similar interests interview applicants. Before this interview, editors prefer applicants to have brought or sent in some sort of creative sample, be it drawings or writing samples. Interns are chosen a few days later.

OVERVIEW

 Just as Marvel characters display both superhuman powers and earthly vulnerability, the Marvel College Internship offers an experience marked by duality. Interns experience the thrill of observing America's top comic book maker in action but in doing so, undertake a large share of mundane assignments. Factor in the inimitably casual atmosphere, the ability to hone writing and drawing skills, and the opportunities for permanent employment—and the internship could be a terrific way to spend a few months. Even if you don't want to make comics your life, interning at Marvel will add a lifelong conversation piece to your resume.

FOR MORE INFORMATION . . .

■ Marvel Comics
Internship Program
387 Park Avenue South
New York, NY 10016
(212) 696-0808

SELECTIVITY	
Approximate applicant pool: 400–500 Interns accepted: 44	🔍 🔍 🔍 🔍

COMPENSATION	
$450–$600/week for undergrads; $700–$900/week for grad students	💲 💲 💲 💲 💲

QUALITY OF LIFE	
Picnic with executives; state-of-the-art gym; 25 percent discount at company store; fun-loving atmosphere	🌴 🌴 🌴 🌴

LOCATION(S)

Los Angeles, CA

FIELD

Consumer goods (toys)

DURATION

12 weeks
Summer

PRE-REQS

Undergrads and grad students
(Market/Finance requires MBA)

DEADLINE(S)

March 31

Barbie. Hot Wheels. See N' Say. Fisher Price toys. You know 'em, you love 'em, you played with 'em when you were little. Nearly every child in America has enjoyed one of these ubiquitous playthings. Parents recognize the name brands for their consistent quality and educational value. Who's behind these objects of childhood delight and edification? Mattel, the largest toy company in the world.

Mattel, Inc., was founded in 1945 by Harold Mattson and Elliott Handler (the company name combines the first letters of their last and first names, respectively), two entrepreneurs who started out making doll furniture in a garage. Today, Mattel is an international corporation employing more than 24,000 people in 36 countries around the world. After merging with Fisher-Price in 1993, Mattel—relying strongly on its base of core products—surpassed rival Hasbro in total sales to become the undisputed leader in the toy industry.

DESCRIPTION

 An internship at Mattel seems like an invitation to play; as one intern puts it, "You think, how can this be real work?" But the billion-dollar toy industry is serious business, and Mattel interns get an unmatched introduction to it. Working in Marketing, Finance, Design, Chem Lab, Human Resources, Planning, or Information Systems, interns experience the different aspects of toy production.

If you think you're going to be playing with Barbies all day or romping with toddlers to test out toys like Tom Hanks did in *Big*, think again: in some departments you "never see the product." A Finance intern

made phone calls, contributed to monthly financial statements, and did "a lot of number-crunching." An intern in Planning collected data from focus group testing—"I sat behind a lot of one-way mirrors, taking notes as mothers talked about what they wanted to see in toys"—and presented the findings to the designers at the design center.

Another intern, who worked in Disney/Infant Products Marketing, spent much of her time doing market research on the pricing and advertising practices of Mattel's competitors. As part of her assignment, she

BUSYWORK METER — LOW · MEDIUM · HIGH — OLDMAN & HAMADEH

was sent incognito to a local Toys "R" Us to do 'price point checks"; she then used that information to do a competitive analysis of the pricing strategies of the leading toy companies.

Mattel interns work at corporate headquarters, a massive complex in El Segundo, CA, which includes the company's Administrative, Finance, and Marketing divisions, as well as the Design and Development Center, where new toys are conceived. Headquarters also boasts its own restaurant, an on-site day care center for employee children, a state-of-the-art gym, a softball field, and basketball and volleyball courts. Of course, there is also a company toy store, where employees receive a sizable discount—25 percent—on Mattel products. One intern took advantage of this opportunity to buy toys for her nephew and herself: "I started my own Barbie doll collection!"

> One intern took advantage of the discount at the company store to start her own Barbie collection.

Many interns have had opportunities to travel. One intern went on a three-day 'brainstorming retreat' with the creative and marketing staff to a resort in Palos Verdes, where "people brought their kids and we tried to think up new toy ideas—it was a ton of fun." Another intern got a trip to New York to scout out a major annual toy fair at Madison Square Garden.

Other special events at Mattel include an intern picnic at the end of the summer, where interns meet and mingle with their bosses and company executives. That is, if they haven't *met* already: one intern "ran into [the Chairman and CEO of Mattel] in the elevator a lot—we used to chat." This top-down friendliness manifests itself in the company culture, which the intern coordinator calls "one of fun—there are toys everywhere, a constant reminder of childhood, and why we're here." Adds one intern: "I love working here—there are huge pictures of Barbie all over the walls, and people are happy."

The professional staff is praised as "always willing to help and take time out to explain things." One intern developed a close mentor relationship with her boss, who was "very supportive—he would talk to me not just about what I was doing at Mattel, but about the future." Another intern said, "I really enjoyed the people—they made it a great atmosphere to work in." Other interns mention being "treated like part of the team, not just an intern" as high points of their experience.

Mattel takes good care of its interns. In addition to a robust salary (as much as $900/week for graduate students), Mattel offers interns close supervision on projects, two detailed evaluations of their work, and a good shot at a permanent job offer. The company also makes a strong commitment to its interns: one intern in Marketing, for example, got to attend a special summer business program at Harvard when Mattel agreed to sponsor her and pay her airfare, fees, *and* salary for the two weeks she was away.

SELECTION

Mattel internships are open to undergraduate and graduate students. There are both paid and academic credit internships available. Mattel is looking for people who are career-oriented, motivated, hard-working, and interested in a permanent career in the toy industry. "We don't want to waste their time or ours," says the intern coordinator. "We want people who will do this type of work when they graduate." Mattel selects its interns carefully, then makes a definite commitment to them: The company focuses on helping interns get the most out of their work experience, and tries to offer most interns permanent positions after graduation. International applicants are eligible. To research Mattel, check out the company's web site at www.mattel.com.

APPLICATION PROCEDURE

 Applications are accepted until March 31. Applicants must submit a resume and cover letter. In early spring, individual departments at Mattel choose the strongest candidates from the pool of applicants; interviews are held in person at the center. Although Mattel tends to draw heavily from the Los Angeles area, especially at UCLA, interns are selected from all over the country.

OVERVIEW

 Mattel's internship program attracts "a very high volume of applicants" for a reason— everyone in the toy industry, and most people outside of it, know Mattel as America's most successful toy manufacturer, the one that made Barbie the best-selling toy of all time. Add that stellar reputation to a "warm and fuzzy" atmosphere, first-rate business training, and a genuine commitment to interns, and you get a internship program that's anything but child's play.

FOR MORE INFORMATION . . .

■ Mattel, Inc.
Corp. Staffing—Internship
333 Continental Blvd.
El Segundo, CA 90245
(310) 252-2000

Merrill Lynch

SELECTIVITY	🔍 🔍 🔍 🔍
Approximate applicant pool: 300	
Interns accepted: 15	

COMPENSATION	💲
None	

QUALITY OF LIFE	🌴 🌴 🌴 🌴
Weekly speaker-luncheons; trips to financial institutions; intern parties, picnics, and trips to sporting events	

LOCATION(S)

Oak Brook, IL, and other offices nationwide

FIELD

Banking; Investment management

DURATION

12 weeks
Summer

PRE-REQS

College seniors in business and related majors
Minimum GPA: 3.3

DEADLINE(S)

March 1

In 1990, Ronald Miller, recently retired from his job of 35 years as an airline mechanic, found himself buried in a mountain of debt. He owed over $1,000 to the mortuary that had taken care of his wife's funeral arrangements. He still had $12,000 left to pay on a home equity loan, which he had taken out to finance his son's college education. He had no monthly income save Social Security. And his IRA contained just over $8,000 in municipal bonds.

So he turned to a professional, financial consultant named Joe Turner. Mr. Turner refinanced the home equity loan, taking advantage of a floating rate that started at three percent below what the former mechanic was now paying, with a cap equal to Mr. Miller's current fixed rate. In addition, Mr. Turner set up a trust that turned over the remaining equity in the home to an insurance company, which then paid Mr. Miller $832 per month for the rest of his life. He also invested Mr. Miller's IRA in a mutual fund that emphasized growth and income.

Within a year, Mr. Miller's finances were on firm ground. Not only was he able to fend off his creditors but his retirement was secure.

Score one for Joe Turner and for his firm, Merrill Lynch.

Helping people like Mr. Miller finance such needs as retirement, a new home purchase, or a child's college education is nothing new to Merrill Lynch, the world's largest provider of retail brokerage services. But servicing individuals is only part of its story. Merrill Lynch is also one of the world's most respected invest-ment banks, advising companies and government institutions on how to raise equity and debt, hedge currency risk, or acquire a competitor, for example. It's no wonder the company ranks number one worldwide in not only lead underwriting of new debt and equity (taking public such companies as Snapple and Boston Chicken) but also total assets held in private clients' accounts (over $500 billion).

BUSYWORK
MEDIUM
LOW HIGH
OLDMAN & HAMADEH
METER

DESCRIPTION

Many of Merrill Lynch's U.S. offices offer internships to undergraduates, although most that do so offer them informally. The company's most structured program can be found at the Oak Brook, IL office. There, interns work as financial consultants in the Finance Department, where they learn stock research techniques, prospecting, selling, and portfolio management. Explained the internship coordinator, "Financial consulting is like an iceberg. The general public just sees the 10 percent [above the surface]—the glamour and the money. Interns experience the 90 percent that's underwater."

At the beginning of the summer, interns are matched with a mentor, with whom they work for the entire summer. Some mentors work with their assigned interns to create a list of goals to fulfill by the end of the summer, covering such topics as "financial planning, managing a portfolio, and how to succeed as a broker." In general, interns learn as they go along, by attending client meetings, following stocks, and performing any tasks that the mentor assigns. A typical day, according to interns, consists of "first talking to a mentor for a half hour. He'll answer any and all questions. Then the mentor will familiarize you with the clients that the two of you will meet later that day."

One intern worked on generating more client business for Merrill Lynch. Besides researching different markets with the in-house computer system, called PRISM, which provides up-to-date financial news, he joined his mentor in discussions with prospective clients. He said: "I enjoyed working with customers on an individual level. I saw how the decisions made by us, the financial consultants, affect them." His work culminated in writing and distributing to all of his customers a letter describing the Mortgage 100 Plan, a program that provides people with investment choices concerning home mortgages.

> At the end of the "Investment Challenge" competition, the winning intern receives a crystal statue.

Praised for its flexibility, Merrill Lynch's internship program is tailored to the specific interests of each intern. One intern commented on her experience, "I'm interested into going into publishing after graduation, so my mentor let me work on the financial writing for the brochures. Furthermore, whenever anyone needed help writing, editing, or revising, they would come to me."

Like full-time financial consultants, Merrill Lynch interns enjoy a substantial degree of responsibility, reading and analyzing personal finance reports, talking to clients, and following stocks. "I got to talk to [my mentor's] biggest clients," said one intern. "Not only did I gain valuable decision-making and people skills but I realized that I represented the firm." The fact that "[interns] are trusted and allowed to do challenging work" inspires them to look favorably even upon the required one week they must spend in the mail room. Regardless, as one intern put it, "[working in the mail room] teaches you a vital part of the business."

Merrill Lynch employees are reportedly "laid-back" and "friendly." Interns and employees alike can be found playing basketball together at lunch or spending a slow afternoon golfing with clients. "After all," joked one intern, "half of our business is done on the greens." Some days, however, the atmosphere in the office can be barometrically related to the rising and falling of the markets: "You can feel the tension when it's a bad day in the stock market."

Located in a quiet, tree-lined suburb of Chicago, the Oak Brook office is decorated "rather austerely," with off-white walls, industrial carpeting, and stainless steel file cabinets. While most interns are assigned partitioned spaces on the main floor, a few get their own offices. Reasonably priced, "better than average" food can be had at the Merrill Lynch cafeteria, although interns report that it is "more fun" to grab a bite at the sprawling mall across the street.

Perks are a strong point with Merrill Lynch's internship. "The mentors can't pay us anything, so they show their appreciation with Sox and Cubs tickets, or gift certificates," one intern said. Participating in occasional field trips, interns visit the Chicago Board of Options and the Chicago Board of Trade, where they see first hand how the markets operate. Moreover, interns are often invited to breakfast meetings with mutual-fund portfolio managers. At these breakfasts, "[y]ou learn a lot about where the economy is going on a global scale. You can see what's going on in Mexico, for example, before it's in the papers. You see how your job impacts the news."

Interns also participate in the "Investment Challenge," in which they build their own stock portfolio. "Given" $200,000, interns compete in a simulation to earn the highest profit. Following the zeal of money-hungry Alex P. Keaton and the teachings of legendary economist John Keynes, they pore over daily figures to find the best investments. At the end of the competition, the winning intern—a recent one, for example, turned her $200,000 into $230,000—receives a crystal statue. Said one intern: "It was electric, seeing the value of your portfolio constantly rising and falling."

SELECTION

 The internship program at Merrill Lynch's Oak Brook office is open to college seniors of any major, provided that they have a demonstrated interest or relevant coursework in finance and business. Opportunities for younger students are occasionally available in other Merrill Lynch offices. Applicants must have a minimum GPA of 3.3. Adds the internship coordinator, "We are looking for people with exceptional communication and research skills." Past interns advise that applicants should be "outgoing," "patient," and "dedicated." International applicants are eligible. To research Merrill Lynch, check out the company's web site at www.ml.com.

APPLICATION PROCEDURE

 The deadline to submit a resume and cover letter is March 1. Prospective interns are typically interviewed in person, although some branches allow telephone interviews for long-distance candidates. Students interested in internship opportunities outside of Chicago should contact the Merrill Lynch office nearest them for an address and phone list and then contact the office of interest directly; there are approximately 420 Merrill Lynch offices nationwide.

OVERVIEW

 Unlike Ivan Boesky, Michael Milken, and other high-profile, high-risk investors, the financial consultants at Merrill Lynch don't gamble on the well-being of their clients. Instead, Merrill Lynch has an enduring tradition of earning fair returns on clients' assets. The firm's internship program can be said to offer a similarly favorable payoff, as interns not only complete meaningful projects and the unique "Investment Challenge," but also benefit from the fact that over 40 percent of interns are offered permanent employment upon graduation.

FOR MORE INFORMATION . . .

■ Internship Coordinator
Merrill Lynch
Commerce Plaza
2001 Spring Rd.
Oak Brook, IL 60523
(630) 954-6325
or contact nearest Merrill Lynch office
www.ml.com

When Egypt resolved to build its high dam at Aswan in 1960, it was faced with a troubling situation. Its celebrated Temple at Dendur, built in 15 B.C. and located in the path of the future dam, would be buried underwater forever. The solution: Find the huge limestone monument a new home. In 1965, the Egyptian government sent the temple to America, stone by painstaking stone. Where did it go? New York's Metropolitan Museum of Art, which houses the largest collection of Egyptian works outside of Cairo, was the logical recipient.

The Met—its abbreviated sobriquet—is the largest and most diverse museum in the Western Hemisphere, containing two million pieces that cover nearly 5,000 years of history. Unlike the majority of the world's museums, which tend to limit their scope to particular styles and periods, the Met satisfies the tastes of everyone, from the aficionado of Impressionist paintings to the pop-culture junkie. Among the Rembrandts, Sumerian stone sculptures, and classical Greek statues, one could find a 1694 Stradivarius violin, a 1973 electric guitar, a 1910 Honus Wagner baseball card reputed to be worth $500,000, and even the pointy-coned corset worn by Madonna during her "Blond Ambition" tour.

DESCRIPTION

In 1973, the Metropolitan Museum of Art first offered summer positions to college students. More than twenty years later, the museum's internship program is still going strong. The ten-week summer internship places graduate students and undergraduates in Administration, Conservation, Library, Development, Communicating, Merchandising, Human Resources and Education, and 19 curatorial departments including the Arts of Africa, Oceania, and the Americas; American Art; Ancient Near Eastern Art; Arms and Armor; Asian Art; the Costume Institute; European Paintings; Greek and Roman Art; Islamic Art; Musical Instruments; Photographs; Prints and Illustrated Art; and Twentieth Century Art. In 1986, the Met's Medieval Arts branch—The Cloisters—decided to offer a formal internship program as well. Every summer, eight students participate

SELECTIVITY	🔍 🔍 🔍 🔍 🔍
Approximate applicant pool: 400 undergrad, 120 grad, Interns accepted: 30 undergrad, 20 grad; varies	

COMPENSATION	$ $
$2,250 for Cloisters undergrads; $2,500 for Met undergrads; $2,750 for grad students	

QUALITY OF LIFE	🕴 🕴 🕴
Monday field trips; Exploratory environment	

LOCATION(S)	
New York, NY	

FIELD	
Art museum	

DURATION	
10 weeks Summer	

PRE-REQS	
College juniors or seniors; grad students; recent grads; See Application Procedure	

DEADLINE(S)	
Application deadlines start mid-January. Contact office for exact date.	

in the branch's nine-week internship in European art of the Middle Ages.

The Met internship program begins with a two-week orientation that introduces the interns to collections and staff members and teaches interns how a world-class museum operates. "It was a wonderful overview," said an intern. "Each curator or assistant curator would give a one-hour gallery talk, explaining the collection and its history while referring to specific pieces." In between curatorial department tours, interns visit the museum's Design department, Legal department, and reproduction studio (where reproductions are prepared for sale). They also meet with Met Director Philippe de Montebello. "We discussed the possible direction the museum will take in the future," said one intern. Graduate students attend the first week of the orientation and afterward begin work in their assigned departments, where they spend the entire summer doing research on specific collections or exhibits, working in conservation, or learning the business side of museum operations.

Where is the _Mona Lisa_? You had better catch the next plane to Paris.

The whirlwind orientation prepares undergraduate interns for the Visitor Information Center. Staffing the desk two half days a week, the Met undergraduates answer visitors' questions that sometimes are not about art at all. "One day we amused ourselves by trying to figure out the most frequently posed question. Unfortunately, it turned out to be 'Where is the bathroom?'" But people ask art-related questions as well, from the very specific ("How much did Mr. Annenberg pay for van Gogh's _Wheat Field with Cypresses_?") to the ingenuous. "We had people ask us to direct them to the _Mona Lisa_ [actually found in the Musée du Louvre, Paris] and the dinosaurs [on display at the American Museum of Natural History, New York]. Boy, were they disappointed."

Near the Information Center is the Tour Board, the starting point of the Met's one-hour highlights and thematic tours, led by the interns. Back in the 1970s, the Met was considerably smaller and more conducive to a tour that started at one end of the museum and ended at the other. "Today, it's impossible," said an intern. Indeed, the Met's two-million-piece collection sits on 1.5 million square feet of floor space. Interns have only enough time to discuss a dozen or so specific works. "But you're given leeway to devise your own tour and choose the pieces that you feel best exemplify the entire collection."

Met interns also spend two full days each week in their respective departments. An intern in Ancient Near Eastern Art helped in the preparation of a 200-object exhibit entitled "The Royal City of Susa: Ancient Near Eastern Treasures in the Louvre." "Sometimes I watched the exhibit being built, occasionally offering my opinion as to the placement of objects. But mostly, I proofread galleys [i.e., drafts] of the exhibit brochure and assigned object numbers to photographs of the pieces, partly to catalog the exhibit and also to prepare pictures to sell out of our gift shop. I also touched up a drawing of a statue; I did a pretty good job and it ended up being published in the brochure."

Over the summer, interns visit all 19 curatorial departments, including The Cloisters. What about The Cloisters, which resembles a 12th-century monastery? It got its name from the sections of four medieval "cloisters"—covered walkways enclosing courtyards and leading to monastic buildings—that are part of the modern architecture of the museum, opened in 1938. Named Cuxa, St.-Guilhem, Bonnefont, and Trie, the four cloisters provide, according to a Cloisters brochure, an "inviting . . . place for rest and contemplation"—the same purpose they served during medieval times. Located several miles north of the Met at Fort Tryon Park, The Cloisters is famous for its Unicorn Tapestries, stained-glass windows, an herb garden containing more than 250 species of medieval plants, and the oldest known complete set of playing cards (circa 1475).

Cloisters interns spend even more time training than their Met counterparts—three weeks. Meeting with curators at the Met and with New York art experts (dealers, curators, etc.), the interns focus on acquiring knowledge of medieval times. They might visit a stained glass workshop downtown and learn how stained glass is made and restored; they might listen to a lecture on reliquaries, containers in which sacred relics, sometimes skulls, are stored; and they meet with Met Director Phillipe de Montebello to hear about museum management.

The three-week orientation readies Cloisters interns for their next task—conducting five weeks of daily tours for groups of young campers, 4 to 12 years old. Limited to two general medieval themes, each intern chooses a few objects to talk about. "My year, the tour topic was 'walls'; I had the kids sit under one of the museum's arches and build a small arch out of wooden blocks. It was a great demonstration of how medieval people created arches without cement."

But there's more to the Met and Cloisters internships than giving tours or helping out in departments. On Mondays, the Met and the Cloisters are closed to the public, so undergraduates at both locations spend the day visiting art institutions and attending lectures. Met interns have perused the Studio Museum in Harlem, observed how works of art are priced for auction at Sotheby's, and visited a private artist's studio to observe art in the making. Cloisters interns listen to William Voelkle (curator of western manuscripts at New York's J. Pierpont Morgan Library) speak on the history of Morgan's manuscript collection, travel to Glencairn Museum (the former mansion of a couple who collected medieval art) outside of Philadelphia, and meet with medieval art dealer Michael Ward, who "allowed us to touch objects without gloves and . . . even let us put a sixth- or seventh-century Byzantine ring on our fingers."

On top of all this, Cloisters and Met undergraduates research art-history topics of interest, which they eventually convert into public tours. Some interns really get into their research. One intern who prepared a talk on Images of Power in African Art said, "I contrasted court art from the Kingdom of Benin to the Minkisi figures popular among 19th-century Congo peoples—royal art symbolic of power versus popular art believed to be powerful."

Whereas Met interns give these tours from mid-summer until the end of the internship, Cloisters interns present their work once (during the last week) to a group of visitors, the staff, and The Cloisters director. Advertised in a flyer that reads "Gallery Talks by College Interns," the talks embrace a variety of medieval subjects. One intern, for example, demonstrated the art of medieval dye making. "I used plants and flowers from the herb garden, mashing chamomile, woad, and madder to make ancient dyes as described in medieval and modern books. I even boiled and crushed hundreds of tiny cochineal insects to make a special red dye. Then I applied the dyes to unspun wool to create a rainbow of colors."

The Met is sometimes described as conservative, probably due to what one intern explains as "the drive to obtain funding from wealthy, conservative donors." The museum is also occasionally labeled as bureaucratic—not hard to believe given its size. "There are thousands of people [2,000 full-time staff and 950 volunteers, to be exact] working on a variety of collections; it's like a small university with many departments, so you might have to go to several places to get the historical information you need."

SELECTION

 The Met internship for graduate students requires at least one year of graduate work in art history or a similar field (e.g., education). The Met internship for undergraduates is open to juniors, seniors, and recent graduates who have yet to attend graduate school. A strong background in art history (eight to twelve courses) is preferred. The Cloisters internship, on the other hand, is open to all undergraduates, but preference is given to freshmen and sophomores. "Applicants to our program must work well with kids," said The Cloisters' coordinator. "They also need to have an affinity for art, even if they have yet to take an art course." In both programs, the coordinators emphasize the importance of "well-thought-out, creative" essays and strong letters of recommendation. In the case of The Cloisters, a glowing letter of recommendation will give even a science student a fair shot at being admitted. International applicants are eligible.

APPLICATION PROCEDURE

 Deadlines are early in the year; they start in mid-January for the Met's undergraduate program. Call the office for exact dates. All candidates must submit two academic recommendations and official college transcripts. Each Met applicant must also send a resume, a separate list of foreign language ability and art-history courses completed, and an essay of no more than 500 words indicating career goals, interest in museum work, and reasons for applying to the internship program. Each Cloisters applicant must also send a page indicating field of interest, academic major, year in class, special honors, and work experience (volunteer or paid) and submit a 500-word essay indicating reasons for applying to the internship program. Except for graduate students, all finalists are required to visit New York (at their own expense) for interviews in March. "Because undergraduate interns must give gallery talks, we want to make sure that they can articulate about art well," explained The Cloisters coordinator.

OVERVIEW

 There's a rich history behind every work at New York's Metropolitan Museum of Art, even behind the museum's logo—it's called the "Leonardo (da Vinci) M." But scholars dispute its origins. Is it from Leonardo, whose style resembles that of the *M* or from Luca Pacioli, a well-known mathematician and Leonardo's contemporary and close friend, in whose book a woodcut version of the *M* appears? No one knows for sure.

This is just a sampling of the type of art history issues in store for students who intern at the internationally prestigious museum. But the Met's well-structured internship programs expose students to more than history. Interns also learn many facets of museum work—documenting objects, setting up exhibits, meeting art dealers, and interacting with the public.

FOR MORE INFORMATION . . .

■ The Metropolitan Museum of Art
1000 Fifth Avenue
New York, NY 10028-0198
Attn: Education Dept., Internship Program
(212) 570-3710
mma-ed@interport.net
www.metmuseum.org

■ The Cloisters
College Internship Program
Fort Tryon Park
New York, NY 10040
(212) 650-2280
www.metmuseum.org

Microsoft ®

Microsoft hasn't had an easy ride lately. The federal anti-trust wrangle went on forever. The incredibly popular Palm personal organizers don't use Microsoft software. Apple's iMac is a one of the best-selling personal computers ever. Alternatives to Windows, from Linux to web browser-allocated software, are cropping up all over. Jini and Java languages also threaten the dominance of Windows.

But these are mere bugs in a computer world that still all but belongs to Microsoft. If you don't know how to use Windows, if you've never regretted *not* buying stock in Bill Gates multi-billion dollar machine, you're nearly alone. It may rain nine months out of the year in Washington State, but the sun never sets on Gates' Seattle-based empire. And if you love computers and lots of hard work, you too might be able to get a piece of the action.

DESCRIPTION

A few Microsoft internships are available at its branches in Bellevue, Washington; Charlotte, North Carolina; and Las Colinas, Texas; and involve working with end-user, enterprise, and developer customers (including *Fortune* 1000 companies). Those who prefer to intern in California should consider the small number of positions available at a variety of Microsoft offices in Cupertino, where Microsoft's Graphics Products Unit develops programs like PowerPoint and OfficeArt; in the Palo Alto complex, where Microsoft operates WebTV (combined Internet and television service); in San Jose, where the Applications and Internet Client Group makes applications for the Macintosh and Internet development tools

(Mac versions of Microsoft Internet Explorer, for example); and in Sunnyvale, the headquarters for Microsoft-owned HotMail. Microsoft now has a comprehensive web site for internship applicants, www.microsoft.com/college/, which provides the latest information on internships available at various Microsoft locations.

SELECTIVITY

Approximate applicant pool: 30,000–40,000+
Interns accepted: 600+ undergrads, 25 MBAs

COMPENSATION

$3050–$3800 per month based on position and year in school; round-trip travel; subsidized rental car or free mountain bike; heavily subsidized housing with biweekly cleaning service

QUALITY OF LIFE

Beautiful Redmond campus; great gym; flexible hours; casual dress; discounts on office software; free classes; seminars; dinner at Bill Gates' house

LOCATION(S)

Cupertino, CA; Palo Alto, CA; San Jose, CA; Sunnyvale, CA; Charlotte, NC; Las Colinas, TX; Redmond, WA (headquarters); Bellevue, WA

FIELD

Computer software

DURATION

12–16 weeks
Summer
Occasionally Fall and Spring

PRE-REQS

College sophomores, juniors, and seniors; MBAs for Finance and Marketing Departments only computer background for most positions

DEADLINE(S)

Rolling

BUSYWORK
MEDIUM
LOW HIGH
OLDMAN & HAMADEH
METER

The Microsoft internship program, like the company's ubiquitous software, is structured to ensure that every intern has the backup necessary to handle extraordinary amounts of responsibility. Interns are welcomed at a day-long orientation, loaded with advice at a company career fair, and regularly invited to luncheon seminars with executives and top-level managers, where they learn about company goals and industry players. Mentors work with managers (senior, and often more distant, employees) to supervise interns on a day-to-day basis. Mentors tend to be workers Microsoft is grooming for management positions who, according to the intern coordinator, have had mandatory "mentor training" to learn "how to give on-the-job feedback as well as give interns their formal performance reviews." Mentors and managers have varying degrees of interaction with interns, but all provide necessary training, dole out assignments, and sign off on evaluations.

Interns are encouraged to take free classes that teach them skills such as different computer languages, how to build software, and the like, as long as the coursework fits in with the intern's work schedule. Despite this structured support system, "there's no hand-holding, no four-week training program for anything really," says a former intern. "You are told what is expected of you, and it's up to you to get it done." Some interns found this approach simply didn't prepare them for their heavy duties, while others relished their independence.

Although mentors and managers review interns' work and check products before they are shipped, Microsoft interns find that they are expected to make hefty contributions to MS software. Interns in the Program Development department often have design-heavy work, writing codes and creating features for the latest software or updates of classics. Some PD interns report developing real code used in the upcoming version of Microsoft Office; another wrote the specifica-

tions for Windows. Program Management allows its interns to do everything from research on competitors to strategy and design. "I was writing the specifications for an add-in for Excel," says one former intern in Program Management. "I was advising the other program managers as to what features we could put into Excel 2000. I mean, me, as a 19-year old having such big control over this thing is just unprecedented—I doubt that Ford interns can directly influence the design of the next Mustang in such a big way."

A number of interns in Product Testing did not find their responsibilities quite as invigorating. Some report being "hideously bored" trying to ferret bugs out of a product, and "deeply stressed" about getting them all out by the shipping date. Others, however, found that "the hours flew by," they learned a lot about each product, and they had to "think like the designers and the users at once, a creative challenge." Most interns in the Finance and Marketing departments are MBA students who, with a total of twenty-five members, form a very small part of the overall internship pool. Interns can change their duties if they don't feel challenged, and can ask for additional responsibilities if they want to test their abilities in an area to which they weren't originally assigned. As one intern remarked, "not once during my whole time there was there 'well, you're just an intern.' . . . The responsibility really charged my experience." There's another parallel to the experience of regular employees: Interns must undergo a casual review mid-way through their internship, and a "corporate-stiff" written evaluation at the close of their stint at Microsoft.

The compensation for Microsoft interns is justifiably legendary. All interns are provided with either free round-trip travel to Microsoft by air, or compensation for expenses incurred by a car trip (including gas, food, and lodging). Even better, Microsoft pays up to $500 for interns to ship their personal necessities to and from the internship location. Microsoft heavily subsidizes fully

> As far as amenities go, Microsoft is the closest one can get to on-the-job nirvana.

furnished apartments convenient to the campus, or in downtown Seattle, where each intern gets a private bedroom and a free biweekly cleaning service. Although interns' apartments are just a short walk away from the campus, to ensure that they don't feel stranded in Seattle's suburbs interns can choose between a free mountain bike or paying for just one third of the monthly cost of an Avis rental car. Some interns opt to share a car, often with roommates (other interns chosen by the company), to cover the entire rental expense.

Interns are paid "about 75 percent of an entry-level salary at Microsoft," says one intern, which means anywhere from $3,050 to $3,800 per month, depending on the intern's department and year in school. There's loot, too. Interns can take home top-notch software at bargain-basement prices (one reports getting Developer Studio for 80 percent off the retail price). The company tries to assuage the fears of anxious parents by reimbursing interns up to $250 per month throughout their internship to cover the cost of health insurance premiums. And this doesn't include interns' free membership to a local health and fitness club, which at the Redmond campus is the sleek PRO Club, an immense facility that includes, according to one intern, "basketball, tennis, and racquetball courts, Jacuzzis, dozens of StairMasters, and even free shampoo in the shower."

The creature comforts at Microsoft's Redmond campus truly make it a home-away-from-home, a necessity considering the long hours interns and employees spend at the complex. The twenty close-knit buildings that make up Microsoft headquarters are appropriately referred to as a campus by everyone, including residents of the surrounding bedroom community. No need for a corporate wardrobe at Microsoft; interns and employees alike can blend in by wearing sandals and T-shirts. Many cubicles and meeting areas are decorated with everything from the usual family photos to Nerf toys, Star Wars posters, and all kinds of interesting accessories.

When meal times come around, take-out is common, although interns report there are a number of decent, cheap eateries in the vicinity sustained in large part by the appetites of Microsoft workers. Every department has at least one kitchen, equipped with free beverages and snacks ("We drank oceans of soda at Bill Gates' ex-

pense," says one intern) for late night work sessions. Lots of people work late and everything from mass take-out to "ice cream and beer for everyone" is provided to sustain interns and employees alike. "Friday Wind-Downs" help everyone do just that through outdoor barbecues and soccer or volleyball games.

One perk mentioned frequently and praised highly by many Microsoft interns is the ability to choose their own work hours. The company believes that night owls and early birds are happiest when laboring on their natural schedules, and is eager to accommodate them. Some arrive at the office at the crack of dawn and leave just after lunch; others arrive when the normal workday ends and don't leave until the wee hours of the morning. As many as a quarter of all interns work in their own offices, while the rest work with one other intern in a shared office. As long as interns fulfill their responsibilities to their assigned teams of five to seven company employees, they can come and go as they please.

Interns located in Washington State can make a mass pilgrimage to meet the man himself, Bill Gates, and munch on catered food in the backyard of his $40 million+ home. If you're willing to wade through "interns who stood around [Gates] in a circle about five to six interns deep," you might even be able to have a word with Gates personally. Bill even gives a speech to his young fans, though it's "usually kind of a lame speech," according to a veteran of two Microsoft internships.

A myriad of entertainment opportunities keep interns from feeling suffocated by their workload: the intern handbook, mail alias for each intern, and newsletter and relocation guide to Redmond help interns have fun in the suburbs of a city that seldom sees the sun except for the few summer months. Some interns turned the Microsoft complex into their very own entertainment center by using the conference rooms as their own late-night theaters, with the help of tapes from the local video store, well-stocked office kitchens, and understanding security guards. The plethora of video games available in every building serve as stress-busters and keep interns happy at the office. Anyone looking for a party need only turn to the "Intern Public Folder," an intern-led newsgroup that organizes trips, parties, and the like. The company actively encourages interns to take advantage of the "spectacular" campus and surrounding area: webs of trails, sports fields, a museum (covering computer as well as company history), the company store, and, just twenty minutes away, all the pleasures of downtown Seattle.

Not all is rosy at Microsoft. Expectations are high and the competition is intense. In the words of one intern: "It is rather fiercely sink-or-swim. . . . If you can't learn very quickly on your own, you won't do well at Microsoft." The hours are very long, with some former interns reporting that they spent late nights and weekends chained to their desks. Although full-timers reportedly encourage interns to keep regular weekday hours, a number of interns find that project requirements and their perfectionist tendencies demanded fifty- to sixty-hour weeks. Complaints about the quality of computers available to interns were voiced by several former participants, but many found that fast machines were plentiful. Socialization with other employees varies widely, with some interns feeling isolated by their reclusive colleagues. On the whole, most interns feel that the majority of employees take an interest in their young co-workers and make an effort to maintain a welcoming office environment. All told, while Microsoft's internship program (like those of other companies) has a few bugs in it, they seem to be few and far between.

SELECTION

 Only undergrads in their sophomore, junior, or senior year are allowed to intern. Those interested in Microsoft's small internship program for MBA students should follow the same application procedure as other interns, and must be aware that they may only intern in the Financial and Marketing Departments. Applicants can have any major, from liberal arts to computer science, as long as they know about the latest computer software, have a record of hard work, and are adept at facing analytical challenges.

APPLICATION PROCEDURE

 Microsoft sends recruiters to more than 140 schools, interviews about 1,900 students on-campus, and provides an application procedure for students (including international students) whose colleges are not visited by the company. While there are technically no set deadlines, applicants for the summer program whose schools are not visited by Microsoft are encouraged to send in their applications prior to winter vacation. Every applicant's resume must have the code CN05i-0101 printed at the top, and should be accompanied by three items: a short statement declaring position and location desired (or a list of positions and locations, in order of preference); a written description of all academic and extra-curricular experiences (including what you learned in each activity and what you contributed); and all computer-related experience (platforms, protocols, and computer languages listed in descending order of proficiency accompanied by years of experience for each).

A Microsoft recruiter will interview by phone only the strongest applicants from colleges not visited by the company. Approximately seven hundred finalists will be flown on the company's dime to Redmond for an interview. According to an applicant who aced the interview, "they didn't just want me to flesh out my resume, like panels at other companies, they threw problems at me. Not just "What if?" questions about potential software, but the sort of math class word problems you either love or hate. I tried to solve them aloud, instead of sitting silently trying to come up with something in my head. Someone told me later that that's what they wanted, to literally hear how I approach problems and analyze material and come to an answer." The application processes for scholarships offered for women and members of minority groups are available on the web at www.microsoft.com/college/.

OVERVIEW

 Doing highly stressful computer stuff 50+ hours per week for three months straight in a Pacific Northwest suburb might not sound like an appealing way to spend your summer vacation. But for the lucky few chosen for Microsoft's internship program, it is a priceless experience. Most bring home strong software development experience, the friendship of some of the brightest computer scientists in the world, memories of meeting not just their peers but Bill Gates himself, and a wad of cash. If you are a workaholic and love computers, Microsoft might just reward you with one of the cushiest internships in the country.

FOR MORE INFORMATION . . .

■ Attn: Recruiting
Microsoft Corporation
One Microsoft Way, Suite 303
Redmond, WA 98052-8303
(425) 882-8080
www.microsoft.com/college
resume@microsoft.com

MUSIC TELEVISION®

The date: August 1, 1981. The time: 12:01 A.M. The video: "Video Killed the Radio Star," by the Buggles.

A characteristically iconoclastic beginning for a cable-television network whose groundbreaking impact cannot be overestimated. Over the years, MTV's ongoing tapestry of music videos has not only defined how the young consume music, but how they talk, dress, and watch television. MTV's willingness to experiment continues to stretch the possibilities of television, giving us shows like Yo! MTV Raps, which has helped bring rap music to the mainstream, and The Real World, which has satisfied voyeurs by capturing the unrehearsed activities of seven housemates. Despite those who blame MTV for corrupting the American mind, the network has attracted more than 60 million subscribers and has even gained the respect of President Clinton, who participated in its "Choose or Lose" forum as a presidential candidate.

SELECTIVITY	🔍 🔍
Approximate applicant pool: 400–600 Interns accepted: 150	

COMPENSATION	$
None	

QUALITY OF LIFE	🌴 🌴 🌴
Speaker luncheons; casual dress in some departments; possible promotional freebies	

LOCATION(S)
New York, NY; Los Angeles, CA; Orlando, FL; Miami, FL; Atlanta, GA; Detroit, MI; Chicago, IL

FIELD
Television; Music

DURATION
10–13 weeks Summer, Fall, and Spring At least 2 days/week

PRE-REQS
High school students; undergrads; grad students Must receive academic credit

DEADLINE(S)
Rolling

DESCRIPTION

MTV has been accepting interns since it hit the airwaves in the early eighties. But up until a few years ago, the internship program wasn't much of a "program"—it was disorganized, decentralized, and inconsistent from department to department. Things haven't gotten a whole lot better, but efforts have been made to improve it with the addition of a full-time intern coordinator, speaker luncheons, and a field trip. Depending on departmental need and intern preference, interns may be placed in a "business" department such as Marketing, Press and Public Relations, Programming, International Programming, and Advertising; a "creative" department such as Art Promotions, Talents Relations, Graphics, On-Air Talent, and Video Library; or a particular MTV program such as *MTV News, Beavis and Butthead,* or *MTV Jams.* Positions are also available at divisions outside of MTV: Music Television, including Nickelodeon, Nick at Nite, and VH-1.

Although responsibilities vary from department to department, a few tasks are common to all. Said one intern: "Working the phones, making photocopies, sending faxes, making more photocopies, running messages, making even more photocopies—these are common denominators for every intern." In addition, few interns leave MTV without becoming an expert in dubbing tapes: "Every day, I was asked to dub

BUSYWORK METER
LOW MEDIUM HIGH
OLDMAN & HAMADEH

beta tapes to 3/4" tapes. It's a simple—and totally boring—job."

Besides enduring "mega amounts" of busywork, interns have assignments unique to their department. Working for *Yo! MTV Raps*, one intern solicited audience members for the show's live performances. "Before a band like Lords of the Underground or M.C. Lyte played live in the studio, I'd round up an audience by calling contacts at other departments. I'd also invite my friends." Another intern, this one in Talent Relations, organized and prepared videos for the weekly "acquisition meeting," where department heads pick which videos will be played on MTV. To her delight, she was invited to observe one of the acquisition meetings: "The meeting was pretty informal. A bunch of executives and department heads watch about 30 videos and make comments about which ones should be shown on the channel. If a video is too violent or sexually explicit, or if it's just not good enough for MTV, the group rejects it."

One of the most popular departments among interns is MTV News. Interns here start the day clipping newspaper articles for the "MTV Daily Digest," a packet of newspaper articles distributed to MTV producers and writers. "Sifting through newspapers isn't exactly a thrill a minute. And photocopying forty sets of articles can be maddening," said one intern. "But [the 'Daily Digest'] is really important as it's often a source of story ideas for the newswriters." News interns also do a lot of "logging tapes," which requires them to watch a particular segment and mark down the time code at various points in the action. For some it's sheer busywork, but for others "it's the rare opportunity to see raw outtakes—stuff that's never aired, like pieces of an interview with Madonna on her 'Blond Ambition Tour.'"

MTV has never been known for offering interns a comprehensive array of extracurriculars—at least not on an official basis. To be sure, recent years have seen a few speaker luncheons, featuring bigwigs like the CEO of Viacom (MTV's parent company), the CEO of MTV, and the MTV creative director. Administrators say there is the "possibility" of a field trip to the Network Operations Center on Long Island—"it's where our signal is sent to the satellite, where MTV technically becomes a TV network."

But the golden opportunities are those that are unsanctioned. Interns might catch the occasional impromptu performance, which some groups are fond of staging when they visit the MTV offices. "It was pretty cool," said one intern. "I'd be dubbing some tapes and find out that the Wildflowers or Blind Melon was downstairs doing an acoustic jam. Needless to say, I bolted down there in a hurry." When they find the time, interns sometimes steal away to the MTV studio on 42nd Street and watch veejays film their segments. Said one intern: "I'd watch the action from the control room or the sound stage. Everything is a lot smaller than it looks on TV." Interns who make the right friends might accompany a producer on a shoot. "I went with the crew to Webster Hall, where I watched [MTV News anchor] Kurt Loder interview Mick Jagger about his new solo album . . . I got to shake Mick's hand . . . [a]nd I stood by as a photographer from *The New York Times* did a photo shoot of Mick playing the harmonica."

As the previous examples suggest, being at MTV offers a smorgasbord of star-scoping. MTV veejays and news anchors are easy game: "You'd see regulars like Kurt Loder, Kennedy, and Daisy Fuentes pretty often—it was no big deal." Appearances by other MTV personalities are less frequent but no less memorable: "Cindy Crawford came in once a month to host *House of Style*, and I declare—she is twice as beautiful in person." But nothing compares to the bevy of artists who visit the offices. Said one intern: "MTV is a magnet for the hottest acts. They'll come by to say hi to executives or discuss a project with producers. One day Aerosmith walked by me in the hall. A week later I shared an elevator with the B-52's." Explain-

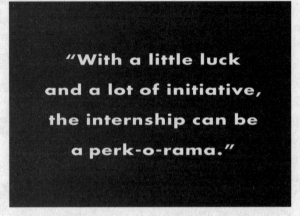

"With a little luck and a lot of initiative, the internship can be a perk-o-rama."

ing the proper celebrity-watching etiquette, another intern advised: "You can't act starstruck—you've got to be cool and contain your bliss."

It's not hard to believe the intern who said that "with a little luck and a lot of initiative, the internship can be a perk-o-rama." Promotional CDs, concert tickets, and party invitations adorn the desk of virtually every high-level employee, and interns who work hard may be rewarded with a few of these spoils. Said one intern: "I got to see some great concerts during my time at MTV—[such as] Keith Richards at the Paramount and Pete Townsend at the Beacon." Added another, "My boss let me have his invitation to a Rick James listening party. It was a funky affair—to get inside, you had to rub a purple butterfly tattoo on your arm." There's also a variety of MTV paraphernalia to be had—if one is "at the right place at the right time." "I picked up an MTV coffee mug, tote bag, and watch," said one intern. "But I was lucky—I became friends with the right people."

Smack dab in the center of New York's honky-tonk Times Square district, MTV commandeers seven floors of a 53-floor skyscraper. The offices are decked out in "Art Deco fashion—sleek, black, and kind of 80s." The decor is suitably funky, with a reception desk "built into a huge rock," a fish tank in the shape of an *M*, and "black rubber floors." Interns are spread out throughout the offices, some with their own desks, others making do with an empty desk or conference table. A few departments devote a common office to interns; MTV News, for example, has an "intern room" described as "small, cramped, windowless, and messy." But what MTV lacks in workspace it makes up for in casualness. It's acceptable for interns to wear jeans, and those in creative departments are given even more sartorial license: "The more you dress like a rock star, the more you fit in."

A few interns are also placed in MTV sales and production offices in Los Angeles, Orlando, Miami, Atlanta, Detroit, and Chicago.

SELECTION

 The internship is open to undergraduates of any level and graduate students; a few exceptionally qualified high school students are also accepted. Applicants must arrange to receive academic credit for the internship. The intern coordinator says that selection is based on an applicant's "previous experience, academic record, proven responsibility, eagerness, and willingness to learn." Past interns advise applicants to "emphasize the personal qualities that make you stand out from the rest of the pack." International applicants are eligible.

APPLICATION PROCEDURE

 Although the application deadline is rolling, applicants are encouraged to apply two to three months prior to the program's start date. Required materials include a cover letter, resume, and written verification of academic credit. The coordinator conducts a mandatory personal interview with the most promising candidates. At the time of the interview, applicants are asked to fill out an application form.

OVERVIEW

 How many internships can boast a write-up in *Seventeen*? The article "I Was an Intern at MTV" appeared in a recent issue of the magazine and described the experiences of a former intern: "I learned more about television [at MTV] than I could have in any course or from any book." A worthy point, but one in need of elaboration. The MTV internship *can* be a terrific learning experience, but perhaps more so than any other program, interns must have the gumption to ensure they don't stagnate in busywork purgatory. Said one intern: "Those who aren't afraid to ask for better assignments can shape their time at MTV into something great."

FOR MORE INFORMATION . . .

■ MTV Networks Internship Program
Human Resources
1515 Broadway, 22nd Floor
New York, NY 11036
(212) 258-8000

SELECTIVITY	N/A
Approximate applicant pool: N/A Interns accepted: est. 1,000	

COMPENSATION	$ $ $
$150–$450/week for undergrads $400–$700/week for grad students	

QUALITY OF LIFE	N/A
N/A	

LOCATION(S)	
Alabama, California, Florida, Maryland, Mississippi, Ohio, Texas, Virgina	

FIELD	
Aerospace and aeronautics	

DURATION	
6 weeks–4 months Summer	

PRE-REQS	
Varies with program—see Selection	

DEADLINE(S)	
Varies with program—see Application Procedure	

What do you need to become a NASA astronaut?

An ability to identify all 88 constellations, the strength to bench-press 250 pounds, and a promise to abstain from any sexual activity for two years.

Just kidding.

In truth, to qualify for NASA's Astronaut Candidate Program, you just need to be between 58.5 and 76 inches in height, pass a thorough physical examination, hold a bachelor's degree in science or engineering, and have at least three years of related work experience.

But don't assume that joining NASA's elite is an easy task—since 1959, only 293 individuals have been selected to become astronauts from over 35,000 applicants. In that time, NASA has done much to advance America's mission "to plan, direct, and conduct aeronautical and space activities." Despite its share of setbacks, NASA has landed Americans on the moon, mapped the surfaces of every planet in the solar system except Pluto, and implemented the world's first reusable system of space shuttles. With an eye toward the 21st century, NASA is making progress on a permanently manned space station, a lunar colony, and a manned Mars expedition.

DESCRIPTION

 There are at least 200 different NASA programs, ranging from high school summer jobs to undergraduate and graduate internships to graduate fellowships. The multitude of programs allows students to work at NASA's 10 facilities (listed below), and within its dozens of university research labs. The federal agency responsible for all of America's aeronautical and space programs, NASA has much to offer students who are interested in airplane design

and outer space technology. Areas of research include robotics, earth sciences (biology, geology, environmental science, etc.), aerodynamics, biomedicine and biotechnology, materials processing, space propulsion, space structures, and satellite communications.

Most NASA programs are specific to each center. The Goddard site (infamous for helping to develop the Hubble space telescope, whose lenses were warped), for example, offers a Summer Institute on Atmospheric and Hydrospheric Sciences, where interns spend the first two weeks of the summer learning about available research projects from Goddard scientists. Afterward, one intern studied atmospheric gravity waves. "They're one of many kinds of gravity waves, all of which induce density and temperature fluctuations in the atmosphere," he explained. "It's important that we understand gravity waves completely because they adversely affect space travel, satellite communications, and radio transmissions."

Because Johnson Space Center designs the manned spacecrafts, acts as "mission control" for all piloted space-flights, and trains astronauts, it's a favorite place among interns. A graduate student intern in the Biotechnology group worked to create an "automated bioreactor" (i.e., a vat used to grow cells) that is able to function in space. "The main problem on Earth," he explained, "is that gravity creates a high shear stress environment for the cells. On Earth, these cells end up against the sides or bottom [of the vat], where they can't grow or differentiate very easily, but in space, they're free-floating." That low shear-stress environment, he explained, will allow scientists to grow whole corneas for use in eye transplants or to generate breast cancer tumors for testing anticancer drugs.

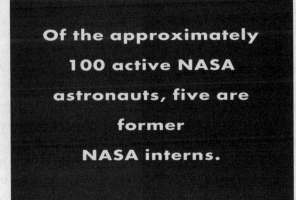

Of the approximately 100 active NASA astronauts, five are former NASA interns.

Another intern at Johnson, this one an undergraduate, worked in the Anthropometrics and Biomechanics Laboratory, where he helped redesign a shuttle treadmill that astronauts use in space to keep their bodies active. "Because there's zero gravity in space," he explained, "we attach the astronauts to the treadmill with bungee cords." But the lab figured that if the tension on the cords was made adjustable, astronauts could simulate their exact body weight. Videotaping several of the astronauts while they ran the treadmill, he helped his lab group create an adjustable model. "It was definitely exciting to work with the astronauts," he concluded. "I learned a lot from them about how the body reacts in space."

Some NASA programs are handled by universities but are open to students nationwide. Managed by Florida A&M University, the Kennedy Space Center's Space Life Sciences Training program (SLST), for example, provides undergraduates with a six-week education in space life sciences. Rotating among departments, SLST interns study how to grow crops in space, how to keep bacteria out of the shuttle's water supply, and how to break down human wastes in space. "For a future space station, lunar colony, or manned mission to Mars (an estimated three years round-trip), we'd need to recycle everything from water to food to fecal matter," explained one intern. But because such research requires that experiments be run in space, where oxygen is nonexistent and gravity's effects are not felt, interns help prepare the experiments for astronauts to perform during shuttle missions. One intern was assigned to a team that worked with sea urchin gametes (i.e., sperm and eggs). "[NASA] wanted to know how zero gravity affects embryonic development," he said, "and our job was to come up with the specifics of the tests. We created customized plastic bags to hold the gametes, determined how the astronauts were to do the experiments, and ran vibration tests to discover what percentage [of gametes] could survive a launch." Because Kennedy is situated on a 140,000-acre wildlife refuge, SLST interns also monitor endangered species, like the indigo snake, to see what impact shuttle launchings have on the animals that inhabit the center's grounds. "What made this program so great overall is that you got to see how engineering and biology come together," concluded one intern. Other Kennedy student programs allow interns to work on the logistics of space shuttle launches and landings, to participate in research to solve operational problems, and to help design shuttle parts in the engineering development labs.

At NASA's Langley Research Center, one of the most popular internships is the Langley Aerospace Research Summer Scholars Program (LARSS), established in 1986. Lasting ten weeks, LARSS chooses 80 to 100 college juniors and seniors as well as first-year grad students to conduct research in engineering, material science, computers, atmospheric science, physics, and chemistry.

NASA also has a contract with the Jet Propulsion Laboratory (JPL), located in Pasadena, CA. JPL designs and explores the solar system with robotic spacecrafts, like *Cassini* and *Galileo* as well as the ill-fated *Mars Pathfinder*. As part of JPL's Summer Employment Program, interns work in business administration and assist with experiments, designs, and tests.

Most NASA locations offer seminars and field trips in addition to social activities. The Space Life Sciences Training Program at Kennedy, for example, has students attend lectures every morning on such topics as "exobiology" (i.e., the search for extraterrestrial life) and the future Mars mission. At Ames, students can log-on to their Email to find a schedule of the week's lectures, from talks on algorithm theory to Cray computers. At other centers, interns may attend speeches on space medicine, fluid-flow analysis, and the effect of cosmic dust on space structures, engines, and suits. Probably one of the most compelling discussions is on the KC-135, a NASA jet flown out of Johnson to simulate zero gravity. Called the "vomit comet" in NASA circles for its ability to nauseate up to 90 percent of its passengers, the plane alternately shoots up toward the heavens and then nosedives, giving a 20-second period of near weightlessness in which NASA may test experiments. But the highlight of any intern's summer is meeting the astronauts, who occasionally stop by the centers to recall the fascinating details of their former missions. "I think that after hearing [astronaut Charles Bolden], we all wanted to become astronauts ourselves," said an intern at Glenn.

Away from their workstations, interns certainly see some "cool stuff." Interns at Ames, for example, may tour the center's 80-by-120-foot wind tunnel, the largest of its kind. At JPL one summer, interns took a trip to Goldstone, approximately three hours northeast of Pasadena by car, to see NASA's 70-meter spacecraft-tracking antenna. "When [the antenna] wasn't transmitting," recalled one intern, "we climbed into the dish and roamed around its smooth vastness." Interns at Johnson may see a mock-up of the astronauts' sleeping quarters on the space station. "Because there's zero gravity [in space], they can sleep upright, downright, or whichever way," said one intern. "[At the mock-up], the beds were against the walls . . . and so the astronauts don't bounce around while they sleep, they Velcro themselves to the bed." At Kennedy, interns tour Space Port USA, a building housing old rockets, astronaut uniforms, and a memorial for the *Challenger* crew. Kennedy interns also see Kennedy's Vehicle Assembly Building (VAB), used to put together rockets and shuttles. "Because [VAB is] hundreds of feet tall," explained an intern, "sometimes rain clouds form in there." What would a summer be without seeing a shuttle launching or landing? At Kennedy, the mother of all shuttle launching sites, interns have an opportunity to see shuttles shoot up into the sky. When it comes to landings, however, the shuttle can touch down at Kennedy or at Edwards Air Force Base, near JPL. "We got up really early and boarded a bus to the base," remembered a JPL intern. "We sat on some bleachers and waited and waited. We weren't too close to the landing strip, but we saw [the shuttle] come in. The whole scene was inspiring—even better than on TV."

With often up to 300 interns at any one center, planned social activities are a real unifying factor. At JPL, interns can join JPL's hiking, fishing, and sailing clubs, among others. Goddard occasionally holds evening receptions for interns—casual gatherings at which hors d'oeuvres, fruits, and vegetables are served. For the fitness-minded, most NASA facilities house fitness centers offering aerobics, StairMasters, stationary bikes, and free weights. In addition, NASA sites often contain volleyball courts, running tracks, and softball diamonds.

Financial compensation for interns varies considerably. Some NASA summer internships for undergrads pay as little as $1,000 for a ten-week period, while other undergraduate summer internships compensate students with as much as $4,000. Graduate students in summer internships earn from $1,600 to over $4,000 a month. Pay depends on major, class level, and experience. Some interns are also provided with travel stipends and free housing.

SELECTION

Each NASA program has its own set of criteria. The Space Life Sciences Training Program, for example, is for only undergraduates (at least sophomore level) studying life sciences, premedicine, bioengineering, or related fields. But NASA has an internship for virtually everyone, from high school students at least 16 years of age to college undergraduates to graduate students (including those studying medicine, business, or law) to faculty members. In general, U.S. citizenship is a requirement; and most programs require a minimum 3.0 GPA. Fields applicable include almost every area of science, mathematics, and engineering. For liberal arts students, there are few internships at the field centers; the largest is a nationwide cooperative-education program in NASA's budgeting, accounting, and procurement departments. Any major is eligible for this program, but business experience is preferred. International applicants are eligible.

APPLICATION PROCEDURE

 NASA deadlines vary, from as early as December 31 for some summer undergraduate programs at the field offices to April 1 for some fellowships. NASA maintains internship program descriptions, eligibility, application access, and points-of-contact information via their main website: www.nasa.gov. Click on "Jobs and Internships" then "Job Information." There are also links to each NASA center. You can explore a number of other source links including *Educational Resources*, *NASA Student Programs*, and *Fellowships/Grants Programs*. There's a bountiful buffet of tasty internship and summer employment opportunities for high school students, undergraduates, grad students, and faculty.

OVERVIEW

 In the words of NASA's head of staffing policy, an experience at NASA is "a chance to work with cutting-edge technology and leading scientific experts." That's right on the mark. Students at NASA can design space shuttle parts, study airplane wings, write computer programs for satellites, investigate the environmental impact of space programs, and research robotics and lasers. Since its creation by Congress in 1958, NASA has hired interns to make a substantial impact in aeronautics and space-related science and technology. Former interns who went on to become NASA employees are currently helping to design a space station, have helped construct *Galileo*, and have even flown in some of America's historic space missions. Of the approximately 135 active NASA astronauts, according to Johnson's Astronaut Selection Office, 8 are former NASA interns.

FOR MORE INFORMATION . . .

NASA internships available at the following sites. See www.nasa.gov for current info and details.

- NASA Ames Research Center
  Moffett Field, CA 94035

- NASA Goddard Space Flight Center
  Greenbelt, MD 20771

- Jet Propulsion Laboratory
  Pasadena, CA 91109-8099

- NASA Johnson Space Center
  Houston, TX 77058

- NASA Kennedy Space Center
  KSC, FL 32899

- NASA Langley Research Center
  Hampton, VA 23681-0001

- NASA Glenn Research Center at Lewis Field
  Cleveland, OH 44135

- NASA Marshall Space Flight Center
  MSFC, AL 35812

- NASA Stennis Space Center
  Mail Code: MAOO
  SSC, MS 39529

- Oryden Flight Research Center
  Edwards, CA 93523-0273

National Audubon Society

SELECTIVITY	🔍 🔍 🔍 🔍
Approximate applicant pool: 50–100 Interns accepted: 6 (Summer), 1–3 (Fall, Winter)	

COMPENSATION	💲
N/A	

QUALITY OF LIFE	🏃 🏃 🏃
Lobbying on Capitol Hill (Washington, D.C.); Intern Alley; "Free and easy" atmosphere; summer softball league	

LOCATION(S)
Washington, D.C., and other cities (see Description)

FIELD
Environmental policy

DURATION
12 weeks (Summer) 12–20 weeks (Fall, Winter)

PRE-REQS
College juniors and seniors; recent grads; grad students

DEADLINE(S)
Rolling

At a recent rally in Washington, D.C., a young man in a wolf costume performed a rap before a crowd of nearly 100 people. With a boom box busting the beat, he declared: "For 50 years he's been under attack. Now it's time to bring the wolf back."

Was this a wannabe musician, a wolf lover, or an intern with the National Audubon Society? Actually, it was all of the above. As a representative of the Audubon Society, he staged the performance to encourage the U.S. Fish and Wildlife Service to place the endangered gray wolf in Yellowstone National Park.

Fighting for the rights of endangered species is only part of the National Audubon Society's mission. Founded in 1886 as an organization to protect the lives of birds, Audubon now also defends wetlands, water sources, and ancient forests. Managing more than 100 sanctuaries nationwide, the society works to restore natural ecosystems "for the benefit of humanity and the Earth's biological diversity." With 516 chapters and more than 600,000 members, the nonprofit National Audubon Society has made a significant impact, helping to establish parks, halt the building of environmentally damaging infrastructures, and create various refuges and preserves.

DESCRIPTION

In the early 1980s, Audubon established an internship program in environmental policy. The Government Affairs Internship Program exposes students to environmental policymaking, grassroots organizing, and lobbying in one of the following departments: Forests, Wetlands, Population, International Fisheries, National Wildlife Refuges, and Agricultural Policy.

Like most internships, Audubon's Government Affairs Internship Program requires interns to do some busywork. In addition to performing clerical tasks, interns respond to the dozens of letters that flow into Audubon's offices every day. "Most were from [Audubon] members or kids asking for information on what they could do [to help out]," explained one intern. "We'd mail them some Audubon pamphlets, which describe the various issues." Interns also update Audubon's various computer databases. Tracking Audubon's staunch supporters of national wildlife refuges, one intern input activists' addresses and phone numbers. "These were people Audubon could count on to go above and beyond the call of duty—get on the phones, write letters, and the like."

There's ample busywork for interns to do outside the office as well. Either alone or as a pack, interns occasionally make "Hill drops," distributing Audubon literature to representatives' and senators' offices. "[Hill drops are] an important part of what we do," explained one intern. "We're here to influence Congress, and one way to do that is by getting materials into the right hands."

When they're not shuffling papers and gofering, interns draft fact sheets and reports that affect congressional legislation. One intern assembled a fact sheet on the California Desert Protection Act. "It was a one-page summary of California's current efforts, dating back to 1976, to create the Mojave National Park," he said. "I described the legislative history, the congressmen and senators who introduced the bill, and what the bill was intended to accomplish." Distributed to members of Congress and other interested parties, fact sheets are used by environmental groups to teach legislators and the public about environmental issues. Another intern wrote a report describing the effect the Endangered Species Act has had on industry. Phoning timber, oil, and chemical companies, he asked senior biologists and public relations officers for examples that showed how their companies had complied with the act. "In one case, a business had set aside a substantial plot of land for endangered animals." The report would come in handy, he explained, because the act is up for reauthorization in 1994. "[The report] showed that business development and protection of endangered animals aren't necessarily mutually exclusive."

Occasionally, interns who gain the confidence of their supervisors are rewarded with "exposure to the front line," where they participate in lobbying efforts. The most effective form of lobbying, according to an Audubon lobbyist, is the grassroots kind, where congressional constituents call and write congress to suggest to their senators and representatives how to vote. On behalf of grassroots campaigns, interns spend a few hours each week on the phone with Audubon members, asking them to contact their congresspeople (by phone or letter) and express their opinions on important environmental legis-

> **Part of an office culture that's "free and easy," interns frequently wear jeans and are even known to traipse around the office barefoot.**

lation. Like Audubon members, interns also write and phone congressional offices. One intern drafted a letter concerning the closing of a military base in Virginia. "I sent the letter to two senators asking them to support converting the base's land to a wildlife refuge."

Interns undoubtedly make the most substantial contributions by lobbying in person. Having secured appointments with legislative assistants (LAs), interns head for the Hill. One intern attempted to convince an LA of the benefits of reauthorizing the Endangered Species Act. "His rep was completely against it for various reasons," he said. "So trying to convince that LA was like talking to a brick wall." Other lobbying efforts are more successful. "I worked very carefully with [Senator] Feinstein's staff . . . [Feinstein] was sponsoring the California Desert Protection Act," said one intern. "Because she and her staff wanted the bill to pass, my role was easy. I provided them with pamphlets and lobbied other senators to support the bill." In rare cases, interns will actually have the opportunity to meet with a senator or representative: "I was talking to the LA, when suddenly the representative came in and asked what we were doing. So I explained the bill's focus on creating a national wildlife refuge system. Surprisingly, he agreed within a few minutes to cosponsor it."

To keep Audubon abreast of the latest developments concerning environmental legislation, interns attend congressional and agency hearings, seminars, and briefings. Taking notes for his supervisor, who was unable to attend, one intern went to a White House briefing on President Clinton's forest plan. Led by executives from the Departments of Agriculture and the Interior, this meeting featured Clinton's commission of scientists who were working to establish a logging plan acceptable to both timbermen and environmentalists. "Most hearings are extremely educational," explained the intern, "because you learn how lawmakers create bills."

Approximately thirty people are employed by Audubon's D.C. office, located in northwest Washington,

D.C., three blocks from the White House. Occupying the top floor of an 11-story building, Audubon has ready access to restaurants, cafes, and a coffee shop. The office is decorated with framed stills of Audubon-sponsored TV specials, featuring spokespersons like Meryl Streep and Robert Redford. Occupying two rows of cubicles in an area known as "intern alley," interns have their own phones and computers. Part of an office culture that's described by a current Audubon lobbyist as "free and easy," interns frequently wear jeans and are even known to traipse around the office barefoot.

Involved in wildlife management as well as environmental policy, Audubon also runs camps and sanctuaries, some of which offer internship programs. These programs allow students to become natural history instructors or student assistants at Audubon camps in CT, ME, and WY. Students may also do field research and give public tours at Audubon's centers in Milwaukee, WI and Sante Fe, NM or at its sanctuaries in Elgin, AZ; Trabuco Canyon, CA; Sharon, CT; Naples, FL; Frankfort, KY; Monson, ME; Garrison and Ithaca, NY; and Harleyville, SC. Interns have the opportunity to do everything from build displays to lead nature walks to collect field data. Positions are generally available year-round.

SELECTION

 Audubon seeks college juniors, seniors, recent graduates, and graduate students. Any major is eligible; no environmental experience whatsoever is necessary, although an interest in the environment is appreciated. Students must possess good verbal and written communication skills. International applicants are eligible.

APPLICATION PROCEDURE

 The deadlines for the Government Affairs Internship Program are rolling. Students must submit a cover letter indicating an environmental issue of interest and a writing sample of fewer than five pages on any subject. After the coordinator screens applications, they're passed along to department managers, who interview top candidates over the phone. Students interested in the wildlife management internship programs should contact the Audubon headquarters office in New York (Attn: Human Resource Department, 700 Broadway, New York,

NY 10003; (212) 979-3000) and request material on positions at Audubon camps, centers, and sanctuaries.

OVERVIEW

 If disappearing habitats and endangered species trouble you and you want to do something about it, then the National Audubon Society's Government Affairs internship is for you. Open to undergraduates, recent graduates, and graduate students—even those with no environmental experience—Audubon's program is an excellent education in resource conservation and wildlife management. Afforded an inside look at how Congress makes laws, interns become versed in the ways of Capitol Hill and the politics of environmentalism—a movement critical to the preservation of the planet.

FOR MORE INFORMATION . . .

■ National Audubon Society
1901 Pennsylvania Avenue, NW
Suite 1100
Washington, DC 20006
(202) 861-2242
www.audubon.org

SELECTIVITY	🔍🔍🔍🔍
Approximate applicant pool: 1,000 + Interns accepted: 30	

COMPENSATION	$ $
$350/week stipend	

QUALITY OF LIFE	🌴🌴🌴
Lunches with NBA execs; attend WNBA games; travel opportunities; basketball mania; tours of NBC studios, Madison Square Garden	

LOCATION(S)
New York, NY; Secaucus, NJ

FIELD
Sports management, TV Production

DURATION
12 weeks Summer

PRE-REQS
See selection

DEADLINE(S)
Summer .... December 15

Who would have imagined that two wooden peach baskets nailed to a gymnasium balcony in 1891 would beget the game that is currently the most played sport in the United States?

Not James Naismith, the Springfield, Massachusetts, divinity professor who asked his school's custodian to put up the baskets. He just wanted to give his pupils something to do indoors during those cold New England winters.

But without Naismith, we wouldn't have basketball or the National Basketball Association (NBA), America's professional basketball league. And without the NBA, we wouldn't have Kareem Abdul-Jabbar's goggles, Pat Riley's slicked-back hair, Michael Jordan's wagging tongue, or Vince Carter's amazing slam-dunks. From Dr. J and the Big Dipper to Air and Magic, NBA players have established the NBA as the world's preeminent basketball league. Nowhere was its dominance in international basketball more recognizable than at the 1992 Barcelona Olympics, where the Dream Team defeated opponents by an average of 43 points per game to win the Gold Medal.

DESCRIPTION

At the time that the NBA was founded in 1946 as the Basketball Association of America, it had only eleven teams. Today, the organization has grown to include twenty-nine teams and worldwide retail sales of NBA-licensed merchandise have reached $2 billion annually, a testament to the NBA's drawing power. In 1982, with its workload burgeoning, the NBA employed one intern in Public Relations, but the next two interns didn't appear until 1984 and 1986. The NBA's internship program was off to a slow start, similar to the evolving history of the NBA itself, which saw so many teams come and go in its first five years that the future of

professional basketball seemed in jeopardy. But in 1999, the NBA organized the current internship program, which assigns about 30 students every summer to NBA Entertainment in Secaucus, NJ, and the following New York departments: Global Merchandising, Marketing Partnerships, Team Operations, WNBA, Human Resources, Finance, Internet Services, E-Commerce, Events and Attractions, and Communications Group.

Busywork is par for the course with sports internships, and the NBA's is no exception—it's a full-court press of unglamorous tasks. In

Broadcasting, interns set up the department's multitide of VCRs, attached to over 15 televisions, to record NBA-related programs such as ESPN's *Sports Center* and during the season, "every single game played on TNT, MSG, TBS, and NBC." NBA Entertainment interns, placed in either the video or photo departments, retrieve videotape footage or photographs of games and players from the department's libraries. Video interns watch programs and commercials come to life in the editing rooms as employees match the selected shots with appropriate music off compact discs. Photo interns assist maga-zines who call in with re-quests for photographs. "When *Sports Illustrated* did the cover story on Reggie Lewis [the late Boston Celtic], I found nearly thirty slides for the magazine to use," explained an intern.

As part of the depart-ment's effort to keep track of the manufacturers that are licensed to use the NBA name, Global Merchandising interns "open all the mail and set aside product sketches and prototypes for review by the department." They also create licensing guideline manuals to assist with licensee requests.

Interns in Team Operations help conduct marketing surveys. "We send each team a 250-page survey asking for information on their PR and Marketing departments, game schedules . . . even how they pick their cheerleaders," said one intern. "I'd get on the phone and make sure the surveys were being completed and sent back to us in a timely manner."

NBA interns (two or three) are placed in the Public Relations department. A big part of their job is "the circ," the daily distribution of articles from major newspapers in NBA-affiliated cities. Interns scan the papers and cut out articles on NBA players, sponsor companies, on teams, and on the other major sports leagues, such as the NFL, NHL, and Major League Baseball. "Every article gets filed," explained an intern, "but only the most important articles are included in the circ, which gets sent to top management." PR interns also assemble press kits and speak with fans on the phone. "Fans asked various questions—who's the shortest player? . . . the tallest player? Others wanted game sched-ules or player files," recalled one intern. The PR department receives its fair share of fan requests, which keeps interns busy mailing stickers and researching trivia questions.

One would expect interns engaged in this much busywork to cry foul, but they are surprisingly accepting, realizing that it's a great way to bone up on the sport. "[Newspaper clipping is] tedious and your fingers get cov-ered in ink," said one intern, "but by reading the articles and talking to people as you deliver the copies, you learn the NBA—its teams and play-ers." Photo interns are equally satisfied: "I don't feel like it's gruntwork at all; I still learn the players, see exciting shots, and learn the various angles for taking pictures."

In exchange for their ef-forts, interns convene over several lunches with NBA executives, such as Chief Op-erating Officer and Presi-dent of NBAE Adam Silver, Deputy Commissioner Russ Granik, and even Commis-sioner David Stern, described by one intern as a "down-to-earth man who's interested in hearing what we have to say about the internship." Overall, interns find the talk at these lunches eye-opening: "Until you listen to these guys, you don't realize the extent to which basketball is a huge busi-ness."

Interns stationed in New Jersey not only participate in these lunches, but also enjoy an additional perk: During the summer, they assist veteran or retired NBA players who come in to create highlight tapes with one of the editors. Said one intern: "I found pictures for Rolando Blackman and Kurt Rambis . . . . It was exciting to help them."

Interns are likely to have other stimulating opportuni-ties. A Broadcasting intern "got to work a Knicks game with NBC out of [the network's] production truck." In Photos, an intern attended several shoots and learned how to use different kinds of cameras: "I took pictures of Ahmad Rashad and Toni Kukoc." A Team Operations intern did the layout and some editing for the NBA's marketing newslet-ter, *Team Talk*. While summer interns in Public Relations wrote "intensive" team previews and player profiles for the

> Lace up your high-tops, grab your wrist bands, and head for New York—it's a great time to intern at the NBA.

preseason, others helped track when and by whom the NBA's one-millionth point was scored: "We had two games going at once. Points were going back and forth, but finally we credited the Utah Jazz's Darrell Griffith with the honor."

Occasionally, interns have the Global Merchandising opportunity to attend out-of-town NBA events. Consumer Products interns, for example, sometimes attend a sporting-goods industry trade show—either February's Super Show in Atlanta or August's National Sporting Goods Association trade show in Chicago—to help set up display booths that show off NBA-licensed products. Interns in Team Operations often attend league-wide marketing meetings, held in March and September in locales such as Palm Springs, CA. Public Relations interns get the chance to help run various press conferences.

Mirroring the increasing popularity of NBA basketball, the number of NBA employees has grown. "We're a hot commodity right now," says an employee, "so we have a tremendous image to uphold. After all, we're trying to make basketball the world's number one sport, and we need as many people as possible behind the effort." This mission breeds an "intense working environment," especially around the time of major events such as the NBA Finals, All-Star Weekend, and McChamps Open, a bi-annual round-robin tournament featuring international teams. "The phones were ringing off the hook with reporters looking for press passes," recalled a Public Relations intern. "I took down requests, had the director of special events verify them, and then called the reporters back with his response."

The NBA's New York headquarters occupies six floors of the 21-story Olympic Towers, located on the corner of Fifth Avenue and 51st Street with second and third buildings in Secaucas, NJ. Decorating the walls are framed photographs of NBA players and displayed in the showroom are NBA-licensed products, from clothing to basketballs. At the end of the summer, the coordinator goes through the showroom to create the intern "going-away gift"—the contents of which are a surprise.

SELECTION

 The NBA seeks undergraduates who have diverse backgrounds and interests. Freshmen, sophomores, and juniors are accepted. The majority of the NBA's past interns have been sports management or TV production majors—the rest study communications, journalism, broadcasting, and marketing. In fact, according to the coordinator, any liberal arts major is eligible so long as he or she has "excellent communication skills" and is "enthusiastic about sports." International applicants are eligible.

APPLICATION PROCEDURE

 The deadline for applications is December 15 for the summer internship. Applicants should submit a resume and cover letter outlining their relevant background and indicating the department to which they're applying. Most candidates who are granted interviews are interviewed over the phone

OVERVIEW

 The NBA's popularity is at an all-time high. Attendance at games is soaring and more Americans are playing basketball than any other sport. So lace up your high-tops, grab your wrist bands, and head for New York—it's a great time to intern at the NBA. Unlike interning with a particular NBA team, working at the NBA exposes sports lovers to the entire roster of NBA teams and also to king-size events—the McChamps Open, the All-Star Weekend, and the NBA Finals. "Once you're on the inside," said one intern, "you can learn all the juice that fans are dying to know. And if you want to get into the sports business, this place teaches it all—licensing, sponsorship, community relations, management, and broadcasting."

FOR MORE INFORMATION . . .

■ National Basketball Association
Intern Coordinator
645 Fifth Avenue
New York, NY 10022
(212) 407-8412

National Institutes Of Health

In 1935, Congress appropriated $100,000 for what was then called the National Institute of Health for a farm to house research animals. The problem was, the NIH had no land. Then along came retired clothing manufacturer Luke Ingalls Wilson, who saved the day by offering half of his Bethesda estate to the U.S. government.

In the Bible, Bethesda is the name of an ancient pool where "whoever got in enjoyed healing, no matter what ailment he suffered" (John 5:4). Is it divine intervention or simply coincidence that the federal government's disease-fighting research center, the National Institutes of Health, is located in the city whose name is synonymous with healing?

Either way, the NIH has been instrumental in disease control. From its humble beginnings as a one-person, one-laboratory operation in 1887 to its current status as the world's largest biomedical research institution, the NIH has made numerous critical medical breakthroughs. It was the first to unravel the genetic code, to develop a vaccine against rubella, and to launch human gene therapy.

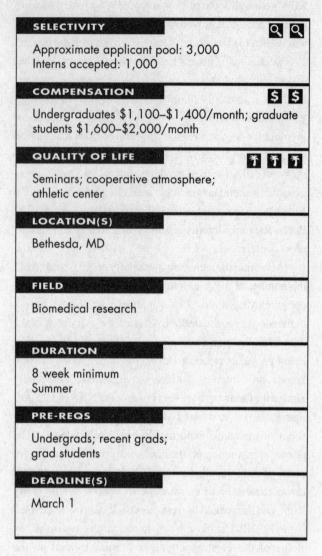

SELECTIVITY

Approximate applicant pool: 3,000
Interns accepted: 1,000

COMPENSATION

Undergraduates $1,100–$1,400/month; graduate students $1,600–$2,000/month

QUALITY OF LIFE

Seminars; cooperative atmosphere; athletic center

LOCATION(S)

Bethesda, MD

FIELD

Biomedical research

DURATION

8 week minimum
Summer

PRE-REQS

Undergrads; recent grads; grad students

DEADLINE(S)

March 1

DESCRIPTION

 Students have been doing summer internships at the NIH for more than 20 years, but in 1990 the NIH established the Office of Education to coordinate postdoctoral research and other educational programs, including a summer internship program. What resulted is a structured opportunity for students to pursue biomedical research in the area of their choice. Every summer over 800 students participate in one of more than 3,000 ongoing research projects within sixteen institutes, including National Cancer Institute (NCI); Office of Research Services (ORS); National Human Genome Research Institute (NHGRI); National Library of Medicine (NLM); National Institute on Aging (NIA); National Institute on Alcohol Abuse and Alcoholism (NIAAA); National Institute of Allergy and Infectious Diseases (NIAID); National Institute of Arthritis and Musculoskeletal and Skin Diseases (NIAMS); National Institute of Child Health and Human Development (NICHD); National Institute on Deafness and other Communication Disorders (NIDCD); National Institute of

Dental and Craniofacial Research (NIDCR); National Institute of Diabetes and Digestive and Kidney Diseases (NIDDK); National Eye Institute (NEI); National Heart, Lung, and Blood Institute (NHLBI); National Institute of Mental Health (NIMH); National Institute of Neurological Disorders and Stroke (NINDS); and The Warren Grant Magnuson Clinical Center (CC).

The breadth of interns' activities at the NIH is enormous. Interns may undertake such tasks as preparing animals for experiments, sequencing proteins, growing cells in incubator rooms, analyzing tissue samples with lasers, building springs for heart valves, or writing computer programs to analyze laboratory data.

At the National Institute of Neurological Disorders and Strokes (NINDS), an intern studied a central nervous system disease called kuru, for whose discovery NINDS scientist Dr. Carleton Gajdusek received the Nobel Prize in 1976. Living among a New Guinea tribe in the 1960s, Gajdusek learned that the disease was due to the slow work of a "latent" infectious protein that tribespeople were contracting from eating dead kinsmen's brains during funeral rites. As part of his research project, the intern took infected and healthy human and monkey brains, cut them up, and then washed them in detergent to break down the membranes. "I had to be careful because the brains . . . still harbored the [active] virus, which can infect you through an open cut . . . or if you get the sudden urge to eat a piece." Using electrophoresis, a lab technique that utilizes electric charges to separate biological materials, he extracted the part of the protein that causes the disease. "Considering that I had no experience doing this kind of research," he said, "it was cool that [the lab director] gave me that much responsibility."

An intern assigned to the National Heart, Lung, and Blood Institute investigated the mechanism of signal transduction—the process by which cells respond to hormones, neurotransmitters, and toxins. Her project focused on human interleukin-2 receptor, which activates the human immune response during infection. After introducing the human genes for a novel version of the receptor into mouse B-cells, she grew the cells in an incubation room. "As the cells grow, the genes create the new receptor, which eventually incorporates into the cell surface," she explained. Using certain lab techniques—"fluorescent antibody tags" and Western Blotting—she then searched cell surfaces for the altered receptors. Her work also included proofreading and revising the project's research paper, which was eventually published. "I feel that I made a significant contribution to an important research effort," she said. "When I apply to medical school, [this experience] will certainly give me an edge."

Like other institutes at the NIH, the National Cancer Institute (NCI) offers internships in its research specialities. But NCI is not a part of the Office of Education, so students interested in working at NCI should apply directly to its offices. An intern at NCI did research on a human protein called transforming growth factor-beta, abbreviated as TGF-Beta. "My mentor and I showed that TGF-Beta can stimulate as well as inhibit [calf heart] cell growth . . . [and that] some forms of TGF-Beta are more powerful than others at inhibiting growth." Because such an inhibitor could prove useful against cancer, in which malignant cells grow out of control, the intern embarked on a mission to "figure out the nuts and bolts of how [TGF-Beta] works." Using a microscope, a radioisotope counter, and a technique called polymerase chain reaction, she discovered that the way she conducted science at the NIH contrasted sharply with the "cookbook labwork" she completed at school.

But not all of NIH's research is about test tubes and incubation chambers, the Institutes also study patients first hand. At the National Institute of Mental Health

> **Well known for his appearances on *Nightline*, Dr. Fauci teaches interns the process by which HIV infection may eventually become full-blown AIDS.**

(NIMH), an intern worked on a "protocol"—the plan of a scientific experiment or treatment—to determine if penicillin can alleviate the symptoms associated with obsessive-compulsive disorder in children. In order to recruit patients, she placed ads in *The Washington Post* and screened potential patients over the phone. At doctor-patient interviews, she recorded patients' medical histories. "The patient interaction got me especially excited," she said. "Now I truly understand how research may be applied to help people."

All of these research projects are conducted in a setting that resembles a college campus with approximately fifty buildings scattered over 300 acres, and with thousands of faculty and postdoctoral fellows, it's not hard to see why. The NIH fosters a friendly, cooperative atmosphere—researchers often stop one another in the hallways to exchange research anecdotes. "In general, scientists are eager to teach people, including interns, about their research," said one intern. Available for interns' use are the NIH athletic center, NIH Library, National Library of Medicine, and four NIH cafeterias "set up like eateries in a mall, with lots of good, medium-priced food." Because parking is described as a "nightmare," most students elect to use the Metro, which stops directly on NIH grounds. Twenty minutes south by subway is downtown Washington, D.C. and only a few minutes west is Great Falls Park, a favorite destination among hikers, canoers, and rock climbers.

For most interns, the NIH experience is the first real research they have done, and they make mistakes any rookie would. To learn proper research techniques, each intern is assigned a mentor who oversees their experiments. "Whenever I mixed up the tubes or cooled when I should have heated, my mentor would say jokingly, 'You've just killed your parents.' I'd get embarrassed, but then he'd show me how to do it right." Mentors frequently alleviate interns' frustrations. "She'd tell me that when you get a different result than expected, it might not be wrong; instead, you may have stumbled on to something," one intern recalled.

Researchers are extremely busy at the NIH and often are reluctant to entrust students with much responsibility. As with most internships, interns must prove their worth. "You'd better read all the recent articles that your lab has published and ask lots of pertinent questions," advised an intern. Students would also do well to attend the weekly lab meetings. "You're certainly not needed, but your presence is appreciated," said one intern. "If you ask a question or two and occasionally put in your intelligent 50 cents, then all the better." If they arrive armed with knowledge and determination, students are often able to convince the head scientist to provide them with challenging work.

While laboratory research is a large part of the program, students don't have to stay holed up in their labs all day long. Interns may attend high-powered lectures on NIH research from studies of current cancer treatments to investigations of obscure genes in frogs. Interns can choose from about ten lectures daily. Interns are also encouraged to attend the Summer Seminar Series, which consists of weekly lectures at a level comprehensible to high school students and college undergraduates by senior NIH investigators. Past speakers have included Dr. Francis Collins, Director of the National Center of Human Genome Research, and obsessive-compulsive disorders expert Dr. Judith Rapoport, author of *The Boy Who Couldn't Stop Washing*. Probably the most well-received speaker has been Dr. Anthony Fauci, considered the country's premier AIDS researcher. Well known for his appearances on *Nightline*, Fauci teaches interns the process by which HIV infection may eventually become full-blown AIDS. In addition to these lectures, students may attend a multitude of workshops on such topics as how to prepare for medical school and how to win fellowships to become MD/PhD students. "It's like a 'what you wish your mother told you but never did' series," explains Dr. Michael Fordis, the director of the Office of Education.

At the end of the summer, students are encouraged to participate in the NIH's two-hour Poster Day, a science meeting featuring interns' work exhibited on 4' x 4' poster boards. While most interns are unable to make major research advances in only eight weeks' time, their contributions are nevertheless important and well received by the scientific community. Subjected to two hours of questioning, which probes the nature of their research, interns learn the shortcomings in their work. "Without Poster Day, I wouldn't have gotten a good grip on my issues," concluded an intern. "You gain confidence in explaining what you've learned to scientists."

SELECTION

 Eligible candidates include college under-graduates, recent graduates attending graduate school in the fall (550 interns) and graduate students (200 interns, which include 125 medical and dental school students). Acceptable majors include biology, biochemistry, chemistry, computer science, engineering, mathematics, psychology, and physics. Liberal arts majors with considerable coursework in one of the aforementioned disciplines are also eligible. According to Dr. Fordis, applicants should be motivated students with good grades and demonstrated academic promise. International applicants are eligible.

APPLICATION PROCEDURE

 The deadline is March 1. Interested students should apply for the NIH summer internship (undergrads and recent college grads) or the NIH Summer Fellowship Program catalog (medical and dental students) electronically at www.training.nih.gov. Students should check the website after mid-November for next summer's deadline.

OVERVIEW

 At the National Institutes of Health, interns contribute in the fight to cure the world's debilitating ailments. Working alongside influential scientists, NIH interns gain in-depth knowledge of an area of health while learning innovative laboratory techniques. When time permits, interns attend lectures by some of America's top researchers on AIDS, the Human Genome Project, and other timely topics. And at an end-of-summer Poster Day, they learn how to present scientific work. Whether interns stay in research or go on to medical school, an NIH experience is a valuable prelude.

FOR MORE INFORMATION . . .

■ Coordinator, NIH Summer Internship Program
Office of Education
(800) 445-8283
www.training.nih.gov

SELECTIVITY	
Approximate applicant pool: 200 Interns accepted: 20–30	

COMPENSATION	
$1,500 stipend if paid; Some internships are unpaid; academic credit possible	

QUALITY OF LIFE	
Creative environment; workshops and event lectures; sketchy neighborhood	

LOCATION(S)	
Washington, D.C	

FIELD	
Radio; Broadcast Journalism	

DURATION	
8–12 weeks Summer, Fall, Winter/Spring Full and part-time opportunities	

PRE-REQS	
College undergraduates; grad students; recent graduates (within 6 months)	

DEADLINE(S)	
Summer .... February 15 Fall...July 15 Winter/Spring .... November 15	

In this time of satellite dishes, virtual reality, and handheld whatchamacallits, the medium of radio is in danger of being cast aside as a quaint holdover from generations past. But National Public Radio (NPR) is still out to prove that radio can be an exciting, provocative, and unpredictable source of information. Crackling to life in 1971, NPR is a radio network dedicated to providing its over 19 million weekly listeners with lively news coverage and alternative cultural programming. Distributing its programs through over 600 member stations, NPR is famous for intellectually rich news-magazines like *All Things Considered* and *Morning Edition*, its talk shows like *Talk of the Nation*, as well as offbeat programs like *Car Talk*. It's home to a group of legendary radio personalities, including Linda Wertheimer and Robert Siegal, longtime hosts of *All Things Considered*, and Nina Totenberg, the legal correspondent who broke the Anita Hill story.

DESCRIPTION

 Interns work in nearly every department, show, and desk of the company. They are involved in everything from copyright law to jazz music, while exploring the world of public radio. Specific information about the different internships opportunities available may be viewed on NPR's website, www.npr.org.

Many interns report that they are actively involved in their departments since the first day. "I've been helping to do research and find archival tape for [*Morning Edition*'s 20th Anniversary]," commented one *Morning Edition* intern. "It's a lot of fun listening to the news of the past 20 years, [and when] the pieces go on the air, I hope to hear some of the tape I dug up from old reels!"

In addition to their duties within their departments, summer interns participate in a wide range of exciting activities. One popular event is the series of weekly brown bag discussions led by NPR employees from different areas of the company. Speakers for these informal presentations have included Jeffrey Dvorkin, Vice President of News and Information, and Murray Horwitz, Vice President of Cultural

Programming, each of whom spoke candidly and humorously about NPR and its listeners.

The NPR internship schedule includes practical education as well with workshops on topics ranging from radio production techniques to writing for radio. These workshops provide hands-on training and experience to interns, many of whom are unfamiliar with the technical aspects of radio and, specifically, NPR. Interns are taught by NPR producers, hosts, newscasters, and editors. Past presenters have included Art Silverman from *All Things Considered*, Alex Chadwick from *Radio Expeditions*, and Korva Coleman from the Newscast unit.

Interns also have the opportunity to visit a member station and the Newseum, a museum of news located in the Washington, D.C., area. "The tour of the member station was worthwhile because it gave us chance to see how NPR is viewed from an outside point of view, and why particular shows are picked [for programming]," observed a *Weekend Edition Saturday* intern. The schedule of events concludes in early August with a press tour of the Capitol.

The interns ultimately use their experiences to research, write, and produce their own radio show. "I think that the intern-produced radio program is an excellent idea," Nolan comments. "It is a great opportunity… to work on issues or stories that interest us." The final product is aired on NPR's Internet site.

The aim of the intern program is to provide students and recent graduates with the chance to be a part of an institution that many have been familiar with for years. One intern mentioned that he chose NPR because he has been a "News junkie [and] Science Friday fanatic" since childhood. Others wanted experience working in a dynamic and challenging business. "Everyone seems to take a large amount of pride in their work and to feel strongly about NPR," said a former intern. "It's a great environment to work in."

The atmosphere at NPR is uniquely casual and energetic. "There are so many cool people at NPR. You walk around the office and there's talk of new books, new films. The mood is progressive and artsy," said an intern. Some interns marvel at their bosses' creativity: "The producer I worked with was a genius—it was hard to follow the track of his mind," said another intern. "Watching the director [of *All Things Considered*] at work was like watching a maestro conduct his orchestra," said another. This creative environment touches all aspects of the job, even dress. For those wondering how to dress for success at NPR, it's time to mothball the Brooks Brothers suits and Laura Ashley dresses. NPR is about as casual as an (indoor) internship can get. "No one would blink if you wore cutoffs," said an intern, "And going barefoot is no big deal, either—one of the executive producers did it all the time."

> "Going barefoot is no big deal—one of the executive producers did it all the time."

NPR recently relocated to a building near Union Station. Interns report that the move is for the better in terms of space and for the worse with regard to location: "The building is triangular like [New York's] Flatiron Building and is a lot roomier than NPR's old headquarters. But the location isn't the best; it's a run-down neighborhood between Union Station and Chinatown." As in the old location, resources are limited, and interns should be prepared to make do with sharing computers and using the desks of vacationing reporters.

SELECTION

 NPR accepts applications from undergraduate and graduate students, as well as individuals who have graduated from college within six months of starting an internship. Individuals of all academic backgrounds are used. Requirements for specific internships are listed on the NPR web page.

APPLICATION PROCEDURE

 The application deadline for the summer internship is February 15; for the fall internship, July 15; and for the winter/spring internship, November 15. Send in a resume, cover letter, completed application form, and writing samples.

OVERVIEW

 An internship at NPR puts students at the heart of a radio network famous for innovative news and cultural programming. Offering hands-on projects, special intern events, and a singularly casual environment, the NPR internship is terrific exposure to the spirit of radio at its intellectual and inventive best.

FOR MORE INFORMATION . . .

■ National Public Radio
Human Resources Staffing Office
635 Massachusetts Avenue
Washington, DC 20001-3753
(202) 414-2909
Fax: (202) 414-3041
internship@npr.org
www.npr.org

SELECTIVITY	🔍 🔍 🔍 🔍 🔍
Approximate applicant pool: 300–400 Interns accepted: 7/session	

COMPENSATION	💲 💲
$275/week (includes health benefits)	

QUALITY OF LIFE	🌴 🌴 🌴
Lobbying on Capitol Hill; brown-bags; environmentally conscious office	

LOCATION(S)
Washington, D.C.

FIELD
Environmental policy

DURATION
24 weeks January to June; July to December

PRE-REQS
College grads of any age; grad students

DEADLINE(S)
January internship........ September 15 July internship............. March 15

Do you know who provides those dark and green recycling bins marked "newspapers," "bottles," and "cans" on your campus, or those special shower heads with trickling water, or your campus tree-planting projects? You probably think they're the work of local earth lovers, but chances are, those projects are sponsored by the National Wildlife Federation's Campus Outreach Program, which funded conservation projects at more than 150 colleges and universities nationwide during the 1992–93 school year.

Since its founding in 1936, the National Wildlife Federation (NWF) has been a powerful force in the protection of natural resources and wildlife. With 46 affiliates and more than one million members nationwide, NWF is the nation's largest not-for-profit, private conservation group. As an organization composed of hunters and conservationists alike, NWF has given its two cents on nearly every major environmentally related piece of congressional legislation, from the Federal Aid in Wildlife Restoration Act of 1937 to current bills proposed to strengthen and reauthorize the Endangered Species Act. Also in the business of conservation education, NWF publishes *National Wildlife* and *Ranger Rick*, which together reach more than one million readers annually. It also manages the Corporate Conservation Council, a cooperative effort between industry executives and environmental leaders to save the environment, and sponsors an annual Wildlife Week, a celebration founded in 1938 to promote nature issues.

DESCRIPTION

Since 1980, NWF has employed interns to work in its Fish and Wildlife Resources, Environmental Quality, and International departments.

By researching existing legislation, lobbying for new legislation, and litigating when necessary, these departments make sure that federal agencies comply with environmental laws and regulations. Positions are also available in the Office of Grassroots Action and the Corporate Conservation Council.

Interns are responsible for answering the dozens of letters and phone calls that pour in to NWF's national office every day. Most inquiries are from members requesting literature or an explanation of NWF's current position on such topics as wetlands, hunting, or whales. In order to keep legislators abreast of NWF's agenda, interns also distribute literature to congresspeople and senators. During these "Hill drops," conducted twice a week, interns walk from one Capitol Hill office to another to hand out such items as reports on wetlands protection or letters urging legislators to vote for various bills.

Assigned to teams that often consist of a scientist, a lawyer, and a lobbyist, interns perform more than administrative work. Because of NWF's broad-based agenda, interns have an opportunity to make an impact on several environmental issues at once. In Fish and Wildlife Resources, interns may concentrate on wetlands, endangered species, public lands, national forests, and regulation of coal, oil, gas, and mineral development. Interns in Environmental Quality focus on global warming, air pollution, acid rain, drinking water, groundwater pollution, oil spills, pesticides, and biotechnology. In International, topics include tropical deforestation and environmental aspects of free trade. Interns may also help NWF in its efforts at grassroots mobilization in the Office of Grassroots Action or push for business accountability as part of the Corporate Conservation Council. For journalism students interested in environmental issues, there's NWF's *EnviroAction*, for which interns write articles.

A must-read among environmentalists is the "fact sheet," a one-page report that establishes the facts behind a specific issue and often makes a case for supporting or rejecting it. Targeting congressional staffers and state government officials, fact sheets help NWF publicize its views on current environmental topics such as the spotted owl, clear-cutting, and grazing fees. One intern analyzed the proposed CAFE (Corporate Average Fuel Economy) bill—legislation slated to improve the nation's automobile fuel-efficiency standards. On a fact sheet, he outlined the main reasons congresspeople should pass the bill. "It will reduce global warming, air pollution, and U.S. de-

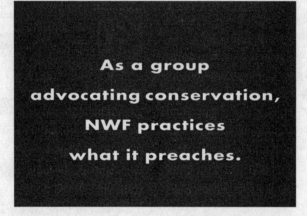

As a group advocating conservation, NWF practices what it preaches.

pendence on foreign oil," he explained. "Moreover, [improved fuel economy] will save consumers money on gas." Another intern composed a fact sheet that emphasized the importance of saving the ancient forests of the Pacific Northwest. "They're America's last virgin forests," she said. "If we lose them, we lose some of the tallest and oldest trees on the planet."

As part of NWF's environmental lobbying efforts, interns sometimes participate in grassroots phone campaigns and write letters to senators and congresspeople. On one occasion, interns sectioned off regions of the country and called NWF members. "We asked them to call their senators and representatives," said an intern. "[Members'] input can often make a difference in how [legislators] vote." On another occasion, an intern wrote a three-page letter highlighting the benefits of fuel efficiency on air pollution. "I got all kinds of environmental groups to sign the letter and then had it distributed to every member of the Senate."

Interns who manage to learn an issue inside and out and impress their supervisor will have an opportunity to do some lobbying in person on the Hill. They meet with legislative aides, hand out literature and talk through the issues. "Sometimes, people aren't interested, and you have to twist their arms," said an intern. "But other times, you talk to someone who wants more information or who gives you assurances of support. Of course, the offices of congressmen [who are] aligned with NWF are easier to deal with."

Interns attend hearings, briefings, and seminars in order to take background notes for supervisors and draft secondary documents and testimony for NWF executives. An intern in the International department, for example, worked on an effort to convince two House committees to influence reform of the World Bank's International Development Association (IDA). "IDA funds Third World development projects such as the building of hydroelectric power plants," she said. "But it does so without taking into account the environmental impact of such projects. Typically, devastation to habitats isn't properly considered." After reading recent papers from governmental and nongovernmental agencies, she and her supervisor came up with a 14-page document that later became part of the committee record. "It was really satisfying to be able to make that kind of contribution," she said. Another intern drafted testimony against a bill that would provide ranchers with federal compensation every time a disease called brucellosis killed their cattle. "I had to write several drafts and get approval at many stages in the process," he said, "but it was well worth it—the testimony was included in the record."

Environmental groups often work together by forming coalitions and holding meetings, which interns may attend. One intern helped organize and attended meetings among D.C. environmental groups who wanted to provide the Clintons with a list of qualified candidates for environmentally related federal positions. "To my surprise, I learned that the transition team relied on environmental groups to float possible names," she said. But often relegated to handing out documents, interns rarely are informed enough to make comments. "Just sit and observe," advised one intern. "You'll still learn plenty on how environmental strategy is formulated."

To familiarize interns with the environmental work outside of their departments, NWF arranges periodic brown-bag luncheons, featuring NWF staffers who speak on their projects. At one luncheon, NWF's peripatetic president, Jay Hair, takes time out from his busy travel schedule to meet the interns. An avid hunter and syndicated environmental columnist with a PhD in zoology, Hair is a renowned conservationist, who is eager to educate interns. "We talked casually about the importance of saving the environment and NWF's role in that effort," said an intern.

Located near Dupont Circle, NWF is about a 15 minute Metro trip from Capitol Hill. The group's offices occupy three floors of a seven-story building that was unveiled in a 1961 dedication ceremony featuring President Kennedy. "By mobilizing private effort through your organization, you are helping not only to develop our wildlife resources," said Kennedy, "but you are helping to create the kind of America that is our common goal—an America of open spaces, fresh water, and green country." Though NWF is a not-for-profit group, it doesn't operate with the informality of most nonprofits. Staffers wear suits and interns receive

their own desks, telephones, and a computer, to share between every two interns. "It has a corporate feel," observed one intern. "It's a fancy building with fancy furniture," said another.

As a group advocating conservation, NWF practices what it preaches. The environmentally conscious organization has solar film on its windows to reduce incoming sunlight and thus retain cool air during the summer and warm air during the winter. In the cafeteria, NWF uses glasses only since paper cups simply increase America's paper use, the coordinator explained. Lights are regulated by motion sensors, and an innovative air-conditioning system keeps the place cool without relying on Freon, one of the dreaded chlorofluorocarbons that destroy the ozone layer; the system uses electricity in off-peak hours to freeze water and then pumps air over the ice during the day. NWF also recycles paper, bottles, and cardboard and makes two-sided copies and faxes. "As you can imagine, we get a lot of mileage out of our office supplies," said an intern.

SELECTION

 NWF seeks college graduates and graduate students with extensive coursework and/or experience in economics, political science, journalism, wildlife biology, fisheries science, ecology, environmental biology, environmental science, biology, chemistry, toxicology, natural resource management, land management, forestry, geology, energy, hydrology, water resources, international environmental issues, and civil engineering. Master's degrees and previous work experience on environmental issues are helpful. International applicants are eligible.

APPLICATION PROCEDURE

 The deadline is September 15 for the January to June internship and March 15 for the July to December internship. Applicants should submit a cover letter indicating their areas of interest, a resume, names and telephone numbers of three to five academic or professional references, and a two- to four-page sample of nontechnical academic or professional writing (aspiring journalism interns must instead submit four writing samples or clips of any length). After the coordinator screens for the best candidates, department directors make final selections. No interviews are conducted.

OVERVIEW

 As an organization committed to a bevy of environmental issues, from acid rain to energy to wetlands, the National Wildlife Federation is an ideal place for college graduates to launch an environmental career. One of the few nonprofit environmental groups with a salaried program, NWF offers interns a well-structured six months in which to experience the life of the environmental policymaker. Whether mobilizing members for phone campaigns or lobbying legislators, NWF interns make vital contacts with influential nature lovers. After an NWF internship, a graduate's chance of landing full-time employment with D.C.'s prominent environmental groups is vastly improved.

FOR MORE INFORMATION . . .

■ National Wildlife Federation
Resources Conservation Internship Program
1400 Sixteenth Street NW
Washington, DC 20036-2266
(202) 797-6800
(202) 797-6819 (intern hotline)
www.nwf.org

SELECTIVITY

SELECTIVITY

Approximate applicant pool: 4,000
Interns accepted: about 20

COMPENSATION $ $

Scholastic program (provides college credit): $100/week
Internship (no college credit): $1,500/month
Those who work 40 hours/week or more may be eligible for benefits

QUALITY OF LIFE

Long hours, hard work during in-season, particularly when the Yankees play at home; two free tickets per intern per game for family members; opportunity to mingle with players, VIPs; possible travel with team to away games

LOCATION(S)

Bronx, NY; Tampa, FL

FIELD

Sports

DURATION

Anywhere from two weeks to ten months

PRE-REQS

Undergrad and graduate students

DEADLINE(S)

Rolling

Babe Ruth gave up his Red Sox uniform for them. Lou Gehrig was a star with them. Joe DiMaggio left the Pacific Coast League to play with them. Reggie Jackson signed on with them. They were the first to wear numbers on their jerseys, had a pitcher who threw the only perfect game in World Series history, and play in arguably the most famous modern sports edifice in the world. Whether or not you're a fan of the National Pastime, you know something about the New York Yankees, the most famous baseball team in the United States—past, present, and probably future.

DESCRIPTION

 The New York Yankees were not the 1999 World Champions for the twenty-fifth time in their long, illustrious history solely due to the abilities of the players and their manager. The players are some of the best in baseball, but they are only helped by playing for an organization that boasts some of the top businesspeople in the industry as part of an extensive apparatus created to support the team—from the executive offices to the media relations department.

Interns are assigned to those departments that request their assistance, and some departments cannot take more than a few interns, if any. Departments that consistently accept interns are the following: Baseball Operations, Community Relations, Marketing, Media Relations, Office Services, Publications, Public Relations, and Tickets. Current and former interns say that most interns are assigned to Marketing, Media Relations, and Public Relations, as these are usually the busiest departments. Occasionally interns are posted to more than one department during their internship, particularly if the intern requests a variety of experiences and it's during the off-season, when the Yankees are not terribly busy and interns can take the time to train with several departments.

Training for interns is informal in every department, to say the least. "I went day-by-day," says one intern, "always learning something new from one person or another in the office. It was pretty random, but it worked." The staff on the whole is regarded as "very friendly" and "helpful" to interns in need of assistance. Interns usually need to work in a department for a week or two to learn how that department operates, and are usually awarded greater responsibility and work on bigger projects if they impress their supervisors. Every department demands that interns perform mundane duties such as copying and filing, but all provide eager interns with the opportunity to do more. And employees also make an effort to learn from their interns. "Once a month we hold an intern meeting," says intern coordinator Harvey Winston, "wherein we discuss how each intern is doing, how their departments are doing, and how the organization as a whole is faring." This is also a time when interns are specifically asked for their suggestions on everything from how to improve interns' training to changes in the ways departments operate.

The Marketing and Public Relations departments have "very similar duties," according to the intern coordinator. Both assist sponsors, work on the distribution of promotional items and "promotional days," coordinate special events, facilitate pre-game ceremonies, and handle charity events. They may also work with the Community Relations department on events like players' visits to local schools, charity drives attended by players, and the like. Both departments involve heavy exposure to VIPs, players, and members of the press, all of which can make those interns posted to other areas of the company a little envious.

Another very popular department that usually needs lots of interns is Media Relations. Interns handle correspondence, issue press credentials, help create game notes (information on players that goes to the media pre-game), clip articles, do statistical research on players' stats, update the Major League Baseball website during the games, and might attend news conferences and go on the occasional trip with the team. One of the biggest projects, particularly during the off-season, is the *Media Guide*, a comprehensive tome for members of the Fourth Estate. Interns often do research, fact check, and proofread for the guide, and learn a lot about the history of the

Yankees and the players in the process. Like Marketing and PR interns, those in Media Relations learn how to deal with the media, "a skill in itself," according to one former intern.

One of the most highly praised perks for interns at the Yankees is the networking possibilities. Interns have the chance to meet and chat with some of the best in the sports business, from the executive level to public relations, and VIPs as well. "I haven't just chatted with players in the clubhouse," says one former intern, "I've been able to hang out with any sort of person you can think of who likes baseball, from Trump to Springsteen." Another intern alumnus advises interns to hustle a little when in the presence of greatness. "When important people can see you at work," he says, "you can make important connections. Don't hesitate to take the opportunity to impress someone."

"I've been able to hang out with any sort of person you can think of who likes baseball, from Trump to Springsteen."

Those who expect to spend most of their internship in the company of the players or VIPs, however, will be disappointed with their experience. "Die-hard fans are sometimes the worst people to be interns," says one alumnus of the intern program. "They are frustrated with the day-to-day work of running a business, don't always take the time to learn how to do their work well, and generally aren't fun to be around during business hours." Making goo-goo eyes whenever someone famous drops by isn't recommended. "If you can't be casual whenever a big name happens to show at the clubhouse," says one intern, "then you can't do your job, and someone else has to do it for you." The internship coordinator agrees. The New York Yankees is "the greatest baseball franchise in the world," he says, "but it's not glamorous from the inside. We look for intern applicants who are interested in the meat-and-potatoes of what we do here, and who will be professional whenever a VIP is around."

Most interns are located in New York, and unlike their counterparts in Tampa, Florida, those assigned to the Yankees headquarters in the Bronx can feel overwhelmed by New York City. Some interns, particularly those getting college credit who don't qualify for the more lucrative $1,500 monthly stipend, feel entirely financially dependent on the assistance of parents or relatives. In fact, those who get the $1,500 per month discover that it goes quickly, even if they don't live in Manhattan.

Social life outside the stadium is variable. "Spending so much time with coworkers already, some people don't want to go out with them outside of work," says a former intern. "But some people get pretty close, and there are always plenty of opportunities to socialize after work and on weekends." Additionally, "Departments take people out to dinner or lunch when they leave, or on their birthdays." Newcomers to one of America's biggest cities can get "carried away," a former intern says. "You need to watch yourself, walking around and on the subway, and not forget that New York can be a crazy city as well as a great tourist attraction."

Anyone who wants to work in the sports business would do well to go for an internship with the New York Yankees. The Yankees eventually hire approximately 10 percent of interns for full-time positions, although this is usually just a case of being in the right place at the right time. One intern can labor indefinitely waiting for a promotion, while a less experienced intern can move up right away if a position suddenly opens in his or her department. "We usually look initially at the intern pool when recruiting for our entry-level positions," says the internship coordinator. "Interns tend to be most familiar with the departments, the personalities involved, and know how we do things here. It's also easier for us to hire interns because it involves less work on our part; we usually already have the best young people for the jobs right here in the stadium."

That's not to mention the fact that the team can pay a lower starting salary when hiring from within. Yankees hiring practices are evident in every department, where at least some members tend to be former interns. "The entry-level pay of about $25,000 sucks, frankly," says one alumnus of the intern program who was hired by the Yankees, "but I know I can get promoted here or in another sports-related business, and my job is a hell of a lot more interesting than anything my old college friends are doing." Interns have been promoted to the executive

level at the Yankees. "Several general and stadium managers are graduates of our internship program," adds the internship coordinator. "That attests to the quality of our interns and the training they receive here."

SELECTION

 Undergraduate and graduate students are encouraged to apply. International students at undergrad and grad institutions may apply, but like their U.S. counterparts must have considerable knowledge of baseball in general and the New York Yankees in particular. Sports fans are welcome, but only if they have demonstrated interest in the business of sports. Applicants who are enthusiastic about, and have some experience in, sports public relations, media relations, publications, etc., as opposed to (for example) just PR or only baseball, are most likely to be chosen for the internship. Those applicants not from the New York City area who are applying to the scholastic internship program, which provides a stipend of just $100 per week, should state in their cover letters that they will be able to secure housing during their internship. As the vast majority of people in the sports business continue to be white males, members of minority groups and women are strongly encouraged to apply. A few interns are brought on at the urging of company executives, an unfortunate fact noted by a number of former Yankees interns and acknowledged by the internship coordinator. This is the case in many prestigious internships, however, and should not dissuade anyone interested in the program from applying.

APPLICATION PROCESS

 Mail an updated resume and a cover letter that includes which departments most interest you, whether you want to intern in the Bronx or in Tampa, and when and for what length of time you would be able to intern. (Do not include recommendations and transcripts, as they will not be considered.) Applicants whose credentials appeal to the intern coordinator will be called for an in-person interview or, if the applicant is not able to travel to New York, for a telephone interview. Interviews are somewhat laid-back, and personal compatibility with the intern coordinator is widely regarded as a significant factor in acceptance. Following the interviews, the directors of those departments in need of interns review the twenty or so resumes and cover letters chosen by the intern coordinator, and talk with the coordinator about the applicants' interview performance. After the departmental directors choose their interns, the intern coordinator contacts only those applicants who have been accepted into the program.

OVERVIEW

 The selectivity of the New York Yankees internship program and the prestige associated with this beloved baseball team make it a dazzling addition to any resume. More than that, the experience interns receive and the contacts they make ensure that interns leave with skills that prepare them for life in a plethora of corporate environments. For those who have a head for business but feel bored by conventional companies, who love sports but can't hit a ball for a living, an internship at the New York Yankees is ideal. The increased possibility of being hired full-time after graduation by the Yankees makes this a gem of an internship. "It's been said before about other intern programs, but it's true about this one: If you can make it here, long hours, hard work, and all," says the intern coordinator, "you really can make it anywhere."

FOR MORE INFORMATION . . .

■ Harvey Winston
Internship Coordinator
New York Yankees
Yankee Stadium
Bronx, NY 10451
718-293-4300
Fax: 718-293-8431
www.yankees.com

NIGHTLINE

NIGHTLINE

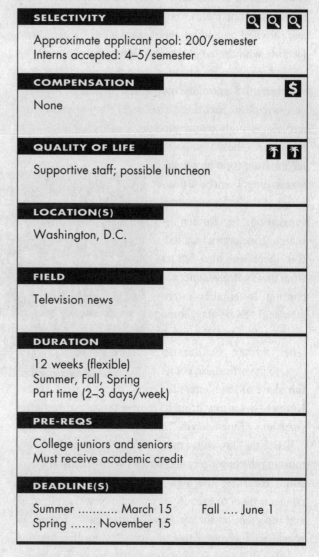

SELECTIVITY 🔍 🔍 🔍

Approximate applicant pool: 200/semester
Interns accepted: 4–5/semester

COMPENSATION $

None

QUALITY OF LIFE ♟ ♟

Supportive staff; possible luncheon

LOCATION(S)

Washington, D.C.

FIELD

Television news

DURATION

12 weeks (flexible)
Summer, Fall, Spring
Part time (2–3 days/week)

PRE-REQS

College juniors and seniors
Must receive academic credit

DEADLINE(S)

Summer .... March 15   Fall .... June 1
Spring .... November 15

"**N**ightline has grown so powerful that it's assumed that any top-shelf newsmaker will do Ted first," wrote the *The Dallas Morning Star*.

Regardless of who "does Ted first," the world's movers and shakers do gravitate to ABC's *Nightline* like barnacles to a hull. Oliver North, Ariel Sharon, Corazon Aquino, Rajiv Gandhi, Nelson Mandela, Mikhail Gorbachev, and Desmond Tutu are just a few of the world-famous guests who've faced the rigors of Koppel's probing questions.

Evolving in 1979 from the ABC News special broadcasts, "The Iran Crisis: America Held Hostage," *Nightline* has become an American institution. Broadcast each weeknight from 11:30 P.M. to midnight, the show covers a major story in the news through a combination of live interviews with newsmakers and reports from *Nightline* correspondents in the field. The show is consistently lauded by critics as the best in daily television journalism. Its long history of journalistic coups includes the first report from Baghdad following Iraq's invasion of Kuwait, the first live television interview of former Chief Justice Warren Burger, and television's first "town meeting" (1987's "A National Town Meeting on AIDS").

DESCRIPTION

Flexibility is king at the *Nightline* internship. Interns generally work 12-week sessions, which coincide with fall, spring, and summer semesters but may adjust the length of their stay by a few weeks, if necessary. *Nightline* uses both part-time and full-time interns. Part-time students work three to four shifts weekly. Each day they may work either the day shift (9:30 A.M.–5:00 P.M.) or the night shift (4:30

P.M.–12:00 A.M.). Full-time students work 40 hours weekly, alternating between day and evening shifts. A few weeks before the internship, interns set a weekly schedule with the program's coordinator.

Of the day and night work periods, the day shift is considered by some to be the less desirable period to work. According to one intern, "The majority of the producers and writers aren't in the office yet, so things are pretty slow." Interns find themselves sending faxes, making photocopies, and scanning newspapers for relevant articles to clip. Answering phones is another part of the "daily grind," as interns field all types of calls, from the legitimate to "the laughable." "Most of the calls were related to the night's show," said one intern, "but sometimes people called up and rambled on and on about story ideas for the show. Dealing with these types was a lesson in diplomacy."

Interns also get a taste of the public when they open viewer mail. Some of the mail is well meaning. "I'd come across requests for information, and I'd try to research an answer. A high school student, [for example], saw a *Nightline* show on abortion and wanted more information for a report she was writing. I sent her a transcript of the show and some suggestions for further research," one intern recalled. But there are also letters from the Twilight Zone, according to another intern who said "Every day, some guy would send Koppel a letter written in Russian . . . . [T]he office also got its fair share of love letters for Koppel—women writing to profess their love and offer snapshots of themselves."

But the day shift is not without its rewards. Every morning the producers and writers get together to brainstorm ideas for the night's show. A conference call connects them to executives from the New York bureau and reporters on the road and Koppel either attends or phones in. Interns are free to watch the morning meeting or listen to it on a speakerphone. "It's amazing to watch how the show gets put together so quickly. The topic is usually chosen the day of the show." If they're lucky, interns also have a few chances to accompany the *Nightline* crew on assignment. One intern went with ABC correspondent Brit Hume to the White House, where they attended a press conference with Treasury Secretary Lloyd Bentsen in the Press Room. Another accompanied the crew to a county jail, where Koppel interviewed Chinese inmates for a show on Chinese immigration. A third intern shadowed Koppel and the crew as they interviewed the public at several Washington locations during Clinton's inaugural ceremonies.

Interns report that the night shift is the key time to be at *Nightline*. "By six o'clock, things start heating up. All the producers and writers are in the building. Everyone is going full throttle to prepare for the show," explained an intern. Busywork is still prevalent, but most find that at night even that's more exciting. "There's not as much phone work and practically all of the calls that come in are directly related to the show," reported one intern. Sometimes interns assist staff researchers in last-minute fact checking: "I searched the LEXIS~NEXIS databases for articles on Hillary Rodham Clinton to double-check certain details." Interns also play the gofer, running messages and scripts down to the control room.

Above all, the night shift is a time to observe. The staff of *Nightline* is unusually receptive to letting interns watch preparations for the show. Said one intern, "I'd visit the editing room a lot. Everyone there was really great about explaining exactly what they were doing. Once they let me look through a series of pictures and pick out the best one for use as the show's backdrop." The Graphics department is also popular among interns. "It's great just to sit there and watch the artists play with pictures and text," said one.

But nothing beats the main attraction—the tapings. The show airs at 11:35 P.M., and interns may watch from the control room or behind the TelePrompTer on the set. "I'd go early and watch [the staff] check the microphones and prep Koppel," said one intern. "[I]t amazed me to see Koppel looking half asleep before the show, and then at 11:35 P.M.—boom—he comes alive and kicks butt." During the interview segment of the show, guests are beamed in by satellite or filmed in the studio. Interns report that before the show Koppel avoids getting too chummy with in-studio guests: "Koppel greets them but keeps his professional distance. There's minimal contact." Even more interesting is how in-studio guests are interviewed: "They're placed in a room adjacent to the studio where Koppel sits. Koppel can see them on the monitor, but they can't see him. Some claim this is just the way the studio is set up, but I think it's done to give [Koppel] an advantage."

> "It amazed me to see Koppel looking half asleep before the show, and then at 11:35— boom—he comes alive and kicks butt."

There are not a whole lot of fringe benefits and extracurriculars at *Nightline*. ABC News often, but not always, holds an intern luncheon for all ABC News interns where executives and producers talk about their jobs. Speaking of food, *Nightline* orders a selection of "finger sandwiches and fruit plates" for guests to enjoy before they go on the air. When a particular show has no in-studio guests, the staff (interns included) has dibs on this "yummy" catered food. Moreover, for those concerned about traveling home after a night shift, interns are reimbursed for taxi fare. Finally, celebrity hounds will be happy (but not surprised) to learn that *Nightline* offers many stargazing opportunities. Interns regularly see such ABC personalities as Peter Jennings, Barbara Walters, Chris Wallace, Cokie Roberts, and Sam Donaldson, as well as an endless stream of politicians, government officials, and academics.

Located on the third floor of the seven-floor ABC News center, *Nightline* shares its building with the offices of *Good Morning America*, *World News Tonight*, and *Weekend Report with David Brinkley*. With decor that offers little more than a few framed pictures of Ted Koppel, the *Nightline* office consists of a large open area surrounded by executive offices. Interns typically work in the open area at one of two large tables. Although *Nightline's* computer system was described as "woefully outdated" a few years ago, recent reports indicate that the computer facilities have been vastly improved. In fact, interns now have access to the ABC newsroom system, Associated Press news wires, America Online, and LEXIS~NEXIS. No cafeteria exists, but if they have the time, interns can grab a bite at one of the many eateries on nearby Connecticut Avenue.

A key reason *Nightline* stands out from the majority of television internships is its supportive and warm-spirited staff. From Ted Koppel down to the secretaries, interns feel welcome and appreciated on the job. Said one intern: "Koppel is a genuine guy. On my first day he walked up to me and introduced himself. I was really impressed." Kudos go to "Nightline" Executive Producer Tom Bettag, too: "[Bettag] was a great inspiration. He sat down with all the interns to answer questions and explain what makes a story newsworthy.... And he has a great ability to make everyone work as a team—which differs markedly from what I've seen at other TV programs, even other ones in this building."

SELECTION

The internship is open to college juniors and seniors. No particular majors are required. All interns, however, must receive academic credit from their colleges. International applicants are eligible.

APPLICATION PROCEDURE

The deadline is March 15 for summer, June 1 for fall, and November 15 for spring. Send a resume, cover letter, two references, a notice of approval of credit, and a completed application form to the address listed below. You may also e-mail niteline@abc.com for internship applications. The intern coordinator conducts interviews (by telephone or in person) with a group of finalists. Successful applicants are usually notified within a month of their start date.

OVERVIEW

Those looking to write news stories or operate video equipment would be well advised to steer clear of the *Nightline* internship or any other big-name internship in broadcast journalism. While *Nightline* provides little in the way of hands-on experience, however, it has much to offer in other areas. Said one intern: "The potential for networking is phenomenal at *Nightline*. If you make a good effort and earn people's respect, they'll be there with valuable job recommendations later. It's a major foot in the door." For those not necessarily planning a future in TV news, however, the internship is still a rare window on what *Time* called "the most indispensable news broadcast on television." Says Executive Producer Tom Bettag: "The *Nightline* internship is like auditing a course. It's a chance to pick up the ambience, the rhythm of the place . . . . [Y]ou get to see experts in their field and what makes them tick."

FOR MORE INFORMATION . . .

■ *Nightline*
 Simone Swink
 Intern Coordinator
 1717 DeSales Street, NW, 3rd Floor
 Washington, DC 20036
 (202) 222-7000
 niteline.abc.com

SELECTIVITY

Approximate applicant pool: 1,200+
Interns accepted: 40+

COMPENSATION

$1,000 stipend allotted at the start,
transportation fees

QUALITY OF LIFE

Awesome campus; immense gym;
weekly speakers

LOCATION(S)

Beaverton, OR

FIELD

Athletic shoes, apparel, and accessories

DURATION

10 weeks
Summer (June–August)

PRE-REQS

College juniors and seniors; grad students

DEADLINE(S)

Mid-January

Take a track star with a Stanford MBA and combine the star with a top track coach, preferably one who designs running shoes. Then add a series of innovative running-shoe designs, including the Waffle Trainer, Tailwind, Air Jordan, Air Pegasus, and Cross Trainer. Mix in dozens of Olympic champions and sprinkle with endorsements by Tiger Woods, John McEnroe, Bo Jackson, Michael Jordan, and Joan Benoit, and garnish it all with a snazzy "swoosh" logo. What do you get? The recipe for a multibillion-dollar athletic-shoe empire named after the Greek goddess of victory, Nike.

Bill Bowerman and Phil Knight joined forces in 1964, and together they parlayed a basement-based sneaker company into the world's first sports and fitness company to surpass $6.5 billion in annual total revenues. A savvy sense of marketing and an unflagging commitment to quality have helped Bowerman and Knight make NIKE synonymous with the best aspects of athletics—vigorous competition, effective teamwork, and uncompromising performance.

DESCRIPTION

NIKE strives to match a student's academic background and vocational interest with a particular area of the company. The following divisions have accepted interns: Sports Marketing, Finance/Accounting, Information Technology, Apparel, Research, Design & Development, Retail, Customer Service, Sales, and Production. Not surprisingly, an intern's experience at NIKE varies considerably, depending on the department and supervisor to which he or she is assigned.

An intern in Sales Operations worked on a development team for sales software. She worked in a team of five people to modify the company's Sales Planning System, a tool used by NIKE sales reps to do forecasts and assortment plans. The highlight of her experience was when she "went to Hawaii for two weeks to deploy SPS to the Japanese reps and train them during the Fall 1997 sales meeting."

Finance interns spend much of their time crunching numbers and solving business problems. One Finance intern undertook such projects as determining why warehouse costs increased and whether hiring more full-time employees would be financially beneficial. Another helped develop a system to monitor how effectively NIKE distributes its merchandise to retail stores.

In other divisions, NIKE interns also find themselves working on projects to boost productivity and improve internal processes. In Marketing, interns helped plan the distribution of custom-designed running shoes to large retailers such as Athlete's Foot and Footlocker. Retail Resources interns spent several weeks evaluating the success of the Gift-with-Purchase program, whereby NIKE sells its products with some sort of freebie, such as a T-shirt, a pair of sunglasses, or a baseball cap. One of the most interesting jobs was assigned to a Records Management intern, who was asked to help organize and catalog NIKE's gargantuan archive system. He ended up sifting through hundreds of shoes, pieces of apparel, watches, cups, mugs—anything that ever came out of the NIKE factory. "It really gave me a product-by-product sense of NIKE's history," he said.

Some interns work with NIKE fabrics and designs. A Research Design intern worked in the apparel lab, determining the extent to which various fabrics were tearable, shrinkable, colorfast, waterproof, and breathable. "There was no busywork in my job," reported the textile major. "They threw me right into it—having me conduct all sorts of experiments on fabrics submitted by different vendors." Other Research Design interns assist in apparel and footwear design. Consulting with professional designers, they brainstorm new ideas and prepare sketches. Sometimes they create for the design team a "presentation board," in which they describe a new design concept and the external influences (logos, cars, animals, etc.) that inspired it. Design interns usually have previous experience in garment construction and drawing.

The wide variety of intern positions means that interns are dispersed throughout several buildings, prompting some to call the program "too spread out" and "not centralized enough." But efforts are made to create

> The Nike campus boasts everything an intern could want .... One intern reported that he bought a fine pair of running shoes for $25.

unity among interns. The summer begins with a two-day orientation program, during which participants are shown the inner workings of every major department at NIKE. To further expose interns to the various roles at the company, the intern coordinator brings all the interns together for a weekly presentation by a NIKE officer. Past speakers include such corporate honchos as the director of Marketing for Europe and the director of Customer Service Administration. The director of Entertainment Promotions was the biggest hit among interns, captivating them with stories of how she oversees the use of NIKE products in movies, arranging for gifts of NIKE products to everyone from Michael J. Fox to Jerry Seinfeld. The final meeting usually finds CEO Philip Knight talking to and mingling with program participants.

NIKE employees do not work at a complex, a corporate headquarters, or an industrial park; they work at the "NIKE World Campus." It's an ambitious name, but one NIKE remarkably lives up to. Ten minutes from downtown Portland, NIKE's physical plant is located in the suburban town of Beaverton and resembles a sprawling, tree-lined college campus. Seven buildings sit on the 74-acre compound, each named after a famous NIKE endorser; when visitors tour NIKE, they find not "Building A" and "Building B," but the "Michael Jordan Building," and the "Mike Schmidt Building." The NIKE campus boasts everything an intern could want: A high-quality cafeteria, dry cleaning, film developing, an employee store selling NIKE products, and even a hair salon. Subsidized by NIKE, goods and services are priced reasonably for employees. The employee store, for example, sells all footwear at cost or lower. One intern reported that he bought a fine pair of NIKE running shoes for $25.

The NIKE World Campus redefines the quality-of-life concept. "This place is like a little city—no—this place is better than a little city," said one intern. For a small monthly fee, interns have full use of the Bo Jackson Sports Center, a state-of-the-art athletic facility offering aerobics, weights, weight trainers, squash, tennis courts, martial arts, Jacuzzis, massage, big-screen TV, an indoor running track, and a day care center.

SELECTION

 NIKE seeks college juniors and seniors, as well as grad students. According to the intern coordinator, desired qualities in applicants include "flexibility," "passion to be the best," "a willingness to ask for additional work," and an "appreciation for sports and fitness." International applicants are eligible.

APPLICATION PROCEDURE

 The application deadline is mid-January. Interested parties should submit a resume with GPA of 3.0 or higher, a cover letter indicating academic achievements and any community and extracurricular involvement. Design students should consult the hotline for portfolio requirements. To apply, you must e-mail your resume and cover letter to jobs@nike.com. The application process at NIKE is 100 percent electronic. Do not mail your resume or call for information—visit the Nike Web site for more information at www.nikebiz.com.

OVERVIEW

 "Love who you are . . . protect your dreams . . . and develop your talents to their fullest extent." "Play to win." "Don't allow anyone to tell you what you can and cannot do." "Tell the truth." "Live off the land." NIKE likes to propagate these maxims among its employees, and the values they refer to reflect the mindset that interns will encounter at the company. The NIKE internship exposes its participants to the machinery of sportswear production and manufacturing also immersing them in a uniquely progressive, athletically minded environment. The NIKE culture is at once dynamic and casual. It is a place where employees bring both an industrious ethic and a duffel bag to work. For those looking for this kind of experience, the answer is clear: Just Do It!

FOR MORE INFORMATION . . .

■ NIKE, Inc.
Internship Program
One Bowerman Drive
Beaverton, OR 97005
(800) 890-6453
www.nikebiz.com

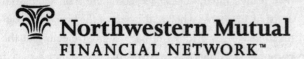

Northwestern Mutual
FINANCIAL NETWORK™

SELECTIVITY	🔍 🔍 🔍 🔍 🔍
Approximate applicant pool: 20,000 Interns accepted: 950 to 1,000	

COMPENSATION	💲 💲 💲 💲
Commission basis; interns earn an average of $8–$12/hour; top ten interns average $26,614; leading intern earned $121,611	

QUALITY OF LIFE	🌴 🌴 🌴 🌴
Weekly classes in life insurance and financial planning; Entrepreneurial spirit; Annual meeting/party; College Awards Show	

LOCATION(S)

350 offices in all 50 states

FIELDS

Life insurance; Financial services

DURATION

One semester to two years
Full-time during the summer; part-time during the school year

PRE-REQS

Undergrads; grad students

DEADLINE(S)

Rolling

"I'm driving to my place in Beverly Hills. I spent my summer selling a product I believe in to my own clients—without a boss breathing down my neck. I make an enviable salary between classes. And I'm confident that I'll have a full-time job doing what I love when I graduate. This is the life."

That introduction is not what you'd expect to hear from an insurance representative talking about his job, let alone a college student bragging about an internship. And although it's true that few college agents who work for Northwestern Mutual reach income levels like that top performer, many take home in one year more than most college students will make during four years of work-study salaries, and none of them say they fit the stereotype of an insurance rep. One alumnus of the internship program says, "We're an entertaining bunch who like people and the good life."

In 1999 *Sales & Marketing Management Magazine* Northwestern Mutual was ranked "number one in the life insurance industry" in the country. Northwestern Mutual has grown exponentially since its inception in 1857 into the fifth largest life insurance company in the United States, with more than $86 billion in assets and over 7,500 agents in 350 offices around the country. "If you want a prestigious name on your resume," says one former Northwestern Mutual intern, "you can't get much better than an internship with Northwestern Mutual."

DESCRIPTION

"For most internships," says one Northwestern Mutual internship alumnus, "you'll file or sit around, but in this program you are a full-fledged business owner, fully licensed." Since the early 1930s, Northwestern's in-

BUSYWORK
LOW MEDIUM HIGH
OLDMAN & HAMADEH
METER

ternship program has graduated more than 16,000 college students from 500 institutions of higher education from its award-winning program. This necessitates that Northwestern Mutual train interns both about the products that interns sell—primarily life insurance—and how to sell those products.

Northwestern Mutual requires that new interns attend courses that outline disability and life income underwriting and detail Northwestern's policies and procedures. It takes approximately two to ten days (depending on the intern's location) of full-time studying to prepare for the state licensing exam that is required for all sales representatives. Techniques for selling are covered in courses that take students through the exam, and typically entail a week of classes on analyzing sales data, establishing a clientele, and methods of executing a successful sale.

Once the classes end, a shadow program commences in which college interns observe how Northwestern Mutual professionals work until they feel comfortable enough to step out on their own. Throughout the internship, Northwestern Mutual offers seminars to interns on various issues in financial planning and life insurance, intended to keep interns informed of its wide variety of insurance policies.

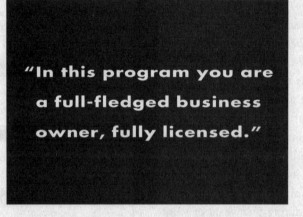

"In this program you are a full-fledged business owner, fully licensed."

The duties of an intern are precisely those of their professional counterparts: zeroing in on markets, finding and nurturing relationships with clients, and achieving sales. There are no production requirements for interns, however. The focus at this level is on ensuring that interns convey concise knowledge about the product and adhere to company philosophy, with the understanding that such abilities will come at different times for different interns. One intern alumnus notes that the pressure to sell would be "overwhelming" otherwise, as the business is not easy and college agents are apt to compete amongst themselves.

Nothwestern Mutual headquarters keeps updated lists of each intern's sales numbers, and in addition to awarding large commissions to the top interns, publicly praises them at regional and national conferences.

The work environment varies with the location and the level of the intern's performance. Most interns spend the majority of their internship meeting clients outside of the local office. Interns are able to work in an office near their hometown or college, and many former interns say they felt quickly incorporated into firms, regardless of whether five or a hundred representatives worked there. Top interns not only receive the usual perks of an internship—a key to the office, use of the computers, and the

knowledge that they are being treated like another member of the business workforce—but they also get their own professional work space complete with secretarial assistance. Interns who are the best of the best are recognized at Northwestern Mutual's annual meeting at the corporate headquarters in Milwaukee.

Despite, or perhaps because of, the independent work of the interns, mentors are crucial to the Northwestern Mutual experience. Most mentor relationships seem to be formed at the beginning of the internship, when the interns are assigned to professional representatives to shadow as a part of their training. Regular meetings are held between interns and their mentors once or twice a week to examine any challenges or difficulties. Many interns report that get-togethers outside of the formal discussions are essential to the enjoyment they got out of the internship. "Sales can be a lonely and discouraging business at times," reports one intern, "and mentors help put it all in perspective. They've been there, and can help you work through it." A few interns say that the mentors kept them in the program when they felt discouraged by the real world of sales, and have since become friends.

The financial benefits of an internship at Northwestern Mutual are considerable. Many interns find themselves bowled over by the compensation possibilities for those who can reap commissions. Northwestern encourages interns to set their own hours to make sales whenever they are not in class, and many interns take advantage of this opportunity. Some interns have worked full-time during the academic year, and others take home more than forty hours a week in pay for their efforts in the summer months. There is another incentive to stay with the internship: Like professional representatives, interns receive generous renewals (i.e., cash rewards for clients who renew Northwestern Mutual products) if they continue to sell life insurance for Northwestern Mutual for more than 12 months. Professional agents who have been at Northwestern Mutual for at least five years often take in 30 to 50 percent of their income from renewal commissions.

Financial benefits aside, one of the perks a number of intern alumni recall fondly is the midsummer meeting and party at the home office. All interns are invited to Milwaukee for what several interns call "an Oscar-like bash." Interns do not usually have trouble paying their way to the party, and most feel that it's worth the trip. "They really go all-out," says one intern, "and it's fun to meet the other interns, hear the speakers, and network."

"One of the best things about this business," says one former intern, "is that you meet and learn to communicate with all sorts of people. If you decide that sales isn't for you, fine—you still have the know-how and contacts, from your co-workers to your clients, that will help you move on" to another career. In 1999 Northwestern Mutual instituted an intern alumni association, which keeps its interns in contact with one another through events at local offices and a newsletter, and affords all former interns with more networking opportunities.

The tremendous responsibilities afforded interns makes this program attractive to a number of employers, who view former Northwestern Mutual interns as extremely mature and self-motivated. Many interns move on to jobs in the sales field, if not within Northwestern Mutual itself, following graduation. About one-third of all former interns become part of Northwestern Mutual, and are hired based on their performance as interns, their demonstrated dedication to sales, and their devotion to the firm. Most interns get to know the business of sales well, and Northwestern Mutual in particular, after a year or more of interning, and Northwestern knows them, so an internship is a pretty good start for those who intend to stay with the company.

Statistically, former Northwestern Mutual interns do measurably better than their peers who also work for Northwestern Mutual but who were not awarded places as interns. A recent study of former Northwestern Mutual interns reveals that the average income of interns ten years out of the program is $140,000 per annum, with the top 25 percent of college agents making $328,000 by their early thirties. In comparison, non-interns go on to make an average of $119,000 at Northwestern Mutual Life and the top 25 percent of agents at Northwestern Mutual earn $259,000 a year.

"If you love sales and aren't bound by the silly stereotype of insurance agents," says one intern, "you will get a lot from being a college agent for Northwestern Mutual."

SELECTION

 National and international undergrads and grad students are eligible, although most Northwestern Mutual interns tend to be juniors and seniors. Approximately one out of twenty applicants is accepted into the internship program on the basis of their demonstrated interest in and gift for sales, previous leadership positions, and overall dedication to hard work. The internship coordinator emphasizes that Northwestern Mutual seeks those who are responsible, mature, and can be trusted to work independently.

APPLICATION PROCESS

 The rolling deadline and rather flexible internship hours means that students can apply when they choose and work hours that suit their academic schedule and professional goals. Candidates must send a cover letter and resume to the national headquarters, at which point Northwestern Mutual will begin a "mutual discovery process" during which the applicant is put through a series of interviews. A preliminary group or individual interview is followed by a 20-minute sales aptitude exam and, providing that the applicant passes both, several sample assignments are to be completed within a week. Some market research and a couple of hours usually are sufficient to complete the samples, which have been likened to a take-home quiz. Finalists participate in a "mutual evaluation and decision conference" with at least one Northwestern Mutual representative to determine their acceptance or rejection. For immediate consideration, e-mail your resume to resume@northwesternmutual.com.

OVERVIEW

 If one can only learn by doing, Northwestern Mutual's internship program is an intense and, according to alumni, unparalleled learning experience. Take away the internship's wages and commissions, resume-boosting ability, assistance in getting a good job right out of college, and pleasant atmosphere, and you're left with a position as a full-fledged life insurance representative. According to one former intern, "every internship pales in comparison to my experiences at Northwestern Mutual. If sales is your goal, this is your dream internship."

FOR MORE INFORMATION . . .

- resume@northwesternmutual.com
  www.northwesternmutual.com/sales

SELECTIVITY 🔍 🔍

Approximate applicant pool: 350 (SS), 40–50 (MS)[2]
Teaching Assistants accepted: 35 (SS), 12–15 (MS)[2]

COMPENSATION 💲 💲 💲 💲

$2,200 plus room & board

QUALITY OF LIFE 🌴 🌴 🌴 🌴

College-caliber facilities; single rooms;
weekend outings; lovely campus

LOCATION(S)

Andover, MA

FIELD

Teaching

DURATION

6 Weeks
Summer

PRE-REQS

Recent grads; grad students

DEADLINE(S)

Summer Session ...... February 15
Math and Science for Minority Students ... February 15

Summer school. Few phrases cause more grief to the adolescent heart. Visions of dark, steamy classrooms, redolent of crayons and floor detergent. A wizened disciplinarian, droning on and on, propagating coffee breath and a thousand lessons better left untaught. The world outside—laughter and blue sky—passing you by.

But at Phillips Academy, summer school doesn't have to be scholastic hell. Every summer, the prestigious Massachusetts boarding school runs two innovative academic programs for high school students. The Summer Session Programs enrolls more than 500 students in a wide range of classes designed to enrich students' secondary education. In addition, the Math and Science for Minority Students (MS)[2] Program offers promising African American, Hispanic/Latino, and Native-American students rigorous coursework in mathematics and science, to prepare them for careers in the medical, engineering, and scientific professions. Students of both programs take advantage of the academy's college-caliber facilities and stunning New England beauty.

DESCRIPTION

 Phillips Academy (or "Andover," as it is commonly called) hires Teaching Assistants (TAs) for both the Summer Session and Math and Science for Minority Students Programs. Those in the Summer Session assist in teaching courses related to their major field of study, from algebra to zoology. Those in the Math and Science for Minority Students Program help teach classes in biology, chemistry, physics, and mathematics as well as English. Both groups of TAs work six days a week for the six-week session. They assist in two different classes, each meeting six days a week from 8:00 A.M. to 1:30 P.M.

All TAs share a basic set of classroom responsibilities. Paired with a master teacher (an adult with several years teaching experience), each assists the teacher in completing administrative work, organizing lesson plans, and grading papers and tests. With regard to the last task, TAs typically share grading responsibilities with the teacher. A TA in English reported: "I had a lot of input in terms of grading. Before assigning a grade, [the teacher] and I would sit down and discuss a grading system: "All the classes use the official grading system, which ranges from six to zero, six being high honors and zero a failing grade. Unfortunately, this system doesn't necessarily correspond to the [letter system] students are used to. It made for some confusion, both on my part and with my students."

TAs in the (MS)^2 Program are also required to lead nightly help and tutorial sessions. In help sessions TAs review the day's concepts and answer questions from students. They also conduct tutorials, which provide a chance for students to meet one on one with the TA. "Tutorials allow students to ask questions and work through problems fully. It was always neat to see the shyer students open up. The individual attention was really good for them," said a TA. Another TA found tutorials personally enlightening: "You really get to know your students. You appreciate how many of them have faced powerful socioeconomic obstacles at home."

Beyond their support duties, TAs are encouraged to teach. "How much you teach depends on the teacher," said one TA. "Most will let you teach at least a few classes alone; others are less willing to give you free rein." Indeed, one TA "got to take over a class for two weeks, teaching an entire novel," while another "worked with a teacher so set in her ways that there never was a chance to address the class alone." As for TAs who do "fly solo," it's an exhilarating and educational experience. "It's pretty amazing," said one TA. "You learn so much in front of a class—how to pace the discussion, how to get everyone to contribute, how to throw out a question and then bring the discussion back to a unifying theme." For many TAs, any initial public speaking anxiety soon gives way to a newfound confidence. "Although I was a bit apprehensive at first, teaching eventually felt no different than explaining something at the dinner table," said one intern.

TAs play an integral role in students' extracurricular activities as well. First of all, Summer Session TAs serve as coaches or supervisors for a variety of afternoon activities, such as volleyball, martial arts, and aerobics. Afternoon supervisory positions are mandatory for Summer Session TAs. All (MS)^2 TAs are also required to chaperon four of the students' weekend activities. Some TAs accompany students on Sunday outings to the movies or the beach. Said one TA: "I went with a group [of students] to the Rockingham Park Mall in New Hampshire. It was pretty mellow. I just made sure they were all accounted for and didn't get into trouble." Other TAs serve as chaperons at the Saturday night dances. "The dances are a big social scene for the kids and are always packed," said a TA. "Most are attended by students from both programs, but (MS)^2 students, many [of whom] prefer more urban music, sometimes hold their own." As in the other activities, TAs play a low-key role: "You're not holding a ruler between couples to make sure the kids aren't dancing too close. It's really casual—you just need to be there, not much else."

Andover administration makes sure TAs are well prepared to do their jobs. Before classes begin, TAs participate in a few days of intensive orientation. "[Administration] made a huge effort. The directors of both programs gave us a pep talk, as did past teachers, TAs, and students. Then they had seminars on TA strategies and how to work effectively with teachers.

The Andover campus is beautiful. Descriptions range from "big and gracious" to "lovely sweeping lawns" to "stately and brick, like the University of Virginia." With a library of more than 100,000 volumes, an arts and communications center, an archaeological museum, and a gallery of American art, Andover definitely has a big-time collegiate feel. One TA said: "I had to repeatedly remind myself that it was just a high school." A 1-hour train ride from Boston, the town of Andover is of the "sleepy New England" sort, with a "little Main Street," "Colonial-style houses," and "quaint shops."

> "I had to repeatedly remind myself that [Andover] was just a high school."

TAs make the ten-minute walk to town several times a week, whether it's to visit the 24-hour CVS pharmacy (for some, "a late-night place to be") or to kick back at Justin's, a popular bar.

All TAs live on campus. Summer Session TAs are required to live in an Andover dormitory, where they have their own room but share bathroom facilities with students. TAs in the (MS)^2 Program reside in faculty-only cottages, which also have single-occupancy bedrooms and common bathrooms. (MS)^2 TAs often relish their time apart from the high schoolers. "To be honest, it was really nice to have a retreat away from the students. At night I went home and had peace of mind," said one (MS)^2 TA. TAs and students eat in one of four dining halls, each with "high ceilings, arched windows, and wooden tables." The food is "good for institutional grub," but one carnivore sniffed: "There were too many things like turkey burgers, tofu, and frozen yogurt, and not enough stuff for us meat eaters." To work off their cafeteria visits, TAs take advantage of the athletic center, a state-of-the-art facility that "rivals any college gym." There's also a huge bird sanctuary adjacent to campus with running trails and shady areas where "students go to break rules."

SELECTION

The Summer Session and (MS)^2 Programs seek college seniors, recent graduates, and graduate students. No other prerequisites exist, except that students should have "a strong academic background in their field and a generosity of spirit." Students of color are strongly urged to apply. International applicants may not be eligible.

APPLICATION PROCEDURE

The application deadline for TA positions with the Summer Session and (MS)^2 Program is February 15. Applications received after the deadlines are still valid, but the applicant's chance for a position is greatly reduced. Candidates should apply directly to either program. Both programs require a completed application and an official undergraduate transcript. The Summer Session also asks for two recent references and a personal essay describing one's most memorable intellectual experience and most challenging personal experience at college. After applications have been read, a number of candidates are invited to Andover (at their own expense) for personal interviews with the director of the program to which they are applying. In rare instances, long-distance applicants may be able to substitute a phone interview for the personal interview. Final decisions are made in late March.

OVERVIEW

Is teaching for you? A summer spent at the Phillips Academy may provide the answer. Teaching Assistants in the Summer Session and (MS)^2 Programs spend six weeks teaching, tutoring, and tending to students. The pace is hectic, the demands are many, but TAs receive a wonderful taste of both teaching and boarding-school life.

FOR MORE INFORMATION . . .

■ Phillips Academy
Director, Summer Session
Andover, MA 01810
(978) 749-4406
summersession@andover.edu

■ Phillips Academy
Director, (MS)^2: Math and Science for
 Minority Students
Andover, MA 01810
(978) 749-4402
ms2@andover.edu

COMPENSATION

Est. $450–$675/week for undergrads
Est. $700–$1,150/week for grad students
Pays relocation expenses and round-trip travel

QUALITY OF LIFE

Dorm housing; social activities;
P & G College; Car for Sales interns

LOCATION

Cincinnati, OH; other U.S. & overseas sites—see Index

FIELD

Consumer goods

DURATION

9–14 weeks
Summer

PRE-REQS

College sophomores, juniors, and seniors; grad
students

DEADLINE(S)

February 1

In 1879, chemist James N. Gamble invented Ivory soap. A few years later, the first ads for the white soap boasted that it was—"99 $\frac{44}{100}$ percent pure." Did you ever wonder just what's in that other $\frac{56}{100}$ percent? Well, according to an independent analysis conducted by the company in 1882, Ivory is 0.11 percent uncombined alkali, 0.28 percent carbonates, and 0.17 percent mineral matter. Nothing scandalous to be certain, this is just an interesting fact about a famous Procter & Gamble product. Founded in 1837 by brothers-in-law William Procter and James Gamble (father of James N.) as a soap and candle business, Procter & Gamble has since grown by leaps and bounds. It's now a $30-billion-a-year consumer-products empire, with approximately 100,000 employees, competing in 44 product categories and operating in more than fifty countries. Its top-selling brands include Tide, Cheer, Clearasil, Cover Girl, Pampers, Charmin, Crest, Folgers, Hawaiian Punch, Jif, Pringles, and Crisco.

DESCRIPTION

Procter & Gamble recruits an army of interns for the following departments and locations: Brand Management (primarily MBA students) at the headquarters in Cincinnati and at the Cosmetics and Fragrances division in Baltimore; Product Supply/Engineering and Research & Product Development at one of the seven technical centers in Cincinnati; Product Supply (Customer Services or Purchases), Financial & Accounting Management, Market Research, and Management Systems in Cincinnati, Norwich, (NY), and Baltimore; Sales & Accounting Management (primarily undergraduates) in field sites throughout the country; and Product Supply/Manufacturing, with positions at almost 50 manufacturing sites nationwide. Overall, two-thirds of the intern class is based in Cincinnati.

Furthermore, another 70 to 100 positions are offered in more than twenty locations to foreign nationals studying in the United States. Preference is given to graduate students who have mastered the local language and culture, and who have the necessary work permits.

In 1879, Harley Procter convinced his partners that P&G should pour money into advertising Ivory as the "99 $\frac{44}{100}$ percent pure" soap that floats. That ad campaign marked P&G as one of the first companies in American business history to advertise its products. Over 100 years later, it's said that P&G, widely recognized as the world's best marketer of products, spends more on advertising than any other U.S. company. Consequently, interns in Brand Management (i.e., Advertising) are in for a real education. Acting as assistant brand managers, they design and execute national promotional events, develop marketing strategies for new products, improve package designs, and identify consumer habits.

A Research and Product Development intern in P&G's Household Products division worked on a project that analyzed how cleaners are distributed on fabric surfaces. "We use an image analyzer—a computer attached to a video camera, which we focus on a piece of fabric with detergent spread on it," he said. "The computer records the level of intensity per pixel, from zero for black to 256 for pure white. [The pixel intensities] are statistically analyzed to determine the distribution of soap on the fabric. It was my job to put together the image analyzer and write computer software for it. Assembling it was relatively easy, but composing the software was more difficult. I bounced ideas off P&G's computer scientists, image experts, and the other members of the project team to determine exactly what was needed."

At the Winton Hill Technical Center, a Product Supply/Engineering intern learned how Charmin and Bounty are made. "Pre-bleached fiber containing water is injected onto a moving wire mesh, which creates a thin, long sheet of fiber . . . . [G]ravity, vacuum, and P&G's proprietary 'predryer process' get rid of most of the water. However, to remove the last traces, the sheet is put on a 'Yankee dryer,' a tube about 20 feet long and 18 feet in diameter. The dry paper is then subjected to 'creping'— the act of scraping it off the Yankee to create two ten-ton rolls about ten feet wide apiece [each called a half-Yankee]."

After learning the paper-making process, he was asked to develop a mathematical model for the predryer. "I made about eighty prototype Bounty and Charmin samples . . . wet them down, and ran them through small-scale machinery at the pilot plant. [The experiments eventually] led us to a simple equation in three variables. It was definitely a good starting point." At the end of the summer, he presented his results, just as all P&G interns do, to a group of about twenty scientists, who posed many challenging questions. "When I couldn't defend myself, my mentor interjected and answered [the scientists'] concerns."

P&G's Product Supply/Purchases department manages the supply of materials and services needed to produce the company's products. A Purchases intern was asked to figure out how much sulfuric acid P&G needed in the next year to meet its laundry detergent output. "I flew out to San Francisco to learn how sulfuric acid is made, and then I researched the raw materials markets. I found out that the price of sulfur was declining, so I asked our five suppliers to fly to headquarters for a meeting, where I suggested that they lower their price and improve delivery and billing services . . . . After appraising each supplier's pros and cons, I redistributed [the volume] of sulfuric acid that each supplier would make. This shuffling saved us $800,000."

Sales interns each sell products to approximately one million dollars' worth of major accounts. As part of the regular sales force, interns get full use of a company car in which to make their rounds and for transportation on weekends. One Sales intern, stationed in Boston with 15 other interns, was responsible for accounts at 14 grocery stores. "You walk in and make sure our products are in stock and are being displayed properly. Afterward, you meet with the manager in order to sell him more inventory or discuss problems with presentation. But sometimes the store manager doesn't want to talk to you because you're a college kid. You have to be pretty persistent." Described as "very demanding" and "intense," the Sales position is more than just a casual visit to grocery stores. One intern

> As part of the regular sales force, each Sales intern gets full use of a company car in which to make his or her rounds.

worked on convincing a grocery store chain to carry a display for a new 16-ounce version of Sunny Delight juice. "I merged data from City Hall and P&G's own database to determine the demographics of our customers and created graphs representing changing market trends. My manager and I made a presentation to the chain's board members, who liked the idea. Two days later, they approved the display and required that all their stores use it."

P&G's internship program is well structured. An apartment-locater service arranges housing for more than 200 Cincinnati-based interns. The program also organizes many social activities, including dinners, a cruise on the Ohio River, and trips to Cincinnati Reds games. Some years, interns are invited to visit King's Island amusement park (paid for by P&G) or a downtown jazz festival. "The company bought each of us a $25 ticket; I got to listen to six hours of Chaka Khan and Jeffrey Osbourne," recalled one intern.

Early in the summer, P&G hosts a one-day orientation at headquarters for all interns (who are flown in from throughout the United States). After attending a half-day of business presentations by vice-presidents, interns enjoy a reception and dinner given by the chairman and president. Sales Management interns stick around and additional day to participate in their own seminars, which teach business ethics and selling strategies. Put up in hotels for a night, Sales interns often spend an evening at a Cincinatti Reds baseball game or at the local amusement park, all of which is paid for by the company. "I hadn't had that much fun or eaten that well in a long time," said one Sales intern.

P&G's Cincinnati headquarters is a sprawling corporate compound. Rippling proudly are the flags of ten countries displayed to remind visitors that P&G is an international company (P&G actually does business with 140 countries and rotates the flags every few weeks). Buildings are spread out over a ten-mile radius, and include the General Offices Complex and five R&D facilities. Each location offers a cafeteria with a convenient payment method—simply slide your ID card through the magnetic card reader and the meal will be deducted automatically from your paycheck.

Interns may join the General Offices' Lifestyle Center, which is equipped with Lifecycles, treadmills, Nautilus and free-weights, for a mere $13 per month.

Seminars and training sessions are scheduled occasionally at P&G. Interns attend such seminars as an R&D lecture on mass spectroscopy and a Purchases workshop on how to analyze consumer trends and forecast prices. They may also take work-related classes like "Memo Writing" and "Total Quality," which range from a half-day to a few days in length and are held at P&G's training center.

SELECTION

 College sophomores, juniors, seniors, and first-year graduate students are eligible to apply. Required fields of study depend on the program to which application is being made. Targeted technical majors include engineering (computer, chemical, electrical, mechanical, and industrial), computer science, information systems, math, statistics, and operations research. Applicants to Sales must demonstrate a clear interest in business, hold a valid driver's license, and pass a pre-employment physical. A brochure lists "leadership qualities, problem-solving abilities, creativity, interpersonal skills, and a strong record of personal achievement" as key selection criteria. International applicants are eligible. To research Proctor & Gamble, check out the company's web site at www.pg.com.

APPLICATION PROCEDURE

 The deadline is February 1. While P&G does almost all of its internship recruiting at approximately 100 campuses nationwide, unsolicited applications from students at other campuses may be considered. Send a cover letter, indicating area of interest, and, resume. Areas of interest include a Brand Management, Sales Management, Market Research, Financial Management, Management Systems, Research & Product Development (BS/MS), and Product Supply (Engineering, Customer Service, Purchases, or Manufacturing). Final selections are made after the company conducts on-campus and on-site interviews.

OVERVIEW

Ever heard of Chipso or Handy Soap? They're discontinued P&G brands. But that doesn't mean that Chipso and Handy Soap failed. Rather, their phaseout illustrates P&G's commitment to constantly improving its already high-quality products. To further that commitment, the company brings college students on board. Working to improve, manufacture, and sell products, they help ensure that consumers worldwide will continue to get the Tide out, squeeze the Charmin, choose Jif, and keep Zestfully clean.

FOR MORE INFORMATION . . .

■ Procter & Gamble
Internship Program Manager
(Area of Interest)
P.O. Box 599
Cincinnati, OH 45201-0599
(513) 983-1100

How would you like to enter a world where chalk wasn't used to write incomprehensible calculus equations but to trace murder victims? Where accused rapists, child abusers, and murderers weren't the characters in last Sunday's television movie with Farrah Fawcett but part of your workaday world? Where "legal internship" meant something more than fetching dry cleaning for some fat-cat lawyer?

All this and more is served up at the Public Defender Service (PDS) for the District of Columbia. PDS provides legal representation to indigent persons charged with criminal offenses, respondents in civil commitment proceedings, and incarcerated individuals in need of legal assistance. Attorneys in the trial division are appointed to represent clients at the outset of legal proceedings and continue representation through the final disposition of a case in trial court. This individualized representation was one of the factors cited by the Law Enforcement Assistance Administration in recently designating PDS as an "exemplary" office—the only defender office in the country so honored.

DESCRIPTION

PDS is comprised of approximately fifty trial attorneys, twelve appellate attorneys, ten to twelve full-time staff investigators, and 100 student interns. When the internship program began in 1976, PDS accepted only law students. PDS soon realized, however, that many law students could not devote enough time to the investigation and preparation of cases. Coordinators of the Criminal Law Internship now seek "sharp, motivated" undergraduates (in addition to recent graduates and graduate students) to help attorneys carry out pretrial investigations.

SELECTIVITY
Approximate applicant pool: 650–700
Interns accepted: 100

COMPENSATION
None; fellowships and stipends may be available

QUALITY OF LIFE
Special lectures and field trips; extensive training; forays into tough neighborhoods

LOCATION
Washington, D.C.

FIELD
Law; government

DURATION
12 weeks minimum
Summer, Fall, Spring

PRE-REQS
Undergrads; recent grads; grad students

DEADLINE(S)
Summer .... April 1
Fall and Spring .... 3 weeks before start of session

Interns undergo one week of training in which they learn basic investigative techniques and receive an overview of the criminal justice system, with an emphasis on the laws governing and shaping the conduct of a criminal investigation. PDS then pairs each "intern-investigator" with an attorney who specializes in Felony 1, Felony 2, Misdemeanor, or Juvenile cases. Interns indicate their preferences for the type of case they want to work on, although it is not always possible to accommodate all interns with their first choice.

Though there is a small amount of

clerical work for interns to do, this is by no means a desk job. Interns spend most of their time out of the office visiting and photographing crime scenes, locating and interviewing witnesses, serving subpoenas, acquiring police reports and criminal records, and visiting penal institutions. Interns also work closely with attorneys in writing reports and correspondence and helping the attorneys prepare for trial.

Many former interns marvel at the amount of responsibility given to interns. The internship coordinator suggests that this program could be considered "more of a job than an internship" based on the indispensable contribution made by the interns. From important investigative interviews to trial preparation, an intern's work becomes an integral part of each case. One former intern noted: "Knowing that you've contributed to an acquittal, for example, is a particularly exciting feeling."

Interns are taken on a series of tours that would fascinate even Hannibal Lecter.

Since conducting investigative interviews is an important part of the work, and because witnesses are often best reached at home, outside of business hours, interns should expect to work some irregular hours. PDS prefers students who can commit to 40 hours per week, but they do accept some part-time interns. Students who intern 20 hours per week at PDS may also be able to hold a part-time job.

Having at least part-time access to a car is an important prerequisite for this internship. Because the locations of crimes scenes, sites for investigative research, and homes at which interviews are conducted are often found in the more urban, or inner-city neighborhoods, and because some work occurs after normal business hours, interns must have the ability to arrive and leave an area on their own schedule, without having to rely on public transportation. PDS therefore gives strong preference to students with access to a car, though they do accept a limited number of interns without cars. Carless interns undergo the same training as other interns and may be paired with interns who do have cars. Otherwise, carless interns function as "case assistants," rather than "intern-investigators," and

are given more clerical tasks and less fieldwork.

Although the thought of spending a lot of time in the tougher parts of D.C. may seem intimidating, several former interns commented that they benefited from seeing "a different side of America." One intern suggested that "those who are least prepared will get the most out of it." Still, PDS does include as part of its training techniques on how to dress and how to approach and talk with people to minimize any potential safety risks.

This program offers an impressive array of perks that will appeal to anyone interested in gaining a first-hand glimpse at the inner workings of our criminal justice system. Interns are taken on a series of tours that would fascinate even Hannibal Lecter, visiting the Police Mobile Crime Unit, the autopsy room at the Chief Medical Examiner's Office, the facility for the criminally insane at St. Elizabeth's, and the lock-down ward at Lorton Penitentiary. Interns also have the opportunity to meet with federal prosecutors, vice squad officers, and judges. Furthermore, PDS encourages student investigators to attend court while in session. The program offers another perk for anyone interested in future graduate study: Interns are eligible for a 15 percent discount on test-prep courses offered in the D.C. area.

Interns do not receive monetary compensation for their work, but PDS does reimburse student investigators for travel by car at 25 cents per mile. Case assistants are similarly reimbursed for on-the-job metro and bus fare.

To help students find housing in Washington, D.C., PDS provides successful applicants with a housing bulletin that lists available housing with short-term leases, information about roommate and apartment search services, and available local dorm housing. PDS only includes housing that members of the staff or former interns have seen and can recommend.

The PDS offices are in Judiciary Square, which is home to the D.C. Superior Court House, the U.S. Federal Courthouse, the U.S. Attorney's Office, and the Metropolitan Police Department. PDS occupies the basement of a "historically old" building, and makes due with somewhat cramped office space, in which two attorneys often share a single office. Interns use attorneys' offices and have access to a single shared intern office, in which each intern keeps a mail box. Though one intern described these close surroundings as "pretty miserable for attorneys of this caliber," most interns spend the majority of their time outside of the office anyway.

The office dress is casual, and jeans and sneakers are the norm. Any court appearances, however, require more formal attire. In general, interns describe the office as having a "very fun," "social," and "close-knit" atmosphere. Interns feel comfortable working with the top-notch attorneys, who are said to be "very sharp" and "supportive."

While PDS attorneys will undoubtedly have graduated from many of the same schools from which the interns have come, PDS encourages diversity in both its intern pool and its full-time staff. A current staff investigator said that many "different walks of life" are represented and that the pervasive attitude is that "everyone is welcome and has something unique to offer."

SELECTION

 This program is open to undergraduates, recent graduates, and graduate students. There is no prerequisite coursework, but most interns have a strong interest in law or public service. According to PDS's literature, an individual who "thrives on the challenges of fast-paced on-the-job learning and interacting with a variety of people in a range of settings, and wants to learn about the law and our legal system by actually working in it" will be a good match for the program. The internship coordinator adds that PDS is looking for "mature" individuals who can handle a "high level of responsibility." PDS selects students who will be able to handle working in an inner-city environment, although few apply who are not prepared for this challenge. International applicants are eligible.

APPLICATION PROCEDURE

 Contact the internship coordinator for an application. The deadline for completed applications for the summer session is April 1. Application deadlines for other semesters are approxi-

mately three weeks prior to the beginning of the training session for that semester. Interviews are conducted either in person or by phone. Two items are of interest: PDS receives by far more applications for the summer session than for other semesters; and PDS accepts a slightly greater number of interns for the summer, meaning attorneys with high caseloads may be assigned more than one intern.

Applicants should indicate any interest in a fellowship on their application, though very few have been offered recently due to budget constraints. And although small stipends are also available, students can apply for stipends only after they have commenced the internship. Therefore, PDS recommends that students seek their own funding for the internship. Public-interest fellowships may be available through colleges. One former intern noted that he received some aid as part of his work-study package through his university.

OVERVIEW

 When shuffling papers at the local law firm just won't do it for you, it's time to seriously consider the Public Defender Service for D.C. The PDS internship is a remarkably hands-on experience, where, in the words of a former intern, "you're out there scrapping—interviewing witnesses, photographing crime scenes, working with attorneys—doing real work for real cases." Add one-of-a-kind field trips, extensive investigative training, and the rush of having the nation's capital as your training ground, and you've got a criminal law internship at its in-your-face best.

FOR MORE INFORMATION . . .

■ Kesha Taylor, Coordinator
Public Defender Service for D.C.
Criminal Law Internship Program
633 Indiana Avenue, NW
Washington, DC 20004
(202) 628-1200
(800) 341-2582
internship@pdsdc.org

QVC®

Imagine this.

It's Sunday afternoon and your favorite rerun of *Three's Company* isn't on for another ten minutes. You grab the remote and start channel surfing. And then you stop—maybe for just a split-second. Your eyes fix on a sparkling Diamonique ring as it spins back and forth on a French-manicured hand. Or you sit mesmerized by an autographed San Francisco 49ers football as it spirals through the air. The voice on the TV beckons you: "Call now." You think to yourself, "I could use one of those." You feel the remote slip from your hand as you reach for the telephone and dial the number on the screen . . .

Well . . . maybe not. But you did stop to look. So what is this thing that kept you from your quest for campy '70s television? Need you ask? It's QVC.

Started in 1986 by the founder of The Franklin Mint, Joseph Segel, QVC, Inc., quickly made itself a spot as cable TV's 24-hour, 7-day-a-week virtual shopping mall. Today, QVC is beamed into more than 73 million households across the country. With just a click of the remote control, home viewers can buy well-known brands like Coca-Cola, Warner Brothers, and RCA. Lest you think people don't actually buy things they see on TV, QVC's customer base is 17 million strong and growing at a rate of one new customer every 18 seconds. Over 60 percent of its customers return to buy again. And if these statistics are not enough to convince you that QVC is a retail force to be reckoned with, it sold over 31,000 Jeff Gordon Star Wars die cast cars in May of 1999. While competitors have hit the television shopping scene over the years, QVC maintains its lead with savvy program hosts, sharp product presentation, and worldwide expan-

SELECTIVITY

Approximate applicant pool: 250
Interns accepted: 50

COMPENSATION

Varies depending on department

QUALITY OF LIFE

Company orientation; Intern luncheons; flexible schedules; company discount for paid interns

LOCATION(S)

West Chester, PA

FIELD

Computer science, fashion merchandising, accounting, finance, information systems, retail management, library science, telecommunications.

DURATION

3–4 months
Year-round; Full- or part-time flexible schedules

PRE-REQS

Undergrads
Must receive academic credit for unpaid positions
Prefer college students who have completed at least 3 academic semesters.

DEADLINE(S)

Fall .... August 1
Spring .... November 1
Summer .... February 15

sion. In addition to opening shop in Germany, Mexico, and the United Kingdom, QVC also has its own music label, QRecords, as well as the very successful iQVC, an interactive online shopping site on the Internet.

BUSYWORK METER
LOW — MEDIUM — HIGH
OLDMAN & HAMADEH

DESCRIPTION

QVC began its formal Internship/Co-op Program in 1994, although it welcomed interns from its inception. Based at QVC headquarters in West Chester, PA, the program offers both paid and unpaid internships in a variety of departments. Interns have worked in the Broadcasting, Merchandising, Internal Communications, Accounting, Tax, Finance, Information Systems and Technology, Human Resources, Creative Services, and Public Relations departments. Said one intern who worked on projects in more than three departments, "I came into the internship wanting to explore various jobs. I didn't know what I would like to do, or even what I would be good at. Not only did I get a chance to try my hand at different tasks, I got to see first-hand how the various groups worked."

While they may be able to "shadow" more than one department, QVC interns don't take this to mean that they should blend in with the scenery. Quite the opposite. QVC engages its interns in hands-on learning. "It's not your basic office job," said the internship coordinator. Unless, that is, you consider running into Joan Rivers in the hallway or trying out a new salsa before the world has ever heard of it routine.

During a stint in the Information Systems and Technology department, one intern discovered the extent to which QVC was willing to go to involve her in challenging projects. "I started . . . writing a manual for some time-accounting software. When this project was temporarily suspended, [my manager] frankly told me that he'd rather have me work on another project—even one for another manager—so I could make the best use of my time." And make use of her time she did. Not only did she work with IQVC executives to help "formalize the vision for the complete overhaul of [its] website," she also created a trio of Lotus Notes databases for tracking project lifecycles that QVC still uses today. She does, however, warn that a QVC internship may not be for everyone. "People who need more structure, or who have a very long learning curve . . . or who feel strongly about carrying a project once started to completion, would probably [be] unhappy here."

One intern in Broadcasting found himself logging tapes for the creation of a video library three weeks into his internship. Determined to salvage what he said could have been the "downfall" of his internship, he asked to be relocated to the Control Room. "While there I was able to run audio, camera, and [graphics] on my own." He even filled in for permanent staff when they were short-handed. Judging from his experience, it pays to speak up if you believe too much of your time is spent on busy-work. There are a myriad of opportunities at QVC for interns who demonstrate initiative and a commitment to hard work. Though some interns may find themselves saddled with a little busy-work every now and then, QVC tries to keep administrative work to a minimum—less than 10 percent of an intern's time.

As ambitious and results-oriented as the QVC program is, interns stress that the atmosphere at QVC is one of respect and genuine concern for others. Interns are made to feel like a part of a close-knit family, albeit a very large one. A supervisor serves as a mentor to each intern, providing guidance, performance feedback, and career development. Interns also have a contact in Human Resources who can help them resolve any problems they might encounter. One intern was particularly impressed with the "infectious enthusiasm" of the people she met. "People seemed delighted to help me learn and obviously cared deeply about the success of the company," she said. "I was even carpooled in to work every day by employees who lived in the city." To enhance the sense of community, QVC provides various opportunities for its interns to meet and interact with one another, as well as with QVC employees. According to the internship coordinator, approximately 30 percent of QVC interns go on to permanent positions in the company.

Studio Park, QVC's headquarters, opened in late 1997. Tours introduce the general public to Studio Park's state-of-the-art digital equipment environment.

> QVC's customer base is 17 million strong and growing at a rate of one new customer every 18 seconds.

Interns at Studio Park will be outfitted with all the necessary office accouterments: cubicle, desk, phone, computer (if necessary) for the job, Email, office supplies, and company directories and manuals.

SELECTION

 QVC seeks currently enrolled college undergraduates of all majors who share its "pioneering spirit" and dedication to teamwork. The program accepts full- and part-time applicants on a rolling basis for its paid and unpaid internships. Applicants for unpaid internships must receive academic credit. International applicants who possess U.S. work authorization are eligible. QVC prides itself on its smoke-free and drug-free work environment and requires all interns to take a pre-employment drug test.

APPLICATION PROCEDURE

 Applicants should submit a resume and cover letter during the semester before they wish to intern. Qualified candidates are invited to QVC for interviews and a tour and fill out applications at that time. Candidates who are unable to interview in person can instead arrange for a phone interview.

OVERVIEW

 In the words of one intern, the QVC internship program is the best way to "hit the ground running" in the real world of television retail. Flexibility, responsibility, and challenging projects go hand-in-hand with exciting opportunities for travel, autonomy, and a back-stage pass to one of TV's most watched television shopping channels. For those not afraid to jump in feet first and work without a formal set of guidelines, a wealth of experience awaits.

FOR MORE INFORMATION . . .

■ College Relations Department
QVC, Inc
1200 Wilson Drive
West Chester, PA 19380
Fax: (610) 701-1150
www.qvc.com
jobs@qvc.com

SELECTIVITY			
Approximate applicant pool: 1000			
Interns accepted: Approx. 30			

COMPENSATION

$300/week

QUALITY OF LIFE

Youthful staff; discounted books;
weekly seminars; trip to Westminster, MD

LOCATION(S)

New York, NY

FIELD

Publishing

DURATION

10 weeks
Summer

PRE-REQS

College juniors; grad students

DEADLINE(S)

March 31

History has given us many famous "houses"—the House of Parliament . . . the House of Usher . . . The House that Babe Ruth built.

In 1927, few would suppose that the new house being contemplated could gain similar recognition. But pals Bennett Cerf and Donald Klopfer, who had acquired a classic-books line called the Modern Library in 1925, were convinced that a publishing house printing original books "on the side at random" was the way to go. "I've got it—Random House," Cerf said, inventing a name that would stand the test of time. An artist present in the room at the time immediately drew a trademark—a three-story house with clouds in the back. His five-minute sketch has been the company's emblem ever since.

Random House, Inc., is now the world's largest general-trade publisher, and its "house" has published authors like John Updike, Toni Morrison, James Joyce, Albert Camus, William Faulkner, Eugene O'Neill and—last, but not least—Dr. Seuss. Owned by Bertelsman AG, Random House, Inc., issues books under numerous imprints, including Alfred A. Knopf, Random House, Crown, Pantheon, Times Books, and Ballantine.

DESCRIPTION

The Random House Internship Program was established in the summer of 1990 to train college students interested in the field of publishing and thereby increase the company's pool of potential employees. In the beginning, some interns worked strictly in editorial positions while others juggled publicity and marketing posts. But in response to interns who wanted to experience both sides of the business, Random House modified the

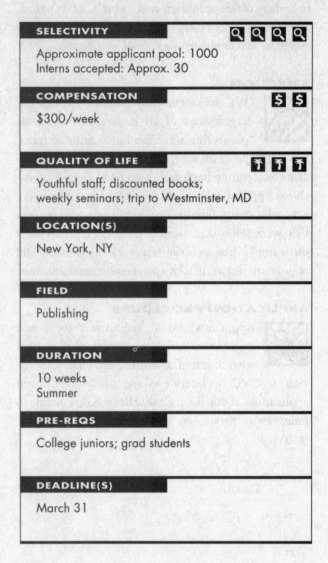

program. Interns are still placed in major publishing groups, as well as trade sales, marketing finance and the legal division.

By the time orientation takes place, interns have already started their tour of duty in one of the publishing groups. At Crown, for example, interns spend equal time with Crown's Harmony, Clarkson Potter, and Crown imprints. Over ten weeks, each intern's experience touches on everything from reading manuscripts to sitting in on book cover meetings. One intern read approximately ten manuscripts in a two-week period and composed a two-page summary for each one. Her analysis included a synopsis and her reasons for rejecting or recommending the manuscript. "My first manuscript was a book already under Crown contract," she said, "but I didn't know it.... I guess [my editor] was testing me, and fortunately I recommended that we publish it." Approximately two years after a book hits the shelves, Random House creates what are called "postmortem" profit-and-loss statements. "They reveal how well the book sold compared with our prediction," explained an intern who completed nearly thirty of them during her time at Harmony. "By doing P-and-Ls, I learned what goes into making a book. During the process, I visited almost all the departments to determine each book's design fees, printing costs, legal payments, publicity expenses, advance, sales, royalties—there's a lot to include."

> Random House's departments are notified from the start that under no circumstances are interns to be given only clerical work.

To generate demand for new books, Random House has interns help crank the company's publicity machine. An intern in Publicity worked on the radio giveaway of a sports book. "I researched in which cities we could best promote the book, looking for strong sports stations. I sent off about fifteen packets, including a picture of the cover and a descriptive page from the catalog, to about five cities." Another intern worked on a promotion for Peter Benchley's *Beast*. He drove to the beach and handed out baseball caps and copies of the book to sunbathers, while planes overhead dragged banners advertising the book.

Random House's departments are notified from the start that under no circumstances are interns to be given only clerical work. This is not to say that interns won't be photocopying the occasional manuscript. "This is a very labor-intensive business," said the coordinator. "They get some busywork just like everyone else." But it does mean that interns won't be engaged in mindless errands at the behest of an editor. Moreover, interns may turn to the coordinator should they find themselves in an awkward situation. "My editor asked me to pick up her laundry and that's not right. I was too intimidated to say anything, so I told [the coordinator] about it," said one intern. By the next day, the coordinator had moved her to a new editor.

The internship is well structured but not rigid. "We create the blueprint," says the coordinator, "but it's loosely defined so that interns with initiative can explore areas of interest." Indeed, some interns observe editors in the later stages of editing, while others work on finance department projects. Interns in editorial positions write "flap copy" (the synopsis on the inside of a hardcover's jacket) and "bound-galley copy" (the description appearing on the back cover of the uncorrected proof given to reviewers for the first critical reading). One editorial intern even wrote a cookbook's "fact sheet," a marketing tool used by publishers to describe a book to booksellers. "It includes information like title, trim size [i.e., the book's dimensions], publishing date, and author's previous works and sales, if any. It also provides a few descriptive selling points and a 'handle,' the one-sentence punch line on why you should buy the book."

In one former intern's estimation, her work was more stimulating and challenging than that of her current position as entry-level editorial assistant: "[The editorial assistants] are more like secretaries, answering the phones at the reception desk two hours each day, dealing with paperwork, and only occasionally reading manuscripts." But for interns, piles of manuscripts sit waiting to be read during those occasional moments when there's a lull in the day. "Even when they're bad," said an intern, "it's an interesting way to spend two hours."

Interns quickly bond, frequenting restaurants, attending Shakespeare in Central Park, and going clubbing on weekends.

Interns also convene once a week at noon to hear various employees speak about their positions within the company. They listen to publishers, editors, people from finance, and Random House's legal counsel, to name a few. "In one talk, a guy from production taught us about the art of typesetting—two people each key a whole manuscript into a computer and then a special program compares the two typeset works for discrepancies. . . . In one talk, Crown's legal counsel [discussed] legal issues in entertainment and then told us how the company decides which books should be scanned for libelous content."

Walking about are predominantly young employees in casual clothes. The informal dress befits what the coordinator says is "far from a stuffy corporate environment"—piles of manuscripts clutter desks, and of course all sorts of books occupy every inch of shelf space.

travel at their own expense to New York for a personal interview.

OVERVIEW

 A first-rate publishing internship with Random House. The selling points? Good pay by publishing industry standards; trip to distribution center in Westminster, MD; and meetings with editors-in-chief and senior executives. The handle? The world's largest book publisher, Random House, Inc., provides students with an excellent training ground in publishing and offers an insider's opportunity to possible full-time regular positions upon graduation.

> About the only thing Random House interns don't do is visit the main distribution center in Westminster, MD.

SELECTION

 Students of all majors are eligible to apply "because we publish books on every subject," said the coordinator. The program is open to college juniors and graduate students who have one year of school left upon completion of the internship. Excellent communications skills, initiative, and a "can-do, make-it-happen attitude" are essential, according to the coordinator. International applicants are eligible.

APPLICATION PROCEDURE

 The deadline to submit materials is March 31, but students may begin applying as soon as January 1. Applicants must send in a resume demonstrating an interest in publishing, and a cover letter indicating what they want out of a book publishing internship and why. "The cover letter gives us a sense of who you are and how well you write," said the coordinator, "and is especially important for people who have no prior publishing-related experience." Top prospects must

FOR MORE INFORMATION . . .

■ Random House, Inc.
Internship Program
1540 Broadway
New York, NY 10036

Raychem

SELECTIVITY

Approximate applicant pool: 2,000
Interns accepted: 40

COMPENSATION

$500–$700/week for undergrads
$700–$1,000/week for grad students;
round-trip travel

QUALITY OF LIFE

Plant tours; intramurals;
dedicated employees

LOCATION(S)

Menlo Park, CA

FIELD

Material science/high-tech

DURATION

10–12 weeks
Summer

PRE-REQS

College juniors and seniors; grad students
Minimum 3.0 GPA

DEADLINE(S)

April 1

What would you call a computer screen that responds to touch? How about a cord that is used on rooftops to automatically melt excess ice and turns off automatically when enough ice has been removed?

What would you call a self-resetting fuse that prevents batteries that short-circuit from starting fires or ruining electronic devices?

Some would say it's magic, but Raychem simply calls it modern technology. Manufacturer extraordinaire of material-science products, Raychem Corporation is on the cutting edge of scientific discovery. In addition to the aforementioned touchscreen technology, IceStop cable, and PolySwitch circuit protector, Raychem has invented more than 10,000 high-performance products, from fiber-optic cable accessories and computer touchscreens to cable TV coaxial-cable connectors and gel sealants. These products bring Raychem more than $1.6 billion in sales every year.

DESCRIPTION

Raychem's Intern Program dates back to the mid-1970s. Opportunities are available in the areas of Engineering, Finance, Manufacturing, Marketing/Product Management, Finance, Human Resources, and Logistics. Three-quarters of all interns are undergraduates.

Every year Raychem's managers submit approximately 150 requests for interns, a number significantly higher than the number of interns Raychem eventually employs. So, the company pares down the requests to the forty most challenging jobs by adhering to a principle articulated by Raychem's president and CEO, Robert Saldich: "The key to a successful internship program rests on who [interns are] working for and what they're working on. If they get a good mentor and an important project, they'll have an excellent experience."

Raychem's R&D division is the company's "primary engine for growth." Spending over 8 percent of sales on R&D annually, Raychem ranks among the top 100 corporations for R&D expenditures. With that much money pumped into the department in which they are placed, interns in R&D have an opportunity to do research on products with excellent commercial potential. An intern assigned to the

Gels group, for example, worked on a project to replace the silicone polymers usually used in gels with ethylene-propylene co-polymers. "The ethylene-propylene co-polymer is roughly $10 per unit less in cost, so if we could make the same gels using the ethylene-propylene co-polymers, we'd get a substantial savings." But first, he had to make sure that the company could get these new kinds of polymers to "crosslink" with one another. "Crosslinking" refers to the process in which high-energy electron beams are focused on a polymer to get the polymers' molecular chains to bond together at random points. The crosslinking results in an elastic yet structurally stable gel that can both adhere well and be easily removed from the surfaces on which it is placed. "Using IR, NMR, and GC techniques, I proved not only that the ethylene-propylene co-polymers crosslink, but also that we could control the reaction to make gels of varying hardness."

The hit-or-miss nature of R&D means that some projects will fail. For example, an intern in R&D worked on creating polymer-based electrodes that could "pull ions out of wastewater." Using a thin piece of metal surrounded by a polymer backing, the electrodes attracted copper and other ions. "We were trying to market it to the photography industry, but the electrode wasn't designed well, and it wasn't sucking up enough ions." Besides learning that "not every project is successful," this intern also realized that R&D work requires "lots of tedious testing; you've got to be willing to try all possibilities and keep plugging away until a solution presents itself."

To support R&D and Manufacturing, the Product Design department builds prototypes, designs assembly tools, and improves manufacturing processes. One intern worked on the company's new surge arresters, those foot-long successions of metal disks attached at the ends of electric lines that protect the lines from overvoltages caused by lightning. "Raychem's hybrid insulator is made out of a ceramic rod wrapped by a silicone cover called a shed. I designed a mold to make the shed, a die to make the rod, and special tools needed to put the surge arrester together. It was a lot of responsibility."

Rigorous projects aren't the only activities in which interns at Raychem participate. Interns are taken on plant tours to gain an overview of the company's ten divisions. Interns also have lunch with Raychem executives including CEO Dick Kashnow. Raychem also recruits university professors to speak on innovation in the field of science (e.g., nonlinear properties of polymers or relaxation times in liquid crystals). And occasionally, managers challenge interns to a softball game or take them to Gordon Biersch microbrewery, where they "toast a few beers."

Raychem's financial package is exemplary. The company covers round-trip airfare or gasoline expenses, if interns drive to Menlo Park. It also pays interns' first week of room and board while they search for an apartment. Weekly pay depends on experience and education. Freshmen typically make $500 per week while seniors can receive up to $700. Master's and Ph.D.-level students, on the other hand, earn $700 to $900 per week, while MBA candidates earn $1,000 per week. One would think that after investing so much money on interns, Raychem would consistently offer most of them permanent jobs. But hire rates vary from year to year. Some years only one intern is hired, while in other years it's five.

Headquartered in Menlo Park, CA, about 30 minutes from San Francisco, Raychem's main campus consists of 26 buildings that sit on an 82-acre site. Raychem has a number of additional buildings within a four-mile radius. On the grounds, easily accessible basketball and volleyball courts mean that summer intramurals are a big part of company athletic life. "If you can handle a challenging bunch of players, the intramurals are a great way to meet employees and other interns," said one intern.

Indoors, student office accommodations are mixed, ranging from cubicles to private offices. Spending most of their time in the laboratory, interns notice that "there's a

> **Easily accessible basketball and volleyball courts mean that summer intramurals are a big part of company athletic life.**

high degree of dedication." Said one intern: "[Employees] love science and technology; it's a positive atmosphere that emphasizes teamwork and communication." One intern found it amazing that "we got to work alongside some top-notch, well-published patent holders. . . . It's like being a batboy in the big leagues."

Students will work on a specific project or set of projects within a particular area and, at the end of the summer, these "batboys" come up to the plate at the Summer Intern Presentation. The presentation of projects (in the form of posters, photographs, or product samples) can either be in a science-fair like format or during a dinner. After answering employees' questions, interns and managers get together for a farewell reception.

SELECTION

 Applicants should have finished their sophomore year in college and should have at least a 3.0 GPA. The company seeks the following majors: engineering (electrical, mechanical, industrial, chemical), materials science, marketing, finance, human resources, logistics, manufacturing operations, and accounting. The internship flyer indicates that "academic record [and] extracurricular activities as well as interpersonal and leadership skills are the basis for selection." International applicants are eligible.

APPLICATION PROCEDURE

 The deadline is March 1. Students should submit a resume and cover letter discussing their work experience (including any other internships completed), leadership activities, and area of interest. After resumes undergo a preliminary screening by College Relations, managers conduct phone interviews to match top candidates to available projects.

OVERVIEW

 Since 1957, Raychem has been making magical products—products that keep pipes from freezing, protect computers from short-circuiting, and seal telephone splices from water and dirt. "The operative word is pioneering technologies," says CEO Saldich. "We don't copy products and try to make them better. We try to be the first to invent products that solve customer problems." Raychem's practice is to intentionally place interns "in the guts of [the company's] businesses," allowing them to work with cutting-edge material-science products.

FOR MORE INFORMATION . . .

■ Raychem
P.O. Box 92016
Los Angeles, CA 90009-2016
Fax: (310) 337-3379
raychem@isearch.com
www.raychem.com

SELECTIVITY	🔍 🔍 🔍 🔍 🔍
Approximate applicant pool: 2,500 Interns accepted: varies	

COMPENSATION	$ $ $ $
$340–460/week for undergraduates $500–$680/week for graduates, NFL players	

QUALITY OF LIFE	♟ ♟ ♟ ♟
Independence; 40 percent discount on shoes; lunchtime basketball games	

LOCATION(S)
Stoughton, MA; Irvine, CA; Atlanta, GA; Chicago, IL

FIELD
Athletic shoes and apparel

DURATION
10–12 weeks Summer

PRE-REQS
College juniors and seniors; recent grads; grad students Minimum 3.0 GPA

DEADLINE(S)
March 15

The rhebok is a small South African gazelle. It is extraordinarily aggressive, agile, and fleet-footed. The image of this animal well-serves the Reebok company, whose humble beginnings go back to 1895. That year, Englishman Joseph William Foster, member of the Bolton Primrose Harriers running club, made himself the world's first pair of spiked running shoes. Though he had sewn the left shoe and nailed the right, his fellow club members all demanded a pair. What started as a curious enterprise soon became J.W. Foster & Sons, hand-crafter of shoes for the world's top sprinters, long-distance runners, soccer players, ruggers, and "footballers." Around 1950, J.W.'s grandsons Joseph and Jeffrey Foster apprenticed at the family business. The experience convinced them to build J.W. Foster & Sons into a new sportswear company, so in 1958 Reebok was born.

Twenty-one years later, an outdoor sporting goods distributor named Paul Fireman spied Reebok's shoes at an international trade show and acquired the North American distribution license. In ten years, Reebok grew from a $1 million- to a $1 billion-per year sporting goods company. Now Reebok International Ltd. comprises Reebok, Rockport, AVIA, Weebok, and BOKS brands and holds 25 percent of the U.S. market, second only to NIKE. Developer and distributor of the world's first aerobic dance shoe, creator of a new exercise movement called Step Reebok, and inventor of The PUMP,™ Reebok is now a $4 billion-per-year operation.

DESCRIPTION

In the summer of 1990, Reebok started the College Relations Internship Program to identify potential employees and to give students experience in the athletic sportswear industry.

Every summer, seven undergraduates and three graduate students are chosen to participate in the program. Placed in the company's Stoughton, Irvine, Atlanta, and Chicago offices, undergraduates work in the company's Reebok division in areas such as Promotions, Human Resources, Retail, Management Information Systems (MIS), Finance, and Sales. Graduate students, usually MBA's, receive assignments within the Reebok division's Marketing unit.

An undergraduate intern in the Sales division's field service group acted as a liaison between Reebok's fitness footwear groups (aerobics, cross training, walking, etc.) and the field representatives. He collected data on each of the new lines being introduced. That summer, for example, Reebok released about ten lines, each featuring two to four shoes. "One such line was the Preseason cross-trainer series featuring the PUMP Paydirt, the Scrimmage Mid, and the Scrimmage Low," he said. "I compiled information on this and every other new line—what sport or activity the shoe targeted, what professional athletes used the shoe, and the shoe's materials." In order to put together such a list of characteristics, the intern had to become well versed in "shoe-ology." "I described what materials made up the upper [visible part of the shoe], the tongue [the flap under the laces], the midsole, and the outsole," he said, "and I learned that Reebok has access to three kinds of leathers and an ingredient called hexalite." Hexalite, a honeycomb like material, is used in space shuttles to absorb the shock a craft experiences upon hitting the earth's atmosphere. Reebok sometimes puts hexalite in a shoe's heel to reduce the shock on an athlete's knees and ankles.

But College Relations interns aren't the only students sniffing around the company. Since 1990, Reebok has hosted a design competition, entitled Designovation,® to ". . . attract the best designers to Reebok." The competition targets design students at nine schools, including the Art Center College of Design (Pasadena), California State University at Long Beach, Carnegie Mellon University, Fashion Institute of Technology (New York), Parson School of Design (New York), Royal College of Art and Design (London), Rhode Island School of Design, and Syracuse University. Each school's top five candidates, determined from footwear/apparel products they create for the competition, are flown to New York, where their work is judged by distinguished designers such as Niels Diffrient and Nicole Miller. The panel of judges eventually christens six finalists Designovation

interns, and provides each with a ten-week summer internship in a Design group at Reebok, Rockport, or AVIA. A former Rockport intern, for example, was told to design a progressive shoe for the women's active lifestyle line. She came up with 12 prototypes, and at the final presentation—featuring Reebok executives, designers, and marketing personnel—Reebok's CEO "was duly impressed." Perks include round-trip airfare, housing, a $3,400 stipend, transportation to and from work, a mentor, and an awards ceremony with "all the glitter usually reserved for the Oscars."

Reebok sponsors a third internship program as well. The company places professional football players in summer account-executive internships at field offices around the country and also at Reebok's headquarters in Stoughton, MA. Past participants include Buford McGee, Jimmy Johnson, Keith Neubert, Stanford Jennings, and Troy Barnett. Though the NFL internship ends one week after the College Relations program begins, exposure to the players is possible. "One time, I shared an elevator with six huge players in slick suits," said a Designovation intern. Another intern found a reason to call Stanford Jennings: "I needed a figure from his department."

Reebok's definition of internship uses words and phrases such as *structured*, *meaningful*, and *impact upon the business group*. Few interns dispute the value of their contributions, but none calls the internship structured. In fact, interns point out that it affords them quite a bit of independence. "I came up with some crazy shoe designs," said one intern. "It seemed like I was free-falling at 100 miles a minute—you do a lot of unplanned projects," said another. One undergraduate collected information from field representatives' surveys of shoe store outlets. "I ranked shoe sales, summarized Reebok's representation at displays, and noted what customers are looking for," he said. "The report went out to management, and I was told that the president of Reebok USA looked at it during

> "I played basketball every day with vice presidents, other interns, and company employees."

strategy sessions."

Reebok's six-story headquarters is located in "sub-urban, woodsy" Stoughton. A mile down the street is the Reebok outlet store, where interns receive a 40 percent discount on blemished shoes and overstocked clothing. The headquarters is home to the divisions (except for Rockport and AVIA, which are located in Marlboro, MA and Portland, OR, respectively), a computer center, two cafeterias (which serve an all-you-can-eat special every Friday during the summer), and an atmosphere described by several interns as "informal," "laid-back," and "family-like." On the last night of the company's summer sales meeting, interns join several hundred "Reebok-ites" as they embark on a cruise of Boston harbor.

As expected, most employees at the company love sports. At lunchtime, employees gather at the company's basketball court—Reebok shoes only, of course. "I played basketball every day with vice presidents, other interns, and company employees. Even guys from the warehouse would come over," said one intern. Interns with no flair for hoops may play Rollerblade hockey and tennis on nearby courts or work out at the company gym. The gym (membership: $3 per week) features weights, aerobics, StairMasters, treadmills, bikes, fitness experts, and cheap massages.

Interns at headquarters attend a two-hour orientation in the third week of the internship. They are introduced to the structure, culture, and mission of the company. "But we are already baptized by then. The introduction should come sooner," complained an intern. Orientation also breaks the ice between interns. "We encourage them to get together socially," said the coordinator, who hands out a list of all interns' names and phone numbers. One year, interns hosted after-hours cookouts that were subsidized by Reebok. Another year, the intern class sponsored a road race for charity.

SELECTION

Undergraduates must have completed their sophomore or junior year by the start of the internship. Recent graduates starting master's-level work in the fall and first-year master's students (including MBA candidates) are eligible for the graduate internship. Applicants must be enrolled in school on a full-time basis at the time of application. Reebok targets liberal arts, business, economics, management information systems, and accounting majors. A minimum 3.0 GPA and excellent communication skills are required. The company looks for well-rounded people: "We want students who have not just excelled in the classroom but also participated in extracurricular activities and held leadership positions." Work experience (volunteer or paid) related to one's academic major or intended profession will also provide an edge. International applicants are eligible.

APPLICATION PROCEDURE

Reebok asks that applicants send in a resume and cover letter during January and February. All resumes will be acknowledged. Students are asked not to call the company. On-site interviews and decisions for finalists take place during March and April.

OVERVIEW

For nearly a hundred years, Reebok has been a purveyor of top-notch athletic footwear and apparel. For the last few of these years, Reebok has provided college students with practical training in the footwear business in a youthful environment that "allows you to run with the ball." Armed with Macintoshes and the freedom to dream, interns attempt to improve Reebok operations. For their efforts, they receive good pay and at least one free pair of shoes. If you love sports and sportswear, then take a lap around the Reebok track. Just remember to give it your heart and sole.

FOR MORE INFORMATION . . .

■ Reebok
   c/o College Relations Program
   100 Technology Center Drive
   Stoughton, MA 02072
   www.reebok.com

Okay music-trivia buffs—Who coined the phrase "rolling stone?" The Rolling Stones, that venerable supergroup headed by weather-beaten showman Mick Jagger, or *Rolling Stone*, that venerable magazine featuring musicians, music reviews, and political commentary? The answer is neither. In 1965, Bob Dylan churned out the rock-and-roll classic, "Like a Rolling Stone." The blues-great Muddy Waters' "I'm a Rollin' Stone" put the phrase in the public's consciousness a few years earlier. And, oh, don't forget the age-old maxim: "A rolling stone gathers no moss."

It may not be the original namesake, but *Rolling Stone* magazine has made a huge contribution to music journalism. Beginning in 1967 as a grassroots publication distributed mostly in Northern California, *Rolling Stone* has become the world's premier music magazine, grossing more than $110 million annually and reaching upwards of 1.2 million readers per issue. Published biweekly and issued twenty-four times a year, it features incisive interviews and photographs of the music world's hottest performers.

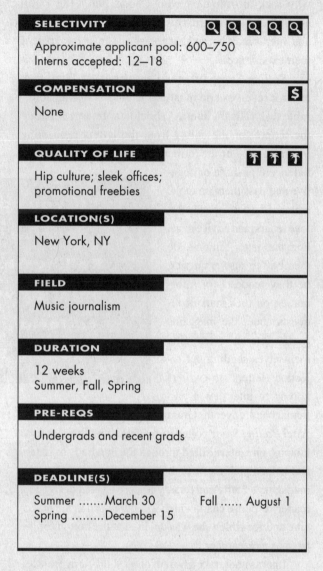

SELECTIVITY

Approximate applicant pool: 600–750
Interns accepted: 12–18

COMPENSATION　$

None

QUALITY OF LIFE

Hip culture; sleek offices; promotional freebies

LOCATION(S)

New York, NY

FIELD

Music journalism

DURATION

12 weeks
Summer, Fall, Spring

PRE-REQS

Undergrads and recent grads

DEADLINE(S)

Summer .... March 30　　Fall ...... August 1
Spring .... December 15

DESCRIPTION

The staff at *Rolling Stone* minces no words about an intern's role at the magazine. Part gofers and part research assistants, interns are not entrusted with the job of writing articles: they receive no bylines, no feature stories, and no literary glory. Participants do, however, gain exposure to all aspects of magazine publishing, from photography to editing. Hundreds of interns have passed through *Rolling Stone* since the program began in the mid-seventies, and most give their experience high marks.

While positions are available in a variety of departments, such as Advertising and Publicity, word has it that the best place to work is the Editorial department. "It's the nerve center of the place. It's where the action is," remarked one intern.

As with most entertainment internships, the Editorial internship at *Rolling Stone* includes a good deal of filing, faxing, photocopying, and phone work. But, as an employee pointed out, unlike phone work at a law firm, phone work at the magazine can be fun. "We deal with a number of 'crazies'—people looking to speak to Mick Jagger, tell us stories about playing guitar with Jimi Hendrix, and offer ideas about why rock-'n'-roll died with Chuck Berry [he's still alive]," said one intern. Busywork is busywork, though, and interns must accept that gofering is an integral part of their experience.

Rolling Stone strives to answer every legitimate letter it receives and most of the burden of this admirable task falls on interns' shoulders. Interns separate the letters for the editor from the letters requesting information. For the former, interns record whether the letters are positive or negative and pass them on to the editor of the correspondence, love letters, and advice page. For the latter, interns do their best to answer queries, be they requests for information on rock stars or requests about the magazine itself. Interns often find themselves sending out rejection letters to writers hoping to interview a particular band, cover the Grammys, or write record reviews. After *Rolling Stone* polled its readers about their favorite albums, one intern sifted through the hundreds of letters and helped pick the ones that would be published in the magazine's 25th Anniversary Issue. She also designed a reader-response chart, which was published in the magazine and for which she was credited at the bottom of the page as a researcher.

Interns undertake a host of other short-term projects. One spent a few days tracking down the publicists of celebrities the magazine wanted to interview. Cold-calling hundreds of agents and production companies, she gained exposure to "the crazy world of celebrities and their agents." Another was asked to call major magazine associations and create a complete list of the awards *Rolling Stone* had won over the years.

Typing and basic computer skills are essential for *Rolling Stone* interns. Interns are responsible for updating the computer index system by entering the titles and dates of recently published articles into the in-house computer files.

> "If you can't be a member of the Rolling Stones, you might as well be an Editorial intern at *Rolling Stone*."

Many intern assignments relate to *Rolling Stone*'s "Campus Issue," a special edition dedicated to college news and trends that is published twice yearly. "I was asked to sift through a variety of college newspapers and find anything offbeat or outrageous that might be of interest to the editors," said an intern. Aware that "interns are in touch with the college scene," editors often consult them for suggestions about stories being written for the college issue. They also encourage interns to call college contacts to find anyone with an interesting story or unusual part-time job.

A few interns remarked that they wished the internship allowed an intern to work closely with a writer on a particular story. Said one: "I would have loved to stay with a particular story for a period of time—brainstorming ideas, doing research, and accompanying a writer on interviews. Instead, it seemed like every few days brought another task, preventing me from getting too involved with any one story." Despite this system, writers and editors try to be accessible to interns, and most are willing to take time out to offer interns words of wisdom.

An undeniable boon of being at *Rolling Stone* is the perks that come with working at a music magazine. Concert tickets, promotional T-shirts, advance movie screenings, and promotional compact discs sometimes float an intern's way. They aren't doled out in a formal manner, rather, when an editor has no need for them, he or she usually passes them along to interns, especially those who have done a good job. Some editors allow interns to borrow their CDs, and interns often have the opportunity to hear new records weeks before they are released to record stores. "I got to put my hot little hands on advance CDs that even radio stations didn't have," gloated an intern. As would be expected, interns also have dibs on free copies of current or past issues.

Although interns attend the occasional in-house birthday or good-bye party, many are disappointed that they aren't invited to magazine or music-industry parties. "Interns are out of the loop on the party scene. It would have been nice to attend a few, especially since we work for free," said an intern. Some were crestfallen at not receiving invites to *Rolling Stone*'s 25th anniversary party, a once-in-a-lifetime blowout attended by every rock-'n'-roll star imaginable. But the employees who attended were not even permitted to bring dates, so it's understandable that invitations were distributed sparingly.

Summer interns are invited to in-house seminars. In each seminar, a department head gives a 30-minute speech exploring his/her job responsibilities. Interns are encouraged to ask questions at the end of the seminar. The first seminar is often hosted by Jann Wenner, the magazine's publisher.

Occupying an entire floor of a midtown skyscraper, *Rolling Stone* shares its space with sister-magazines *US* and *Men's Journal*. The office is sleek, with an abundance of natural wood and glass. Some windows overlook the famous neon marquee of Radio City Music Hall. A variety of artwork decorates the walls of the spacious office, including an assortment of distorted rock-star illustrations by Philip Burke, whose sketches normally appear on the contents page of the magazine. Nearby on display is the paint-splotched suit Steve Martin wore on a 1981 *Rolling Stone* cover. Line sketches by John Lennon adorn an adjacent wall, and an entire alcove is devoted to displaying, in chronological sequence, every *Rolling Stone* cover since the magazine's inception.

Interns like their workspace. Each occupies a fully equipped cubicle, similar to those used by the editorial staff. All of the cubicles are situated near each other and not far from the cushy office of Jann Wenner. "Our location was choice. We had a good view of Jann's office and scoped out the celebs who came in to visit him," an intern said. Interns also enjoy the music that often fills their workspace, as several members of the editorial staff have boom boxes, which they play when the mood strikes them. One intern's "productivity increased threefold with reggae jamming in the background." If on-the-job visual and auditory stimulation aren't enough, free coffee and tea are a short walk away.

SELECTION

 Although the program looks for college juniors, seniors, and recent graduates, a few of the interns surveyed worked at *Rolling Stone* as college freshmen or sophomores. No prereqs apply, but past interns stress the importance of being outgoing and self-motivated. An avid interest in rock and roll helps, too. According to the intern coordinator, the best interns "want to learn every aspect of magazine publishing" and are "inquisitive and enthusiastic, even when carrying out clerical work." International applicants are eligible.

APPLICATION PROCEDURE

 The deadline is August 1 for fall, December 15 for spring, and March 30 for summer. A complete application includes a resume, a transcript, a letter of recommendation from a professor or professional, and a cover letter stating the session to which the student is applying and the reasons for wanting to work at *Rolling Stone*. Local applicants are requested to interview in person, but phone interviews are also conducted.

OVERVIEW

 Abandon all (editorial) hope ye who enter here. Although *Rolling Stone* interns rarely, if ever, do any actual writing for the magazine, they rave about just being *at* a place like *Rolling Stone*. "If I did the same work at a drier magazine, the internship would have been completely different. Being at a hip, progressive place like *Rolling Stone* made it all worthwhile," said one intern. Several former interns have made their mark in the publishing world, including one who's an editor of *Sassy* magazine and another who's the music editor at *Vibe*. For music fans who wish to spend a semester on the cutting edge of the music industry, an intern advised, "If you can't be a member of the Rolling Stones, you might as well be an Editorial intern at *Rolling Stone*."

FOR MORE INFORMATION . . .

■ Rolling Stone
Internship Coordinator
1290 Avenue of the Americas
New York, NY 10104
(212) 484-1616

It swims with hooked jaw. It swims in cold, clear waters. But most important, as far as Rosenbluth is concerned, it swims against the stream.

Rosenbluth International chose a salmon as its mascot to reflect the company's willingness to buck tradition. CEO Hal Rosenbluth outlined the company's unconventional "customer comes second" policy in an article he wrote for the *Harvard Business Review*. In it, he said, "What we have is a hierarchy of concerns: people, service, profits. We focus on our people, our people focus on service, and profits result—a by-product, you might say, of putting our associates [Rosenbluth-talk for "employees"] ahead of our customers." Whether it is training its workforce with games like Rosenopoly and Travel Jeopardy, employing managers (called "leaders") who go out of their way to encourage associates, or planning festive events like Hawaiian Shirt Gonzo Friday to boost morale, Rosenbluth leads the corporate pack in employee satisfaction. Its motivated workforce has helped make it the nation's third largest travel agency. But the term "travel agency" doesn't do this company justice. Rosenbluth is a worldwide travel management empire, arranging the travel for more than 1,500 corporate clients, including Oracle, Eastman Kodak, Compaq Computer, DuPont, and Westinghouse.

SELECTIVITY
Approximate applicant pool: 300–400
Interns accepted: 10

COMPENSATION
None

QUALITY OF LIFE
Friendly, upbeat culture; unique orientation; intern events

LOCATION(S)
Philadelphia, PA

FIELD
Corporate travel management

DURATION
10–15 weeks
Summer, Fall, Spring

PRE-REQS
Undergrads; recent grads; grad students

DEADLINE(S)
August/September for fall
December/January for spring
April/May for summer

DESCRIPTION

Although positions are available in a variety of areas, including Information Technology, Learning and Development, Supplier Relations, Travel Reservations, Accounting, Marketing, and Human Resources, sources say that the Corporate Communications department offers the juiciest work. Corporate Communications coordinates the activities related to Rosenbluth's corporate identity—advertising, public relations, and internal communications. As the company does not rely on outside ad agencies or PR firms, there's extensive marketing work to be done.

Corporate Communications interns are entrusted with a wide range of marketing projects. Some research or write articles for *Executive Traveller* magazine, a publication Rosenbluth sends to its corporate clients. Said one: "I wrote the CEOs of top travel companies, asking them to submit to *Executive Traveller* a brief article about the travel industry. I found about six executives willing to write articles, including the CEOs of Marriott and USAir." Chances are that interns will also write press releases, work one on one with suppliers (printers, designers, etc.), and attend client meetings. One intern designed a "Rosenbluth Rolodex card" to give the company better exposure among local businesses. "I put together a special Rolodex card, figuring out everything from a color scheme to a catchy slogan."

The internship, however, is not always a day at the park. A modest amount of administrative work awaits the Rosenbluth intern. "Sure, there was some monkey work," said one intern. "But it wasn't all-consuming." Interns may be asked to fax press releases to the media, drop off media kits to locations around Philadelphia, update the media list in the company's database, fill out Fed Ex forms, and stuff envelopes with the *K.I.T.* ("Keep in Touch") internal newsletter. Even so, Rosenbluth has a support staff that keeps clerical work to a minimum for interns.

If anything makes Rosenbluth stand out, it's the company's remarkably warm-spirited atmosphere, one that brings to mind the REM song "Shiny Happy People." Hal Rosenbluth said as much in an October 1990 interview in *Inc.* magazine: "A company has an obligation to the people it employs to make that part of life pleasant and happy." The 42-year-old Rosenbluth sets the tone with his power-of-positive-thinking attitude. Once, for example, he sent crayons to 100 employees and asked them to draw a picture of what the company meant to them. This touchy-feely spirit trickles down to interns. "The attitude at Rosenbluth is very tolerant and upbeat. People here care about each other," said one intern. Birthdays are celebrated with "miniparties" in a conference room—"expect lots of bagels and doughnuts." At the end of the internship,

> **"The attitude at Rosenbluth is very tolerant and upbeat. People here care about each other."**

interns are given a surprise (shhh) going-away party, where one should (again) "expect lots of bagels and doughnuts."

The end of the internship may be enjoyable, but the beginning is even better. New interns don't just experience a few hours of orientation, they participate in the two-day, no-holds-barred New Associate Orientation Program. Designed for all new employees, from interns to new vice presidents, the program steeps them in the Rosenbluth mindset. "[Orientation leaders speak about] one of the most important facets of quality customer service, one that is rarely emphasized: listening. We talk about teamwork, or more specifically, barriers to successful teamwork . . . [like] stubbornness, lack of a clear goal, and preconceived notions," an associate reported in *Travel Weekly* magazine. Not content with conveying their message by lecture alone, orientation organizers ask new associates to dream up and act out a bad-service scenario, such as a careless barber giving a client a botched haircut. Orientation culminates in a visit to the executive offices, where new associates chat with Hal Rosenbluth. "Mr. Rosenbluth took off his jacket and served us tea in expensive china," said an intern. "I had to ask myself, 'Is the president of the company really serving us tea?' I was blown away by his willingness to take time out to talk to us."

All interns are assigned a mentor. During the first week of the internship, the mentors sit down with the interns to determine the objectives of the experience. The mentor and intern meet on a regular basis to determine if the intern is meeting his or her objectives.

While the logical fringe benefit, travel packages, are reserved for permanent employees, interns have their fill of smaller perks, namely Rosenbluth knickknacks. As one intern put it, "They're big on corporate culture here." A few months at Rosenbluth will yield a fine wardrobe of salmon-emblazoned merchandise, not the least of which includes Rosenbluth T-shirts, golf caps, key chains, sweatshirts, and windbreakers. If interns want more items, they can always order from the aptly named "Upstreamer" catalog.

SELECTION

 While Rosenbluth relies on the Great Lakes College Association to find many of its interns, unsolicited applications are also welcome. Undergraduates of any level, recent graduates, and graduate students are eligible to apply. The program looks for students "with excellent writing skills, poise, maturity, and the ability to handle pressure, responsibility, and meet deadlines," according to a coordinator. International applicants are eligible.

APPLICATION PROCEDURE

 Applications are accepted on a rolling basis. Interested parties should submit a cover letter, resume, and creative writing samples. After an initial screening of applications, the intern coordinators invite the applicants they are interested in to interview at Rosenbluth.

OVERVIEW

 Haven't heard of Rosenbluth before? Don't worry if you haven't; virtually all of its clients are corporations. While Rosenbluth may not be a household name, there's more to a top internship than immediate name recognition. Not only does Rosenbluth expose students to the nuts and bolts of travel management, it also offers one-of-a-kind opportunities in marketing, communications, and many other areas. Rosenbluth staff members seem sincerely committed to having interns squeeze as much as possible out of their jobs; some associates even assist interns in creating a portfolio of their work. Only the most cynical curmudgeon could resist the company's warm and fuzzy culture. Hal Rosenbluth said it best in *Inc.* magazine: "We look at human resources the way others look at financial assets."

FOR MORE INFORMATION . . .

■ Internship Coordinator
Rosenbluth International
2401 Walnut Street
Philadelphia, PA 19103-4390
(215) 977-5429
www.rosenbluth.com

RUDER·FINN

As the saying goes, "In the modern world, propaganda is as important as ammunition. Nobody understands this principle better than Ruder Finn—one of the world's leading public relations agencies for over 50 years. The privately held, family-owned company has been a pioneer in using new strategies, tactics, and technologies of communication to help sustain recognition, cultivate good will, and motivate customer purchases for its clients. The agency is widely recognized for its work with arts and cultural institutions, and it has an impressive roster of corporate clients, including Ford, the Four Seasons hotel, Pfizer, and the country of Barbados.

The New York-based public relations firm handled publicity for the republics of Croatia and Bosnia during the late 1990s, drawing international media attention to the human rights violations in the former Yugoslavia. With Ruder Finn communicating the message, the world became very aware of Serbian attempts at ethnic cleansing, prompting everyone from the Clinton administration to Jewish lobby groups to condemn the Serbs.

SELECTIVITY	🔍🔍🔍🔍🔍
Approximate applicant pool: 200 Interns accepted: 6–15	

COMPENSATION	$ $ $
Pro-rated weekly, based on a $21,000 yearly salary	

QUALITY OF LIFE	🧍🧍🧍
Educational curriculum; office meetings	

LOCATION(S)
New York, NY (HQ); Washington, D.C.

FIELD
Public relations

DURATION
4 months Summer, Fall/Winter, Winter/Spring

PRE-REQS
College seniors; college juniors (summer); grad students

DEADLINE(S)
Summer .... April 1   Fall/Winter .... August 1 Winter/Spring .... December 1

DESCRIPTION

Established in 1978, Ruder Finn's Executive Training Program assigns entrants to client service groups or has them serve as "floaters" to assist groups across the Agency. Client service groups are specialized — some by the industry they serve, others by the communications approach emphasized in the work. Groups include technology (hardware and software), telecommunications, Internet (infrastructure, services, websites), prescription pharmaceuticals, over-the-counter drugs, consumer products, luxury products, travel and hospitality, corporate and institutional identity, arts & culture, publishing, event marketing, and social responsibility. Communications service specialties include knowledge management, Internet marketing, Web development, graphic design, and video production.

All trainees have a basic set of responsibilities, no matter where they work. Creating and updating media lists are trainees' least favorite chore, but "it's elemental to the public relations process, so it has to be done." While one trainee warned that spending hours on media lists can "make one cross-eyed with boredom," another emphasized a benefit of such work: "By making the dozens of calls needed to assemble a media list, you learn not to fear talking on the phone . . . . [I]t teaches you professional savvy." Trainees also spend a lot of time writing pitch letters in hopes of convincing journalists to cover a particular client. "I'd pull my hair out trying to be creative," said a trainee. After writing a pitch letter, trainees typically submit them to a supervisor for editing and reediting. A corollary to pitch letters are pitch calls, for which trainees dial up news organizations and ask them to "run a client's public service announcement or cover a client's activities."

Other responsibilities vary from department to department. A trainee in Visual Technology was asked to conduct on-the-street interviews to test public opinion of a local hospital. "Microphone in hand, I approached passersby and asked if they knew about the hospital. Not everyone was willing to be interviewed—it sometimes took some coaxing and joking around to warm them up." Working for the Glad Bag-a-thon Clean-Up & Recycling Program, a trainee in the Environmental Communications group traveled to Newport News, VA, where he solicited news coverage for the town's massive cleanup effort. "I drove to a series of newspapers and TV stations and tried to generate interest in the final day of the Bag-a-thon." A trainee in the same department helped out at a press conference for a Citibank Visa Card promotion. "When reporters arrived, I told them where to sit and answered their questions . . . . [M]ost questions were pretty basic, but occasionally a reporter threw me a curve like 'How will all this impact the Dow Jones?'"

A telltale sign of how an organization views its trainees is its willingness to include them in office meetings. Ruder Finn comes through with flying colors in this regard. Trainees are encouraged not only to attend creative sessions but also to participate. "At creative sessions, executives would sit around and think of innovative publicity ideas for a client," said a trainee. "These meetings always had an open, unintimidating feel. Trainee input was enthusiastically encouraged."

One session was held to brainstorm ways of spicing up Mr. World's American Tour, a geography program sponsored by Citibank and the National Geographic Society that traveled the country visiting elementary schools. A trainee thought up a way to increase student involvement by having students at every school draw a "map" of the important elements in their lives. Management liked the proposal so much that they implemented it, and according to the trainee, "Young students across the country sent in maps of their lives, drawing their bus stops, families, pets, and so forth . . . . [W]e attached these maps to the back pages of a 6" × 4" book, which went on tour with Mr. World."

> During the first week, trainees attend all-day classes on the public relations profession.

A unique feature of this program is the educational curriculum. During the first week of the program, trainees attend all-day classes on the public relations profession; thereafter, they have class once a week. Classes feature lectures by staff experts and group discussions emphasizing journalistic writing skills and various practical components of the profession. The curriculum covers such topics as "Strategic Thinking in Public Relations," "Basic Newswriting," "Introduction to Major National Broadcast Press," and "Ethical Issues in Public Relations." Every week, trainees are given a homework assignment relating to the week's topic. They might be asked to write a press release, draft an article announcing an employee promotion, or think up possible headlines for a hypothetical story. Assignments are critiqued by the week's speaker or the trainee coordinator, but "no grades are given—it's a low-key, constructive process."

Ruder Finn's headquarters are located on three floors of an office building in midtown New York. The decor is described by trainees as "unimpressive" and "nothing to write home about," except for the abundance of photographs taken by president David Finn, about which one trainee said, "Finn is a big photography buff, so he hangs his work all over the agency. The photos are of people, street scenes, statues—things like that. I think they make neat decorations—they add a common thread to the agency." Once grouped together in an isolated trainee area referred to as the "playpen," trainees are now assigned cubicles near their assigned groups. This new seating plan has reportedly helped trainees feel more integrated within their respective groups.

SELECTION

 Applicants must be college graduates at the time the session for which they are applying begins. The program accepts candidates from any academic background, including those with graduate degrees. Note: Part-time summer positions are available to college seniors, who are paid $10 per hour. According to the intern coordinator, undergrad interns perform the same work as trainees.

APPLICATION PROCEDURE

 The deadline for the summer program (mid-June to mid-October) is April 1; for the fall/winter program (mid-October to mid-February), August 1; and for the winter/spring program (mid-February to mid-June), December 1. Required materials include an application form, resume, writing samples, names and addresses of two references, and, for those who have graduated within the past six months, an unofficial transcript. In addition, applicants must submit responses to two writing assignments, which typically require 300-word essays on hypothetical public relations situations. Applicants to the D.C. office should apply through the New York headquarters.

Approximately one month after the deadline, the Executive Training Committee arranges interviews with selected applicants. The interview period runs the fifth and fourth weeks before the beginning of the program. Interviews are conducted by account team members of the group(s) you have expressed an interest in working for either in person or by phone. Candidates selected for interviews are notified by phone and receive a case history to analyze prior to the interview. A portion of the interview session is devoted to discussion of the case study.

OVERVIEW

 For the lucky few, Ruder Finn offers a one-of-a-kind introduction to the public relations profession: practical experience combined with a structured training program. Although an average of 50 percent of participants are hired as permanent employees, trainees warn against going into the program expecting permanent employment: "It's a gamble. You can work your tail off as a trainee and still be passed over for a job." But even if it fails to lead to a job offer with Ruder Finn, the program shines because—in one trainee's words—"it's so respected in the profession that it will open several other doors."

FOR MORE INFORMATION . . .

■ Ruder Finn
Trainee Coordinator
301 East 57th Street
New York, NY 10022
(212) 593-6332
degnd@ruderfinn.com
www.ruderfinn.com

SKADDEN ARPS SLATE MEAGHER & FLOM

Scene: *A high-powered New York law office, walled in huge glass windows that offer a stunning view of the nighttime skyline of Manhattan. Two interns, in white shirts with rolled-up sleeves, sit at a desk, eating a late dinner.*

Intern One: (looks up, chopsticks in one hand, take-out carton in the other) Rough week, huh?

Intern Two: Yeah, crazy—but good. I'm excited about this new trademark legalization case I'm doing; it's going well. I'll probably come in tomorrow to work on it.

Intern One: No rest for the weary—and that would be us.

Intern Two: But you know what they say:

Intern One and Two: (in unison) Thank God it's Friday—only two more work days left!"

This last line captures the spirit of Skadden, Arps, Slate, Meagher & Flom. Founded in 1948, Skadden, Arps is one of the nation's leading law firms, best known for its corporate and litigation work. With more than 1,000 lawyers and nearly 450 legal assistants in thirteen countries, Skadden, Arps represents all twenty of the world's largest banks and about one-third of the Fortune 500 companies.

SELECTIVITY 🔍 🔍 🔍

Approximate applicant pool: 150
Interns accepted: 20–25

COMPENSATION 💲 💲 💲 💲

$400/week

QUALITY OF LIFE 🔼 🔼 🔼

Occasional travel to client site; seminars with partners; long hours

LOCATION(S)

Boston, MA; New York, NY; Washington, D.C.

FIELD

Law

DURATION

10–12 weeks
Fall, Winter, Spring

PRE-REQS

College juniors and seniors

DEADLINE(S)

Fall .... August 1   Winter .... December 1
Spring .... February 1

DESCRIPTION

Assisting legal assistants and attorneys, interns at Skadden, Arps work in various departments, including Corporate Finance, Banking, Labor, Intellectual Property, Mergers & Acquisitions, Litigation, Bankruptcy, and Products Liability. Wherever they end up, most interns do what one former intern in Washington calls "a lot of paper shuffling." This ranges from making lists and filing, coding, and indexing casework to more challenging duties like proofreading reports and preparing documents for presentation. Interns also conduct non-legal research on clients and clients' competitors. While this would seem to score high on the busywork meter (one intern calls the work "often tedious and very repetitive") another intern defends the job: "It's not just copying and filing—we do everything legal assistants do, and that involves a lot of responsibility."

Interns often become closely involved with the work of a particular lawyer, who usually assigns more complicated tasks like producing legal briefs. In conjunction with such work, interns are often sent out to cover important meetings. One New York intern, on his first day on the job, was sent to consulate offices all over the city to find out the visa requirements for Khazakstan. A Washington intern gathered data for a case by attending a series of Department of Energy hearings on efficiency improvement, an assignment she recalled as "very cool."

Skadden interns join the firm on the lowest rung of the corporate ladder. As one intern reports, "There's a saying around here that s--- runs downhill—well, we're at the bottom of the hill." When something goes wrong, another intern says, "You don't get blamed, but you're expected to fix it!" Interns have to learn to "be flexible, and do whatever, whenever." Their low status notwithstanding, most interns find Skadden's culture encouraging. Says one intern, "The legal assistants treated me like an equal, which really helped me adjust to the job." The staff gets raves for being "so friendly, and incredibly willing to accommodate you or help you with anything you need." A New York intern stresses the importance of developing a close relationship with one of the firm's lawyers, saying that "if he or she believes in you, the sky's the limit—you can do anything."

Although interns might be able to do anything, they work hard to earn that kind of trust: long hours are the rule, not the exception. Sixty-hour weeks are common; one New York Finance intern boasted, "One guy in my department's been here six days straight!" But another puts a positive spin on it: "When you stay overnight, you can see the sun rise over Manhattan." Workaholics thrive in this high-powered, high-pressure environment. An intern in Litigation explains it this way: "People here have a desire to prove themselves—there is a very high level of expectation for your work." Another intern, who worked in the Antitrust division in the Washington office, says, "Once you work so much on a project that it becomes yours, you *want* to come in and make it perfect."

The high expectations and fast pace have their benefits and drawbacks. One intern says, "You always have to do your best work, because everyone's on the ball," while another called the spirit of Skadden "very driven" and said, "Some people get turned on by that, but I've seen others become complete basketcases from the stress." The pressure trickles down to the interns, creating an atmosphere where "you feel like you have to be constantly trying to get ahead, that you should be out there meeting people, making contacts, and getting assignments."

> The intern office is nicknamed the "Romper Room"—"it's like an extension of college."

For those who can take the intensity of the environment, working at Skadden offers many rewards. Interns share office space, but each gets his or her own phone line, voice mail, extensive access to computers, and even "notepads with your name on them!" In New York, where Skadden occupies twenty-four floors of an imposing 47-story skyscraper in midtown Manhattan, interns and legal assistants take up the entire 23rd floor. Nicknamed the "Romper Room" by one recent intern, it's a high-energy place filled with people under thirty, where college sweatshirts are draped over chairs and "it's like an extension of college." The company cafeteria, Cafe 21, "not consistently good," says one intern—is often no match for the order-out offerings of midtown Manhattan. There is a gym, but it is open to attorneys only.

Skadden's offices are described as "sparsely decorated" but "dripping with power" and are located in prime areas: in Washington, the firm is squarely in the middle of the political scene, while in New York interns are walking distance from world-famous Central Park and the Museum of Modern Art. Interns, in their limited time off, can visit the Guggenheim, see *The Marriage of Figaro* at the Met, or go shopping and clubbing in SoHo.

Generous monetary compensation is another benefit: interns make $10 per hour and $15 per hour for overtime (anything above 40 hours/week). "The firm really takes care of you," says one intern, who notes that if you stay after 8 P.M., the firm provides a meal allowance for dinner and a free ride home. Each month, Skadden also sponsors a few intern lunches, where partners and junior attorneys speak about job opportunities in the legal field.

SELECTION

 Skadden internships are open to college juniors and seniors. While many interns treat the job as a "training ground for law school," the internship is also a good place to experience the corporate legal environment and decide if it's really for you. The ideal intern, says the coordinator, is aggressive, independent, creative, self-motivated, ambitious, and focused— a personality profile that fits the firm as a whole. International applicants are eligible.

APPLICATION PROCEDURE

 Deadlines are August 1 for the fall internship, December 1 for winter, and February 1 for spring (during the summer, Skadden's internship programs are reserved for first- and second-year law students). Applicants must submit a resume and cover letter to the New York office regardless of the location in which they wish to intern. Those whose resumes and cover letters meet Skadden's requirements are asked to sit for interviews, conducted in person in Washington, Boston, or New York to introduce prospective interns to the firm.

OVERVIEW

 In three major American cities—New York, Boston, and Washington—is a law firm that doesn't slow down. Skadden, Arps, Slate, Meagher & Flom, headquartered in New York and one of the nation's premier corporate law firms, has a reputation for high-powered, fast-paced intensity. Interns agree with this picture, and speak of the incredible opportunities and learning potential that the internship offers. Says one intern, "If you perform well and aren't scared to work hard and achieve, your experience can benefit you for years to come." And another calls this the best internship he's ever had, saying, "After being at Skadden, I feel like I can handle anything the legal world throws at me."

FOR MORE INFORMATION . . .

■ Manager, Legal Assistant Services
Skadden, Arps, Slate, Meagher & Flom
4 Times Square
New York, NY 10036
(212) 735-3000
Fax: (212) 735-2000
csprague@skadden.com
www.sasmf.com

SELECTIVITY	N/A
Approximate applicant pool: N/A Interns accepted: 700	

COMPENSATION	$
None, but a few positions may offer stipends	

QUALITY OF LIFE	⬆ ⬆ ⬆
Seminars and workshops; gift-shop discounts; gym available	

LOCATION(S)
Washington, D.C.; New York, NY (Cooper Hewitt Museum, National Museum of the American Indian)

FIELD
Museums

DURATION
2 months–1 year at least 20 hours/week; may vary Summer, Fall, Winter, Spring

PRE-REQS
Varies with position

DEADLINE(S)
Varies with program. Central Referral Service deadlines are: Summer ...... February 15   Fall .... June 15 Spring .... October 15 (Subject to change)

For a painting, a sculpture, a musical instrument, a coin, or even a locomotive, there's no greater honor than to be accepted into the Smithsonian Institution. To become part of the Smithsonian, an artifact is judged for its physical condition, exhibit potential, size, and "readability" (whether a visitor can understand the artifact by looking at it). Pieces that pass muster are incorporated into the world's largest museum complex, the Smithsonian Institution, composed of sixteen museums, the National Zoo, and several research facilities. With upwards of 25 million visitors each year, the Smithsonian is a wonderland of things valuable and collectible.

DESCRIPTION

The Smithsonian Internship places interns among 40 museums, administrative offices, and research programs. "There's truly something for everyone," as the internship brochure points out, and it's no overstatement. Animal lovers may work the National Zoo, and art aficionados have the National Portrait Gallery, the National Museum of American Art, and the Hirshhorn Museum, among others. *Jurassic Park* groupies can get their ya-yas out at the National Museum of Natural History and the Smithsonian Environmental Research Center is a natural choice for environmentalists. Budding librarians may hit the books at the Smithsonian Institution Libraries—the list goes on and on.

One of the most popular museums in which to intern is the National Museum of American History (NMAH), where the majority of interns help prepare for upcoming exhibitions. An intern in the African-American Cultures department, for instance, worked with a curator to acquire materials for a Wade in the Water, a 1995 exhibition on the African-American sacred-music tradition of the 19th and 20th centuries. On one of her assignments she visited the National Archives and Library of Congress, where, among other relevant artifacts, she "found pictures of fugitive slaves [for whom] music was a means of survival." She arranged for the Smithsonian to purchase prints of these photographs, which were incorporated into an exhibition.

But not all interns at NMAH work directly on exhibitions. In the Department of

Social and Cultural History, an intern worked with inner-city high school students on a theatrical presentation relating to one of the museum's exhibitions. To augment an exhibition on the African-American migration to the North between 1840 and 1940, the intern and her group of students staged *A Man of Letters*, a play that dealt with the issue of "passing" (i.e., light-skinned African Americans who tried to "pass" for white). Involved in all aspects of the production, she oversaw the students, designed costumes, and even played three roles in the performance.

Another intern, this one in NMAH'S Division of Public Programs, conducted research for the museum's concert series. "Part of my job [entailed] calling agents to find music groups who would amplify the themes of the exhibitions," she explained. "The museum looks for a wide variety of top-notch but lesser-known musicians, from Native American bands to singing cowboys from Texas." Conducting this research and dubbing tapes of past concerts, she learned that a culture's musical traditions often transcend those stereotypically attributed to it: "There's so much [musical] diversity [within a culture] that most people aren't aware of. Native Americans [for example] not only have the traditional drum and chant, but also songwriters and guitar-and-harmonica groups."

For those seeking experience in artifact conservation or those enrolled in a graduate conservation training program, the Smithsonian offers intern positions in its Conservation Analytical Laboratory (CAL). Interns at CAL help preserve a variety of paintings, textiles, furniture, and other objects. An intern assigned to the "objects lab," for example, participated in an ongoing project to excavate and restore a group of 8,500-year-old Jordanian statues. "Jordan doesn't have the facilities to recover the statues . . . so the Jordanian government asked the Smithsonian to help," she explained. The statues were in pieces and buried in the original block of dirt in which they were found, so she documented the exact location of the fragments as she removed them. "You had to be very careful and photograph where each piece was being taken from. The process was very tedious." After excavating the fragments, the intern strengthened the pieces with a resin and set about reassembling them into statues. "It was really neat to see the figures regain their original shape. . . . [One particular statute] was very strange—it turned out to have two heads."

With its awesome collection of historic airplanes hanging overhead, the National Air and Space Museum is a perennial favorite of the public. Interns here have done everything from photographing the ongoing restoration of airplanes to assisting in the creation of new curriculum packages to writing the museum's first intern handbook. Assigned to the Library, one intern found herself organizing a collection of rare books on aviation. "I went through and recorded the bibliographic data for dozens of fascinating books—some on ballooning, others on the Wright brothers, and even one autographed by Amelia Earhart, which displayed a miniature American flag she carried with her in flight." The intern was also asked to look over another collection of books and make recommendations as to which should be included in the museum's rare-book collection. "I rated each book in terms of its age, exhibition potential, rarity, and uniqueness (e.g., if it's autographed by a famous aviator)."

No intern leaves the Smithsonian without the chance to attend a variety of seminars. Most museums have their own program for interns. The National Air and Space Museum, for example, holds luncheons during which each intern makes a presentation on his or her project. Alternatively, the National Museum of American History runs a weekly brown-bag luncheon with one of the

> Choosing where to intern at the Smithsonian is a little like drinking from a fire hose— overwhelming.

museum's curators. Said an intern about the luncheons: "They were top-notch. One week we had Lonnie Bunch, a well-known curator who spoke about being commissioned by Japanese companies to create an American history exhibition in Japan. [Another week] we listened to a curator who put together the First Lady exhibition and how he went about [procuring] Hillary Rodham Clinton's briefcase and headband for it." Beyond events unique to each museum, there's a workshop on museum careers that is open to all Smithsonian interns. Gathering four times during the summer and once during the fall and spring, interns hear presentations by museum directors, curators, and education staff. They also attend a workshop on resume building and meet with representatives from graduate programs in museum studies.

As for other perks, the most useful is a 20 percent discount at museum gift shops. Interns take full advantage of this privilege, buying oodles of postcards, posters, ceramics, and for one intern at the Air and Space Museum, "*Star Trek* paraphernalia, especially punch-out paper models of the new *Enterprise*." Interns may apply for a full tuition scholarship to take a Smithsonian Institution summer course. Taught by local professors and museum experts, courses are open to the public and cover topics in areas such as art history, music history and American history.

The museums of the Smithsonian Institution line the perimeter of The Mall, a rectangular expanse of grass bordered by the Washington Monument at one end and the U.S. Capitol at the other. Tourists are everywhere, which for one intern presented the opportunity to make new friends. "It was easy to meet visitors from all over the world during lunch breaks and after work." Intern accommodations vary with each museum and each office therein, ranging from "a conference table but not much else" to "my own cubicle—including a desk, IBM computer, and voice mail." A cafeteria exists in every museum, but some eating facilities receive higher marks than others: "Having done several Smithsonian internships, I think the best food is at [the] Air and Space [Museum]. There are just better cooks over

there. . . . The lasagna was *really* good." For those looking to get physical, the Interstate Commerce Building (a ten-minute walk) has a weight room and aerobics classes open to federal employees (including Smithsonian interns). The National Air and Space Museum has a limited physical fitness facility. It includes an exercise room equipped with treadmills, rowing machines, stationary bicycles, leg press, sit-up benches and a universal gym.

SELECTION

 Just about anyone is welcome to apply to the Smithsonian Internship including high school seniors, undergraduates of any level, recent graduates, graduate students, and career changers. Prerequisites vary with each position. Interested parties may write to the Center for Museum Studies (CMS) for "Internships and Fellowships," a free brochure listing museum addresses and position descriptions, or send the CMS a $5.00 check for *Internship Opportunities at the Smithsonian Institution,* a book providing detailed information on each museum's internship.

APPLICATION PROCEDURE

 Candidates may apply to one or more office/ museum on their own. CMS administers the Central Referral Service, which may be used by individuals who are submitting multiple applications or those desiring assistance in matching their interests with appropriate offices/museums.

Application deadlines may vary. The Central Referral Service and some offices/museums use the following dates: summer internship, February 15; fall internship, June 15; and spring internship, October 15.

The completed Intern Application consists of an application form, a two-page essay on reasons for seeking an internship, two letters of recommendation, undergraduate and graduate transcripts (as applicable). Forms, details, and assistance with the application process may be obtained from the CMS. Personal interviews are not required.

OVERVIEW

 Choosing where to intern at the Smithsonian is a little like drinking from a firehose—overwhelming. But once the choice is made, interns can count on an internship filled with rewarding projects and edifying seminars. Whether or not they go on to pursue a museum-related career, interns leave the Smithsonian with a "quantum-leap increase in cultural awareness" and a name "you put in boldface on your resume."

FOR MORE INFORMATION . . .

■ Intern Services Coordinator
Smithsonian Center for Education
    and Museum Studies
900 Jefferson Drive, SW
Suite 2235
Washington, DC 20560-0427
(202) 357-3102
siintern.cms.si edu

Sony Music

SELECTIVITY	
Approximate applicant pool: 500 (Credit), 800 (Minority) Interns accepted: 100 (Credit), 80 (Minority)	

COMPENSATION	N/A
None (Credit) Varies with position (Minority)	

QUALITY OF LIFE	
Promotional freebies; cafeteria; seminars and trips (Minority)	

LOCATION(S)	
Santa Monica, CA; New York, NY (HQ); and field offices in CA, GA, IL, MA, MD, NY, OH, and TX	

FIELD	
Music	

DURATION	
10 weeks (Summer, Fall, Spring) Credit 10 weeks (Summer) Minority	

PRE-REQS	
See Selection	

DEADLINE	
Rolling (Credit) for fall/spring semesters; March 31 for summer and Minority Internships	

If Martians were to visit America and take a good look around, what would they think was important to the human race—love, honesty, trust? Perhaps, but if they judged our values by the labels appearing most often in our households, they might think our most prized ideal was "Sony." After all, it's rare to find a household without a few televisions, stereos, and radios emblazoned with the distinctive Sony logo.

But Sony is much more than electronics. In 1986, the company acquired CBS Records, arguably the world's most successful record empire. The resulting division, Sony Music Entertainment, Inc. (SMEI), took over CBS Records, Columbia, and Epic record labels and also established new labels such as Chaos Recordings and TriStar Music Group. The upshot for SMEI has been an impossibly rich roster of artists, including the likes of Michael Jackson, Bruce Springsteen, Sade, Mary Chapin-Carpenter, Harry Connick, Jr., Mariah Carey, Michael Bolton, Pearl Jam, and Spin Doctors.

DESCRIPTION

 Sony Music Entertainment, Inc., runs two internships. The Credited Internship is open to undergraduate and graduate students who are able to secure academic credit for their work. The Summer Minority Internship Program is a paid experience for minority undergraduate and graduate students that is augmented by a number of seminars, trips, and training sessions. Both internships place students in a full range of SMEI departments, including Promotions, Publicity, Retail Marketing, Artists and Repertoire (A&R), A&R Administration, Business Affairs, Finance, and MIS.

Interns in Publicity help keep artists in the public eye. Assigned to Epic Records' Black Music division, a Publicity intern spent much of her time putting together press kits. "The basic way we publicize an artist is through press kits," she said. "They consist of a brief biography of the artist, an 8" × 10" glossy, and a CD or tape of the artist's new album. I was in charge of assembling these kits and sending them to various publications." Her most exciting job involved assisting with the department's "press day," a "mini news conference" where an artist would answer questions from a group of reporters and magazine editors. Whether creating a special booklet to brief the press on a particular artist or calling journalists to invite them to the conference, she had a finger in all aspects of press-day preparations. She also attended the event, and even escorted journalists to the conference room before the meeting began. "Press days were a great way to hype a band, to create a buzz. We had them for groups like Patra, Hoodratz, and Shakim. And a good showing of publications would be represented, including *USA Today*, *Ebony*, *Vibe*, and *Rap Sheet*."

An intern in Video Production worked as an assistant on video shoots. "On a Sony soundstage or on location around New York, the producers in my department created artist-profile videos with established artists like Tony Bennett and Tom Chapin," she explained. "I accompanied the production team on shoots and did a little of everything—running errands, setting up props, working with the lighting people . . ." Happy to volunteer for any assignment, she once found herself driving downtown to pick up soul food for rapper LL Cool J, who "loved the chicken and grits." For her efforts, she was allowed to spend hours in the edit room watching editors put together video footage. "[The editors] were great about letting me see how they transform the clips into a finished video—I learned a lot of technical stuff . . . I also got to see all sorts of outtakes and raw footage. They really give you insight into the personality of an artist."

Not all interns work in creative departments. An intern in A&R Administration, for example, worked with record contracts. Despite having "no previous experience with contracts," she was asked to read several contracts, glean their essential points, and enter the information into a computer database. She described: "It was not easy. I had to cut through the confusing language and determine an artist's rights in terms of things like royalties, artwork, and budgets for music videos." She eventually became a pro at reading record contracts, learning the nuts and bolts of legal jargon like "override royalties" and "leaving-member options." She also got to read the confidential deals worked out with various artists. "I wasn't given the really big-name contracts, but I did get to see the details in contracts for [Bruce Springsteen's wife] Patti Scialfa and [the group] Bad Brains."

Participants in the Minority Internship Program participate in several special events. Every Thursday they attend a brown-bag luncheon featuring a senior-level executive. One week they may meet with the director of A&R at the luncheon, the next week it may be a senior VP from Columbia or Epic Records. The coordinator also likes to plan a get-together with interns and Minority Internship alumni currently working at Sony Music; says the coordinator, "It's the chance for interns to meet people who've been in their positions . . . and it's the ideal time for networking." The coordinator then takes interns' education a step further by spending an afternoon watching and discussing a video adaptation of Steven Covey's bestseller *Seven Habits of Highly Effective People*. No summer would be complete without a field trip to Sony Music Studio ("a veritable shrine of high-tech equipment") and a Sony CD-manufacturing plant in Pitman, NJ.

Although interns receive no official perks, working at a thriving record company is bound to yield a few unexpected rewards. A few interns, for example, were asked to help pick the winners of the *Poetic Justice* competition, a poetry and rap contest publicizing the soundtrack of Janet Jackson's *Poetic Justice* movie. "We reviewed all of the poetry and rap submissions and picked three finalists for each category," said one of the interns. "The rap songs were especially fun to screen. We looked for originality (the fewer samples, the better) and professionalism (a clean-cut sound that was good enough for radio)." In addition to the possibility of receiving a "cool assignment," interns can usually get their mitts on some promotional goodies.

"Among my friends who applied to [music industry] internships, Sony was everybody's first choice."

Past interns have tapped into free CDs ("although you can't go shopping and clean out the whole place"), T-shirts, concert tickets ("I saw Billy Joel and Terence Trent D'Arby"), and free movie passes to Sony Pictures films. Invitations to listening parties are also a possibility, one intern reports attending listening parties for Columbia Records stars Kris Kross and Baby Face.

Located in a skyscraper whose roof is "curved like a scoop," Sony headquarters has the "extremely modern" black-and-white decor one would expect of a Japanese electronics company. Everything in the building is sleek and streamlined, from the fifth-floor "sky lobby" to the omnipresent modular furniture. The offices of Sony Music Entertainment are decorated with gold and platinum albums, posters of different artists, and various plaques. The majority of desks have a stereo, all of which, of course, sport the Sony logo. Intern accommodations vary from "a cubicle equipped with voice mail and a typewriter" to "my own desk in a secretarial bay" to "a chair on the side of my supervisor's desk." The sky lobby has a cafeteria with a variety of pasta, grilled foods, pizzas, and salad bar offerings.

SELECTION

 The Credited Internship is open to undergraduates and graduate students who are currently enrolled in a college or university. Participants in this program must receive academic credit for their work. The Minority Internship targets undergraduates and graduate students who are African American, Latino, Asian American, and American Indian. Minority Interns must have at least a 3.0 GPA in their majors and be entering or returning to school after the internship. Both programs accept students from any academic background, but in the brochure's words, "an interest in the music business is an asset." International applicants are eligible.

APPLICATION PROCEDURE

 The deadline to submit materials for the Minority Internship is March 31; the Credited Internship has a rolling application deadline for the fall/spring semester and March 31 for the summer. Applicants should submit a cover letter and resume to the appropriate address. Finalists are invited to Sony for personal interviews with the Recruiting and Placement Department and, in exceptional cases, long-distance applicants may substitute a phone interview for an on-site visit.

OVERVIEW

 What has the Sony Music Entertainment internship got that the others don't? A well-organized program in which it's possible to be something other than a copy room beast of burden, a record company flush with big-name artists (and the cash to make sure they remain big-name artists), and a minority internship that goes out of its way to acclimate students to an industry traditionally underrepresented by minorities. The word is out that Sony has a top-notch program, as one intern reports: "Among my friends who applied to [music industry] internships, Sony was everybody's first choice."

FOR MORE INFORMATION . . .

■ Sony Music Entertainment, Inc.
  Credited Internship
  550 Madison Avenue,
  2nd Floor
  New York, NY 10022-3211

■ Sony Music Entertainment, Inc.
  Minority Internship
  550 Madison Avenue,
  13th Floor
  New York, NY 10022-3211
  Attn: Department 13-5

■ Internship Hotline: (212) 833-7980

SOTHEBY'S
FOUNDED 1744

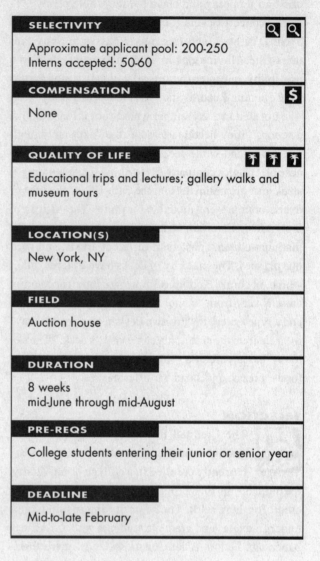

SELECTIVITY

Approximate applicant pool: 200-250
Interns accepted: 50-60

COMPENSATION

None

QUALITY OF LIFE

Educational trips and lectures; gallery walks and museum tours

LOCATION(S)

New York, NY

FIELD

Auction house

DURATION

8 weeks
mid-June through mid-August

PRE-REQS

College students entering their junior or senior year

DEADLINE

Mid-to-late February

Winking and nodding. Glasses on, glasses off. Pencil in pocket, pencil in hand. Tugging the earlobe . . .

What's happening here? Is someone having a nervous fit, or in desperate need of a bathroom? No, these are just a few of the signals bidders use when they wish to remain anonymous at a Sotheby's auction. Explains Sotheby's CEO and auctioneer (and former intern, '78) Bill Ruprecht: "Some people like to participate discreetly, so they prearrange with me a certain signal."

"Mystery bidding" is just one factor in the mystique that pervades the hallowed halls of Sotheby's, arguably the world's most famous and respected auction house. Founded in 1744 so British citizens could exchange property without the burden of face-to-face bargaining, Sotheby's today is known the world over as *the* place to sell property of great value and interest. Recent Sotheby's auctions have featured the Duchess of Windsor's jewelry collection, Andy Warhol's art collection, paintings by Georgia O'Keeffe, Vincent van Gogh's *Irises* (sold for $53.9 million, making it one of the most expensive paintings in history), and even Elton John's collection of jewelry and clothes (read: enormous sunglasses, Doc Martens boots, and sequined stage-suits).

DESCRIPTION

You better not blink or you might miss the Sotheby's internship—it lasts only a scant eight weeks. Interns don't seem to mind, though: "It's enough time to decide if the auction business is for you." Interns are placed either in a client-service department like the Press Office, Graphics, or Marketing, or in one of many expert departments like American Paintings or Chinese Works of Art.

The advantage of working in a client-service department is that it provides exposure to all areas of the organization. Interns in Marketing, for example, help put together newspaper and magazine advertisements for upcoming sales, and in doing so, work with expert departments to highlight their pieces. Explained a Marketing Intern: "When a department—say,

Watches and Clocks—was running a sale, I'd collect the vital information—date, viewing time, the pieces being sold, and any photographs. The Graphics department would design the actual ad, but I'd arrange for the ad to run in an appropriate publication, such as *Watch and Clock Review* or *The New York Times*." Similarly, interns in the Press Office assist the expert departments in notifying the press about past and future auctions. "I did the legwork for press releases, researching how a certain piece sold or was predicted to sell at an upcoming auction. The best part was that I got to deal with all of the other departments—which gave me a broad view of the auction business," said a Press Office intern.

The benefit of being in an expert department is that it familiarizes interns with a particular period of art or type of antique. Virtually everything interns do increases their knowledge about an area of art, whether they tag pieces for identification purposes, record how much was paid for an item, or file pictures of the art in the department's archives. In addition to these tasks, an intern in American Paintings was asked to run paintings over to the offices of art dealers, who would verify the paintings' authenticity. Although this assignment was essentially gofer work, it was still edifying: "After interacting with these [art dealers], I really got a sense of how experts judge whether a painting is genuine. Sometimes it's a matter of what corner of the painting the artist signs his name or whether the artist signs his full name or just his initials."

Paintings are but one specialty interns are exposed to at Sotheby's. Interns work in a remarkable variety of departments, including Books and Manuscripts, Jewelry, Rugs and Carpets, and Silver.

Interns typically spend a major portion of their time typing, phoning, and faxing—most see gruntwork as a necessary evil in order to "get a foot in the door at one of the world's most prestigious auction houses."

Interns participate in an excellent orientation day during the first week of the program. A few hours are spent taking care of business—"you learn the corporate structure and the phone system, and you get an ID card," reported an intern. Interns are then welcomed by members of Sotheby's senior management. Best of all, interns have ample opportunity to meet each other. "It was obvious that [the intern coordinator] wanted us to build a sense of community." Day one of the program is an organized orientation that includes an outing, lunch for the group, and a number of speakers. "It was a great way of making a friend right off the bat," said one intern.

One intern spied Madonna looking at old European paintings of madonnas.

Sotheby's is interested in educating interns about the art world. They receive guided tours of New York art museums and galleries. Recent summers have found interns visiting museums like The Cloisters, the Whitney, the Cooper Hewitt, and the Brooklyn Museum, as well as more unusual sites like the sculpture garden at the headquarters of PepsiCo. Said one intern of the trips: "It was a chance to glimpse eight widely differing art worlds in New York. And it was interesting to contrast galleries and museums with the much faster-paced auction world." In addition, interns attend a lecture led by a Sotheby's executive or art expert. The speaker, who could be anyone from the president to the head of Decorative Arts to an auctioneer, talks about his or her background in the arts and how it led to Sotheby's. Sometimes the presentations get the interns involved, like the expert who challenged interns to appraise various objects he displayed. "Great fun! We'd inspect and attempt to put a dollar value on a variety of pieces," an intern recalled. "The only catch was that some of the pieces were fake. We found out later, for example, that an Asian porcelain bowl was actually a soup bowl someone swiped from a Chinese restaurant!"

In the week prior to a sale, Sotheby's holds exhibitions at which the public can inspect the items up for auction. Whenever possible, interns are taken on a "gallery walk" through the exhibitions. A department specialist responsible for the exhibit leads them through the exhibition room and highlights important pieces. Said one intern: "The gallery walks were a great way to learn about another type of art. The specialists are very thorough and easy to understand." When they have the chance, interns are also welcome to check out the exhibitions without a guide. Some go just to spy on visiting celebrities. One intern reported seeing Nancy Reagan, Bruce Willis, John McEnroe, and Madonna ("who [appropriately enough] was looking at old European paintings of madonnas").

A wise philosopher once said that there's nothing like watching a baseball game to learn the ropes of baseball. In a similar vein, there's nothing like watching a Sotheby's auction to learn the art of the auction. Although summer is "off-season," with far fewer auctions than in the spring and fall, interns are still able take in a few auctions when they have the time. Items sold at a Sotheby's auction, are rare, historic, or owned by someone who habitually bathes in Dom Pérignon. Although the majority of auctions do not cause a sensation, every now and then there's an adrenaline-charger. A former intern who was hired on as a permanent employee witnessed the sale of one of twenty-four copies of the Declaration of Independence. (How much is freedom worth? A cool $2.4 million). Another intern was around when a gold and enamel Imperial Fabergé Egg went for $2.3 million.

But auctions need not involve millions of dollars to be enjoyable. One intern dropped by auctions for sheer people watching. "It's fun to check out the type of people each kind of auction attracts. French furniture auctions bring in a very well-heeled, predominantly female group. On the other hand, sales of watches attract a mostly male audience of watch dealers." Sometimes it's not the audience but the auction itself that's entertaining. Comic book and cartoon companies, for example, sometimes send costumed representatives of their characters to promote a sale. An auction of a vintage Marvel comic book featured a Spider-Man who "got up on the stage and struck spiderlike poses." At a reception after the sale of *Beauty and the Beast* cartoon cels, Disney had a decked-out Beauty and Beast "greet guests and generate excitement."

SELECTION

 The internship is open to college students entering their junior or senior year. Successful candidates must arrange for academic credit through their schools and furnish this documentation. Unlike most internships in the auction business (e.g., Christie's), Sotheby's accepts students of any major, not just those studying art history or fine arts. According to the coordinator, successful interns have "a genuine interest in some area of art" and are "outgoing," "polite," and accepting of all assignments, no matter how mundane. International applicants are eligible, however they must provide proof of valid working papers that permit them to work in the United States prior to their arrival at Sotheby's. Successful candidates must make arrangements for their own living accommodations and transportation to and from Sotheby's.

APPLICATION PROCEDURE

 Interested candidates should send an introductory letter and resume to the Internship Coordinator at Sotheby's Human Resources department in January. Sotheby's will send back an application in February. The application asks for department preferences and reasons the applicant wants to work at Sotheby's. The strongest applicants are interviewed by the individual departments in March and earlyApril. Phone interviews are acceptable for most departments, although some require an in-person interview (at applicant's expense).

OVERVIEW

 Sotheby's interns get a taste of what it's like to be knee-deep in the excitement and the workaday details of a top auction house. Despite being served a generous helping of busywork, interns end up learning a great deal about the auction business, be it through projects or a wonderful array of field trips and in-house speakers. In the hand signals of an auctioneer, the Sotheby's internship gets two thumbs up.

FOR MORE INFORMATION . . .

■ Internship Coordinator
Sotheby's Inc.
Human Resources
1334 York Avenue, 8th Floor
New York, NY 10021
(212) 606-7000
Fax: (212) 606-7028

SELECTIVITY	🔍 🔍 🔍
Approximate applicant pool: 1,500–2,000 Interns accepted: 250	

COMPENSATION	$ $ $ $ $
$500–$850/week	

QUALITY OF LIFE	↑ ↑ ↑ ↑
Weekly seminars; mentors; professional training	

LOCATION(S)

New York, NY (95%)

FIELDS

Investment banking; Asset management; Management consulting; Corporate law; Accounting

DURATION

10 weeks minimum
Summer

PRE-REQS

Undergraduates of color, academic excellence, leadership, and commitment to community service.

DEADLINE(S)

February 15

It's a long-standing dilemma: Corporate recruiters want talented students of color, but talented students of color have difficulty breaking into the established channels at law firms, investment banks, consulting companies, and accounting firms. Is there any hope?

Call in Sponsors for Educational Opportunity (SEO), founded in 1963 to help "motivated, but underserved" elementary and high school students of color get into college and in doing so improve their chances of landing corporate jobs. Thirty years later, approximately 85 percent of the 4,000 New York City youths of color who have gone through SEO's programs have received college degrees.

In 1980, SEO decided to tackle the lack of diversity on New York's Wall Street by establishing its Career Program. More than 15 years later, SEO has made a tremendous impact. In addition to two Fulbright and four Rhodes Scholars, SEO counts among its alumni one of the "25 Hottest Blacks on Wall Street" (*Black Enterprise*, 1992), the CEO and president of the former Cisneros Asset Management firm, and the former 24-year-old mayor of Baldwin Park, CA.

DESCRIPTION

In 1980, 11 college students of color gathered at SEO's office, a renovated brownstone on East 31st Street in New York City. Before them stood an opportunity to explode an invidious myth: There are few talented students of color capable of working on Wall Street. As the first interns in SEO's newly formed investment banking program, they were each about to spend the summer at a Wall Street investment bank. Nineteen years later, SEO targets additional business fields in need of diverse talent, offering internships in six pro-

grams: Investment Banking (100 to 150 interns), Corporate Law (30), Management Consulting (15–20), Accounting (15–20), Asset Management (10–20), and Information Technology (12–15). In total, forty-one firms participate in these career programs (contact SEO for a complete listing).

Since the emphasis in the eighties upon *Wall Street* (the movie), junk bonds, and huge takeover deals, Wall Street has generated a lot of press. "The awareness of the financial services industry was low in the early eighties," says a current SEO board member who interned with SEO in 1981. "But by 1985, Wall Street came of age in popular culture. Consequently, students are interested in becoming the next great financier." In keeping with this demand, SEO's Investment Banking program is by far the organization's largest internship, with more than 1,300 alumni. Placed in 15 heavy-hitter firms like Goldman Sachs, Morgan Stanley, Salomon Smith Barney, Merrill Lynch, J.P. Morgan, and Credit Suisse First Boston, interns work in such areas as corporate or public finance, sales and trading, and research. Besides compiling financial figures or building financial models on computers, interns may travel nationwide to interview employees of companies targeted for acquisition. In a rare move, one intern flew to London with his supervisor to an insurance conference to gather information for a research report analyzing the impact of AIDS on insurance companies. Another intern read business plans as part of his firm's venture-capital group and spent time on his firm's hectic trading floor. After attending a "condom conference" in Chicago, a third intern analyzed trends in the condom market and wrote a report on how those trends affect the stock prices of such companies as Carter-Wallace, the manufacturer of Trojans.

> **"It doesn't matter if you're black, white, yellow, or red. There's only one color on Wall Street, and that's green."**

Management Consulting interns work at firms like Monitor, Booz Allen & Hamilton, BCG, and McKinsey & Company. Creating financial models on spreadsheets and interacting with clients "just as a full-time analyst would," interns help consultants come up with recommendations to solve client business problems. One Consulting intern helped improve the distribution channels for a toy manufacturing company. For an appliance-leasing company, he assessed the market potential for an expansion into Mexico, traveling to New Jersey and to Mexico City to speak with department store managers about the company's products. "It was especially neat to speak Spanish with the Mexican credit managers," he said, "and it was really challenging to pull together all the information I had gathered and come up with the recommendation."

In Accounting, interns are divided among a few firms. Starting off with one to two weeks of training, interns learn the nature of "auditing," the process of formally reviewing an organization's financial books. "My firm placed all of its interns in one room for a week of self-study followed by a week of instruction from managers and [senior accountants]," recalled an Accounting intern. Afterward, interns are assigned to various work areas. There they "sit waiting like relief pitchers in a bullpen for managers to call with assignments." Most assignments take interns off-site to help with audits. One intern spent two weeks at a New York publishing house auditing cash and fixed assets. "It was typical staff work . . . what you'd expect to do as a first year," he said. "But on top of that, you learn how to interact with a client's employees and how to confidently approach CFOs and VPs of Finance for financial information."

Corporate Law interns are placed in some of the biggest law firms in New York—Skadden, Arps, Slate, Meagher & Flom; Sullivan & Cromwell; and Paul, Weiss, Rifkind, Wharton & Garrison, to name a few. Because undergraduates have had no legal training, however, interns must immerse themselves in a great deal of clerical work. Assisting attorneys with whatever tasks need to be done, interns copy cases out of the library or type documents, occasionally putting in 12- or 13-hour days. For their efforts, interns are invited to client meetings, where they witness partners and clients discussing the legalities of such transactions as stock issues or asset acquisitions. Concluded one intern: "I didn't learn much about the law per se, but by the end [of the summer], I understood the role of litigation in corporate law and I learned that the law is incredibly diverse—there's room for specialization."

In 1993, SEO started the Asset Management Program, which provides interns with an opportunity to see the "buy side" world of financial services. Recent interns have worked in marketing to identify potential clients and as research assistants to portfolio managers. According to

SEO literature, "[t]he emphasis on quantitative analytical skills is at a premium in this program, where work demands are similar to those of the research positions in the Investment Banking Program."

In response to client interest, SEO started an Information Technology internship. Six investment banking firms are charter members of this initiative: Chase, Goldman Sachs, J.P. Morgan, Merrill Lynch, Morgan Stanley Dean Witter, and Prudential. The Program, which began in the summer of 2000, allows interns to work with the most advanced technologies to develop, enhance and support software from mainframe and distributed architectures. Responsibilities may include developing, testing, maintaining, installing and/or deploying third party proprietary technologies. Interns may choose a highly technical career path, or one that's more business or management focused. Providing students of color with coveted Wall Street, corporate law, accounting, and management consulting jobs is not enough for SEO. To give minorities a leg up during their job hunts later on, each program also runs a weekly seminar series, hosted by a different firm in the field. Seminar speakers are investment bank chairmen and presidents, law firm and accounting firm senior partners, and managers of recruiting. Following a discussion of issues in the field—such as real estate, bankruptcy, and the legal issues of mergers and acquisitions for Law interns—interns and hosts mingle. With the 55 to 100 high-level people present, the seminars provide an ideal opportunity to make a contact: "When you're interviewing for jobs later, you'll not only have a connection at each firm but you'll also already have a feel for the type of personalities working there."

All interns are assigned mentors at their firms and SEO Alumni mentors to assist in career planning and to provide a perspective on the industry. "Your mentor can show you how to negotiate a more reasonable project deadline or how to approach your bosses for more work," explained one intern. "It's the kind of guidance you want when you're a college grad coming to the firm for the first time," said an SEO board member and alumnus. Many mentors not only provide guidance but also help interns create their own personal network of contacts inside and outside the firm. "My mentor introduced me to a director at [one of the other banks]," said one intern. More than a dozen years later, he still turns to that director for advice.

SEO teaches interns the unwritten rules of corporate America at an early June orientation. Besides listening to former SEO interns and board members speak about their experiences, interns learn proper business etiquette and behavior. SEO also stresses the significance of the seminars: "They told us that VPs are there to meet us and that we should be aggressive, but palatably so, when approaching them." Emphasizing the importance of setting goals, the orientation conveys that as minorities, interns must work harder to prove themselves. "Some people were intimidated," said an intern.

In addition to the orientation, Investment Banking and Asset Management interns experience a week-long series of training seminars, where they obtain knowledge of the basic framework of investment banking. Besides teaching stocks and bonds, currency trades, and LBOs (leveraged buy-outs), the workshop instructors reiterate the message from the orientation: "Be palatably aggressive, strive for excellence, exhibit a superhuman work ethic, and have unimpeachable integrity." The SEO graduate who started the training program in 1986 explains that, although this philosophy is directed at minorities, it really applies to everyone on Wall Street. "It doesn't matter if you're black, white, yellow, or red," he says. "There's only one color on Wall Street, and that's green."

SELECTION

 SEO targets students of color. Applicants should have at least a 3.0 GPA. Though the Investment Banking, Management Consulting, and Asset Management programs are open only to college juniors and seniors who will have one semester to complete at the time of the internship, sophomores are occasionally accepted. And while the Corporate Law program accepts juniors and seniors, the vast majority of Law interns are spring graduates who will be attending law school in the fall. The Accounting Program is open only to students who have completed a minimum of three accounting courses. The five other programs require no particular major.

To apply for the Technology Program, applicants should have taken courses in computer science, information systems, or engineering. The Information Technology internship is open to college sophomores, juniors and seniors who will have one semester to complete at the time of the internship. SEO cites leadership, professionalism, academic excellence, participation in community service, and maturity as important qualifications. International applicants are eligible.

APPLICATION PROCEDURE

 The deadline is February 15 of every year. SEO encourages students to begin submitting their applications during the fall and early winter. SEO reserves the option to consider candidates for early admission action at any point after their applications are received. The majority of candidates will still be evaluated after February 15 and they will accept all application materials until this final deadline.

Students should submit a resume, a one-page typed essay explaining their interest in the SEO program, a completed application form (available at many college career centers or www.seo-ny.org), two recommendations from professors, an official transcript, two self-addressed stamped envelopes, and a passport-sized photo. After SEO reviews application materials, top candidates are either invited to New York for on-site interviews or interviewed at designated locations throughout the country by SEO alumni and staff members. Note: Students must apply to one program only and cannot indicate a preference for a specific firm.

OVERVIEW

 Landing an internship on Wall Street or with a corporate law firm as an undergraduate is next to impossible. "Unless your dad is a partner or a major client," said an intern, "you can't easily get one." But if you're a college student of color, you can call on a guiding light named SEO. A "new network for people who have been denied access to the old-boy network," SEO offers structured internships in corporate law and all areas of investment banking as well as internships in management consulting, accounting, asset management, and information technology. Through weekly seminars with the movers and shakers in their fields, interns make valuable connec-

tions for the future. Such connections help over 80 percent of Investment Banking interns secure full-time job offers upon graduation from college.

FOR MORE INFORMATION . . .

- Sponsors for Educational Opportunity
  Career Program
  23 Gramercy Park South
  New York, NY 10003
  (212) 979-2040
  www.seo-ny.org

"We were tracking sheep hunters in the Kenai Peninsula Wildlife Refuge in Alaska. We flew into a lake valley on floatplanes, landed on the lake, and camped in the valley. Every day we made peak ascents to patrol the area. One day, after a particularly hard climb, we got to the top of this gorgeous peak with incredible views stretching out forever. We actually met a sheep hunter up there; he turned to us and said, 'Look at this place—it's so worth it!'"

This story, told by a recent intern in Alaska, encapsulates the appeal of an internship with the Student Conservation Association: breathtaking scenery, backcountry wilderness work, and the unforgettable experience of a lifetime.

Founded in 1957, the Student Conservation Association (SCA) is a nonprofit, 17,000-member organization that fosters long-term stewardship of the environment. In addition to offering education and leadership programs, SCA marshalls volunteers of all ages to perform public service in natural resource management, endangered-species protection, and ecological restoration on America's public lands. Through the years, more than 30,000 volunteers have participated, including helping to restore Yellowstone after ravaging fires and the Everglades after Hurricane Andrew.

DESCRIPTION

Since SCA's founding, the goal of the organization has been to provide students with an opportunity to restore the wilderness and, at the same time, experience the outdoors, explore environmental careers, and serve the community. Under the auspices of the SCA's Re-

source Assistant (RA), Conservation Career Development (CCD), and High School (HS) Programs, interns work in national parks, forests, wildlife refuges, and conservation centers under the jurisdiction of private organizations, state agencies, the U.S. Navy's Natural Resources Program, and such Federal agencies as the U.S. Forest Service, Bureau of Land Management, and National Park Service.

Targeting urban youth, the Conservation Career Development Program offers minority high school and college students year-round conservation training, 5-week

SELECTIVITY	🔍 🔍
Approximate applicant pool: 6,000 Interns accepted: 1,100 (RA), 200 (CCD), 450 (HS)	

COMPENSATION	💲 💲
RA: $50/week, round trip travel, free housing, accident insurance; CCD: see Description; HS: free tent and food	

QUALITY OF LIFE	🌴 🌴 🌴 🌴
Stunning natural beauty; intensive, on-site training (RA); mentors & career counseling (CCD)	

LOCATION(S)
CCD (h.s. students)—Los Angeles and San Francisco, CA; Newark, NJ; Seattle, WA; Washington, D.C. CCD (undergrads), RA, & HS—43 states in the United States, Washington, D.C., and Canada—see Index

FIELDS
Archaeology; Environment; Park/forest management; Recreation

DURATION
RA: 12 weeks (Summer, Fall, Early Winter, Late Winter, Spring) CCD: see Description; HS: 4–5 weeks (Summer)

PRE-REQS
See Selection

DEADLINE(S)
RA .... Rolling (at least two months before starting date preferred); CCD .... Rolling; HS .... March 1

BUSYWORK METER
LOW MEDIUM HIGH
N/A
OLDMAN & HAMADEH

summer internships, career counseling, mentoring, and $1,000–$2,000 scholarships. Seeking to improve their community's historical, cultural, and environmental resources, CCD college interns spend the summer working on projects that range from outdoor fieldwork like restoring a riverbank in Seattle to urban horticulture training in New Jersey. CCD high school interns participate in six- to ten-person environmental work groups on projects that include backcountry living, outdoor field projects, and recreational opportunities.

In the High School Program, which lasts up to five weeks, groups of six to ten students live in outdoor camps on public lands near their worksite, and complete different backcountry conservation projects like improving hiking trails, constructing cabins, and restoring vegetation at heavily impacted campsites. Although there is no cost for participating in the program—food, shelter, and group equipment are provided—interns are responsible for their own gear and transportation to and from the site. Financial aid is available, and at the end of the program, participants take a one-week camping trip to enjoy their newly gained skills. Says the internship coordinator: The High School Program, as well as the high school component of the CCD Program, offer high school students an unparalleled opportunity to "see a beautiful part of the country, give something back to their communities, and do service for the country and for the earth."

The jewel in SCA's crown, though, is the Resource Assistant Program. Spread out over more than 290 federal lands across the country, RA's work with natural resource professionals as part of programs in land stewardship and wildlife conservation. According to an SCA brochure, jobs in Alaska and Hawaii are the most popular among interns and therefore the most selective. On average, RA positions last three months.

RA's find themselves doing a wide variety of tasks related to land management. One RA in Montana did

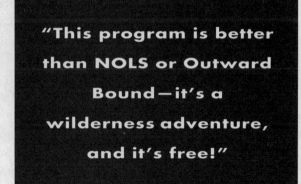

"This program is better than NOLS or Outward Bound—it's a wilderness adventure, and it's free!"

"extensive backcountry ranger work, like clearing, patrolling, and maintaining trails." An RA at Denali National Park in Alaska "monitored the area for illegally built cabins—we knocked them down by whatever methods we could." In Klamath National Forest in California, another RA "spent a lot of time walking around, looking at the sky" to monitor the goshawk and spotted owl populations. Other RA assignments include rafting down the Colorado river to oversee riverbank campsites, patrolling backcountry trails on horseback, and flying into a canyon to take soil samples.

Positions vary greatly in terms of training, background required, and physical difficulty. The RA at Donner Memorial State Park in the Sierras, who helps run the visitor center, must have a background in public speaking and the conservation of cultural objects, while the RA position at Tongass National Forest in Alaska requires a person in excellent physical condition, who is willing to do very physical labor and has extensive backpacking, kayaking, and climbing experience. For those who didn't grow up making peak ascents in the Himalayas, rest assured: SCA provides all the training you need for the position to which you are accepted. In fact, one to two weeks at the start of each RA internship is devoted to intensive on-site training that can include aviation safety, water survival, or proper firearms handling. One RA in Alaska found herself learning how to use a shotgun: "You have to carry a gun—for the grizzly bears." Faint hearts need not apply.

One RA found herself immediately incorporated into the public parks system: "I was amazed at how much responsibility they gave me—right after training, they sent me out to patrol trails or do whatever was needed." Another RA confirmed: "I had a lot of camping experience, but I'd never done any trail work before. Yet I was asked to monitor trails almost immediately. Boy, did I learn fast." But not all RA positions involve backcountry trail work, or what SCA calls "resource management."

There are many RA positions, like the one at Little Bighorn National Park, which involve researching the cultural history of the park and running educational programs for visitors. Other RA positions, many of which require a natural sciences background, focus on data collection and field research.

Almost all former RAs give glowing reports of the people in the program—supervisors and other RAs. Said one RA: "The permanent staff couldn't have been nicer—I was treated like a queen." The co-workers of another RA regularly sprang for pizza whenever she returned from trips into the backcountry. "The people are great," reports another RA, who interned in Hawaii. "Both the RA's and the professional staff have a great attitude and are very easy to get along with."

RAs come from a wide variety of backgrounds: "Many people interested in law or environmental policy do the program for the experience," says the internship coordinator. Academic majors range from accounting to humanities to natural science. While most RAs have some camping background and knowledge of wilderness skills, "you don't need them—in fact, doing the program is a great way to get wilderness experience that you never would otherwise," says a former RA in California. Technically volunteers, RAs do not receive a salary, but SCA pays for food, housing, and transportation to and from the site. One RA calls it "better than NOLS [i.e., the National Outdoor Leadership School] or Outward Bound—it's a wilderness adventure, and it's free!"

As might be expected, RAs get numerous and unparalleled opportunities to explore the wilderness. One RA in Alaska "found that [her supervisors] were always encouraging [her] to go out and take trips" on days off, resulting in camping expeditions to Denali National Park and the Kenai Peninsula Wildlife Refuge. Another RA said that the exploration was the best part of his experience: "It's amazing how much you learn when you're actually out there on your own—it's an education like nothing else."

Despite its get-back-to-nature appeal, there are some downsides to the RA experience. Many RAs work with two or three other people in very isolated areas (Flathead National Forest in Montana, for example, is described as "a very primitive setting") with few oppor-

tunities to interact with the outside world. Trips to town for supplies are very limited when the nearest town is 500 miles away. Also, there are the rigors of living in the wilderness for three months: Accommodations range from dormitories to camper/RVs to sleeping bags in tents for the hard core backcountry positions. The work, depending on the position, can be strenuous and even dangerous: fighting fires, maintaining trails in isolated areas, and dealing with wild animals like bears and wolves are just some of the possibilities. While many RA positions involve perfectly safe ranger duties like advising visitors and maintaining campsites, there is an element of risk in any wilderness experience.

After completing the internship, many RAs end up in "professional-level park service positions," like one former intern in the Rocky Mountains who is now the chief ranger at Isle Royale National Park. As it is becoming "very difficult to get into [agencies like] the National Park Service," an SCA internship offers invaluable wilderness experience and training. In a recent survey, 67 percent of respondents in professional land and resource management positions credited SCA with helping them get their first job. And even if you don't want to be a professional park ranger, an SCA internship "looks great on a resume," says one former RA who is now in law school.

SELECTION

 The CCD Program is open to minority high school students and undergrads from urban centers. The HS program is open to 16–18-year-old high school students, while the RA program is open to any high school graduate over 18, although most RAs are college students. What SCA looks for in applicants, says the internship coordinator, is "enthusiasm and an interest in learning everything they can—we want people who want to be there." International applicants are eligible.

APPLICATION PROCEDURE

 The deadline to apply to the RA Program is approximately two months before one wishes to start (summer, fall, early winter, late winter, and spring). For the CCD Program, interested students may apply anytime. The HS Program's deadline falls on March 1. Prospective interns must complete a detailed application form. For a description of available positions, contact SCA for a catalog. Upon receipt of applications, SCA distributes them to the individual sites, where the professionals (park rangers, etc.) do the actual selection of RAs. Interviews to flesh out the information on the application, ensure compatibility, and answer applicants' questions are conducted over the phone.

OVERVIEW

Imagine yourself working on the North Rim of the Grand Canyon and waking up every morning to the spectacular sight of sunlight flooding the canyon walls. Or fighting fires in Montana's Glacier National Park. Or climbing to the top of a mountain in Denali National Park in Alaska and witnessing a magnificent vista of mountains, glaciers, and rivers spread out before you. SCA offers this as well as the chance to serve the country, learn and use practical wilderness skills, and gain valuable professional experience in land and resource management. It's an amazing experience, one that many former SCA interns consider the best three months of their lives. As one RA put it, "Grab it and do it—you'll never regret it!" And apparently many don't, as 25 percent of RAs return to their sponsoring agencies for full-time entry-level employment.

FOR MORE INFORMATION . . .

■ Student Conservation Association
P.O. Box 550
Charlestown, NH 03603-0550
(603) 543-1700
Fax: (603) 543-1828
www.sca-inc.org

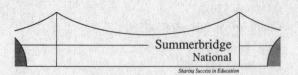

Summerbridge
National

Sharing Success in Education

To teach or not to teach?

That is the question that many college students face. The established route requires a degree in education, state certification, and a long-term commitment.

College graduates can sidestep these requirements by joining Teach for America, a corps of nearly 2,000 noncertified teachers from various academic backgrounds, each working a minimum of two years in underresourced urban or rural public schools.

But what about undergraduates who are interested in teaching but who want to find out before they graduate if teaching is for them?

Summerbridge National helps many of these students make up their minds about teaching. Founded in 1978 at San Francisco University High School, Summerbridge allows high school students and college undergraduates to spend eight weeks in the summer teaching a group of predominantly underprivileged kids. With thirty-six outposts nationwide, Summerbridge has rapidly become a national institution. Given that the high schoolers and college undergraduates not only teach the classes but also manage the entire program, it's as much teaching responsibility as a student could hope for.

SELECTIVITY

Approximate applicant pool: 1,500
Interns accepted: 850

COMPENSATION

$750 stipend & up to $1,250 aid available for undergrads; $500 stipend for high school students

QUALITY OF LIFE

Independence; creative environment; workshops on teaching; long workdays

LOCATION(S)

Nationwide (See Description)

FIELD

Education

DURATION

8 weeks
Summer

PRE-REQS

High school sophomores, juniors and seniors; undergrads; recent grads

DEADLINE(S)

New Applicants ....March 1
Returning/Veterans ..... February 1

DESCRIPTION

Summerbridge is a two- to three-year "Workshop in Education" for "talented students with limited educational opportunities" in the fourth through eighth grades. Nationwide, approximately 2,000 students participate in Summerbridge's two- to three-year program of six-week summer sessions, school-year tutorials, and year-round counseling. Having older students teach courses that prepare middle-school

students for high school is not Summerbridge's only innovation—the school is also tuition-free.

From 1978 to 1990, the Summerbridge program was run in conjunction with San Francisco University High School only. Its success in preparing often economically and academically disadvantaged middle school students for the rigors of college-prep high school programs was so widely acclaimed that thirty new programs were established in the early 1990s, at schools in Los Angeles, Sacramento, San Francisco (two schools), San Diego, and Ross, CA; Denver, CO; New

Haven, CT; Miami, FL; Atlanta, GA; Honolulu, HI; Louisville, KY; New Orleans, LA (two schools); Cambridge and Concord, MA; Kansas City, MO; Raleigh, NC; Manchester, NH; the Bronx and Locust Valley, NY; Cincinnati, (three schools) OH; Portland, OR; Lehigh Valley, Philadephia, and Pittsburgh, PA; Providence, RI; Fort Worth and Houston, TX; Norfolk, VA; and Hong Kong. The thirty-six schools hire nearly 850 teachers every summer, employing an equal number of high school and college students.

Summerbridge's mission was acknowledged in a recent *Newsweek* article on "alternative training programs." "[Summerbridge] attack[s] the lack of minority educators on a more local level . . . " explained the piece, "[and] is designed to get the younger kids into learning and the older kids into teaching." It does so by putting only three to eight students in each class and by giving the young teachers, half of whom are minorities, free rein over the entire program, from creating their own classes to chairing the academic departments. Teachers are typically assigned to three academic classes related to their interests from a wide range of courses in literature, math, science, foreign language, and social studies. Teachers also design one elective course. But there's more to the teachers' work than developing unique lesson plans. Teachers also advise students, take care of administrative matters, and organize field trips.

From 8:30 A.M. to 3:30 P.M., students take seven classes—five academic courses such as Speech and Debate, Geography, and Spanish, as well as two electives in arts, sports, or drama. Uninspired methods of teaching are tossed out the window in favor of more interactive and creative styles. Drawing a baseball diamond on the blackboard, a teacher instructs her students to come forward one at a time to respond to various math questions. With every correct response, the students get closer to "home plate," eventually earning a run for their team. In a Writing Through Literature class, students play a game of

> Teachers work from 7:30 A.M. to 6:00 P.M. on campus and then well into the evening to correct homework assignments.

Jeopardy! Hitting their desks in lieu of pressing the buttons used on the game show, students respond to the clues provided with a question—in this case, "What is proofreading?" is the correct answer to "The act of marking corrections in writing." When students read college-level plays such as Lorraine Hansberry's *A Raisin in the Sun* or Shakespeare's *A Midsummer Night's Dream*, they act out scenes on a nearby grassy area or the cafeteria stage. "Acting out the plays increases students' understanding of them," explained a teacher. These academic classes are offered alongside unusual student-designed courses such as American Sign Language, Fantasy Role-Playing Games, and Animation. Taught in the afternoon, these "mini-courses," are educational but focused on fun. A teacher at the San Francisco school, for example, designed a Cooking class: "I brought in recipes and had the students try them out. Everything we made—wontons, pizzas, cakes—we naturally got to eat afterward."

Teachers also organize field trips, workshops, clubs, and school dances. Designed to teach students about real life, they take trips to meet local businesspeople, participate in scavenger hunts, or go to City Hall. Back at school, a business workshop teaches resume writing, business dress, and the art of the handshake. For socializing, groups of students and teachers form clubs with imaginative titles such as Purple Smurf Cult, Dennis the Menace to Society, and the Hyperactive Hysterics. Every other Friday, students may tango at the school dance. The summer culminates with the "Olympics," a day of mental as well as physical challenges. In one of many competitions, a 50-yard dash requires students to stop every 10 yards and answer questions such as "What is the name of the president's daughter?"

The young teachers, committed to increasing the knowledge of their impressionable pupils, have high expectations for themselves and their students. Teachers often ride "an emotional roller coaster," feeling more elated certain days about their work than others. "Some days the kids just don't get it," said a teacher. But such frustration is often swept away by a sense of accomplishment. "When the students seem to be catching on, it's wonderful." And teachers' hard work does not go unnoticed by the students. For example, because a Spanish teacher consistently brought in props, prepared special lessons, and tutored her pupils after school, her students presented her with a bouquet of flowers and a certificate of appreciation.

Summerbridge teachers are more than classroom lecturers; they are also role models. Admirably, many have overcome difficult circumstances, such as having grown up in dangerous neighborhoods or having been raised by non-English-speaking parents. Usually only a few years older than their students, teachers are in the unique position of being able to relate to the students. "We feel that we can talk to them," said a student. That's important in a school where many of the students contend with problems at home or violence in the neighborhood. "We give them hope and direction and excite them about the possibility of going to college," said a teacher.

Teachers accomplish all of these tasks after ample training and with continuing guidance. The week before the program begins, Master Teachers (professional adult teachers) spend hours conducting workshops on lesson planning and diversity. Once the program gets under way, teachers attend additional workshops on managing classrooms, grading and commenting on students' work, and writing formal evaluations. There are also weekly staff meetings for interns and one-on-one consultations with the program director. The faculty lounge is also open throughout the day for teachers to meet and go over teaching strategies. Fortunately, problem kids are few. "These students want to be here," said a teacher, "so motivating them is not too difficult."

If it sounds like teachers are deluged with responsibilities, you've heard right. Most teachers report working from 8:00 A.M. to 6:00 P.M. on campus and then well into the evening, as late as 9:00 P.M., to correct homework assignments and create lesson plans. Teachers also make themselves available to answer students' questions by phone. "We want them to call us if they need any sort of clarification about what we've done in class," explained a teacher, "because it's important that they understand the material."

Teachers must be willing to accept what is described by many as "really low pay." Fortunately, Summerbridge offers ways to alleviate this problem. Many teachers win grants from third parties such as the Ford Foundation, the J.W. Saxe Memorial Fund, and campus work-study programs. Summerbridge itself awards a few college students already on financial aid with additional stipends of up to $1,250. For teachers from out-of-town, Summerbridge can arrange free room and board with families of the program's students.

The "workshop" is so short-lived that before they know it, teachers are evaluating final exams (there are no grades at Summerbridge) and it's time to say goodbye. Sprawled out on a floor in a lounge, the teachers are amazed at the impact they've made in just six weeks. A few students have picked up a whole new language. Some are more outgoing while others are more motivated to learn. "But it's not long enough," said a disappointed teacher. "You just start to see changes, and then the program is over." On the last day, it's common to find an outpouring of emotion, often resulting in a free flow of tears. "I look back now and smile," said a teacher, "because I know that we helped those kids make it."

SELECTION

 High school applicants must be sophomores, juniors, or seniors. College applicants must be undergraduates or recent college grads (those who graduate in May or June before the start of the internship). While there is neither a minimum GPA nor a particular major required, all applicants must have the "heart and desire to teach." Summerbridge seeks students who have done well academically and who "want to work with young motivated students." International applicants are eligible.

APPLICATION PROCEDURE

 The application must be postmarked by March 1. Students must submit the written application and a resume or list of skills and previous experience. Send away for the application in November because it is extensive: ten pages asking for desired Summerbridge location(s), general information, short essays, a personal statement, and sample lesson plans. "Some of our teachers say that [the application] is more difficult than a final exam," says the coordinator. High school students are required to sit for "station interviews" (where they must spontaneously come up with solutions to hypothetical staff situations) and give a 15-minute teaching presentation to a group of adult teachers. College students, however, receive less formal yet challenging in-person or phone interviews by program directors.

OVERVIEW

 How would you like to spend the summer teaching chemistry, English, geography, or Chinese to 9- to 14-year-olds? Throw in some "extra cool" classes, too, such as The History of Rap or Jogging for Fun. Did we mention that you'll also help run the entire school? Now add school dances, an "Olympics," parent-teacher conferences, and field trips. You're hooked? That's Summerbridge—utter immersion in the teaching experience. Playing role model, confidant, and—yes—educator, Summerbridge's student-teachers are making an impact on America's declining public-education system.

FOR MORE INFORMATION . . .

■ Summerbridge National
361 Oak St.
San Francisco, CA 94102
(415) 865-2970
Fax: (415) 865-2979
info@summerbridge.org
www.summerbridge.org

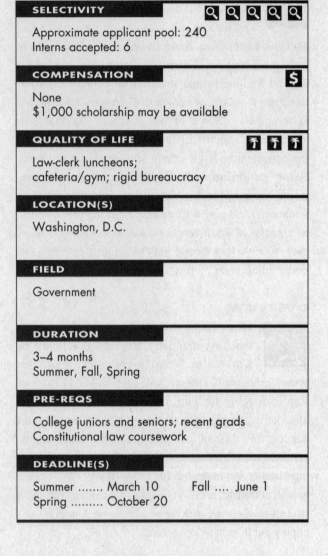

SELECTIVITY	🔍 🔍 🔍 🔍 🔍
Approximate applicant pool: 240 Interns accepted: 6	

COMPENSATION	$
None $1,000 scholarship may be available	

QUALITY OF LIFE	⬆ ⬆ ⬆
Law-clerk luncheons; cafeteria/gym; rigid bureaucracy	

LOCATION(S)
Washington, D.C.

FIELD
Government

DURATION
3–4 months Summer, Fall, Spring

PRE-REQS
College juniors and seniors; recent grads Constitutional law coursework

DEADLINE(S)
Summer .... March 10   Fall .... June 1 Spring .... October 20

Corinthian columns. Marble halls. The aura of history and of great thinkers of years past. No, it is not a mausoleum—far from it. The Supreme Court of the United States sits like a Greek temple atop Capitol Hill in Washington, D.C., and its stately grandeur never fails to impress passersby. This architectural magnificence provides a fitting home to America's highest judicial body. The nine justices of the Supreme Court meet to discuss and issue decisions on our nation's most important jurisprudential issues. The Supreme Court is the solemn interpreter of the Constitution, the source of controversial policy decisions, the eleventh-hour provider of stays of execution, and home to immensely powerful but publicly invisible jurists.

DESCRIPTION

In 1972, the Office of the Administrative Assistant to the Chief Justice established the Judicial Internship Program, enabling college students to work under the auspices of the administrative assistant, who serves as the chief justice's right-hand man or woman. While each session's two Judicial interns answer ultimately to the administrative assistant, they work primarily with the Judicial Fellow, typically a lawyer or professor serving the year-long Judicial Fellowship at the Court. The Judicial Fellow oversees the interns' daily activities and long-term projects.

A typical day for the Judicial intern includes mundane and substantive tasks. The least appealing daily task requires interns to clip, categorize, and file articles from four newspapers, adding to the office's extensive archives of law-related news articles. While article-clipping keeps interns abreast

of current events, it can be time-consuming and monotonous: "There were always more newspapers to clip. We'd spend entire mornings cutting out and filing articles. Real brainy stuff—not!" But the Judicial Internship brochure warns applicants that interns must have a "willingness to shoulder one's share of less glamorous tasks." Even so, there are interns who become frustrated when their jobs are not the apprentice justiceships they were expecting: "I was insulted to spend an afternoon stuffing information booklets into envelopes." On the whole, however, most interns willingly accept the requisite busywork in exchange for the opportunity to work at America's most prestigious legal institutions.

Other facets of the Judicial Internship are more exciting. Every few days the Judicial Fellow assigns each intern a project. Contrary to the expectations of many interns, these assignments never involve cases pending before the Court; such are the exclusive province of the justices and their immediate staff. Nevertheless, interns have the opportunity to research and write memorandums on a variety of relevant subjects; past topics have focused on such areas as judicial confirmation, problems of civil procedure, legal ethics, jury reform, and alternatives to litigation. An intern's research is submitted in memorandum form to the administrative assistant or Judicial Fellow, and it may even serve as background information for the chief justice's speeches. The latter outcome no doubt brings exhilaration to an intern's experience; as a past intern emphasized: "When [Chief Justice] Rehnquist delivered a speech on the judiciary to a group of visiting dignitaries, he made reference to a congressional bill I had spent three days researching . . . it was gratifying to know that I made a contribution to the chief's speech, albeit a small contribution!"

Interns acknowledge the rigid bureaucracy in place at the Court: "You are the lowest link on the institutional food chain." But strict hierarchies are nothing new in government, and alumni of the program rave about the advantages of being one of only two interns, as opposed to one of hundreds of congressional interns. "You may be a small fish, but you are one of two small fish in a prestigious, marble-lined pond," said one intern. "With a little luck, you'll gain great insight into the inner workings of the judiciary." Indeed, Judicial interns are exposed to a wealth of experiences. They receive special tours of the Court's internal offices, observing the outer reaches of places like the clerk's office and the commo-

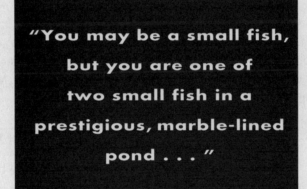

"You may be a small fish, but you are one of two small fish in a prestigious, marble-lined pond . . . "

dious, chandelier-filled library. During days when oral arguments are heard (typically Monday through Wednesday, from October to April) interns are encouraged to observe the hour-long exchanges between justices and lawyers. Interns are also invited to several "law-clerk luncheons," where they dine with the 30-odd law clerks and hear a distinguished speaker, such as the chief justice, an associate or retired justice, or a government honcho like the attorney general. As one alumnus puts it, "This is heady stuff for an undergrad."

Interns give respectable ratings to quality of life. The Court's cafeteria serves up an array of hot and cold meals, as well as a salad bar, and is frequented by tourists, staff, and occasionally even a hungry justice. For those athletically inclined, the Court's top floor features a modest weight room, allegedly the site of Justice O'Connor's aerobics class and a full-size basketball court, affectionately referred to as the "highest court in the land." Playing hoops is an ideal way to get to know a broad mix of Court personnel such as law clerks, policemen, and various staff members. On the Court's first floor there's a collection of fascinating exhibits on Supreme Court history, arranged with loving care by the curator's office for those seeking a bit of culture.

Judicial Internships are held three times a year. While summer is often the easiest time for students to complete the internship, interns reveal that a fall or winter tenure allows students to experience the Court in session, with its oral arguments and daily influx of lawyers and reporters. One intern warned that the summer internship is like "working at a football stadium during off-season!" Whichever term interns work, however, the Judicial intern workweek leaves little room for other employment, as interns work eight-hour days, five days a week.

Until 1991, the Judicial Internship program offered students no financial compensation. But recently it seems to have loosened the purse strings a bit, as program coordinators report the possibility of granting a $1,000 scholarship to interns who successfully complete the internship and return to academic studies. The program also helps students receive academic credit through work-study programs affiliated with their universities.

SELECTION

The Judicial Internship Program is open to college juniors and seniors as well as recent graduates. While students from any academic major are welcome, program coordinators say applicants should have taken some coursework on constitutional law or the Supreme Court. After an initial screening, the Judicial Fellow winnows the pool to a handful of applicants, each of whom are then given a phone interview. You may want to keep in mind that the fall and winter internships occur during the academic year, and therefore usually have fewer applicants than the summer internship and thus are slightly less competitive. International applicants are eligible.

APPLICATION PROCEDURE

Application deadlines are as follows: summer, March 10; fall, June 1; spring, October 20. The application procedure is nothing short of laborious. Required materials include a resume, an official transcript, a statement explaining the applicant's reasons for seeking the internship, a short writing sample, three letters of recommendation, and a two-page essay on the American constitutional system. Past interns stress the importance of the applicant's personal statement: "Use it to explain why you can offer the Supreme Court something extraordinary. Cite examples. Don't exaggerate."

OVERVIEW

The Judicial Internship Program offers an unmatched opportunity to become immersed in the inner workings of the U.S. Supreme Court. Limited to only two interns, the program offers an intimate working environment of substantial responsibility, learning, and collegiality. Students who enjoy the program are able to accept their low-profile role within the Court's rigid bureaucracy, while taking advantage of enriching research projects and luncheons. The sheer luster of the Supreme Court attracts top-notch interns who tend to end up in prestigious jobs and graduate schools. A recent reunion of Judicial interns included several graduates of top law and business schools, an award-winning journalist, a White House Fellow, a Marshall Scholar, and four Rhodes Scholars.

FOR MORE INFORMATION . . .

■ Supreme Court of the United States
Judicial Internship Program
Office of the Administrative Assistant
to the Chief Justice
Room 5
Washington, DC 20543
(202) 479-3374

A group of surfers dedicated to environmental activism? Whoaaa. *Dude!* What do they do, wax their boards with organic paste?

The Surfrider Foundation blows away the misconception that all surfers care about is shredding waves. Fed up with Southern California's increasingly polluted waters, a circle of surfers banded together in 1984 to create a group dedicated to the preservation of coastal waters and beaches. Today, Surfrider is an international organization with more than 25,000 members. Its track record as a coastal watchdog is impressive: It helped divert storm drain waters from Santa Monica Bay to the city's sewage treatment system, settled the second largest Clean Water Act enforcement lawsuit in U.S. history, and stopped the California Coastal Commission from building a $200 million beach-destroying breakwater at Bolsa Chica State Beach in Southern California. These are just a few of its triumphs. Surfrider also spends time educating local students and lifeguard associations about ocean pollution and coastal ecology.

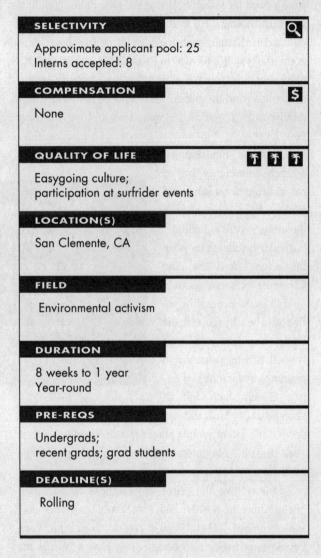

SELECTIVITY

Approximate applicant pool: 25
Interns accepted: 8

COMPENSATION

None

QUALITY OF LIFE

Easygoing culture;
participation at surfrider events

LOCATION(S)

San Clemente, CA

FIELD

Environmental activism

DURATION

8 weeks to 1 year
Year-round

PRE-REQS

Undergrads;
recent grads; grad students

DEADLINE(S)

Rolling

DESCRIPTION

Surfrider believes in making good use of its interns' capabilities. Sure, there's a lot of busywork to be done—phone work, faxing, stuffing envelopes, and the like—but that's par for the course at a nonprofit group. Over the past few years, Surfrider has made a concerted effort to have interns carry out important projects.

One intern's project involved analyzing the effectiveness of Surfrider's Blue Water Task Force, a program encouraging people across the country to test samples of ocean water for pollution and send in the results to Surfrider. Using the data these testers submit, the organization keeps track of pollution patterns and attempts to pinpoint where the pollution originates. Another intern was involved in a project that assessed the environmental impact of tollways on the land and waterways they disturb. Describing the damage that automobiles on one tollway have caused to the surrounding environment.

Another intern researched the "coastal reserves" section of California's Proposition 132. Designed to set aside areas for scientific research, the coastal reserves policy bans recreational use of four ocean sites. He investigated the implications of this prohibition, weighing the state's need for research sites against the public's right to access the ocean. He said: "After weeks of research, I concluded that although the idea of coastal reserves is good, the way it's worded in Prop 132 is ambiguous. It's open to interpretation in a way that may unfairly restrict ocean use from the public." Excerpts of his report were published in *Longboarder* magazine and the Surfrider newsletter.

Surfrider Foundation is based in San Clemente, a beach community known for its health food stores and trinket shops. Located in a three-story office building, Surfrider headquarters is up the street from the San Clemente pier but about a mile from the ocean. The office has a beachy feel to it; the walls are decorated with framed surfing posters and paintings by famous surf artists. Conch shells and an abundance of plants and windows complete the laid-back decor. "It's a comfortable place to work," said one intern. "But since it's nonprofit, expect to share computers and make do with few amenities."

Interns love the office environment at Surfrider. "People here are positive and, for the most part, relaxed," said an intern. "There's not a profit-driven ethic here. People come to Surfrider because they have a love for the California coastline." Interns say that the positive energy at Surfrider is directed their way: "The staff bends over backward to show that they think interns are important. Working hours, for example, are flexible. If you come in late because you're working on your project at the library, no problem . . . . They trust you."

One is not likely to forget that Surfrider is an organization founded by surfers. Although the Jeff Spicoli surfer-dude persona is "an exaggeration," Surfrider employees definitely do surf. One intern estimates that at least 80 percent of the employees at Surfrider actually "ride the surf." In fact, when the surf is unusually good, it's acceptable for staff to take time out to hit the waves.

> **When the surf is unusually good, it's acceptable for staff to take time out to hit the waves.**

"It doesn't happen a lot, but occasionally you'll see people grabbing their boards and heading out to the ocean," said an intern. For those who have never had the chance to hang ten, a veteran Surfrider is usually willing to offer an early morning lesson.

Interns are encouraged to help out at the informational booths Surfrider sets up at events throughout Southern California. In return, they get to enjoy the events for free. Interns work the booth at surfing competitions, environmental-awareness expositions, and even the Lollapalooza concert. They also participate in cleanup days held at Bolsa Chica and other nearby beaches. Parties are another extracurricular option to interns who help out at such soireés as the Surfing Industry Manufacturers Association Ball. Said one intern about the SIMA Ball: "In exchange for selling drink tickets part of the time, I enjoyed an elaborate ball in a beautiful sculpture garden. Celebrities like Ted Danson were milling around. It was pretty cool."

SELECTION

 Surfrider welcomes applications from college students, graduate students, and recent graduates. According to the intern coordinator, the program looks for applicants who are "outgoing" and "environmentally aware." Knowledge of the surf industry and computer proficiency help, too. International applicants are eligible.

APPLICATION PROCEDURE

 Although applications are accepted on a rolling basis, applicants are advised to submit their materials at least three weeks before the date on which they wish to start. Send in a cover letter explaining the reasons for wanting to work at Surfrider; also enclose a resume or listing of relevant skills. The intern coordinator prefers to conduct in-person interviews but is willing to use phone interviews for long-distance applicants.

OVERVIEW

Ponytails, goatees, and easygoing attitudes may be the standard at the Surfrider Foundation, but get one thing straight—Surfrider is an effective lobby that's here to stay. Combining a passion for surfing with an inclination for environmental activism, Surfrider is committed to protecting the coastal environment. Whether carrying out badly needed administrative work or completing projects central to Surfrider's mission, interns are key players in the organization's success. For diehard surfers or mere ocean enthusiasts, interning at Surfrider is a means of ensuring that the endless summer lives on.

FOR MORE INFORMATION . . .

■ Surfrider Foundation
Internship Program
122 South El Camino Real
P.M.B. #67
San Clemente, CA 92672
(800) 743-SURF

SYMANTEC.

SELECTIVITY:

Approximate applicant pool: 1000
Interns Selected: 50–70

COMPENSATION:

$12–$20/hour, depending on class level and background

QUALITY OF LIFE:

Structured mentor program;
warm, friendly atmosphere;
company parties

LOCATION(S):

Cupertino, CA; Santa Monica, CA; Eugene OR;
Beaverton, OR; Toronto, ON; International Sites

FIELD:

Computer software design, Sales, Marketing,
Finance, MIS, Human Resources

DURATION:

3 months full-time during the summer
Part-time and full-time during the school year

PRE-REQS:

Undergrads and grad students

DEADLINES:

March 7 for summer, rolling the rest of the year

What was once the office of the future is now a reality. The following is now not uncommon: You're on the road, traveling to another business meeting in Jakarta. While sitting on the plane, you pull out your handheld PC and check your Email while scanning the latest headlines on the Web. Or you're at your office workstation at the beginning of the day: You leave a voice mail message for your assistant while sending a fax to the Tokyo office, then download a file you need for the 9:00 A.M. meeting while paging your team for a last-minute update on your presentation.

This vision of the working environment is reality today, brought to you by Symantec Corporation, whose products are pushing the limit of the possible in communications and computer technology. Symantec products can help you stop viruses at the point of entry, stay in touch and work productively from remote locations, and build, manage, and use software across complex computer networks. The future is now in the Symantec software world.

Symantec is a global corporation devoted to the development, manufacture, marketing, and support of computer software for individuals and business. Founded in 1982, Symantec is best known as the industry leader in utility and communication software for keeping individuals and businesses working productively in the Internet world. Today Symantec offers a wide range of products in three categories: Internet tools, security and assistance, and remote productivity solutions. With more than 2,400 employees at over forty locations worldwide and $75 million in revenues in the last fiscal year, Symantec is clearly a major player on the international software scene.

DESCRIPTION

Symantec's internship program began with ten interns in 1994 and is expected to reach sixty interns in 1999; this number is expected to grow in years to come. Interns work in all departments of the corporation, including Engineering, Quality Assurance, Marketing, Sales, Human Resources, Finance, and MIS (management information systems).

Most interns work in the Engineering group. For those with a computer science background, interning with the engineers at Symantec is a techie dream come true. "It's so exciting," said one intern who worked in software development/testing. "It's the cutting edge of technology—you can't be bored here." In his time at Symantec, he worked on developing Internet tools and Java compilers, "basically, programming languages for the Internet." "It was a fantastic experience," he said. "This is where everything is happening!"

Other interns are just as enthusiastic about the company. "It was great—I hope I get another internship just like it!" said one Human Resources intern. Although technically in the staffing department, she was allowed to "go around to all the departments to learn how they worked."

Symantec works hard to make its interns feel comfortable. The average age of the company is "about 31," people wear "jeans and T-shirts to work," and "you can always hear people laughing," says a staff representative. "It's an atmosphere where creativity and innovation just thrive." One intern in Marketing fondly remembered the fresh bagels in her department every Friday morning.

Symantec employees work hard, especially the engineering/product development groups— "When shipment dates and deadlines come up, it gets really crazy around here," said one engineering intern—but they play hard, too. Summer evenings are the scene for rooftop parties, where employees can relax and unwind after work.

Full-time employees help the integration process by having tremendously positive attitudes toward interns. "People here are so friendly," said one engineering intern. A Sales intern praised the feel of corporate headquarters, saying, "It's a great atmosphere: very friendly, and a fun crowd to be around. Everyone works hard, but they work together as a team, and they also have fun."

Most interns are based at Symantec's corporate headquarters in Cupertino, CA. Departments including Human Resources, Marketing and Finance are located there; Engi-

neering has its own building. Cupertino has been rated one of the most livable cities in the country; the affluent area offers a high living standard (accompanied by a high cost of living), excellent public schools, and a diverse population. Authentic ethnic food offerings include Indian, Vietnamese, Japanese, Chinese, and Mexican. The clubs, bars, and excitement of San Francisco are a one-hour drive to the north; the Pacific ocean and the wooded mountains of Santa Cruz are both less than an hour away.

Compensation for interns is generous, ranging from $12 to $20 an hour.

For those with a computer science background, interning with the engineers at Symantec is a techie dream come true

SELECTION

The internship program is open to undergraduate and graduate students in all fields, but especially computer science and engineering. Symantec is looking for interns with previous internship or relevant project experience and the "initiative to do things on their own." To survive in the fast-paced software industry, says a senior staff representative, "you need a full set of skills: personal and technical." For this reason, Symantec seeks interns who are well-rounded, and who will be able to contribute in a variety of ways in the long term.

APPLICATION PROCEDURE

The quickest and most efficient way to apply to Symantec is on the Web. The company's web site (www.symantec.com) lists all the latest job opportunities. Interested job-seekers can submit their resume to the company electronically. Those without Internet access can mail or fax a resume and cover letter.

Job openings for summer internships are posted on the Web throughout the year. The applications are then put through a three-round screening process. Selected applicants are interviewed either on-site or, for international applicants, on-screen through video conferencing.

OVERVIEW

 Want to talk Java? C++? Internet? Find reliable cross-platform interoperable solutions? If you're interested in being on the cutting edge of computer systems technology, Symantec's internship is for you.

Symantec's internship program offers an unparalleled opportunity to dive headfirst into the competitive waters of the software industry and start swimming right away. A strong support structure gives interns the opportunity to do substantive work with the latest technology. Especially noteworthy is Symantec's commitment to hiring interns full-time: The company developed its internship program in order to "aggressively recruit" young, full-time employees. An internship at Symatec is a kick-start into the fast-moving world of the software industry. As one Sales intern put it, "The internship was great—it was the best work experience I've ever had."

FOR MORE INFORMATION . . .

■ Symantec College Relations Program
20330 Steven's Creek Blvd.
Cupertino, CA 95014-2132
(408) 253-9600
Fax: (408) 446-8136
jobs@symantec.com
www.symantec.com

Every month it seems there's a new one. As a ski slope. A swimming pool in L.A. An Art Deco building in Miami. Carved out of a wheat field. A peeled lemon. Painted by Andy Warhol. Keith Haring. Configured in gold, steel, stone, and light bulbs. As a Christmas tree. Twice.

The mighty Absolut Vodka bottle has been etched into the minds of millions of consumers, thanks to an ingenious advertising campaign featuring the sleek Absolut bottle in more than 300 different ads. The mastermind behind this campaign is TBWA/Chiat/Day, a high-quality, medium-sized advertising house in New York. With $1.2 billion in billings, TBWA/Chiat/Day ranks among the world's top twenty advertising agencies. Besides Absolut, its clients include such high-profile companies as Wonderbra, Evian water, Timberland shoes, and Nivea skin cream.

It also created the recent award-winning, *Toy Story*–esque ad for Nissan that featured Van Halen's stomping cover of the Kinks "You Really Got Me" in the background; in a clever move to secure permission to use the song, word has it that the agency scored Eddie Van Halen and each of his band mates a limited-edition Nissan 300ZX.

SELECTIVITY	🔍🔍🔍
Approximate applicant pool: 900 Interns accepted: 24–36	

COMPENSATION	$
$75–225/week	

QUALITY OF LIFE	🌴🌴🌴🌴
Hip atmosphere; luncheon seminars international flavor; parties/picnic	

LOCATION(S)
New York, NY; Overseas—see Description

FIELD
Advertising

DURATION
10 weeks Summer

PRE-REQS
College juniors and seniors

DEADLINE(S)
March 1

DESCRIPTION

 At TBWA/Chiat/Day each intern is assigned a job in one of three work areas: Strategic Planning, Creative, Account Management, or Media. Strategic Planning interns spend their days investigating potential clients and figuring out what the agency can do for them. "An agency can't rest on its current accounts," said one intern. "It must progress and find new clients. As interns, we help it do so." Interns examine all sorts of markets and companies. Baby products, Swiss Army knives, the U.S. Army, an Italian import company—all are fair game for an intern's research. Sometimes interns in Planning carry out projects suggesting new directions for a current client. One intern, for example, spent three weeks studying and writing about how companies like Nissan can become more socially responsible. To carry out their research, interns do everything from searching computer databases to combing the AAAA Library, a midtown library that is exclusively used by ad agencies.

In Account Management, interns contact clients, attend client meetings, and help out with the agency's billing and budgeting. "I have no creative ability," said an intern in response to why Account Management was the best department for her. "As an Account Management intern, I carried out side projects for account executives, doing research and writing reports . . . I wrote a binder full." Among other papers, she wrote a detailed report exploring whether outdoor advertising would be beneficial for Carvel ice cream.

Like Strategic Planning and Account Management, the Media department assigns its interns a host of research projects. These projects often focus on determining the best medium (TV, newspaper, magazines, etc.) for TBWA/Chiat/Day's clients. While carrying out research for Evian, one intern, for example, investigated whether *Vanity Fair* readers have a higher propensity to drink mineral water than readers of other magazines. Computer databases prove immensely helpful in this kind of research, and by the end of the summer interns have a great deal of experience searching them to find appropriate statistics.

> The Woolite group jamm[ed] Aretha Franklin's "Respect" while it unveiled its stain pump's motto: "Stains need no respect, but your clothes do."

While interns generally find their daily work rewarding, they rave about their other main task during the internship—the marketing project. At the beginning of the summer, interns are divided into teams of five or six and are asked to develop complete marketing and communications plans for a TBWA/Chiat/Day client. With guidance from an assigned mentor, each team must create specific marketing, advertising, and media plans for a real product or service that is complete with creative examples. One group was asked to identify stronger brand and growth opportunities for Wonderbra. Another worked on a stain pump for Woolite. The year before, a group of interns created a Club Med campaign targeting Hispanic communities. Still another developed an advertising plan to sell Carvel ice cream in Texas.

The marketing project requires a concerted effort throughout the term of internship. Meeting after work and on the weekends, the teams research the market for their particular product. All along, interns have access to the agency's editorial and art resources, and they use them to write detailed reports and construct creative supplements like storyboards and sketches.

The marketing project culminates in a final exam of sorts at the end of the summer. Each team presents its work to the senior management of TBWA/Chiat/Day and then shows it to representatives of the actual client. "We, a bunch of college students, had the full attention of a group of Wonderbra managers. It was something!" said one team member. After two months of preparation, interns are ready to strut their stuff, making use of overhead projections, storyboards, on-the-street interviews, and sample products. The Woolite group even worked music into its presentation, jamming Aretha Franklin's "Respect" while it unveiled its stain pump's motto: "Stains need no respect, but your clothes do." The client representatives are often duly impressed, and many take the groups' projects to heart, carrying the information back to the home office for further consideration. Interns cannot say enough good things about the experience: "We acted as a bona-fide advertising unit, doing everything real advertising professionals would. And [TBWA/Chiat/Day's senior management] trusted us to present our plan to real clients. I'll never forget it."

Every week, interns attend special two-hour luncheon seminars designed to teach them about advertising subjects (media, creative, production, direct marketing, interactive media) and other areas like corporate brand identity promotion, public relations, and presentation techniques. Past speakers include the creative director, copywriters, art directors, client representatives, and even the president. The last, Bill Tragos, got stellar reviews. "In one sense, it was really humbling. After all, he is the [CEO] of the fifth largest privately held advertising agency in the world," one intern said. "But he was totally unpretentious and direct. He answered all our questions."

TBWA/Chiat/Day's headquarters is located on Madison Avenue, a street synonymous with advertising the world over. The agency occupies four floors of its building, and every floor has a different feel, though all are modern and inviting. The executive floor, for example, has a handsome, Japanese look, while the creative floor is less chic, with everything from basketball hoops to advertising awards affixed to the walls. Interns sit in cubicles decked out with all the office supplies one could want—"a real professional setup," in one intern's estimation.

The office atmosphere at TBWA/Chiat/Day gets high ratings. "Even more hip than I imagined," said an intern. "It's youthful, energetic, and stimulating." Another attributes the mood to the agency's president, saying, "Mr. Tragos is very charismatic and friendly. His attitude filters down to everyone, even the interns." Interns enjoy hanging around together and they learn a lot from each other's different cultural backgrounds. TBWA/Chiat/Day has outposts in every major capital in Europe, so it's no surprise that its internship attracts international students. American interns are often surprised (and pleased) to find that several of the interns are foreign students: "Our group looked like a meeting of a mini United Nations." Recent years have attracted students from England, France, Italy, Germany, Japan, Korea, Sweden, Austria, and Tahiti.

Interns are satisfied with the fringe benefits that come their way at TBWA/Chiat/Day. Parties are an occasional treat, periodically thrown and hosted by clients like Absolut. The agency annually sponsors a mid-summer picnic at a New Jersey park, and, at the end of the internship, the executive vice president holds a lunch at which a student is chosen as the "Intern of the Year." This honor is presented to the intern who has made the best impression on TBWA/Chiat/Day management. In addition to the in-house announcement, the executive vice president takes the Intern of the Year out to a celebratory lunch at a posh restaurant.

Students interested in interning overseas will be happy to learn that TBWA/Chiat/Day has offices in more than thirty countries. While the majority of these offices accept an intern or two, TBWA/Chiat/Day management reports that the strongest internship opportunities can be found at TBWA/Chiat/Day outposts in Amsterdam, Barcelona, Frankfurt, London, Paris, and Johannesburg.

In most respects, TBWA/Chiat/Day is an intern's dream. "This is a full-fledged, knock-'em-dead internship program. Big commitment, bigger reward," an intern concluded. But there are a few gripes. Workdays are long, especially when interns stay late to work on their marketing projects. Some wished their supervisors were around more often to offer guidance with daily tasks. Others groaned that the lunchtime seminars were postponed too often.

SELECTION

 TBWA/Chiat/Day seeks interns who are entering their junior or senior year of college. No particular majors are favored, but the program brochure states that successful applicants demonstrate "a consuming interest in the advertising business" and "have a point of view about it." The brochure adds that "extracurricular activities, work experience, and personal interests are also taken into account since all of these provide insight into the candidate's leadership qualities and overall personality." According to past interns, those who thrive in the program have "high self-esteem, as advertising is a business of big egos," "positive attitudes, because you're not working in a funeral home," and "good public speaking skills—you'll need them when presenting your final project." Adds the internship coordinator: "We want self-assured, tireless people who have agile minds, a sense of humor, and who are terrified of being bored." International applicants are eligible.

APPLICATION PROCEDURE

 Applicants should submit their materials by March 1. The procedure is relatively simple: Send in a resume and cover letter explaining your reasons for seeking the job. Live interviews are mandatory for all but overseas students, who can interview at one of TBWA/Chiat/Day's European outposts. TBWA/Chiat/Day selects its interns in late April. Students interested in interviewing at one of TBWA/Chiat/Day's overseas offices should write to the New York office for a contact or to have New York forward their application. Applicants must be fluent in the local language.

OVERVIEW

 If you're looking for a career in advertising, TBWA/Chiat/Day's internship is hard to beat with its substantive work, stimulating environment, and a "real-world" marketing project. TBWA/Chiat/Day believes strongly in its internship program, and it shows. In the program's brochure, the agency even enumerates its reasons for hiring interns, not the least of which is the desire to offer "participants a hands-on work experience that generates a real understanding of what agency 'life' is really about." Another dividend of the internship is the opportunity to work closely with a highly talented and delightfully international group of interns. Chances are an intern will leave TBWA/Chiat/Day with a network of friends from around the world. A summer at TBWA/Chiat/Day is absolutely worthwhile.

FOR MORE INFORMATION . . .

■ TBWA/Chiat/Day
Internship Program
488 Madison Avenue
New York, NY 10022
(212) 804-1000

3M

SELECTIVITY	
Approximate applicant pool: 4,000 Interns accepted: 200	🔍 🔍 🔍 🔍

COMPENSATION	
$440–$540/week for undergraduates $550–$680/week for graduate students	💲 💲 💲 💲

QUALITY OF LIFE	
Employee camaraderie; social activities; 3M Center	🌴 🌴 🌴 🌴

LOCATION(S)
St. Paul, MN; Austin, TX; and 80 plants nationwide—see Index

FIELD
Consumer, health care, commercial, and industrial goods

DURATION
14 weeks Summer

PRE-REQS
College sophomores, juniors and seniors; grad students; Minimum 3.0 GPA

DEADLINE
December 31

Don't you hate it when your bookmark falls out and you've lost the page you were on? Back in 1974 so did Art Fry, a Division Scientist at 3M. A member of his church choir, he would mark his hymnal with bookmarks, but the bookmarks would often fall out, leaving him unable to keep his place. Taking advantage of 3M's "15 percent policy" (whereby the company's engineers and scientists may spend up to 15 percent of their time on projects of their choice), Fry worked to create a sticky bookmark. He sought out a semi-sticky adhesive invented by a 3M employee four years earlier and started applying it to various types of paper. "At first, the adhesive left some residue on the hymnal . . . [but] I finally figured it out . . . and started making [sticky paper] for other employees, who used it as notepaper. After about ten sheets, they were all addicts," Fry told us. The invention? 3M Post-it notes. Introduced nationally in 1980, they were an instant success.

Besides Post-it notes, 3M's "15 percent policy" has spawned a host of classics, including masking tape and Scotch Brand transparent tape. These innovative products have made 3M, which stands for Minnesota Mining & Manufacturing, a world-recognized company with yearly sales of over $15 billion and an employee base of 85,000 people. Founded in 1902 as a maker of sandpaper, 3M now manufactures more than 60,000 office, household, and industrial goods from sponges, videotapes, and computer disks to overhead projectors, medical laser imagers, and surgical masks.

DESCRIPTION

3M started its summer program in 1951, making it one of the oldest internship programs in corporate America. Today, more than 200 college undergraduate and graduate-student interns from around the country participate in a variety of programs, including minority-only programs that target students nationwide. The Summer Intern Program places 140 to 160 students in laboratory, engineering, and manufacturing positions, where they help improve old products and create new ones. Approximately 80 interns are also placed in finance, marketing, and administrative positions. About 70 percent of the students work in St.

BUSYWORK METER
LOW MEDIUM HIGH
OLDMAN & HAMADEH

Paul, the rest in Austin, TX, or one of the 80 plants throughout the country. Ninety percent of 3M interns are undergraduates.

Each intern starts the summer by going through a small-group training session, administered to all new 3M hires. In Corporate Accounting, the session educates interns on profit-and-loss statements and teaches them how to read production summaries. After the session, one Accounting intern was placed in the Specialty Adhesives and Chemicals Division. She worked on two projects, one analyzing the cost of incinerating 3M's toxic wastes and another involving 3M's Distributive Unit Cost System (referred to as DUCS, pronounced "ducks"). "DUCS is an in-house computer system we use to determine the unit cost for each chemical produced in our division. It takes into account the labor, the material, the packaging, and many other variables. Some of the numbers generated seemed too high and others too low, so I was charged with going through it." Scour it she did, finding that some of the data were old, that other data were incorrectly input, and that a third problem was so complex that "even after talking to 3M's best programmers, I could not solve it in the short time I was there."

But making products is what 3M is all about. "One intern could work on sandpaper and another on diaper tape," said the coordinator. "The variety of jobs is endless!" One intern worked on a digital imager, a machine that transforms electronic data from X-rays and CAT scans, for example, into photograph-quality pictures. "3M had already figured out how to produce the images. I was there to help figure out the mechanics." Accordingly, he broke the task down into discrete projects with workable deadlines. He tinkered with an old imager to determine if any of the parts or processes could be improved. "We realized that the circuit board would need a protective cover to prevent certain components from touching each other. But the cover also had to cool the components. I sat down with design engineers to figure

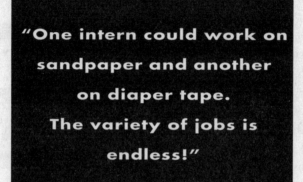

"One intern could work on sandpaper and another on diaper tape. The variety of jobs is endless!"

out how we could do that. By the time I left, I had designed a fan and specified its location and air flow."

Another intern worked in Dental Products on dental clay, that plasterlike guck orthodontists use to make impressions of your teeth. Assigned to the product development group, she worked on a new and improved version to address dentists' concerns. "I used a Brookfield viscometer to measure the viscosity of [the clay] and make sure that it was within the range specified by the engineers who designed it. Once a statistical test confirmed that the [new clay] met the specifications, I worked with labeling and marketing to get it into dentists' hands."

Interns cannot choose which products they want to work on. If they could, "[they'd] all ask to work on Post-it Notes and wouldn't learn anything about other products," said an intern who ended up testing adhesives for medical dressings, and in the end optimized the hold and release properties of a particular 3M medical adhesive. "I mixed the chemicals together to create new formulations, spread them onto dressings, and then did the initial tests, which consisted of putting two dressings against one another and recording how well they stuck." Once he found a few formulations that adhered well and were also easily removable, it was time for the human trials. "At 3M, employees are willing to test your products so long as you test theirs. My test was unfortunately a little painful; some of the dressings tended to pull off arm and leg hair!"

Interns report that 3M's projects are "challenging" and come with "very little supervision." The combination frustrates some interns at first. "My supervisor didn't know how to help a student—he wasn't able to respond adequately to questions I had on my project." But most interns find that their frustration eventually gives way to a sense of accomplishment: "It forced me to go through the project on my own, and it was rewarding because I actually solved a 3M problem." Tackling a project alone also prepares them for the presentations they must give at a two-day affair in front of managers and employees at the end of the summer. "I was so nervous at the time," remarked one intern, "but in hindsight, I am happy that 3M made me give one. I learned that I could stand in front of a group and defend my work."

3M works with an apartment locator service to help students find housing for the summer. Within a mile and a half of work, two apartment buildings house nearly three quarters of the summer interns. Some students are pleased with their assignments: "It was fairly cheap and much like living in a big dorm—lots of parties." Others are disappointed: "My apartment was located in East St. Paul, right off the highway. I also didn't hit it off with my two roommates, both 3M interns."

Most interns work at the 3M Center, the company's headquarters in St. Paul, MN, described by the College Relations Manager as "a marvelous place to live, a cultural center with everything from sports to theater." With 25 buildings on more than 400 acres, the 3M Center is "an easy place to get lost." In front of the complex are several office buildings and behind are orange-brick R&D facilities. On-site are also a barber, bakery, convenience store, and gift shop, all for 3M employees. With fountains, a well-manicured lawn, and lots of shady trees, it's like a minicommunity, nicknamed "the campus" for its university-like setting. The only thing missing is an on-site gym, a fact one intern deemed "a big disadvantage." But there are subsidized cafeterias, where interns and employees rarely stop talking about 3M products. "We are continuously improving things and developing ideas. You can't help but get excited. When you see your friends in the 'caf,' you feel like telling them what you've been up to."

The camaraderie usually continues off-hours as well. Departments frequently organize picnics at a nearby park, also the site of the company-wide welcome and farewell intern picnics. Staffing also plans trips to Twins games, dinners with management, and a riverboat cruise. For athletes, there are company intramural leagues in volleyball, softball, tennis, and golf—played on the 3M-owned golf course.

But the company can't arrange every social and recreational event, so interns take it upon themselves to make their own fun. They keep each other abreast of activities like trips to the dog track, zoo, and Valley Fair amusement park. For those who love the outdoors, St. Paul is full of biking and running trails. Roller blading is popular among residents, and tubing down the calm Apple River, 40 minutes away, is a popular 3M intern event, described by one as "an inexpensive day in the sun."

SELECTION

 For the Summer Intern Program, although the majority of positions require interns to be seniors, there are a few opportunities for sophomores and juniors. Eligible majors include chemistry, engineering (chemical, electrical, mechanical, industrial, and ceramic), computer science, materials science, biology, and physics. For finance positions, applicants must be seniors in accounting or business, though a few sophomores, juniors, and MBA candidates have been accepted in the past. For marketing positions, applicants must be seniors pursuing marketing-related degrees, including communications, journalism, or advertising; MBA candidates are also eligible. All applicants must have at least a 3.0 GPA. International applicants are eligible. To research 3M, check out the company's web site at www.mmm.com.

APPLICATION PROCEDURE

 The deadline is December 31. Students must submit a resume and cover letter. Interviews with Staffing or specific departments, by phone or on-site, are arranged as needed.

OVERVIEW

 Life without 3M products would be life in the Dark Ages—no Post-it notes, no Scotch-Brite cleaning pads, and no Scotch brand transparent tape. But there's no need to entertain such a thought, since the scientists and engineers at 3M continue to churn out products that make modern life easier. As 3M interns, students get to contribute to the mission and carry out projects of significance. Some interns improve processes, while others help to create new products. Either way, every year the program launches a good 50 percent of graduating interns into full-time employment with 3M. It did so with Art Fry, the Post-it notes inventor, who completed his 3M internship in 1955.

FOR MORE INFORMATION . . .

- 3M
  Student Programs
  224-1W-02
  3M Center
  St. Paul, MN 55144-1000
  (800) 328-1343

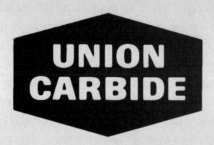

"**U**nion Carbide"—to the average person, the name doesn't exactly drip with corporate sexiness.

The word "union" brings to mind a musty, timeworn union hall, squatting in the shadow of dark factories and billowing smokestacks. Or perhaps it suggests a stout, cigar-chomping labor organizer, dressed in greasy overalls, yelling into a microphone.

And what about "carbide"? Is it the black, sooty film which soils the uniforms of brick-oven cooks and chimney sweeps? Or is it a lonely, little-known element, so lowly that scientists have never bothered to include it on the Periodic Table?

Taken together, "Union Carbide" might seem like the fast track to Dullsville.

Happily, it isn't.

In fact, Union Carbide is one of the world's leading manufacturers of chemicals and polymers, with over 12,000 employees and annual sales of approximately $6.5 billion. Founded in 1917, it is also the world's largest producer of ethylene oxide, which is used to make ethylene glycol, a component of polyester and antifreeze. As a major industrial supplier of chemicals, plastics, industrial gases, and polymers, Union Carbide is not a consumer-goods company. Yet its products end up in everything from food preservatives, bandages, and floor coverings to chewing gum, pharmaceuticals, and cosmetics.

DESCRIPTION

Established in 1990, Union Carbide's Student Employment Program offers internship and co-op positions in Production, Technology Improvements, Distribution, Engineering, Management Information Systems, Finance, Research and Development, and Sales. Because the program seeks "to find good, strong student employees, and nurture them into becoming good, strong full-time Union Carbide employees," interns are afforded a large degree of responsibility, support, and, as one intern put it, "respect": "They treat you like one of them . . . everything from having lunch with you to talking with you about projects going on in the plant."

An intern in Research and Development spent his summer developing polymers for use in plastics applications.

SELECTIVITY	🔍 🔍 🔍
Approximate applicant pool: 1,000 Interns accepted: 135–150	

COMPENSATION	💲 💲 💲 💲 💲
$1,900/month for recent high school grads; $2,000–$3,000/month for undergrads; $3,200–$3,600/month for grad students; round-trip travel; housing benefits; health & life insurance	

QUALITY OF LIFE	🚶 🚶 🚶 🚶
Brown-bag luncheons; organized social activities; city survival kits; orientation	

LOCATION(S)

Danbury, CT; New Orleans, LA; Bound Brook and Somerset, NJ; Cary, NC; Houston, Texas City, & Victoria, TX; South Charleston, WV

FIELD

Chemicals

DURATION

12 weeks
Summer, Fall, Spring

PRE-REQS

See Selection

DEADLINE

Summer ...... March 31   Spring ..... November 30
Fall .... May 31

BUSYWORK METER
OLDMAN & HAMADEH
MEDIUM
LOW HIGH

Helping to create a special plastic for various automobile components, as well as foam for automobile seat cushions, he said: "I was able to see how everything fit together—the theory in my classes with how research is done in industry, how ideas are generated, and how a project is developed from its initial stages up to the final product."

A Production intern spent part of his summer creating a spreadsheet and diagrams which helped Carbide monitor the performance of its plants' heat exchangers. This allowed engineers to determine the best times for "backflushing" (chemical-speak for cleaning) the exchangers, and to schedule the cleanings at convenient times. He reported: "I had to use my own brain. I had to create something of my own. The supervisor had no idea how to do it either. He left it up to me."

Many interns prize the fact that they often work on several projects over the summer. "A lot of companies give you only one assignment, but at Carbide when they give you three or four, like most interns here get, you get a real sense of responsibility. You feel like you're a full-time engineer," said an Engineering intern who worked on three different projects. Besides updating blueprints of the plant structure and collecting and performing safety valve calculations, she was asked to modify an industrial fan in the plant. She spoke with everyone from the maintenance crew, to the engineers, to the vendors, before passing on her recommendations. Attesting to the importance of her work, Union Carbide followed her recommendations "almost exactly."

Another Research and Development intern spent her first summer out of high school working on two projects for Carbide. Her first was to help devise a new chemical test which plant operators could use to estimate the amount of organic carbon in the plant's waste water. The current test, she explained, required too much time to run. After creating a suitable test, she made a graph correlating the test's results with the amount of organic carbon in the water distributed to the plant operators. Later in the summer, she worked on a project that required going into the field to collect samples from waste water ponds and then conducting lab experiments on the samples to determine the levels of solid waste in the ponds. "I enjoyed working independently," she said. "My superiors were not always looking over my shoulder, so the work was challenging."

Although most interns work on their own, they sometimes convene in teams to tackle an assignment. One group of twelve interns at the Taft, LA, plant, for example, was charged with analyzing a sewer system. After receiving training in how to work as a group and meeting with an engineering adviser, the group set off on its own. Described one member: "We held regular meetings and turned in weekly reports detailing our progress."

Treated like regular employees, Carbide interns receive superlative benefits compared to interns at most companies. Except for profit sharing, interns enjoy an allowance for travel to and from the work site, medical and dental plans, savings programs, and life insurance. Out-of-town students also receive housing benefits, which vary from site to site. "[The housing benefits] are outstanding," said one intern. "You have to pay 250 to 300 dollars a month for some apartment near work, and Union Carbide covers the rest."

At the start of the summer, interns attend a "Student Orientation," where they undergo safety training and are assigned a supervisor as well as a "business advisor" who serves as a year-round mentor. Advisers counsel students on different issues, including grades and courses, job concerns, and future career options both within and outside Carbide. "I didn't realize how crucial my advisor would be . . . ," said one intern. "As a graduating senior, I relied on him to explain all of my options within the chemical industry."

> **Union Carbide is proof positive that you can't judge a company (or an internship) by the sound of its name.**

Throughout the summer, on-site training and personal development programs are offered to all interns. The mainstay of this training is the "brown-bag luncheon," usually held every other week to enable students to interact with management. Bringing in an instructor from the Continuing Education Center, a Carbide training center located at each site, a typical brown-bag lunch might involve a presentation and discussion on a technical subject or a topic such as time management, interviewing, presentation techniques, communication skills, or problem analysis. In addition, all interns receive feedback on their work by participating in two summer work performance evaluations.

Intern social activities are plentiful. Arranged by the internship coordinator, such events as cook-outs, movies, and pizza parties are common, with a trip to a Six Flags amusement park, dinner at an exclusive restaurant, or deep-sea fishing occasionally thrown in. But many interns also plan their own group outings. Students at the Taft, LA, plant, for example, find plenty to do in nearby New Orleans, especially since Carbide provides them with "city survival kits," replete with maps and lists of "things to do." Said one intern: "There were many nights we went into town to go clubbing, or out to dinner, or to watch a show at one of the comedy clubs. I made a lot of good friends that way."

Carbide's atmosphere is, in the words of one intern, "a warm, fuzzy one," where everyone watches out for everyone else. "My first week there," said one intern, "a few of my co-workers pulled me out of my office and said, 'Come eat lunch with us.' I was surprised that they genuinely cared about getting to know me." Another commented, "People really listened to what I had to say. If I asked to work in a certain area, my supervisor did her best to accommodate me. [I was] treated as a professional." Another intern cited how helpful Carbide employees are. "I didn't know what some of the symbols I was analyzing meant or how certain equipment worked," she said. "But it was no problem. My supervisor took me out to look at the equipment and explained it all to me."

SELECTION

 Union Carbide's Student Employment Program is open to recent high school graduates (summer before college), undergraduates, and graduate students with a BS in engineering who are working on an MS/MBA UC students studying chemical engineering are particularly sought after. Applicants must have a minimum GPA of 3.0. In keeping with Carbide's friendly, team atmosphere, students who have, through participation in campus activities or part-time work, displayed leadership and an ability to work with a team have a slight edge. Interns suggest that applicants must also be able to "accept criticism," "ask questions," and "take something and run with it." International applicants are eligible.

APPLICATION PROCEDURE

 The deadline is March 31 for summer positions, May 31 for fall, and November 30 for spring. Although Carbide's recruiting is concentrated at twenty-five colleges and universities in the Gulf Coast and Eastern Regions—including Penn State, Howard University, and North Carolina State—all interested students are encouraged to send in their resumes. Students are first interviewed by a Carbide representative (an engineer) on campus either at a formal interview or during an informal career fair. Their resumes (as well as other, unsolicited resumes) are then passed on to the regional recruiting skills center. The centers are responsible for matching students with different sites, according to descriptions of positions the sites provide. Students then undergo another interview before selection by site managers.

OVERVIEW

 Union Carbide is proof positive that you can't judge a company (or an internship) by the sound of its name. Carbide offers an experience that should excite anybody interested in working for a leading chemical manufacturer. Plum projects, sweet pay, brown-bag luncheons with executives, housing benefits, well-planned extracurriculars, and an astounding 90 percent rehire rate make Carbide a star internship program. Add to that a uniquely supportive atmosphere, enhanced by an extensive mentoring network and career counseling, and you've got an internship that fires on all cylinders.

FOR MORE INFORMATION . . .

■ Internship Coordinator
Union Carbide Corporation
Eastern Region Skill Center
P.O. Box 8004
South Charleston, WV 25303

Students interested in gaining exposure to the United Nations are faced with a bewildering array of options. UN headquarters used to offer the Ad Hoc Internship Program and now has the Headquarters Programme, administered through its Human Resources department. Once eligible for these programs, undergraduates are no longer accepted. Furthermore, American citizens comprise only about one-third of the graduate students accepted. Added to the morass is the fact that UN organizations have their own internship programs, each independent of the others—UNICEF, UNIFEM, UNIDO—what a UNI-*pain!*

The United Nations Association of the United States of America (UNA) stands as a beacon in this dark night of internship confusion. A private, nonprofit organization, the UNA dedicates itself to enhancing U.S. participation in the UN system through programs in public outreach, policy analysis, and international dialogue. Though not officially a part of the UN, it is a bastion of information about and analysis on the UN, disseminating its work through 175 UNA chapters, 135 affiliated organizations, and a wide variety of publications. Most importantly, the UNA offers an internship that gives motivated students the opportunity to gain a comprehensive understanding of the United Nations.

SELECTIVITY	🔍 🔍 🔍
Approximate applicant pool: 245 Interns accepted: 25 (summer), 10 (fall/winter)	

COMPENSATION	$
Paid fellowships and unpaid positions	

QUALITY OF LIFE	🕊 🕊 🕊
Access to UN; brown-bags; free books/posters	

LOCATION(S)
New York, NY; Washington D.C. (a few)

FIELD
International affairs

DURATION
10–12 weeks Summer, Fall, Spring Part-time available

PRE-REQS
Undergrads; recent grads; grad students; high school (Model U.N.)

DEADLINE
Summer .... before March 15   Fall .... August 15 Spring .... before November 15
Applications are also accepted on a rolling basis for special programs and conventions that may arise.

DESCRIPTION

Internships are available in the Communications Department, Corporate Affairs, Policy Studies Programs, Model U.N. and Education, Development, Executive Office, Media, National Programs, and Council of Organizations. The UNA internship application describes the role of each department and interns' responsibilities therein. Nevertheless, a few positions are worth elaborating on here.

Interns in the Communications Department research, fact check, and write small articles for various UNA publications. Some interns are assigned to the *InterDependent*, an eleven- to twenty-two-page quarterly newsletter distributed to UNA members, the international affairs community, and journalists. Interns research and analyze

BUSYWORK METER

LOW MEDIUM HIGH

OLDMAN & HAMADEH

such UN-related issues as arms control, international trade, human rights, and environmental protection. Writing assignments aren't always as dry as one might expect; one intern wrote a short piece for the *InterDependent* on the "hairy potato," a fuzzy, insect-trapping spud that needs no insecticide. Other interns do research or proofreading for *A Global Agenda: Issues Before the General Assembly of the United Nations*, an annual volume that offers an overview of global political issues (e.g., disarmament) and the complex UN agenda.

The Model U.N. and Education department assists the many Model United Nations conferences held around the world. Thousands of high school and college students attend these conferences to participate in simulated UN meetings. Interns research and write chapters for UNA's *Guide to Delegate Preparation*, a book that briefs conference participants about how to prepare for a Model UN conference. The book describes that specific nature of diplomacy and provides in-depth information about specific global issues and the countries involved. Combing the stacks of the UN's Dag Hammarskjöld Library and the New York Public Library, interns research a particular country or group of countries, digging up statistics and analyzing governments. They also try to interview a representative of the appropriate country's "mission" (i.e., embassy) to the UN. Most interviews take place by phone, but sometimes diplomats are willing to meet with interns in person. One intern, for instance, arranged a luncheon interview with a press officer from the British mission to the UN. She elaborated: "[The *Guide to Delegate Preparation*] circulates throughout the UN. Diplomats care about what we say about their country. They want interns to get it right. Every so often, they'll grant you a live interview."

The Policy Studies department assigns interns to one of its Parallel Studies Programs. In the Asian Security program, for example, interns study such topics as North Korea's nuclear potential, the growing tension in Indian-Pakistani relations, and the establishment of a new political and economic order in the Asia-Pacific region. Alternatively, the East and Central Europe program finds interns analyzing the region's integration into the international economy, the implementation of human rights standards, and the management of security issues.

Approximately one-fifth of an intern's work is administrative. Interns must deal with the daily "three *ph*'s": photocopying, phone work, and (ph)axing. "It was never as boring as it could have been," said an intern. "We made the best of it . . . . We played a radio in the background." Interns may also be asked to pick up and deliver documents to UN headquarters, a chore that isn't as dull as it may seem: "It taught you the ins and outs of headquarters—which is valuable when you need to do research there later on."

A brief orientation program marks the beginning of the internship. Interns receive a special handbook that goes over the mechanics of their jobs and lists a series of do's and don'ts ("don't make long-distance personal calls," "don't stay in the office after-hours," etc.). They also get together to plan which speakers they want to invite for the summer's weekly brown-bag luncheons. Past interns have arranged luncheons with such big shots as the president of the UNA and UN delegates from the Netherlands and Malta.

The UNA experience is at once formal and flexible. Interns must adhere to a conservative dress code—suit and tie for men, dresses for women; "sloppy jeans don't go over well here," says the intern coordinator. At the same time, however, interns are afforded a lot of freedom. "There's no strict nine-to-five law at the UNA. They let you do your own thing." No one minds if an intern occasionally takes time out for a personal matter or takes a break to get some fresh air.

Located one block from the United Nations, UNA occupies the second floor of a midtown office building. The elevator opens up to an attractive waiting room, decked out with glass walls and official flags. Inside are

> The Delegate's Lounge "crackled with energy—you didn't actually hear anything, but you knew by people's faces that important discussions were going on."

several offices, two full kitchens, and a conference room resembling "an anteroom to the Oval Office." Interns work together, often three to an office. The UNA-USA has recently provided interns with new computer equipment.

When life grows tiresome at the UNA office, interns are free to take a walk to UN Headquarters. Armed with a prized UN pass, they have easy access to UN territory. As one intern commented, "although it's in New York, UN headquarters feels like a world unto itself." Indeed it should, for the compound is an international zone, complete with its own laws, flag, and postage stamps. Interns are free to roam through the 39-story glass-and-marble Secretariat tower and the low-domed General Assembly Building. At the latter, they may observe the General Assembly, which is the primary meeting of UN member countries that is held for several months in autumn. Interns may also dine at the Delegate's Lounge, a private, red-carpeted dining room overlooking the East River. A hotbed of "behind-the-scenes diplomatic discussion," the Delegate's Lounge, "crackled with energy—you didn't actually hear anything, but you knew by people's faces that important discussions were going on," said one intern.

Don't count on leaving the internship with a bag full of UNA key chains and windbreakers (if they existed). But there are a few excellent souvenirs to be had. Free copies of books and pamphlets circulate through the office. "I took home all sorts of literature on the UN and international affairs. These reports—especially one on the UN and disarmament—would have come in handy for my senior thesis," said one intern. The Non-Governmental Organization (NGO) Resource Center at UN headquarters is another treasure trove of UN literature. But if a sea of UN pamphlets isn't enough, NGO/DPI also stocks an assortment of posters, all free for the asking. "Among others, I snagged a sharp-looking poster commemorating the Year of the Indigenous Person," said an intern. By virtue of their internship, interns also receive free membership in the UNA Network, which distributes a bimonthly newsletter and sponsors conferences on international affairs.

SELECTION

 The UNA welcomes applications from undergraduates of any level, recent graduates, and graduate students from all countries. There are two exceptions; Communications and Policy Studies prefer only college seniors and older. Also, the UNA occasionally takes on a few high school students who are, as the coordinator put it, "really sharp." Ideal applicants have strong backgrounds in international affairs as well as good writing and research skills. Although most departments have no hard-and-fast prerequisites, Policy Studies requires foreign language skill and familiarity with a particular country's foreign policy; Corporate Affairs requires proficiency with computers. Before applying, check the UNA internship application for more details. International applicants are eligible.

APPLICATION PROCEDURE

 Final selections for summer internships are made on March 15; for fall internships, August 15; and for spring internships, November 15. The earlier applicants apply, the better their chances of securing the position they desire. Submit a resume, a writing sample (any brief academic paper), and a UNA application. In addition to asking applicants to name the dates they are available and the department they prefer, the UNA application requires three brief essays explaining one's background in international affairs, special qualifications for the internship, and impressions of the UN and its effectiveness in the international system. Application materials are circulated to the director of the department in which applicants indicate interest. Interviews are not required and are rare. Occasionally, program directors will conduct an interview over the phone.

OVERVIEW

 If interning at UN Headquarters is like being in the dugout during a baseball game, then interning at the UNA is like having a seat behind home plate. The former may get one closer to the players, but the latter yields a better view of the game. By virtue of the UNA's nonpartisan commitment to education and analysis on the UN, interns leave the UNA with a broad understanding of how the UN works and the issues it faces. Besides important research and writing assignments, UNA interns are given a coveted UN pass with which they may observe UN meetings and briefings. In the summer, they also have the unique opportunity of selecting their own speakers for a weekly luncheon seminar. In all the right ways, the UNA internship is designed with its interns' education in mind.

FOR MORE INFORMATION . . .

■ United Nations Association of the USA
Internship Coordinator
801 Second Avenue
New York, NY 10017
unahq@unausa.org
www.unausa.org

There's something impossibly frightening about the thought of being arrested and unfairly punished in a foreign land. Most Americans can only imagine that heart-wrenching feeling of helplessness that comes with the realization that one is subject to a strange land's laws (or lack thereof). From the steamy Turkish dungeon in *Midnight Express* to the Singaporean caning of Michael Fay, we are riveted by the drama of foreign punishments for crime.

But when an American faces such a fate, working behind the scenes is the U.S. Department of State, the agency responsible for the nation's foreign policy. Though not always successful, the State Department works with foreign governments to ensure the fair and equitable treatment of accused U.S. citizens.

Even so, engineering the fair treatment of Americans abroad is only one of the State Department's functions. Established in 1789 by President George Washington, the State Department also issues visas and passports, negotiates treaties and trade agreements, controls the proliferation of nuclear weapons, combats drug trafficking, and helps foreign nations establish viable political and economic systems, among other endeavors. Developing and implementing these policies are 24,000 full-time employees, who serve in Washington, D.C., and more than 250 embassies and consulates worldwide.

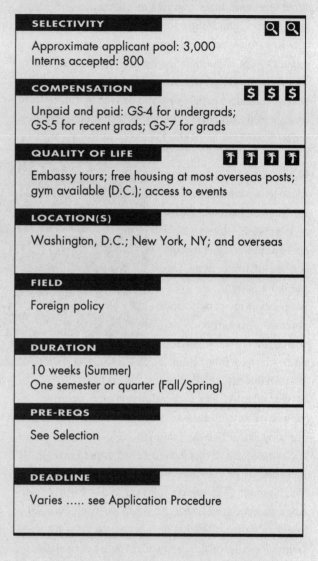

SELECTIVITY

Approximate applicant pool: 3,000
Interns accepted: 800

COMPENSATION

Unpaid and paid: GS-4 for undergrads;
GS-5 for recent grads; GS-7 for grads

QUALITY OF LIFE

Embassy tours; free housing at most overseas posts;
gym available (D.C.); access to events

LOCATION(S)

Washington, D.C.; New York, NY; and overseas

FIELD

Foreign policy

DURATION

10 weeks (Summer)
One semester or quarter (Fall/Spring)

PRE-REQS

See Selection

DEADLINE

Varies ..... see Application Procedure

DESCRIPTION

The U.S. Department of State offers interns positions all year long. The State Department places 800 students annually in internships, about 150 of whom work in fall and spring the rest in summer. The Student Intern Program offers opportunities year-round, the majority in Washington, D.C. Most of the positions are unpaid; in fact, a paltry 5 percent pay. Yet while paid positions are scarce, there are no less than thirty-one bureaus and offices to choose from, covering every region of the world and topic of international affairs, including Art in Embassies Program, Consular Affairs, Diplomatic Security, Information Management, Economic and Business Affairs, European and Canadian Affairs, Human Rights and Humanitarian Affairs, Intelligence and Research, International Narcotics Matters, Office of

BUSYWORK
MEDIUM
LOW HIGH
OLDMAN &
HAMADEH
METER
?

the Legal Advisor, Near Eastern and South Asian Affairs, Oceans & International Environmental and Scientific Affairs, and Politico-Military Affairs.

Regardless of where they are placed, interns should expect to log some time on the busywork bandwagon. The daily grind may involve anything from sorting passport documents to collecting and delivering cables from foreign embassies to (in the case of two undergrad interns) loading bags on the Secretary of State's airplane prior to an overseas trip. Other interns answer some of the letters which pour into the State Department daily.

Because they often serve as junior-level foreign service officers, State Department interns also prepare briefing papers and conduct background research on cases involving domestic and international law. An intern in the Bureau of Consular Affairs in Washington, for example, reviewed nationality cases—"people overseas who stop by our consulate offices and claim to be U.S. citizens." Since U.S. consulates do not have the resources to investigate these claims, he explained, all such cases must go through Washington. "I'd search relevant files—birth certificates, passports, and other records to verify citizenship—and then write an opinion on whether the person should be granted citizenship." They might be asked to update an evacuation plan, which the State Department keeps at each U.S. embassy in case of collapsing public security.

The Office of the Secretary keeps the Secretary of State abreast of important global activities and oversees preparations for her diplomatic trips. Besides scanning cables from embassies overseas and passing them on to the appropriate departments, an intern in this office prepared briefing books, which contain information on foreign countries and policies and are used by U.S. diplomats in advance of a trip abroad.

Working in counter-terrorism and counter-narcotics trafficking, an intern in the Bureau of Inter-American Affairs helped write assessments of terrorist groups and drug cartels operating out of South America. "I had to get a higher security clearance [in order] to use some of the resources available at CIA Headquarters in Langley," he said. "Once cleared, I met with analysts and pored through sensitive documents. There was a lot of cooperation going on." He also assisted in the preparations for a three-day meeting among the five Andean nations, Mexico, and the U.S., convening to discuss strategies for collective action against drug trafficking. "Beforehand, I helped write progress reports, sent off some cables, and made sure the translation equipment was set up," he said. "Once everyone showed up, I stood in the greeting line and seated the drug czars and foreign ministers in attendance ... I even did some translating."

> "One summer, the embassy in New Delhi sent its intern as the American representative to the Dalai Lama's birthday party."

Not all intern positions are in Washington, D.C. The Student Intern Program places about forty percent of its interns in U.S. embassies and consulates around the globe as well as at the U.S. Mission to the United Nations in New York City. Overseas interns help maintain friendly American-foreign relations and coordinate U.S. Government activities. An intern stationed in New Delhi, India (one of the few overseas posts where English is the primary language), focused on human rights. When one Pakistani-American woman was arrested in New Delhi and imprisoned, for example, the Consular officer asked the intern to make some inquiries. "I went down to the prison and walked into the courthouse next door," he recalled. "But the judge in charge of this woman's case insisted that I leave ... [yet] I persisted, respectfully explaining our interest. I don't know if I had anything to do with it, but she was released later that day."

An intern in Santiago interviewed Chileans and other foreign nationals seeking "non-immigration" (that is, temporary) visas. "Most of it involved simple fact-checking, but we sometimes saw a few suspected terrorists, drug dealers, and criminals," he said. "Obviously, we rejected them." Admittedly routine, visa work, he noted, is primarily what 95 percent of all first-year foreign service officers do anyway. But visas did not occupy his entire summer. He also had the opportunity to write a cable to Washington updating Chilean adoption laws and procedures. "I interviewed directors at adoption agencies, compiled statistics, and reviewed legislation," he said.

While interns in D.C. must make their own arrangements for housing (the State Department merely provides a listing of available dorms and apartment complexes), overseas interns often receive free housing, usually at embassy apartments.

The U.S. Department of State makes its home in Washington D.C.'s Foggy Bottom district, home also to the World Bank and George Washington University. To enter the main building (there are several satellite offices around Washington and one in Rosslyn, VA), interns must flash their ID card past metal detectors, cameras, and a phalanx of armed guards. The first six floors of the eight-story complex house the bureaus and offices; floor seven is occupied by the Secretary and Deputy Secretary; and the eighth floor contains the Diplomatic Reception Room and the State Rooms, used for formal ceremonies and decorated with such priceless American antiques as Thomas Jefferson's furniture, Paul Revere's silver set, and an original Gilbert Stuart painting of George Washington. In the basement are a second-hand bookstore, a cafeteria, and a barber shop—but at $18 per haircut, one intern recommended using the Pentagon's hairstylist instead (only $6 per visit)—and the Foreign Affairs Recreation Association, known as FARA. An annual membership fee of $12 gets interns unlimited access to the spa and weight room; FARA members may also purchase aerobics classes, piano lessons, and heavily discounted State Department paraphernalia.

The State Department internship starts with an orientation, where interns learn the State Department missions, take the oath of office, and undergo a security briefing. "We're told what we can and cannot leave on our desks and shown how to open the safes [where the classified materials go every night]," described an intern.

The State Department also affords interns occasional access to other events. Past D.C. interns have attended Al Gore's "Reinventing Government" speech, the swearing-in ceremony for Ambassador Mondale, and former Secretary of State James Baker's resignation announcement. Overseas interns also have an opportunity to attend various briefings and receptions, such as the intern in Chile who went to a reception for Fulbright scholars. One summer, the embassy in New Delhi sent its intern as the American representative to the Dalai Lama's birthday party. "I met all sorts of power brokers within the Indian government," he reported. Briefed on what to say, he also delivered a three-minute address on U.S. policy in India. "I walked up to the microphone with an interpreter, and when I finished, the audience clapped and gave me presents," he described. "I received rice, spices, and about 15 white scarves—a sign of gratitude and fertility, I think."

The 5 percent of interns receiving checks under the Student Intern Program are paid at GS-4 to GS-7 rates, depending on their year in school.

SELECTION

 Every major of study is applicable to a State Department internship; even those studying art history, architecture, engineering, and nursing are eligible. The Student Intern program takes college juniors, seniors, and graduate students (including second- and third-year law school students); recent grads (from college or graduate school) are eligible so long as they plan to return to school in the semester or quarter immediately following the internship.

APPLICATION PROCEDURE

 The deadline for the Student Intern Program is November 1 for summer, March 1 for fall, and July 1 for spring. After the Recruitment Division screens intern applications for completeness, it passes them on to the bureaus, which sometimes conduct phone interviews. Those chosen by the bureaus are asked to fill out Form SF-86, used to conduct a background investigation. Final acceptance into a program is contingent upon receiving a security clearance.

OVERVIEW

 If the State Department's internships had their own flag, they might incorporate four elements: a globe, a spyglass, clasping hands, and an eagle. The globe symbolizes opportunities overseas, where interns gain a greater understanding of foreign cultures and languages. The spyglass represents the security clearances that afford interns access to sensitive documents with international-security implications. The clasping hands stand for the opportunity for interns to occasionally interact with ambassadors and assistant secretaries as well as attend receptions, swearings-in, and briefings. And finally, the eagle, an American icon, reflects the chance for interns to serve as junior-level U.S. foreign service officers, observing first-hand that career opportunity.

FOR MORE INFORMATION . . .

■ U.S. Department of State
Office of Recruitment
Student Programs
P.O. Box 9317
Arlington, VA 22219

■ Director
Department of State Foreign Affairs
Fellowship Program
The Woodrow Wilson National
Fellowship Foundation
Box 2437
Princeton, NJ 08543-2437

■ Phone: (703) 875-7490

SELECTIVITY	🔍 🔍 🔍 🔍
Approximate applicant pool: 250–300 (Fall, Spring), 500–600 (Summer); Interns accepted: 30–35	

COMPENSATION	$ $
$78/week, plus room and board	

QUALITY OF LIFE	🌴 🌴 🌴 🌴 🌴
Intern seminars; stunning recreational facilities; excellent food; freebies; travel opportunities	

LOCATION(S)

Colorado Springs, CO; Lake Placid, NY; San Diego, CA

FIELD

Sports Administration, Journalism, Broadcasting, Computer Science, Marketing, Sport Science, Accounting

DURATION

18 weeks (Winter/Spring)
10 weeks (Summer)
15 weeks (Fall)

PRE-REQS

College juniors and seniors; grad students

DEADLINE

Spring .... October 1   Summer ... February 15
Fall .... June 1

Johnny Weissmuller snares an amazing five golds in swimming and one bronze in water polo at the 1924 and 1928 Olympics and then plays Tarzan in the 1932 Hollywood classic *Tarzan, the Ape Man*. American Jesse Owens battles racial stereotypes and baffles Adolf Hitler by winning four track-and-field gold medals at the 1936 Olympic Games in Berlin. Prancing pugilist Cassius Clay, later boxing as Muhammad Ali, dazzles the crowds with his punching might and strikes gold at the 1960 Olympics in Rome. A little-known 1980 U.S. ice hockey team upsets the Soviet titans in an inspiring semifinal round match-up at Lake Placid and then defeats Finland to win the gold. A virtual unknown and teenage underdog, Mary Lou Retton captures an all-around gymnastics gold, in addition to two silver and two bronze medals, at 1984's contests in Los Angeles. Since 1896, the modern-day Olympic Games have represented the ultimate athletic contest, testing the strength and will of its participants. Initially a meeting of thirteen nations, the Olympic Games now hosts more than 190 countries' premier athletes, each intent on returning home, with a medal swinging proudly around his or her neck.

DESCRIPTION

Founded in 1896 by James E. Sullivan as an informal association, the United States Olympic Committee (USOC), as it became known in 1961, served as the major promoter of amateur athletics in America. As the United States' sole coordinating body for the Olympic and Pan American Games competitions, the USOC quickly rose to prominence and attracted such presidents as Major General Douglas MacArthur and sporting goods manufacturer A. G. Spalding. In 1977, the committee unveiled the first-of-its-kind Olympic Training Center in Colorado Springs. One year later, it named the Colorado Springs facility its headquarters as well and hosted the U.S. Olympic Festival.

Today, the USOC has numerous divisions, including Broadcasting, Accounting, Journalism, Computer Science, Sports Administration, Marketing/Fundraising, and Sport Science (Weightroom), and houses the national governing bodies (NGBs) of 14 sports associations. Internships have been available in most of these areas since the early 1980s. While nearly every intern works out of Colorado Springs, there are a few positions in Lake Placid, NY, and San Diego, CA.

Because of the unique nature of each division and NGB, interns' experiences vary considerably. One former intern, working for Coaching Development, became heavily involved in writing for the quarterly magazine *Olympic Coach*. "I wrote research articles, mostly for coaches and physiologists," said the intern. "The stories were usually technical, on subjects like altitude training, banned substances, or time management." He also worked on a special project analyzing whether old military bases could be used as training facilities for future athletes, and attended the annual coaching symposium, hosted by the USOC for coaches from around the world. "I helped out in every way," he said. "I even drove to the airport to pick up the symposium speaker, Digger Phelps, the television sports analyst and former Notre Dame basketball head coach."

Another intern, assigned to Information Services within the U.S. Swimming NGB, sat down with the director her first day to discuss the long- and short-term goals of her public relations internship. For the next three months, she not only answered phones and wrote correspondence but also created a central database of swimming information. "I downloaded facts from the USOC main computer and arranged them in a way that was accessible to the media," she explained. "And I went down into the Archives, a huge vault in the USOC basement, to find old articles and handwritten notes and diaries that described, often in foreign languages, the environment surrounding various swimming meets." She also wrote press releases and articles for *U.S. Swimming*. "I interviewed [such famous swimmers as] Jeff Rouse, Matt Biondi, and Janet Evans," she said. "I was hooked in to the national team."

An intern for the U.S. Volleyball Association helped run the association-sponsored volleyball camps. "I scheduled gym and training times, provided keys, arranged transportation, and collected money," she said. Beyond administrative tasks, this intern wrote a manual and worked with sports scientists to design exercise programs for high school and college volleyball players.

Through the gates of the USOC compound, an athlete's paradise awaits. Gymnasiums, weight room, pool, and recreational facilities—this place has it all. A former Air Force base, the center houses athletes and interns in dormitories. Rent is deducted directly from interns' paychecks. Gluttons, rejoice, for the USOC provides copious amounts of quality food at the on-site cafeteria. "The dining hall was open from 7:00 A.M. to 8:00 P.M. every day," said an intern. "Some of the food was donated by sponsors and we could eat all we wanted." In recent years interns have also received free haircuts from a Supercuts booth.

The USOC holds intern seminars designed for personal and professional growth. The intern manager also plans events like Broomball Night, whitewater rafting trips, and an end-of-term intern dinner and show.

Depending on the office and time of year, interns may also travel to meetings or events. Interns at the Wrestling NGB once went to North Dakota for the Nationals. The Swimming NGB once flew its intern to Minneapolis for a two-week international swimming competition. Another intern at U.S. Swimming was sent to Olympic Trials in Indianapolis to run the press office: "Here I was, 21 years old, telling people from ABC, CBS, and NBC camera crews where to go and what to do." In a rare fit of adventurousness, the USOC, after listening to a business proposal, sent a Spanish-speaking intern to Barcelona for the '92 Games, where she hired interpreters and set up the hospitality program for corporate sponsors.

But not all is gold in Olympic country. Some interns complain that there is too much secretarial work: "It's frustrating to answer so many phone calls and do so much filing." Others groan about the low pay. And a few complain about the delays inherent in the bureaucracy: "People are always traveling, so if a person whose ap-

> "[It's] America;
> it's red, white, and blue,
> an opportunity to
> meet sports figures
> from around the world."

proval you need is out of town, a project can be put on hold for weeks."

Overall, though, former interns glow about the 10- to 18-week experience. "What you do at the USOC is important and relevant," said an intern. "And the recreational opportunities are terrific." Indeed, in winter months interns ski in Vail. They also attend rock concerts, hike up Pike's Peak, and ride bikes through the nearby Garden of the Gods. Less outdoorsy interns, like the one who described Colorado Springs as "the cultural black hole of America," will find metropolitan Denver a one-hour drive away.

SELECTION

 Undergraduate and graduate students currently working on a degree are eligible to apply. The former must have finished at least two years of college by the start of the program. Recent college graduates will not be considered unless they have been accepted into a graduate program. Because all of the USOC groups utilize computers in their work, familiarity with IBM and/or Macintosh computers and Microsoft Word, Power Point, and/or Excel is highly desirable. Good writing skills as well as a GPA of 3.0 or better give one an edge. After the intern manager screens the applications, "to see how well the applicant followed directions," the materials get passed on to specific departments for review.

APPLICATION PROCEDURE

 Applicants must submit the necessary materials by June 1 for the fall semester, February 15 for the summer term, and October 1 for the winter/spring semester. Write for the Student Intern Program Application, which must be included. The form requires a faculty advisor signature. A resume and official transcript must also accompany the completed application form. Students may also enclose up to three letters of recommendation and other information that might be relevant, so long as none of it is placed in page protectors or binders. Note: Applicants to the Journalism program must submit six recent writing samples as well. The samples must be on 8 1/2" x 11" paper; newspaper, magazine, booklet, or brochure pieces must be photocopied. The USOC does not return submitted materials.

OVERVIEW

 Representing the major continents, five interlocked rings—blue, black, red, yellow, and green—have stood for nearly 100 years as a symbol of the meeting of world athletes. For over a decade, the USOC's internship program has stood as a symbol of student involvement in the Olympic movement and spirit. Indeed, the manager boasts: "The environment here is America; it's red, white, and blue, an opportunity to meet sports figures from around the world." Indeed, this one-of-a-kind program's alumni hold all sorts of positions: Academic Counselor for athletes at Rutgers University, Executive Director of USA Cycling, USOC Associate Director of Finance and Risk Management, Director of Media and Public Relations for USA Boxing, Senior Account Representative with Advantage International, and producer with CNN. All in the tradition of *Citius, Altius, Fortius,* the Olympic motto meaning "Swifter, Higher, Stronger."

FOR MORE INFORMATION . . .

■ United States Olympic Committee
Student Intern Program
One Olympic Plaza
Colorado Springs, CO 80909-5760
(719) 632-5551, ext. 2597
Fax: (719) 578-4817
internprog@usoc.org
www.olympic-usa.org

Imagine working among some of the most creative and innovative minds in the entertainment business. Tucked away in the Hollywood Hills, you're a short jaunt from the famous Hollywood sign. Or, perhaps you'll find yourself in the growing media haven of Orlando, Florida. You're part of the glamour. The glitz. You're at the center of the entertainment business. It's your chance to gain hands-on experience that will mold you into a valuable prospect for future employment. It's your chance to be part of a team that entertains hundreds of millions of people, in just about every spot on the planet. Welcome to the Universal Internship Program.

Although it's a diverse entertainment company today, the Universal Studios story began with movies. In 1912, Bavarian immigrant Carl Laemmle founded Universal and in the following years turned out a torrent of silent westerns, comedies, and action-adventure films. But it was the horror film that distinguished Universal: *The Hunchback of Notre Dame*, *Dracula*, *Frankenstein*, and *The Bride of Frankenstein* to name a few.

Universal has been responsible for some of the industry's biggest modern hits, too, including *Jaws*, *Jurassic Park*, and *Schindler's List*. In addition to movies, Universal produces entertainment in virtually every form: television, interactive, recreation, consumer products, and music. It boasts operations worldwide.

An industry leader in every sense of the word, Universal is a driving force in entertainment innovations.

DESCRIPTION

 Overall, an internship with Universal Studios equals a chance for students to raise their level of professionalism, get a better understand-

SELECTIVITY	
Approximate applicant pool: 5,000 Interns accepted: 200	

COMPENSATION	
About half are paid, amount varies	

QUALITY OF LIFE

Team-oriented atmosphere; intern orientation; wrap-up party; professional development seminar

LOCATION(S)

Universal City, CA; Orlando, FL

FIELD

Film; Television; Music

DURATION

12–15 weeks
Summer, Fall, Spring
Part-time available

PRE-REQS

Undergrad students; grad students
Must receive academic credit for unpaid positions

DEADLINE(S)

Rolling

ing of daily operations and long-term strategies of a major corporation, and learn more about the entertainment business. With its variety of entertainment divisions and expanding global reach, Universal offers nearly limitless internship possibilities.

One division of Universal, Universal Music Group, made headlines recently when it acquired PolyGram, becoming the largest music group in the world. Music lovers interested in the entertainment business can explore this group's diverse mix of music by working as an intern under labels like A&M,

Geffen, MCA, Universal, Interscope, or Mercury, to name a few. Other departments within the Music Group are active in live entertainment, bringing the world's top artists to stages across the country. As if that weren't enough, interns at Universal Music Group have been known to "walk away from their internship with more CDs than you can shake a stick at." An internship with the music group not only has the glamour appeal, but offers solid work experience. One intern reports being "involved in every aspect of music video. I read treatments submitted by directors. I dealt with artists, production personnel, and other Universal employees. I traveled to sets and music showcases. In all I was involved in everything that came through the office."

The legendary Universal Pictures has been home to many of the world's greatest filmmakers, and has a film library that is overflowing with more than eighty-five years of phenomenal productions. Within this group is Universal Home Video, which creates and distributes films, television properties, and products for direct-to-video markets. Universal Family and Home Entertainment oversees all direct-to-video, live action, and animated television (Universal Cartoon Studios). An internship with the motion pictures division of Universal Pictures can be quite exciting, according to one intern, and offers opportunities to see the process outside the office. "I was invited by other members of the department to publicity events," says one intern. "First I was taken to a press interview with a star of *BASEketball* where I was able to see how international press junkets work. Later I was invited to attend a TV/Press junket for *Small Soldiers* focusing on the 'behind-the-scenes' aspects of the film. At the junket, instead of feeling as though I was just an observer on the side, I was able to participate and help with the junket by working with the international journalists." Working as a Home Video Marketing intern is another way to soak in the "biz" while being exposed to

> Interns at MCA Records "walk away from their internship with more free CDs than you can shake a stick at."

the professional side of the film industry. One intern found that, "To be honest, the 'glamour'—for lack of a better word—I associate with this internship stems from the level of professionalism associated with it. When I arrived, I had a phone, a computer, a cubicle, and supplies waiting for me. I was never asked to answer phones or to file. Each and every project I worked on had some learning experience tied into it and never once did I feel that I had wasted my time."

Another division of Universal is the Universal Studios Recreation Group, which features major revenue-generating businesses that also hire interns. Universal Studios Hollywood, the original movie-based theme park, entertains visitors with rides, live shows, and a behind-the-scenes tour of a major film and television studio. Another part of the fun is Universal CityWalk, a shopping/dining venue. In Orlando, Florida, interns work for Universal Studios Escape—The Orlando Entertainment Destination for the 21st Century, which features two theme parks: Universal Studios Florida and Universal Studios Islands of Adventure, an all-new theme park.

Universal Studios Online Services Group is the business unit where properties go digital and harness the power of the Internet. "My main duties revolved around research and marketing," says one intern. "I created an online database full of facts, charts, and articles, as well as making marketing presentations that were used by the entire staff." This division also has a young staff and fun, cutting-edge attitude. "Because the New Media division is so young," explains our intern, "I never felt intimidated or uncomfortable. Everyone in the office was extremely friendly and quite supportive."

The Universal Consumer Products Group creates toys, clothing, books, gifts, and interactive products that represent Universal's films, TV shows, and other properties—it all gets licensed here. The interns who work for this division have the opportunity to get hands-on experience on real projects. One reported, "The project that I worked on this summer will be implemented throughout the upcoming year and will contribute very positively to the increased growth of the distribution company. Having total autonomy over my projects, being able to carry them out from start to finish, and having a stipulated budget made this experience all the more meaningful."

The Universal Internship perks and benefits are huge. On a daily basis, interns get a behind-the-scenes look at some of the most recognized entertainment properties in the world. They are involved with movies, TV shows, music, and attractions that entertain millions every year. Interns also have a chance to attend an intern orientation and professional development seminars, and to interact with Universal managers who lecture about the tremendous opportunities within the company. Interns also get discounts on merchandise and studio attractions, but, they report, the biggest perk is access to movie screenings. In true Hollywood fashion, Universal likes to conclude its internships by hosting wrap-up parties in honor of the interns.

Despite all of this, interns at Universal are not completely without criticism of the program. Several interns expressed a desire to have more unity among interns and to learn more about Universal as a whole: "The program needs more internship programs such as speakers and social gatherings to introduce interns to the different departments of Universal, as well as to the other interns we are working around."

Living in pricey Los Angeles is difficult, driving many interns to seek other part-time jobs to support themselves. Still, working for one of the largest entertainment groups in the world is not a prison sentence by any stretch. As one intern pointed out, "You have access to new releases, CDs, and free movie tickets, not to mention more contacts than you ever dreamed of." In fact, those contacts lead to permanent employment at Universal for approximately 25 percent of interns. According to one intern, "Universal's representatives stated that the company would love to hire back interns summer after summer in the hopes of eventually hiring them after graduation. It really makes perfect sense. After seeing the impression that Universal has made on me this summer, I see little reason to stray from it in the future when I begin my career search."

SELECTION

 Universal seeks exceptional people with diversified backgrounds and interests for their internship programs. To think that Universal internships are geared strictly toward creative backgrounds would be a mistake. Just as important are interns with interests in legal, finance, and marketing careers. All potential interns, however, should have the desire to learn more about the entertainment business. Out of 5,000 applicants, only 200 interns are accepted. Needless to say, competition for positions in the movie and television groups is especially competitive. While some of the Universal Studios positions are paid internships, others are unpaid positions which require students to receive academic credit. The Universal Internship Program is open to undergraduate as well as graduate students.

APPLICATION PROCEDURE

 Internships are available in the fall, spring, and summer, and generally last from twelve to fifteen weeks. Application materials may be submitted at any time. To apply, submit a resume and cover letter stating your specific area of interest and availability.

Resume submission process: Students interested in internships at Universal Studios in California should submit resumes and cover letters electronically to Universal's National Resume Processing Center at universal@webhire.com. Or you can mail your resume with a cover letter that references "Ad Code: PRR99-INTN" in the subject line to:

Universal Studios National Resume Processing
    Center
P.O. Box 385
Burlington, MA 01803

If you are interested in opportunities at Universal Studios Escape in Orlando, Florida, mail your resume to:

Universal Studios Escape
Internship Program
1000 Universal Studios Plaza
Building B-111
Orlando, FL 32819

OVERVIEW

 Universal is a diversified entertainment company and a worldwide leader in music, motion pictures, television, and home and location-based entertainment. No matter what your area of interest, this is a good place to intern if you're interested in a career in entertainment industry. Whoever said there's anything wrong with soaking up a little excitement while you are interning? It doesn't have to be all photocopies and filing. By participating in the Universal internship program, you'll be running far ahead of the pack.

FOR MORE INFORMATION . . .

www.universalstudios.com

The City of New York

John Williams is 35 years old, has a prison record, is a possible substance abuser, perhaps is mentally ill, and is living on the streets.

By one New York City agency's estimate, there are thousands of people like John Williams walking the city's streets every day. Until recently, the City's Department of Social Services was responsible for providing housing and income support to such individuals. But this approach hadn't yielded sufficient results. That's why in February of 1992, the Cuomo Commission recommended that the city create an autonomous agency to focus upon the city's homelessness problem. One of several people in charge of implementing the recommendation was a 22-year-old city employee and a recent college graduate. Working out of the Mayor's Office of Operations, she drafted parts of the implementation plan, organized meetings with the Department of Social Services, and analyzed the new agency's request for vehicles to transport homeless individuals, food, and clothing. She was part of the city's quarter-century-old Urban Fellows Program, a nine-month internship in city management.

SELECTIVITY	🔍 🔍 🔍 🔍
Approximate applicant pool: 1200 (UF), 200 (GS) Interns accepted: 125 (UF), 25(GS)	

COMPENSATION	$ $ $
Government Scholars—$3000 taxable stipend Urban Fellows—$18,000 taxable stipend	

QUALITY OF LIFE	🌴 🌴 🌴
High-powered atmosphere; Weekly seminars Government bureaucracy	

LOCATION(S)
New York, NY

FIELD
City government

DURATION
GS: 10 weeks, Summer UF: 9 months, Academic Year

PRE-REQS
GS: College sophomores, juniors, and seniors; UF: Recent grads

DEADLINE
Government Scholars............January 12 Urban Fellows.....................January 19

DESCRIPTION

In 1968, an administrator at the office of Mayor John Lindsay made a proposal: "Why don't we give 20 students the opportunity to work full-time in city management?" The city agreed; the Alfred P. Sloan Foundation donated two years' worth of stipends, and the Urban Fellows (UF) Program was born. It soon evolved into a nationwide competition for the country's brightest college students. "This was the late 1960s," said founder Sigmund Ginsburg, now vice president of business development at the American Museum of Natural History. "It was a period of hope, and the charisma of Mayor Lindsay attracted the best students. We placed them in his office back then—as assistants to the commissioner, budget director, superintendent, and the like."

But the desire for direct contact with citizens became greater and greater. "Not every student wanted to sit behind a desk all day long. Some wanted 'street work,'" explained Ginsburg. "So we made available up to 100 meaningful jobs from which the Fellows could choose—jobs affording daily contact with people." The Fellows were also exposed to various big-shots at weekly off-the-record seminars, featuring such guests as the police commissioner, the mayor, political commentator William F. Buckley, and columnist Jimmy Breslin.

Little has changed since that promising beginning. The Urban Fellows Program still starts with an orientation, though the original two weeks have been expanded to nearly four. Fellows spend a week exploring a borough and then make presentations on their findings. They attend lectures. They take tours of the city, to observe how city policy affects the city's residents and sometimes ride along in patrol cars with on-duty police officers. "Over four or five hours, we ran across vandalism . . . and even the scene of a shooting," said a ride-along participant. Other interns have toured Rikers Island, a state maximum-security penitentiary. "I talked to some inmates and learned how complex our whole penal system is," said one. "It was a chilling experience. To this day, I can still hear the checkpoint gates slamming behind me as we left."

During orientation, Fellows explore as many as two hundred placement possibilities within the mayor's office and its agencies. On the basis of a dozen to several dozen interviews, Fellows select positions best suiting their interests and needs. "You get to decide where you want to go—a sleepy old office or the firing line," said an Urban Fellow. Once Fellows are placed, their tasks are many and varied. Working on short- and long-term projects, they do everything from policy consultation and planning to administrative problem solving and delivery of services.

One Fellow, working as an assistant commissioner to Personnel, helped to reshape the entire 3,000-member Human Resources department. "I evaluated the goals of the department, changed the way performance evaluations are conducted, added recognition awards, established training and development programs, and set up an internship program," he said. Twelve years later, many of the programs he implemented are still in place.

A Fellow with the Economic Policy and Marketing group worked on several research projects with the chief economist. One project dealt with recycling. "I tried to develop a strategy to dispose of the large volume of waste collected," he said. "We figured out ways to entice businesses to come into the city and create jobs in waste management." Another project analyzed Business Improvement Districts (BID), areas in which property owners have agreed to pay additional fees in exchange for extra security and sanitation services. "I reworked the 24 different formulas that determine how much each BID should pay," he said.

Like the two previous examples, most Fellows occupy bureaucratic positions. Some Fellows, however, get involved with the public. A Fellow at the Center for Collaborative Education co-taught an elective course at a local high school. Titled *Power New York City*, the class provided an insider's view of the history and politics of the city. The experience was particularly relevant to a Board of Education project upon which he worked—the construction of 12 new high schools. "I helped find space, teachers, and funds," he said.

Committed to providing the Fellows with a broad overview of city management, program administrators arrange weekly seminars with high-level city officials. Since Mayor Lindsay's administration, officials from a host of departments like the Department of Corrections, the Police Department, the Center for Collaborative Education, and the Board of Education, have made appearances. In unofficial one- to three-hour meetings, Fellows comment on city policies. "I'd go for the guts and ask politically challenging questions, putting the speaker on the defensive," said one Fellow.

Urban Fellows make two formal out-of-town visits—one to the state capital in Albany, the other to the nation's capital in Washington. In Albany, Urban Fellows tour government buildings and meet legislators and

> "You get to decide where you want to go— a sleepy old office or the firing line."

state officials. In Washington, Fellows evaluate the federal government's obligations to America's cities, particularly New York City. In recent years, Fellows have met with senators and representatives, talked with officials from Housing and Urban Development, Labor and Education, convened with advocacy groups and met with Health and Human Services Secretary Donna Shalala.

Because the goal of the program is to promote learning and to offer a beneficial experience, unhappy Urban Fellows may request a transfer to another city department. Though rare, these transfers have occurred. One Fellow felt that he was spending too much time transcribing notes, so he switched departments to relocate to the New York City Transit Authority, which runs the city's subways and bus lines. "I worked in the Special Events unit and helped arrange the filming of subways for movies like *Ghost*," he said. "Sometimes I staffed the night filmings, making sure that the producers adhered to safety considerations as laid out in the contracts." Transferring doesn't guarantee happiness, however. "Because the Transit Authority is such a huge organization, I did almost as much memo writing and paper pushing as before," he said.

In 1980, then–Deputy Mayor Ronay Menschel decided that college undergraduates would benefit from a full-time introduction to city management as well. Modeled after the Urban Fellows Program, the Government Scholars Program began placing students that year.

Government Scholars (GS) participate in a shorter orientation than Urban Fellows. During this time, they interview with potential supervisors in order to best match their interests and needs. Like Urban Fellows, they work on short- and long-term projects in such areas as human services, criminal justice, health, housing, transportation, and economic development. They also analyze and review policy and do fieldwork.

One Government Scholar worked for the deputy chancellor of New York City public schools. "I wrote a lot of letters explaining school-wide policy to parents and matched corporate resources to school programs," he said. "But I benefited most by watching rather than doing—observing task force briefings and participating in seminars." Another researched AIDS-discrimination cases, writing reports and making recommendations.

"Some of my work even got incorporated into policy," she said.

Focusing on homeless shelters, a Scholar in Social Services found that the city's transitional housing was not being allocated efficiently. "I would visit the three shelters in our charge and talk to homeless people so I could understand their point of view," she stated. Out of these first-hand glimpses, she developed a guide for case workers that is still used today.

Government Scholars have the opportunity to attend weekly seminars. Though some say these seminars do not provide as in-depth a look at the issues as the Urban Fellow seminars, Government Scholars speak well of them. "We met many high-powered commissioners, usually politically astute people we'd read about in the papers," said a former Scholar.

Government Scholars and Urban Fellows work throughout the city, in buildings described mostly as needing major renovation. Interns are often afforded their own cubicle space, equipped with a computer and a phone. They have access to municipal libraries and New York University research facilities.

Government Scholars work ten weeks while Urban Fellows serve nine-month tenures. "[We] can't get very involved in that short amount of time," commented one Scholar. "Urban Fellows' yearlong commitment and direct contact with the mayor, on the other hand, elevate them to a whole new level." Affirmed another: "If the Urban Fellows Program is the main course, then the Government Scholars Program is the appetizer." Nevertheless, the Government Scholars experience heightens many participants' awareness to sensitive urban issues. "It got me addicted to city government," one scholar said.

Many Government Scholars go back to school optimistic about their ability to make a difference. But many Urban Fellows finish the program frustrated at their difficulty in breaking through an entrenched bureaucracy. "Agencies are too slow to respond," said one. "City administration is neither effective nor efficient," added another. "Moreover, the inflexible nine-to-five work schedule often makes our job routine." However, many fight back in creative ways. "My year, the 24 Urban Fellows created a network," said one of them. "We finished projects faster by collaborating and by sidestepping formal channels."

SELECTION

By the start of the internship in September, Urban Fellows must have received their BA degrees, but must not have been out of college for more than two years. Government Scholars must be sophomores, juniors, or seniors. College graduates less than a year out of college by the start of the Government Scholars Program may apply as well. So long as they are interested in pursuing public service careers, students of any academic major are eligible. Applicants must display demonstrated leadership, whether as elected campus officials or as heads of organizations. The director mentions "intellectual ability and flexibility," "scholastic aptitude," and "willingness to look at issues with an open mind" as additional helpful traits.

APPLICATION PROCEDURE

Deadlines are as follows: January 19 postmark for Urban Fellows; January 12 postmark for Government Scholars. (Note: Personnel requests that applicants check these program deadlines, as they vary from year to year.) Applicants must submit a completed original application form, a resume, an official transcript, three (two for Government Scholars) letters of recommendation from academic or professional sources, and two essays—a description of goals and an autobiographical statement. A panel of readers, consisting of Urban Fellow and Government Scholar alumni, and city managers, scores all applications. While Government Scholars are selected solely on the highest scores, Urban Fellows are selected on the highest scorers' completion of a half-day of interviews in New York. The interview process includes two one-on-one interviews and one panel interview. Insider's tip: The panel interview consists of a public policy exercise in which the applicant recommends some solution to a social problem.

The Department of Personnel manages another internship program as well, the Public Service Corps. It places hundreds of undergraduates and graduate students in public sector internships for academic credit, for federal work-study stipends, or as volunteers. Write or call to get more information (New York City Public Service Corps, (212) 487-5663).

OVERVIEW

New York, New York—city of possibility and opportunity. "If I can make it there, I'll make it anywhere," as the song goes. That city, in fact, is the only city in the United States to offer a comprehensive government internship to young people. If interns can make a dent in the problems ravaging America's largest city, then there's hope for cities nationwide. Challenging officials at weekly meetings, these college students and graduates—Government Scholars and Urban Fellows—help the impoverished, analyze AIDS policies, and tackle problems in recycling, education, transportation, and many other areas. Now many of them are making it in the Big Apple and elsewhere as assemblymen, vice presidents on Wall Street, and directors of public service organizations. Most of the former Urban Fellows are also part of the Urban Fellows Alumni Association, which volunteers time at homeless shelters, drug rehab clinics, and the like. "We made an impact then," said an alumnus, "we feel that we should make an impact now, too." Now that sounds like the determination and optimism characteristic of someone who has lived in the "city that never sleeps."

FOR MORE INFORMATION . . .

■ City of New York
Department of Personnel
Fellowship Program
1 Centre Street, Room 2425
New York, NY 10007
(212) 669-3695
Fax: (212) 669-3688
www.ci.nyc.ny.us/html/dcas/html/intern.html

VAULT.com

> the insider career network™

You've got a job interview next week—and a knot in your stomach. Or maybe you're frustrated because your parents want you to be an investment banker and you want to try your luck at a burgeoning dot-com. Don't know where to begin? If you're savvy, you'll head for www.vault.com—the home of Vault.com— the premier source of career information on the web.

In addition to its career guides to popular industries (banking, law, consulting, the Internet, etc.) and employers (you name it, they probably cover it), Vault.com boasts an interactive community that attracts the nation's most ambitious students and professionals. Clearly, a smart way to kick-start your own career is to intern at the company that knows the most about high-powered professions.

Launched in 1997 (by a team that includes the authors of this book), Vault.com has grown into a useful destination for young professionals as well as the companies that want to recruit them. The company offers a broad array of resources and tools for career management, but its core concern has always been providing the most accurate and timely information culled through independent research in addition to input from actual company insiders.

Media giants including *The Wall Street Journal, Forbes, Newsweek* and CNN have recognized Vault as a "fun" and "edgy read" that delivers accurate, incisive information about top employers. Vault.com offers profiles of more than 3,000 leading companies, with information on corporate history, the interview process, and corporate culture. Vault's editorial staff interviews thousands of insider company contacts and recruiters each year. In addition to providing company and industry guides, Vault.com also offers

job postings, employee message boards, a proprietary search-and-match recruitment service, and online courses.

SELECTIVITY	🔍 🔍 🔍 🔍 🔍
Approximate applicant pool: 800 Interns accepted: 30	

COMPENSATION	$
Travel stipend	

QUALITY OF LIFE	🌴 🌴 🌴
Free books; comfortable offices; casual dress; democratic environment; "Show-and-tells"	

LOCATION(S)	
New York, NY	

FIELD	
Publishing; Internet	

DURATION	
Approximately 12 weeks	

PRE-REQS	
High school students; college students; recent grads; grad students	

DEADLINE	
Rolling	

DESCRIPTION

Vault.com is one of those companies that "those in the know always know," which is why so many students from the nation's top schools send their resumes in each year. Each summer alone, more than 800 students from high schools, colleges and universities, and graduate programs apply for internships at Vault.com. Less than 30 get the chance. The company hires interns in editorial, research, marketing, business development, and IT—but these categories can be very fluid. "What I loved about Vault," says a former intern, "is that if you've been admitted into the internship program, everyone knows that you're smart. That means you have a lot of leeway."

While interns often start with basic work such as Web research or responding to customer inquiries, once they've established a level of trust, they get more responsibility. Interns like the fact that they "don't have to stay in one department," and can "do everything from working on the Vault Web site, to making customer service decisions, to writing parts of the *Vault.com Industry Guides*."

One longtime intern reports that his experience was "definitely different than other internships. Once, we were trying to get one of our books to the printer on time. Around four in the afternoon, I volunteered to stay and help put the book together. I did everything from proofreading to helping with layout to running out for pizza. It was a fantastic experience to witness and help out in the final stages of putting a book together." Another intern interviewed "insiders" at law firms to learn about their experiences for the *Vault.com Guide to America's Top 50 Law Firms*, and catalogues survey results.

Interns feel that they "really impact what goes into Vault's books," and are credited for their hard work by getting their names in the Vault.com publications. "I went into Barnes and Noble in Boston," says one intern, "and I saw some of our books in the store. I opened it up and there was my name. It was weird seeing my name in another state like that." Unlike large publishing companies, say interns, Vault.com offers them the chance to "get into the guts" of a company and "make an immediate contribution" of real value. "When I first arrived," says a college senior, "I was immediately put to testing the new

web site. Not only did I make editorial changes, I beta tested crucial components of the VaultMatch recruiting service."

All interns work in Vault.com's sunny headquarters in Manhattan's hip Chelsea neighborhood. The "airy," "window-filled" office takes up three floors of a converted industrial loft. One intern recommends spending lunch hours at the Greenmarket in nearby Union Square, where local farmers sell fresh produce and baked goods during the spring and summer. Another preferred to "pick up a sandwich at a nearby deli and eat in Madison Square Park," also nearby, with fellow interns and Vault.com staff.

Vault.com uses an open seating plan – no offices, no cubicles. Interns get their own desks, just like editors, partners, and programmers. According to insiders, this makes the office feel more like a "newsroom, like in *All the President's Men*. People are always telling jokes and playing music," one intern explains, "so if you're easily distracted or you can't work with noise, you might have to go into one of the conference rooms to concentrate." The upside of the chaos and the open seating plan? "You get to bring in whatever music you want to listen to," says one college junior, "they play everything from Beck, to the Beastie Boys, to the soundtrack to *Strictly Ballroom*."

Vault.com is perhaps most unique among publishing companies for its youthful and non-hierarchical culture. One intern recounts his surprise after interviewing with one of the cofounders of the company: "I thought he'd be about 60, since he was a CEO, but he was in his late twenties." Not only do interns sit next to other employees and partners, but they work with them and attend company meetings, held every Monday morning. "It is definitely not a monkey suit environment," remarks a veteran intern. Vaulties dress casually and "jeans and t-shirts" are typical. Even partners at the company dress down (unless they've got important meetings); one is occasionally said

> "...if you've been admitted into the internship program, everyone knows that you're smart. That means you have a lot of leeway."

to come to the office wearing "really shiny track pants." On the other hand, interns on marketing projects will sometimes attend corporate presentations or job fairs. For such occasions, business suits are necessary—it's almost like "a non-casual Friday."

Work hours are flexible and can range from five hours a week (during the school year) to 50—though most interns work 35 to 40 hours during the summer. Many interns become "lifers," working shortened hours during the school year and vacations, returning full time during the summers. Insiders report "a level of flexibility" that comes in very handy and "is part of the trust and appreciation that the company has for interns." Interns are compensated with stipends, in addition to Vault.com publications and "all the T-shirts they can carry"—which are sure to become collectors items in the coming years. Interns are often pleased to find that at Vault.com, they are also "part of the team" socially. Interns participate in the company's trademark "show and tells," where employees show off their talents – which have ranged in the past from Macedonian cooking to juggling. During the summer of 1999, one intern brought in his cello and treated a rapt audience of Vaulties to a recital. Interns are invited to all corporate events and holiday parties, and coworkers usually throw birthday parties for them as well.

One major benefit of working at Vault.com, say interns, is that it's an opportunity to learn how companies and careers really work. In addition to learning about what Vault.com does, they get that trademark "inside look" at every industry and career issue the company covers. "I like learning about the business world," one intern remarks, "I didn't even know what a fiscal quarter was until I showed up." Interns may speak and correspond with hundreds of employees from companies in industries ranging from fashion to investment banking, as well as recruiters and executives at those firms. This means that when it comes time for interns to make their own way into the working world, they will not only be intimately familiar with the best companies and how to interview, they will be sure that Vault.com will be an impressive line on their resumes. One former intern credits part of his admission to law school with his work at Vault.com.

SELECTION

Vault.com hires high school, college and graduate students, as well as recent college graduates. In the past, most interns have come from top colleges and high schools, with majors ranging from English to computer science. Ideally, interns should exhibit knowledge and interest in business issues and a familiarity with the Internet and computer applications. All Vault.com interns should be enthusiastic, diligent and eager to learn, and have excellent communication skills. A good sense of humor (and musical taste) is a must, too.

APPLICATION

The deadline for application is rolling. Prospective interns should send a resume, cover letter, and two references. If you are applying for a position in the editorial department, writing samples are also necessary. Selected candidates will interview at Vault.com HQ in New York City, where all internship positions are based.

OVERVIEW

If you're interested in business and want to work for a flourishing dot-com, take a long hard look at Vault.com. It gives its interns the rare opportunity to work side-by-side with the leaders of a company and make contributions that show up on its website, books, and reports. Interning at Vault.com may be your ticket to a feast of career insight and opportunities.

FOR MORE INFORMATION . . .

■ Intern Coordinator
Vault.com
150 West 22nd Street, 5th Floor
New York, NY 10011
Fax: (212) 366-6117
jobs@staff.vault.com

SELECTIVITY	
Approximate applicant pool: 500 Interns accepted: 30–40	

COMPENSATION	$
Michigan—$360–$540/wk; Germany—DM200/wk (approximately $150/wk) and subsidized housing	

QUALITY OF LIFE	
Monthly intern meetings; international flavor	

LOCATION(S)	
Auburn Hills, MI; Wolfsburg, Germany	

FIELD	
Automobiles	

DURATION	
3–6 months Year-round	

PRE-REQS	
College juniors and seniors; grad students	

DEADLINE	
Rolling	

It is 1969, and Disney Studios wants to feature a car in its upcoming movie. After filling the parking lot with suitable candidates, Disney employees examine each automobile, scrutinizing the frame, fondling the upholstery, beeping the horn, and kicking the tires. But when they come to one car—a Volkswagen Beetle—they simply pat it. They don't have to subject the Beetle to any tests—they've found their star. That Beetle would eventually play Herbie, the hero of 1969's *The Love Bug* and its sequel, *Herbie Rides Again*. A few years later, on reflection, producer Bill Walsh (not the football coach) would say: "The VW had a personality of its own, which reached out and embraced people."

Interestingly enough, that's just what the Beetle's inventor intended back in the 1930s when he dreamed up his peculiar-looking auto, calling it Volkswagen—"people's car" in German. But the first Beetles, built in 1935, were used solely by the German military for World War II. Dr. Ferdinand Porsche (the first "modern" Porsche sports car was his brainchild) had to wait until 1945 to make his first commercial Beetle. Nevertheless, it was a hit; within two years his factory had built more than 10,000 Beetles and had also introduced the Microbus, a.k.a., the VW Bus. By the end of the 1960s, Volkswagen was selling nearly 500,000 Beetles per year in the United States alone, and their owners were in love with their car. This prompted *Life* to write: "A VW is a member of the family that just happens to live in the garage." Volkswagen sold more than 21 million of the original Beetles (a world record for a single model), and you don't have to look past your nearest street corner to notice the immense popularity of their new Beetle. Manufacturing more than 3 million vehicles per year, it is the world's fourth largest passenger car maker.

DESCRIPTION

Volkswagen of America (VWoA) has improved their already top-notch internship program in the past few years by adding one important element: money. As the umbrella organization of Volkswagen and Audi, VWoA now offers their interns between $9 and $13.50 per hour, depending on the years of university education completed (seniors and grad students receive $11 or more). Besides adding a stipend, VWoA still provides one of the best hands-on internships, allowing interns to work on real-life projects and learn how theory is successfully put into practice.

Your personal interests are taken into account as you are initially placed into either

Volkswagen Marketing, Audi of American Sales and Marketing, Product Strategy, Public Relations, Service Engineering, Parts, Learning and Transformation, Human Resources, Finances, Information Technology, or VW Credit Inc. Each division promises interns the same work of its regular full-time employees. "This is a real job with real responsibilities," confirmed a former intern. "There's no coddling going on here."

An intern in Audi Marketing worked on a project stemming from Audi's European golf tournament. "Audi wanted to start a tourney somewhere in the United States, perhaps Chicago or Dallas," he said. "I went over rules and regulations and analyzed the advantages and disadvantages of making it pro or amateur." In another project he analyzed Audi's auto show budgets. "In 1993, over ten million people attended the United States' twenty-four auto shows . . . . [W]e wanted to make an impact on that many people, but our costs were too high relative to returns." Breaking down the previous year's figures into costs for transportation, setup, take-down, warehousing, and space, he helped determine where cuts should be made. "I worked side by side with VW's special promotions manager," he said.

A Public Relations intern wrote articles for VW and Audi newsletters. Sometimes he searched for auto industry news in major newspapers. Other times, he wrote serious stories on management changes, new technologies, and new services. "Of course, some pieces were more fun to do than others," he said, "like the one about all the special effort that went into delivering Michael Keaton's customized van to his Montana home, or another about my two-day trip to Oklahoma City to cover Auto Cross, a road race pitting two VW Corrados against each other."

Like employees, interns are encouraged to offer suggestions to management. "Maybe because we aren't paid, managers feel obligated to include us as much as possible," said an intern. "They make us feel like part of the team." The president of VWA, Gerd Klaus, for example, makes it a point to know all interns on a first-name basis. He is often seen walking up to interns and asking them how their projects are going. "When he asks, he means it," said an intern. "VW wants everyone, including interns, to help improve operations."

In order to streamline business operations, the company frequently asks interns to transform their ideas into actions. For example, an Audi Marketing intern attended a meeting of field sales and marketing employees from around the country. "They pointed out that all of VW's incentive and advertising programs are described in separate booklets, perhaps twenty in all," said the intern. "Many expressed how inefficient that was and said that they were often missing information, especially since they didn't always get every booklet. I thought to myself, this is a situation ripe for consolidation." After the meeting, he went up to the division head and proposed putting together a guide. "The guide would provide a reference for VW's zone and district managers and consultants. Impressed, his boss gave him the go-ahead. "I interviewed people and pored through booklets to find out what information should be included," he said. "Now the company has a guide that shows managers what kinds of ads are acceptable for local campaigns, tells them how to do a direct mailing, and describes in detail all of VW's dealer incentive programs." The intern pointed out that VW's outside consultant would have charged $50,000 to undertake such a project. "My bid—free of charge—obviously saved the company a lot of money."

Interns work out of fully furnished, PC–equipped cubicles in a four-story building shaped like an *L*. "It looks like a boomerang or like a Pac-Man getting ready to chomp down on some dots," said an intern. On sunny days,

> On sunny days, interns can often be found eating their lunch on the company picnic tables in the backyard, near a spouting fountain and a man-made pond.

interns can often be found eating their lunch on the company picnic tables in the backyard, amidst a spouting fountain, a river, a walking path, and a man-made pond "containing six families of geese."

Interns are treated no differently than VW employees. Both groups get security cards for access into the building, security clearances to use computers, and computer files for e-mail, spreadsheets, and word processing. Interns are also offered the opportunity to attend computer training classes, various workshops, and seminars.

About once a month, interns get together on their own. "These occasional meetings are the only things that distinguish us from regular employees," said one intern. Interns tour a Detroit VW and Audi dealership in order to witness the retail sales, marketing, and service experience. "We would have loved to see VW cars being manufactured," said one disappointed intern, "but unfortunately, the nearest VW plant is in Mexico." Other gatherings introduce new products or discuss how to handle VW's German employees calling from overseas with questions: "We were reminded to take our conversations slowly and not get frustrated by the broken English." Interns also plan weekend excursions to nearby cities such as Chicago or Toronto.

International interns at VW of America, mostly German and some selected by the company's international headquarters in Germany join their American counterparts in rare occassions. Engaged in the same type of work as American interns, the few overseas students are also assigned housing by VW, either with an employee's family or in an apartment with several other interns. Fortunately, American interns may also tap VW for these housing arrangements. But the similarities stop there. Unlike Americans, some international students are provided with funds for housing, living, and transportation expenses. One might think that this salary policy is as acceptable to Volkswagen's American interns as Wiener schnitzel in a burger joint. Maybe so, were the two kinds of students working under the same program. However, some of the overseas students situated in Detroit work under the auspices of the German parent's more rigorous trainee program.

Administered out of Wolfsburg, or Ingolstadt for Audi, the program places some majority of them in permanent positions upon completion of the internship. No matter, the Americans say, because the Germans infuse the company with that famous Bavarian work ethic and teach interns about another culture.

Through intern evaluations, which are written at the conclusion of students' internships, VW gets its fill of feedback that helps to improve the program.

Like VW of America, Volkswagen's world headquarters also hires a few interns—these in Manufacturing and in Business. Interns receive a modest salary of 200 Deutschemarks a week and subsidized housing. Because interns (undergrads) must be fluent in German, applicants must submit a resume and cover letter in German.

SELECTION

 Undergraduates in their junior or senior year are eligible to apply, and grad students are accepted as well. No particular major is required, but a business or related major is desired. While the company does not adhere to a minimum GPA, the coordinator says that successful applicants tend to have at least a 3.0 GPA. "Applicants must show something in their backgrounds—a focus or some experience relevant to a VW department," she adds. "That helps us to make a good match." International applicants are eligible.

APPLICATION PROCEDURE

 The deadline for the VWoA internship is rolling. Applicants should submit a resume and a cover letter to the Human Resources Intern Coordinator in the HR Department at the Auburn Hills, Michigan, headquarters. Students should include in their cover letter their area of career interest and the dates they would be available to work. Potential candidates will be contacted by department managers for interviews. Preference is given to applicants who are available for six months with three months as the minimum.

OVERVIEW

The needs of the people—this was VW's driving concern when it designed the Beetle. After 50 years, the company still focuses on the common consumer. VW also realizes that self-motivated employees are critical to its success. Because interns are a potential source of such employees, the company creates an atmosphere that allows the ablest interns to have an impact upon the business. They're regular employees, working on team projects, under the eyes of managers who hold high expectations. "If you think about it, I'm just an everyday student," said one intern. "But VW treated my ideas with the utmost seriousness." No doubt a policy Dr. Porsche, "people's car" inventor, would have endorsed.

FOR MORE INFORMATION . . .

- Volkswagen of America, Inc.
  Human Resources Group
  3800 Hamlin Road
  Auburn Hills, MI 48326
  www.vw.com

- Ms. Regina Peldszus
  Human Recources Group
  Volkswagen, A.G.
  Berliner Ring 2
  38436 Wolfsburg, Germany
  49-53-6192-1245
  Fax: 49-53-6192-2294

THE WALL STREET JOURNAL.

SELECTIVITY

Approximate applicant pool: 600–800
Interns accepted: 15–18

COMPENSATION

$600/week

QUALITY OF LIFE

Demanding pace; formal dress;
low-key newsroom

LOCATION(S)

New York and various major cities (including
Chicago, Atlanta, Dallas, and Washington, D.C.)

FIELD

Newspaper journalism

DURATION

10 weeks
Summer

PRE-REQS

Undergrads; graduating seniors; grad students
Previous journalism internships and/or college
newspaper experience

DEADLINE

Thanksgiving

What do Spam and the Pulitzer Prize have in common? If you ask Tom Knudson, he might tell you that if you write about the former, you may eventually win the latter. A tenuous connection at best, but Knudson got his journalistic feet wet as an intern with *The Wall Street Journal*, where he wrote, among other stories, a witty piece on the history of that lunch-box favorite, Spam. In the 12 years that followed, Knudson reported for the *Des Moines Register*, *The New York Times*, and the *Sacramento Bee*, and won two Pulitzer Prizes in the process.

Interning at *The Wall Street Journal* does not destine a person to win the Pulitzer Prize, even if that person has an abiding interest in canned pork shoulder. It does, however, expose one to the inner workings of what many deem America's most influential newspaper. Founded in 1889 as a four-page bulletin pledging to offer "a faithful picture of the rapidly shifting panorama of [Wall] Street," the *Journal* has grown into an international daily with a circulation larger than that of any other U.S. newspaper. Despite this stature, it strives to adhere to old values, namely "accuracy, independence, and fairness." If the independent surveys that consistently show the *Journal* to be America's most trusted publication are any indication, it is doing an admirable job.

DESCRIPTION

Wall Street Journal interns concur: The internship begins fast and furious. "A story was assigned to me at noon on my first day. It was panic city! But I made it through relatively unscathed," said one intern. His experience sums up a distinctive feature of the *Journal* internship: An intern's work is completely substantive and demanding, particularly in the sense that interns are not coddled through it. "You do the kind of work a regular reporter does," stated an intern. "The editors give you direction, but there isn't much hand-holding. They throw you into the fire, expecting you to write from day one."

Interns spend a good deal of time working on "spot news," meaning they man phones and watch news wires for the latest news on companies. Fielding press releases as soon as the news comes in, interns determine which pieces are appropriate as small stories

BUSYWORK
MEDIUM
LOW HIGH
OLDMAN & HAMADEH
METER

for the paper. Spot news also provides information for the Dow Jones News Wire, a financial news service used by investment banks, brokerage houses, and private investors. "I'd constantly call the New York office to report headlines like 'Company X Fires 100 People.' You'd need good judgment—an ability to evaluate whether business dealings were newsworthy."

Spot news notwithstanding, interns find themselves working on meaty writing assignments. On average, interns write about three front-page or front-section stories during their stay. As expected of a newspaper named for New York's financial district, business stories are prevalent. Whether they're writing about tobacco tax, commodities markets, or corporate mergers, interns find themselves doing a good deal of business reporting. For many, writing about business news is foreign territory, which takes some getting used to. "I was a blank slate when it came to writing about financial issues," said an intern. "But my editors were patient. They gave me materials to augment my business background. Gradually, I got better." In general, interns rave about the business education they receive working at the *Journal*: "You leave there feeling very comfortable talking and writing about financial issues."

But, as one intern pointed out, the "scope of the *Journal* exceeds mere business journalism," and thus interns write a fair share of feature and medium-length stories that are not directly business related. One intern wrote a feature story analyzing whether 900-number legal help services provide valuable advice. Another wrote about men who have chosen the priesthood as a second career, his story focusing on how the traditionalists of one seminary viewed these second-career clergymen. Stories are many and varied: "At the *Journal* I wrote on a different topic every few days . . . things stayed fresh and involving." One intern remembers reporting on the decline in Chicago's housing market one week and the

perils of pig farming another.

Many interns have ample opportunity to work on so-called softer news. Some write "orphans," the small, offbeat stories appearing in the lower left-hand corner on page one of the paper's Marketplace section. "I had a lot of fun writing an orphan about a whitewater rafting trip executives take in West Virginia," recalled one intern. Others write "a-heds," the quirky stories found on the middle of the front page. A-hed topics are many and varied and have covered everything from old-fashioned sporting goods stores to Memphis barbecue stands to a man who spends his life retrieving and re-selling used golf balls. One enterprising intern convinced an editor that he should write an a-hed about rock musicians who engage in social activism; he ended up being flown to Philadelphia, where, armed with a press pass, he covered the historic Live Aid concert. "It was a kick," he said. "I mingled backstage with rock stars, talked with all sorts of music industry bigwigs, and was invited back to Jackson Browne's house, where I interviewed him over lunch."

While the Live Aid piece demonstrates the editors' receptivity to self-generated stories, the majority of stories are assigned by the editors. After writing a story, an intern submits it to an editor, who critiques it and often allows the intern to make revisions. "After an editor read your story, you'd get to do your own editing, which differs from other newspapers I've worked on, where once you wrote the first draft, it was out of your hands," recalled one intern. Reworking their stories, interns hone their writing skills, learning journalism under the guidance of some of the best newswriters in the business. Interns also learn the inimitable style of the *Journal*, which, some say, is sharp, punchy, and more analytical than most newspapers. Said one intern: "Unlike the vast majority of papers, which tell what happened and little more, the *Journal* strives to provide analysis of what

> "This is not a fluff internship—it's a real working experience. You are a *Wall Street Journal* reporter for a summer . . . . Come back with a story or fall flat on your face."

happened. Its reporters try to link situations together and draw conclusions."

Just as the perspective of the *Journal* differs from most newspapers, so does its office environment. At the New York office, one finds not a frenetic Lou Grant–style sweatshop, but a relatively low-key newsroom, more reminiscent of an insurance office than a major newspaper. One intern likened the feel of the New York office to that of a university, populated by reporters who debate issues and write books in their spare time. Most of the staff in New York dress formally; "jackets and ties were commonplace among men," observed one intern. Situated on New York Harbor, *Journal* headquarters stands across from the World Trade Center, with a view of the Statue of Liberty. Interns get their own desks, although in recent years a lack of space has necessitated that some use the desks of vacationing reporters.

In addition to the seven or so interns who work in the New York office, interns are placed in bureaus across the country. *Journal* outposts in such cities as Washington, D.C., Chicago, Atlanta, and Dallas accept interns, with usually one intern per bureau, although the bureaus hiring interns vary from year to year. Bureaus are considerably smaller than the New York office, and are thus more conducive to meeting people. They also tend to be roomier, as most are located in cities where space is not such a scarce commodity. Happily, the dress code is usually looser in the bureaus, too.

The *Journal* has no special programs for interns. It's a no-frills experience: no orientation, no weekly speaker series, and no parkside picnics. Perhaps the intern coordinator said it best: "This is not a fluff internship—it's a real working experience. You are a *Wall Street Journal* reporter for a summer. Come back with a story or fall flat on your face." Interns generally appreciate the *Journal*'s no-nonsense attitude, seeing it as an opportunity for responsibility and freedom: "The permanent staff respected [the interns]. They didn't need to indulge us with a lot of extra activities because there was so much meaningful work to do. They wanted us to learn to be better reporters." Even so, the *Journal*'s relatively unstructured program does not garner unanimous praise. "Some interns during my tenure at the *Journal* felt lost," remarked an intern. "They weren't getting much to do and

they didn't have gumption to demand more action." Another intern echoed the same problem: "It's a fast-paced place. Some interns floundered when they did not receive enough guidance." On the whole, however, interns are more than satisfied with their work and the way in which it was assigned.

This satisfaction is evident in the large number of interns who seek permanent positions at the *Journal*, although openings are scarce. According to the coordinator, in one year five former interns were hired out of an intern class of fifteen; in other years, none were hired. On the average, the *Journal* taps one former intern about every other year.

SELECTION

The internship is open to undergraduates, recent graduates, and graduate students. About half of the internships go to minority applicants. The application bulletin states that "in-depth reporting and writing experience on campus papers and previous internships at other newspapers are essential." While the majority of interns surveyed had solid journalistic backgrounds before applying, a few had relatively little experience; said one intern: "It varies; most interns my summer were well-credentialed journalists, but I knew a few without much experience, especially when it came to reporting on business. There's a sense that the *Journal* will take a chance on a few applicants who lack a lot of experience but demonstrate great enthusiasm." Besides having a passion for their work, interns should be "adaptable," "assertive," and "enterprising." Said one intern: "This job is 90 percent attitude. You've got to soak up everything you can from the permanent reporters. You must be open to their guidance." International applicants are eligible.

APPLICATION PROCEDURE

Procrastinators, take note: Application materials must be submitted before Thanksgiving. Applicants should send a cover letter, resume, and clips of journalistic work to Carolyn Phillips, an assistant managing editor at the *Journal*. She and a few other staff members comprise a committee that whittles the applicant pool down to a final group of about 40 applicants. Finalists are interviewed in person or over the phone. The bureau chiefs in various cities then choose whom they want as interns, selecting a total of about 18 applicants.

OVERVIEW

 Interning at *The Wall Street Journal* is no toe-dip in a bubble bath, it's a full-body plunge into a chilly sea of journalistic responsibility and prestige. Although coddling is about as likely as a "Dear Abby" column's appearing in the *Journal*, interns receive an unmatched initiation into the world of big-time reporting. With a *Journal* internship under one's belt, there's no limit to what one can do professionally.

Just ask Derek Dingle. After interning in the *Journal*'s Chicago bureau, he eventually became managing editor of *Black Enterprise* magazine. He now runs a company that makes comic books featuring black superheroes, and when recently the *Journal* described his venture in its Business and Race section, he remarked: "In ten years, I went from writing *for* the *Journal* to being written about *by* the *Journal*."

FOR MORE INFORMATION . . .

■ *The Wall Street Journal*
Internship Program
c/o Carolyn Phillips, Assistant Managing Editor
200 Liberty Street
New York, NY 10281

Washington **I**nternships for **S**tudents of **E**ngineering

At many colleges, students are divided into two camps—"techies" and "fuzzies." The former are number-crunching, formula-figuring, laboratory-dwelling science lovers, while the latter are politically minded, java-drinking, essay-writing, liberal arts students. But have you ever run across a "fuzzy techy"? They're a rare breed, particularly when it comes to engineering students who have a solid grasp of government. Yet, in our increasingly technological society, the need for people conversant in both science and policy cannot be overemphasized: The Washington Internships for Students of Engineering (WISE) was created to address this necessity.

DESCRIPTION

In 1973, University of Washington Engineering Professor Barry Hyman served a one-year tenure as a congressional Fellow. Through this experience, he realized that undergraduate engineering students would benefit from a similar experience; he founded WISE in 1978. Supported by a generous National Science Foundation grant and funds from private engineering societies, the program welcomed its first class of interns in 1980. About ten professional engineering societies sponsor one or two students each, providing WISE with around $6,000 per student. A portion of this money goes to the faculty-in-residence, an engineering professor chosen each year to oversee the interns and their work.

WISE introduces students to Washington and the technical public policy issues debated there. Students attend 20 to 30 meetings organized by their faculty-in-residence. One to two hours in length, the meetings begin with a presentation followed by a question and answer period. One year, for example, saw sessions with Senators David Pryor (D-Ark.) and John Glenn (D-Ohio) as well as the heads of the Office of Technology Assessment, the House Committee on Science, Space, and Technology, the National Academy of Sciences, and the Office of Science and Technology Policy. The same year, interns were treated to a meeting with President Bush's science adviser. "We took a tour of the Executive Office Building and then discussed Bush's science policy," said one intern. "Although we had heard a rumor that the adviser disapproved of Bush's science policy, none of us dared to bring it up."

SELECTIVITY	🔍 🔍 🔍 🔍
Approximate applicant pool: 75 Interns accepted: 14–16	

COMPENSATION	💲 💲 💲
$1,800 stipend, lodging, and round-trip travel allowance	

QUALITY OF LIFE	🌴 🌴 🌴 🌴
Independence; meetings with political bigwigs; dorm housing; faculty-in-residence	

LOCATION(S)

Washington, D.C.

FIELD

Engineering and public policy research

DURATION

10 weeks
Summer

PRE-REQS

Engineering students apply in their junior year; Must be U.S. citizen

DEADLINE

Early December

But discussions with government officials do not constitute the entire experience. The primary objective of the program obligates each student to write a research paper "that analyzes specific engineering public policy issues of concern to the sponsoring society," as the brochure explains. Papers explore topics like global environmental governance, free-trade policy, U.S. industrial competitiveness, and defense downsizing. One student, who analyzed the Nuclear Regulatory Commission's response to the Three Mile Island disaster, read briefs and interviewed several of the people involved. "In Washington, the most valuable information comes from the people currently wrestling with the issues," he said. "So I talked to decision makers at NASA and the Department of Defense, and to lobbyists and technical assistants. By the end of the summer, I understood nuclear policy better than I ever thought I could."

Another intern, exploring the government's control of unclassified information, combed through books and journals in an attempt to familiarize herself with current policies. She soon learned that the timeliness of the issues demanded an investigation of the committees and legislators themselves. "This was no ordinary research paper," she said. "Because my topic was current, I needed to interview those people helping to shape policy, particularly aides to the top brass at the Defense Department."

Aware that the average college student has little access to high-level officials, the full-time faculty-in-residence often helps track down important policymakers. When an intern needed to speak with the person in charge of nuclear plant licensing but couldn't arrange an interview, he turned to the faculty-in-residence. "The professor knew some important people at the Nuclear Regulatory Commission," he said. "His connections helped me land several meetings."

Sponsored by the American Institute of Chemical Engineers, an intern researched hazardous waste minimization in the United States. Starting at the Georgetown

library, he read many articles on his topic to gain insight into the issue. "Once I had done that," he said, "I talked extensively to staff members in all three branches of government in order to understand the government's policy toward hazardous waste." By the end, interns often amass so much material that a gargantuan task awaits. Some feel rushed to complete the write-up on time. Even so, one ambitious intern wrote 100 pages on his topic. While few interns go to such extreme lengths, final papers average forty pages and are comparable in scope, the director says, to an undergraduate thesis.

Current organizations participating in the WISE program include: The American Institute of Chemical Engineers (AIChE); the American Nuclear Society (ANS); the American Society of Civil Engineers (ASCE); the American Society of Mechanical Engineers (ASME); the Institute of Electrical & Electronics Engineers (IEEE); the National Society of Professional Engineers (NSPE); the Society of Automotive Engineers (SAE); and the National Science Foundation (NSF). Each organization sponsors one, two, or three Interns.

Housed together in a George Washington University dormitory, interns can't help but interact with each other daily. Though the faculty-in-residence does not live in the dorm, interns are able to discuss research issues and paper ideas with the professor at daily morning meetings. "The faculty-in-residence," said one, "is an integral part of the program." Besides the in-house professor, students take advantage of Washington resources like the Library of Congress and the Congressional Research Service. Interns typically analyze the information derived from these sources in the privacy of their communal office, which is equipped with computers and a laser printer.

In addition to the meetings organized by the faculty-in-residence, WISE arranges a few special luncheons and dinners. Interns congregate on The Mall for a picnic. They also travel to various points beyond the Beltway. One year, for example, interns toured the infamous

> "If you are an engineer interested in the broader implications of engineering, in understanding how technology plays a role in public policy, then WISE up—this program is for you."

Three Mile Island nuclear power plant. Occasionally, a sponsoring society sends an intern to its annual convention, where the intern presents his or her summer paper.

Some interns are unhappy with the stipend, especially since they must earmark half of it for rent. "The pay may be sufficient to live on," said one intern, "but it's still not enough." WISE eases some of the financial burden by covering round-trip travel, whether students fly or drive. At the end of the summer, interns receive an overall grade and three units of credit from Florida State University, which they can transfer to their respective institutions, offsetting graduating requirements in some cases.

SELECTION

To qualify for consideration, applicants must be engineering students, apply during their junior year, be a citizen of the United States, and if seeking sponsorship by ANS, ASCE, ASME, or IEEE, the student is required to be a member of that society. Applications for WISE are sought from outstanding engineering students who display evidence of leadership skills and have a keen interest in public policy. Minority students are encouraged to apply.

APPLICATION PROCEDURE

The deadline is in early December. Students must turn in a completed application form, two short essays, resume, an official transcript, and two letters of recommendation. WISE administrators screen the initial pool of applicants. Finalists are then chosen by the sponsoring engineering societies, who assist the interns in choosing research paper topics.

OVERVIEW

Engineering students, think big. Abandon the classroom and spend a summer discovering how science can contribute to public policy decisions. WISE invites a troop of talented techies to the nation's capital and brings them face to face with top policymakers. Factor in the required research paper, and interns have one heck of a learning experience. At the very least, a summer with WISE will heighten students' overall interest in politics. And some may even be inspired to incorporate government into their technical careers. One WISE intern went on to assist President Bush's domestic policy adviser. Another was inspired to augment his engineering background with a law degree, and he ended up clerking for Supreme Court Justice Sandra Day O'Connor. As a WISE alumnus puts it: "If you are an engineer interested in the broader implications of engineering, in understanding how technology plays a role in public policy, then WISE up—this program is for you."

FOR MORE INFORMATION . . .

■ Anne Hickox
   Washington Internships for Students
      of Engineering Program
   c/o SAE
   400 Commonwealth Drive
   Warrendale, PA 15096-0001
   (724) 776-4841, ext. 7476
   Fax: (724) 776-2103
   anne@sae.org

The Washington Post

SELECTIVITY 🔍 🔍 🔍 🔍 🔍 🔍

Approximate applicant pool: 400–800
Interns accepted: 20

COMPENSATION $ $ $ $ $

$803/week

QUALITY OF LIFE ☂ ☂ ☂

Speaker luncheons; mentors;
strenuous workload

LOCATION(S)

Washington, D.C.; VA; MD

FIELD

Newspaper journalism

DURATION

12 weeks
Summer

PRE-REQS

College juniors and seniors; grad students
Previous journalism experience

DEADLINE

November 1

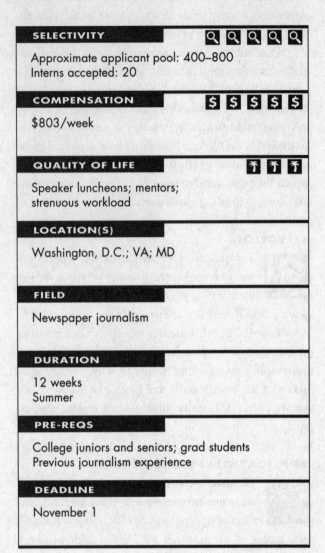

Take a walk in the history section of your local bookstore. Chances are you'll come across *All the President's Men*, perhaps the greatest political detective story of the century. It reveals how two newspaper reporters, Carl Bernstein and Bob Woodward, blew open the Watergate scandal, delivering revelations that led to Richard Nixon's political demise. Where did these men do this Pulitzer Prize–winning reporting? *The Washington Post*, of course. You might also encounter another work in your bookstore—*Power, Privilege, and the Post*, the story of Katharine Graham, a woman who helped build a spectacularly profitable, internationally renowned newspaper empire. What paper did she command? You guessed it: *The Washington Post*. One of the world's most respected newspapers, the *Post* is a locus of power in the United States, reporting on, and in some instances shaping, the course of American history.

DESCRIPTION

The Washington Post assigns its interns to the Metro, Business, Sports, Style, Photo, or News Art departments. Wherever they go, one constant holds true in every department: There's little busywork. "[The *Post*] assumes you are there to be a reporter—photocopying, answering phones, and the like are unheard of," a former intern reported. Indeed, the closest a *Post* intern gets to busywork is occasionally doing the legwork for a staff reporter's story.

Mostly, interns are expected to report and write their own stories. Responsibility is the operative word and *Post* interns get a lot of it, so much so that newly arrived interns sometimes underestimate the amount of responsibility they are afforded from day one. "On my first day on the job my supervising editor had me travel the then unfamiliar streets of Washington and report a story on a lawyer who had been censured by a judge for wearing a West African shawl in the courtroom. After scrambling for courtroom interviews and searching computer databases for background information, I wrote the story—and it ended up on the front page of the paper! If that wasn't heady enough,

John Chancellor [of NBC News] called me the next day to ask a few other details about my story."

The above experience is obviously not representative of every intern's first day, but it indicates the potential for adventurous and substantive work at the *Post*. Interns often write more than one story a week. Most see at least one of their stories appear on the front page of the newspaper or the front page of a section and some pen as many as five or six front-page stories during the internship. Story ideas come from one of the editors or reporters with whom an intern works and from an intern's own ability to brainstorm new ideas. "We would report and write about a tremendous variety of people and events," said an intern.

Indeed, the scope of topics interns cover is breathtaking. Metro interns report on everything from local crime stories to Washington politics to plane crashes. One even covered a Boy Scout jamboree in Virginia, where she was one of a few women among 40,000 Boy Scouts. Sports interns find themselves in the locker rooms and press boxes of such professional sports teams as the Washington Redskins and the Baltimore Orioles. A Style intern spent a night with a group of LSD-using high school students and wrote a story about it which went on to win the D.C. Press Association's Best Feature Story Award. But the rewarding stories are not always the splashy ones. A Metro intern spent an afternoon interviewing random people on the streets of D.C. about the abundance of rain the city was receiving. "This assignment helped me get over my fear of working a crowd," he recalled, "and tackling a deceptively simple subject like rain taught me how to appreciate the subtle, finer points of a story."

While the wealth of reporting opportunities makes the *Post* an intensely educational and enriching internship, such work carries certain pressures. "This is a high-octane place," warns an intern. "It is strenuous, definitely not for someone who wants a relaxing job between tough semesters." Long days and strict deadlines surprise new interns who underestimate the extent to which they will be treated as capable reporters. Said one: "When I started, I was a bit unnerved at the demanding routine reporters follow at the *Post*. No matter how early I arrived for work, it seemed like my supervisor came earlier." The newspaper's fast pace and ability to attract overachieving interns gives it an environment of competition that some even describe as cutthroat. "You feel a little envious when your fellow intern gets assigned a better story," reported an intern. "Sometimes it seems as if some interns jockey for power, striving to impress their editors in hopes as being invited back for permanent employment." As an average of only one or two interns are asked back each year, some interns can't help but feel pangs of competition. A few conclude that this environment stifles camaraderie among interns. But, as one intern pointed out, "Every class of interns has a different complexion, and intern unity varies from summer to summer."

The majority of interns work at the *Post*'s 15th Street headquarters, located in the heart of downtown Washington. Comments on the office's appearance range from "spacious" to "grungy" to "just what you'd expect—a sea of desks, right out of *All the President's Men*." The *Post* assigns a few Metro interns to its bureaus in Virginia and Maryland, which for some is "a bit isolated, especially because you are usually the only intern there" and for others is "less competitive and just as substantive as working in downtown Washington."

Perks abound at the *Post*. Pay is terrific, commensurate with the salary of a beginning-level reporter; in recent summers, interns were paid around $800 a week. Interns enjoy a daylong orientation program including a bus tour of D.C. and a lunchtime picnic. Virtually every week the newspaper holds a special intern luncheon, at which interns hobnob with a *Post* editor or reporter, often

> For those willing to follow a hectic, demanding schedule, a treasure trove of journalistic opportunity awaits.

a "mythical figure in the world of journalism"; past lunch guests have included Bob Woodward, executive editor Len Downie, former editor Ben Bradlee, and syndicated columnists David Broder and Richard Cohen. The *Post* also conducts an informal mentor program in which each intern is paired with a staff member; in one intern's estimation, "this buddy system is a great way of learning about the newspaper business on a more personal level."

SELECTION

The program accepts college juniors and seniors as well as graduate students. Although the application states that previous journalism work is "preferred," a survey of past interns suggests that previous internships or college newspaper experience is virtually required. Said a former intern: "It seemed like all of my fellow interns had strong journalism backgrounds—everything from part-time work with local newspapers to previous internships with *Time*, *The Wall Street Journal*, and *Newsday* to editorial experience on college papers." Besides experience, the *Post* looks for individuals with initiative and self-confidence, able to vigorously pursue a story and see it through to fruition; "relentless" is how one former intern described the desired ethic. International applicants are eligible.

APPLICATION PROCEDURE

The application deadline is November 1. This date is earlier than most other prestigious newspaper internships, in part, according to a past intern, to give the *Post* first dibs on the best applicants. Applicants should write for an application well in advance of the deadline, or see www.washingtonpost.com/intern. Besides returning a completed application, applicants must send two letters of recommendation, a 500-word typewritten autobiography, half a dozen clips of journalistic work (e.g., clips from a college paper), and a college transcript.

OVERVIEW

Interning at *The Washington Post* is not merely a three-month observer's post at a pinnacle of American journalism. It is a chance to learn the art of reporting and writing under the supervision of professional journalists in one of the world's most powerful and newsworthy cities. For those willing to follow a hectic, demanding schedule, a treasure trove of journalistic opportunity awaits. In the last three years, seven summer interns were hired into the two-year copy editor program. The internship program has been in existence for more than a quarter of a century and it has produced a star-spangled array of alumni. In fact, about 90 current staffers launched their careers as *Post* interns, including the newspaper's executive editor.

FOR MORE INFORMATION . . .

■ www.washingtonpost.com/intern

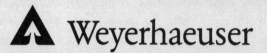

Weyerhaeuser

SELECTIVITY	🔍 🔍 🔍 🔍
Approximate applicant pool: 500 Interns accepted: approximately 60	

COMPENSATION	$ $ $ $
$560–$680/week for undergrads; $700–$900/week for grad students; company benefits	

QUALITY OF LIFE	🌴 🌴 🌴 🌴
Mentors; career development; seminars/tours; social activities	

LOCATION(S)
Federal Way, WA, and at some of the 250 facilities in the United States and Canada

FIELD
Technology and business areas of forest products

DURATION
6–8 months Summer/Fall; Winter/Spring

PRE-REQS
Varies with position—see Selection

DEADLINE
Winter/Spring .... October 10 Summer/Fall .... January 20

Think working at a Fortune 100 company's corporate headquarters means toiling away in a windowless cubbyhole on the 34th floor of a downtown high-rise? Think again. Weyerhaeuser, one of the world's largest manufacturers of products made from wood and paper, is based in the natural beauty of Washington State. Its headquarters—an architectural marvel of glass and ivy gardens—is surrounded by a 600-acre campus that includes forests, meadows and a lake. It isn't unusual to see a bald eagle dive for fish while looking out the cafeteria windows!

And if you expect a culture as old-fashioned as a logging camp, you're in for a pleasant surprise. Open communications, high ethics, and a respect for the individual are the keystones of Weyerhaeuser's values. It's a place where you can ask the CEO any question you like by mail or in person at one of the frequent employee forums—and get an honest answer.

You don't have to be a forester to work at Weyerhaeuser, either. Jobs run the gamut from accountants to zoologists. Weyerhaeuser's vision is to be the best forest products company in the world—and it's looking for motivated young people with fresh ideas to help it get there.

DESCRIPTION

In 1975, Weyerhaeuser's Information Technology (IT) unit established its own internship program for about a half-dozen students. Now, having grown in size and popularity, the program attracts a group of about 60 IT interns yearly. These interns are dispersed throughout the company's headquarters to further IT's mission: to achieve a sustainable, competitive advantage for Weyerhaeuser through improved business processes and information technology. Assigned to teams, interns plan, analyze, design, and develop business application sysytems; evaluate software; engineer and implement system test plans; develop tools for data interchange between systems; and maintain local area networks. But according to the coordinator, the internship requires "as much use of soft skills and teamwork as knowledge of computers."

An IT intern in Containerboard Packaging worked on developing a database to track the company's huge PC (personal computer) inventory. "Company PCs move around a lot," she explained. "Cataloging them decreases the chance of misplacing them." Using a commercial program, she created the database. "I set up fields for the serial number, type of computer, make, and model," she said. "And I also wrote some code so that people working with the database could delete, add, or print information."

Another IT intern worked with the Customer Support Team. "As an intern with this group," he said, "I helped IT keep tabs on all of its capital projects, much like Capital Management does for the corporate offices." He helped create a computer system to consolidate project information. "Each business unit had a project that it wanted to do," he explained. "We input each project's duration, total cost, benefits—nearly 100 elements for about 300 projects. It was a lot of information to track. I was in charge of maintaining the system, by creating new functions and removing bugs."

The IT internship, however, is not as old as other internships available at Weyerhaeuser. In the 1950s, the company provided Forestry internships to students interested in agriculture. Decades and scores of alumni later, the company offers experiences not only in Forestry but also in Accounting and Engineering—approximately 50 spots at corporate headquarters and over 100 positions with many of the 250 offices and plants across North America.

Company-wide interns work with mentors to develop projects related to the forest products industry. Technology interns (generally engineering) apply technology to help Weyerhaeuser businesses achieve a competitive advantage. They contribute to a wide variety of projects, including implementing mill process control systems; evaluating mill equipment and processes to improve air and water quality; collecting and analyzing data for water reduction in mills; analyzing fiber properties of changing wood supplies; evaluating methods for strength enhancements of recycled fibers; finding nondestructive means to predict log quality; and evaluating materials to improve fiber length and strength for papermaking.

Timberlands (generally forestry and forest engineering) interns gain valuable experience in commercial forestry activities of growing, harvesting, and marketing timber. Strong emphasis is placed on business and financial elements of commercial forestry and on hands-on application of Weyerhaeuser's environmental and public resource protection standards and strategies.

Controllership Development (accounting) interns provide accounting, analytical or audit support to a business unit or staff group.

Just as Weyerhaeuser nurtures its trees, so it nurtures its interns. Each week, IT interns congregate for development programs—activities into which IT puts a lot of thought and effort, plus a free lunch. In fact, the entire year's activities—workshops, videos, and tours— are scheduled before IT interns even arrive. One to five hours in length, the programs teach IT interns how to become Weyerhaeuser professionals. Considering that most IT interns return after graduation to be full-time employees, it's no surprise that the company spends a considerable amount of time training them.

Workshops address such topics as business ethics, website development guidelines, career planning, informational interviewing, corporate culture, and project management. A communication skills workshop focuses on listening and questioning skills. "One key development area for our interns is communication skills—listening, speaking, and writing," says the IT internship coordinator, "and the communication skills workshop helps them out."

Videos teach IT interns interpersonal, telephone,

> **Employees and interns are often seen jogging on the area's snakelike running trails or pumping iron at one of the corporate fitness centers.**

and meeting skills. With flicks like *If Looks Could Kill* (a half-hour British mystery about interpersonal behavior) and *Meetings, Bloody Meetings*, interns rarely become bored. Other videos discuss Weyerhaeuser's vision and values.

Videos and workshops probably don't provide as much insight into the company as tours, conducted every month or so for interns throughout the company. Interns visit The Weyerhaeuser Technology Center, which houses engineers, scientists, and their research and development projects. They also take organized field tours of company facilities such as a tree farm, a seedling nursery, a log export facility, a sawmill, and a recycling plant. Recalled one: "We spent a whole day traveling from one mill site to another, where boards, paper, and pulp are manufactured. We watched paper get turned into corrugated boxes at the box plant and observed employees caring for seedlings at the nursery. And we saw that every part of the tree is used to make something, from fuel for the boilers to fine printing paper."

At the end of the internship, interns share what they have learned with a group of Weyerhaeuser employees. In front of supervisors, mentors, and management—50 to 60 people in all—each intern makes a five-minute presentation of his or her work.

Weyerhaeuser's corporate headquarters is located in Federal Way, Washington. The five-story corporate building is flanked on one side by a meadow and on the other by a lake that is home to ducks, geese, and swans. Employees and interns are often seen jogging on the 600-acre area's snakelike running trails or pumping iron at one of the corporate fitness centers.

The headquarter's grounds also serve as the setting for a multitide of outdoor activities and games. Interns at Weyerhauser can be involved with the annual intern picnic or can organize their own events. Previous activites that interns have planned include laser tag, white water-rafting, hiking, camping, softball, volleyball, and bowling.

SELECTION

 The IT program targets college sophomores and juniors studying computer science or information systems. The Controllership Development Intern Program seeks college juniors majoring in accounting. Typically, engineering and science interns are college sophomores though graduate students in engineering (chemical, environmental, electrical, mechanical, and civil), pulp and paper science, and wood science are also sought after. Other areas using interns include Timberlands and Health/Fitness.

The list of key selection criteria (or core competencies) Weyerhaeuser looks for includes:
* Commitment to continuous learning
* Technical competence
* Problem-solving skills
* Initiative
* Flexibility
* Communication skills
* Customer Focus
* Quality orientation

APPLICATION PROCEDURE

 The deadline is January 20 for June to December internships and October 10 for January to June internships. The latter internships may sometimes be extended to August. The preferred method to apply is to submit a resume and cover letter directly to the specific intern program of interest, as described on the company website, www.weyerhaeuser.com/careers/college. Alternatively, applicants may submit resumes and cover letters to College Relations at the address on the opposing page. Well-qualified candidates receive on-campus or phone interviews. Those garnering highest marks in the interviews are brought to headquarters or one of the plants for final interviews. Selections are made a few days later. Offers are contingent upon satisfactory pre-employment drug testing.

OVERVIEW

 In the early 1800s, daring pioneers ventured west to claim their fortunes in the American forests. Legend has it that Paul Bunyan, a mythical lumberjack, hovered closely above in spirit while they axed trees and sawed lumber. Students who venture into Weyerhaeuser territory will find a Paul Bunyan watching over them, too. Caring mentors and supervisors ensure that interns work on projects of value to the company. Videos, workshops, and tours help interns develop professional skills. Coordinators make sure interns balance hard work with recreational and social activities. Just as Bunyan, patron saint of the American lumber industry, protected early loggers, so Weyerhaeuser grooms its interns for roles as future wood-industry professionals.

FOR MORE INFORMATION . . .

■ College Relations-CCB5D7
Weyerhaeuser
PO Box 9777
Federal Way, WA 98063-9777
www.weyerhaeuser.com/careers/college
college@weyerhaeuser.com

THE WHITE HOUSE
WASHINGTON

We named the White House one of *America's Top Internships* way back in the 1994 edition of this book, and now we know one thing for sure: Monica listened!

The White House offered a terrific internship pre-Monica. And let it be known, the internship remains a winner post-Monica. While brushes with the Prez are few and far between, an internship at the White House can provide access to bigwigs and big jobs in a way that few other programs can match.

DESCRIPTION

Despite the scandal, the White House still offers one of Washington's strongest internship programs. In fact, *The Rocky Mountain News* recently testified to the program's continued strength by declaring in a feature story: "Interns Sidestep Scandal. Focus on Lewinsky Case Doesn't Hinder Program."

Students may apply for the fall, spring, or summer internship. Applicants for the summer internship must choose either session I (early June to early July) or session II (mid-July to late August). Twenty-two White House offices take on interns, including Advance, Cabinet Affairs, Chief of Staff, Communications, Correspondence, Domestic Policy, Office of the Executive Clerk, First Lady's Office, General Counsel, Intergovernmental Affairs, Legislative Affairs, Management/Administration/Operations, National Economic Council, Office of National Service, Photography Office, Political Affairs, Presidential Personnel, Public Liaison, Scheduling, Staff Secretary, Vice President's Office, and Visitor's Office.

The substance of interns' work varies greatly from office to office. Some positions, for example, consist of assignments relating to a specific issue. An intern in Domestic

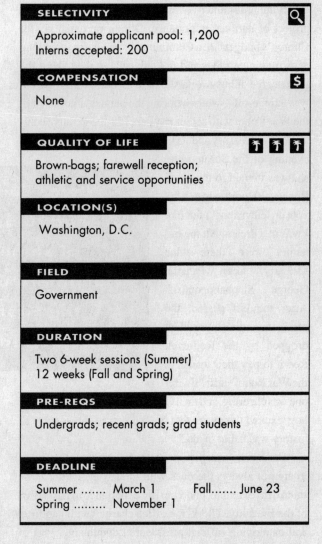

SELECTIVITY	🔍
Approximate applicant pool: 1,200 Interns accepted: 200	

COMPENSATION	$
None	

QUALITY OF LIFE	🏆 🏆 🏆
Brown-bags; farewell reception; athletic and service opportunities	

LOCATION(S)
Washington, D.C.

FIELD
Government

DURATION
Two 6-week sessions (Summer) 12 weeks (Fall and Spring)

PRE-REQS
Undergrads; recent grads; grad students

DEADLINE
Summer .... March 1   Fall....... June 23 Spring .... November 1

Policy collected background material on health care reform and incorporated it into a briefing book for senior adviser Ira Magaziner; he also drafted letters to citizens who had written Magaziner about health care issues. Other positions are a bit of a grind. Correspondence interns, for example, spend most of their time responding to the president's huge volume of mail, phone calls, and faxes. Some positions are just plain old fun. Visitor's Office interns help coordinate requests for White House tours and plan special events such as the Pageant of Peace and the Easter Egg Roll. Helping out at Clinton's Georgetown Class of '68 reunion,

BUSYWORK
MEDIUM
LOW HIGH
OLDMAN & HAMADEH
METER

one Visitor's Office intern "got to hang out with [musical guest] Chuck Berry."

Sometimes interns find themselves assigned to a project of national importance. During preparations for Clinton's budget bill, a Communications intern spent long days running errands and fielding calls. Asked about the high degree of busywork, she said: "I didn't mind at all. It was a trade-off—while working the phones, I got to sit in the War Room with senior advisers like the deputy secretary of the Treasury and Al Gore's press secretary." On the evening of the Senate vote, she was invited to the plush Roosevelt Room to watch the vote on television: "I felt like I was in a dream. All the big names were there—Mac McLarty, Leon Panetta, George Stephanopoulos." After the bill passed, the president and vice president dropped by the Roosevelt Room to pay their thanks to the War Room staff: "Everyone was cheering, and then Clinton and Gore came in to say how excited they were that the bill passed. I was there as history was being made."

As in many internships, the best departments to work in are not always the ones with the sexiest names. One intern, for example, had a terrific experience in the Office of the Executive Clerk, the office charged with handling and cataloging official presidential documents. Part of his time was spent on the phone fielding inquiries about bills and nominations signed by the president. He also filed documents in the office's archives—a rewarding task "if only because you got to see valuable presidential papers dating back to 1890." But nothing could compare to his other responsibility: hand-delivering presidential messages and nominations to Congress. Twenty or so times during the summer he went to Capitol Hill to deliver presidential papers, each document in a special envelope sealed with an official wax stamp. The highlight of this job was delivering the Supreme Court nomination of Ruth Bader Ginsburg: "A military car took me up to Capitol Hill, where I was escorted to the Senate floor and was introduced to the Senate as one of the president's

secretaries. I bowed, then handed over the envelope and said, 'I am directed by the President of the United States to deliver a message in writing.'" The delivery was filmed on C-SPAN and immortalized on the pages of the *Congressional Record*.

While some experiences are simply awesome, others are delightfully silly. An intern in the Visitor's Office, for example, once had the rare opportunity to meet Socks the cat. "Socks' caretaker came by and dropped him off for an hour. Everyone in the office played with him. I even had my picture taken with the cat." But events soon took a turn for the worse: "About ten minutes later, I had an allergic reaction. I started sneezing and itching. My supervisor had to take me to the White House's doctor." Laughing all the way to the doctor's office, he contemplated his crazy luck: "I was convinced it had to be a first of some sort—an intern allergic to the First Pet of the United States."

> "I was convinced it had to be a first of some sort— an intern allergic to the First Pet of the United States."

The internship kicks off with a daylong orientation. The early part of the day is spent with representatives of the Secret Service, who brief interns on security issues. Said an intern: "They basically scare you out of doing what you're not supposed to do." Afterward, interns receive an official welcome and "major pep talk" from a VIP (Tipper Gore did the honors in 1993). Following the VIP's welcome, the director of the Office of National Service takes to the podium and speaks on the importance of public service.

The focus of interns' extracurricular life is a weekly series of brown-bag luncheons with presidential assistants, Cabinet secretaries, and congressional leaders. The luncheons are held in the Old Executive Office's Indian Treaty Room, a marble-and-tile chamber with an intricately decorated balcony overhead. Recent speakers have comprised a constellation of Washington stars: Dee Dee Myers (former White House press secretary), David Wilhelm (Democratic party chairman), Janet Reno (U.S. Attorney General), Joan Baggett (White House political director), and George Stephanopoulos (former White

House senior adviser). One of the interns' favorite speakers was political consultant James Carville, who peppered his remarks with "genuinely funny" jokes and finished to a standing ovation.

A variety of other activities keep interns busy. Intern-jocks run the bases in an intern softball league. Service-oriented interns participate in D.C. Cares, a program that pairs students with underprivileged children. Curious interns may arrange to watch a presidential helicopter arrival or departure on the White House's South Lawn. The South Lawn is also the site of the White House's Fourth of July party, where interns may watch fireworks with White House staff and their families. (Paparazzi, take note: One recent partygoer spied Chelsea Clinton hanging out on the roof with her friends.) Last but certainly not least, interns get to meet Bubba himself, when Bill, Hillary, and Al Gore host a good-bye reception at the end of the internship. Described an intern: "[Bill] gave us a two-minute thank-you speech. We each then got to shake his hand, and we all posed together for a group picture."

Contrary to common expectations, few interns actually work in the White House itself. With the exception of East and West Wing offices such as Staff Secretary, Chief of Staff, and Legislative Affairs, most interns are situated in the Old Executive Office Building. Next door to the White House, the Old Executive Office Building has four floors of handsome, scrubbed-clean corridors and black-and-white diamond tiles. Interns' accommodations vary—some interns have their own desks; others make do with "floating between open desks." In the coordinator's words, "facilities and equipment are well shared."

SELECTION

The program is open to undergraduates of any level, recent graduate students, of any major are welcome, as are conservatives. Says the intern coordinator: "As this is a nonpartisan White House, the program is open to everyone, even those of the opposite political persuasion."

APPLICATION PROCEDURE

The application deadline for the summer internship is March 1; for the fall internship, June 23; and for the spring internship, October 15. Submit a resume, two letters of recommendation (preferably one from a college professor and one from a political/professional source), writing sample (two to three pages), and unofficial transcript. In a cover letter, applicants may describe any interesting, unusual, or significant information about their family, upbringing, or heritage. Applicants must also fill out and submit the one-page White House Internship Application, which asks for personal and academic data as well as four department preferences. No interviews are given. Applicants should hear a decision from the coordinator at least a month before the start date of the internship.

OVERVIEW

If this book had a "prestige meter," the White House internship would shatter its limit. But the program offers more than mere resume radiance; it is the rare chance to experience life on the doorstep of the world's power center. Some offices are more substantive and exciting than others, but all interns should expect some busywork, some projects, and a whole lot of exposure, both formal and informal, to Washington's movers and shakers. An intern who had previously served three other government internships said it best: "The White House—there is no substitute."

FOR MORE INFORMATION . . .

■ The White House
Intern Program
Old Executive Office Building
Room 84
Washington, DC 20502
(202) 456-2742
Fax: (202) 456-5123
www.whitehouse.gov/internship

Whitney Museum of American Art

"Cultural War at the Whitney," declared the headline in a recent issue of *U.S. News & World Report*.

This was not the first time the Whitney was lambasted for its Biennial exhibition, and it was certainly not the last. Since 1932, the museum's Biennials have showcased the work of living American artists, providing a forum for unconventional art that is often displayed provocatively. Biennials of years past have been criticized for transgressions like underrepresenting female artists, combining paintings and sculpture, and overdosing on political correctness. But no matter how feisty or radical or infuriating they are, Biennials fulfill founder Gertrude Vanderbilt Whitney's desire to support American artists, regardless of whether their art is accepted at the time of exhibition.

But judging the Whitney by its Biennials is like judging a bookstore by its unconventional book festival. With all the hoopla generated by the Biennials, it's easy to lose sight of the fact that the Whitney is arguably the world's most comprehensive museum of 20th-century American art. Its permanent collection of more than 10,000 works reads like a who's who of modern American artists, including the likes of Joseph Stella, Georgia O'Keeffe, Charles Demuth, Edward Hopper, Max Weber, and George Bellows.

DESCRIPTION

Interns are placed in the following departments: Curatorial, Development, Education, Film and Video, Library, Operations, Communications/PR, Publications, and Registrar. Positions are also available in the two Whitney branches, located at the Philip Morris building in Manhattan and the Champion International Corporation in Stamford, CT.

SELECTIVITY

Approximate applicant pool: 125
Interns accepted: 25

COMPENSATION

$500 + two monthly Metrocards

QUALITY OF LIFE

Cozy atmosphere; weekly trip & lectures; exhibition openings; Sarabeth's

LOCATION(S)

New York, NY and Stamford, CT

FIELD

Art museum

DURATION

9 weeks full time (Summer)
10–16 weeks part time (Fall and Spring)

PRE-REQS

College juniors and seniors; grad students

DEADLINE

Summer .... March 1
Fall and Spring .... Rolling

Those who desire exposure to new exhibitions should head for the Curatorial Department. Interns here spend their time helping the curator track down paintings for upcoming exhibitions. Said one intern: "Locating paintings is detective's work. I was constantly on the phone with other museums, galleries, auction houses, and private owners . . . . Sometimes it was necessary to consult the archives of art magazines to determine the artists and locations of lesser-known paintings." Exhibition preparation also requires interns to do extensive bibliographic research on the featured artist or group of artists. "The curator wanted me to find out what everyone else had said on a particular artist, so I searched [the curator's] archives for every article that had been written about the artist," one intern said. "It was the type of thorough research that one does for a paper in graduate school."

Interns in the Education department perform research for a variety of exhibitions, seminars, symposiums, gallery tours, and films. One intern, for instance, put together material that prepared docents for talks they give to the public. "I spent a lot of time in the Whitney's library gathering background material on artists that the docents would lecture on. [It] gave me a great background in American and contemporary art." Later in her internship, she was asked to create a collection of news articles on the then-raging Robert Mapplethorpe controversy. "After searching dozens of magazines and newspapers, I put together a substantial collection of articles. They were later used for a Whitney symposium on censorship."

Publications and New Media has eleven staff members with the big responsibility of editing and producing all of the Whitney publications, including catalogs, brochures, posters, and calenders of events. Interns here work on a mixed bag of projects—one day they're creating wall labels, the next they're helping with brochures. Working on the production of a postcard book, one intern did everything from organizing the captions to helping select which prints to make into postcards. She also assisted in the publication of an Edward Hopper poster, a Charles Demuth catalog, and program notes for the Film and Video department. "I had no background in creating brochures and catalogs," she said. "But my summer at Whitney was incredibly productive. I left with a good grasp of what publishing is all about."

Housed in an angular building that looks like an "upside-down wedding cake," the Whitney has five floors of galleries in the main Breuer building. The adminstrative offices are housed in three converted brownstones adjacent to the Breuer building on 74th Street. The offices take up five floors and are referred to as the Annex where the interns work. This casual atmosphere is largely due to the museum's relatively small staff of 210, as compared with "Pentagon-size" museums in New York like the Metropolitan Museum of Art, which has two thousand employees. Said one intern: "At other museums, people talk in whispers and are uptight. At the Whitney, the mood is relatively relaxed. Its small size makes for a cozy atmosphere where making friends is easy."

Membership
in Whitney's Internship
Program
has its privileges.

Nothing enhances an internship like seminars and field trips—and fortunately for interns, the Whitney agrees. Every week the Human Resources department arranges a half-day presentation to provide interns with an overview of the museum and career possibilities. Past seminars have featured lectures from department heads as well as films and panel discussions about art. Observed one intern: "The seminars really gave you a sense of the different pieces that work together to make the museum run."

In addition to attending the seminars, interns embark on several afternoon field trips. One week it might be to Sotheby's. The next, to the Studio Museum of Harlem. Next on the agenda is a tour of the Whitney's Permanent Collection storage facility. One of the most influential trips is to the Whitney's Independent Study Program in lower Manhattan, where interns meet with the artists and curatorial fellows who are completing this prestigious fellowship. A number of interns have applied to and completed the Independent Study Program after having been introduced to it during their internship. Said one: "I would never have heard of the Independent Study Program if I hadn't been an intern. I saw how great it could be."

Whenever the Whitney launches a new exhibition, it holds a private "opening" to introduce the artists and their work to selected guests. There's plenty of schmoozing, wine, and hors d'oeuvres—and best of all, interns are invited. It's a heady experience for some: "Openings are definitely a scene—artists and critics abound. It's exciting to know that you're seeing an exhibition before virtually everyone else in the city does." Others see openings through a more cynical lens: "There's a good bit of pretension . . . sometimes it seems that few guests are there to actually look at the artwork." Interns typically get to go to a wide assortment of openings during the internship; one intern, for example, attended openings for exhibitions featuring Jasper Johns and Agnes Martin as well as a Biennial opening.

Membership in Whitney's Internship Program has its privileges. A Whitney Intern ID card is good for free admission to most New York museums; says one intern, "I loved not having to pay the admission fee to the Museum of Modern Art." Interns receive a 33 percent discount at the museum sales desk where they may purchase Whitney-produced items like posters, books, T-shirts, and postcards. They also get 20 percent off on merchandise in the Store Next Door, which stocks hand-crafted items designed by American artists (e.g., ceramics, jewelry, quilts, and watches). Food-seeking interns will be satiated at Sarabeth's at the Whitney, an in-house gourmet restaurant offering a 10 percent discount to museum employees and interns. Best of all, interns receive free admission to museum talks held for the public in the fall and spring. The talks are given by an artist or art critic and have featured such notables as Elizabeth Murray, Yoko Ono, Ross Bleckner, Laurie Anderson, and Barbara Kruger.

SELECTION

 The program primarily looks for college juniors and seniors, though graduate students are selected for appropriate projects. While there are no other pre-reqs save for having "a strong background and interest in American art and/or museum studies," the Curatorial department gives preference to art history majors. International applicants are eligible.

APPLICATION PROCEDURE

 The deadline for the summer internship is March 1; the fall and spring internships have rolling application deadlines. An eight-part application procedure awaits: a resume, a letter of recommendation from a college professor or employer, college transcripts, a list of three museum departments, in order of work preference, proposed beginning and ending dates of internship, housing arrangements, availability for an in-person interview (give dates), and a one-page statement of purpose stating one's reasons for requesting the internship and what one hopes to gain from and contribute to the experience. After reviewing applications, the Human Resources office calls selected applicants for personal interviews; in rare cases, phone interviews may be substituted for live interviews. Since last-minute openings sometimes occur, those not selected for an initial interview, or who are interviewed but not initially accepted, are placed on a waiting list.

OVERVIEW

 In an admirable display of initiative, a recent group of Whitney interns designed and wrote their own four-page "Whitney Interns Newsletter," because—in their words—they "wished to create something that was truly by, for, and interesting to the interns as a group." Things like this happen at the Whitney because by and large interns are happy and staff members are supportive. The Whitney offers interns a unique environment in which to learn the ropes of the museum world—it is a place of ferment, a place unafraid of experimentation. It is also a place where interns are well appreciated. Said one intern: "To the Whitney, interns aren't temporary observers—they're the future. Staff treat interns like protégés and try to get as much knowledge into them as possible. Why? They know some of the interns will return as permanent staff."

FOR MORE INFORMATION . . .

- Whitney Museum of American Art
  Internship Program
  Human Resources
  945 Madison Avenue
  New York, NY 10021
  (212) 570-3600
  Fax: (212) 570-1807

THE WIDMEYER GROUP, INC.

Sometimes slang words capture the essence of meaning in a way conventional words never could. So it is with "spin doctor," a fashionable term defined by the *Random House Webster's Dictionary* as a "press agent skilled at spin control," which is the "attempt to give bias to news coverage, especially a political event."

The Widmeyer Group is a spin doctor extraordinaire. As Washington's fastest-growing independent public relations agency, Widmeyer creates media strategies for leading corporations, foundations, and nonprofit advocacy groups. The realm of public policy and government is one of Widmeyer's specialties. It has written speeches for political candidates and members of Congress, organized national forums for everyone from Ronald Reagan to Bill Clinton, and conducted research for groups like the Rockefeller Foundation and the Secretary of Labor's Commission on Achieving Necessary Skills.

DESCRIPTION

Political scientist or poet, engineer or English major—the Widmeyer internship wants you. The only requirement is an enthusiastic interest in the public relations profession. And for older candidates with previous PR experience, there's a Fellowship program. Fellows do the same type of work as interns but receive a stipend for their efforts.

An internship in public relations is almost sure to include some busywork, and Widmeyer's does. Interns may find themselves photocopying a 400-page report, faxing dozens of press releases, and covering the phones for the receptionist. Every day interns spend the morning clipping and photocopying newspaper articles to keep senior staff abreast of events relevant to Widmeyer's clients. A definite no-brainer, but one that offers some reward: "It kept me clued in to the daily news. Where else do you get to read newspapers as part of your job?"

After their daily two to three hours of mundane work, interns dive into assignments directly related to public relations. Common to all interns is the making of media lists and pitch calls. The former requires one to compile a list of news organizations that may be interested in a client's activities. Consulting news

SELECTIVITY	
Approximate applicant pool: 400	
Interns and Fellows accepted: 15	

COMPENSATION	
Internship: None	
Fellowship: $200/week	

QUALITY OF LIFE	
Upbeat, tightly knit culture; youthful staff; strategy meetings	

LOCATION(S)
Washington, D.C.

FIELD
Public relations

DURATION
12–16 weeks
Summer, Fall, Winter/Spring

PRE-REQS
Internship: Undergrad
Fellowship: Recent grads or grad students w/PR experience.

DEADLINE	
Summer .... April 15	Fall......... August 1
Winter/Spring .... December 1	

industry resource books, interns update the vital statistics (contact person, address, and phone numbers) of various magazines, TV stations, and radio stations. After putting a list together, interns make "pitch calls" to persuade news agencies that a Widmeyer client is worth covering. "I'd telephone a TV station and say, for example, 'So-and-so client has a public service announcement in which your viewers would be interested. Will you use it?'"

Elemental to the work of a public relations firm is putting together the press release—a document sent out to news agencies announcing the activities of a client. Interns are taught how to write an effective press release and then given the chance to compose a few. "I'd first find out everything I could about a client—using background information in the office and phone interviewing representatives of the client. Once I got a complete picture of the client's mission, I'd write it up in press release format . . . . I did this for such clients as Trans Africa and the National Commission to Prevent Infant Mortality." After interns write a press release, it is edited by the staff member assigned to that particular client. "My supervisor made excellent suggestions on how to improve the press releases I wrote," said an intern. "With his guidance, I quickly became proficient at putting together high-quality press releases."

When clients want widespread exposure on television or radio, Widmeyer will often arrange a satellite media-tour. This tactic involves having a spokesperson for the client answer questions via satellite transmission from reporters around the country. It's a complicated production—one that definitely benefits from the help of interns. Spending hours on the phone, interns make pitch calls to get news organizations to participate. They also help out at the video studio where the actual satellite interviews take place. "At one [satellite media tour], I'd call the reporters who were scheduled to participate and let them know they were on. And I'd sometimes hold up

> **Widmeyer is a positive, forward-moving place. There is delightfully little of the office politics and backbiting you see at larger, mass-production firms.**

cue cards for the client if he needed to be reminded of a fact or statistic."

Sometimes interns' work is as simple as distributing press passes at an event. As humdrum as it seems, this task puts interns in some exciting settings. One intern attended a few press conferences, where in addition to signing in members of the press, he handed out press kits and background bulletins about the client sponsoring the conference. "Checking in the reporters as they arrived, I stood in the doorway and tried to look important. Playing the gatekeeper was fun." Another intern was asked to distribute press passes at the HFStival, a rock concert sponsored by one of Widmeyer's clients, Washington radio station WHFS. "Over a few hours, I handed out [the passes] to reporters from MTV, ABC, and the like. But for the most part, I watched a great concert—which featured such bands as INXS and the Posies—and roamed around backstage, where there was plenty of free food and free compact discs."

The Widmeyer experience is augmented by a few extracurricular opportunities. Interns are welcome to sit in on company strategy meetings, where account executives discuss how they should approach a client's publicity needs. "I mostly watched," said an intern. "But I made a few suggestions—which were warmly received. The permanent staff was excited that I wanted to make a contribution." And on rare occasions, interns get to travel, like the two who were sent on a four-day trip to Pittsburgh to help out at a convention of the American Federation of Teachers.

Widmeyer has the dubious distinction of being situated only paces away from the Washington Hilton, the hotel where President Ronald Reagan was shot. Infamy aside, the neighborhood—Dupont Circle—happens to be one of Washington's liveliest, with a plethora of cafes, ethnic restaurants, and movie theaters. The Widmeyer office is located in a modern, ten-floor office building.

Senior staff have their own offices, but interns and young associates work at six-person pods, where each worker has his or her own desk space, phone, and computer. The office keeps a refrigerator stocked with free soda and mineral water. There's also a concierge in the lobby of the building with whom employees can leave their dry cleaning.

A definite advantage to working at Widmeyer is the agency's small size. Said one intern, "There are only about 25 employees, including the interns. It makes for a homey atmosphere. Everyone seems happy working here." Relative to other public relations firms, Widmeyer is young—with regard to both the age of its employees and its corporate philosophy. "It's a youthful, social place," said an intern. "Many of the executives I worked with weren't much older than me." Added another: "Widmeyer is a positive, forward-moving place. There is delightfully little of the office politics and backbiting you see at larger, mass-production firms." Office morale is sustained in part by opportunities to loosen up. Every Friday is a "casual day," where employees dress in comfortable clothes (no jeans, though). Some Friday afternoons find the office holding a happy hour— "Around five or so, we'd kick back with a beer. It was a great way to start the weekend."

The one recurrent complaint among Widmeyer interns involves the long days they work. Said one intern: "You work from 9:00 to 5:30—technically. In reality, you sometimes stay as late as seven o'clock. That's a long day to be putting in without being paid any salary." Added another: "It was assumed that we'd stay as late as it took to get a project done. At times staying late became tiring."

SELECTION

 The internship program is open to undergraduates of any level; no previous experience in public relations is required. The Fellowship program is geared toward recent graduates with prior public relations experience or graduate students in journalism, media relations, political science, marketing, or communications. International applicants are eligible.

APPLICATION PROCEDURE

 The application deadline for summer internships is April 15; for fall internships, August 1; and for winter/spring internships, December 1. A word to the tardy: The internship coordinator may accept applications a few days after the deadline; call for details. The application process is relatively simple: Send in a cover letter, resume, and a few brief writing samples. Interviews are conducted in person or over the phone.

OVERVIEW

 Scott Widmeyer, the 39-year-old president of the Widmeyer Group, is no stranger to internships. Before founding the agency that bears his name, he worked for both President Carter's re-election campaign, which hired "a lot of excellent interns," and the American Federation of Teachers, where he started its internship program. Widmeyer was even once an intern himself, beginning his career interning for a Maryland newspaper. There he "gain[ed] valuable practical experience" and realized how "internships can raise a person's level of understanding about an industry."

Widmeyer's appreciation for interns comes through in his agency's program. Interns are made to feel part of the Widmeyer family, whether working directly on public relations projects or taking care of clerical work. Said one intern: "The fact that Widmeyer is not a multicity public relations giant is clearly a virtue. Interns get to break into the field of public relations in an intimate, progressive setting."

FOR MORE INFORMATION . . .

■ Paul Stilp, Internship Coordinator
The Widmeyer Group
1825 Connecticut Avenue, NW
5th Floor
Washington, DC 20009
(202) 667-0901
Fax: (202) 667-0902
fellowships@twbg.com

WOLF TRAP FOUNDATION
FOR THE PERFORMING ARTS

SELECTIVITY 🔍🔍🔍

Approximate applicant pool: 150
Interns accepted: 20

COMPENSATION 💲

$150/week stipend

QUALITY OF LIFE 🌴🌴🌴🌴

Park setting; free tickets; brown-bag lunches with guest speakers; diverse intern class; field trip

LOCATION(S)

Vienna, VA

FIELD

Theater production and arts management

DURATION

12 weeks
Summer (full time); Fall and Spring (part time)

PRE-REQS

College sophomores, juniors, seniors;
recent grads; grad students

DEADLINE

Summer ...... March 1   Fall .... July 1
Spring .... November 1

The Wolf Trap Foundation for the Performing Arts does things a little differently. Whereas major performance centers are typically found wedged in the canyons of an urban landscape, Wolf Trap is situated on an expanse of Virginia farmland. While most prestigious arts organizations stage their performances in stuffy, chandelier-lined theaters, Wolf Trap has an open-air amphitheater with thousands of lawn seats. Despite the fact that the majority of performance centers focus primarily, if not entirely, on programming events, Wolf Trap performs public service through a variety of educational programs for children.

But just because Wolf Trap prefers moonlight to chandeliers and retains a social conscience doesn't mean it's minor league. Since its founding in 1968, the organization has attracted performers of every kind, including Bob Dylan, James Brown, Leonard Bernstein, Beverly Sills, Sammy Davis, Jr., Johnny Cash, and Dolly Parton. It is also home to the Wolf Trap Opera Company, one of America's outstanding career-entry programs for young singers.

DESCRIPTION

While Wolf Trap offers a few part-time intern positions in the fall and spring, the vast majority of students complete the full-time summer internship. During the summer, the organization places a few interns in each of the following departments: the Wolf Trap Opera Company, Opera Administration, Institute for Education (Early Learning Through the Arts), Development and Special Events, Accounting, Public Affairs, Human Resources, Special Programs, and Public Affairs.

BUSYWORK METER
LOW — MEDIUM — HIGH
OLDMAN & HAMADEH

Only one department gives interns hands-on experience in theater production—the Wolf Trap Opera Company. In season from June to August, the company assigns interns tasks in stage management, carpentry, scenic painting, lighting, props, costuming, wigs, and makeup. Those who lack experience in technical theater but still yearn for close contact with the opera may intern in Opera Administration. Here, interns perform jobs that help keep the opera running, such as assisting in the development and distribution of promotional materials, coordinating housing and transportation arrangements for singers and staff, updating repertoire lists, and assisting in the procurement and distribution of orchestra music.

While interns in other departments do not have direct contact with the theater, they are still given important assignments. Development interns, for example, research and prepare reports on potential donors. Said one: "This wasn't the typical empty-the-trash internship—I had to use real skills. My supervisor asked me to investigate the giving histories of various donors and prospects. I consulted reference materials and made a lot of calls." After the intern researched potential donors, the director of Development would call some of them and make a formal solicitation. Every so often, a prospect he researched panned out: "I did background research on the Virginia Commission for the Arts—and they ended up giving Wolf Trap a grant . . . . It was good to see that some of my work paid off."

If one had to pick the least glamorous department at Wolf Trap, it would have be Accounting. Accounting interns "do a little of everything" with the foundation's financial activities, whether it be writing financial reports, maintaining a computerized deposit log of ticket receipts, or—for lack of a jazzier phrase—counting cash. Despite these dry tasks, Accounting interns sometimes have direct contact with the public, which may add a little zest to an otherwise monotonous day. One intern was asked to call ticket buyers who had used bad checks or credit cards. "It was kind of fun. A few people would come up with the darnedest stories as to why their payment didn't go through. One guy practically gave me his life's story, complete with the details of how his ex-girlfriend was responsible for his lack of funds."

A unique aspect of Wolf Trap is its Institute for Education. Established in 1981 under a grant from the federal government's Head Start program, the Institute trains teachers in the use of performing arts techniques that help young children learn basic academic concepts (e.g., shapes and colors) as well as life skills (e.g., hand washing, sharing, and problem solving). Interns in this department assist the professional actors, musicians, and storytellers who run such innovative workshops as "Singable Songs for Non-Singers," "Using Gestures and Drama for Language Development," and "Songs and Stories about Science and Nature." They also help plan special performances attended by preschool students from the Washington, D.C., area.

Interns are often struck by the academic and geographic diversity of their peers. As there are no academic prerequisites (except for positions with the Opera Company), the program attracts students from all disciplines, some with a vocational interest in arts management, others just curious about what makes an arts center tick. Because Wolf Trap is nationally known, students come from all over the country to complete the internship. In recent years students have come from a majority of states, including Wisconsin, Iowa, Alabama, Maine, and New Mexico.

There's plenty of entertainment when interns want it. First and foremost, they receive two complimentary tickets to every performance and they're sure to be pleased with at least one, as Wolf Trap "endeavors to schedule something for everyone." Past interns not only have had access to first-rate operas but also have been able to take in a range of shows, from Bill Cosby to symphonies. If pre- or post-performance discussions are held in conjunction with the show, interns are welcome to attend. They may also view dress rehearsals of the Wolf Trap Opera Company, where the company "performs without stops—unless a major problem arises." About three times during the summer, the intern coordinator schedules brown-bag lunches, where interns may cross-examine a department head about his or her role in the organization.

If skyscrapers, subways, and concrete are requisite surroundings, then read no farther. But if a "glorious"

> If a "glorious" wooded wonderland stocked with wildlife sounds alluring, then Wolf Trap hits the target.

wooded wonderland stocked with wildlife sounds alluring, then Wolf Trap hits the target. Wolf Trap doesn't just seem like a park—it is one. A half-hour's drive from Washington, D.C., the organization is nestled among the flora and fauna of the Wolf Trap Farm Park, the country's only national park for the performing arts. On the park's 168 acres are the Filene Center, a cedar-wood amphitheater seating more than 7,000, and the Barns of Wolf Trap, a performance facility that houses the Wolf Trap Opera Company during the summer months. Joining the theaters is a motley assortment of farm houses that have been converted into administration buildings. Interns are spread out among these "kooky little houses," some of which are log cabins. The setting has a distinct *Green Acres* feel to it: "From a window in my office I'd see all sorts of wildlife . . . deer, rabbits, groundhogs. Once I even saw a stray goat."

SELECTION

 The Wolf Trap internship is for college sophomores, juniors, and seniors, as well as recent graduates and graduate students. Most departments have no prerequisites save for strong writing skills and familiarity with computers. The Wolf Trap Opera Company, however, requires prior experience in technical theater, and Public Affairs–Photography expects its interns to have access to basic camera equipment. Consult the internship brochure for more details. International applicants are eligible.

APPLICATION PROCEDURE

 The application deadline for the summer internship is March 1; for the fall, July 1; and for spring, November 1. Submit a cover letter (including a brief personal statement and outline of career goals), resume, two references (academic or professional), and two contrasting samples of writing. After the coordinator screens the initial applicant pool, each department head chooses a handful of interns to interview. The majority of interviews take place over the phone, but in-person meetings can be arranged.

OVERVIEW

 Wolf Trap is the type of venue that encourages its patrons to kick off their shoes, quaff a few glasses of wine, and enjoy first-rate performances in a parklike setting. Similarly, interns at Wolf Trap gain valuable theater-operations experience in a hassle-free and uniquely pastoral environment. Unlike the plethora of performing arts organizations who've suffered in these uneven economic times, Wolf Trap remains robust financially, so its interns can be sure that the organization has the resources to ensure students a rewarding internship. For aspiring arts administrators or those who just want a taste of the footlights, the Wolf Trap internship is a worthy backstage pass to the world of arts management.

FOR MORE INFORMATION . . .

■ Wolf Trap Foundation for the Performing Arts
Intern Coordinator
1624 Trap Road
Vienna, VA 22182
(703) 255-1933
www.wolf-trap.org

APPENDIX

HIGHEST COMPENSATION

J.P. Morgan & Co.
The Washington Post
Microsoft
Sponsors for Educational Opportunity
Hallmark Cards
Ford Motor Company
Raychem
Union Carbide
The Wall Street Journal
Symantec
Hewlett-Packard
Arthur Andersen
Procter & Gamble
Chevron
Mattel, Inc.
Frito-Lay
Boeing
Kraft Foods, Inc.
Abbott Laboratories

MOST SELECTIVE

New York Yankees
Reebok
Lincoln Center for the Performing Arts
Late Show with David Letterman
Microsoft
Raychem
Kraft Foods, Inc.
Hallmark Cards
John Wiley & Sons
Rolling Stone
Supreme Court of the United States
The Wall Street Journal
Academy of Television Arts & Sciences
Hill and Knowlton
NBA
Boeing
Coors Brewing Company
NIKE
The Washington Post
The Widmeyer Group
Vault.com
Abbott Laboratories
National Wildlife Federation
Federal Bureau of Investigation
Creamer Dickson Basford
Northwestern Mutual Financial Network
Ruder Finn

HIGHEST QUALITY OF LIFE

Abbott Laboratories
American Association of Advertising Agencies
Aspen Center for Environmental Studies
Boeing
Ford Motor Company
Hewlett-Packard
Microsoft
NIKE
Symantec
United States Olympic Committee

DEADLINES BEFORE JANUARY 1 (FOR SUMMER)

Federal Bureau of Investigation (November 1)
United States Department of State
     (November 1—Student Intern Program)
The Washington Post (November 1)
The Wall Street Journal (Thanksgiving)
Central Intelligence Agency (November 30)
Environmental Protection Agency (December)
Washington Internships for Students of Engineering
     (December)
Lucent Technologies Bell Laboratories (December 1—
     SRP only)
National Aeronautics and Space Administration
     (December 31≠—a few programs only)
3M (December 31)

DEADLINES AFTER MARCH 1 (FOR SUMMER)

Summerbridge National (March 1)
Crow Canyon Archaeological Center (Early
     March—same for the two fall and one winter
     programs)
Symantec (March 7)
Supreme Court of the United States (March 10)
Academy of Television Arts & Sciences (March 15)
The Carter Center (March 15)
Genentech (March 15)
Reebok (March 15)
National Wildlife Federation (March 15—July to
     December internship)
Butterfield & Butterfield (March 30)
Lucasfilm/Lucas Digital (March 30)
Rolling Stone (March 30)
Frito-Lay (March 31)
Kraft Foods, Inc. (March 31)
Mattel, Inc. (March 31)
Random House (March 31)

Sony Music Entertainment (March 31—Minority
    Internship only)
Union Carbide (March 31)
United Nations Association of the United States of
    America (March 31)
American Enterprise Institute (April 1)
Ford Motor Company (April 1)
Georgetown Criminal Justice Clinic (April 1)
Library of Congress (April 1)
Public Defender Service for D.C. (April 1)
Raychem (April 1)
National Aeronautics and Space Administration
    (April 1—a few programs only)
Ruder Finn (April 1)
Rosenbluth International (April/May)
The Hermitage (April 10)
American Conservatory Theater (April 15)
The Widmeyer Group (April 15)
Hewlett-Packard (April 30)
Center for Investigative Reporting (May 1)
Liz Claiborne (May 1)
See also Rolling Deadlines

ROLLING DEADLINES

Atlantic Records (Internship only)
Bates USA
Bertelsmann Music Group
Chevron (until January)
Central Intelligence Agency (grad students)
Creamer Dickson Basford (fall and spring)
Elite Model Management
The Environmental Careers Organization
The Feminist Majority
Frontier Nursing Service
Hill, Holliday, Connors, Cosmopulos, Inc. Advertising
Intel
Marvel Comics
Microsoft
MTV: Music Television
National Audubon Society
New York Yankees
Northwestern Mutual Financial Network
QVC
Rosenbluth International
Sony Music Entertainment (Credited Internship only)
Student Conservation Association
Surfrider Foundation
Symantec
Universal Studios
Vault.com
Volkswagen
Whitney Museum of American Art (fall and spring
    only)

INTERNSHIPS OPEN TO HIGH SCHOOL STUDENTS

Atlantic Records
The Feminist Majority
Hewlett-Packard
Inroads
MTV: Music Television
National Aeronautics and Space Administration
Smithsonian Institution
Student Conservation Association
Summerbridge National
Vault.com

INTERNSHIPS OPEN TO COLLEGE FRESHMEN

American Civil Liberties Union
American Enterprise Institute
Atlantic Records
Bertelsmann Music Group
Center for Investigative Reporting
Chevron
Elite Model Management
The Environmental Careers Organization (DI only)
Environmental Protection Agency
The Feminist Majority
Ford Motor Company
Frontier Nursing Service
Inroads
Johns Hopkins University Center for Talented Youth
Intel
The Kennedy Center
Late Show with David Letterman
Liz Claiborne
Mattel, Inc.
The Metropolitan Museum of Art (The Cloisters only)
MTV: Music Television
National Aeronautics and Space Administration
National Institutes of Health
National Public Radio
New York Yankees
Northwestern Mutual Financial Network
Public Defender Service for D.C.
QVC
Rolling Stone
Rosenbluth International
Smithsonian Institution
Sony Music Entertainment
Student Conservation Association
Summerbridge National
Surfrider Foundation
Symantec
Union Carbide
United Nations Association of the United States of
    America

Universal Studios
Vault.com
Volkswagen
The Wall Street Journal
Weyerhaeuser
The White House
The Widmeyer Group

INTERNSHIPS OPEN TO COLLEGE SOPHOMORES

Abbott Laboratories
Academy of Television Arts & Sciences
American Association of Advertising Agencies
American Civil Liberties Union
American Conservatory Theater
American Enterprise Institute
Atlantic Records
Bertelsmann Music Group
Boeing
Center for Investigative Reporting
Chevron
Coors Brewing Company (Public Relations only)
Elite Model Management
The Environmental Careers Organization (DI only)
Environmental Protection Agency
The Feminist Majority
Ford Motor Company
Frontier Nursing Service
Genentech
Hewlett-Packard
Hill, Holliday, Connors, Cosmopulos, Inc. Advertising
Inroads
Johns Hopkins University Center for Talented Youth
Intel
J.P. Morgan & Co.
The Kennedy Center
Kraft Foods, Inc.
Late Show with David Letterman
Liz Claiborne
Lucent Technologies Bell Laboratories (SRP only)
Mattel, Inc.
The Metropolitan Museum of Art (The Cloisters only)
Microsoft
MTV: Music Television
National Aeronautics and Space Administration
National Basketball Association
National Institutes of Health
National Public Radio
New York Yankees
Northwestern Mutual Financial Network
Procter & Gamble
Public Defender Service for D.C.

QVC
Rolling Stone
Rosenbluth International
Smithsonian Institution
Sony Music Entertainment
Sponsors for Educational Opportunity
Student Conservation Association
Summerbridge National
Surfrider Foundation
Symantec
3M
Union Carbide
United Nations Association of the United States of
    America
Universal Studios
Urban Fellows/Government Scholars Programs
Vault.com
Volkswagen
The Wall Street Journal
Weyerhaeuser
The White House
The Widmeyer Group
Wolf Trap Foundation for the Performing Arts

INTERNSHIPS OPEN TO COLLEGE JUNIORS

Every program, except:
The Coro Foundation
Creamer Dickson Basford
Lincoln Center for the Performing Arts
Merrill Lynch
National Wildlife Federation
Phillips Academy
Washington Internships for Students of Engineering

INTERNSHIPS OPEN TO COLLEGE SENIORS

Every program, except:
The Coro Foundation
Federal Bureau of Investigation
Hallmark Cards
Inroads
John Wiley & Sons
Lincoln Center for the Performing Arts
National Basketball Association
National Wildlife Federation
Phillips Academy
Random House

INTERNSHIPS OPEN TO RECENT COLLEGE GRADUATES

Academy of Television Arts & Sciences
American Civil Liberties Union
American Conservatory Theater

American Enterprise Institute
Aspen Center for Environmental Studies
Brookfield Zoo
Butterfield & Butterfield
The Carter Center
Center for Investigative Reporting
Chevron
The Coro Foundation
Creamer Dickson Basford
The Environmental Careers Organization
Frontier Nursing Service
Georgetown Criminal Justice Clinic
The Hermitage
The Kennedy Center
The Library of Congress
The Metropolitan Museum of Art
National Audubon Society
National Institutes of Health
National Public Radio
National Wildlife Federation
Phillips Academy
Public Defender Service for D.C.
Reebok
Rolling Stone
Rosenbluth International
Ruder Finn
Smithsonian Institution
Sponsors for Educational Opportunity (Corporate
     Law program only)
Student Conservation Association
Summerbridge National
Supreme Court of the United States
Surfrider Foundation
United Nations Association of the United States of
     America
United States Department of State
Urban Fellows/Government Scholars Programs
Vault.com
The Wall Street Journal (graduating seniors)
The White House
The Widmeyer Group
Wolf Trap Foundation for the Performing Arts

INTERNSHIPS OPEN TO GRADUATE STUDENTS

Abbott Laboratories
Academy of Television Arts & Sciences
American Association of Advertising Agencies
American Civil Liberties Union
American Enterprise Institute
AT&T Bell Laboratories (UR only)
Aspen Center for Environmental Studies
Atlantic Records

Bates USA
Bertelsmann Music Group
Brookfield Zoo
The Brookings Institution
Butterfield & Butterfield
The Carter Center
Center for Investigative Reporting
Central Intelligence Agency
Chevron
CNN
Coors Brewing Company
Creamer Dickson Basford
Crow Canyon Archaeological Center
The Environmental Careers Organization
Environmental Protection Agency
Federal Bureau of Investigation
The Feminist Majority
Ford Motor Company
Frito-Lay
Frontier Nursing Service
Genentech
Georgetown Criminal Justice Clinic
Hallmark Cards
The Hermitage
Hewlett-Packard
Hill and Knowlton
Hill, Holliday, Connors, Cosmopulos, Inc. Advertising
Johns Hopkins University Center for Talented Youth
Intel
The Kennedy Center
Kraft Foods, Inc.
The Library of Congress
Lincoln Center for the Performing Arts
Lucasfilm/Lucas Digital
Mattel, Inc.
The Metropolitan Museum of Art
Microsoft
MTV: Music Television
National Aeronautics and Space Administration
National Audubon Society
National Institutes of Health
National Public Radio
National Wildlife Federation
New York Yankees
NIKE
Northwestern Mutual Financial Network
Phillips Academy
Procter & Gamble
Public Defender Service for D.C.
Random House
Raychem
Reebok

Rosenbluth International
Smithsonian Institution
Sony Music Entertainment
Sponsors for Educational Opportunity
Student Conservation Association
Surfrider Foundation
Symantec
3M
Union Carbide
United Nations Association of the United States of
    America
United States Department of State
United States Olympic Committee
Universal Studios
Vault.com
The Wall Street Journal
The Washington Post
Weyerhaeuser
The White House
Whitney Museum of American Art
The Widmeyer Group
Wolf Trap Foundation for the Performing Arts

INTERNSHIPS OPEN TO COLLEGE GRADUATES OF ANY AGE

American Civil Liberties Union
American Conservatory Theater
Brookfield Zoo
Butterfield & Butterfield
Center for Investigative Reporting
Chevron
The Coro Foundation
Creamer Dickson Basford
The Environmental Careers Organization
Frontier Nursing Service (high school graduates of
    any age)
Georgetown Criminal Justice Clinic
National Wildlife Federation
Smithsonian Institution
Student Conservation Association

INTERNSHIPS OPEN TO INTERNATIONAL APPLICANTS (NON—U.S. CITIZENS)

Every program, except:
Central Intelligence Agency
Federal Bureau of Investigation
Inroads
Phillips Academy
United States Department of State
The White House

INTERNSHIPS WITH MINORITY PROGRAMS

(M = Minority Internship is the only program available)
American Association of Advertising Agencies (M)
Central Intelligence Agency
The Environmental Careers Organization
Hallmark Cards
Inroads (M)
Intel
J.P. Morgan & Co.
Lucent Technologies Bell Laboratories
National Aeronautics and Space Administration
Sony Music Entertainment
Sponsors for Educational Opportunity (M)
Student Conservation Association (M)

INTERNSHIPS AVAILABLE DURING THE SUMMER

Every program, except:
American Conservatory Theater
The Coro Foundation
Skadden, Arps, Slate, Meagher & Flom

INTERNSHIPS AVAILABLE DURING THE ACADEMIC YEAR

American Civil Liberties Union
American Conservatory Theater
American Enterprise Institute
Arthur Andersen
Atlantic Records
Bates USA
Bertelsmann Music Group
Boeing
Brookfield Zoo
The Brookings Institution
Butterfield & Butterfield
The Carter Center
Center for Investigative Reporting
Central Intelligence Agency (grad students)
CNN
The Coro Foundation
Creamer Dickson Basford
Crow Canyon Archaeological Center
Elite Model Management
The Environmental Careers Organization
Environmental Protection Agency
The Feminist Majority
Frontier Nursing Service
Hill and Knowlton
Hill, Holliday, Connors, Cosmopulos, Inc. Advertising
Intel
The Kennedy Center
Late Show with David Letterman

Liz Claiborne
Lucasfilm/Lucas Digital
Marvel Comics
Microsoft
MTV: Music Television
National Audubon Society
National Basketball Association
National Public Radio
National Wildlife Federation
New York Yankees
Nightline
Northwestern Mutual Financial Network
Public Defender Service for D.C.
QVC
Rolling Stone
Rosenbluth International
Ruder Finn
Skadden, Arps, Slate, Meaghers & Flom
Smithsonian Institution
Sony Music Entertainment (Credited Internship only)
Student Conservation Association
Supreme Court of the United States
Surfrider Foundation
Symantec
Union Carbide
United Nations Association of the United States of
     America
United States Department of State
United States Olympic Committee
Urban Fellows/Government Scholars Programs
     (Urban Fellows Program only)
Vault.com
Volkswagen
Weyerhaeuser
The White House
Whitney Museum of American Art
The Widmeyer Group
Wolf Trap Foundation for the Performing Arts

FREE HOUSING

Abbott Laboratories
Aspen Center for Environmental Studies
Crow Canyon Archaeological Center
Ford Motor Company
Frontier Nursing Service
The Hermitage
Johns Hopkins University Center for Talented Youth
Microsoft (first two weeks only)
National Aeronautics and Space Administration
     (some programs only)
Phillips Academy
Student Conservation Association

Summerbridge National
Union Carbide
United States Department of State
     (overseas interns only)
United States Olympic Committee

HOUSING ARRANGEMENTS AVAILABLE

AT&T Bell Laboratories
Boeing
Central Intelligence Agency
Federal Bureau of Investigation
Intel
Lincoln Center for the Performing Arts
Microsoft
Procter & Gamble
3M
Volkswagen
Washington Internships for Students of Engineering

FREE MEALS

American Enterprise Institute
Aspen Center for Environmental Studies
Crow Canyon Archaeological Center
Frontier Nursing Service
The Hermitage
Johns Hopkins University Center for Talented Youth
Phillips Academy
Public Defender Service for D.C.
Student Conservation Association
Summerbridge National
United States Olympic Committee

CARS PROVIDED

Frontier Nursing Service
Microsoft
National Aeronautics and Space Administration
     (Goddard's Summer Institute)
Procter & Gamble (Sales interns only)

ROUND-TRIP TRAVEL COVERED

Abbott Laboratories
Academy of Television Arts and Sciences
Boeing
Central Intelligence Agency
Chevron
Ford Motor Company
Frito-Lay
Hewlett-Packard
Intel
Lucent Technologies Bell Laboratories
Microsoft

NIKE
National Aeronautics and Space Administration
    (some programs only)
Procter & Gamble
Raychem
Union Carbide
United States Department of State
    (some programs only)
Vault.com
Weyerhaeuser
Washington Internships for Students of Engineering

SCHOLARSHIPS AVAILABLE

The Coro Foundation
Hewlett-Packard (high school students only)
Lucent Technologies Bell Laboratories
Smithsonian Institution
Student Conservation Association
Summerbridge National
Supreme Court of the United States
United States Department of State

FITNESS FACILITIES AVAILABLE

Abbott Laboratories
Boeing
The Carter Center
Central Intelligence Agency
Chevron
Coors Brewing Company
Federal Bureau of Investigation
Ford Motor Company
Frito-Lay
Frontier Nursing Service
Hallmark Cards
Hewlett-Packard
Hill, Holliday, Connors, Cosmopulos, Inc. Advertising
Genentech
Intel
Johns Hopkins University Center for Talented Youth
Kraft Foods, Inc.
Lucasfilm/Lucas Digital
Lucent Technologies Bell Laboratories
Mattel, Inc.
Microsoft
National Aeronautics and Space Administration
National Institutes of Health
NIKE
Phillips Academy
Procter & Gamble
Reebok
Smithsonian Institution

Supreme Court of the United States
United States Department of State
United States Olympic Committee
Weyerhaeuser

PART-TIME AVAILABLE

Atlantic Records (college reps)
Bates USA
Bertelsmann Music Group
Brookfield Zoo
The Brookings Institution
Butterfield & Butterfield
The Carter Center
Center for Investigative Reporting
Elite Model Management
Environmental Protection Agency
The Feminist Majority
Hill, Holliday, Connors, Cosmopulos, Inc. Advertising
    (fall and spring)
Liz Claiborne
MTV: Music Television
National Public Radio
Nightline
Northwestern Mutual Financial Network
QVC
Smithsonian Institution
Symatec
United Nations Association of the United States of
    America
Universal Studios
Vault.com
Wolf Trap Foundation for the Performing Arts

CASUAL DRESS ALLOWED

Academy of Television Arts & Sciences
American Civil Liberties Union
Aspen Center for Environmental Studies
Brookfield Zoo
Crow Canyon Archaeological Center
Elite Model Management
Frontier Nursing Service
Genentech
The Hermitage
Hewlett-Packard
Intel
Johns Hopkins University Center for Talented Youth
The Library of Congress
Marvel Comics
The Metropolitan Museum of Art
Microsoft
MTV: Music Television

National Audubon Society
National Institutes of Health
National Public Radio
National Wildlife Federation
NIKE
Procter & Gamble
Random House
Raychem
Reebok
Rolling Stone
Summerbridge National
Surfrider Foundation
Vault.com
Washington Internships for Students of Engineering

HIGH PROPORTION OF MALES OR FEMALES

The Feminist Majority (female)
Marvel Comics (male)
The Metropolitan Museum of Art (female)
Random House (female)
Whitney Museum of American Art (female)

OPPORTUNITIES FOR STAR-GAZING

Academy of Television Arts & Sciences
American Conservatory Theater
American Enterprise Institute
Aspen Center for Environmental Studies
Academy of Television Arts & Sciences
The Brookings Institution
Butterfield & Butterfield
CNN
The Kennedy Center
Late Show with David Letterman
Lincoln Center for the Performing Arts
Lucasfilm/Lucas Digital
MTV: Music Television
National Basketball Association
New York Yankees
Nightline
Sotheby's
United States Olympic Committee
The White House

GOOD PROSPECTS FOR PERMANENT EMPLOYMENT

(Approximately 50 Percent or More of Former Interns
    Offered Jobs)
Academy of Television Arts & Sciences
Atlantic Records
Bertelsmann Music Group
Chevron
Ford Motor Company

Frito-Lay
Hewlett-Packard
Inroads
Intel
J.P. Morgan & Co.
Kraft Foods, Inc.
Marvel Comics
Procter & Gamble
Random House
Reebok
Ruder Finn
Sponsors for Educational Opportunity
3M
Union Carbide
Weyerhaeuser

INTERNSHIPS BY INTEREST

ACCOUNTING

Abbott Laboratories
Arthur Andersen
Boeing
Chevron
Coors Brewing Company
Federal Bureau of Investigation
Hallmark Cards
Hewlett-Packard
Hill, Holliday, Connors, Cosmopulos, Inc. Advertising
Inroads
Intel
J.P. Morgan & Co.
Lucasfilm/Lucas Digital
Mattel, Inc.
National Aeronautics and Space Administration
NIKE
Procter & Gamble
QVC
Raychem
Reebok
Sponsors for Educational Opportunity
United States Department of State
United States Olympic Committee
Weyerhaeuser
Wolf Trap Foundation for the Performing Arts

ADVERTISING

American Association of Advertising Agencies
Bates USA
Hill, Holliday, Connors, Cosmopulos, Inc. Advertising
The Kennedy Center
MTV: Music Television

Procter & Gamble
QVC
Rolling Stone
Rosenbluth International
TBWA/Chiat/Day

AEROSPACE
Boeing
Inroads
National Aeronautics and Space Administration
Smithsonian Institution

AIDS
Abbott Laboratories (science research)
American Civil Liberties Union
Genentech (science research)
National Institutes of Health (science research)
Urban Fellows/Government Scholars Programs
    (policy)

ARCHITECTURE
United States Department of State

ARCHAEOLOGY
Crow Canyon Archaeological Center
The Hermitage
Student Conservation Association

ART
See Museums/Auction Houses

AUCTION HOUSES
See Museums/Auction Houses

AUTOMOBILES
Ford Motor Company
Volkswagen

BANKING/MANAGEMENT/
CONSULTING/ECONOMICS/FINANCE
Abbott Laboratories
American Enterprise Institute
Arthur Andersen
Central Intelligence Agency
Frito-Lay
Genentech
Hallmark Cards
Hewlett-Packard
Inroads
Intel

J.P. Morgan & Co.
John Wiley & Sons
Kraft Foods, Inc.
Lincoln Center for the Performing Arts
Liz Claiborne
Lucasfilm/Lucas Digital
Merrill Lynch
Microsoft
National Aeronautics and Space Administration
NIKE
Procter & Gamble
QVC
Raychem
Reebok
Sony Music Entertainment
Sponsors for Educational Opportunity
3M
Urban Fellows/Government Scholars Programs
United States Department of State
Volkswagen
The Wall Street Journal
The Washington Post
Weyerhaeuser
The White House

BIOTECHNOLOGY
Genentech
Inroads
National Aeronautics and Space Administration
Washington Internships for Students of Engineering
    (policy)

CAREER DEVELOPMENT
The Coro Foundation
The Environmental Careers Organization
Inroads
Sponsors for Educational Opportunity

CHEMICALS/PHARMACEUTICALS
Abbott Laboratories
Chevron
Genentech
Inroads
Union Carbide

CLOTHING
Inroads
Liz Claiborne
NIKE
Reebok

COMPUTERS/INFORMATION SYSTEMS/ELECTRONICS

Abbott Laboratories
Boeing
Central Intelligence Agency
Environmental Protection Agency
Frito-Lay
Hallmark Cards
Hewlett-Packard
Inroads
Intel
Kraft Foods, Inc.
Liz Claiborne
Lucasfilm/Lucas Digital
Lucent Technologies Bell Laboratories
Microsoft
National Aeronautics and Space Administration
National Institutes of Health
Procter & Gamble
QVC
Raychem
Reebok
Symantec
3M
United States Department of State
United States Olympic Committee
Vault.com
Washington Internships for Students of Engineering (policy)
Weyerhaeuser

CONSUMER GOODS

Coors Brewing Company
Frito-Lay
Hallmark Cards
Inroads
Kraft Foods, Inc.
Mattel, Inc.
Procter & Gamble
3M

DESIGN (ART, GRAPHIC, AND/OR TEXTILE)

Brookfield Zoo
Central Intelligence Agency
Hallmark Cards (minority programs only)
Hill, Holliday, Connors, Cosmopulos, Inc. Advertising
Liz Claiborne
Lucasfilm/Lucas Digital
Marvel Comics
Mattel, Inc.

MTV: Music Television
NIKE
Reebok
Sotheby's

ECONOMICS

See Banking/Management Consulting/Economics/Finance

EDUCATION

See Teaching/Education

ELECTRONICS

See Computers/Information Systems/Electronics

ENGINEERING/HIGH TECHNOLOGY/MANUFACTURING

Abbott Laboratories
Boeing
Central Intelligence Agency
The Coro Foundation
Coors Brewing Company
The Environmental Careers Organization
Federal Bureau of Investigation
Frito-Lay
Genentech
Hallmark Cards
Hewlett-Packard
Inroads
Intel
Kraft Foods, Inc.
Lucent Technologies Bell Laboratories
Microsoft
National Aeronautics and Space Administration
National Institutes of Health
National Public Radio
Procter & Gamble
Raychem
Ruder Finn (High Tech account)
3M
United States Department of State
Washington Internships for Students in Engineering
Weyerhaeuser

ENTERTAINMENT/FILM/TELEVISION

Academy of Television Arts & Sciences
Atlantic Records
Bertelsmann Music Group
CNN
Late Show with David Letterman

Lucasfilm/Lucas Digital
Marvel Comics
MTV: Music Television
National Basketball Association
National Public Radio
New York Yankees
Nightline
QVC
Rolling Stone
Ruder Finn (Translink account)
Sony Music Entertainment
United States Olympic Committee
Universal Studios

ENVIRONMENT/NATURE
Aspen Center for Environmental Studies
Brookfield Zoo
The Coro Foundation
The Environmental Careers Organization
Environmental Protection Agency
National Audubon Society
National Wildlife Federation
Ruder Finn
Smithsonian Institution
Student Conservation Association
Surfrider Foundation
Urban Fellows/Government Scholars Programs
United States Department of State
Washington Internships for Students of Engineering
Weyerhaeuser

FILM
See Entertainment/Film/Television

FINANCE
See Banking/Management Consulting/Finance

FOREIGN AFFAIRS
American Enterprise Institute
The Brookings Institution
The Carter Center
Central Intelligence Agency
United Nations Association of the United States of
    America
United States Department of State

GOVERNMENT
The Carter Center
Central Intelligence Agency
The Coro Foundation
The Environmental Careers Organization

Federal Bureau of Investigation
The Library of Congress
National Aeronautics and Space Administration
National Institutes of Health
Public Defender Service for D.C.
Supreme Court of the United States
United States Department of State
Urban Fellows/Government Scholars Programs
Washington Internships for Students of Engineering
The White House

HEALTH CARE/MEDICINE/NURSING
Abbott Laboratories
American Heart Association
The Carter Center
Frontier Nursing Service
Genentech
National Aeronautics and Space Administration
National Institutes of Health
Ruder Finn
3M
United States Department of State
Urban Fellows/Government Scholars Programs
The White House

HIGH TECHNOLOGY
See Engineering/High Technology/Manufacturing

HUMAN RESOURCES
Abbott Laboratories
Boeing
Frito-Lay
Hallmark Cards
Hewlett-Packard
Hill, Holliday, Connors, Cosmopulos Advertising
Intel
Kraft Foods, Inc.
Lucasfilm/Lucas Digital
National Aeronautics and Space Administration
NIKE
Raychem
Reebok
Rosenbluth International
United States Department of State
Weyerhaeuser
Wolf Trap Foundation for the Performing Arts

INFORMATION SYSTEMS
See Computers/Information Systems/Electronics

INSURANCE
Northwestern Mutual Financial Network

JOURNALISM
American Enterprise Institute
Center for Investigative Reporting
Central Intelligence Agency
Coors Brewing Company
CNN
MTV: Music Television
National Public Radio
National Wildlife Federation
Nightline
Rolling Stone
Rosenbluth International
United Nations Association of the United States of America
United States Department of State
United States Olympic Committee
The Wall Street Journal
The Washington Post

LAW
American Civil Liberties Union
Central Intelligence Agency
The Coro Foundation
The Environmental Careers Organization
Environmental Protection Agency
Federal Bureau of Investigation
National Aeronautics and Space Administration
National Audubon Society
National Public Radio
National Wildlife Federation
Public Defender Service for D.C.
Skadden, Arps, Slate, Meagher & Flom
Sony Music Entertainment
Sponsors for Educational Opportunity
Supreme Court of the United States
Surfrider Foundation
United Nations Association of the United States of America
United States Department of State
United States Olympic Committee
Urban Fellows/Government Scholars Programs
Washington Internships for Students in Engineering
The White House

LIBRARIES
The Library of Congress
The Metropolitan Museum of Art

MTV: Music Television
Smithsonian Institution
Whitney Museum of American Art

MAGAZINES
See Newspapers/Magazines

MANAGEMENT CONSULTING
See Banking/Management Consulting/Finance

MANUFACTURING
See Engineering/High Technology/Manufacturing

MARKETING
See Advertising
See Public Relations/Marketing

MEDICINE
See Health Care/Medicine/Nursing

MODEL MANAGEMENT
Elite Model Management

MUSEUMS/AUCTION HOUSES
Butterfield & Butterfield
The Metropolitan Museum of Art
Ruder Finn (Arts & Communication account)
Smithsonian Institution
Sotheby's
Whitney Museum of American Art

MUSIC
See Entertainment/Film/Television

NATURE
See Environment/Nature

NEWSPAPERS/MAGAZINES
Rolling Stone
The Wall Street Journal
The Washington Post

NURSING
See Health Care/Medicine/Nursing

OIL/GAS
Chevron
Inroads

PERFORMING ARTS/THEATER
American Conservatory Theater
The Kennedy Center
Lincoln Center for the Performing Arts
Wolf Trap Foundation for the Performing Arts

PHOTOGRAPHY
Butterfield & Butterfield
Central Intelligence Agency
The Library of Congress
National Basketball Association
Smithsonian Institution
Sotheby's
The White House
Wolf Trap Foundation for the Performing Arts

PUBLIC POLICY
American Civil Liberties Union
American Enterprise Institute
The Brookings Institution
The Carter Center
The Coro Foundation
The Environmental Careers Organization
Environmental Protection Agency
The Feminist Majority
National Audubon Society
National Wildlife Federation
Surfrider Foundation
United Nations Association of the United States of
America
United States Department of State
Urban Fellows/Government Scholars Programs
Washington Internships for Students in Engineering
The White House

PUBLIC RELATIONS/MARKETING
Academy of Television Arts & Sciences
American Enterprise Institute
Bertelsmann Music Group
Boeing
Brookfield Zoo
Butterfield & Butterfield
The Carter Center
Coors Brewing Company
Creamer Dickson Basford
Environmental Protection Agency
Frito-Lay
Genentech
Hallmark Cards
Hewlett-Packard
Hill and Knowlton

Hill, Holliday, Connors, Cosmopulos, Inc. Advertising
John Wiley & Sons
The Kennedy Center
Kraft Foods, Inc.
Lucasfilm/Lucas Digital
Microsoft
MTV: Music Television
National Basketball Association
National Public Radio
New York Yankees
NIKE
Procter & Gamble
Raychem
Reebok
Rolling Stone
Rosenbluth International
Ruder Finn
Sony Music Entertainment
Sotheby's
3M
United States Department of State
United States Olympic Committee
Volkswagen
The Walt Disney Studios
Weyerhaeuser
The White House
Whitney Museum of American Art
The Widmeyer Group
Wolf Trap Foundation for the Performing Arts

PUBLIC SERVICE
The Carter Center
The Coro Foundation
Inroads
Urban Fellows/Government Scholars Programs
The White House

PUBLISHING
John Wiley & Sons
Random House
Vault.com

RADIO
See Entertainment/Film/Television

SALES
Abbott Laboratories
Ford Motor Company
Frito-Lay
Hallmark Cards

Hewlett-Packard
Kraft Foods, Inc.
Liz Claiborne
Northwestern Mutual Financial Network
Procter & Gamble
Reebok
Volkswagen
Union Carbide
Weyerhaeuser
Whitney Museum of American Art

SCIENCE
Abbott Laboratories
Central Intelligence Agency
Coors Brewing Company
The Environmental Careers Organization
Environmental Protection Agency
Federal Bureau of Investigation
Genentech
Inroads
Johns Hopkins University Center for Talented Youth
Kraft Foods, Inc.
Lucent Technologies Bell Laboratories
National Aeronautics and Space Administration
National Institutes of Health
Raychem
3M
United States Department of State
Weyerhaeuser

SPORTS
Coors Brewing Company (Wellness Center/
    Recreation)
National Basketball Association
New York Yankees
NIKE
Reebok
United States Olympic Committee
The Washington Post

TEACHING/EDUCATION
Aspen Center for Environmental Studies
Brookfield Zoo
Crow Canyon
Frontier Nursing Service
Johns Hopkins University Center for Talented Youth
The Kennedy Center
Lincoln Center for the Performing Arts
The Metropolitan Museum of Art
Phillips Academy
Smithsonian Institution

Summerbridge National
Urban Fellows/Government Scholars Programs
Whitney Museum of American Art
Wolf Trap Foundation for the Performing Arts

TELEVISION
See Entertainment/Film/Television

THEATER
See Performing Arts/Theater

TRAVEL MANAGEMENT
Rosenbluth International

ZOOKEEPING
Brookfield Zoo
Smithsonian Institution

INTERNSHIPS BY LOCATION

ALABAMA
American Civil Liberties Union
Arthur Andersen
Boeing
Environmental Careers Organization
Inroads
National Aeronautics and Space Administration
Northwestern Mutual Financial Network
Procter & Gamble
Student Conservation Association
3M
Weyerhaeuser

ALASKA
American Civil Liberties Union
Environmental Careers Organization
Northwestern Mutual Financial Network
Student Conservation Association

ARIZONA
American Civil Liberties Union
Arthur Andersen
Atlantic Records
Frito-Lay
Inroads
Intel
National Audubon Society
Northwestern Mutual Financial Nework
Procter & Gamble

Student Conservation Association
3M

ARKANSAS
American Civil Liberties Union
Environmental Careers Organization
Northwestern Mutual Financial Network
Procter & Gamble
Student Conservation Association
3M
Weyerhaeuser

CALIFORNIA
Academy of Television Arts & Sciences
American Association of Advertising Agencies
American Civil Liberties Union
American Conservatory Theater
Arthur Andersen
Atlantic Records
Bertelsmann Music Group
Boeing
Butterfield & Butterfield
Center for Investigative Reporting
Chevron
CNN
The Coro Foundation
Creamer Dickson Basford
Elite Model Management
Environmental Careers Organization
Environmental Protection Agency
The Feminist Majority
Genentech
Hewlett-Packard
Inroads
Intel
Johns Hopkins University Center for Talented Youth
The LEK/Alcar Consulting Group
Lucasfilm/Lucas Digital
Mattel, Inc.
MTV: Music Television
National Aeronautics and Space Administration
National Audubon Society
Northwestern Mutual Financial Network
Procter & Gamble
Raychem
Reebok
Sony Music Entertainment
Student Conservation Association
Summerbridge National
Surfrider Foundation
Symantec

3M
Universal Studios
U.S. Olympic Committee
Weyerhaeuser

COLORADO
Arthur Andersen
Aspen Center for Environmental Studies
Atlantic Records
Bertelsmann Music Group
Coors Brewing Company
Crow Canyon Archaeological Center
Environmental Protection Agency
Hewlett-Packard
Inroads
Northwestern Mutual Financial Network
Procter & Gamble
Student Conservation Association
Summerbridge National
3M
United States Olympic Committee

CONNECTICUT
American Civil Liberties Union
Arthur Andersen
Atlantic Records
Environmental Careers Organization
Inroads
National Audubon Society
Northwestern Mutual Financial Network
Student Conservation Association
Summerbridge National
Union Carbide
Whitney Museum of American Art

DELAWARE
American Civil Liberties Union
Environmental Careers Organization
Hewlett-Packard
J.P. Morgan & Co.
Northwestern Mutual Financial Network

FLORIDA
American Civil Liberties Union
Arthur Andersen
Atlantic Records
Bertelsmann Music Group
CNN
Elite Model Management
Environmental Careers Organization

Environmental Protection Agency
Inroads
MTV: Music Television
National Aeronautics and Space Administration
National Audubon Society
New York Yankees
Northwestern Mutual Financial Network
Procter & Gamble
Student Conservation Association
Summerbridge National
Universal Studios

GEORGIA
American Civil Liberties Union
Arthur Andersen
Atlantic Records
Bertelsmann Music Group
The Carter Center
CNN
Elite Model Management
Environmental Careers Organization
Environmental Protection Agency
Hewlett-Packard
Inroads
MTV: Music Television
Northwestern Mutual Financial Network
Procter & Gamble
Reebok
Sony Music Entertainment
Summerbridge National
3M
The Wall Street Journal

HAWAII
American Civil Liberties Union
Environmental Careers Organization
Northwestern Mutual Financial Network
Procter & Gamble
Student Conservation Association
Summerbridge National

IDAHO
American Civil Liberties Union
Environmental Careers Organization
Hewlett-Packard
Northwestern Mutual Financial Network
Student Conservation Association

ILLINOIS
Abbott Laboratories
American Association of Advertising Agencies

American Civil Liberties Union
Arthur Andersen
Atlantic Records
Bertelsmann Music Group
Brookfield Zoo
Butterfield & Butterfield
CNN
Elite Model Management
Environmental Careers Organization
Environmental Protection Agency
Frito-Lay
Inroads
Kraft Foods, Inc.
Merrill Lynch
MTV: Music Television
Northwestern Mutual Financial Network
Procter & Gamble
Reebok
Sony Music Entertainment
Student Conservation Association
3M
The Wall Street Journal

INDIANA
American Civil Liberties Union
Arthur Andersen
Atlantic Records
Environmental Careers Organization
Inroads
Northwestern Mutual Financial Network
Procter & Gamble
Student Conservation Association
3M

IOWA
American Civil Liberties Union
Procter & Gamble
Northwestern Mutual Financial Network
3M

KANSAS
American Civil Liberties Union
Atlantic Records
Boeing
Environmental Protection Agency
Hallmark Cards
Northwestern Mutual Financial Network
Procter & Gamble

KENTUCKY
American Civil Liberties Union

Arthur Andersen
Environmental Careers Organization
Frontier Nursing Service
National Audubon Society
Northwestern Mutual Financial Network
Procter & Gamble
Student Conservation Association
Summerbridge National
3M

LOUISIANA
American Civil Liberties Union
Arthur Andersen
Atlantic Records
Chevron
Environmental Careers Organization
Inroads
Northwestern Mutual Financial Network
Procter & Gamble
Student Conservation Association
Summerbridge National
Union Carbide

MAINE
American Civil Liberties Union
Environmental Careers Organization
National Audubon Society
Northwestern Mutual Financial Network
Student Conservation Association

MARYLAND
American Civil Liberties Union
Arthur Andersen
Atlantic Records
Environmental Careers Organization
Inroads
Johns Hopkins University Center for Talented Youth
National Aeronautics and Space Administration
National Institutes of Health
Northwestern Mutual Financial Network
Procter & Gamble
Sony Music Entertainment
Student Conservation Association
3M
The Washington Post

MASSACHUSETTS
American Association of Advertising Agencies
American Civil Liberties Union
Arthur Andersen

Atlantic Records
Bertelsmann Music Group
CNN
Environmental Careers Organization
Environmental Protection Agency
Hewlett-Packard
Hill, Holliday, Connors, Cosmopulos, Inc. Advertising
Inroads
Intel
Johns Hopkins University Center for Talented Youth
Northwestern Mutual Financial Network
Phillips Academy
Procter & Gamble
Reebok
Skadden, Arps, Slate, Meagher & Flom
Sony Music Entertainment
Student Conservation Association
Summerbridge National
3M

MICHIGAN
American Association of Advertising Agencies
American Civil Liberties Union
Arthur Andersen
Atlantic Records
Bertelsmann Music Group
CNN
Environmental Careers Organization
Environmental Protection Agency
Ford Motor Company
Inroads
MTV: Music Television
Northwestern Mutual Financial Network
Procter & Gamble
Student Conservation Association
3M
Volkswagen
Weyerhaeuser

MINNESOTA
American Civil Liberties Union
Arthur Andersen
Atlantic Records
Bertelsmann Music Group
Environmental Protection Agency
Inroads
Northwestern Mutual Financial Network
Procter & Gamble
Student Conservation Association
3M

MISSISSIPPI
American Civil Liberties Union
Chevron
National Aeronautics and Space Administration
Northwestern Mutual Financial Network

MISSOURI
American Civil Liberties Union
Arthur Andersen
Atlantic Records
Bertelsmann Music Group
Boeing
The Coro Foundation
Hallmark Cards
Inroads
Northwestern Mutual Financial Network
Student Conservation Association
Summerbridge National
3M

NEBRASKA
American Civil Liberties Union
Arthur Andersen
Northwestern Mutual Financial Network
3M

NEVADA
American Civil Liberties Union
Atlantic Records
Environmental Protection Agency
Northwestern Mutual Financial Network
Student Conservation Association

NEW HAMPSHIRE
American Civil Liberties Union
Environmental Careers Organization
Hewlett-Packard
Northwestern Mutual Financial Network
Student Conservation Association
Summerbridge National

NEW JERSEY
American Civil Liberties Union
Arthur Andersen
Atlantic Records
Environmental Careers Organization
Hewlett-Packard
Inroads
Liz Claiborne
Lucent Technologies Bell Laboratories

National Basketball Association
Northwestern Mutual Financial Network
Procter & Gamble
Student Conservation Association
3M
Union Carbide

NEW MEXICO
American Civil Liberties Union
Arthur Andersen
Intel
National Audubon Society
Northwestern Mutual Financial Network
Student Conservation Association

NEW YORK
American Association of Advertising Agencies
American Civil Liberties Union
Arthur Andersen
Atlantic Records
Bertelsmann Music Group
Bates USA
CNN
The Coro Foundation
Creamer Dickson Basford
Elite Model Management
Environmental Careers Organization
Environmental Protection Agency
Hill and Knowlton
Inroads
J.P. Morgan & Co.
John Wiley & Sons
Johns Hopkins University Center for Talented Youth
Kraft Foods, Inc.
Late Show with David Letterman
Lincoln Center for the Performing Arts
Liz Claiborne
Marvel Comics
The Metropolitan Museum of Art
MTV: Music Television
National Audubon Society
National Basketball Association
New York Yankees
Northwestern Mutual Financial Network
Procter & Gamble
Random House
Rolling Stone
Ruder Finn
Skadden, Arps, Slate, Meagher & Flom
Sony Music Entertainment
Sotheby's

Sponsors for Educational Opportunity
Student Conservation Association
Summerbridge National
TBWA/Chiat, Day
3M
Union Carbide
United Nations Association of the United States of
        America
United States Department of State
United States Olympic Committee
Urban Fellows/Government Scholars Programs
Vault.com
The Wall Street Journal
Whitney Museum of American Art

NORTH CAROLINA
American Civil Liberties Union
Arthur Andersen
Atlantic Records
Bertelsmann Music Group
Environmental Careers Organization
Environmental Protection Agency
Inroads
Northwestern Mutual Financial Network
Procter & Gamble
3M
Student Conservation Association
Summerbridge National
Union Carbide
Weyerhaeuser

NORTH DAKOTA
American Civil Liberties Union
Student Conservation Association
3M

OHIO
American Association of Advertising Agencies
American Civil Liberties Union
Arthur Andersen
Environmental Careers Organization
Inroads
National Aeronautics and Space Administration
Northwestern Mutual Financial Network
Procter & Gamble
Sony Music Entertainment
Student Conservation Association
Summerbridge National
3M

OKLAHOMA
American Civil Liberties Union
Arthur Andersen
Environmental Careers Organization
Environmental Protection Agency
Northwestern Mutual Financial Network
Student Conservation Association
3M
Weyerhaeuser

OREGON
American Association of Advertising Agencies
American Civil Liberties Union
Bertelsmann Music Group
Environmental Careers Organization
Environmental Protection Agency
Hewlett-Packard
Intel
NIKE
Northwestern Mutual Financial Network
Procter & Gamble
Student Conservation Association
Summerbridge National
3M
Weyerhaeuser

PENNSYLVANIA
American Association of Advertising Agencies
American Civil Liberties Union
Arthur Andersen
Atlantic Records
Bertelsmann Music Group
Boeing
The Coro Foundation
Creamer Dickson Basford
Environmental Careers Organization
Environmental Protection Agency
Inroads
Johns Hopkins University Center for Talented Youth
Lucent Technologies Bell Laboratories
Northwestern Mutual Financial Network
Procter & Gamble
QVC
Rosenbluth International
Student Conservation Association

RHODE ISLAND
American Civil Liberties Union
Environmental Careers Organization
Northwestern Mutual Financial Network
Summerbridge National

SOUTH CAROLINA
American Civil Liberties Union
National Audubon Society
Northwestern Mutual Financial Network
Procter & Gamble
Student Conservation Association
3M

SOUTH DAKOTA
American Civil Liberties Union
Northwestern Mutual Financial Network
Student Conservation Association
3M

TENNESSEE
American Civil Liberties Union
Arthur Andersen
Atlantic Records
Environmental Careers Organization
The Hermitage
Inroads
Northwestern Mutual Financial Network
Procter & Gamble
Student Conservation Association

TEXAS
American Association of Advertising Agencies
American Civil Liberties Union
Arthur Andersen
Atlantic Records
Bertelsmann Music Group
Chevron
CNN
Environmental Careers Organization
Environmental Protection Agency
Frito-Lay
Inroads
Intel
National Aeronautics and Space Administration
Northwestern Mutual Financial Network
Procter & Gamble
Sony Music Entertainment
Student Conservation Association
Summerbridge National

3M
Union Carbide
The Wall Street Journal

UTAH
American Civil Liberties Union
Atlantic Records
Northwestern Mutual Financial Network
Student Conservation Association
3M

VERMONT
American Civil Liberties Union
Atlantic Records
Environmental Careers Organization
Northwestern Mutual Financial Network
Student Conservation Association

VIRGINIA
American Civil Liberties Union
Atlantic Records
Central Intelligence Agency
Federal Bureau of Investigation
The Feminist Majority
Inroads
National Aeronautics and Space Administration
Northwestern Mutual Financial Network
Procter & Gamble
Student Conservation Association
Summerbridge National
The Washington Post
Wolf Trap Foundation for the Performing Arts

WASHINGTON
American Association of Advertising Agencies
American Civil Liberties Union
Arthur Andersen
Atlantic Records
Bertelsmann Music Group
Boeing
Environmental Careers Organization
Environmental Protection Agency
Hewlett-Packard
Intel
Microsoft
Northwestern Mutual Financial Network
Procter & Gamble
Student Conservation Association
3M
Weyerhaeuser

WASHINGTON, D.C.
American Civil Liberties Union
American Enterprise Institute
Arthur Andersen
Bertelsmann Music Group
The Brookings Institution
Central Intelligence Agency
CNN
Environmental Careers Organization
Environmental Protection Agency
Federal Bureau of Investigation
Georgetown Criminal Justice Clinic
Inroads
The Kennedy Center
The Library of Congress
National Audubon Society
National Public Radio
National Wildlife Federation
Nightline
Northwestern Mutual Financial Network
Public Defender Service for D.C.
Ruder Finn
Skadden, Arps, Slate, Meagher & Flom
Smithsonian Institution
Student Conservation Association
Supreme Court of the United States
United Nations Association of the U.S.
United States Department of State
The Wall Street Journal
Washington Internships for Students of Engineering
The Washington Post
The White House
The Widmeyer Group

WEST VIRGINIA
American Civil Liberties Union
Inroads
Northwestern Mutual Financial Network
Student Conservation Association
3M

WISCONSIN
American Civil Liberties Union
Arthur Andersen
Atlantic Records
Frito-Lay
Inroads
Kraft Foods, Inc.
National Audubon Society
Northwestern Mutual Financial Network
Procter & Gamble
Student Conservation Association
3M
Weyerhaeuser

WYOMING
American Civil Liberties Union
National Audubon Society
Northwestern Mutual Financial Network
Student Conservation Association

NOTES

NOTES

NOTES

NOTES

NOTES

NOTES

NOTES

NOTES

We Want To Hear From You!

Please tell us about your internship experience. If you've participated in one of the programs listed in *The Best 106 Internships*, tell us how it compares with our description. Or, if your program's not in the book, tell us whether it deserves to be a "Best Internship." Then mail this form (feel free to attach additional sheets if necessary) to the address listed below. Thanks!

Name of organization: _____

City in which internship is located: _____

Phone number and contact person (if available): _____
_____

What did you do? _____
_____
_____
_____
_____
_____

Describe any extracurricular activities (seminars, field trips, etc.) and perks: _____
_____
_____
_____

Your name: _____

Phone: _____

School: _____

Year in school during internship: _____

■ **The Best 106 Internships—9th Edition**
150 West 22nd Street, 5th Floor
New York, NY 10011
Fax: (212) 366-6117

Mark Oldman and **Samer Hamadeh** are **The Internship Informants™**, the only nationally recognized experts on the subject of internships. They are authors of *The Best 106 Internships* and *The Internship Bible,* as well as nationally syndicated columnists on internships and career education. They are also the founders of Vault.com, the leading Internet site for career information.

Mark Oldman (at left) graduated Phi Beta Kappa with BA and an MA in English from Stanford University as well as a JD from Stanford Law School. At Stanford, he designed and taught an undergraduate course on the U.S. Supreme Court, ran the Stanford Wine Circle, and spent a term at Oxford University. He has completed internships in government, law, television, music, and advertising.

Samer Hamadeh (at right) graduated with a BS in Chemistry and an MS in Chemical Engineering from Stanford University. At Stanford, he managed his own printing company, played rugby, and served a teaching assistantship in the Chemistry Department. He has served internships in engineering, management consulting, and public policy.

Expert Advice

www.review.com

Talk About It

www.review.com

Pop Surveys

Paying for it

www.review.com

www.review.com

The Princeton Review

Getting in

Word du Jour

www.review.com

Find-O-Rama School & Career Search

www.review.com

Finding it

Best Schools

www.review.com

FIND US...

International

Hong Kong
4/F Sun Hung Kai Centre
30 Harbour Road, Wan Chai,
Hong Kong
Tel: (011)85-2-517-3016

Japan
Fuji Building 40, 15-14
Sakuragaokacho, Shibuya Ku,
Tokyo 150, Japan
Tel: (011)81-3-3463-1343

Korea
Tae Young Bldg, 944-24,
Daechi- Dong, Kangnam-Ku
The Princeton Review—ANC
Seoul, Korea 135-280,
South Korea
Tel: (011)82-2-554-7763

Mexico City
PR Mex S De RL De Cv
Guanajuato 228 Col. Roma
06700 Mexico D.F., Mexico
Tel: 525-564-9468

Montreal
666 Sherbrooke St.
West, Suite 202
Montreal, QC H3A 1E7 Canada
Tel: 514-499-0870

Pakistan
1 Bawa Park - 90 Upper Mall
Lahore, Pakistan
Tel: (011)92-42-571-2315

Spain
Pza. Castilla, 3 - 5º A, 28046
Madrid, Spain
Tel: (011)341-323-4212

Taiwan
155 Chung Hsiao East Road
Section 4 - 4th Floor,
Taipei R.O.C., Taiwan
Tel: (011)886-2-751-1243

Thailand
Building One, 99 Wireless Road
Bangkok, Thailand 10330
Tel: 662-256-7080

Toronto
1240 Bay Street, Suite 300
Toronto M5R 2A7 Canada
Tel: 800-495-7737
Tel: 716-839-4391

Vancouver
4215 University Way NE
Seattle, WA 98105
Tel: 206-548-1100

National (U.S.)

We have more than 60 offices around the U.S. and run courses at over 400 sites. For courses and locations within the U.S. call 1-800-2-Review and you will be routed to the nearest office.

WHERE DO I GO FROM HERE?

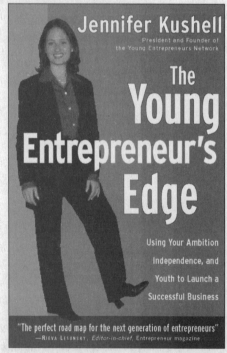

"The perfect road map for the next generation of entrepreneurs"
—RIEVA LESONSKY, Editor-in-chief, Entrepreneur magazine

GUIDE TO YOUR CAREER
4TH EDITION
0-375-75620-5 • $21.00

JOB NOTES: COVER LETTERS
0-679-77873-X • $4.95

JOB NOTES: INTERVIEWS
0-679-77875-6 • $4.95

JOB NOTES: NETWORKING
0-679-77877-2 • $4.95

JOB NOTES: RESUMES
0-679-77872-1 • $4.95

JOB SMART
JOB HUNTING MADE EASY
0-679-77355-X • $12.00

TRASHPROOF RESUMES
YOUR GUIDE TO CRACKING
THE JOB MARKET
0-679-75911-5 • $12.00

NEGOTIATE SMART
0-679-77871-3 • $12.00

SPEAK SMART
0-679-77868-3 • $10.00

**THE YOUNG
ENTREPRENEUR'S EDGE**
USING YOUR AMBITION,
INDEPENDENCE, AND YOUTH TO
LAUNCH A SUCCESSFUL BUSINESS
0-375-75349-4 • $12.00

WORK SMART
0-679-78388-1 • $12.00

Available at bookstores, or call (800) 733-3000

www.randomhouse.com/princetonreview